Teaching The
Mentally Retarded

Teaching The Mentally Retarded

ALAN C. REPP

Department of Learning, Development and Special Education
Northern Illinois University
DeKalb, Illinois

PRENTICE-HALL, INC.

Englewood Cliffs, N.J. 07632

Library of Congress Cataloging in Publication Data

REPP, ALAN C.
  Teaching the mentally retarded.

  Includes bibliographies and index.
    1. Mentally handicapped children—Education.
  2. Mentally handicapped—Education—History.
  I. Title.
  LC4601.R43   371.92'8   81-21123
  ISBN 0-13-893867-9   AACR2

© 1983 by Prentice-Hall, Inc., Englewood Cliffs, New Jersey 07632

Printed in the United States of America

10 9 8 7 6 5 4 3 2 1

Editorial/production supervision: Nicholas Romanelli
Manufacturing buyer: Edmund Leone
Cover design: Zimmerman/Foyster

ISBN 0-13-893867-9

PRENTICE-HALL INTERNATIONAL, INC., *London*
PRENTICE-HALL OF AUSTRALIA PTY, LIMITED, *Sydney*
PRENTICE-HALL OF CANADA, LTD., *Toronto*
PRENTICE-HALL OF INDIA PRIVATE LIMITED, *New Delhi*
PRENTICE-HALL OF JAPAN, INC., *Tokyo*
PRENTICE-HALL OF SOUTHEAST ASIA PTD. LTD., *Singapore*
WHITEHALL BOOKS LIMITED, *Wellington, New Zealand*

Contents

PART   IV

Chapter 7 *Reinforcement* 178

Chapter 8 *The Effective Use of Reinforcers in Reinforcement Programs* 214

Chapter 9 *Schedules of Reinforcement* 241

Preface

The opportunities for treatment available to retarded individuals have undergone extraordinary change during this century, in both an ethical and an educational sense. During the first few decades of the twentieth century, the major thrust was toward institutionalizing retarded people so that they could be separated from society. Educational opportunities were virtually nonexistent, and the most that generally could be hoped for was that custodial treatment would at least be humane. Most efforts today are directed toward deinstitutionalization, with various living alternatives such as the natural home, foster home, group home (houses where a few retarded persons live together), or independent living are stressed. Frequently, educational opportunities are extensive, with input from diverse disciplines such as speech pathology, psychology, special education, recreation, and medicine. With the passage of Public Law 94-142, the social movement toward improved services is now supported by law.

Although there are many approaches for providing services for retarded persons, the one stressed and explained in this book is the behavioral approach. This approach requires that we carefully monitor the success of our programs, make changes when the data so suggest, and base our work concerning procedures on principles of learning that have been established through research. Although this approach may sometimes seem a cold one, it is not; rather, it suggests that if you care enough, you will do the additional reading and take the extra care required to find what will best serve the retarded person you are teaching.

This book represents many years of work with retarded individuals by the author and his colleagues. During that time, we have learned many new ways to help teach them, and hopefully that learning progress will continue for us in the future. A.C.R.

PART

I

CHAPTER

1

A History of
Mental Retardation

But what then am I? A thing which thinks. What is a thing which thinks? It is a thing which doubts, understands, (conceives), affirms, denies, wills, refuses, which also imagines and feels. (Descartes)

And what is a retarded person? Too often such a person has been considered to be one who does not think, or feel, or imagine, but rather, one who exists at the will of society, and one who exists in a condition totally determined by *other* members of society, a condition generally disgraceful and often despicable, a condition generally ignored by a society which, until very recent adjudications, has not considered retarded persons worthy of membership.

We seem now, in the last two decades, to be in a technological period where we do include retarded persons in our society and provide educational (in the widest sense) opportunities for them. Since John F. Kennedy's action in 1961 to create the President's Panel on Mental Retardation, we seem to be in a social period in which we are concerned with the humanness of the conditions in which they live. Perhaps this era, prodded through the results of federal and common laws and through the normalization and mainstreaming movements, is just collateral to the general concern with an improved quality of life for all of us through large-scale and personal environmental control. If it is, it is susceptible to the quixotic changes that government and unpredicted events can cause. Or perhaps it is a movement unto itself, with its own supporters innured to external pressures—we hope so. The conditions described by Blatt (1976), Rivera (1972), and others are not appreciably different from the conditions that exist in some states today.

Progress is not evident for these persons; but there has been some progress for others. New institutions and new community centers provide improved living conditions that are available for some retarded persons. A small portion of the changes in this (possible) era of concern is demonstrated by the improvements in physical environments; another portion is demonstrated by the slow but successful movement of institutionalized persons back to the communities through the increase in group homes, foster-care placements, and other alternative living situations. But a major portion of the change has come through the beginnings of the technology of measuring, of changing, and of maintaining human behavior. The majority of this book will present the components of this technology and the issues surrounding them. But, first, we will examine the antecedents of our present practices, and we shall do so in three areas: (1) mental retardation, (2) issues, and (3) applied behavior analysis.

EARLY CHRONICLES

There is extemely little written information about retarded persons prior to the nineteenth century, with only spare references available. Many of the descriptions are, in fact, not verbal; they are pictorial, e.g., the "fools" of King Phillip IV of Spain as painted by Velasquez. While there could be many reasons, the major one seems to be that the topic was not of much interest either to writers or to those concerned with the health of societies.

The earliest written reference to mental retardation appears to have been the Papyrus of Thebes (1552 B.C.) which discussed the treatment of persons whose exceptionality was intellectual. That some treatment was attempted is suggested by the various remains in Europe, South America, and Central America of skulls with crude surgery, generally intended to allow spirits to escape from the body. As there was no distinction between mental illness and mental retardation at that time, some of the victims were probably mentally retarded persons.

The treatment of retarded persons during this period and during the Greek and Roman civilizations has been characterized by Kolstoe and Frey (1965) as the *era of extermination,* a reaction they attribute to society's quest for survival. Apparently, in both nomadic and static societies, there was little time, supplies, or understanding for the handicapped. Early Greece appears to have been contemptuous of the handicapped and applied the term "idiot" to all types of deviancy from the norm (L'Abate & Curtis, 1975). As we remember from *Oedipus Rex* and other accounts, many deformed children were removed from the community and left to perish, although some apparently retarded persons survived when a use could be found for them, e.g., as a physician's slave (Keramidas, 1976).

Rome continued Greece's program of genocide, and the practice of leaving children in open sewers was common (Kaufman & Payne, 1975). But Rome became an empire of excesses and indulgences for the wealthy and, in so doing, it found a use for some handicapped persons and reinstated a function originated in Ancient Egypt—that of court jester. Prominent Romans such as Seneca used some deformed persons, and particularly dwarfs, as means of amusement; and some of those providing the amusement, such as Gabba the "fool" of Emperor Augustus, became famous themselves (Mainford & Love, 1973).

But there did seem to be a growing foundation over the centuries for recognizing the retarded. Keramidas (1976) credits the written acknowledgment of retardation in Thebes with having set the stage for a movement from supernaturalism to scientific explanations and methods of treatment. He goes on to cite the physician Hippocrates as mentioning the retarded and describing deformities of the skull, but Greece's concern for ideal human form prevented dissection of and further understanding of the human body. This disinclination was continued by the Romans, although the physician Galen noted differing mental acuities while he treated gladiators. The only concern for treatment of the retarded appears to have been suggested in the East by Confucius (500 B.C.) and Zoroaster (400 B.C.), who advocated tender care for retarded persons, and by Justinian, whose often ignored code sought some care and treatment (L'Abate & Curtis, 1975).

From the next millenium, there are few references to the retarded, although some syndromes presently identified seem to have been recognized during this period. Jordan (1972) discusses both a report of a hydrocephalic skull recovered below the second cataract of the Nile (dating A.D. 350–550) and an account of hydrocephalus in an Egyptian living during the Roman times. Some recognition of care seems to have occurred as Pope Gregory decreed that those handicapped by virtue of being crippled should be helped (Chin, Drew & Logan, 1975), and El Kendy, a ninth-century Arab scholar, discussed simple-minded and epileptic children (Jordan, 1972). Although there was no remarkable progress for the retarded during this period, there was a considerable change—an inclination by society to allow the deviant to live. Kolstoe and Frey (1965) surmise that during this agrarian period a caste system developed around the nobleman-serf relationship in which the serf received protection and the nobleman received workers. With survival easier, society could afford not to kill the retarded and replaced that practice with one of ridicule.

In the Middle Ages treatment was ambivalent. Some of the deformed were still being used as court jesters, while the less fortunate were thought to be possessed by the devil and were scourged to drive him out. But the period did contain movements of protection. Gheel, Belgium, began the first community approach to the retarded; the church in general became more lenient and constructed monasteries and asylums for the handicapped, who were made wards of the church; and Henry II of England enacted legislation known as the *de praerogitive regis*, which made "natural fools" wards of the king (and in doing so made an interesting distinction between mentally retarded and mentally ill persons, with the latter not being regarded as *natural* fools).

Little change occurred until the 1500s during which there was an interesting array of conflicting attitudes. Spain maintained the *status quo* to some extent, with the Catholic Church developing sympathy and compassion for the handicapped and for others regarded as unfortunate. Dwarfs continued to be employed as jesters, this time by Philip IV, who had a retarded son, Charles II, whose adult behavior was described as comparable to that of a six-year-old. Some members of the Court believed that the retarded were "divinely compensated" for their handicap, and that they may have possessed a mentality not comprehended by the nondivine (Keramidas, 1976). Some of the "possessed" were kept by persons of station, and one is reported to have been a companion and adviser to Tycho Brahe, a sixteenth-century astronomer who believed the incomprehensible mutterings to be a divine revelation (Mainford & Love, 1973). Others who were intellectually handicapped were provided homes founded by St. Vincent de Paul (1576–1660) and the Sisters of Charity (L'Abate & Curtis, 1975).

Another attitude of the 1500s was also translated to treatment. It is related to the concept of possession and presents an interesting irony for the tolerance expressed by religions during the European Reformation. Reports indicate that the "uncivilized" sections of Northern Europe generally left the retarded alone to wander, continuing to believe them to be "blessed infants." But the "civilized" sections persecuted the retarded for two reasons: (1) they could not comprehend Christian teaching, and (2) they were possessed by the devil and should have the spirit beaten out of them. Paracelsus, who was the first medical authority to attempt to point out a causal relationship between cretinism and environmental effects (and was thus a forerunner of a very important nineteenth-century factor in the education of the retarded), continued this retreat in humanity by supporting the concept of devil possession (Keramidas, 1976), a philosophy well expressed by Martin Luther (1483–1546):

> Eight years ago, there was one at Dessau whom I, Martinus Luther, saw and grappled with. He was twelve years old, had the use of his eyes and all his senses, so that one might think he was a normal child. But he did nothing but gorge himself as much as four peasants or threshers. He ate, defecated, and drooled, and if anyone tackled him, he screamed. If things didn't go well, he wept. So I said to the Prince of Anhalt: "If I were the Prince, I should take this child to the Moldau River which flows near Dessau *and drown him.*" But the Prince of Anhalt and the Prince of Saxony, who happened to be present, refused to follow my advice. Thereupon I said: "Well, then the Christians shall order the Lord's Prayer to be said in church and pray that the dear Lord take the Devil away." (Kanner, 1964, p. 7)

Counter to the intent of Luther and others, and interesting with today's important and extraordinary concern with the law and constitutional rights as they relate to the mentally retarded, is Jordan's (1972) reference to Fitzherbert's *De Natura Brevium* (1534) as an early recognition of the need to define mental retardation to the satisfaction of the law. Jordan also noted that he has found in the state papers of Henry VIII (1491–1547) a remark that "William Paulet conducted the affairs of the 'King's Widows and Idiots,' meaning those dependent persons who were wards of the crown" (p. 5). Although the treatment certainly has varied between and within centuries, Henry II's recognition of the need for governmental intervention into the affairs of some of those who are disadvantaged seemed to have been ahead of his time.

1600–1800

The 1600s and, in particular, the 1700s broke with the "possessed" theory of retardation and developed very basic theories of learning that were translated in the 1800s into treatment programs. The age of Rousseau, Locke, and the Encyclopedists led to the humanitarian treatment of the oppressed, begun in the last decade of the eighteenth century, a movement without which the theories would never have so soon after been tested. In the 1600s, there were a few attempts to determine the reasons for deficiencies. For example, early in the century, the Italian Tassoni discussed mental deficiency, stating that it was not due solely to heredity—progenitive of the 1930s in the United States, and a step forward—but that it was also due to the sensual excesses of the parents (Jordan, 1972), a remark that seems plausible hundreds of years ago, but, incredibly, a cause also advocated by the leading experts on mental retardation at the beginning of the twentieth century. More alternation between progress and entrenchment occurred in the latter part of the seventeenth century when Thomas Willis, who pioneered work on the circulatory system, published *De Anima Brutorum* which included a chapter on mental deficiency. He differentiated between congential "stupidity" and that which occurred from a blow and, as such, began a simple system of classification according to etiology. Discussing properties of the brain, Willis remained consistent with his other work by suggesting that deficiencies were due to irregularities within the body. In the case of mental deficiency, he believed "stupidity" to be a result of too much moisture or coldness and advocated blood-purifying methods such as bleeding (Jordan, 1972).

As strange as they seem today, purifying methods are understandable in the context of the middle of these two centuries, which were affected by the conflict between powerful religious groups—the Protestant Reformation and the Roman Catholic Church with its intense Counter-Reformation. While there were advances in science during this period, individuals had to be careful when the advances became involved in any way with God, nature, spirits, and demons. Even Galileo, who invented the scientific method, and who was the most powerful scientist at the height of the conflict, did not escape. For his support of the theory of Copernicus, he was brought to the Inquisition, found guilty on the basis of a document that Bronowski (1973) describes as "manifestly a forgery—or, at the most charitable, a draft for some suggested meeting which was rejected" (p. 214), was twice threatened with the tortures of the day, and, finally, was forced to recant any prior teachings, defenses, or beliefs that the earth is not the center of the world.

But, despite the power of the forces within the Reformation and the Counter-Reformation, there were societal, philosophical, and scientific movements that would radically change the focus of society on itself. In his analysis of the cultural factors affecting the study of mental retardation, Keramidas (1976) chronicles some of these events and finds that the immense popularity of the Baroque style of art had an interesting relation to the declining authority of the Church. This style, with its emphasis on grandeur, became so popular that rivals began to use it to exalt themselves rather than God, and the Church, with its previously unchallenged dominance as a cultural power, was unable to contain it. As such, the Church signaled its own decline in power. Contrasted with the activities of the wealthy was a recognition by them of the activities of the poor. Louis XIV (1638–1715) constructed a hospital for disadvantaged and/or retarded persons that, while not providing educational treatment, did at least offer a place to stay. As such, it continued the intervention of government into this area. Further advance was contributed by St. Vincent de Paul, an ex-peasant who developed the first general hospital and who also began in Paris an orphanage whose clients included the retarded.

The power of the Church continued to decline in Protestant Holland and England, where capitalism and experimentation dominated the rise of the middle class and provided the final separation from the authoritarian control of religion. Descartes (1596–1650) laid a foundation for learning theories when he studied perception, a concept characterized as central to these centuries (Keramidas, 1976), for without some understanding and speculation of how the average person learned, there probably would not have been Itard's later attempt to test current theory on the behavior of the "wild boy of Aveyron."

Newton's (1642–1727) work in science highlighted the years following Galileo and epitomized the *zeitgeist*. Science was expanding astronomically, and during the Enlightenment, fashionable men and women purchased for display and some use scientific instruments such as telescopes. Interest in medically related areas was high: Willis issued his book; Hoefer discussed cretinism and suggested it was related to poor food and education; and interest in anatomy caused graverobbing to be a profitable undertaking.

Collateral to the interest and advance in science were three other series of occurrences that exerted considerable influence on the later education of the retarded. *One was the development of education for identifiable special populations*. In the latter part of this period, embossed line print was developed for the blind (1786), and Valentine Hauy (1745–1822), who was the first to organize work with the blind, founded in 1785 a school in Paris for the blind. Developments for deaf persons were also occurring, and the work of one man, Jacob Rodrique Pereire (1715–1780), was extremely influential in the development of teaching techniques in the next century. During these two centuries, the earlier work of Pedro de Ponce (1520–1584) was continued; a manual alphabet was developed in 1620; the oral method was developed in 1740; treatment of the deaf was studied by the Royal Society of England; Heinicke (1727–1790) borrowed from the philosophy of Locke and taught his deaf pupils to remember vowel sounds by combining the sense of taste and smell; and the work of Jacob Pereire, a Spanish physician whose interest in deaf education may have been stimulated by the handicap of his deaf sister, began.

Pereire, who began his work in 1743 with deaf mutes, developed principles of teaching that were adopted by Itard and Seguin in the initial systematic teachings of the retarded. Referred to by Doll as principles which have become embedded in special education, they included "scientific observation, use of the case history, adaptation of methods to the individuality of the pupil, sensory substitution and sensory reinforcement, progress through developmental sequences, education in terms of social needs, and the principle of proceeding from the known to the unknown" (Doll, 1967, p. 176). After studying anatomy for 10 years, Pereire extended the perceptual theories of Descartes and Locke by focusing on the associations of sound and touch and words. Noting that a baby born deaf understands speech as he lies on the vibrating chest of his mother (Mainford & Love, 1973), he taught his deaf pupils to perceive vibrations and to match them to words, and in doing so was the first educator reported to have systematically employed the senses in teaching handicapped persons.

A *second major influence was philosophical* and included (1) the theory of perception begun by Descartes and discussed in different fashions by Locke (1632–1704) and de Condillac (1715–1780), and (2) the radical social theory of Rousseau (1712–1778), whose *Emile* (1762) presented a noble savage uncorrupted by society and by the political profiteers. Locke, who described in 1690 a clear distinction between idiocy and insanity (Keramidas, 1976), discussed the rationality of man and argued that the intellect was a storehouse for information gathered by the senses and that it was affected by the "laws of association." De Condillac stressed the concept of perception but argued that sensations alone, without associations, are the basis of mental life. The doctrine became known as "sensationalism" and, in 1799, a perfect test for his theory arrived adventitiously, a living "noble savage."

A *third major influence was the change in philosophy toward man* that surrounded the French Revolution. Rousseau's famous "man is born free, but everywhere he is in chains" was the theme of the Revolution resulting in the death of Louis XVI and his wife, Marie Antoinette. The aftermath of the Revolution was even more horrendous than its preceding period, and Robespierre's reign of terror (1793–1794) has been regarded as a "massive guillotine" for suspected traitors. The period became marked by a growing concern for humanity and for the plight of the oppressed, and by a general reassessment of man's relation to man. In 1794, at the close of the reign of terror, Pinel was appointed to the directorship of Saltpetriere and, becoming disgusted with the abuses, "threw aside the whips, the chains, and the stocks, with which they (the insane) had hitherto been controlled, and in their stead substituted the power of kindness, gentleness, and love" (Brockett, 1856, reprinted on p. 73 of Rosen, Clark & Kivitz, 1976, Vol. 1).

THE NOBLE SAVAGE

With the interest in a theory of perception, with the foundations of techniques for educating special populations, and with increasing concern for the humanness of treatment, the closing of the century was an excellent period for progress, and the period was met with a most propitious discovery and combination: (1) a wild boy, Rousseau's savage untainted by society and de Condillac's perfect subject for the test of his theory of perception, was found by hunters in the French woods of Aveyron; and (2) Jean Marc Itard (1775–1838), a physician who was working in an institution in Paris for the deaf, and who had adopted the "sensationalist" theory that learning is acquired through the senses and that all persons could learn given the proper sense training. M. Bonaterre, something of a professor of natural history, marveled over the possibilities of using this pure specimen as an empirical test of the "sensationalist" theory. The boy was brought to the French Academy of Science, Itard was challenged, and the first scientific attempt at educating a retarded person was about to begin (Keramidas, 1976).

Described as an 11- or 12-year-old boy who responded to the sound of a nut falling from a tree but not to the sound of a pistol, who discriminated neither hot from cold nor foul from pleasant smells, and who had uncontrollable moods fluctuating from excitement to depression (Mainford & Love, 1973), Victor was declared to be an incurable idiot by Pinel, who then challenged Itard. Through repetitious "sense" training, Itard taught Victor to wear clothes, to dress and undress with some aid, to drink from a cup and to eat with some implements, to make some sensory discriminations, to develop a three-word vocabulary, and to understand the meaning of a large number of words. But Itard had adopted a philosophy that, if true and if approached with the correct teaching methods, would result in Victor developing into a "normal" boy. In so doing, Itard was, of course, sentenced to fail. After five years of work, and after Victor broke out in a wild storm of passion attributed to puberty, Itard terminated his work and concluded that he was a failure. But the French Academy of Science disagreed and honored him for his work. Later, Itard regained his interest and wanted to instruct a class of incurables, but because of his age, he sought and found a younger man—his pupil Edouard Seguin (1812–1880).

ANOTHER ATTEMPT

Seguin sought counsel on his methods from Jean Esquirol (1772–1840), a French pioneer in mental health who organized the first educational program in psychiatry, who was the first to describe two grades of mental retardation (idiocy and imbecility), and who determined that idiocy was not a disease but rather a condition originating before the complete development of the intellect.[1] With Esquirol's and Itard's suggestions that idiocy could be improved, Seguin sought to improve the behavior of those in his care to a higher level of independence in a manner discussed in his book, translated as *The Moral Treatment, Hygiene, and Education of Idiots and Other Backward Children.*

Seguin was a St. Simonist and adopted a strong philosophy of dedication to elevating the poorest and lowest members of society's hierarchy. Education of the retarded was generally considered a moral obligation that Seguin believed was not completed until the idiot could help a neighbor with some type of meaningful labor. His theory combined the embryonic knowledge of neurology with the ever-present homunculus theory (still maintained today, but with varying descriptors), and Seguin viewed human behavior as a functional circle held together by a peripheral and a central nervous system with active and passive functions activated by the will. Those believed to have peripheral nervous system dysfunction were called by Seguin superficial types, while those with central nervous system damage were called profound types (Mainford & Love, 1973). Idiocy was believed to result from an interruption in the functional circle, which then isolated the will from the world of moral choice. The objective of treatment was to break the idiot's "negative will of total passivity" by the methods of training—psychological, physical, and sensory methods, all addressed to what Seguin termed "moral training."

Seguin worked with several senses, unlike Itard who concentrated first only on hearing, and considered touch, hearing, and sight as the most important. His work, while certainly indigenous to his era, is remarkably current in his anticipation of gradually increasing the difficulty of tasks (now called shaping) and of gradually making discriminations less obvious (now called fading). Seguin clearly understood B. F. Skinner's century-later concept of contingencies, the relation of environmental events to responding, and demonstrated this under-

---

[1] An interesting parallel to the American Association on Mental Deficiency's 1973 definition of mental retardation, one criterion of which is manifestation during the developmental period.

standing through the use of antecedent stimuli such as the formboard, which he developed, the use of antecedent procedures such as fading, and the use of pro-grammed consequences of responding. Although choosing a consequence infre-quently used in today's applied programs, Seguin demonstrated the use of response-produced events by applying fear training (now called avoidance conditioning) in which idiots were taught to avoid punishment by performing tasks sequenced carefully for increasing difficulty.

Seguin had studied the work of and had written a book about Pereire, who had argued that touch was the first and most important sense to teach. Although determined not to limit his teaching predominantly to one modality as Itard had, Seguin did emphasize physical movement to achieve very specific motoric objec-tives. Respected as an amateur gymnast, he enlisted the aid of Colonel Amoros, a renowned gymnast, to employ every gymnastic aid to teach idiots to stand, climb, and control body movements. He considered learning a task the demonstration of the active extention of the will that could be developed once the senses were developed. And the training of the senses prior to the training of the will is a central difference between Itard's and Seguin's theories, the former theorizing one only had to train the senses, the latter theorizing one had to train the senses before training the will.

THE SCHOOL MOVEMENT: SEGUIN

The importance of Seguin's influence for the century, however, went beyond his theory of instruction. In 1837 (Mainford & Love, 1973) or 1838 (Rosen, Clark & Kivitz, 1976), the first successful public residential institution for retarded persons was established. In 1842, a portion of the Bicêtre was set aside for in-structing idiots, and Seguin was appointed its director. After a short period, he left the Bicêtre to establish a private school, and finally, with the revolution of 1848 and his distrust of those involved, Seguin saw no hope of free thought and action in France and moved to Ohio (Wilbur, 1880). But Seguin's work had become known in Europe and was one of the two major contributions to the establishment of institutions, the other being the threat of cretinism. Seguin's influence spread through replications of the school movement in various countries. In Germany, two schools were begun during the decade. In England, after reports of Seguin's and Guggenbuhl's works became known, a school was established in 1846 in Bath. This was followed rapidly in Highgate by the Park House (1848), which was formerly a nobleman's residence; in Colchester, by Essex Hall, which was provided by Sir S. M. Petro; and in 1853 by Earlswood, near Reigate, Surrey, which was dedicated by Prince Albert. The latter was a large institution for 400 residents and cost $175,000, in addition to the price of the 100-acre estate (Rosen, Clark & Kivitz, 1976).

Some work on a small-scale basis had been occurring in the United States prior to this period. For example, in 1818, an idiot girl was admitted to the American Asylum for the Deaf and Dumb and remained there until 1824. The trial must have been considered at least partially successful as others were admit-ted gradually until 34 girls had been treated. In 1839, an idiot boy was admitted for three years to the New York institution of the Deaf and Dumb; and in the same year, Samuel Gridley Howe (1801–1876) instructed a blind idiot at the Perkins Institution for the Blind in South Boston (Brockett, 1856). But the movement toward larger programs awaited a visit to Seguin and translation of his works, and some social provocations. In her famous 1843 "Memorial to the Legislature of Massachusetts," Dorothea Dix attacked our treatment of persons in asylums, prisons, and almshouses. Then, on January 13, 1846, the Honorable F. F. Backus introduced a bill for an institution for the retarded in New York, which was defeated because of a lack of appropriations and which was suspended until the legislature opened an experimental school in Albany three years later. Concurrently, the Massachusetts House of Representatives received on January 22, 1846, a resolution from the Honorable Horatio Byington for a commission to study idiots within the state. Within the year, two programs had begun. Dr. H. B. Wilbur, who had sent to Paris for copies of Seguin's work and who has been credited by Seguin with successfully adopting his methods to classrooms, began in July a private institution in Barre, Massachusetts. Then Howe, himself, took directorship of a wing of the Perkins Institute that was dedicated to testing the capacity of idiots for instruction (Brockett, 1856). A few years later, the success lead to the establishment of the first state school for the mentally retarded. Originally known as the Massachusetts School for Idiots and Feeble-Minded Youth, its name was later changed to the Walter E. Fernald State School at Waverly.

These developments presaged the era of institutionalization that was intended primarily to provide treatment for the retarded. New York passed its resolution, and Wilbur was appointed director of an experimental school at Albany. In 1855, the school was moved to Syracuse and renamed the State Asylum for Idiots. In 1852, J. B. Richards, who had gone to Paris to learn from Seguin and who had worked a few years at the experimental school in Massachusetts, went to Philadelphia to open a school in Germantown. The program received support from Dr. Alfred Elwyn, expanded and moved to another section of Philadelphia, and, in 1859, moved 15 miles south to Media. In the same year that Richards left, Seguin arrived and worked with Howe. But, although the two men agreed in their philosophies of helping the retarded, they did not agree on the method of instruction; they argued and soon dissolved their working relationship. With the influence of Seguin and Howe, schools continued to propagate so that by 1898 there were 24 state schools operated by 19 states and one school operated by the City of New York.

With these occurrences, the residential status of retarded persons was changed for a century until the National Association of Retarded Children (now Citizens) and others began the deinstitutionalization program in the 1950s. While institutions are now believed by many to be an anachronism, they did provide treatment for the remainder of the nineteenth century before moving completely to the custodial model. Wolfensberger (1975) reminds us of the care for mentally handicapped persons in the first portion of the nineteenth century with two perspectives: (1) that as late as the 1820s, mentally retarded persons were grouped with other dependent deviants and sold to the *lowest* bidder (i.e., those willing to take them for the least amount of public support), and (2) that during this period, those declared mentally handicapped were denied many privileges and rights (e.g., thought to be without basic sensory acuities to the point that they were presumed to lack the ability to discriminate hot from cold, some of the retarded were not even provided heat in their cells during the cold New England winters).

THE MOVE AGAINST CRETINISM

Another factor that added to the change from the general treatment described by Wolfensberger to the educated treatment adopted in some of the early schools was the attempt by Johann Guggenbuhl (1816–1863) and others to control cretinism, then described as a form of idiocy, with the affected usually "retaining the goitre, . . . suffering from feeble and swollen limbs, distorted and deformed features, pale, bloodless and tumid skin, and almost entire helplessness" (Brockett, 1856, p. 74). In some sectors of Europe and Asia, the extent of the problem leaves one almost incredulous. Brockett describes four "departments" of Europe in which, in 1850, 54,000 of the 958,000 inhabitants were cretins, and a hamlet, referred to as Bozel, in which 1,011 of the 1,472 inhabitants were affected either with goiter or cretinism.

This problem had certainly been recognized for many years, and after centuries of concern, governments began to become involved. King Victor Amedee of Savoy commissioned a study of cretinism in the 1790s; Napoleon ordered a census in 1811; and King Charles Albert of Sardinia called the prototype of today's task force to study the problem (Keramidas, 1976). But the first major effort to control cretinism awaited the work of Guggenbuhl, a young physician who pledged himself to a "God-chosen" objective of full-time residential treatment of cretins. After two years of experimental work, he purchased in 1841 a tract of land "on the Abendberg near Interlachen, about four thousand feet above the level of the sea, (which) commanded a view of one of the finest landscapes in Switzerland" (Brockett, 1856, p. 74), a description that suggests an inordinantly different perspective by European society of some of its handicapped members than that which outraged Pinel and others at the end of the prior century. Guggenbuhl himself encountered poor health, traveled too much through Europe persuading others to open training schools, became the first director of a training school to be closed due to poor management (Keramidas, 1976), and died in disgrace; but his contributions to the treatment of retarded persons were exceptional: (1) his choice of a location of apparent charm rather than disgrace was important for bringing retarded persons to attractive residencies, (2) his propaganda greatly increased the rate at which training schools propagated in the United States and Europe, and (3) his combination of a special diet with special education methods of sensory training furthered the relatively peaceful coexistence of medicine and education during that period.

FROM SCHOOLS TO INSTITUTIONS

The period from 1850–1900 is probably considered by many readers to be better for the retarded than the preceding decades and considerably better than the two or three that followed it. But while it may have been for the immediate movement, it certainly was not when the influences on the future are considered. The first 40 years of the century contained little progress, but the leaders who would make a contribution in the next two decades were being educated. The sixth, seventh, and eighth decades contained progress in medical, social, and educational areas, but the leaders who would destroy the progress in the next decades were being educated. The last few years of the nineteenth century and the first quarter of the next century represent a shameful and shocking period whose influences are subtly present and still forceful. But, interestingly, the inhumaneness of that period prepared the anger and enthusiasm of today's leaders and the promise that we can have for the next critical decades.

Howe's goals when he opened the experimental wing of Perkins for retarded persons were to teach his pupils to be as self-sufficient as possible in three areas: (1) cleanliness and decency, (2) dressing, feeding, and ambulation, and (3) speech and reading (Kanner, 1964). These seem to be reasonable goals, all aimed toward teaching self-sufficiency for the community, not self-sufficiency for the residential school. Indeed, during this and the next two decades, residential programs were generally directed to community care rather than to life-long custodial care. Some set maximum time periods of residency; all anticipated the return of the client to the community; all were schools rather than custodial institutions (Stevens, 1976).

But there was an interesting combination brewing that seems to make the stated objective of release a "paper objective." The two sources of the combination were (1) society's general belief that retarded persons were immoral and incapable of sustained prudent judgment, and (2) the suspected relation of retardation, immoral behavior, and the natural laws of God. Howe expressed the temper of this belief quite eloquently:

> The moral to be drawn from the prevalent existence of idiocy in society is that a very large class of persons . . . sin in various ways; they disregard the conditions which should be observed in intermarriage; they overlook the hereditary transmission of certain morbid tendencies; or they pervert the natural appetites of the body into lusts of diverse kinds,—the natural emotions of the minds into fearful passions,—and thus bring down the awful consequences of their own ignorance and sin upon the heads of their unoffending children.
>
> It [idiocy] is not an accident; . . . it is merely the result of a violation of natural laws, . . . which, if strictly observed for two or three generations, would totally remove from any family, however strongly predisposed to insanity or idiocy, all possibility of its recurrence. (Howe, 1848, p. 34)

The control of behavior for "two or three generations" is the suggested solution to decreasing the incidence of mental retardation; and this is the suggestion of clearly one of the three or four most powerful persons in the field; it is not the isolated proposal of a radical unlikely to see his suggestions followed. Above all, it is a proposal simply incompatible with releasing persons society believed could neither control themselves nor be controlled.

The movement to support the growth of institutions has been chronicled by C. T. Wilbur, brother of H. B. Wilbur, and a supporter of institutions. Wilbur recalled in his writings of 1888 that:

> In 1848, two were organized in Massachusetts, one private and one public school; in 1851, the State Asylum of New York; in 1852, a private corporation in Penn-

sylvania; in 1857, the State Asylum in Ohio; in 1858, a private institution in Connecticut, which has since become a private corporation receiving state aid; in 1860, the State Asylum of Kentucky; in 1865, the State Asylum of Illinois; in 1868, the County Asylum on Randall's Island in New York Harbor; in 1870, a private school at Fayville, Massachusetts; in 1876, the Iowa State Asylum; in 1878, a State Asylum for females at Newark, New Jersey; in 1879, the Minnesota State Asylum, the school in Indiana, and Dr. Edward Seguin's private school in New York City; in 1881, the Kansas State Asylum; in 1882, one at Baldwinsville, Massachusetts; in 1883, a private school at Amherst, Massachusetts; in 1884, a State Asylum in California and private schools in Michigan and Maryland; in 1885, a State Asylum in Nebraska and a private institution in Brooklyn, New York. There are two institutions (a private one at Lyme, Connecticut and a public one at Orillia, Ontario) whose date of establishment I am unable to give. Efforts have been made to establish public institutions in Michigan, Wisconsin, Colorado, Missouri, Texas, New Jersey, Delaware, Maryland, Virginia, and Georgia. (C. T. Wilbur, 1888, p. 296)

With a good deal of enthusiasm, Wilbur goes on to report that beyond the listed additions, many of the older establishments had increased the number of buildings so that by 1888 there were 4,000 "inmates," housed at a cost of $3 million for grounds and $800,000 per year for tuition, shelter, support, and maintenance. With this last reference to money, Wilbur identified one of the major reasons for the demise of schools and the conversion to custodial institutions, the latter requiring fewer staff and less costs than the schools required to educate. The economics converted the goals of the schools from teaching self-sufficiency outside the school in the community to teaching self-sufficiency inside the institution for the sake of the institution. Fernald, superintendent of the Massachusetts School for the Feeble-Minded from 1887 to 1924, expressed the change when he discussed a Pennsylvania institution where "the per capita cost for all the inmates has been reduced from $300 to a little over $100 per annum, largely from the fact that the work of caring for the low-grade children in the custodial department is done to a very large extent by the inmates themselves" (Fernald, 1893).

A second reason for the change from teaching schools to custodial institutions was that the institutions had simply failed in their efforts to teach the skills of self-independence necessary to cope in the community, and the state found maintaining persons within the institution cheaper than maintaining them in the community (Stevens, 1976). Fernald summarized this admission when he stated that:

where the lower-grade cases are received, . . . it is safe to say that not over 10 to 15 percent of our inmates can be made self-supporting in the sense of going out into the community and securing and retaining a situation and prudently spending their earnings. With all our training we cannot give our pupils that indispensable something known as good, plain "common sense." (Fernald, 1893)

A third factor in this movement was the foundation for segregation and eugenics, a foundation being created by several separate findings. Certainly one of the most famous was a paper in 1877 by R. L. Dugdale who described "hereditary pauperism as illustrated in the 'Juke' family," the "Jukes" being a pseudonym for a family in Ulster County, New York. The various papers Dugdale published on the subject described five generations of this family, totaling 709 persons, in which "crimes against society" were transmitted through family lines. Although only one of the 709 was certified as mentally retarded, public reaction was against the family and tended to equate poverty, asocial behavior, and mental retardation. The conclusion was that the transmission was hereditary, a conclusion not reached by Dugdale himself, who instead concluded that:

> [more information on members of the "Juke" family that moved from Ulster] would help settle which factor is most potent in forming human character, heredity or environment; and if both contribute, to what degree, and in what form, for we could make a comparison between those who have lived under continuous conditions in the old home and those who now live under altered circumstances in the new. I had hoped to make this addition, . . . but the study stands still; for how long it will continue to do so, I know not. (Dugdale, 1877, p. 282)

Dugdale's study continued to "stand still" for almost 60 years, until the "Iowa studies" and others of a like nature.

But the public did not remain still, and the concept that retardation was synonymous with social misfits *by nature* grew. Some of the separate contributions were (1) the theory of Benedict Morel, a French psychiatrist who proposed in 1853 that retardation was evolutionary regression and evolutionary degeneration (Jordan, 1972); (2) the conclusions of the 1854 study of the Worcester Mental Hospital of Massachusetts (a hospital that was failing because of its increasing size) that idiocy, insanity, and crime were highest among the poor, that the incidence was due to imperfectly organized brains, that Irish immigrants should be segregated, and that blacks were mentally inferior (Keramidas, 1976); (3) interpretations of Darwin's theory of evolution and Sir Francis Galton's study of individual differences. Galton's study in 1869 of the lineage of genius in royal families led to a conclusion that mental superiority was inherited. From that conclusion, an inference that mental deficiency was inheritable and hence inevitable was not difficult to support, and the means to prevent the inevitable is obvious and would be proposed shortly; and (4) the Victorian era of protection of the fit from the unfit, a movement that was reflected by an 1876 London meeting of mental retardation professionals who suggested that the mentally deficient be separated from society at a young age and that idiots were to be kept "quietly, safely, away from the world, living as angels in heaven, neither marrying nor given in marriage" (Keramidas, 1976). This solution was also supported in the United States by many, including M. W. Barr, who wrote the first American textbook on mental retardation: "I think we need to write it very large, in characters that he who runs may read, to convince the world that by permanent separation only is the imbecile to be safeguarded from certain deterioration and society from depredation, contamination, and increase of a pernicious element" (Barr, 1902, p. 101).

SOME SIGNIFICANT PROGRESSIONS

Despite the retreat from attempts to provide better living and teaching environments for the retarded, there were several advances in disparate areas. One of these advances was the continuing clarity in classifications and etiology. Although this movement has had little historically to offer those who teach retarded persons, it did lead to increasingly successful identification of syndromes and to remarkable medical intervention for such syndromes as phenylketonuria. Most classification statements around 1850 were unitary; i.e., all were classified as idiots. Seguin's descriptor that an idiot is one who "knows nothing, can do nothing, cannot even desire to do anything" (Howe, 1848, p. 37) reflects this classification quite well. Howe, while deferring attempts to "establish a scientific classification of idiots," does offer a descriptive account of those with whom he had worked—and, in reality, a classification schema that is no less useless programmatically than the present classification of profound, severe, moderate, and mild retardation—that is reflective of his era:

> [Pure] idiots of the lowest class are mere organisms, masses of flesh and bone in human shape, in which the brain and nervous system have no command over the system of voluntary muscles; and which consequently are without power of locomotion, without speech, without any manifestation of intellectual or affective faculties.
>
> Fools are a higher class of idiots, in whom the brain and nervous system are so far developed as to give partial command of the voluntary muscles; who have consequently considerable power of locomotion and animal action; partial development of the affective and intellectual faculties, but only the faintest glimmer of reason, and very imperfect speech.
>
> Simpletons (or imbeciles) are the highest class of idiots, in whom the harmony of the nervous and muscular system is nearly perfect; who consequently have normal powers of locomotion and animal action; considerable activity of the perceptive and affective faculties; and reason enough for their simple individual guidance, but not enough for their social relations. (Howe, 1848, p. 37)

Classification continued to be based either on observed behavioral and physiognomic differences or on presumed physiological differences, but the classification systems within the fields of mental deficiency and mental illness continued to make a clearer distinction between these two areas that were by the turn of the century to lead to two very separate areas of study. In 1866, when he began to discuss his discovery of a particular syndrome later to be labeled Down's syndrome, Langdown Down offered four classifications of idiocy, which were Caucasian, Ethiopian, Negroid, and Mongolian. Quickly realizing the mistake of a racially based classification system, Down issued another that was more attractive to his colleagues: (1) congenital idiocy, which included microcephaly and hydrocephaly; (2) developmental idiocy, which was a function of one's proclivity to mental breakdowns and to anxiety associated with such events as cutting teeth and puberty; and (3) accidental idiocy, which is caused by events like injuries and illnesses. Rather than a classification based on the behaviors of idiots, Down's system was an attempt to classify by etiology, i.e. to identify the causes of idiocy and to classify as such. This system was clearly an attempt to classify by "disease" and to make alterations through disease-prevention methods, a movement that became known as the medical model of treatment. Although several high-incidence or pronounced syndromes had been isolated and treated before, e.g., the first known attempt to treat hydrocephalus by tapping the ventricles is reported to have been done by a Dr. Conquest around 1830 (Jordan, 1972), the major breakthrough in understanding a medical syndrome occurred in the latter part of the century when Courneville introduced in 1880 the entity that has since come to be called tuberous sclerosis, and in 1881 when the American neurologist Sachs published studies of a disease now known as Tay-Sachs disease (Kanner, 1964). These advances began the pursuit of specific structural anomalies and marked the beginning of participation of the medical community as medical scientists rather than as teaching theorists (e.g., Itard & Seguin).

   Another significant advance during that period resulted from a meeting of medical officers on June 6, 1876, at which the Association of Medical Officers of American Institutions for Idiotic and Feeble-Minded Persons was formed. Electing Seguin as its first president, the association assured some distribution of information by publishing its proceedings and assured itself wider distribution and political influence by allowing membership to include persons who were not medical doctors. Later known as the American Association for the Study of the Feeble-Minded (1906) and the American Association of Mental Deficiency (1933 to the present), its discussion of research and issues through annual meetings, political and judicial activity, and publications (*American Journal of Mental Deficiency* and, more recently, *Mental Retardation*) has had continuing influence on the field.

   An interesting educational and social advance occurred with the advent of special classes in public-based schools. The retarded began to be educated rather than being held in custodial placements, and they were being educated in public rather than in wards from which the public was sheltered. Although special public schools and classes were not a new concept in this country, none for the retarded existed prior to the close of the century. Public instruction for the deaf began in 1869 in Boston, and public training of refractory and truant boys began in New York in 1874, in Cleveland in 1879, and in France and Prussia in 1879 (Wallin, 1924). After decades of use in France, Prussia, and England, public classes for the retarded began in the United States and helped address several problems, three of which were (1) the disruption of the family unit caused by institutionalization, (2) the lack of education of the mentally deficient caused by the change from educational to custodial treatment, and (3) the rising costs of institutions that were themselves growing rapidly both in number and size. The movement for special classes went from Europe to the United States in 1896, when a special class in Providence, Rhode Island, was begun for students who were said to be disciplinary problems and who were judged by a neurologist to be retarded (Keramidas, 1976). Although followed the next year by special classes in Springfield, Massachusetts, the success of the class in Providence was severely damaged when a newspaper reporter called it a "fools class" and suggested no one would want to be in it (Mainford & Love, 1973).

The Baltimore Plan, in 1898, divided children into groups judged normal, bright, and dull; the Batavia, New York, plan added a teacher to classrooms with slow learners; the Cambridge, Massachusetts, plan of a decade later divided children into average and gifted; while the Elizabeth, New Jersey, plan of the same period divided students in three or more sections. Even at the beginning, there were concerns for the flexibility and lack of stigma that special classes should afford; and these suggestions for a good special class program were later offered by Wallin (1924): (1) children with IQ scores of 65 or 70 should first be placed in the class for higher-grade pupils, and only after failing a trial of one or two years should they be placed in a special class (a suggestion that was, unfortunately, not consistently followed); (2) the class organization should be flexible, allowing students to move in both directions—from regular classes to special classes *and* from special classes to regular classes; (3) in all forms of classes, instruction should be individualized, and in special classes instruction should be centered on "concrete, practical activities"; and (4) the terms feeble-minded, mentally defective, imbecilic, and moronic should be dropped from use in the classes.

At the same time, special classes made their way into the university setting when, in 1896, the eminent psychologist Lightner Witmer began a special school at the University of Pennsylvania. Doll (1967) characterizes his study as including physical defects, aphasia, disturbed laterality, postencephalitic behavioral difficulties, as well as topics one finds today still in need of study—parental neglect and environmental deprivation. Witmer's work included two historical contributions generally unrecognized, one that was to have no direct effect and one that was. The former was his choice of the label "children with mental defects" rather than mentally defective children," a seemingly minor distinction, but in reality a very significant one that was not adopted until decades later by B. F. Skinner and his followers in their attempts not to label children but rather to focus on their behavioral deficits and surpluses.[2] The second contribution by Witmer was a lasting one, and that was the beginning of the union between universities and the field of mental retardation, a union that was solidified six decades later with public laws for teacher training, with research centers, and with university-affiliated facilities.

Another influence, frequently unrecognized because of disagreements with her teaching methods, was the work of Maria Montessori, who had served in the asylums for the mentally ill in Rome, studied the methods of Itard and Seguin, and opened in Rome the Orthophrenic School for the Cure of the Feeble-Minded. Two of Montessori's lasting contributions were her emphasis on well-trained, qualified teachers and her emphasis that mental retardation was an

---

[2] This distinction was verbalized eloquently by O. R. Lindsley (1964) with a simplicity that belied its implications: "Children are not retarded. Only their behavior in average environments is sometimes retarded. In fact, it is modern science's ability to design suitable environments for these children that is retarded. We design environments to maintain life, but not to maintain dignified behavior."

educational rather than a medical problem (Mainford & Love, 1973). Her demand for training is still the major problem for universities, many of which certify teachers but few of which graduate teachers with skills necessary for teaching environments; and her demand that mental retardation is an educational problem is still true and is still unsolved. The group of persons labeled mildly retarded, educable mentally retarded, or educable mentally handicapped form by far the majority of those called mentally retarded, and they do not have medically based disabilities. They also, however, often do not have adequate programs for their educational, vocational, social, and recreational needs. In the twentieth century, public fears of the retarded culminated and the eugenics movement began during a period characterized by Stevens (1976) as one in which "society demonstrated its true concern for the mentally retarded through public apathy, political interference, inadequate fiscal support, and by enacting specific laws and regulations disqualifying the mentally retarded from generic health and social services" (p. 4).

EUGENICS, OR THE PROFESSIONALS MOVE AGAINST THE RETARDED

There were many factors contributing to the eugenics alarm, and many seemed to come to fruition around 1900. The power of heredity was being felt as a theory for the first time in history by the masses. Galton's explanation of royal breeding leading to genius provided the suggestion that "inferior" breeding led to mental deficiency, and that only a cessation of breeding for certain classes would prevent deficiency. The situation was exacerbated when superintendent Kerlin of the Pennsylvania Training School, because of his belief that idiocy, mental illness, pauperism, and crime were generally synonymous, recommended that the retarded be detained for life and be prevented from marrying or multiplying (Rosen, Clark & Kivitz, 1976, Vol. 1).

Further support for the theory of hereditability came from misinterpretations of the work of Drs. Blin and Damaye in 1904 and of Alfred Binet, who was commissioned by the French Ministry of Public Instruction to organize special classes in public schools. Binet sought a means of determining which students would be best suited for academic programs and which would be best suited for self-care instruction. He issued with his co-worker the Binet-Simon Intelligence Test, which was translated by Goddard in 1910 and revised by Terman in 1916 as the Stanford-Binet. Although Binet supported the modifiability of intelligent quotients through environmental intervention, his work was seized by those who advocated eugenics and who cited it as support for the constancy of intelligence, a basis of the "once-retarded-always-retarded" syndrome and a necessary principle for a successful eugenics program.

Finally came the social-biological interpretations of retardation, and these seemed to have been the finishing touches for large numbers of Americans who had not previously been affected by low-circulation journal articles. In 1911, C. B. Davenport claimed that the children of two retarded persons would definitely be retarded, and that all defectives other than mongoloids were due either to a defective parent or to a parent with idiocy in their "germ plasma" (Mainford & Love, 1973). In 1915, Eastbrook reanalyzed Dugdale's study of the "Jukes," a study in which one of 709 persons was certified deficient, and concluded that half the "Jukes" were feeble-minded and that all the Juke criminals were feeble-minded. Thus what was considered by Dugdale 38 years earlier to be a study of social degeneracy became a study of mental deficiency (Rosen, Clark & Kivitz, 1976, Vol. 2). Goddard's *The Kallikak Family, a Study in the Heredity of Feeble-Mindedness* was the comparison of two groups of descendants of Martin Kallikak, a revolutionary war soldier. The first group, the progeny of an illegitimate child of Kallikak and a barmaid, was characterized as a group of thieves, prostitutes, and other "undesirables." The second group, the progeny of Kallikak and a woman with normal intelligence and higher social status, was characterized as a collection mostly of average persons but with some superior persons. The conclusion that genetics was the cause led Goddard to support the role of heredity in crime, guessing that 90% of intelligence was hereditary and that half the persons in prison were mentally deficient. Goddard's conclusion to the third chapter of his book summarizes the fervency of his belief:

> From this comparison [of Kallikak blood kept pure and of Kallikak blood contaminated by the nameless feeble-minded girl], the conclusion is inevitable that *all this degeneracy* [italics added] has come as a result of the defective mentality and bad blood having been brought into the normal family of good blood, first from the nameless feeble-minded girl and later by additional contaminations from other sources.

The eugenics movement was terrifying for its intensity and consequences. In 1897, Congress passed a sterilization bill. In 1902, the chief physician of the Pennsylvania Training School from 1893 to 1930, M. W. Barr, concluded that teaching coeducational classes resulted in excessive "nerve strain" and was useless; that those judged mentally and morally deficient should undergo "asexualization upon admission"; that we should "address ourselves to the task of weeding the garden of humanity from the tares [of the unimprovable imbecile] which a highly nervous age has sown broadcast. Not only weeding out, but garnering so safely that no untoward accident or chance may scatter seed that can produce only imperfection and ill," and that "an ideal spot might be found—either on one of the newly acquired islands, the unoccupied lands of the Atlantic seaboard, or the far West which, under proper regulations, could be made a true haven of irresponsibility, and deriving its population as it would from the trained workers from the institutions throughout the country, might become in time almost, if not entirely, self-sustaining" (from Rosen, Clark & Kivitz, 1976, Vol. 2, p. 103-104). In 1907, Indiana was the first state to pass sterilization laws, and by 1926, 23 states had passed such laws. In 1911, Lamborse discussed the proposition that criminals were born to be criminals and could be identified by "stigmata of degeneracy." The issue was extended, and alcoholism, tuberculosis, paralysis, and prostitution were all believed to be rooted in mental deficiency (Rosen, Clark & Kivitz, 1976, Vol. 2). In 1913, Fernald concluded that the "feeble-minded are a parasitic predatory class never capable of self-support or of managing their own affairs. They cause unutterable sorrow at home and are a menace and danger to the community. Feeble-minded women are almost invariably immoral and if at large usually become carriers of venereal disease or give birth to children who are as defective as themselves. . . . *Every feeble-minded person, especially the high grade* [italics added], is a potential criminal needing only the proper environment and opportunity for the development and expression of his criminal tendencies" (Rosen, Clark & Kivitz, 1976, Vol. 2, p. 145). Although Fernald's statement seems to be the rhetoric of the era, it is extraordinarily different from Barr's in one way; it included the high-grade defective that Barr excluded from sterilization and incarceration. The scare was increasing in its pervasiveness.

Fernald's exhortations were continued by some through the end of the next decade with the same intensity. In 1929, just before becoming the superintendent of the Elwyn Training School for 30 years, E. A. Whitney wrote that "eugenical sterilization is the only means whereby we may be sure of eliminating hereditary feeble-mindedness. However, at the present time there are only 23 states that have legalized eugenical sterilization. In these states, but about 7,000 sterilizations have been performed. We know that there are 656,000 avowed feeble-minded. The sterilization of all these should be our goal—a large order to be sure, but one well worth fulfilling" (Rosen, Clark & Kivitz, 1976, Vol. 2, p. 204). Whitney's plan solidified Fernald's earlier proposal, capturing an incredible 656,000 humans, arguing that high-grade defectives should be serilized to prevent propagation and that low-grade deficients should be sterilized *to eliminate obscene habits.*

The eugenics movement in this country—led not by persons disassociated from the field of retardation, arguing against costs, drain on resource pools, etc., but rather led by the professionals in whose care the retarded were placed by society presumably for humane care and treatment—resulted in (1) more and larger institutions directed toward custodial care, (2) restrictive immigration laws directed toward protecting our society from the increasing numbers of foreign "inferior stock" (20,000,000 immigrants had come to the United States between 1890 and 1930), and (3) the sterilization movement and laws. But sterilization could be considered ineffective in that it only prevented progeny and, thus, only affected the drain on the next generations of society. A more direct solution was proposed in 1933; simply exterminate the retarded now so that the effect will be felt by the present generation; and with the Act for the Prevention of Hereditary Diseased Offspring, Nazi Germany did just that. Designed for the sterilization and "mercy killing" of mental defectives, physically deformed, and incurables, the act resulted in the death of 100,000 persons and yet remains curiously unannounced (Rosen, Clark & Kivitz, 1976, Vol. 1).

While there were many supporters of the eugenics movement, there were some dissidents. Wallin reviewed the research supporting the concept that every feeble-minded child is a potential criminal and argued that the studies' diagnostic and sampling methods and, hence, conclusions, were inaccurate. S. P. Davies supported Wallin's summary, citing overgeneralizations by Goddard and inaccurate conclusions from the prison studies. Davies discussed alternative means of social control and advocated colonies, parole systems, and community programs instead of sterilization and institutionalization, the latter being viewed as appropriate only for a small number (Rosen, Clark & Kivitz, 1976, Vol. 1). The antieugenics group also received support from a convert—Fernald, himself. In his 1919 study of 646 persons discharged over a 25-year period from the State

School at Waverly, Massachusetts, Fernald found to his surprise that more than half had made a successful adjustment and presented no threat to the community. Finding that studies showed that more than half the residents at Wrentham State School and Letchworth Village had parents who were not mentally retarded, he admitted his prior excesses and argued against the "twin ogres of heredity and criminality" in his 1924 presidential address to the American Association for the Study of the Feeble-Minded.

Overshadowed by the eugenics movement were other developments during the period. Public day school classes increased rapidly from 1915 through 1930, and by 1920 there were 200 classes in this country (Stevens, 1976). The trend slowed, however, during the next decade, and by 1940 there were probably fewer special classes than in 1930. Public education continued to receive some support through mandatory education legislation in New Jersey in 1911. The acceptance of public education continued to gain acceptance in several states, with legislation also being passed in Minnesota in 1915; in New York in 1917; in Illinois, Missouri, Pennsylvania, Massachusetts, and Wyoming in 1919; and in California and Connecticut in 1921; so by 1952 all states except Nevada and Montana had passed mandatory or permissive legislation for the education of mentally retarded persons (L'Abate & Curtis, 1975).

The concept of work-related activities rather than, or in some cases in addition to, academic-related training continued to be supported. In 1882, Stewart began what Doll (1967) calls the first mature vocational program. The Kentucky institution trained women in the afternoon for whole trades, or for useful labor, or for specific limited job operations, the program selection being a function of the women's capabilities. The colony program, promoted as a solution to overcrowding in and excessive costs of the institutions, continued to be in vogue, and the successes and difficulties of beginning a farm colony are journaled by Fernald (1903). The Birmingham Plan of England, begun in 1916, advocated part-time training on the job under school-based supervision, and it was soon adopted in the United States (Doll, 1967). Specific, detailed analysis of the job, and hence training objectives, was promoted by Buhl in 1928 and is the precursor of today's task analysis. Buhl's curriculum for the retarded was divided into self-help, occupational, physical and mental development, and recreation. These were further divided into activities and specific tasks numbering about 500, and each was further divided into the number of steps necessary to complete each task (Doll, 1967).

While an academic program for the retarded was being further delineated following the suggestions of Seguin and other early workers, academicians were becoming increasingly interested in studying problems associated with the retarded through developing scientific methodology. The Vineland Training School, directed by E. R. Johnstone, became a serious center of research and propaganda for the field when the "Feeble-minded Club" developed into a research laboratory under Goddard, whose list of publications was extensive. Following Goddard's resignation, the tradition of excellence was continued by the appointments of S. D. Porteus, developer of the Porteus Maze Test, in 1919 and E. A. Doll, developer of the Vineland Social Maturity Scale, in 1925. Excellence in research was continued by a group at the Child Welfare Research Station and the Institution for Feeble-Minded Children at Glenwood, Iowa. Known for its very unpopular challenge of Goddard's assertion that intelligence is at most minimally modifiable, the group included H. M. Skeels, H. B. Dye, B. Wellman, and M. Skodak, all of whom became quite well known for their work. The most important study was that published by Skeels and Dye (1939), which followed a group of children transferred from an orphanage nursery to a school for the feeble-minded with a resulting increase in IQ scores. The question and the effect of the answer was put quite well by the authors:

> If, on the one hand, intelligence is static, a fixed entity and relatively unmodifiable by changes in environmental impact, then changes in living conditions and amount and kind of education can be expected to have little influence on the mental level of individuals. On the other hand, if intelligence shows change in relation to shifts in environmental influence, then our concept must include modifiability, and the implications for child welfare become more challenging. (p. 114)

The Iowa group, of course, chose the latter option and education once again became an important concept for the retarded. The third group of researchers assembled at the Wayne County Training Center in Northville, Michigan, under the leadership of the center's superintendent, R. H. Haskell. Making significant contributions at the center was an extraordinary group of individuals that included S. A. Kirk, N. C. Kephart, B. McCandless, A. A. Strauss, T. Hegge, H. Werner, M. H. Ainsworth, Z. P. Hoakley, and S. W. Bijou.

The question of the scope and role of institutions continued to be asked, but the answer came rather adventitiously to the movement itself. When America entered World War I, a group intelligence test had been designed, and its final organization and proofreading were being done at the Training School at Vineland. The test was to determine those who should not be taken to Europe on the presumption that they would not adjust well. Administered in two forms— Alpha, the language test, and Beta, the nonlanguage test—the army tests found enormous numbers of young men with low mental age scores, and hence IQ's, who still functioned well. The numbers of these people who would be considered retarded by Terman's 1916 criteria of less than a score of 79 on the Stanford-Binet was far too large to allow institutionalization, and their suitable adaptation to their environments precluded the necessity of institutionalization. During this period, Davies (1925) reviewed the functions of institutions historically in this country, concluding that they were (1) initially, as boarding schools that were a branch of the public school system, a link in a chain of common schools, (2) then, a focus of custodial care, and (3) after the enormity of the mental deficiency problem was revealed by the army tests, a center of social rehabilitation, designed to return persons to the community.

A PAUSE IN MOVEMENTS

Davies continued his opposition to a large-scale institutionalization program for the nation, arguing that special classes should take precedence over institutions because (1) there is no substitute for the love and individual attention that is available in good, average home care, (2) institutions are at best an artificial environment, and (3) expecting taxpayers of states to support such costs is unreasonable. Davies's remarks, published in 1925, are interesting historically: his second reason is the basis for judging environments put forth by the normalization movement four and five decades later, and his third reason presaged the next two decades.

The fervor of the incarceration movement was lessening but that, by itself, would not have been sufficient to bring such a rapid decrease in expansion, for institutions and buildings are funded and commissioned by legislatures five and ten years before they open. But, the Depression brought a sudden decline in mental-health programs and plans for progress. Funding programs for relatively few disadvantaged persons could simply no longer be a priority when a relatively large number of persons had become economically disadvantaged. The general lack of excitement on a wide, not individualistic or small group, basis continued through the next decade and was supported, of course, by World War II. Again, state and/or federal monies were simply not available for programs affecting a small minority, who were, in addition, disadvantaged, two reasons generally hard to overcome in arguments for progress.

A RETURN TO AWARENESS

A few events in the 1930s and 1940s, although not garnering large public support, gave some basis for the movements in the next three decades to define and then protect the rights of retarded persons. In 1934, Fôlling discovered that phenylketonuria was a metabolic disorder and, in so doing, provided a model for studying biochemical causes of a hereditary nature. Credited by the medical doctor and historian Kanner as "one of the great discoveries in medical history" (Kanner, 1964), Folling's work also contributed hope that some forms of mental retardation might be arrested and even cured if identified within various critical periods. In addition, although not traditionally credited with doing so, his work may have begun to define a role for medical doctors as experts in medicine through their specified training, rather than as experts in special forms of education. Other contributions were educational or social in nature, and these included the continued work on environmentally modified intelligence, the work of Kirk on early childhood education as a force to combat retardation associated with poverty, and programs directed by Franklin Roosevelt to combat poverty—certainly not programs to combat retardation, but at least a federal recognition of the disadvantages an environment of poverty would produce.

Then, at the beginning of the next decade, two sources of information developed and became very important in promoting interest in mental retardation. One influence was a report released in 1953 by Ginzberg and Bray that 716,000 men were rejected from service in World War II because their scores on entrance examinations resulted in a classification of mental deficiency. The authors further emphasized the relation between poverty and retardation, and the public was made aware of the incidence and the pervasiveness of mental retardation. A second influence, one that has been enduring and that has been perhaps the single most important force for establishing the rights of mentally retarded persons, was the formation of the National Association for Retarded Children (now the National Association for Retarded Citizens, NARC).

Established in Minneapolis, in 1950, by 42 parents, the association expanded rapidly into other states so that within 15 years the membership exceeded 100,000. The effect of this group in generating legislative support in this formative decade was considerable (Boggs, 1971), and its success in marshaling wide public support has been unequaled. Its eminent success was continued in the next decade, one in which it met a president genuinely and personally interested in the retarded, and one in which it was joined by another organization in effecting considerable impact on national legislation (Boggs, 1971). Although the Council for Exceptional Children (CEC) has a longer history, its Division on Mental Retardation (CEC-MR) was not established until 1963. Adroitly located near Washington, D.C., CEC has had considerable success in the legislative area, but its goals go beyond that single one, with the MR section having as its purposes

> the education and welfare of the mentally retarded, research in the education of the mentally retarded, competency of education in this field, public understanding of mental retardation, and legislation needed to help accomplish these goals; to encourage and promote professional growth, research, and the dissemination and utilization of research findings. (CEC, 1963)

Although there are many other organizations working for retarded persons (e.g., American Psychological Association, American Medical Association), NARC, AAMD, and CEC have become three powerful groups clearly and immediately identified with improving conditions for retarded persons.

SOME RECENT FACTORS

Public concern for the retarded has been considerable since 1950, and our present era represents the second such development of widespread public attention, the first such development being focused on eugenics. Although there are many contributions to the present *zeitgeist*, six are of interest to this discussion: (1) attention to the incidence of retardation and its social consequences, (2) the role of John F. Kennedy, (3) congressional action, (4) civil rights, (5) the normalization movement, and (6) the effect of behavioral principles on programming for the retarded.

Incidence and Consequences of Retardation

Attention to the retarded has been in various forms. The report that about half the men tested during World War I had mental age scores of less than 12 years was certainly astonishing, but many interpreted this finding correctly as a statement that adaptive behavior was more important than intelligence test scores in classifying a person as mentally retarded. Others interpreted this as a condemnation of the present validity of intelligence tests. Still others interpreted the results as an indication that the number of intellectually disadvantaged persons was far greater than anticipated; some of these advocated an inhumane solution, while others proposed a humane educative solution. The report that 716,000 men were rejected from World War II because of mental deficiency restated the problem as a significant one. The concept of adaptive behaviors was still germane, but intelligence tests were in vogue and attacking their validity was not. The only conclusion available, that there were many persons in this country with intellectual deficits, could not be denied and apparently aided the legislative successes of these decades. Active campaigns attempted to relate to the public the incidence of mental retardation in numerical and relative terms. While the incidence of retardation is certainly debated (Tarjan, Wright, Eyman & Keeran, 1973), the public has generally been told that 3% of our population could at some time in their lives be so classified. The present argument for attention and funding has been expressed by Mainford and Love (1973) when they state that "there are twice as many mentally retarded cases than there are of blindness, polio, cerebral palsy, and rheumatic heart disease combined. Only four disabling conditions have a higher incidence: arthritis, cancer, cardiac disease, and mental illness" (p. 24).

Influence of Kennedy

Individualized reports and reactions have also been important, and the report that one of President Kennedy's sisters was retarded has been the most important in demonstrating the pervasiveness of retardation. The continued support from the Kennedy family has been important in many aspects, and the outrage of Robert Kennedy upon his visit in 1965 to several state institutions gained considerable publicity. Additional outrage was presented graphically by Blatt and Kaplan in *Christmas in Purgatory*, which was distributed free to leaders of the parent movement in mental retardation, prominent legislators, commissioners of mental health, and university professors. Discussing his visits to state institutions during the filmings by Kaplan with a hidden camera, Blatt (1976) recalls that

> as I entered the dormitory, . . . it was the sickening, suffocating smell of feces and urine, decay, dirt, and filth, of such strength as to hang in the air and, I thought then and am still not dissuaded, solid enough to be cut or shoveled away. But as things turned out, the odors were among the gentlest assaults on my sensibilities. I was soon to learn about the decaying humanity that caused them. . . . In every institution I visited, with the exception of The Seaside, I found incredible overcrowding. Beds are so arranged—side by side and head to head—that it is impossible, in some dormitories, to cross parts of the rooms without actually walking over beds; oftentimes the beds are without pillows. I have seen mattresses so sagged by the weight of the bodies that they were scraping the floor. . . . In some checking that I have done recently, I learned that in our better zoos, the larger animals require a higher per capita expenditure [than do persons in many state institutions]. (p. 350-351)

The work by Blatt was continued a few years later by Geraldo Rivera, who similarly presented a pictorial essay of conditions (Rivera, 1972), but who shocked the usually placid television audiences with pictures in his television program of the conditions at the Willowbrook Institution in New York.

The actions of John Kennedy as president were also singularly significant. Shortly after he assumed office, the Joint Commission on Mental Illness and Health, a five-year effort funded under the Mental Health Study Act of 1955, gave its final report, a report that only incidentally discussed the problems of mental retardation. Apparently urged by his sister Eunice Kennedy Shriver, President Kennedy assembled a 27-member President's Panel on Mental Retardation in October of 1961, and presented the following opening address:

> The manner in which our Nation cares for its citizens and conserves its manpower resources is more than an index to its concern for its less fortunate. It is a key to its future. Both wisdom and humanity dictate a deep interest in the physically handicapped, the mentally ill, and the mentally retarded. Yet, although we have made considerable progress in the treatment of physical handicaps, although we have attacked on a broad front the problems of mental illness, although we have made great strides in the battle against disease, we as a nation have for too long postponed an intensive search for solutions to the problems of the mentally retarded. That failure should be corrected. (Boggs, 1971, p. 113)

Congressional Action

Congressional activity has also become more concerned with the retarded recently, although there have been many historical contributions in associated areas. Boggs (1971) reviewed some of the congressional activities relative to retarded persons and noted the suppressive effects of the Depression and World War II, although there were some developments during these periods. The Social Security Act of 1935 provided federal grants-in-aid to states for maternal and child health and welfare and services to crippled children. The National Mental Health Acts of 1946 and 1950 created the National Institute of Mental Health (NIMH) and the National Institute of Neurological Diseases and Blindness (NINDB), both of which began sponsoring activities in mental retardation. The Vocational Rehabilitation Act, amended during World War II to include mentally handicapped persons, provided funds and continues to do so while, through additional amendments, broadening its coverage of the retarded.

In the late 1950s, congressional action began to provide increased funding for various efforts directed toward the handicapped. In the Cooperative Research Act of 1957 (Public Law 83-531), Congress provided $675,000 to support research related to the education of handicapped children. In the next year, Public Law 85-926 recognized that relatively few professionals were dedicated to research or to training, and it provided aid to universities and colleges to prepare teachers and leaders in mental retardation. Public Law 88-164, passed in 1963, extended Public Law 85-926 to include all handicapped children. An expansive law, it has had seven amendments, one of which was Edward Kennedy's amendment, which provided funds for training personnel in physical education and recreation. The next Congress passed several bills related to retardation. Passed as the first amendment to Public Law 88-164, Public Law 89-105 provided for an increase and extension of the funding authorizations, including the construction and support of facilities for research and support for research and related purposes. Public-Law 89-10, the Elementary and Secondary Education Act, declared that, for the purposes of the bill, mentally retarded and other handicapped children would be considered educationally disadvantaged and eligible for programming funds. Public Law 89-97, the Medicare bill, increased benefits and the number of persons eligible for payments. Public Law 89-313 amended the Elementary and Secondary Education Act and included among the disadvantaged who are eligible for project aid those who are school-aged and who live either in state residential institutions or in state-supported private schools. Public Law 89-333 also dealt in part with housing, as it authorized construction of community residences for retarded adults undergoing rehabilitation. A vocational rehabilitation bill, it also increased the varieties of improvements and expansions of sheltered workshops for training and long-term employment and funded technical consultation, construction funds, training stipends, and initial staffing.

Returning to research, the next Congress passed Public Laws 90-170 and 90-247. The former expanded the original research authorization to include support of research and related activities in physical education, recreation, and the training of leadership personnel, supervisors, and researchers for the handicapped, while the latter authorized entrance into contracts to conduct research, surveys, or demonstrations. That Congress also passed Public Law 90-576, which authorized awarding grants to agencies in addition to states, colleges, and universities. Two years later, in 1970, Public Law 91-230 amended the Elementary and Secondary Act and reinforced the federal commitment to the preparation of personnel to educate handicapped children. Public Law 93-380 continued the increased emphasis by authorizing higher levels of aid to the states, but is perhaps more singular for beginning to protect the rights of handicapped children. The bill specified due process requirements to protect the rights of handicapped children, supported the principle of placing a child in the least restrictive educational environment, and required the states to have as a goal educational services to handicapped children and to state how and when a state expects to achieve that goal. The next year, 1975, Congress reacted to the *zeitgeist* set by the courts and passed Public Law 94-142, the Education for All Handicapped Children Act, calling for a massive expansion of the authorized levels of basic state grants, perhaps to an annual budget of $3 billion by 1982. This bill is unlike others in that it has no expiration date, being regarded instead as a permanent instrument, and in that it established the proposition that education must be extended to handicapped persons as their fundamental right. This law may be the most powerful legislation ever to affect handicapped persons. It deplores the lack of services for handicapped persons and addresses these needs in many areas, including (1) free special education services to all handicapped persons, (2) free related services (including speech pathology and audiology, psychological services, and medical diagnoses and evaluations), (3) free appropriate public education, and (4) a written individualized education plan specifically stating the goals for each student. If the intent of this law is met, a real revolution in the extensiveness of services for mentally retarded persons could take place.[4]

Rights

In some cases during this last decade, Congress was reinforcing the decisions within another branch of government, the judicial, that have changed the treatment of the retarded in a way that should be irrevocable. Truly landmark decisions have been made in the areas of rights to treatment (*Wyatt* v. *Stickney*), to education (*Pennsylvania Association for Retarded Children* v. *Pennsylvania*), to freedom from peonage (*Souder* v. *Brennan*), to freedom from cruel and unusual punishment (*Horacek* v. *Exon*), and to protection from deterioration (*New York State Association for Retarded Children* v. *Rockefeller*). Many other products of the common law system have either established or indicated the prior existence of rights of persons in mental health systems. But the rights suggested by the various decisions and by nonjudicial presumptions have been summarized by the President's Committee on Mental Retardation (1976) and provide an understanding of current legal, civil rights, and habilitation progress. The committee adopted several basic premises and based their statement of rights upon these; these premises are that

> retarded persons have the same rights, legal and constitutional, as every other United States citizen, including the rights of due process and equal protection of the laws; retarded persons can be more independent and can function more competently and responsibly than is commonly believed; and full citizenship exercised by a retarded person in a community setting is possible and is in the public interest. (p. 58)

Based upon these premises, the rights can be summarized as follows:

(a) Right to equal access to quality health and social services adapted to the individual's needs.
(b) Right to residential programs and other services in the setting most conducive to development and independence, to a least restrictive living environment, and to individual habilitation programs.
(c) Right to educational opportunities, including free public education without age limitations, periodic review of individualized goals, and due process.
(d) Right to equal employment opportunity, including job training and freedom from architectual barriers in buildings and transportation systems.
(e) Right to marry and bear children.
(f) Right to equal protection in the criminal justice system, including qualified counsel with sufficient background in mental retardation, individually determined levels of responsibility, and rehabilitation.
(g) Right to vote.

Normalization

Interwoven within the arguments for basic rights, decisions of common law, and directives of public law is the concept of normalization, which

> refers to a cluster of ideas, methods, and experiences expressed in practical work for the mentally retarded in the Scandinavian countries, as well as in some other parts of the world . . . and means making available to the mentally retarded patterns and

conditions of everyday life which are as close as possible to the norms and patterns of the mainstream of society. (Nirje, 1969, p. 363)

Central to the concept of normalization is the thesis, expressed in Section 1 of the 1968 Swedish law on mental retardation, that mental retardation is not necessarily a life-long condition, and that with special training one can manage to live in the community without continued care and specialized services. Nirje (1969), in one of his several explanations of this principle, listed eight components of normalization that are particularly relevant to the abnormal living conditions within institutions, a seeming anachronism that in 1976 still housed 176,000 citizens (Stevens, 1976); these components are as follows:

(a) A normal rhythm of the day, with a normal time to go to bed and to get up, eating many meals in a family-size group, and some access to solitude.

(b) A normal routine of life, with schooling in one place, residency in another, and recreation in several others.

(c) A normal rhythm of the year, with holidays and family days of personal significance.

(d) An opportunity to undergo normal patterns of developmental periods within a life cycle. Children should have a warm atmosphere, with rich sensory stimulation and settings of proper proportions. Youths should live in a world structured for them and learn significant social experiences outside the classroom; mentally retarded youths should never live in a confined setting along with mentally retarded adults, because experiences should be gained through interaction with a normal society. Growing from adolescence to adulthood should be accompanied with significant environmental changes, and with an opportunity to develop attitudes toward oneself and others unrestricted by the same environment from year to year.

(e) Choices and wishes of the mentally retarded should be taken into consideration and respected.

(f) Freedom to live in a bisexual world.

(g) Freedom to operate under normal economic standards, such as child allowances, personal pensions, old-age allowances, or minimum wages.

(h) Right to live in facilities that have the same standards as other facilities in the rest of society.

Normalization will certainly continue to have major effects on programming, living alternatives, etc., but it has already had many effects, some of which are (1) fostering programs to depopulate institutions, (2) helping redefine admission and release criteria, (3) encouraging integration of residential programs into the community, (4) increasing short-term respite care, (5) improving health, education, and social services, (6) increasing interaction with universities, and (7) facilitating use of institutional staff as consultants for the community (Stevens, 1976).

Effects of Behaviorism

Another recent influence on the field of mental retardation has been the intervention of a science of behavior in applied settings, that being the theory of behaviorism alternately called behavior modification or applied behavior analysis. With many principles, it introduced the seemingly obvious and simple concept that conditions antecedent to and subsequent to behavior would affect the likelihood that the behavior would recur. Through careful analyses of these effects, behaviorists have moved from the laboratory to applied situations and, with particular relish, to the field of mental retardation. Today, there are programs for all levels of self-help training, for language, for various academic objectives, for decreasing aberrant behaviors, for increasing social behaviors, for implementing systems of accountability, and for an inordinate number of other objectives, some of which will be discussed throughout the ensuing chapters.

SOME DEFINITIONS OF MENTAL RETARDATION

But before we discuss applied behavior analysis in an historical and then a present, detailed fashion in the following chapters, we will discuss definitions of the subject of our inquiry—mental retardation. There are, of course, many definitions of mental retardation; after all, anyone publishing an article has some license to proffer one, and many of those who write a book on mental retardation seem to find the offer of a new definition to be a requisite. We may find some of the historical definitions interesting and expectantly quaint, indigenous to the past century. For example, Brockett (1856) repeated Seguin's description of an idiot as "an individual who knows nothing, can do nothing, and wishes nothing; and every idiot approaches more or less to this maximum of incapacity," and then decided that "we should define idiocy as the result of an infirmity of the body which prevents, to a greater or less extent, the development of the physical, moral, and intellectual powers" (p. 78).

These definitions were perhaps not "sophisticated" in that they did not connect numbers, which generally bring an aura of fact, of certainty, of science, to the definitions. Terman took care of this omission in 1916 when he classified persons as retarded based upon their scores on the adaptation of the Binet-Simon intelligence test. People were retarded if they scored 79 or less and were called borderline, morons, imbeciles, or idiots depending upon their score ranges. Not an idea to die easily, this classification schema was repeated by Wechsler in 1958 with score ranges appropriate to his own intelligence test. Even AAMD, with its apparent care not to classify persons as retarded solely on the basis of intelligence test scores, labels persons as profoundly retarded solely on the basis of a score of less than 20 on the Stanford-Binet, and continues by labeling others as severely, moderately, or mildly retarded if they have scored 20 to 35, 36 to 51, or 52 to 67 on this test.

During the first half of the present century, other definitions were as important as the test-score definitions but were with different bases. Two of these were by Tredgold and Doll, the former's being that amentia is "a state of incomplete mental development of such a kind and degree that the individual is incapable of adapting himself to the normal environment of his fellows in such a way as to maintain existence independently of supervision, control or external support" (Tredgold, 1937, p. 4). Influenced by England's Mental Deficiency Act of 1913, Tredgold eschewed the reliance on intelligence test scores as the sole criterion for defining mental deficiency and referred to some persons with intelligence test scores of 90 to 100 as mentally defective and others with scores below 70 as not defective (Sarason, 1949). But there was also an American who strongly opposed the intelligence quotient approach, and that was Doll, who argued that

> it employs an illogical and unvalidated statistical concept without safeguarding the welfare of the individual, his family, or society . . . . It stops short at an arbitrary statistical gate-post and does not concern itself with the many ramifications of the conditions which if adequately explored would reveal the absurdity of its point of view. (Doll, 1947, p. 42)

Doll (1941) offered instead a definition that, like Tredgold's, was directed more toward one's adaptation to his environment. Doll considered six statements to be essential to an adequate definition: "(a) social incompetence, (b) due to mental subnormality, (c) what has been developmentally arrested, (d) which obtains at maturity, (e) is of constitutional origin, and (f) is essentially incurable" (Doll, 1941, p. 215). Doll developed the Vineland Social Maturity Scale to make the definition of social incompetence more explicit, valid, and consistent. Giving evidence of motor, social, and linguistic aspects of development, the scale forces the clinician to consider what the person does every day in his environment, rather than just his performance on an intelligence test. But Tredgold's definition has been criticized for not offering a valid way of differentiating defectives from nondefectives and for not offering an explicit definition of "normal environment," and Doll's definition has been criticized because low test scores cannot lead to the conclusion that they are a function of constitutional origin, essentially incurable, and obtaining at maturity (Sarason, 1949).

In 1957, AAMD, as part of the Project on Technical Planning in Mental Retardation, began to develop a manual on definition and classification terminology. It resulted in a definition, generally credited to Heber, that emphasized a score on an intelligence test, repeated Doll's inclusion of an age criterion, adopted the concept of adaptive behavior, and read "mental retardation refers to subaverage intellectual functioning which originates during the developmental period and is associated with impairment in one or more of the following: (a) maturation, (b) learning, and (c) social adjustment." This definition, with the phrase "subaverage intellectual functioning," included those who, in addition to meeting the age and adaptive behavior criteria, scored between 68 and 83 on the revised Stanford-Binet. The incorporation of this group, as borderline retarded, raised considerable objections from many individuals and organizations in the United States, as well as objections from two committees of the World Health Organization's Mental Health Unit. The major complaint was that most of these persons functioned well enough in their environment not to be discredited by a label of mental retardation, and that with those individuals not functioning well enough, the dysfunction was not due solely to their intellectual levels. Finally, responding to the criticism, AAMD produced another "Manual on Terminology and Classification in Mental Retardation" (Grossman, 1973), and in doing so offered another definition: "mental retardation refers to significantly subaverage general intellectual functioning existing concurrently with deficits in adaptive behavior, and manifested during the developmental period." This definition lowered the upper limit of retardation to a score of 67 on the Stanford-Binet and 69 on the Wechsler by adding the word "significantly," extended the development period from 16 to 18, and strengthened the association of concurrent deficits in adaptive behavior. The manual goes on to provide examples of areas of adaptive behaviors at different age levels, and several attempts to produce standardized measures of adaptive behavior have been offered.

AAMD's definition has been quite influential, and most current definitions from individuals and from organizations either explicitly or implicitly include a reference to intelligence test scores, to adaptive behavior, and to age of onset. There are several, however, who disagree with it. Clausen (1967, 1972) has argued that there are no adequate measures of adaptive behavior, so using it in the definition of mental retardation brings a great deal of subjectivity to the area. He suggests instead that IQ test scores alone be used in the definition of mental retardation. Mercer (1971, 1973a, b) agrees that there are no good measures of adaptive behaviors for mildly retarded persons, but she has adopted an alternative approach. She has developed a sociological model in which a person is considered retarded if he or she has failed to meet the expectations that society has developed for the role that person has. So, although two people have the same scores on an IQ test, only one may be labeled retarded because only he has failed in his role in his society. Another exception to the AAMD definition is the behavioral definition of Bijou (1966), who uses the term developmental retardation instead of mental retardation or mental deficiency in order to stress the philosophy that it is a person's behaviors, both surpluses and deficits, that cause him or her to be called retarded. Bijou suggests

> that developmental retardation be treated as observable, objectively defined stimulus-response relationships without recourse to hypothetical mental concepts such as "defective intelligence" and to hypothetical biological abnormalities such as "clinically inferred brain injury." *From this point of view, a retarded individual is one who has a limited repertory of behavior shaped by events that constitute his history.* (p. 2)

Bijou finds that the principles of development are the same for normal and for "deviant" individuals, and he calls for research in retardation to analyze those observable conditions that produce retarded behavior.

Bijou's definition is that which we shall follow in this book because it is isomorphic with the basis tenet of behaviorism, i.e., that behavior is lawful. This statement means (1) that there are principles discovered and still remaining to be discovered that explain why behavior occurs, (2) that behavior can be understood in the context of its relationship to the environment, and (3) that we, as psychologists, educators, therapists, social workers, and so forth, have only the environment at our disposal to effect *planned* educative changes in retarded behavior, so we should learn how environments can best be arranged to enhance learning performance. Before providing a discussion of how one can plan those changes, we shall describe applied behavior analysis in a manner that will certainly be extended in the ensuing chapters, but in a manner that may allow the reader to determine why certain directions are provided in the first few chapters. This description will be in two sections: What Is Applied Behavior Analysis? and A Brief History of Applied Behavior Analysis.

REFERENCES

Barr, M. W. [The imperative call of our present to our future.] In M. Rosen, G. R. Clark & M. S. Kivitz (Eds.), *The history of mental retardation* (Vol. 2). Baltimore: University Park Press, 1976. [Reprinted from *Journal of Psycho-Asthenics*, 1902, 7(1), 5-8.]

Benda, C. E. Psychopathology of childhood. In C. Mussen (Ed.), *Manual of child psychology* (2nd ed.). New York: John Wiley & Sons, Inc., 1954.

Bijou, S. W. A functional analysis of retarded development. In N. R. Ellis (Ed.), *International review of research in mental retardation* (Vol. 1). New York: Academic Press, Inc., 1966.

Blatt, B. Purgatory. In M. Rosen, G. R. Clark & M. S. Kivitz (Eds.), *The history of mental retardation* (Vol. 2). Baltimore: University Park Press, 1976.

Boggs, E. M. Federal legislation: 1955-1965. In J. Wortis, M. D. (Ed.), *Mental retardation* (Vol. 3), 1971.

Boggs, E. M. Federal legislation: Conclusion. In J. Wortis, M. D. (Ed.), *Mental retardation* (Vol. 4), 1972.

Brockett, L. P. [Idiots and the efforts for their improvement.] In M. Rosen, G. R. Clark & M. S. Kivitz (Eds.), *The history of mental retardation* (Vol. 1). Baltimore: University Park Press, 1976. (Reprinted from *American Journal of Education*, 1856.)

Bronowski, J. *The ascent of man.* Boston: Little, Brown and Co., 1973.

Chin, P. C., Drew, C. J., & Logan, D. R. *Mental retardation: A life cycle approach.* St. Louis: C. V. Mosby Co., 1975.

Clausen, J. A. Mental deficiency: Development of a concept. *American Journal of Mental Deficiency*, 1967, **71**, 727-745.

Clausen, J. A. Quo Vadis, AAMD? *Journal of Special Education*, 1972, 6, 51-60.

Davies, S. P. The institution in relation to the school system. *Journal of Psycho-Asthenics*, 1925, 30, 210-226.

Descartes, R. Meditations on first philosophy. In D. J. Bronstein, Y. H. Krikorian & P. P. Weiner (Eds.), *Basic problems of philosophy* (2nd ed.) Englewood Cliffs, NJ: Prentice-Hall, Inc., 1955.

Doll, E. A. The essentials of an inclusive concept of mental deficiency. *American Journal of Mental Deficiency*, 1941, 46, 214-219.

Doll, E. A. Is mental deficiency curable? *American Journal of Mental Deficiency*, 1947, **51**, 420-428.

Doll, E. A. Trends and problems in the education of the mentally retarded: 1800-1940, *American Journal of Mental Deficiency*, 1967, **72**, 175-183.

Dugdale, R. L. [Hereditary pauperism as illustrated in the "Juke" family.] In M. Rosen, G. R. Clark & M. S. Kivitz (Eds.), *The history of mental retardation* (Vol. 1). Baltimore: University Park Press, 1976. (Reprinted from Proceedings of Conference of Charatics, 1877, 81-95.)

Education and Training of the Mentally Retarded. Reston, VA: Division on Mental Retardation, The Council for Exceptional Children, 1966-present.

Fernald, W. E. Description of American institutions, 1893. In M. Rosen, G. R. Clark & M. S. Kivitz (Eds.), *The history of mental retardation*. Baltimore: University Park Press, 1976.

Fernald, W. E. Farm colony in Massachusetts. *Journal of Psycho-Asthenics*, 1903, 7, 74-80.

Grossman, H. J. (Ed.) *Manual on terminology and classification in mental retardation*. Washington, D.C.: American Association on Mental Deficiency, 1973.

Horacek v. Exon, 375 F. Supp. 71 (Nebraska); U.S. District Court, D. Nebraska, 1973.

Howe, S. G. [Report of commission to inquire into the conditions of idiots of the Commonwealth of Massachusetts.] In M. Rosen, G. R. Clark & M. S. Kivitz (Eds.), *The history of mental retardation* (Vol. 1). Baltimore: University Park Press, 1976. (Reprinted in Senate Document No. 51, 1848, 1-37.)

Ireland, W. W. *On idiocy and imbecility*. London: J. & A. Churchill Ltd., 1877.

Jordan, T. E. *The mentally retarded* (3rd ed.). Columbus, OH: Charles E. Merrill Publishing Co., 1972.

Kanner, L. A. *A history of the care and study of the mentally retarded*. Springfield, IL: Charles C Thomas, Publisher, 1964.

Kaufman, J. M., & Payne, J. S. (Eds.) *Mental retardation: Introduction and personal perspectives*. Columbus, OH: Charles E. Merrill Publishing Co., 1975.

Keramidas, C. *Mental retardation: A cultural concept*. Washington D.C.: American Association on Mental Deficiency, 1976.

Kolstoe, O. P., & Frey, R. M. *A high school work study program for mentally subnormal students*. Carbondale, IL: Southern Illinois University Press, 1965.

L'Abate, L., & Curtis, L. T. *Teaching the exceptional child*. Philadelphia: W. B. Saunders Co., 1975.

Lindsley, O. R. Direct measurement and prothesis of retarded children. *Journal of Education*, 1964, 147, 62-81.

Mainford, J. C., & Love, H. D. *Teaching educable mentally retarded children*. Springfield, IL: Charles C Thomas, Publisher, 1973.

McCulloch, T. L. Reformulation of the problem of mental deficiency. *American Journal of Mental Deficiency*, 1947, 52, 139.

Mercer, J. R. The meaning of mental retardation. In R. Koch & J. C. Dobson (Eds.), *The mentally retarded child and his family: A multidisciplinary handbook*, pp. 23-46. New York: Brunner/Mazel, Inc., 1971.

Mercer, J. R. *Labeling the mentally retarded*. Berkeley: University of California Press, 1973a.

Mercer, J. R. The myth of 3% prevalence. In R. K. Eyman, C. E. Meyers & G. Tarjan (Eds.), Sociobehavioral studies in mental retardation. *Monographs of the American Association on Mental Deficiency*, No. 1 1973b.

New York State Association for Retarded Children v. Rockefeller, 357 F. Supp. 752 (E.D.N.Y., 1973).

Nirje, B. The normalization principle and its human management implications. In M. Rosen, G. R. Clark & M. S. Kivitz (Eds.), *The history of mental retardation* (Vol. 2). Baltimore: University Park Press, 1976. [Reprinted from R. B. Kugel and W. Wolfensberger (Eds.), *Changing patterns in residential services for the mentally retarded*. Washington, D.C.: President's Committee on Mental Retardation, 1969.]

Pennsylvania Association for Retarded Children v. Pennsylvania, 334 F. Supp. 1257 (E.D. Pa. 1971); 343 F. Supp. 279 (E.D. Pa. 1972).

President's Committee on Mental Retardation. *Mental retardation: Century of decision.* Washington, D.C.: U.S. Government Printing Office, 1976.

Rivera, G. *Willowbrook: A report on how it is and why it doesn't have to be that way.* New York: Random House, Inc., 1972.

Rosen, M., Clark, G. R., & Kivitz, M. S. (Eds.), *The history of mental retardation* (Vols. 1 and 2). Baltimore: University Park Press, 1976.

Sarason, S. B. *Psychological problems in mental deficiency.* New York: Harper & Row, Publishers, Inc., 1949.

Skeels, H. M., & Dye, H. B. A study of the effects of differential stimulation on mentally retarded children. *Journal of Psycho-Asthenics,* 1939, **29,** 166-182.

Souder v. Brennan, 42 U.S.L.W. 2271 (D.D.C., 1973); 367 F. Supp. 808 (D.F.C., 1973).

Stevens, H. A. *Residential services for the mentally retarded in the U.S.A.: A historical perspective.* Washington, D.C.: American Association on Mental Deficiency, 1976.

Tarjan, G., Wright, S. W., Eyman, R. K., & Keeran, C. V. Natural history of mental retardation: Some aspects of epidemiology. *American Journal of Mental Deficiency,* 1973, **77,** 369-379.

Tredgold, A. F. *A textbook of mental deficiency* (6th ed.). Baltimore: William Wood & Co., 1937.

Wallin, J. E. W. Classification of mentally deficient and retarded children for instruction. *Journal of Psycho-Asthenics,* 1924, **29,** 166-182.

Wilbur, C. T. Institutions for the feeble-minded, 1888. In M. Rosen, G. R. Clark & M. Kivitz (Eds.), *The history of mental retardation* (Vol. 1). Baltimore: University Park Press, 1976.

Wilbur, H. E. Eulogy to Edouard Seguin: Remarks by Dr. H. B. Wilbur, Oct. 31, 1880. In M. Rosen, G. R. Clark & M. S. Kivitz (Eds.), *The history of mental retardation* (Vol. 1). Baltimore: University Park Press, 1976.

Wolfensberger, W. [The origin and nature of our institutional models.] Syracuse, NY: Human Policy Press, 1975. (Originally published, 1968.)

Wyatt v. Stickney, 344 F. Supp. 373 343 F. Supp. 387 (M.D. Ala. 1972) aff'd *sub nom. Wyatt v. Aderholt,* 503 F. 2d 1305 (5th Cir. 1974).

CHAPTER

2

History of
Applied Behavior Analysis

In the last chapter, we concentrated on the concept of mental retardation in an historical and in a present context. In this chapter, we shall concentrate on two areas. The first, What Is Applied Behavior Analysis?, is an introduction to the approach on which this book is based. In it, you will be offered a working definition of applied behavior analysis (ABA), as well as various characteristics of this approach, the latter being offered to provide you an introductory overview of the ensuing chapters. The second area of this chapter is a brief and selective historical account of the entry ABA into the field of mental retardation. This section should indicate to you, the youth of this area of inquiry, that we are neophytes in the technology of improving retarded behavior, and that there are still enough time and unanswered (or unasked) questions for you to make significant contributions to our efforts to improve the living conditions and response repertoires of those we are servicing.

WHAT IS APPLIED BEHAVIOR ANALYSIS?

There are a large number of names for the systems that use principles of learning in applied settings. Day (1974) refers to some of these as "Skinnerism, behavioral technology, operant conditioning, behavior modification, behavior training, contingency management, programmed instruction, accountability, performance-based instruction, and competency-based instruction"; to this list, one may readily add precision teaching, behavior therapy, and applied behavior analysis. In this book, we use the term applied behavior analysis for three reasons: (1) it is a term that is consistently used today to describe the approach presented here, (2) it is a term that, unlike many others, is infrequently used to describe practices other than those which the field itself uses, and (3) it is the term adopted by the Society for the Experimental Analysis of Behavior in its publication, the *Journal of Applied Behavior Analysis*, the leading publication of articles solely related to the methodology presented in this book.

Applied behavior analysis is primarily a system by which one asks a question and attempts to answer it through the use of numbers. While there is basically only one guideline to presenting the question, that it be asked objectively, there are many guidelines to the way in which the questions can be answered. Other areas of psychology, education, sociology, etc., may choose to answer the questions differently, and that choice is fine. As a result, these studies do not meet the criteria necessary to be labeled examples of ABA, and that consequence is fine to all concerned. But some areas of those and other disciplines answer questions according to these guidelines, so they provide examples of applied behavior analysis in their fields. Before those guidelines are discussed under Characteristics of Applied Behavior Analysis, some of the basic concepts of this approach are presented.

Some Basic Concepts in Applied Behavior Analysis

While the roots of applied behaviorism can be traced to Watson, Pavlov, Thorndike and others in experimental psychology at the beginning of this century, certainly the most influential and important person in this field has been B. F. Skinner. In a monumental series of books (1938, 1948, 1953, 1958, 1961, 1968, 1969, 1973), he has argued for a laboratory analysis of behavior radically separated from the dominant methodology in psychology through the first 60 years of the century. He has then applied his methodology to a variety of topics, most of which concern an analysis of ways by which one can improve oneself and one's society. Certainly, with the thousands of pages he has written, Skinner has continued through the years to develop basic premises through his judgments, suggestions, and guidelines in answering questions we ask about how behavior can be improved. However, throughout all these books is a basic approach to psychology that was offered in *Science and Human Behavior* (1953), a book that presented his rationale for interpreting human behavior and his fundamental assumptions for the field that evolved as applied behavior analysis. In this and in ensuing treatises, Skinner presented above all a faith in science and a faith that humanity can learn to use science for its betterment. His characterization of science in this book and throughout the others has been that science (1) is an organized accumulation of information, (2) develops and refines particular instruments for research, (3) argues for precise measurements, (4) obtains a set of attitudes that includes both a propensity for facts rather than opinions and wishes and a willingness to withhold judgments until the facts are analyzed, (5) searches for order and for relations among events, and (6) is an attempt to systematize collected facts.

The scientific portion of psychology embodies these activities and separates itself from other sciences in its subject for study, which is typically said to be the prediction and control of behavior. Skinner's approach is separated from the rest of psychology by the assumptions it makes about behavior and by the manner in which it seeks to learn how to predict behavior. While both will be presented throughout this book, the basic assumptions will be presented here, prior to the introduction of ABA.

Skinner, along with the rest of psychology, has chosen to study two types of events and has classified these as dependent and independent variables. In our work, dependent variables are behaviors; independent variables are environmental events which sometimes include behaviors of other persons. In this schema, the dependent variable is said to *depend* upon the independent variable; i.e., behavior depends upon, or is a function of, the environment.[1] This is the fundamental assumption of Skinner's behaviorism, which today seems so "unremarkable" that one would hardly expect arguments about it; but this assumption has nevertheless generalized a number of criticisms. Some persons view it as an argument against heredity—but it is not; some view it as an argument against humanity—but it is not, being instead an argument for a more human humanity. Given the first assumption that behavior is a function of the environment, the second assumption is that we should deal with behavior in its present context. Behaviorists assume that behavior is a function of (1) the immediate environment, (2) the past environment, and (3) genetic contributions. In the applied analysis of behavior, we do not study the origin of genetic contributions—that study remains for physiologists, medical doctors, histologists, geneticists, and so forth.[2] In addition, we do not dwell on the historical environment. We might question what events contributed to the present behavior and whether these events are continuing; or we might question the interpretation a person has of past events, the way he or she talks about those events, and the way the person's interpretation affects present behavior; but, unlike several forms of psychotherapy, we do not *dwell* on the historical environment. We dwell, instead, on the present environment and how it can be arranged to promote and maintain appropriate, healthy, and adaptive behaviors.

In this analysis of the interaction of the environment and behavior, Skinner has defined three classes of events: (1) the *response*, which describes a single occurrence of behavior, (2) *antecedent stimuli*, which describe those events that affect responding and that antecede the response, and (3) *subsequent stimuli* or *consequences*, which describe those events that affect responding and are subsequent to the response. Although much of the research and programming in ABA has focused on arranging subsequent events, all the temporal relations of stimuli

---

[1] For example, let's consider my behavior of "dressing to go for a 20-minute walk." Today, the sky is brilliant and the sun is direct, there is only a breeze, and the temperature is 15°C. Through my behavior in my past environment with the same conditions, I might wear my lightweight jacket, lightweight pants, etc., and be quite comfortable; my present behavior is then appropriate to my present environment. On the other hand, the temperatures last month were often -35°C and the winds were often 25 mph. Through my past experiences with that type of environment, I dressed considerably differently than I would today. I dressed according to the environment present on those days, and my behavior was a function of that environment.

[2] For example, if we are faced with a child shown to have trisomy 21, we are not concerned with altering his genes, that is impossible and is not our area of study. We are not concerned with learning how to prevent trisomy 21; again, that is simply not in our domain of study and should be left to those whose expertise is in this area. We are, however, concerned with why he does not tie his shoes, or why he does not correctly add 1 + 1, or why he does not interact with his peers; those are all behaviors, and they can be studied as a function of the child's environment.

to responding are important and have been called by Skinner the "three-term contingency," i.e., the interrelation of antecedent stimuli, the response, and the consequences of responding. To all of us in this field, teaching is the proper arrangement of antecedent and subsequent stimuli. As Skinner has said,

> teaching is the arrangement of contingencies . . . under which students learn. They learn without teaching in their natural environments, but teachers arrange special contingencies which expedite learning, either hastening the appearance of behavior which would otherwise be acquired slowly or making sure of the appearance of behavior which otherwise might never have occurred. (1968, pp. 64-65)

Some Definitions of Behavior Modification

Because behavior modification has historically been the most used term, we present those definitions rather than definitions of ABA to offer some background for what those in the field define as their area of study. Early definitions related behavior modification primarily to clinical treatment and are characterized by those offered by Watson (1962) and by Ullmann and Krasner (1965). Watson referred to it as a system which "includes many different techniques, all broadly related to the field of learning, but learning with a particular intent, namely clinical treatment and change" (1962, p. 19). In their timely presentation of case histories and short studies, Ullmann and Krasner referred to it as an "explicit, systematic application of learning concepts to achieve a particular behavior goal selected at the start of the treatment" (1965, p. 37). These definitions rested on the assumption that behavior itself is neutral; i.e., it is neither bad nor good in and of itself. Whatever it is to be called is simply determined by society. A second assumption was that most behavior, whether maladaptive or adaptive, is learned and is subject to particular laws of learning. As the field began to move from a relatively restricted analysis of either therapy-based or treatment-based situations to include nontherapeutic situations such as camps, public schools, and universities, the definition became more pervasive and is characterized by those offered by (1) Sulzer and Mayer (1972), who considered it to be in use "when the methods of behavioral science and its experimental findings are systematically applied with the intent of altering behavior" (p. 2), and (2) Thompson and Grabowski (1972), who labeled it "the systematic application of conditioning principles to the improvement of human behavior" (p. 8).

Brown, Wienckowski, and Stolz (1976) provide more extensive definitions and differentiate between behavior influence and behavior modification. The former occurs whenever one person exerts some degree of control over another in such situations as schools, advertising, and child rearing. The latter they consider to be "a special form of behavior influence that involves primarily the application of principles derived from research to experimental psychology to alleviate human suffering and human functioning" (p. 1). The authors go on to write that it "involves the systematic variation of behavioral and environmental factors thought to be associated with an individual's difficulties, with the primary goal of modifying his behavior in the direction that, ideally, he himself (or his agent) has chosen" (p. 4) . . . [and that it] . . . "specifically excludes psychosurgery, electroconvulsive therapy, and the administration of drugs independent of any specific behavior of the person receiving the medication" (p. 3). Brown, Wienckowski, and Stolz continue that it refers to "procedures that are based on the explicit and systematic application of principles and technology derived from research in experimental psychology, procedures that involve some change in the social or environmental context of a person's behavior" (p. 3).

The Relation of the Definitions of Applied Behavior Analysis to Mental Retardation

Although the definitions of ABA vary slightly, they are generally quite similar and are all based on the importance of carefully arranging events antecedent or subsequent to responding in order to maximize the effects of programs. Earlier in this chapter, several definitions of mental retardation were cited, and, although they presumably discussed the same subject, they differed considerably. Perhaps the most deviant of those was offered by Bijou (1966), who argued (1) that "a retarded individual is one who has a limited repertory of behavior shaped by events that constitute his history" (p. 2), (2) that we should concentrate on altering behaviors we label retarded, and (3) that we should examine the observable conditions that produce retarded behaviors. In summary, Bijou states that "in our view, retarded behavior is a function of observable social, physical, and biological conditions, all with the status of independent variables" (p. 3).

While important to psychology and education for varying reasons, Bijou's definition is important to the study of mental retardation for two reasons. The first is that it is the only definition that addresses the problem with a solution. If behavior (the dependent variable) is a function of environmental conditions (the independent variable), then retarded behavior can be improved through careful manipulations of antecedent and subsequent events. This is the crux of the behavioral approach to mental retardation, and the belief in this basic assumption, an assumption supported literally by thousands of demonstrations, is the reason behaviorists are so fanatical in their investigations of the conditions under which responding occurs. Compare Bijou's definition with that offered by AAMD: "mental retardation refers to significantly subaverage general intellectual functioning existing concurrently with deficits in adaptive behavior, and manifested during the developmental period" (Grossman, 1973). Does AAMD's definition suggest a model for improving intellectual functioning? Does it suggest a means to improve adaptive behavior? Does it suggest anything you can do to alter the age of onset? A second important aspect of Bijou's definition is that it presumes that all learned behavior, whether it be adaptive or maladaptive, is developed and maintained by the same principles of learning. This approach means that a person we call retarded *is* a human being, that he or she learns according to the same rules by which we learn—perhaps more slowly, but by the same rules. The behavioral approach argues strongly against other approaches that hold the retarded incapable of learning or capable of learning only according to principles other than those by which you and I learn—other approaches that do not view the retarded in this context as a human being.

Because we assume that the principles of learning apply to all of us, all the principles from research with nonretarded populations can be applied to retarded populations. The responsibility of those who write journal articles, books, etc., is to provide reliable information in a very objective manner; our responsibility is to be well read and to apply what we read to our work.

Read the applied articles from *Mental Retardation*, suitable articles from the *Journal of Applied Behavior Analysis, Behavior Therapy, Behavior Research and Therapy, Behavior Modification, Applied Research in Mental Retardation*, the applied articles that occasionally appear in the *American Journal of Mental Retardation*, and selected articles from the many other psychology and education journals; read books on the topic (they really are not all the same, and each may contribute something you previously had not read); and attend lectures from courses in applied behavior analysis. If your school does not have more than one course but does have different lecturers, repeat the course, or repeat it at another university; you may be astounded at the differences in the quality and quantity of information presented to you by different professors. In the life of retarded persons, in their learning to respond in ways that will allow them not to be called retarded, you are the independent variable, and the degree to which you are an effective independent variable is a function of your own learning behavior.

Some Characteristics of Applied Behavior Analysis

In this book, we consider ABA to be an educational and evaluative system based on principles of learning and characterized by the following: (1) Programs in which diagnosis of the presenting problem, analysis of the data, and the treatment are *individualized*. Treatment is not prescribed for a specific etiological group, e.g., "dyslexics," "brain damaged," or "retarded"; rather, programs are implemented according to the characteristics and behaviors of the individual and according to the total environment of the individual, including such considerations as parents, school, home environment.

(2) A definition of the presenting problem in terms that allow *direct observation and measurement*. For example, aggression in a classroom could be initially defined as throwing objects; hitting, biting, kicking, or pinching others; tearing papers; spitting; and knocking over furniture. Then, if two observers who were given these lists did not agree that responding was occurring, each term would be more fully explained through a number of sentences, clarifying the definition of the response.

(3) Direct observation that occurs *in the setting* in which the behavior is defined. An indirect approach such as an interview or a standardized test is not used unless "verbalizations in an interview" or "correct responding on the WISC" is the behavior in question. In the preceding example, the child's aggressive behavior would not be measured on and/or inferred from a Rorschach or any other psychological test. It would be measured in the classroom and any other portion of the natural environment in which observation was appropriate.

(4) Behavioral measurement in a *continuous* manner. For example, instead of assessing the effectiveness of a special reading program by testing a child today and four months later on the Wide Range Achievement Test, one would measure the child's performance each day during the reading program (and perhaps many of the ensuing days to measure the continuing effect of the

program). When inventories[3] are used, they should be employed as auxiliary information and they should be used as frequently as is administratively possible.

(5) *Data* that are presented *in numerical form* directly related to the behavior in question. We would not report that the aggressive child "harbored hostile feelings toward siblings and displaced them toward other members of his class." Instead, we would report that on Monday the child emitted 3, 8, 2, 2, 0, 1, 6, and 9 of each of the following responses by throwing objects; hitting, biting, kicking, or pinching others; tearing papers; spitting; and knocking over furniture, respectively. Summary statements could be made, but they would still be in numerical form; e.g., Charles averaged 4, 7, 2, 5, 1, 4, 3, and 6 responses per hour for each of the eight behavioral classifications during the two-week baseline period; or Charles's eight aggressive behaviors reduced 25, 75, 8, 12, 37, 62, 31, and 52% during the period in which the teacher praised his good behavior.

(6) An emphasis on *individual* rather than on group *analysis of the effectiveness of programs.* Traditional experimental design has employed "group" as opposed to "single-subject"[4] designs. Although there are many variants of the group design, a basic educational one has been to implement a special program for an experimental group and to make no changes in the program for a control group. Increases in appropriate behavior, decreases in inappropriate behavior, etc., are then compared between the two groups. The behavioral approach does not follow this design, but rather chooses to allow each child to respond under the control condition that was occurring before intervention and then to allow each child to respond under the special program. Certainly there are variations to this design, but most ABA designs compare a person's progress under both the regular and the special conditions and then present data on each individual's progress.[5]

(7) An *introduction of independent variables,* like a special reading program, in *a systematic manner* that allows us to believe that the independent variables caused the reported effect. To approach credulity, ABA typically uses one of the four designs (all of which will be explained in Chapter 6): reversal, multiple baseline, multielement, or changing criterion.

(8) A *continuing assessment* of the reliability of measurement of the dependent variable *that allow us to be relatively certain* that the behavior did change as a result of the program. Called interobserver agreement, this assessment requires two people to measure or record responding and reports the extent to which they agree on the occurrence of responding. If they do not, then the behavior is not said to be reliably measured, and changes in responding are not attributed to the independent variables.

(9) An explanation of the independent variables and the manner in which they are used that *allows someone else* to *repeat* the procedure in exactly the

---

[3] Discussed in Chapter 6.

[4] Discussed in Chapter 6.

[5] Occasionally, a group rather than an individual will be studied because of the nature of the problem. However, the "spirit" of the design remains the same as the group is studied under varying conditions. For example, Schnelle, Kirchner, McNees, and Lawler (1975) measured the crime reported to Nashville police when police patrols did not walk and did walk the areas in which the residents' calls to police were being counted. In this case, the community experienced *both* the regular (did not walk) and the special (did walk) conditions.

same way if she or he so chooses. While this statement is true for all experimental work, the necessity for clear, nontechnical reports of procedures is more important in ABA than in many other fields. Most published research in psychology, education, etc., is published for a peer audience of academicians who have developed particular research skills and vocabularies. Research in ABA should be, but is not always, written for the consumer of importance who regularly works with the population described. In our case, those persons would be teachers, direct-care staff, aides, nurses, recreation therapists, music educators, etc., and others who work with retarded persons.

(10) The work is *applied*. Whether or not it is applied is determined by society, by its interest in and perceived importance of the problem. A primary question is "how immediately important is this behavior or these stimuli to this person?" (Baer, Wolf & Risley, 1968). Whether or not the behavior is socially significant is one of the factors separating basic research (called The Experimental Analysis of Behavior, TEAB, when it is in the Skinnerian paradigm) from applied research (ABA when in the Skinnerian paradigm).

(11) An effort to develop *conceptual systems*. As ABA is based on principles of learning, results of studies should be discussed in terms of principles. For example, we should not just present the steps in moving from one color discrimination to another for a child; we should discuss the principle of *fading* as it applied to the problem in general. If we did not, we would be developing only a cookbook approach, one lacking generality (Baer, Wolf & Risley, 1968).

These are some of the basic tendencies for the approach called applied behavior analysis. As we progress through this book, we will find many examples of these tendencies or characterizations. But before those examples are presented, a brief discussion of the history of this approach as it relates to mental retardates will be presented.

HISTORY OF APPLIED BEHAVIOR ANALYSIS IN MENTAL RETARDATION

Some Historical Roots

Historically, there are, of course, countless examples of persons attempting to influence the behavior of handicapped persons, and some of these have adopted philosophies similar to that held by those associated with operant learning theory. When Pinel introduced the concept of moral treatment, he argued that the insane are not animals to be chained, but rather that they are humans who when treated normally would respond normally. In this approach, Pinel presaged the behavioral philosophy that most behavior, whether we call it adaptive or maladaptive, is learned, and that some behaviors can be altered by changes in the environment. In his work, Pinel was contending that the behaviors of those called insane were animalistic when the persons were treated like animals, and that the behaviors were human when the persons were treated like humans. Other workers used teaching methods that were later to be included among the principles of operant conditioning. For example, when Itard taught Victor to spell *lait* (milk), he arranged antecedent events in a particular way by pointing to the board with the word *lait*, by pronouncing it, and by asking him to respond. When Victor responded correctly, Itard consequated his behavior with a particular subsequent event—milk (MacMillan, 1973). Seguin continued Itard's work, but arranged antecedent events more carefully by breaking some complex tasks into their more easily learned components. While neither these men nor their colleagues can be considered behaviorists, they did employ what psychologists later found to be consistent rules (i.e., principles) of learning. Like so many others in this and in various other fields, they considered the approaches that might reasonably work, selected from those the single approach which seemed most reasonable, and applied it. Applying principles of learning certainly did not have to await the late 1800s, when psychology, the science that studied behavior, was formed; the application of principles was simply less frequent and less systematic than it now is.

In the first half of this century, several theories of learning were developed that were intended to explain considerable portions, if not all, of behavior. Pavlov developed a model of neurophysiology designed to study learning in a manner that is called classical conditioning. J. B. Watson adopted this model, attempted to explain all of human behavior, and began the school of "radical behaviorism." In the 1950s, Wolpe, Lazarus, and Eysenck popularized the systematic and extensive application of classical conditioning to clinical problems and developed that branch of behavior modification known as behavior therapy.

While Pavlov, Watson, and others were concerned with the effect on behavior of stimuli antecedent to a response, Thorndike was concerned about the effect of stimuli occurring subsequent to a response. When he found that consequences affected behavior, he described the relation as the "law of effect." Two decades later, Skinner began his prolific and long-term study of the effects of behavioral consequences, agreeing essentially with the concept of a "law of effect" but disagreeing substantially with the methodology of Thorndike and all other experimental psychologists. Beginning early in the development of behavioral psychology was the predilection to study behavior as it occurs in relation to a trial (e.g., the number of trials necessary for an animal to run ten consecutive times through the correct portions of a maze). But Skinner objected to this approach, because he believed that it did not correctly describe the manner in which one learns. He turned instead to what he called the "free operant" approach in which the laboratory animal is left free to respond in the experimental chamber. This approach was considered quite radical and was opposed by a large majority of experimental psychologists for several decades. It has, however, become a standard procedure today, and Skinner's perseverance is quite important to our study of applied behavior analysis. A basic premise in this branch of psychology has been that we should develop methodology and principles on infrahumans; in essence, to err is human, but one should not err on humans. The methodology and principles, once established, are then transferred to applied situations and to human problems, and this overall intent is exactly the manner in which we have learned to develop social behaviors as reinforcers for asocial persons, or to analyze a dressing task so that a profoundly retarded youngster can be aided in learning self-help skills, or the many other techniques we shall discuss. If Skinner had not argued for the "free operant" approach, we would not have developed the understanding of human behavior that we have today, for very little of our behavior is similar to the trial paradigm. If we could only go to the store when someone freed us to do so and could not go at any other time, then our behavior could be studied through the trial paradigm. But this is not the case; we could go if a friend asked us, or after we read two more pages of a magazine, or right now, or tomorrow. In the vast majority of our experiences, we have had the choice of whether or not to behave, and our choice has not been predictated.

While Skinner was continuing to develop his arguments for the analysis of relations between environmental events and behavior, a very simple but interesting study began the conjoining of operant behaviorism and retardation. Fuller (1949) sought to determine whether the operant methodology could be used to teach an essentially inactive 18-year-old labeled a "vegetative idiot" to move. Fuller's description provides some understanding of the problem: the boy weighed 30 pounds a year earlier, and, at the time of the study, "he lay on his back and could not roll over; he could, however, open his mouth, blink, and move his arms, head, and shoulders to a slight extent. He never moved his trunk or legs . . . . He had been fed liquids and semi-solids all his life. While being fed, he sometimes choked and would cough vigorously" (p. 587). Fuller arranged a syringe filled with a warm sugar-milk solution that could provide small amounts for the boy to drink, and used this as a consequence for a discrete response— lifting his right arm while not appreciably moving his head or shoulders. For 20 minutes, the syringe was placed next to the youth but not operated. Fuller counted the number of right-arm movements and found they occurred less than once per minute. The syringe was then made operable for four sessions, the solution was delivered when he moved his right arm, and the behavior inceased in rate to more than three times per minute. The author then made the syringe inoperable, and the behavioral rate decreased. The experiment was short; it was simple; but it did clearly demonstrate that a profoundly retarded child, whom the attending physician described as incapable of learning anything, could rapidly be taught a discrete response.

Unfortunately, the implications for a systematic extension of this work to applied situations with retarded persons was ignored for the next decade while the operant methodology continued to be explored and refined in the laboratory, with the primary examples being Ferster and Skinner's *Schedules of Reinforcement* (1957), a monumental summary of work in the Harvard laboratory, and the *Journal of the Experimental Analysis of Behavior* (1958), a large journal devoted solely to operant studies. In the 1950s, however, there was a continuing discussion about the operant analysis of children's behavior in laboratory situations (e.g., Bijou, 1955, 1957a, b; 1958a, b; Bijou & Sturges, 1959). The late 1950s and the early 1960s saw little application of behavioral principles to the practical problems of retarded persons, although the Experimental Class at the Ranier School in Buckley, Washington, was established in 1961. This group studied the relationship between antecedent events and academic responding, developing the Ranier Reading Program while relying heavily on programmed instruction (Bijou, Birnbrauer, Kidder & Tague, 1966; Birnbrauer, Bijou, Wolf & Kidder,

1965; Birnbrauer, Kidder & Tague, 1964). This group also studied the relation of subsequent events to responding and was among the first to publish results of token studies with the retarded (Birnbrauer & Lawler, 1964; Birnbrauer, Wolf, Kidder & Tague, 1965). However, the majority of the operant work with retarded persons at that time was laboratory based, and was either a direct or a systematic replication of the basic research with infrahumans according to the methods developed by Skinner and his associates and articulated by Sidman (1960).

Illustrative[6] of that period is the work of Ellis, Barnett, and Pryor (1960) and Orlando and Bijou (1960), who replicated laboratory experiments by studying the behavior of retarded people who were reinforced according to elementary schedules of reinforcement presented in the manner described by Ferster and Skinner (1957). Further studies by Barrett and Lindsley (1962) and Orlando (1961) indicated that retarded persons would apportion their responses to experimental conditions in the same manner as the laboratory animals had in earlier studies. As a result of this work, a major premise of Skinner, that relations between behavior and environmental events would hold across phylogenetic orders, was being firmly supported. The application of the principles to problem situations then began to be discussed more fully.

Almost all the research performed in the later 1950s and early 1960s was basic laboratory experimentation, and it has been distinguished from later applied research in that its primary intent was not the direct solution of behavioral problems characteristic to the retarded persons that were employed as subjects (see Baer, Wolf & Risley, 1968, for an elaboration of this distinction). Rather, the purpose of this early research was to extend the basic principles which had been derived from Skinner's initial experiments with animals (1938) and, more recently, from his work with Ferster (Ferster & Skinner, 1957) to the area of human behavior. Thus, the early research was crucial in establishing a solid base for conceptualizing the behavior of retardates as operant in nature, and for laying the methodological groundwork for the later application of operant procedures to the problems of retardation.

A Beginning to Systematic Research

In 1963, Bijou urged researchers to investigate the observable or potentially observable conditions that may produce retarded behavior. In this and a subsequent paper published in 1966, he suggested a functional analysis approach to the study of retardation. Such an approach would take into account the biological, physical, and social interactions of an organism with its environment, and would empirically investigate the effects of the following variables on behavioral development: (1) abnormal anatomical structure and physiological functioning, (2) inadequate reinforcement and discrimination histories (including extinction), (3) contingent aversive stimulation, and (4) reinforcement of aversive behavior.

---

[6] Extensive reviews of this literature are offered by Spradlin and Girardeau (1966) and by Watson and Lawson (1966).

Lindsley (1964) made a more radical proposal. He contended that it was not "children" who were retarded; rather, it was our ability to provide environments in which these children could behave effectively. Thus, he called for the development of procedures and environments which would increase the control functions that should be performed by discriminative stimuli, reduce the effort and probability of error for responding, and increase the probability of correct responding through the use of reinforcement contingencies. In this way, Lindsley concluded, exceptional children will behave efficiently and with full human dignity. It is now apparent that Bijou and Lindsley accurately reflected the outlook of many of their contemporary operant conditioners working in the area of retardation, for it was that period which marked the explosive beginnings of applied research.

Self-Help Skills. A majority of the early applications investigated the extent to which retarded persons could be taught various self-help behaviors, or what are now usually called "activities of daily living." In 1963, Ellis developed a theoretical analysis and a model program for toilet training, and subsequent studies demonstrated that various (though not necessarily all) aspects of toileting could be shaped using a variety of operant approaches (e.g., Baumeister & Klosowski, 1965; Dayan, 1964; Giles & Wolf, 1966). Self-feeding procedures were developed not only to increase the incidence of appropriate eating (Spradlin, 1964; Zeiler & Jervey, 1968), but also to reduce disruptive mealtime behavior (Edwards & Lilly, 1966; Henriksen & Doughty, 1967). The use of operant techniques in developing and maintaining other behaviors such as ambulation (Meyerson, Kerr & Michael, 1967), dressing (Minge & Ball, 1967), and functional sight (Stolz & Wolf, 1969) were also reported.

In addition to the rapidly accumulating studies concerned with the modification of single behaviors, the same period saw the development of a number of large-scale programs. The most notable of these were the research efforts at Parsons State Hospital in Kansas, where the use of tokens in cottage programs for the retarded was first implemented (e.g., Girardeau & Spradlin, 1964; Gorton & Hollis, 1965). During this period, John Hollis continued his excellent series of basic research studies (1965a, b, c, 1966, 1967a, b, c), but also published with Gorton (1965) a description of their applied work at Parsons. Residents were in feeding, self-care, perceptual motor, and communication programs based on procedures in which the staff were trained and which are illustrative of the transfer of principles from the laboratory to applied situations:

> (a) concentrating on the use of positive reinforcement following appropriate behavior . . . , (b) delivering reinforcement immediately . . . , (c) using continuous reinforcement while establishing certain behavior and then using intermittent reinforcement to maintain it, (d) using large amounts of reinforcement at first and then reducing the amount slowly after the behavior is established, (e) rewarding small improvements and building toward a more complicated, gross chain of responses, (f) ignoring undesirable behavior, thus extinguishing such behavior, and (g) individual programming of rewards and requirements. (p. 19)

The work at Parsons was continued (Lent, 1968; Lent, Cotter, Spradlin & Devine, 1968; Lent, LeBlanc & Spradlin, 1967), and it remained a stalwart example of the application of behavioral technology to problems of retarded persons.

These and other studies demonstrated the effectiveness of operant procedures with many subjects over a wide range of both basic (e.g., Bensberg, Colwell & Cassel, 1965; Burchard, 1967) and vocational self-help skills (e.g., Crosson, 1969; Hunt & Zimmerman, 1969) across a number of different settings. Many of the more basic and earlier developed procedures were included in the first training manual for use by ward staff (Bensberg, 1965).

Inappropriate Behavior.   Highly destructive and aggressive behavior has been a frequently occurring and serious problem among the institutionalized retarded. Such behavior was often both physically and environmentally damaging, and it prevented many residents from receiving adequate stimulation (due to the control procedures of physical restraint and sedation), much less the opportunity to benefit from training. Furthermore, poor staff training and staff-resident ratios created conditions whereby inappropriate behavior was actually reinforced as a result of inadvertent differential attention.

In the late 1960s a number of procedures were investigated in an effort to reduce various forms of inappropriate behavior exhibited by institutionalized retardates. The least damaging of these behaviors were stereotypic movements, such as excessive rocking and repetitive arm or hand waving. Mulhern and Baumeister (1969) were able to reduce stereotypic rocking by using DRL[7] procedures. White and Taylor (1967) and Luckey, Watson, and Musick (1968) demonstrated that more serious behaviors, rumination and vomiting, could be virtually eliminated through the use of response contingent shock. Lovaas and Simmons (1969) and Tate and Baroff (1966) also found shock to be effective in controlling self-destructive behavior, while Bailey and Meyerson (1969) and Peterson and Peterson (1968) treated the same types of behavior using non-contingent vibration and DRO[8] procedures, respectively.

Classroom Applications.   Most of the research described in the previous categories was conducted in institutional settings. Yet most retarded persons did not require residential placement; instead, their behavioral deficits it was hoped could be remediated through various types of day training programs. However, as with any educational endeavor, the existence of a program did not ensure learning on the part of the student. Special education classrooms were especially prone to problems, since traditional disciplinary and educational procedures were not very effective with children who had less sophisticated social and academic repertoires.

In light of the promising results obtained in institutions through the use of operant procedures, the special education classroom appeared to be a likely area of extension. Several early studies focused entirely on the elimination of disruptive behavior. Patterson, Jones, Whittier, and Wright (1965) employed a DRO procedure to eliminate the excessive movements of a hyperactive boy using

---

[7] DRL is a procedure designed to reduce the frequency of responding by delivering reinforcement only when responding is occurring at a low rate. It is discussed in detail in Chapter 11.

[8] DRO is a procedure in which the frequency of behavior is reduced by reinforcing its absence for specified periods of time.

candy and toys as reinforcers, and Perline and Levinsky (1968) produced similar results with an entire class using tokens. Free time was also used as a reinforcing event by Osborne (1969), who made additional recess contingent upon "in seat" behavior by individual children, and by Sulzbacher and Houser (1968), who employed a group response cost procedure whereby minutes of a special recess were subtracted contingent upon display or discussion of an obscene gesture.

A more comprehensive approach was taken by Birnbrauer and his associates, in that they dealt with both social and academic behavior. In one of the earliest classroom token programs reported, Birnbrauer and Lawler (1964) were able to produce improvements in a number of areas such as entering and leaving the room quietly, in-seat and on-task behavior, and working at a task for extended periods of time. These results were replicated and extended in subsequent work utilizing both token reinforcement and programmed-instruction techniques. Birnbrauer, Bijou, Wolf, and Kidder (1965) and Birnbrauer, Wolf, Kidder, and Tague (1965) demonstrated the effectiveness of these procedures in accelerating academic productivity, reducing error rates, and decreasing disruptive behavior.

Staff Training and Maintenance.   Given an increasing emphasis on both quality care and training in residential facilities, administrative and supervisory staff have recently become more concerned with the training and maintenance of staff behavior. Applied operant researchers have approached this formidable problem in a fairly straightforward manner: by identifying the specific problem, assessing the relevant aspects of both the behavior and the environment, and manipulating one or more aspects of the environment to bring about a behavior change.

Research on training has mainly concerned itself with the acquisition of new skills. Although several program descriptions have been published in the areas of both general skill (Bensberg & Barrett, 1966) and behavior modification training (Thompson & Grabowski, 1972), and although several studies have demonstrated the short-term effectiveness of training, there is no indication at the current time that training alone will maintain staff behavior on a long-term basis. In fact, quite the opposite has been found (Panyan, Boozer & Morris, 1970; Quilitch, 1975). In an effort to maintain appropriate levels of staff behavior, a number of studies investigated the effects of different procedures on a number of staff performance measures. Feedback to staff regarding their performance was found to be an economical, yet effective maintenance procedure (Panyan, Boozer & Morris, 1970; Quilitch, 1975). These studies illustrate the importance of taking into consideration not only the ability of staff to perform, but also the contingencies under which they respond. Such a consideration will lead to the development of procedures to maintain newly acquired training skills.

SUMMARY

This chapter presents (1) a number of basic concepts, including the interactive effect of stimuli on behavior, (2) some definitions of behavior modification and applied behavior analysis, (3) the relation of these definitions to definitions of mental retardation, and (4) some characteristics of applied behavior analysis including:

1. Use of individualized programs.
2. Response definitions that allow direct observation and measurement.
3. Direct observation in the setting in which the behavior occurs.
4. Continuous measurement of behavior.
5. Data presented in numerical form.
6. An emphasis on individual rather than on group analysis of data.
7. A systematic introduction of independent variables.
8. A continuing assessment of the reliability of measurement.
9. A detailed explanation of the procedures, thus allowing replication.
10. Work that is concerned with socially important behaviors.
11. An effort to develop conceptual systems.

This chapter also contains an historical introduction to applied behavior analysis including (1) a discussion of its experimental underpinnings and (2) a review of its work as related to mental retardation in the areas of self-help, social behaviors, inappropriate behaviors, classroom applications, staff training, community living, and some potential problems.

The next chapter will conclude the introductory section of the remainder of this book and will present a discussion of some of the major issues related to applied behavior analysis and mental retardation. These will include (1) the use and misuse of behavior-modifying drugs, (2) the use and misuse of behavioral technology, (3) labeling, (4) exclusionary policies, (5) the transfer of institutional abuses to community programs, (6) accountability, (7) the need for additional trained personnel, and (8) deinstitutionalization, mainstreaming, and normalization.

REFERENCES

Baer, D. M., Wolf, M. M., & Risley, T. R. Some current dimensions of applied behavior analysis. *Journal of Applied Behavior Analysis*, 1968, **1**, 91-97.

Bailey, J., & Meyerson, L. Vibration as a reinforcer with a profoundly retarded child. *Journal of Applied Behavior Analysis*, 1969, **2**, 135-137.

Barrett, B. H., & Lindsley, O. R. Deficits in acquisition of operant discrimination and differentiation shown by institutionalized retarded children. *American Journal of Mental Deficiency*, 1962, **67**, 424-436.

Baumeister, A. A., & Klostowski, R. An attempt to group toilet train severely retarded patients. *Mental Retardation*, 1965. 3, 24-26.

Bensberg, G. J. (Ed.) *Teaching the mentally retarded: A handbook for ward personnel.* Atlanta, GA: Southern Regional Education Board, 1965.

Bensberg, G. J., & Barrett, C. D. *Attendant training in southern residential facilities for the mentally retarded.* Atlanta, GA: Southern Regional Education Board, 1966.

Bensberg, G. J., Colwell, C. N., & Cassel, R. H. Teaching the profoundly retarded self-help activities by behavior shaping techniques. *American Journal of Mental Deficiency*, 1965, **69**, 674-679.

Bijou, S. W. A systematic approach to an experimental analysis of young children. *Child Development*, 1955, **26**, 161-168.

Bijou, S. W. Patterns of reinforcement and resistence to extinction in young children. *Child Development*, 1957a, **28**, 47-54.

Bijou, S. W. Methodology for an experimental analysis of child behavior. *Psychological Reports*, 1957b, **3**, 243-250.

Bijou, S. W. Operant extinction after fixed interval schedules with young children. *Journal of the Experimental Analysis of Behavior*, 1958a, **1**, 25-29.

Bijou, S. W. A child study laboratory on wheels. *Child Development*, 1958b, **29**, 425-427.

Bijou, S. W. Theory and research in mental (developmental) retardation. *Psychological Record*, 1963, **13**, 95-110.

Bijou, S. W. A functional analysis of retarded development. In N. R. Ellis (Ed.), *International review of research in mental retardation*, Vol. I. New York: Academic Press,Inc., 1966.

Bijou, S. W., & Sturges, P. T. Positive reinforcers for experimental studies with children—consumables and manipulatables. *Child Development*, 1959, **30**, 151-170.

Bijou, S. W., Birnbrauer, J. S., Kidder, J. D., & Tague, C. E. Programmed instruction as an approach to teaching of reading, writing, and arithmetic to retarded children. *Psychological Record*, 1966, **16**, 505-522.

Birnbrauer, J. S., & Lawler, J. Token reinforcement for learning. *Mental Retardation*, 1964, **2**, 275-279.

Birnbrauer, J. S., Bijou, S. W., Wolf, M. M., & Kidder, J. D. Programmed instruction in the classroom. In L. P. Ullmann & L. Krasner (Eds.), *Case studies in behavior modification*. New York: Holt, Rinehart and Winston, 1965.

Birnbrauer, J. S., Kidder, J. D., & Tague, C. F. Programming reading from the teachers' point of view. *Programmed Instruction*, 1964, **3**, 1-2.

Birnbrauer, J. S., Wolf, M. M., Kidder, J. D., & Tague, C. E. Classroom behavior of retarded pupils with token reinforcement. *Journal of Experimental Child Psychology*, 1965, **2**, 219-235.

Brown, B. S., Wienckowski, L. A., & Stolz, S. B. Behavior modification: Perspective on a current issue. Washington, D.C.: U.S. Department of Health, Education, and Welfare, 1976.

Burchard, J. D. Systematic socialization: A programmed environment for the habilitation of anti-social retardates. *Psychological Record*, 1967, **17**, 461-476.

Crosson, J. E. A technique for programming sheltered workshop environments for training severely retarded workers. *American Journal of Mental Deficiency*, 1969, **73**, 814-818.

Day, J. F. Behavioral technology: A negative stand. *Intellect*, 1974, **102**(2355), 304-306.

Dayan, M. Toilet training retarded children in a state residential institute. *Mental Retardation*, 1964, **2**, 116-117.

Edwards, M., & Lilly, R. T. Operant conditioning: An application to behavioral problems in groups. *Mental Retardation*, 1966, **4**, 18-20.

Ellis, N. R. Toilet training the severely defective patient: An S-R reinforcement analysis. *American Journal of Mental Deficiency*, 1963, **68**, 98-103.

Ellis, N. R., Barnett, C. D., & Pryor, M. W. Operant behavior in mental defectives: Exploratory studies. *Journal of the Experimental Analysis of Behavior*, 1960, **3**, 63-69.

Ferster, C. B., & Skinner, B. F. *Schedules of reinforcement*. New York: Appleton-Century-Crofts, Inc., 1957.

Fuller, P. R. Operant conditioning of a vegetative human organism. *American Journal of Psychology*, 1949, **62**, 587-590.

Giles, D. K., & Wolf, M. M. Toilet training institutionalized, severe retardates: An application of operant behavior modification techniques. *American Journal of Mental Deficiency*, 1966, **70**, 766-780.

Girardeau, F. L., & Spradlin, J. E. Token rewards on a cottage program. *Mental Retardation*, 1964, **2**, 345-351.

Gorton, C. E., & Hollis, J. H. Redesigning a cottage unit for better programming and research for the severely retarded. *Mental Retardation*, 1965, **3**, 16-21.

Grossman, H. (Ed.) *Manual on terminology and classification in mental retardation.* Washington, D.C.: American Association on Mental Deficiency, 1973.

Henriksen, K., & Doughty, R. Decelerating undesired mealtime behavior in a group of profoundly retarded boys. *American Journal of Mental Deficiency*, 1967, **72**, 40-44.

Hollis, J. H. Effects of reinforcement shifts on best-wire performance of severely retarded children. *American Journal of Mental Deficiency*, 1965a, **69**, 531-535.

Hollis, J. H. The effects of social and nonsocial stimuli on the behavior of profoundly retarded children: Part I. *American Journal of Mental Deficiency*, 1965b, **69**, 755-771.

Hollis, J. H. The effects of social and nonsocial stimuli on the behavior of profoundly retarded children: Part II. *American Journal of Mental Deficiency*, 1965c, **69**, 772-789.

Hollis, J. H. Communication within dyads of severely retarded children. *American Journal of Mental Deficiency*, 1966, **70**, 729-744.

Hollis, J. H. Development of perceptual motor skills in a profoundly retarded child: Part I: Prosthesis. *American Journal of Mental Deficiency*, 1967a, **71**, 941-952.

Hollis, J. H. Development of perceptual motor skills in a profoundly retarded child: Part II: Consequence, change and transfer. *American Journal of Mental Deficiency*, 1967b, **71**, 953-963.

Hollis, J. H. Vertical operant manipulandum for profoundly retarded children. *Perceptual and Motor Skills*, 1967c, **24**, 156.

Hunt, J. G., & Zimmerman, J. Stimulating productivity in a simulated sheltered workshop setting. *American Journal of Mental Deficiency*, 1969, **74**, 43-49.

Lent, J. R. Mimosa cottage: Experiment in hope. *Psychology Today*, 1968, **2**, 50-58.

Lent, J. R., Cotter, V., Spradlin, J., & Devine, P. Progress report: A demonstration program for intensive training of institutionalized mentally retarded girls. HEW Grant. January 1967–January 1968.

Lent, J. R., LeBlanc, J., & Spradlin, J. E. Designing a rehabilitative culture for moderately retarded adolescent girls. Parsons Research Center, Working Paper 174, 1967.

Lindsley, O. R. Direct measurement and prosthesis of retarded behavior. *Journal of Education*, 1964, **147**, 62-81.

Lovaas, O. I., & Simmons, J. Manipulation of self-destruction in three retarded children. *Journal of Applied Behavior Analysis*, 1969, **2**, 143-157.

Luckey, R. E., Watson, C. M., & Musick, K. Aversive conditioning as a means of inhibiting vomiting and rumination. *American Journal of Mental Deficiency*, 1968, **73**, 139-142.

MacMillan, D. L. *Behavior modification in education*. New York: Macmillan, Inc., 1973.

Meyerson, L., Kerr, N., & Michael, J. L. Behavior modification in rehabilitation. In S. W. Bijou & D. M. Baer (Eds.), *Child development: Readings in experimental analysis*. New York: Appleton-Century-Crofts. 1967.

Minge, M. R., & Ball, T. S. Teaching of self-help skills to profoundly retarded patients. *American Journal of Mental Deficiency,*, 1967, **71**, 864-868.

Mulhern, T., & Baumeister, A. A. An experimental attempt to reduce stereotypy by reinforcement procedures. *American Journal of Mental Deficiency*, 1969, **74**, 69-74.

Orlando, R. The functional role of discriminative stimuli in free operant performance of developmentally retarded children. *Psychological Record*, 1961, **11**, 153-161.

Orlando, R., & Bijou, S. W. Single and multiple schedules of reinforcement in developmentally retarded children. *Journal of Experimental Analysis of Behavior*, 1960, **3**, 339-348.

Osborne, J. G. Free time as a reinforcer in the management of classroom behavior. *Journal of Applied Behavior Analysis*, 1969, **2**, 113-118.

Panyan, M., Boozer, H., & Morris, N. Feedback to attendants as a reinforcer for applying operant techniques. *Journal of Applied Behavior Analysis*, 1970, **3**, 1-4.

Patterson, G. R., Jones, R., Whittier, J., & Wright, M. A. A behavior modification technique for the hyperactive child. *Behaviour Research and Therapy*, 1965, **2**, 217-226.

Perline, I. H., & Levinsky, D. An inexpensive device to measure activity in crib-confined subjects. *Psychological Record*, 1968, **18**, 51-52.

Peterson, R. F., & Peterson, L. R. The use of positive reinforcement in the control of self-destructive behavior in a retarded boy. *Journal of Experimental Child Psychology*, 1968, **6**, 351-360.

Quilitch, R. A comparison of three staff-management procedures. *Journal of Applied Behavior Analysis*, 1975, **8**, 59-66.

Schnelle, J. F., Kirchner, R. E., McNees, M. P., and Lawler, J. M. Social evaluation research: the evaluation of two police patrolling strategies. *Journal of Applied Behavior Analysis*, 1975, **8**, 353-366.

Sidman, M. *Tactics of scientific research*. New York: Basic Books, Inc., 1960.

Skinner, B. F. *The behavior of organisms*. New York: Appleton-Century-Crofts, Inc., 1938.

Skinner, B. F. *Walden two*. New York: Macmillan, Inc., 1948.

Skinner, B. F. *Science and human behavior*. New York: Macmillan, Inc., 1953.

Skinner, B. F. *Journal of the Experimental Analysis of Behavior*, 1958-present—A journal published by the "Society for the Experimental Analysis of Behavior," Bloomington, IN.

Skinner, B. F. *Cumulative record*. New York: Macmillan, Inc., 1961.

Skinner, B. F. *The technology of teaching*. New York: Appleton-Century-Crofts, Inc., 1968.

Skinner, B. F. *Contingencies of reinforcement: A theoretical analysis*. New York: Appleton-Century-Crofts, Inc., 1969.

Skinner, B. F. Answers for my critics. In H. Wheeler (Ed.), *Beyond the punitive society*. San Francisco: W. H. Freeman & Co., 1973.

Spradlin, J. E. The Premack hypothesis and self-feeding by profoundly retarded children: A case report. Parsons Research Center, Working Paper 79, 1964.

Spradlin, J. E., & Girardeau, F. L. The behavior of moderately and severely retarded persons. In N. R. Ellis (Ed.), *International review of research in mental retardation*, Vol. 1. New York; Academic Press, Inc., 1966.

Stolz, S. B., & Wolf, M. M. Visually discriminated behavior in a "blind" adolescent retardate. *Journal of Applied Behavior Analysis*, 1969, **2**, 65-77.

Sulzbacher, S. I., & Houser, J. E. A tactic to eliminate disruptive behaviors in the classroom: Group contingent consequences. *American Journal of Mental Deficiency*, 1968, **73**, 88-90.

Sulzer, B., & Mayer, G. R. *Behavior modification procedures for school personnel.* Hinsdale, IL: Dryden Press, 1972.

Tate, B. G., & Baroff, G. S. Aversive control of self-injurious behavior in a psychotic boy. *Behavior Research and Therapy*, 1966, **4**, 281-287.

Thompson, T., & Grabowski, J. (Eds.) *Behavior modification of the mentally retarded.* New York: Oxford University Press, Inc., 1972.

Ullmann, L. P., & Krasner, L. (Eds.) *Case studies in behavior modification.* New York: Holt, Rinehart and Winston, Inc., 1965.

Watson, L. S., & Lawson, R. Instrumental learning in mental retardates. *Mental Retardation Abstracts*, 1966, **3**, 1-20.

Watson, R. I. The experimental tradition and clinical psychology. In A. J. Bachrach (Ed.), *Experimental foundations of clinical psychology.* New York: Basic Books, Inc., 1962.

White, J. C., & Taylor, D. J. Noxious conditioning as a treatment for rumination. *Mental Retardation*, 1967, **5**, 30-33.

Zeiler, M. D., & Jervey, S. Development of behavior: Self-feeding. *Journal of Consulting and Clinical Psychology*, 1968, **32**, 164-168.

CHAPTER

3

Issues in Mental
Retardation and Applied
Behavior Analysis

For the welfare of his Ideal Commonwealth, Plato suggested a law which should provide: "That the wives of our guardians are to be common, and their children are to be common, and no parent is to know his own child, nor any child his parent. . . . The proper officers will take the offspring of the good parents to the pen or fold, and . . . will deposit them with certain nurses . . . , but the offspring of the inferior, or of the better when they chance to be deformed, will be put away in some mysterious, unknown place, as they should be."[1]

Although Justice McReynolds finds that restrictions such as those proposed by Plato would violate both the letter and the spirit of the Constitution, our history has been to treat retarded persons in this fashion. They have often been detained or infirmed against their will, and few thought that they had a right to protest. They have been denied treatment and education; they have been forced into peonage; they have often been denied the right to marry; they have been forced to live in environments which are more restrictive than necessary for their own health and safety. The list goes on, but it reduces to the fact that, for the

---

[1] Attributed to Justice McReynolds by Gilhool and Stutman (in press).

century and a half since we have recognized that some people learn much more slowly than others, we have denied those individuals both due process and equal protection under the law.

But two movements have had an immense impact on our conservative approach toward retarded persons, and perhaps the fact that they coincided in time brought to them the force that they have. One movement has been the impressive educational results achieved by those who have believed that teaching could be more a science and less a laissez-faire. Whether the methods used by these educators and psychologists were or could even be called behaviorally based is really irrelevant. What is relevant is the idea that through careful measurement we could learn which procedures were effective and which were ineffective, and that such information could be passed to others through journals, meetings, and informal correspondence. Beginning in earnest in the late 1950s, we adopted that approach and began to show that retarded individuals could learn useful self-management skills that would allow them to lead freer lives. When we adopted that approach and achieved those results, we showed that retarded persons were not individuals to be pitied and segregated; they were humans who should be educated and integrated into our societies.

The other significant movement, also beginning in earnest in the 1950s, was the movement toward social consciousness and equal rights. These confrontations were begun in many areas, of course, and one of those areas was retardation. There is probably no issue today that has any pervasiveness to it in our field that is not concerned with establishing or protecting the rights of retarded persons. This movement included the many court cases of the 1950s and 1960s that attempted to ensure that all citizens were afforded the same rights. Perhaps the most germinal of all these was *Brown* v. *Board of Education*, a case that was the basis for racial integration in schools, but a case that also led to the presumption that, if we were not to deny access to education because of race, then perhaps we should not deny access to education because of intellectual limitations.

Prior to the 1950s, there were of course some self-contained classrooms and some self-contained centers that did provide educational services. But these were limited in number and often in quality. Mentally retarded persons were treated in accord with the basic public educational objective of the times, which was to educate the masses. If a child deviated (by being either retarded or gifted), he or she either was denied either any services at all or any additional services that might be required. The burden was on the individual, who was to conform to the school; the school could not conform to individual needs. Fortunately, some parents fought this approach and began to enlist the aid of influential politicians. From just such a parents' group came the National Association of Retarded Citizens. One of the most influential politicians was John F. Kennedy. When the public became aware that a member of his family was retarded, some of the fear and some of the stigma seemed to lessen. When he formed the President's Panel on Mental Retardation, the public became more informed, and resistance seemed to lessen a little more.

One of the first expressions of the panel concerned the rights of retarded persons. In an eloquently direct statement, it declared that "Our basic position is that all rights normally held by anyone are also held by the retarded" (1963).

Other groups then became more interested in making similar statements. The International League of Societies for the Mentally Handicapped met in 1967 and issued as its first general principle the statement that

> The mentally retarded person has the same rights as other citizens of the same country, same age, family status . . . unless a specific . . . determination has been made by appropriate procedures, that his exercise of some or all of such rights will place his own interests or those of others in undue jeopardy. (Sterner, 1967)

As rights for retarded persons have been stated by important organizations, they have become more and more real in the sense that we have come to abide by them more each year. But following these has not been so easy as it sounds, as some of them are not "black and white." Others appear to be more objective, but their pursuit seems to involve a shaping process. Each year we progress closer to the goal, but some steps require longer than others to declare what is correct. So with these rights we have a number of issues, all of which have some degree of ambiguity. In this chapter, we shall discuss these issues in several ways. For some issues (e.g., legal rights), there is a history, so they will be discussed briefly from that perspective. For others, there is little or no history, so they will be discussed simply in the present. For most, there will be a brief discussion from a behavioral viewpoint, that being the perspective of this book. These viewpoints, however, should be considered those of the author, reflecting his experiences. They should not be construed as the position of all behaviorists, for although we who call ourselves behaviorists agree on many things, we certainly do not agree on all.

The number of issues that can be discussed is of course large. But in this chapter the issues to be discussed will be limited to most of those ascribed by the President's Committee on Mental Retardation (1976) to CEC and AAMD. They represent what these organizations consider to be the major issues of the present and the near future. They include (1) the use and misuse of behavior-modifying drugs, (2) the use and misuse of behavioral techniques, (3) labeling, (4) exclusionary policies in service delivery, (5) institutional problems and abuses being transferred to community programs, (6) drastic changes in both institutional and community programs, (7) accountability and demonstration of effectiveness in service systems, and (8) changes in attitudes to allow normalization and mainstreaming.

THE USE AND MISUSE OF BEHAVIOR-MODIFYING DRUGS

The use of behavior-modifying drugs has been an issue that has many underpinnings. The problem is that there have been two classes of behaviors which have been treated by drugs. One type has been medical in nature and has included such overt and covert behaviors as seizures, blood pressure, and heart rate. The other type is more psychological in nature, being concerned with what we more readily use the term "behavior" to describe. This has included such labels as aggression, hyperactivity, and lack of attention. Both of these classes have been treated with drugs for some time for at least four reasons: (1) Whether they were considered medical or psychological problems, physicians had something to offer that produced demonstrable changes. So our behavior of asking physicians for help and their behavior of prescribing help were reinforced in a symbiotic relationship. (2) Funding was generally so low that client-to-staff ratios were very high. So whether the clients were in an institution or in a school, there was usually insufficient staff to provide a special individualized program. The alternative, giving a child a pill or an injection, was much more viable. (3) Behavioral technology in the applied area was virtually nonexistent, and other approaches did not offer successful procedures to meet these needs. (4) The retarded client was generally not regarded competent to make a decision either alone or through parents. The doctrine of *in loco parentis* was adopted instead, with the idea being that whatever the state did it was entitled to do, because it would always be acting in the best interests of the client.

Three of these reasons for relying on drugs have changed considerably. Behavioral (and nonbehavioral) methods have been developed which can successfully address many of the problems presented by retarded persons. Many of these procedures were developed in research settings or programs, and they were staffed more densely than most community or institutional settings. But with the increased funding that has occurred in some places recently, these procedures have been shown to be effective time and again. As such, they have become for some settings viable alternatives to drug treatment. In addition, the right of retarded persons either to say for themselves or through advocates that they do not want to be drugged, and that they would rather learn to behave in a normal fashion, has been supported. But these three changes have certainly not been enough. There continue to be drug abuses, although more and more administrators and physicians are learning that alternatives do exist.

As the dilemma over "psychological" behaviors is becoming more clear, the dilemma over "medical" behaviors may be about to surface. There now is no question that conditions for which we have been using medication can in some cases be eliminated. Through biofeedback and other methods, we can reduce headaches, seizures, blood pressure, gastric acidity, and many other conditions formerly thought to be treatable only through medical procedures. As we find in the next decade that these methods are available to us as an alternative to medication, and that we do not have to use medication, one wonders how long it will be before retarded individuals are presented the same option.

THE USE AND MISUSE OF BEHAVIORAL TECHNOLOGY

For the last several decades, in novels such as *Animal Farm, Brave New World,* and *1984,* our society has been depicted as uncovering a technology of human behavior that would surely bring our social destruction. But Skinner (1953) addressed this issue quite clearly. The technology is neither good nor bad; it is neutral. It is our use of this technology that can be good or bad. To deny that we should continue our pursuit of learning why people behave as they do is to deny the possibility that we could learn a great deal that could help us all. To deny, however, that there should be certain constraints on our technological use is foolish.

In the last few years, guidelines of national importance have appeared from the American Association on Mental Deficiency, *Wyatt v. Stickney*, Joint Commission on Accreditation of Hospitals, and the National Association of Retarded Citizens (May, Risley, Twardosz, Friedman, Bijou, Wexler, et al., 1975). By far the most important, because it is the longest and the most explicit, is that adopted by NARC. These guidelines are divided into three sections: (1) an introduction describing what behavior modification is; (2) a very specific discussion of types and uses of behavioral techniques; and (3) procedures for advice, review, and consent. The NARC guidelines are specific and make many very good suggestions; they do, however, present some problems. Although written by some of the most competent and renowned behaviorists (Bijou, Risley, Twardosz) and lawyers (Friedman, Wexler) in the field, they have by no means gained universal acceptance. Both Sajwaj (1977) and Stolz (1977) have made very pointed comments about the vagaries of such guidelines. Stolz, perhaps subtly, has listed her interpretation of the content of the document. It

(a) involves the establishment of elaborate systems of committees to monitor the behavioral procedures;
(b) emphasizes the involvement of persons whose behavior is to be changed, their representatives, or their attorneys, as well as citizen representatives;
(c) involves potentially long delays between the planning of a new intervention and its implementation in practice;
(d) is based on legal rulings current at the time they were formulated;
(e) is based on the scientific knowledge current at the time the guidelines were formulated;
(f) prescribes or proscribes specific procedures in specific circumstances;
(g) describes in detail the qualifications of intervention personnel;
(h) emphasizes a legalistic approach, such as extensive, explicit procedures for informed consent. (p. 542)

Stolz offers three reasons for not having guidelines for behavior modification. The first is that they will produce unfortunate side effects. She supports Goldiamond's (1975) argument that regulating behavior modification, while no other procedures are regulated, will lead to the demise of this technology. The analysis is of course behavioral. When we have two options, (1) choose a behavioral procedure, write a proposal, and wait a month for a committee to convene and give us permission, or (2) do anything else we wish, as long as it is not labeled behavioral, and to be able to do it without delay, we will choose the latter. The second reason is that a list of approved procedures may have a limiting effect on the development of new procedures. If we can only use those that were approved in a formal national document, how could we ever develop new procedures? The third reason is that guidelines may give unwarranted protection to certain procedures. Those "meeting the letter, but not the spirit, of a set of guidelines may be sheltered from criticism because of the guidelines" (p. 543).

Sajwaj (1977) provides other criticisms. A very telling one is adopted from Roos's (1974) discussion of statements of fact and statements of opinion. An example of a statement of fact is that timeout, when appropriately used, can reduce certain undesirable behaviors. A statement of opinion is that timeout will not be used because it impinges on the freedom of retarded individuals. Sajwaj points out several cases in which fact has been confused with opinion. One is that in overcorrection[2] the behavior to be practiced must be topographically (i.e., physically), related to the inappropriate behavior. From Sajwaj's own work (Epstein, Doke, Sajwaj, Sorrell & Rimmer, 1974), we know that this is a statement of opinion and not a statement of fact. Sajwaj further argues that statements such as "problem behaviors occur *primarily* when people are not involved in goal-directed activities" (p. 16) suggest that we know a great deal about the etiology of behavior, when we do not. Actually, we have more opinion than fact. His main point, as he notes, is that, when recognized leaders in our field interweave fact and opinion, the thousands with less experience and expertise who follow the guidelines are likely to accept opinions as facts. A second argument that Sajwaj offers against these guidelines is that, while they have done a commendable job of specifying some competencies of levels of programming staff, they have also been somewhat vague in order to be more generic and to cover more situations. As a result, he thinks (and from our experiences we cannot agree more strongly) that "there is considerable danger that state merit systems, employee unions, or civil service boards will define criteria in terms simply of *time* on a previous job. Thus, a merit system might define 'successfully supervised' as holding a job title containing the word 'supervisor' for one year, or 'practicum experience' as mere attendance for a minimum number of hours at inservice training lectures and demonstrations" (p. 534). The behavioral criteria will be lost. In another paper, we (Repp & Deitz, 1978) discussed how the bureaucracy suggested by such guidelines impinges on the rights of retarded persons to receive treatment promptly.

Both Sajwaj and Stolz argue for an alternative to these guidelines. In general, Stolz prefers a code of ethics similar to those of other professions. Among those suggested are the Revised Ethical Standards of Psychologists (American Psychological Association, 1977), Standards for Providers of Psychological Services (American Psychological Association, 1974), and Ethical Principles in the Conduct of Research with Human Participants (American Psychological Association, 1973). Although these standards are for psychologists, there is no reason they could not be modified so that they are relevant to all of us whether we be direct-care personnel, teachers, or speech therapists.

Stolz, like Sajwaj, suggests the use of checklists that evaluate one's ethics regardless of the type of intervention. A checklist of this type has been adopted by the Association for Advancement of Behavior Therapy, and Stolz has listed the heading of the checklist's eight sections:

Have the goals of treatment been adequately considered? Had the choice of treatment methods been adequately considered? Is the client's participation voluntary? Does the therapist refer the clients to other therapists when necessary? Has the adequacy of treatment been evaluated? Has the confidentiality of the treatment rela-

---

[2] Timeout and overcorrection are procedures used to decrease responding; they are discussed in detail in Chapter 12.

tionship been protected? Is the therapist qualified to provide treatment? When another person or agency is empowered to arrange for therapy, have the interests of the subordinated client been sufficiently considered? (p. 545)

The issue of whether to provide guidelines for the use of behavioral technology seems to be resolved; most agree that there should be guidelines of some sort. But the issue of what form the guidelines take is very alive. Although the division is somewhat simplistic, there seem to be two different approaches to this topic. One is to discuss the methods that are appropriate or inappropriate for certain situations. The other is to discuss what constitutes ethical behavior on the part of the person using behavioral methods. Regardless of how this issue is settled, behaviorists are quite concerned that a high degree of ethical behavior be attained and maintained. Interestingly and fortunately, pursuit of this objective should help meet the concerns of those who have feared that the more we know of behavior, the more likely we are to abuse that knowledge. Instead, with concerns like those shown, the more we know, the more likely we are to help our society solve some of its problems.

LABELING

Officially labeling persons as "mentally retarded" has certainly been a practice in which we have engaged with great eagerness this century. When the intelligence test was invented, we seemed to have found an objective means for estimating someone's intelligence. As "mental retardation" was indeed considered to be a deficit in mental abilities, tests such as the Stanford-Binet or the Wechsler Intelligence Scale for Children seemed to be just what we needed. To make our decision to use intelligence tests even more reinforcing, several people developed tests that were easier to administer, required less training to administer, took less time to administer, and required less time to analyze and to write a summary of the results. We had developed the best of both worlds and had become both objective and more efficient.

There were, however, a few who objected to this approach. Skinner argued that understanding how an individual behaved in a natural environment was a key to understanding both normal and underdeveloped behavior. Special education workers, whether they were called teachers, therapists, or direct-care staff, began to discuss the idea that the critical issue was how well a person adapted to the environment rather than how well he or she performed on a 1-hour test. While philosophers and service providers may be provided the foreground for what was to come, the issue of labeling based on a test did not emerge as critical until the era of litigation. The decision in Brown v. Board of Education indicated that separate education was inherently unequal. Yet retarded children were educated separately if they were educated at all; and their educational placement was determined primarily by their performance on a test. Slowly, however, arguments were developed against labeling and against placement that was primarily based on testing. Ross, DeYoung, and Cohen (1971) have summarized five of these arguments:

(1) *Most tests have middle-class children as their norm[3] population.* These tests contain questions appropriate for that sector of society, but they also contain items that are inappropriate for some Mexican-Americans, some Indians, some poverty-level children, and other ethnic groups whose primary language and experiences simply are not those of middle-class children. For these individuals, test scores do not accurately reflect their cognitive competencies; these test scores do, however, provide either the sole or the primary basis for the label of retardation.

(2) *The administration of the tests is often incompetent.* Sometimes the administrator has not been well versed in the cultural background and native language of the children being tested. Sometimes the individual has been poorly trained in the administration of the test, if she or he has been trained at all (some state systems do not require that psychologists demonstrate competencies in testing; they require instead only that certain university courses appear on that person's transcript). Other times, the test is not so much a measure of particular knowledges as it is a measure of the extent to which test-taking behaviors have been developed. Hyperactivity, withdrawal, shyness in novel situations, and many such problems can produce a lower score than would be obtained if these interfering behaviors did not exist (Lovaas, Koegel, Simmons & Long, 1973, provide a very nice example of this effect with children who have been labeled autistic). To label a student retarded because this type of behavior has produced a depressed score is to provide a disservice to the student.

(3) *Parental involvement is often avoided.* Students are often tested without the parent's knowledge, scores are considered, and a placement decision is made. The data are then presented to the parents as if they were indisputable. To encourage placements, some administrators emphasize the positive aspects, such as smaller classes and more attention. They may not, however, emphasize the possibility that once a child is labeled and placed in a class for retarded persons, he or she may be in such a class the rest of their school life. Even though PL 94-142 provides for parental involvement, one can still avoid opposition through skillful and pointed advice to the parents. Only the more assertive tend to be willing to oppose a school or a school district, and the effort required to go through such a confrontation is often considerable.

(4) *Special education is inadequate.* Plaintiffs have argued that placement tends to be permanent, that the special education classes do not emphasize appropriate vocational skills, and that as a result the student is ensured of a low socioeconomic status the rest of his or her life.

(5) *Improper placement stigmatizes the student and causes irreparable harm.* The presumption is that the label alters the way schoolmates, teachers,

---

[3] On norm-referenced tests, the summary score received is based on one's performance compared with other persons who have taken the test either at the same time (e.g., college board tests) or in prior years (e.g., intelligence tests).

and other adults treat the student. They tend to expect less and concomitantly provide less for the student. Generally, the less one is expected to do, the less one does. The relation becomes circular, and the stigma applies.

The behavioral viewpoint on the question of labeling has been longstanding. It has considered tests to be an inadequate basis for such major decisions as placement when used alone. Certainly IQ tests provide some information, and certainly, unless the circumstances are quite bizarre, a score of 30 indicates a far different level of functioning than a score of 60. But IQ tests do not tell us where the levels of weakness are, and where we should emphasize programming in order to provide an individual with the experiences necessary to make a successful adaptation to life. Such information can come only from analyzing the living and working situations for the behaviors they require, analyzing the present level of functioning, and teaching the student the skills necessary to progress from the latter to the former.

EXCLUSIONARY POLICIES ON SERVICE DELIVERY

The history of mental retardation has been one in which varying levels of treatment and education were available. At one time or another, the *zeitgeist* has been for (1) no education, (2) education in institutions, (3) education in segregated schools, (4) education in special classes located in regular schools, or (5) education in regular classes. Today's *zeitgeist* is for education in the least restrictive environment possible, i.e., in a setting as close to the regular integrated classroom as possible. The burden of proof today seems to be shifting from the client to the school; i.e., the client is not so much required to prove that he or she could function as well in a less restrictive environment, as the school is required to prove that the client would be hurt educationally if she or he were in one environment instead of a more restrictive one. Public Laws 93-380 and 94-142 both support the right to education in the least restrictive environment, and they seem to imply that unless the school proves otherwise, a student is entitled to an education in an integrated environment.

While a number of court cases have been concerned with the right to treatment and the right to education, several have been particularly significant, and these will be discussed here. These two rights are often commingled, but they are considered separately by some. "Education" is often used to refer to the right to have access to nonrestrictive educational programming. "Treatment" often refers to the right of someone who has been deprived of liberty through institutionalization of some sort to a treatment program directed toward the reason for that deprivation. The "right to treatment" was first publicly discussed by Morton Birnbaum in 1960 (Friedman, 1975), and an important and early case in this area was *In Re Gault*. Gault was a 15-year-old confined to a state school for making obscene telephone calls. He argued that he had not been accorded full due process rights; the state argued that full due process was not required because the proceedings were not criminal in nature and were intended to benefit the individual (precisely the argument facilities have long used in exercising independent authority over placements). The Supreme Court, however, held that due process was warranted. A later case, *Rouse* v. *Cameron*, is often cited as the first to hold that the right to treatment was a constitutional right. Rouse was committed to a mental institution at which he received no treatment. He contended that treatment was the basis for his confinement, and that since he was not being treated he should be released. Judge Bazelon agreed and indicated that there might be a constitutional right to treatment. The court extended the significance of this concept by refusing to allow the lack of treatment to be excused by an insufficiency of resources (Stone, 1975). This is a very important statement, used in later cases such as those at Partlow and Willowbrook. The court also asked for a legitimate effort to provide an individualized treatment program and periodic review, a concept that would be repeated in other cases and in public laws.

In 1970, action began on an extremely important case that involved several state hospitals in Alabama and came to be known as *Wyatt* v. *Stickney*. Because of a budget deficit, the commissioner of mental health in Alabama fired many professionals and paraprofessionals at Bryce State Hospital. The employees filed suit on the lack of due process and, secondarily, on the fact that, if this hospital, which was already understaffed, lost 99 more employees, the residents would be severely damaged. Other hospitals joined in the suit, and the right-to-treatment principle was advanced in force. Funding was pitiful; there were two social workers, three part-time psychiatrists, and one psychologist for a population of 5,000; $0.50 a day per person was spent for food, a finding that led the U.S. Department of Health, Education, and Welfare to testify that malnutrition was being programmed. When the state protested that it did not have sufficient funds for proper staffing, the court ruled that on legal precedent lack of fiscal resources was not an acceptable excuse when constitutional rights were being withheld. The reply to the state by George Dean, the plaintiffs' attorney, was particularly apt and has been described by Friedman (1975):

> [he] combed the legislative record for a list of monies already appropriated for the next fiscal year. He found appropriations for a Miss Alabama Pageant, a football hall of fame, and a livestock coliseum, among others. He observed that more money was spent on individual animals at the local zoo than on his own clients and quipped wryly that his clients would be better cared for in Alabama if they were "athletic or photogenic cows of Confederate ancestry." Since the Alabama Code described the delivery of state mental health services as an "essential function" of the state, why shouldn't the treasurer be enjoined from expending monies on such non-essential functions, at least until the mental institutions were brought up to snuff? This question was not an easy one to answer. (p. 4)

The decision in *Wyatt* was a far-reaching decision, as it went beyond the issue of right to treatment. As such, it has become one of the most pervasive cases in our history. Martin (1975) has summarized the findings:

> The court focused on *three fundamental conditions* for *effective and adequate* treatment: a *humane physical* and *psychological environment, qualified staff in numbers* sufficient to *administer adequate treatment,* and *individualized treatment plans.* The court enumerated many rights which must be met. Among them are: *A right to the least restrictive conditions necessary for treatment. The right to be free from isolation* (with one hour as the time limit on therapeutically justifiable

isolation). A *right not to be subjected to experimental research without consent* (with Human Rights Committees formed to approve any experimentation). A *right not to be subjected to treatment procedures such as lobotomy, electroconvulsive treatment, adversive* [sic] *reinforcement conditioning,* or *other unusual or hazardous treatment procedures without express and informed consent after consultation with counsel. The right to keep and use personal possessions. The right not to be required to perform institutional maintenance work, and to receive the minimum wage if they volunteer for such work; residents may be required to perform therapeutic work tasks if those tasks do not involve the operation or maintenance of the institution. A right to a comfortable bed and privacy. The right to access to a day room with television and other recreational facilities. The right to adequate meals—the denial of an adequate diet shall not be used as punishment. The right to adequate staff. The right to an individualized treatment plan with a projected timetable for meeting specific goals, criteria for release to less restrictive treatment conditions, and criteria for discharge.* (p. 178-179)

As the Wyatt case was being tried in the courts, another case involving an institution was begun. Willowbrook, an enormous institution in New York, was the subject of a suit in a case begun as the *New York Association of Retarded Children* v. *Rockefeller.* Noted witnesses "told stories of bruised and beaten children, maggot-infested wounds, assembly-line bathing, inadequate medical care, cruel and inappropriate use of restraints, and inadequate clothing. They testified that children has deteriorated physically, mentally, and emotionally during treatment" (Friedman, 1975, p. 6). Like the *Wyatt* case, the Willowbrook court set standards for the ratios of staff to clients; it forbid such practices as seclusion, corporal punishment, medical experimenation; and the routine use of restraints; it required individual education plans on a number of areas; and it created several boards to oversee the implementation of all the new developments. The court in this case took a different approach to the "right to treatment" as it discussed the relation of this term to those of "protection from harm" and "need for care." "The consent judgment reflects the fact that protection from harm requires relief more extensive than this court originally contemplated, because harm can result not only from neglect but also from conditions which cause regression or which prevent development of an individual's capabilities." The adoption of the "protection from harm" doctrine, based on the Eighth Amendment's protection from cruel and unusual punishment, is interesting. The concept is that, in order to be protected from harm, one must be provided the range of services directed by such cases as *Wyatt.* If one is not given full treatment, one cannot be protected from harm.

The only "treatment" case to be decided by the Supreme Court was *O'Connor* v. *Donaldson,* a case which has solidified the argument brought by so many others. Donaldson, who was committed to a mental institution in Florida, refused for religious reasons the two therapies offered to him: electroshock therapy and tranquilizing drugs. Virtually nothing was done for him in terms of treatment for 15 years. The court decided in favor of Donaldson, and the basis for the decision has been well summarized by Martin (1975): "Where the justification for commitment is treatment, it violates due process if the treatment is not provided. If the justification for commitment is dangerousness to self or others, treatment is the *quid pro quo* society must pay as the price of the extra safety it derives from the denial of the individual's liberty" (p. 170).

While these cases were deciding whether an individual who was in an institution of some nature could be denied treatment, another case reached an entirely different conclusion. The Pennhurst decision, put forth by Judge Broderick, was that the institution should be closed and the mentally retarded persons should receive services in the community. The conditions described by Judge Broderick in his opinion are shocking indeed, whether they are statements of specifics or of generalities:

> 43% of the residents have had no family contact within the last three years . . . one vocational adjustment service report every ten years. . . . On the basis of this test [the Vineland], they have shown a decline rather than an increase in social skills while at Pennhurst. . . . As professionals leave the staff, they are often not replaced. . . . If one factors out those programs that are considered beneficial, the average treatment per resident drops to about fifteen minutes per day. . . . 511 residents are on the referral list for occupational therapy. . . . 51 (of 300) have been fitted with hearing aids . . . only 143 (of 300-400) are receiving physical therapy needed to prevent physical deterioration . . . the muscles in the limbs of these youths will contract and become useless. . . . None of the (1200) residents had a full multi-discipline assessment . . . physical restraints are used due to staff shortages. An extreme example . . . was in a physical restraint for 651 hours in June; 720 hours in August; 674 hours in September; 647 hours in October. . . . Outbreaks of pinworms and infectious disease are common . . . the noise level in the day rooms is often so high that many residents simply stop speaking. . . . Injuries to residents by other residents, and through self-abuse are common . . . one resident pushed a second to the floor, resulting in the death of the second resident. . . . In addition, there is some staff abuse of residents. . . . (pp. 17-34)

Each of the plaintiffs also has a list of injuries and grievances. Those of Robert _____ are typical:

> He was placed in a ward with forty-five other residents. His parents visited him two and one-half weeks after his admission and found that he was badly bruised, his mouth was cut, he was heavily drugged and did not recognize his mother. On this visit, the parents observed twenty-five residents walking the ward naked, others were only partially dressed. During this short period of time, Robert has lost skills that he had possessed prior to his admission. The parents promptly removed Robert from the institution, the mother commenting that she "wouldn't leave a dog in conditions like that." (p. 35)

In issuing his directives, Judge Broderick discussed several bases for his actions. These included (1) a constitutional right to minimally adequate habilitation, (2) a constitutional right to be free from harm, (3) a constitutional right to nondiscriminatory habilitation (i.e., education), and (4) a federal statutory right to nondiscriminatory habilitation.

The importance of this case may be extraordinary, not only for Judge Broderick's support of prior decisions, but also for the forcefulness of his description of what should be done with Pennhurst:

> All desire to improve the education, training and care provided the retarded in Pennsylvania and believe that *Pennhurst should be closed* and that all residents should be educated, trained and cared for in the community. All agree that institutions such as Pennhurst are inappropriate and inadequate for the habilitation of the retarded. (p. 45)

While these cases have been related to whether an individual who is in some type of institution can be excluded from treatment, another case was related to whether a state could exclude some of its residents from educational programs. This case was the quite famous PARC case in which the Pennsylvania Association for Retarded Children brought suit against the Commonwealth, because it excluded many retarded persons from educational programs. The premise of this case was that these children had a constitutional guarantee, provided by the Equal Protection Clause of the Fourteenth Amendment, to receive as much education and training as Pennsylvania provided for its other residents. The Pennsylvania statutes had said that it would provide education for all its handicapped conditions, yet a few paragraphs later it excluded uneducable and untrainable children, as well as those who have not yet reached a mental age of five before they are 16 years old (they were in effect excluded for life). The argument in this case was first based on the *Brown* decision of 1954, which provided a very compelling statement:

> If education is a principal instrument in helping the child to adjust normally to his environment, it is doubtful that any child may reasonably be expected to succeed in life if he is denied the opportunity of an education. The opportunity of an education, *where the state has undertaken to provide it to any, is a right which must be made available to all* on equal terms [italics added]. (Gilhool, 1973, p. 603)

The second basis for the argument was that with proper training most retarded persons could achieve self-sufficiency. Before all the witnesses for the plaintiffs could testify, the attorney general for the Commonwealth yielded to the evidence and agreed that all retarded children in Pennsylvania had the right to an education. The court ordered that the Commonwealth should provide access to a free public education according to the capabilities of each individual. It further suggested that education should be in the least restricted environment possible: that education in a regular class is preferable to education in a special class, and so forth.

The PARC case was an extraordinarily important case that has had effects on later court rulings, as well as on the procedures adopted by school districts without court directives. It has also had, of course, tremendous personal significance for retarded persons, their parents, and their friends. Gilhool (1973) relates an experience of one of the plaintiffs and uses it to describe an improving situation:

> . . . another school official defendant came to the house of another plaintiff and said, "We have the order, we will obey it, of course, if you want us to. We have a class for Felix. It is the same class that we had 2 years ago, and we will put him in it if you want us to. You remember, however, what happened a few years ago. Felix went into the class, but the class wasn't the class for him. In 2 weeks he began to act up. We had to call you and tell you to come and take Felix home. Well, if you want us to, we will obey the order and put him in that class, but we expect that in another 2 weeks we will have to call you again and say, 'Felix is acting up; come and get him and take him home.' Of course, we will tell you about your rights to a hearing and all the rest. We will do it if you want us to, but what good parent would put his child through all of that?" The parents said many things to that school official, none of which I will repeat, at least not in exact terms. But essentially what they said was, "Sir, you're talking the wrong language. It is no longer the case that the child must fit the class. It is now the case that the class must fit the child." (pp. 608-609)

Gilhool's paraphrasing points out the hopes of all those involved in this movement. But one wonders whether it does not confuse two things; (1) the right of access to educational placements, and (2) the quality of that education. To believe that future cases in other districts will not uphold the right to treatment and to education is unwarranted. To believe that access to placement and quality education are the same is, however, also unwarranted. We have seen far too many examples of students in their least restrictive environment who are not receiving a good education. Indeed, we know that in our country *in toto* we are not providing good education for students whether they be in public schools or in universities. Why should we expect any more for retarded persons? We must be quite careful at this time to distinguish between being in a classroom and learning in that classroom. Various public laws and legal decisions have addressed the former; they have not, however, even broached the latter in a significant way. While all of us are quite proud of the accomplishments of the judges, lawyers, associations, parents, and retarded citizens, we have only seen the first objective being approached. The second may be far more difficult.

INSTITUTIONAL PROBLEMS AND ABUSES BEING TRANSFERRED TO COMMUNITY PROGRAMS

Our first problem, as more of our citizens become involved in community programs, is to eliminate the abuse of inadequate education. As a community of professionals and paraprofessionals, we still know neither how nor what to teach retarded persons. Certainly, we have learned that some methods, whether they be called behavioral or not, are more successful than others. But to presume that we have identified truly efficient ways of teaching retarded persons is to delude ourselves. From the perspective of this book, the strong approach to advocate is not the exclusive use of behavioral methods so popular today, but rather the *analysis* of the effectiveness of ways to teach people. Perhaps the adoption of the term "applied behavior analysis" in lieu of the term "behavior modification" supports this point quite well. Too many of us are concerned with the modification of behavior, and too few of us are concerned with the analysis of behavior. Acceptance of the former approach leads to the automated adoption of methods, rather than to the analysis of what is supporting current levels of behavior and what could support improved levels. Many of us have been quite pleased with the significant adoption of behaviorism by so many workers in our field. But we should not be complacent, as we have so much more to learn. Ironically, by its significant growth, current behavioral practices may be signaling the demise of the field's popularity. We simply have too many people in token programs, in overcorrection, in timeout, etc. When teachers begin to recognize that situation, and when they see that many of these programs fail, they will turn to other options. We hope that behaviorists will be able to provide those options.

We also do not know enough about what to teach retarded persons, at least in a systematic sense, and we have this problem in two areas. The first is that we have not identified the terminal skills appropriate for various levels of functioning at various ages. Certainly, many of us have identified terminal skills for programs, but they vary across programs, and the information is not available to all in a usable format. We know that certain self-help skills and certain vocational skills should be developed, but we have still not identified and matched them to our client's needs in a way that would be helpful to the many who provide educational programs. We have also not yet identified hierarchies of tasks in terms of prerequisites. There is some information that certain arithmetic skills, for example, are necessary before other skills can be learned; but there must be a great deal more that can be learned about prerequisites within skills, as well as between skills. Our task of teaching persons who are slow in the rate at which they acquire skills could certainly be helped if we knew what skill acquisitions would speed the rate of learning other skills.

While our lack of educational expertise may be a subtle abuse that transfers across situations, others are not so subtle. One of these is institutional peonage, a practice well developed in the 1800s, when there were attempts to make institutions as self-sufficient as possible. The practice has been continued. Stone (1975) discussed one study of three-quarters of all our institutions which found that (1) 20% of the residents were engaged in nontherapeutic labor, (2) 30% of these received no wages while 50% were paid less than $10 per week, (3) many worked more than 40 hours per week, and (4) the work was primarily dull, negative, and without therapeutic value.

There is also no reason to suspect that community programs will prevent occurrences of staff abuse of clients. Certainly, in more public programs there should be fewer opportunities for covert abuse, but it will not be totally prevented, nor should we expect that it can be. Staff who work with retarded persons are, after all, members of a society that has a great problem with crimes of all types. To presume that teachers will only be from that group of society not so inclined is unrealistic. We can only attempt to develop effective standards and penalties that will decrease the likelihood that such abuses will occur.

There are, of course, enumerable problems that will be transferred from institutional to community programs, and we should be prepared for them. Adoption of the community approach really only tends to produce two results: (1) services are decentralized, and (2) living and programming groups are smaller. The vigor with which some proponents advocate community services makes one wish that as much attention would be directed toward ensuring that the community programs deliver the services they promise.

ACCOUNTABILITY AND DEMONSTRATION OF EFFECTIVENESS IN SERVICE SYSTEMS

During the 1970s, we were supposed to have been in an era of accountability, a concept that means we are responsible for our actions. At one level, acountability refers to our responsibility to provide services to our retarded citizens. Legally, it is based primarily on due process, freedom from cruel and unusual punishment, and equal protection. Morally, it is based on much, much more. As Turnbull (1975) writes, "this is an age of egalitarianism, an age that is capable of adopting as its tenets the indivisibility of human and constitutional rights and the essential quality of all persons" (p. 428).

Accountability in this sense is inextricably related to the right to treatment and the right to education. Each of the court cases has suggested that there should be standards of some type for service providers. Most recent cases have required some sort of individualized educational plan. This approach has, of course, also been promoted by Public Law 94-142. The extent to which service providers are required to be accountable has been discussed by Martin (1978): (1) an individualized educational plan must be written in cooperation by representatives of both the service providers and the client; (2) the plan should contain objective descriptions of the individual's needs based on objective assessments of his or her physical condition, physical development and motor coordination, language skills, academic skills, social skills, and vocational skills where appropriate; (3) long- and short-term goals should be stated in objective terms that allow measurement of progress; (4) dates for the initiation and proposed duration of programming for each goal should be stated; (5) all goals should interrelate to produce a total program for the individual; (6) the plan should specify each agency delivering services, as well as each individual and that person's qualifications to deliver the service; and (7) the agency should involve persons from the client's normal environment.

In discussing to what one should be held responsible, Turnbull (1975) refers to various standards, such as those of the Joint Commission on the Accreditation of Hospitals (ACFMR), Department of Health, Education, and Welfare (ICF-MR), and the guidelines of *Wyatt* v. *Stickney*. While one would not argue with the intent of any of these, there still remain problems of bureaucracy and interpretation. We (Repp & Barton, 1980) recently studied in depth one state's largest residential facility and compared the amount of programming in the units that did and did not meet that state's licensing requirements (basically the same as the JCAH and ICF-MR standards). Presumably, one should find a difference between the amount of programming in the units that were licensed and the units that were not licensed. We did not; instead, we found that in more than 90% of the observations between 9:00 A.M. and 3:30 P.M., Monday through Friday, there was no programming in the units comprising either the licensed or the nonlicensed units. This finding was quite disappointing to our hopes that licensing would be a reliable indication that services were indeed being programmed. The results should not be interpreted, however, as meaning that we cannot hold people accountable for abiding by the appropriate standards. They could be interpreted as meaning (1) that the standards should include guidelines for measuring programming, and (2) that occasional and superficial inspections are not adequate.

We also have data, collected from a number of facilities, that indicate that the spirit of individualized educational plans is not being upheld. Many facilities have eight or ten objectives per client per year and consider that amount to be sufficient. Such presumptions, however, degrade this concept. Although writing and monitoring a large number of long- and short-term goals can be very time consuming, there are systems by which one can have long, complicated, and individualized educational plans (e.g., see Repp & Lazarus, 1979). When we were providing services for severely and moderately retarded persons, each client had a minimum of 50 six-month goals which were programmed by at least six professional disciplines; many clients had as many as 100 goals. While these numbers may be inappropriately large for some people, they do represent a reasonable effort by staff to be held accountable for providing educational programs.

DEINSTITUTIONALIZATION, MAINSTREAMING, AND NORMALIZATION

Deinstitutionalization, mainstreaming, and normalization are three separate concepts which, nevertheless, are so interrelated that a discussion of one is difficult without reference to the other two. Deinstitutionalization means that we shall remove retarded persons from institutions and place them in other environments. Mainstreaming means that retarded persons will be educated as much as possible in classes with nonretarded persons. Normalization means that the individual's total environment should be as close as possible to that of nonhandicapped person's environment. The extent to which these concepts are related is expressed in the language of PL 93-380, the Education Amendment of 1974. This amendment is quite direct and requires that, in order to receive federal funds for the education of handicapped persons, a state must develop a plan that contains

> procedures to insure that, to the maximum extent appropriate, handicapped children, including children in public or private institutions or other care facilities, are educated with children who are not handicapped, and that special classes, separate schooling, or other removal of handicapped children from the regular education environment occurs only when the nature of severity of the handicap is such that education in regular classes with the use of supplementary aids and services cannot be achieved satisfactorily. [Public Law 93-380, Title VIB, Sec. 612(d)(13B)]

Deinstitutionalization, mainstreaming, and normalization are such power-ful concepts that we might presume each has been a resounding success the last few years. In truth, however, none has been, for each has advocated particular physical changes without taking a hard stance on the quality of programming provided in the situation each advocates. Perhaps that approach is as it should be, and quality should be a philosophy separate from those advocated. The persons involved in each of these movements may have realized that to discuss the life of retarded persons in terms that could be easily quantified (e.g., achievement) would slow the movement. To base the movements instead on the less quantifiable belief in one's sense of humanity was much wiser, for who could disagree (with or without data) that we should provide the opportunity for as wonderful a life as possible for those who are less able to provide it for themselves. Our belief, however, is that the time has come for us to slip past rhetoric, to presume that the movements to place handicapped persons in least restrictive environments will continue, and to begin to concern ourselves more with what is happening to the retarded student, whether all or none of the other students sitting in his classroom are handicapped.

Deinstitutionalization

Deinstitutionalization is, or course, a movement in reaction to institutionaliza-tion and perhaps can best be understood in that context. As discussed in Chapter 1, several hundred years ago retarded persons were not categorized separately, but were combined with the mentally ill, and sometimes with persons with other handicaps. Since the church was omnipotent, a religious explanation was offered for their deviancy. As nonhandicapped persons were regarded as the province of God, handicapped persons came to be regarded as the province of the devil. Then the power of the church decreased, and mentally retarded and ill persons were regarded as examples of moral deviance. Then as Pinel began his revolution for the basis of treatment at Hôpital Salpêtrière in Paris, a more humane ap-proach began, and institutions began in part to help these individuals. However, in the later 1800s, institutions grew to great sizes, became conscious of cost-effectiveness measures, and began to house people without a great deal of care for treatment. While there certainly are exceptions, that trend continued until relatively recently. Then in the 1950s and 1960s a number of social movements began that were to help retarded persons. One of the more important to this issue was President Kennedy's approach to mental illness, which was more com-munity based than institution based. The U.S. Department of Health, Educa-tion, and Welfare brought forth mental health guidelines for the "mentally ill" and promised funding for community centers that provided in-patient and out-patient care, emergency treatment, partial hospitalization, and consultation and education (Bassuk & Gerson, 1978).

This approach certainly influenced those governing the lives of retarded persons, and they began to consider community placements a viable and more humane effort. The horrors of our institutions became the basis for some biting social commentary (Blatt & Kaplan, 1966; Rivera, 1972), and the movement gained more impetus. Similarly, we seemed unable to identify any reason (except for the convenience of other members of society) why retarded persons should be segregated from the rest of us. Finally, various legal decisions required that institutions either be decreased greatly in population or that they be closed entirely.

Today, deinstitutionalization should include three processes: (1) preventing institutionalization by finding appropriate alternative placements, (2) returning to the community all residents who have developed the skills necessary for a successful transition, and (3) establishing residential environments that protect rights and that produce a rapid transition to the community (Vitello, 1977). While these do not seem to be insurmountable goals, and while society does not seem at all to be opposed to it, deinstitutionalization has not been a profound success.

Burda (1977) reports several investigations in Pennsylvania which produced the typical list of inadequate and often atrocious living conditions. She then reports the work of PARC, which called for and received plans for improvements in these facilities. Reports from PARC's well-trained observers, who initiated unannounced visits, however, included "lack of programming or sporadic programming, excessive drug usage, overcrowding, . . . staff shortages, unsanitary conditions, lack of personal clothing supply, . . ." (p. 36). The list continues, and the point is well made: many residents are not being prepared for a transition to the community. In fact, according to Burda, a program of reinstitutionalization rather than deinstitutionalization is actually being practiced.

—200 residents were transferred to a mental health institution in the eastern part of the state.

—150 residents were transferred to a nursing home in the eastern part of the state.

—174 residents were transferred to a converted tuberculosis hospital in the western part of the state.

—264 residents were placed in two nursing homes in the western part of the state, one of which has had six administrators in three years and as of this writing is still not delivering adequate services to residents.

—142 residents were transferred to a building designed and built as a geriatric center. Children in this building are still denied access to education in the community in spite of Public Law 94-142, the Education for All Handicapped Children Act.

—Two of these facilities have been termed "transitional" facilities. However, less than 100 of the residents placed in these facilities in the last four years have been transferred to a community service or less restrictive setting.

—In 1973, Pennsylvania operated nine institutions for mentally retarded persons. In 1977, Pennsylvania operates 13 institutions for mentally retarded persons and three nursing homes housing more than 100 mentally retarded persons. This is scarcely a trend toward deinstitutionalization. (p. 37)

Vitello (1977) also describes some negative reports on deinstitutionalization. A 1977 U.S. Comptroller report to the U.S. Congress contained the following: (1) placements were to nursing homes where the quality of care was worse than in institutions, (2) treatment consisted primarily of medication, and (3) readmissions to institutions were occurring because community facilities were unavailable. Collins and Hussain (1977) found (1) 36 persons placed who were *not* retarded, (2) overmedication, (3) poor medical diagnosis, (4) inadequate educational and medical plans, (5) regression in adaptive behaviors, (6) incompetent staff, and so forth. Skarnulis (1976) reported on the Nebraska effort to use community facilities (an effort initiated by Wolfensberger and reported by his followers as evidence for the success of normalization), and found that (1) adults had difficulty adjusting, (2) inappropriate behaviors increased, (3) adults were placed in shoddy rooms in the community, and (4) neighbors opposed the placements.

Vitello goes on to report other negative results, but he counterbalances that information with some positive results. Scheerenberger and Felsenthal (1976) found successful placements and preferences by the clients for living in the community. Aaner and Moen (1976) found increases in functioning as measured by the AAMD Adaptive Behavior Scale. O'Connor (1976), in her monograph on group homes, found that many community facilities were better placements than institutions had been. She warned, however, that

> The philosophy that anything is better than an institutional placement must be seriously questioned, at least on a short-term basis. With sufficient planning, appropriate program implementation, and careful monitoring, community placement can provide excellent opportunities for our handicapped citizens. Without these precautions, hundreds even thousands of individuals could end up in mini institutions without public attention and resources now available in public institutions. (p. 68)

Mainstreaming

Mainstreaming is an approach that emphasizes integration, and as such it is the antithesis of the earlier institutionalization movements, which emphasized segregation. At various times in our educational history, we have had less restrictive educational plans in which students were educated in special classes or even in the same classroom as nonhandicapped students (the one-room schoolhouse is the ultimate in architectural integration). But not until the early 1960s did we begin to recover from the late-1800 program of segregating retarded persons as much as possible. Today's program, which emphasizes integrating retarded persons as much as possible, has had many forebearers. Three forces in this movement have been (1) the fact that special classes were often racially imbalanced, (2) lawsuits that were litigated for students whose test scores resulted in misclassification, and (3) the failure of research to demonstrate that special classes produced greater achievements for retarded persons.

Dunn (1968), in his farewell address to the Council for Exceptional Children, provided a major impetus to this program. He asserted that special classes were not superior to regular classes and that placement in a special class stigmatized those children. Since the intent of special classes (to provide better education) was not being met, there really seemed to be little reason to retain them. The efforts then came to be directed toward a less restrictive educational environment.

Various models advocate certain interpretations or plans for mainstreaming, and they propose different degrees of intervention. But we really should not expect there to be one unitary concept of mainstreaming, as many thousands of people are contributing to what this philosophy will become 10 and 20 years from now. The Council for Exceptional Children (Caster, 1975) has provided some guidelines for what it considers to be the central themes of mainstreaming programs. Their view is that mainstreaming means (1) providing the most appropriate education for each child in the least restrictive environment, (2) concentrating on specific educational needs rather than on labels, such as mentally retarded or learning disabled, (3) developing means by which regular classroom personnel can service students with learning or adjustment problems, and (4) uniting the skills of regular and special educators in an effort to best serve the students. The council's view is also that mainstreaming is not (1) a wholesale return of handicapped children to the regular classroom, (2) allowing students to be in regular classes without having the special services they require, or (3) a less costly procedure than servicing students in special classes.

Today, there is a lot of rhetoric concerning mainstreaming. Some argue that the only acceptable approach is to have all students of the same chronological age, regardless of developmental age, in the same classroom. Others argue that such a plan would only provide a disservice to handicapped persons. Unfortunately, many of these people have missed the more important point of our educational problem today. Because our research over the decades has produced so few significant results in teaching academic and social behaviors, we are not doing a particularly good job of teaching, whether our students are in a preschool program or in a doctoral program. Our public schools are failing, and we simply have not solved that problem. Our major concern should not be with where a child sits; it should be with how well she or he is being taught.

Normalization

Normalization is a principle that interestingly is based on institutionalization and its alternatives. It is a concept that has only recently been articulated, yet it is a very powerful principle. Some people interpret it to mean that retarded persons should be treated normally, just as you and I are treated. This approach is a misguided (or unguided) one, however. Normalization should mean that all the skills one needs to acquire to live most successfully should be addressed by service providers. Some of these skills can be developed in a "normal" fashion, and they should be. Some of these skills can be developed only through specialized atypical means, and they should be. Ways of life, aside from skill development, should also be as normal as possible. Architectural and social barriers should be removed. Precisely for these reasons, normalization has been instrumental as a principle in removing people from institutions when communities can serve them as well.

The first formal discussion of normalization, published by Nirje in 1969, was an attempt to provide goals and guidelines for providing an institutional or a community life that was as much like a nonretarded person's life as possible. In this work, Nirje provided the eight components which were discussed in Chapter 1.

Others began discussing this principle also. Roos (1969) concluded that it was a sound principle on which to develop residential services for retarded persons. In the same year, the National Association for Retarded Children adopted a policy statement on the need to base services on humanistic and developmental principles (Mesibov, 1976). Nirje also wrote of the need to develop community services, so the principle of normalization began to develop a deserved foundation in both residential and community services. Wolfensberger (1972) also wrote about normalization, developed the Nebraska Plan, which was based on this principle, and became the name identified in our country with this movement.

The principle of normalization, in its basic form, is hardly an idea with which one could argue. It is basically an approach to help an individual live in as humane and respectful an environment as possible. Unfortunately, however, some people have used this concept to promote the idea itself without regard to the individual who is being affected. Mesibov (1976) warns us of this problem, and urges a rational approach:

> We should determine the efficacy of any treatment program based upon the progress made by the individual client and we should not be afraid to use the program that proves itself to be most effective. This does not require or preclude normalization, institutionalization, mainstreaming, special education, or anything else. All it says is that a service delivery system has an obligation to measure client growth and to determine treatment strategies and programs based on that growth. To the extent that normalization agrees with this approach, . . . I have no arguments. But to the extent that normalization is used as a justification for mainstreaming *all* EMR children in certain states (and it is); and to the extent that the only measure of the effectiveness of certain Group Homes is the degree to which they conform to what is considered normal (and it is); and to the extent that normalization is used to argue that absolutely *no one* should *ever* be in *any* institution (and it is); I must say let's step back and reconsider what is happening and how the clients are progressing in these "normal" settings. Certainly let those who are doing well remain, but let's find something else for those who are not. I have seen too many examples of children (and adults) suffering in normalized environments that were obviously detrimental for all concerned. These examples suggest that all is not well with normalization. Whether these examples arise because many misunderstand the philosophy of normalization is not the question. The point is that these things are happening, and normalization is being used as their justification. If this is because the principle is misunderstood, perhaps people . . . [should take the time to respond to those who are in error]. (pp. 373-374)

SUMMARY

The summary of these issues is really the same point that a summary of this book would make. We have two objectives: (1) to provide better services and better lives for retarded persons, and (2) to learn how best to reach that objective. From a behavioral viewpoint, these goals are intertwined. We should seek humane goals, and we should record data that can tell us how well we are reaching these goals. We are in an era of science and of humanity that should allow us to progress, but there are some cautions. The primary one, from my viewpoint, has been well stated by an eminent scholar, Edward Zigler, who has called upon research to help us avoid the errors we have made before:

> Research takes an added importance at this particularly critical juncture in constructing social policy for the retarded. At the social policy level, the mental retardation field is in a state of flux and disarray. Some years ago, experts convinced decision-makers that special education was the solution to the problem of training the retarded. This view is now suspect and decision-makers are committing themselves to such concepts as normalization and deinstitutionalization. I join with those many senior workers in the field who view these concepts as little more than slogans that are badly in need of an empirical data base. (1976, p. 6)

In this chapter, we discuss many issues that will be with us throughout the 1980s. Although only one of these (the misuse of behavioral technology) is directly related to applied behavior analysis, all can be addressed through this system of evaluation and teaching. In the last two parts of this book, we will consider how the methods of measurement, evaluation, and behavior change relate to each of these issues. We will find, for example, (1) alternatives to drugs that can reduce inappropriate responding; (2) ways of using natural, unobtrusive, and nonaversive procedures to change behavior that will be fully in accord with any guidelines; (3) methods to make learning easier so that some people will never be labeled retarded, while others who are labeled will be better educated; and (4) methods of teaching and evaluation that allow you to direct your efforts toward the student rather than toward slogans that, while helpful to retarded persons, are more social than educational in purpose.

In the next part of this book, we will introduce procedures that will help define, measure, record, and evaluate behavior. Although these procedures are not teaching procedures, they are at the heart of any behavior change procedure; for once we learn to use them, we will be able to learn whether we are using the behavior change procedures discussed in this book correctly, and, perhaps even more importantly, whether we are correctly using novel procedures or procedures not mentioned in this book. In this way, we will learn even more about educating retarded persons.

REFERENCES

Aaner, D., & Moen, M. Adaptive behavior change of group home residents. *Mental Retardation*, 1976, **14**, 36-40.

Accreditation Council for Facilities for the Mentally Retarded. *Standards for Residential Facilities for the Mentally Retarded*. Chicago: Joint Commission on Accreditation of Hospitals, 1971 (5th printing, 1975).

American Psychological Association. *Ethical principles in the conduct of research with human participants*. Washington, D.C.: The Association, 1973.

American Psychological Association. *Standards for providers of psychological services*. Washington, D.C.: The Association, 1974.

Arnold v. Tampalpais Union High School District, Civil Action No. 61215 (Superior Ct. Marin Cty., Cal. 1972).

Bassuk, E. L., & Gerson, S. Deinstitutionalization and mental health services. *Scientific American*, 1978, **238**, 46-53.

Birnbum, M. The right to treatment. *American Bar Association Journal*, 1960, **46**, 499-503.

Blatt, B., & Kaplan, F. *Christmas in purgatory*. Boston: Allyn & Bacon, Inc., 1966.

Brown v. Board of Education, 347 U.S. 483, 74 S. Ct. 686, 98 L. Ed. 873 (1954).

Burda, M. Residential services: The Pennsylvania paradox. *Amicus*, 1977, 34-39.

Burton, T. A., Burton, S. F., & Hirshoren, A. For sale: The state of Alabama. *Journal of Special Education*, 1977a, **11**, 59-64.

Burton, T. A., Burton, S. F., & Hirshoren, A. Rhetoric versus reality. *Journal of Special Education*, 1977b, **11**, 70-72.

Caster, J. Share our specialty: What is "mainstreaming"? *Exceptional Children*, 1975, **42**, 174.

Cleland, C. C., & Sluyter, G. V. The Alabama decision: Unequivocal blessing? *Community Mental Health Journal*, 1974, **10**, 409-413.

Cohen, J. S., & DeYoung, H. The role of litigation in the improvement of programming for the handicapped. In L. Mann & D. A. Sabatino (Eds.), *The first review of special education*, Vol. 2, pp. 261-286. Philadelphia: Buttonwood Farms, Inc., 1973.

Collings, G. D. Case review: Rights of the retarded. *Journal of Special Education*, 1973, **7**, 27-37.

Collins, S. H., & Hussain, S. B. Can communities provide all services to the retarded? Paper presented at a meeting of the American Association of Mental Deficiency, 1977.

Comptroller General of the United States, Report to the Congress, Returning the mentally disabled to the community: Government needs to do more. Department of Health, Education, and Welfare, January 7, 1977.

Covarrubias v. San Diego Unified School District, Civil Action No. 70-30d (S.D. Cal. 1971).

Davis v. Watkins, 384 F. Supp. 1196 (N.D. Ohio 1974).

Diana v. Board of Education, Civil Action No. C-70-37 (N.D. Cal. 1970).

Donaldson v. O'Connor, 493 F. 2d. 507 (5th Cir. 1974). *Vacated*, 422 U.S. 804 (1975). *O'-Connor v. Donaldson*, 422 U.S. 563 (1975).

Dunn, L. M. Special education for the mildly retarded: Is much of it justifiable? *Exceptional Children*, 1968, **35**, 5-22.

Epstein, L. H., Doke, L. A., Sajwaj, T. E., Sorrell, S., & Rimmer, B. Generality and side effects of overcorrection. *Journal of Applied Behavior Analysis*, 1974, **7**, 385-390.

Friedman, P. R. The right to treatment comes of age. Unpublished manuscript, Mental Health Law Project, 1975.

Gilhool, T. K. Education: An inalienable right. *Exceptional Children*, 1973, **39**, 597-609.

Gilhool, T. K., & Stutman, E. A. Integration of severely handicapped students toward criteria for implementing and enforcing the integration of PL 94-142 and Section 504. In S. Sarason, D. Geller, & M. Klaber (Eds.), *Least restrictive alternatives: Moral, legal, and administrative dilemmas*. New York: Free Press, in press.

Goldiamond, I. Singling out behavior modification for legal regulation: Some effects on patient care, psychotherapy, and research in general. *Arizona Law Review*, 1975, **17**, 105-126.

Halderman, et al. v. Pennhurst State School, et al. Civil Action No. 74-1345 (E.D. Pa. 1978).

In Re Gault, 387 U.S. 1 (1967).

Larry P. v. Riles, Civil Action No. 71-2270 (N. D. Cal. 1971).

Lovaas, O. I., Koegel, R., Simmons, J. Q., & Long, J. S. Some generalization and follow-up measures on autistic children in behavior therapy. *Journal of Applied Behavior Analysis,* 1973, **6**, 131-164.

Martin, R. *Legal challenges to behavior modification: Trends in schools, corrections, and mental health.* Champaign, IL: Research Press, 1975.

Martin, R. Legal regulation of services to the developmentally disabled. In M. S. Berkler, G. H. Bible, S. M. Boles, D. E. D. Deitz, & A. C. Repp (Eds.), *Current trends for the developmentally disabled.* Baltimore: University Park Press, 1978.

May, J. G., Risley, T. R., Twardosz, S., Friedman, P., Bijou, S. W., Wexler, D., *et al.* Guidelines for the use of behavioral procedures in state programs for retarded persons. *M. R. Research,* 1975, **1**.

New York Association of Retarded Children v. Rockefeller, 357 F. Supp. 752 (E.D. N.Y. 1973).

Nirje, B. The normalization principle and its human management implications. In R. B. Kugel & W. Wolfensberger (Eds.), *Changing patterns in residential services for the mentally retarded.* Washington, D.C.: President's Committee on Mental Retardation, 1969.

O'Connor, G. Home is a good place. Monograph of the American Association of Mental Deficiency, Number 2, 1976.

O'Connor v. Donaldson, 493 F. 2d 507 (5th Cir. 1974).

Pennsylvania Association for Retarded Children v. Commonwealth of Pennsylvania, 343 F. Supp. 279 (E.D. Pa. 1972).

President's Committee on Mental Retardation. *Mental retardation: Century of decision.* Washington, D.C.: U.S. Government Printing Office, 1976.

President's Panel on Mental Retardation. Washington, D.C.: U.S. Government Printing Office, 1963.

Repp, A. C., & Barton, L. E. Naturalistic observations of institutionalized retarded persons: A comparison of licensure decisions and behavioral observations. *Journal of Applied Behavior Analysis,* 1980, **13**, 333-341.

Repp. A. C., & Deitz, D. E. D. Ethical responsibilities in reductive programs for the retarded. In M.S. Berkler, G. H. Bible, S. M. Boles, D. E. D. Deitz, & A. C. Repp (Eds.), *Current trends for the developmentally disabled.* Baltimore: University Park Press, 1978.

Repp, A. C., & Lazarus, S. G. An accountability system for institutions with mentally retarded persons. *Education and Training of the Mentally Retarded,* 1979.

Revised ethical standards of psychologists. *APA Monitors,* March, 1977, pp. 22-23.

Rivera, G. *Willowbrook: A report on how it is and why it doesn't have to be that way.* New York: Random House, Inc., 1972.

Roos, P. Current issues in residential care with special reference to the problems of institutional care. Paper presented at the meeting of the International League of Societies for the Mentally Handicapped, 1969.

Roos, P. Human rights and behavior modification. *Mental Retardation,* 1974, **12**, 3-6.

Ross, S., DeYoung, H., & Cohen, J. S. Confrontation: Special education and the law. *Exceptional Children,* 1971, **7**(4), 5-12.

Rouse v. *Cameron*, 373 F. 2d 451 (D.C. Cir. 1966).

Sajwaj, T. Issues and implications of establishing guidelines for the use of behavioral techniques. *Journal of Applied Behavior Analysis*, 1977, **10**, 531-540.

Scheerenberger, R. C., & Felsenthal, D. A study of alternative community placements. Unpublished manuscript, 1976.

Skarnulis, L. Less restrictive alternatives in residential services. *American Association for the Education of the Severely and Profoundly Handicapped Review*, 1976, 3, 42-84.

Skinner, B. F. *Science and human behavior*. New York: Macmillan, Inc., 1953.

Sterner, R. (Ed.), *Legislative aspects of mental retardation*. Stockholm, Sweden: International League of Societies for the Mentally Handicapped, 1967.

Stolz, S. B. Why no guidelines for behavior modification? *Journal of Applied Behavior Analysis*, 1977, **10**, 541-547.

Stone, A. A. *Mental health and law: A system in transition*. Rockville, Md.: National Institute of Mental Health, 1975.

Turnbull, H. R. Accountability: An overview of the impact of litigation on professionals. *Exceptional Children*, 1975, **41**, 427-433.

Vitello, S. J. Beyond institutionalization: What's happening to the people? *Amicus*, 1977, 40-44.

Wolfensberger, W. *The principle of normalization in human services*. Toronto: National Institute on Mental Retardation, 1972.

Wyatt v. *Stickney*, 325 F. Supp. 781 (M.D. Ala. 1971), 334 F. Supp. 1341 (M.D. Ala. 1971), 344 F. Supp. 373, 344 F. Supp. 387 (M.D. Ala. 1972), 368 F. Supp. 1383 (M.D. Ala. 1974), affirmed in part, modified in part sub. nom. *Wyatt* v. *Aderholt*, 503 F. 2d 1305 (5 Cir., 1974).

Zigler, E. NICHHD appropriations for mental retardation. Unpublished manuscript. Yale University, New Haven, Conn., 1976.

PART

II

CHAPTER

4

Defining and Measuring Behavior

Teaching retarded persons—all persons, for that matter—consists of deciding what is to be taught, determining a goal, arranging conditions that are optimal for reaching the goal, and measuring whether the goal has been reached. One of the differences between the behavioral approach and others is the choice of what is to be taught. Most approaches advocate teaching subjects like arithmetic or self-help skills, but a behavioral approach does not; it chooses instead to teach an *individual*, to teach the *individual to behave* in certain ways (e.g., to say "three" when asked "what number is this (3)?"); it chooses to use curricula as antecedent events for teaching the appropriate behaviors, and it chooses to use subsequent events for maintaining appropriate behaviors.

Defining Behavior

The purpose of this chapter is to focus on the beginning point of any teaching or behavior change program, that being definition of the response in question. We will discuss reasons for careful definitions and the means by which we write definitions. In the second portion of the chapter, we will discuss the measurement of behavior, both the purposes and the types of measurement. From this chapter, we will learn to define behavior and to choose a method by which to measure it. In the following chapter, we will learn methods of recording behavior. Then we will be prepared to consider alternatives for changing behavior and for evaluating the effectiveness of a behavior change procedure.

THE CONCERN FOR ACCURATE DESCRIPTIONS

Chapter 2 contained a description of some of the characteristics of the field of applied behavior analysis, but of all those characteristics, the primary one is an insistence on an objective description of behavior and of conditions related to its occurrence and nonoccurrence. As such, the beginning point of all behavioral programs is the identification and definition of responding. Identifying merely involves labeling the behavior in an objective manner that will allow a detailed definition (e.g., head-banging, or correctly completing arithmetic problems, or acting friendly). Defining, on the other hand, involves writing a detailed description of behavior that will allow two or more people to agree consistently that a response[1] has occurred.[2] Throughout the literature of applied behavior analysis, you will find a continuing concern with writing thorough behavioral definitions. While the reasons for this concern are many, several are particularly relevant to teaching retarded persons: (1) to direct the teacher's attention to the behavior, (2) to provide an accurate base for setting goals, (3) to reduce errors in judgment, (4) to provide a base for accountability, and (5) to help produce a science of teaching.

Directing the Attention of Teachers

While we might presume that teachers know, *a priori*, to direct their attention toward children acting appropriately and not toward students who are acting inappropriately, there is considerable evidence that this relationship is not so. Patterson, Cobb, and Ray (1972) have discussed the issue of teacher attention, citing several studies that have shown that the majority of teacher attention actually follows nonstudy rather than study behavior (Hall, Lund & Jackson, 1968; Walker & Buckley, 1971; Werry & Quay, 1968). The study by Walker and Buckley found particularly interesting results: (1) 77% of the teacher's attention was contingent upon responding of problem children, while only 23% was directed toward properly behaving children; (2) of the attention directed toward the problem children. 89% was for inappropriate responding, while only 11% was for appropriate. While there can be many reasons for this disproportionate distribution of attention, the teacher's behavior of attending can best be changed after a proper definition of appropriate and inappropriate student behaviors has been made.

Providing a Base for Setting Goals

All programs should state goals, but when the response is not properly defined, we cannot accurately tell when the goal has been reached, because we can never measure the behavior in the same manner from day to day; as a result there sim-

---

[1] In this book, the distinction between *behavior* and *response* made by Skinner (1953) will be maintained; i.e., *behavior* refers to that which we say that a person does, while *response* refers to a particular instance of observable behavior.

[2] The means by which the agreement between people is assessed is quite exacting and will be discussed in the section on interobserver agreement.

ply will be no consistency. We all know that when we set goals we generally try to attain them; and we all know that the more subjective we allow that goal to be, the more likely we are to allow the goal to become "achieving the goal" rather than "emitting the behaviors appropriate to reaching the goal." When the former becomes the case, we find it far easier to *say* we succeeded than to do all the things necessary actually to have succeeded.[3] But when there is accurate definition and measurement of all behaviors necessary to achieve the goal, we are more likely to do the proper work necessary to reach the goal. When the matter is related to retarded students, the need for unbiased and unvarying appraisal of their success is important so that we can know we are teaching them to cope with the demands of their environment.

Reducing Errors in Judgment

When we do not make complete behavior definitions, and when as a result definitions vary over time, we can make errors of three types: (1) We can believe that the behavior changed when it did not and go on to something else in its place. For example, if we are working with a child who has an "attention deficit" and begin praising him for attending, we may believe we succeeded when we did not simply because we did not carefully define and measure "attending." To move to another task as a result of this error in judgment is unfortunate. (2) We can believe we found a procedure that worked (e.g., praising behavior) and use it in other situations to help the child learn other behaviors. But if we erred in judging the effect of the procedure and it really was not effective, then we will probably be wasting both the student's time and our time when we try to improve the other behavior. (3) We can believe a procedure was effective when it was not and then use it to improve the behavior of other students. This type of judgmental error becomes even more serious than others, because the error affects so many other students.

Providing a Base for Accountability

While there are many definitions of accountability, common elements to most are setting goals, measuring the degree to which they are achieved, determining how they were achieved or why they were not, identifying how long it took to reach the goal, and identifying what was done during other periods of the workday. Inherent in all attempts at accountability is a careful definition of what one does, for accountability means "holding one accountable for what one does." But if there is an unclear and a varying definition of what we do, there can be no system of accountability.

---

[3] For example, it is far easier for you to tell your friends you received an A in this course, when you did not, than for you to have done all the work necessary to earn that grade.

Producing a Science of Teaching

Behaviorists are very interested in making teaching a science so that it can be more efficient and effective, thus allowing us more time to pursue arts, recreation, and other work. The first requisite of a science is that its methods allow replication; i.e., the same results can be reproduced with the same people (*direct replication*) or the same results can be produced with different people or responses, or with different but identifiable conditions (*systematic replication*). The fascination with replication is inherent to all science; whether the study be physics, psychology, or podiatry, it cannot be science unless its methods are replicable. The ubiquitous support for this concept is expressed in the old bromide, so familiar in textbooks of all disciplines: the basic canon of science is that its methods be replicable. While there are many rules designed to ensure replication in the science of educating the retarded, and while we will discuss many, the most basic is that, if the response definition varies, the measurement of behavior will vary, the behavior change will not be a function of the treatment instituted, and the conclusions reached will not be accurate. In the science of educating the retarded, this type of error is catastrophic, because (1) the time lost in applying an incorrect conclusion to teaching a retarded person can never be regained, and as people are generally called retarded because they require more time to learn, time is essential; and (2) all the information we have today on methods to help teach retarded persons would be lost, and we would find ourselves more involved with custodial treatment than with educating, an era to which we should never return.

DEFINING THE OCCURRENCE OF A RESPONSE

There are two principal ways in which the occurrence of a response is defined in ABA: (1) by machine, or (2) by human observers. Machine definitions are a very important carryover from laboratory studies in which electrical equipment defines, records, and sometimes analyzes responding, while human definitions are the heart of the applied system, as machine use is usually too expensive, impractical, or simply impossible in much of the work in applied settings.

Machine Definitions

In the original laboratory work with retarded persons (e.g., Barrett & Lindsley, 1962; Bijou, 1955, 1957a, b, 1958a, b, 1959; Bijou & Sturges, 1959; Orlando & Bijou, 1960), each individual would press a lever, a panel, or a telegraph key and be reinforced according to some schedule. Generally, electromechanical equipment was used to define whether or not a response occurred.

In later applied work, excellent use was made of mechanical definitions of responses in a number of settings. For example, Azrin and Foxx (1971) developed very simple devices for defining urinary and fecal responses by the severely or profoundly retarded adults they were toilet training. Inappropriate responding was defined by a moisture-detection device consisting of (1) two clothing snaps fastened in the crotch of ordinary men's briefs; (2) two flexible wires leading from the snaps to a circuit box worn around the client's waist (the wires had snaps at one end so that the apparatus could easily be removed when pants were soiled); and (3) a circuit box which sounded a tone whenever urine or feces moistened the area between the clothing snaps.[4] A second device measured appropriate responding and consisted of (1) a toilet with a malleable plastic bowl fitted to the normal toilet bowl, (2) two detachable wires leading from the bowl to a circuit box on the floor, and (3) a circuit box which sounded a tone when moisture connected the ends of the two wires.

Other mechanical definitions of responding have been offered by Tom Ball in an inventive series of studies addressing a wide variety of behaviors. While these devices generally allowed immediate consequences of responding, only their role in providing immediate response definitions will be discussed here. Ball, Sibbach, Jones, Steele, and Frazier (1975) were concerned with the behaviors of five retarded persons, which consisted of repetitive body movements, including frantic shaking of the arms, hitting all parts of the body with fists, face slapping, body slapping, head-banging, severely assaultive behavior toward others (e.g., breaking the noses of two attendants), and a number of other similar behaviors. To define (and then consequate) responding, Ball and his associates designed an accelerometer[5] that would be activated only when a forceful movement was stopped suddenly, such as a client hitting herself with her fist. The authors addressed the generalized usefulness of the device when they stated that "because the accelerometers can be set to respond only to the violent movements or impact forces associated with assaultive or self-destructive behaviors, the subject can move freely through the environment and engage in a normal range of activities without receiving" the contingency (p. 224). A very different type of behavior was the subject of another study (Ball, McCrady & Hart, 1975) in which the sitting behavior of two mentally retarded and cerebral palsied children was automatically defined, recorded, and consequated. Because the head-up response is often infrequent in cerebral palsied retarded children, and because it is often necessary for learning social and other behaviors, the authors sought to teach the two children to hold their heads in an upright position and consequated this response by providing music the children appeared to enjoy. To define the response, Ball attached a mercury switch to a miniature earphone held in place on each child's left ear. When the child's head was held upright, the switch was closed, a timer was operated, and music was played through the earphone. When the child's head dropped forward, the circuit was broken, and

---

[4] While this device is presented here as an example of a machine definition of responding, it really has many advantages, including (1) a reliable definition of initial responding, (2) an automated definition that allows the programming staff to direct their efforts toward other teaching tasks instead of continually checking for a response, and (3) a procedure that removes some of the aversiveness associated with toilet training youngsters and adults.

[5] Although the device is described as an accelerometer, it may be more meaningful to consider it to be a decelerative device, as the circuit was activated not when a rapid movement was initiated, but rather when a rapid movement stopped extremely quickly, as when a client hit her leg with her fist.

both the timer and the music stopped. The use of a device like this, which provides definition, recording, and consequation of a response, and which fits into the natural environment so unobtrusively, is really quite elegant in terms of its simplicity and usefulness.

Observer Definitions

Although machine definitions are quite useful, being consistent and serving to free the teacher for other work, most response definitions in applied behavior analysis involve observers who define and then record each instance of responding. In this case, there arises a new set of problems, *viz.*, all those variables other than the target response which affect the observer's recording behaviors. These variables include observer motivation, fatigue as the observation session becomes longer, distracting stimuli, knowing someone else is watching us observe and record the target behavior, and many other variables. While there have been a number of studies on factors affecting accuracy in recording, Hawkins and Dobes (1973) have shown that writing accurate and complete behavior definitions may be the most important factor in promoting a consistent day-to-day definition of a response. In their study, pairs of observers were given nine definitions of behaviors and were asked to record whether or not the children and teachers they were observing engaged in these behaviors. Results showed that, when definitions did not meet Hawkins and Dobes's criterion of being *objective, clear, and complete*, there was little agreement between two observers on the occurrence of responding.

DIMENSIONS OF BEHAVIOR

Dimensions of behavior refer to those characteristics which are important to the definition of a response. Some of those that are common in applied behavior analysis are (1) frequency, (2) duration, (3) latency, (4) magnitude, and (5) topography.

Frequency

Frequency[6] refers to the number of responses emitted per unit time. While many studies count each occurrence of a response as a unit, some count it only as a subunit. For example, if a teacher were interested in how many assignments a stu-

---

[6] There is considerable inconsistency in the use of the word *frequency* in applied behavior analysis. One group uses it to refer to the "average number of responses per unit time," and then uses the word *count* to refer to that number. Another group uses the word *rate* to refer to the "average number of responses per unit time," and then uses the word *frequency* to refer to that number. In this book, the former reference will be used for two reasons: (1) the standard use of the word in our language implies a time base. For example, "it snows *frequently*" implies a relatively large number of days with snow each winter; and (2) the word is used in other sciences such as physics to mean the number of occurrences per unit time.

dent completed, and if each assignment consisted of 10 problems and 20 minutes in which to complete them, 10 completed problems would constitute one response, while fewer than 10 would constitute zero responses. In cases of this type, frequency of the subunits of responding would be critical to the definition.

Duration

Duration is often an important dimension to the definition of a response. Its most typical use is in defining the length of an episode of behavior before it is defined as a response. For example, *on-task* might be counted as occurring only if it were present for 30 consecutive seconds. If it were present for only 29 seconds, a response would not be defined as having occurred. A second and less typical use of duration is to define the absence of at least one of the characteristics of the response for some period of time as the termination of one response occurrence and the precondition to the beginning of another. For example, one common definition of *verbalization* is "any appropriate verbalization from a child to a teacher or to another child, whether in response to a question, command, request, or suggestion, or whether initiating the verbalization not in response to such behaviors. The observer should count it as a separate response if it follows a prior response by at least four seconds. The observer should exclude laughing, humming, and singing." Note that if a verbalization occurs for 3 seconds, does not occur for 12 seconds, and then occurs for 8 seconds, the definition requires a count of two responses. On the other hand, if the behavior occurs for 1,000 seconds without the absence of at least one characteristic of the definition for at least 4 consecutive seconds, then only one response can be defined as having occurred.

Latency

Latency is another dimension that can have two different functions in the definition of a response. The most typical is to define a response as having to occur within a period of time. For example, in a large project with a group of initially uncontrolled, profoundly retarded adolescents, a group of teachers taught the students to line up on command. The definition of the response was "while sitting on a chair at a work table, a student will rise, walk to the front of the room, have at least one foot on a 3-inch wide tape, be behind the person who last lined up, and complete all the behaviors within 10 seconds of the command '[name], line up, and stand quietly for 30 seconds without touching other students.' " In this example, the response had to be completed within 10 seconds of the request, so the latency is 10 seconds. If the behaviors were completed 12 seconds after the teacher's request, then the behavior would not have met the latency dimension of 10 seconds that was included in the definition.

Another less typical use of latency is to describe the time that must pass before behavior can occur in order to meet the response definition. For example, in an early childhood program, we were concerned with a child's *remembering* two-step commands. In this case the response was defined as "at least 10 seconds after the teacher gives [name] a two-step command, the student will begin to comply with the first step. Within 45 seconds of the command, both steps will be correctly completed, one time each, and in the proper sequence." In this example, we could consider latency to be that period before the response was to occur (10 seconds), as well as the length of time the behavior could not exceed and be counted as having met the requirements of the response definition (45 − 10 seconds = 35 seconds).

Magnitude

Magnitude is another dimension of behavior that is occasionally considered in the response definition. It is used independently when the amount or intensity of a response varies and when the other dimensions of behavior, such as topography and duration, are constant. When these dimensions are not constant, it is used in combination with them in order to provide a complete definition. While magnitude can certainly be an important dimension in a retarded person's behavior, published studies using it in the response definition have generally been with nonretarded populations. In one study, Wilson and Hopkins (1973) sought to reduce noise levels in four secondary school classrooms and defined the response in terms of its magnitude, which was "greater than 76 dB" in one classroom and "greater than 70 dB" in each of three other classrooms. To obtain objective and reliable definitions of responding, the authors set a voice-operated relay to operate at 76 and at 70 decibels, the magnitude of noise necessary for a response to be counted as occurring. Other electrical equipment recorded the frequency and duration of responding, but all recording was a function of the definition of responding that was based on the magnitude of responding.

Other studies have investigated changing the magnitude of autonomic responding in a variety of ways that indicates the possible usefulness of this dimension in studying similar behaviors of retarded persons. For example, some (Benson, Shapiro, Tursky & Schwartz, 1971; Elder, Ruiz, Deabler, & Dillenkoffer, 1973) have successfully reduced blood pressure in essential hypertension; others have reduced cardiac arrhythmias (Weiss & Engel, 1971); others have altered the gastric pH in duodenal ulcer and in nonulcerative persons (e.g., Gorman & Kamiya, 1972; Welgan, 1974; and Whitehead, Renault, & Goldiamond, 1975). Each of these defines a response in terms of its magnitude and then programs the consequences. While none of these studies has been with retarded persons, similar procedures could easily be used with retarded persons having hypertension, cardiac problems, and ulcers.

Topography

Topography refers to a description of the physical components of the response considered requisite to the definition. Often implicit, frequently explicit, topography is always within the definition. For example, in one study (Deitz, Repp, Mitchell, Deitz, & Repp, 1975), we were concerned with the extent to which severely retarded persons praised each other for correct responding. If praise were limited just to vocal praise, the topography would be related only to verbalizations; but it also included hand-clapping and pats on the back, so the topography also became related to these physical actions. In many other projects, we were interested in teaching retarded persons to eat independently. While the definitions varied across groups, there were definite topographies that were related to the response, e.g., putting food in the mouth from a spoon, rather than from the hand, or passing food during family-style dining from left to right only. The role played by topography in a response definition is always important, but the ease with which a topographical description can be made varies enormously as a function of the complexity and/or of the numbers of ways in which the response can be made.

A MODEL FOR DEFINITIONS

While frequency, duration, latency, magnitude, and topography form the basis of the response *description*, there are other characteristics of a response *definition*, and these are that the definition (1) is objective, (2) allows measurement, (3) is clear, (4) is complete, and (5) describes a movement cycle.

Is Objective

In applied behavior analysis, objectivity refers either to definitions that allow *direct observation* of the behavior or to definitions that allow observation of a *direct translation* of the behavior; in either case, definitions that allow only subjective information are not used as primary data in this field.[7] Examples of direct translations that are objective include the pH electrode, electronic equipment, and meter to show relative changes in pH as used by Whitehead, Renault, and Goldiamond (1975); the pressureometer, electronic equipment, and strip-chart recorder used by Elder and others (1973) to measure diastolic blood pressure in essential hypertensive patients; or *Mobat*, the mobile breath alcohol test equipment, used by Sobell and Sobell (1975) to measure blood alcohol concentrations. Behaviors that allow definitions in the direct-observation category are far more numerous and include teacher instructions, compliance, self-stimulation, non-interaction, seizures, speaking, writing letter reversals, praising, oral reading, and thousands of others. In the following section, there will be several examples of behavioral definitions, each of which is in the direct-observation category.

Allows Measurement

In Chapter 2, several of the described characteristics of applied behavior analysis referred to measurement (behavioral measurement in a quasi-continuous

---

[7] Occasionally, some work will involve subjective *ratings* of behaviors, but these are never used in lieu of objective data; they are used instead to provide interesting additional data. For example, Hersen and Bellack (1976) examined the eye contact, speech duration, verbal requests, verbal compliances, disruptions of one's own speech, words spoken, and smiles of patients with the psychiatric diagnosis of schizophrenia. To measure the effectiveness of the program, the authors objectively defined each of the behaviors and collected direct data on each before, during, and after treatment. In addition, the authors sought to determine the subjective impressions one would have when meeting the patients, so they asked colleagues to rate appropriate affect and overall assertiveness. If Hersen and Bellack had provided information only on the subjective ratings, the study would not be an example of ABA; but because they relied primarily on the objective definitions and data, the study is an example of ABA.

manner, data that are presented in numerical form, an emphasis on the analysis of each individual client's progress, and a continuing assessment of the dependent variable). Each of these characteristics stresses the importance of measurement in our field. Because subjective data are often (but not always) unreliable or invalid, there is an insistence on objective definitions that allow the collection of objective data. A major, perhaps the major, contribution of this field has been its critical insistence on self-accounting, i.e., on determining the state of events before and after we have worked on a problem which we are being paid to solve. This insistence on accountability toward employers, supervisors, or peers for our actions cannot be supported unless we measure our successes and failures (in behavior analysis, we know that we will succeed on some occasions and will fail on others, but a primary insistence is that we at least ought to be able to identify *when* we have succeeded or failed, and we ought to *try* to determine *why* we have succeeded or failed; only measurement will let us approach the answers to all these situations). While ABA generally uses four methods of recording behavior,[8] the common element of each of these is that behavior must be measured by a count of some sort, whether that be counting the number of times something happens, or how long something happens, or simply whether or not something is happening. As such, the requirement that a behavioral definition must allow measurement means that a behavioral definition must allow us to *count* some aspect of the behavior that is being defined.

Is Clear

The requisite of clarity is described by Hawkins and Dobes (1973) in this manner: "the definition should be *clear* in that it should be so readable and unambiguous that experienced observers could read it and readily paraphrase it accurately" (p. 4). This is an important requirement that often becomes salient shortly after we begin to write definitions. During that period, a writer often attempts to have definitions cover all possible situations and, as a result, produces a definition so long and obscure that an observer attempting to record whether or not responding occurred simply cannot accurately remember the definition. The definition should be inclusive, but it should be written so that it can be readily paraphrased.

Is Complete

Complete definitions are described by Hawkins and Dobes (1973) as those that "delineate the 'boundaries' of what is to be included and what is to be excluded, thereby directing the observers in all situations that are likely to occur and leaving little [variance] to their judgment" (p. 4). In this sense, "out-of-seat behavior" is a clear and an objective response definition, but it is not a complete one, because it does not delineate the boundaries of the behavior. For example, if we were simply interested in how much time a student sat in his or her chair during a class period, then we would time the durations of the student's out-of-seat

---

[8] Frequency recording, interval recording, duration recording, and time sampling will be discussed later in this chapter.

responding. However, if we were interested in the amount of time a student was out of his or her seat inappropriately, then we would have to list those situations that would be excluded from the definition of the response (e.g., whenever the teacher asked the student to leave his or her chair or during free period). In this situation, defining the behavior as "out-of-seat" is incomplete.

Describes a Movement Cycle

A movement cycle refers to that part of a definition which indicates when one response ends and another one can begin. Sometimes the movement cycle is inherent in the definition; e.g., the movement cycle for "out-of-seat" behavior begins when the student leaves his chair and ends when he sits down, for only then can another out-of-seat response occur. Sometimes, however, the movement cycle needs to be explicitly stated. For example, one child involved in a study on reducing stereotypic responding of retarded children (Repp, Deitz, & Speir, 1974) engaged in a great deal of rocking behavior. In defining her rocking behavior, we observed that her response consisted of rocking in a forward and backward direction while sitting on the floor. To describe a movement cycle, "a single response was defined as a movement greater than 15 degrees from the starting position and a return to the starting position. When movement was forward, then backward (or vice versa), and then forward to the starting position, it was counted as two responses" (p. 280). Another student in the study continuously engaged in "lip-flapping" which "was defined as a vertical movement of her fingers across her lips and a return to the starting position" (p. 280). Both these definitions offer explicit descriptions of movement cycles, as they indicate the point at which one response ended and another response began.

EXAMPLES OF DEFINITIONS

There are, of course, thousands of behavioral definitions in use today, many hundreds of which have been published. Although we will give definitions of responses throughout the chapters that describe methods for changing responding, a few definitions of related behaviors may be useful at this point. Mealtime behaviors represent a series of related behaviors that generally become training objectives at one time or another for retarded persons. Barton, Guess, Garcia, and Baer (1970) successfully increased appropriate and decreased inappropriate eating behaviors of 16 retarded persons at the Kansas Neurological Institute. Their preliminary observations resulted in their writing seven behavior categories described as mutually exclusive and functionally exhaustive of all behavior observed in the situation. Table 4-1 provides definitions of *stealing*, *fingers*, *messy utensil*, *neat utensil*, *pigging*, *other behavior*, and *no behavior*. The seven one- and two-word descriptions listed here are good examples of the *identification* process in defining responding, resulting in short descriptions that can be easily remembered but which, by themselves, are highly ambiguous. The definitions in Table 4-1, on the other hand, are clear and complete for most eating situations with retarded persons; they also allow direct observation and measurement; and, with the accompanying rules for recording behavioral occurrences, they have either implicit or explicit statements of movement cycles. As such, with appropriate alterations for anything indigenous to the situation, they should prove useful to us if this type of mealtime behavior is an objective in our program.

TABLE 4-1

Mealtime Behaviors of Severely or Profoundly Retarded Persons[a]

DEFINITIONS

Stealing: Removal of food or other object from another resident's tray.

Fingers: Eating food (from a dish) with fingers (excepting use of fingers to hold hamburger buns, bread, rolls, potato chips, celery sticks, and other foods properly eaten with fingers).

Messy utensil: Pushing food off dish with utensil, using fingers to place food on utensil, spilling food off utensil or cup en route to mouth, or using utensil with face closer than 2 in. to the dish.

Neat utensil: Use of utensil to eat, excluding those behaviors defined as "Messy Utensil."

Pigging: Eating food spilled on table, floor, clothing, or own tray; and eating food by placing the mouth directly on it (without use of fingers or utensil).

Other behavior: Engaging in behavior not defined above (requesting, being taught to use spoon, appropriate use of fingers, and being timed-out).

No behavior: Absence of gross behavior, e.g., looking about, sitting quietly, chewing or swallowing.

RECORDING PROCEDURE

Observations were made during the noon and evening meals, beginning only when all subjects were seated, and ending when the last subject had finished his meal. Each subject was observed until one of the defined behaviors occurred, or for 10 seconds; however, "No Behavior" or "Other Behavior" were recorded for a subject only after 10 seconds of observation had failed to produce a different recording.[b] Subjects were observed in turn, starting with the resident who had been seated first and continuing once around the table in clockwise fashion. The observer then recorded the behavior of the subjects seated at the second table, in the same manner; he then returned to observe the table again.

[a] From Barton, Guess, Garcia, and Baer (1970), p. 78.

[b] This sentence in effect defines movement cycle, in an admittedly different fashion than usual, because it indicates to the observer when the next response could be recorded, which in this case is after each of the other 15 residents has been observed once.

WRITING AND ASSESSING DEFINITIONS

Writing Definitions

The first step in writing a definition is identifying the behavior of interest and attaching a short and relevant label to it. The second step is to write a definition. The third is to give any situation in which the behaviors should not be recorded; the fourth is to assess the definition by recording the subject's behaviors; and the fifth is to rewrite weaknesses pointed out by the assessment. An example of this procedure can be found from our work with a group of retarded students who were noncompliant, engaging in many stereotypes, sleeping, and who were not working during a group task at a table. We decided to concentrate on these and many associated behaviors, one of which was working while at a table. The teacher believed a prerequisite to correct responding included both sitting erect and not making responses incompatible with the task, so we (1) labeled the response "correct student sitting behavior"; (2) listed correct sitting behaviors, which included head up and facing teacher, with both feet on the floor and with buttocks on chair regardless of posture; (3) listed behaviors which voided correct sitting, including (a) hands in mouth, above head, in front of eyes, or in general anywhere but on the table, on teaching materials, in lap, or by one's side; or (b) elbows and forearms on table unless demanded by task, or (c) stereotypes such as groaning, head-weaving, humming, or hitting; (4) assessed the definition; and (5) made any changes necessary in the definition.

Assessing Definitions

There are two ways to assess definitions. The first is an informal way and requires that someone else observe with you for anywhere from a few minutes to a few hours, depending upon the complexity of the response and the frequency with which it is occurring. During the observation period, both people should talk about each response that one or both observers believe occurred. Differences in the implicit definitions under which the two observers are operating can be made explicit, and the definition can be refined. The second manner of assessing definitions[9] is a formal one and involves conducting interobserver agreement checks while recording the behavior(s) of the target subject(s). Interobserver agreement, like many of the terms in applied behavior analysis, is essentially self-explanatory; it is the agreement between (thus *inter*) observers and can be defined as the extent to which a pair of observers independently agree that responding has or has not occurred. It is very much a technical procedure which varies in practice as a function of the method of recording responding; as such, ways of calculating agreement will be described after a complete discussion of the various methods of recording behavior.

Measuring Behavior

MEASUREMENT

Measurement is basic to applied behavior analysis, and the field's insistence on direct measurement and evaluation may be its most important contribution to the study of mentally retarded persons. As a result of this insistence, behavioral programs have produced data that have allowed both self-correction and accountability. Self-correction in this sense describes a system providing

---

[9] And of assessing the consistency with which observers are recording responding; i.e., the *reliability* of the observer.

continuous information that allows changes to be data based. For example, if a child's arithmetic behavior is measured both prior to and during a token program, and the results indicate that responding did not improve, the system offers information that will allow correction through the adoption of another program of rewarding the child, such as praise. If there were no data available, an accurate decision may not have been possible. Similarly, the social behavior of a child could be measured when she or he is with different teachers. Results could show that differences in "good" and "bad" behaviors are related to the teachers instructing the child. Such information can allow teachers to try to identify the situations that help the child behave appropriately, and the situations in which the child behaves inappropriately could perhaps be corrected. Applied behavior analysis stresses the measurement of behavior across treatment conditions so that several basic questions can be asked and answered. Among these are how much improvement did the program produce? At what cost? How much time was required to institute the change? Was the amount of change sufficient, or should another intervention be tried? The questions we can ask are numerous, and they are often situation specific. But with proper measurement, most can be answered.

Purposes of Measurement

Measurement is generally considered to have three purposes in education, and these are to provide information for description, comparison, and prediction. In describing someone's behavior, we usually offer comments like "he's very friendly," or "she's good at arithmetic." In dealing with educational objectives, however, we need to have more precise descriptions of the behavior in order to provide a starting point for determining goals. By measuring a child's responding and by learning that she correctly identified the numbers 1 to 10 on 100 of 100 trials, the descriptor "she's good at arithmetic" becomes more precise and meaningful. While descriptive information can be provided by knowing how many times a child does something, or how long it takes the child to finish a task, comparative information allows us to differentiate between responses or conditions leading to responding. For example, by measuring a student's "talk-outs," we might learn that he "talks-out" three times per class period when Mrs. Smith is the teacher and 20 times per class period when Mr. Johnson is the teacher. With this information, we can compare the student's behavior under two conditions and make some judgments based upon the comparisons. In this case, we would find that we do not have a child who is generally disruptive, but rather one who is selectively so, and we can begin to develop a suitable program for him. Another type of comparison could be between people. For example, we might find that Jerry hit the student next to him 12 times during the first class period Monday, while Sally hit the student next to her 5 times during the same period. With this information, we can compare the two students' hitting behaviors during that class period.

   Single measurements of behavior provide information for description and some comparisons, but repeated measurements provide information for more complete descriptions, more certain comparisons, and more accurate predictions. Because the more often measurement is repeated, the more likely comparisons and predictions are to be correct, applied behavior analysis stresses repeated measurements of each person's performance. From the data of the last example, we might have predicted that Jerry would hit the student next to him 12 times during Tuesday's class period. But repeated measurements might have indicated that he hit others only twice on Tuesday, once on Wednesday, and not at all on Thursday or Friday. Further repeated measurements might indicate a similar pattern, with much more inappropriate responding on Monday than on other days of the week. With this added information, we are more likely to place the problem in perspective (e.g., Jerry is not a "behaviorally disturbed" child) and to determine both the conditions under which he acts appropriately and the conditions under which he acts inappropriately.

Direct and Indirect Measurement

Two types of measurement systems have been used for many years, and these are usually categorized as indirect and direct measurement. While the former has a much longer history in psychology and education, applied behavior analysts have chosen not to continue its use and, by so doing, have made a decision that has allowed them to pursue another means of investigating human behavior. While there are very definite mathematical differences between these two systems, the important one for practitioners is that indirect measurement assesses performance on one continuum and makes statements about performance on *another*, while direct measurement assesses performance along one continuum and makes statements about performance on the *same* continuum. While the difference may at first seem basically semantic, it is much more than that, for only with the latter are we identifying the objectives for a teacher. Tests of "mental abilities" account for much of the indirect measurement in mental retardation, presumably because the common definitions require some measurement of intelligence. All these tests measure behavior along one continuum and then discuss behavior along another. For example, all intelligence tests directly measure the behavior of the test subjects on a particular set of problems, i.e., those problems on the test. The results, however, are discussed by most psychologists on a continuum far larger than that particular set of problems. The persons taking the test are given scores and are then ranked along a supposed continuum of mental ability based upon those scores. While such information can be useful in comparing different groups of persons, it does not provide the teacher direct information on the child's progress on learning tasks in class—only direct measurement provides that information.

Achievement tests are similarly used as indirect measures of performance. While the test is a direct measure of the child's performance in answering the questions on the test, it is used as an indirect measure of his or her performance on many other and on many different kinds of problems. Again, students are assigned scores based upon their correct and incorrect answers, and they are then ranked according to their scores. For example, a child who correctly answered 50% of the problems on an arithmetic test (a direct measure) might be assigned a score of "fifth grade, sixth month" (an indirect measure), which, of course, is a descriptor of a far different continuum of skills. A direct measure, on the other hand, would test a particular behavior and then discuss only *that* behavior in its results. For example, if a child were given 10 minutes to add correctly every two-number combination from the set of numbers 1, 2, 3, 4, and 5, and if the only errors were on the problems $3 + 5$, $4 + 5$, and $3 + 3$, the results could be discussed only in terms of the test itself, along the same continuum as the set of test problems; i.e., in 10 minutes, Johnny wrote correct answers to all problems except $3 + 5$, $4 + 5$, and $3 + 3$ from the list $1 + 1$, $1 + 2$, $1 + 3$, ..., $5 + 5$. With the achievement test score, the teacher has the problem of translating a generality into a specific, the generality being the test score and the specific being those arithmetic problems the student completes correctly, as well as those problems the student does not complete correctly. With the latter type of measurement, the teacher has a direct measure of the student's performance in adding certain numbers and can immediately identify problems with which the student needs additional work. It is at this level that the distinction between direct and indirect measurement becomes important for those who are working with retarded individuals, trying to design effective teaching programs.

TYPES OF MEASUREMENT IN APPLIED BEHAVIOR ANALYSIS

There are three types of measurements used in applied behavior analysis: measurements of (1) a permanent product automatically generated by a machine, (2) a permanent product generated by the client, and (3) a permanent product generated by an observer. Each measurement has similarities and differences with the other methods in terms of summarizing the measurements that are made, but the primary similarity is that each involves a permanent product, and the primary difference is that each produces the permanent product in a different way.

Permanent Product Automatically Generated by a Machine

The work by Ball and his associates (e.g., Ball & McCrady, 1975; Ball, McCrady, & Hart, 1975; Ball, Sibbach, Jones, Steele & Frazier, 1975) is an excellent example of the use of equipment to measure responding and to provide permanent products of those measurements. In each case, self-injurious responding, aggressive responding toward others, finger praxis, and sitting behavior were measured by a machine which provided permanent records through counters that indicated the duration of responding. Similar use of equipment to provide permanent products of the measurement of behavior was made by Tate (1968), who was concerned with the work behavior of retarded persons in a sheltered workshop. One of the tasks involved loading 20 brass cylinders into 20 fuse holders mounted on a plastic disc. To count the number of discs completed, Tate wired the fuse holders so that (1) a counter would operate each time an entire disc was completed, and (2) a timer would indicate how long the client was at the work station. These simple devices provided permanent records on the counters and timers of the client's responding on this task, and, as consequences for good working were planned throughout the day, eliminated the need for someone to count the work units for each person in the workshop; the equipment had already counted the units.

Permanent Product Generated by the Client

While machine measurement is quite useful in many settings, it is impractical in most; so measurement is usually left to permanent products generated by other means. The most common product in teaching situations is that generated by the student and consists of writing words, numbers, etc., or of completing puzzles, or of constructing toys. The examples, of course, seem endless, and this type of permanent product is usually easy for the teacher, an aide, or the student to measure and record.

Permanent Product Generated by an Observer

Certainly, most of the responding we do does not result in a permanent product in the sense described here. We eat, sleep, listen to music, read, walk, play games, and so on, and there is no permanent record of the responding. As such, the predominant means of measuring behavior in our field involves the use of an observer who decides when responding meets the definition of occurrence, who then measures it, and who then makes a record of its occurrence either by writing on recording sheets or by operating equipment[10] which provides the record. This type of measurement is included within an observation system and is the basis for most of the work with retarded persons. Such observation systems always include definitions of the behaviors in question, choice of a datum to be used in measurement, and a method of recording. Definitions have been discussed in the first part of this chapter; the other two topics follow.

CHOICE OF DATUM

In applied behavior analysis, as well as in many other sciences, datum refers to the unit in which the measurement is expressed, and data refers to the numbers expressed in those units. In this field, the most common datum are count, rate, and percent, all of which are described by numbers. For example, if we were concerned only with how long a child sat in isolation, we might count and find that he sat 60, 80, 90, and 30 minutes. If we then became concerned with how long the child sat in isolation *relative to* the length of time we observed him each day, and we found that of the 120 minutes we recorded each day, he sat alone 30, 20, 30, 60, and 30 minutes, the datum would be *percent* and the *data* would be 25% (from 30 ÷ 120), 17% (from 20 ÷ 120), 25%, 50%, and 25%. In another situation, we might be concerned with how many pages a child reads, and we might find that she read 20, 26, 31, 18, and 22 pages. If we were concerned instead with how fast the child read and found that in one hour she read 12, 16, 9,

---

[10] Such as an event recorder.

11, and 14 pages, then the datum would be *rate*, and the *data* would be 12, 16, 9, 11, and 14 pages per hour.

Count

Count refers only to number and, as such, is the simplest datum. We can use it to provide a measure of how many responses are made by simply counting the number of responses; or we can use it to provide a measurement unit for the duration of responding by simply counting how long each response occurred; or we can use it to provide a measurement unit for the latency of responding by counting the time between when a response could start and when a response did start; or we can use it to provide a measurement unit for the magnitude of responding by counting how many units of a response occurred (e.g., the number of decibels of noise). While frequently used, count is not always the appropriate datum. For example, it is appropriate when the length of time we measure behavior remains the same from session to session, but it is not appropriate when this length of time varies.

As an example of the latter, consider a situation in which the attending behavior of a child is recorded under two conditions termed baseline[11] and intervention. If responding occurred 9, 6, 15, 12, and 9 times during baseline and 12, 8, 20, 16, and 12 during intervention, we might conclude that the intervention program was moderately successful. As a result, we might continue to use it in this situation and continue its use in other situations. But suppose that the person who recorded the behavior mentioned that he thought the class was longer the first week than the second, and that upon questioning the teacher we found that his class was 45 minutes the first week and 60 minutes the second week. As the data from the second set of days are 0.75 times the data the first set of days, and as the recording period the second week is 0.75 times the recording period the first week, we could no longer conclude that intervention was moderately successful; instead, we would conclude that it resulted in no measured change. Clearly, count was an inappropriate unit of measurement, and another should have been chosen.

Count is an appropriate datum when the duration of responding is relatively constant, but it is generally not appropriate when the duration of responding varies considerably. For example, if the 10 sessions of data on attending were all of the same length, count may still not have been the appropriate unit of measurement. This type of responding usually varies in length and a count of "1" does not convey the same meaning each time. The first time the child might have been attending for 10 seconds, while the second time, he might have been attending for 30 minutes; clearly, these two responses vary considerably and should not be counted as equivalent. In cases like this, we might want to know how many responses the child made, but we would also want to know the total time the child was attending or the percent of the class period he was attending. In the latter case, we would use percent, as well as count, as units of measurement to express the data.

---

[11] Baseline is the first phase in a behavioral program and provides a standard against which one can assess the change in behavior produced by manipulation of the independent variable.

In this example, we could use count to indicate the number of responses and a separate count to indicate the number of minutes responding lasted provided the recording period was of the same duration from day to day. Another situation in which two counts may be necessary occurs daily in all classrooms, that being a count of correct *and* incorrect responding. Given either that the duration of responding is unimportant to the teacher or that the length of time in which to do the work remains the same from day to day, we might at first believe that a count of correct *or* incorrect responding would *always* be sufficient, but that assumption is incorrect. For example, if we were concerned with correct answers to arithmetic problems and found that the child answered 10, 12, 14, 12, and 12 problems correctly during baseline, and 20, 24, 28, 24, and 24 problems correctly during an intervention phase, we might conclude that our program was successful and we might use it with other students. But if the number of problems increased twofold during the intervention program, the conclusion would have been incorrect. In this case, data on correct and incorrect responding should have been provided, and these two counts would have offered information on the success of the program. A single count would have been correct if the total number of responses remained the same (and if the difficulty was constant from week to week), but it is inappropriate when the total opportunities for responding vary over time.

In each case in which count is an incorrect datum, it is so because it does not give equal weight to each response. When the session length varies, the count *within* each session has equal weight, but the count *between* sessions does not; when the duration of responding varies, a count of "1" for each response occurrence is not equivalent *across each response;* and when the number of opportunities to respond varies from session to session, the count *within* each session can have equal weight, but the count *between* sessions does not because the opportunity for responding has varied.

Rate of Responding

Rate or frequency of responding is simply the count per unit time and is usually expressed as responses per minute (rpm), responses per hour (rph), or as responses per day (rpd). Rate is an attempt to reduce the description of responding to a common unit of time (e.g., minutes) and is accomplished by dividing the number of responses counted by the length of the recording period. For example, if we recorded 12 responses in 30 minutes, we could express the rate of responding as 0.4 rpm (from $12 \div 30$ minutes); similarly, if we recorded 6 responses in 6 hours, we could express the rate of responding as 1.0 rph (from $6 \div 6$ hours) or as 24 rpd (from $6 \div .025$ days).

Because rate does account for the period of time during which recording occurs, it is generally a more sensitive measure than count. The attending responses in a prior example that were recorded for 45 or for 60 minutes could have been made equivalent insofar as the session length is concerned by converting all data to a common base such as responses per hour. In that case, the data for the first five sessions would have been 12, 8, 20, 16, and 12 rph, and the data for the second five sessions would have been 12, 8, 20, 16, and 12 rph. If the duration of responding had been the same for each response, then rate would have been an appropriate datum by which to express the measurement of attending behaviors. Although rate is more sensitive than count, the caution in expressing the attending behaviors solely in terms of rate suggests that, because rate is *count* per unit time, it is susceptible to some of the same problems to which count is susceptible.

Percent

Percent is a very common unit of measurement which summarizes the relation of one event to another (e.g., correct answers to total number of answers, or time attending to time in class). To determine percent, we divide one number by another and then multiply by 100. Because behavior never occurs as a percentage but is only summarized as such, percent is often criticized as a unit that does not reflect behavior as it occurs. Percent does, however, have its uses in describing behavior and some of these are (1) when a description of the percent of the total time a client responded is important, (2) when use of rate or count is impossible, (3) when the measurement system only allows percent, or (4) when we want to report the proportion of responses that fall into a certain category.

In many cases, the duration of responding varies, so in addition to reporting the number of responses, we should report the percent of the total recording period in which the target response occurred. In looking at parallel play behavior, for example, we found that one child responded for 12, 88, 37, 360, 130, and 310 seconds during a 60-minute period. The behavior could be described in terms of count, i.e., it occurred six times, but it should also be described in terms of the percent of time in which responding occurred, which in this case is 26% from (12 + 88 + 37 + 360 + 130 + 310 seconds) ÷ 3,600 seconds).

Percent is also used when rate or count is impossible either because of the nature of the response or because of the recording procedure. An example of the former case is certain types of stereotypic responding. One student, who came to our program after being at home for more than 15 years, engaged in finger movements that we found to occur 816 times in a randomly selected 15-minute period. Rates of this type are so high that observer fatigue is rapid, so we recorded the percent of time in which the student engaged in responding, which could be counted simply by timing each response with a stopwatch during the recording session. In this example, the recording procedure was adjusted to the nature of the response, but in some situations, the recording procedure is chosen because it is the only one possible in the situation. When a teacher is the only person in the classroom, timing the duration of each response is generally impossible, so another procedure[12] is to observe only for an instant every 10, 20 minutes, etc., and then to record whether or not responding was occurring at that moment. In this case, we count both the number of observations during which responding was occurring and the total number of observations. When the number of observations varies across days, the only datum that can be used is percent, and in this case the teaching environment dictated the choice of the datum.

---

[12] This procedure is labeled momentary time sampling; it will be discussed in Chapter 5.

Percent is often used to report the proportion of responses that fall into certain categories; often this use is correct, but sometimes it is not. Percent is not a good unit of measurement for correct responding when the number of problems varies across days or when there are more than two categories of responding. If a student answers 12, 8, and 4 problems correctly in 10 minutes on each of three days, and there are 24, 16, and 8 problems presented to him, correct responding would be expressed as 50%, 50%, and 50%. But, responding is clearly different each day, and rate or count would have been a more appropriate datum. In this case and in all others as well, percent reduces data to a common base, and in so doing it loses considerable information. If the number of problems were constant from day to day, percent could be an appropriate datum. If, however, there were another classification of responding, then just reporting percent correct would be inappropriate (the other class in this situation would, of course, be "problems attempted"). If we were just interested in correct problem solving, then percent correct alone could be an appropriate choice. If, however, we wanted to differentiate between the child who had 10 correct and none incorrect out of 20 problems, and the child who had 10 correct and 6 incorrect out of the same 20 problems, then we could report the percent correct and the percent incorrect, all other things being equal.

Percent is an appropriate datum when one wants to report the relation of responses to each other when the response categories exhaust all possible occurrences of responding. In the last example, correct responses, incorrect responses, and responses completed out of 20 possible problems exhausts all possibilities, so we could report the percent correct, percent incorrect, and, if desired, the percent attempted (the last is, of course, simply the sum of the first two and may be redundant in some cases). Another example is provided by Barton, Guess, Garcia, and Baer (1970), whose seven response classes of mealtime behaviors were discussed earlier. These classes were defined in such a way that anything that a person was or was not doing that was not included in the first five categories had to be included in the sixth or seventh. As such, the definitions exhausted all possible occurrences of behavior, and each classification could be compared with all others. For example, during a 10-day period, each of these seven might have constituted 10, 20, 20, 10, 5, 15, and 20%, respectively, of the mealtime behaviors. Regardless of the datum by which responding was originally presented, each response class could be compared with the other when percent is used as the datum.

SUMMARY

In the section on defining behavior, this chapter presents (1) five advantages of accurate descriptions, including directing the attention of teachers to target behaviors, providing a base for setting goals, providing a base for accountability, producing a science of teaching, and reducing errors in judgment; (2) two means of defining the occurrence of a response—by machine or by observer; (3) five dimensions of behavior, including frequency, duration, latency, magnitude, and topography; (4) five requirements of a response definition, including being objective, allowing measurement, being clear and complete, and describing a movement cycle; (5) examples of definitions; and (6) information on writing and assessing definitions.

In the section on measuring behavior, this chapter presents (1) the purposes of measurement, which were to provide information for description, comparison, and prediction, (2) the difference between direct and indirect measurement, (3) the types of measurement in applied behavior analysis, including permanent products generated by machine, client, or any observer, and (4) the types of datum used in applied behavior analysis, including count, rate, and percent.

Chapter 5 will present information on (1) means of observing and recording the behavior of retarded persons and (2) methods of assessing the extent to which observers agree on what they have recorded. The first section describes three methods of recording behavior through continuous observations: frequency recording, interval recording, and duration recording; the second section describes two methods of recording behavior through discontinuous observations, and these include time sampling and task sampling. The third section indicates how to assess interobserver agreement on data from continuous observations, the fourth section indicates how to assess agreement on data from discontinuous observations, and the fifth section covers data-collection methods.

REFERENCES

Azrin, N. H., & Foxx, R. M. A rapid method of toilet training the institutionalized retarded. *Journal of Applied Behavior Analysis*, 1971, 4, 89-99.

Ball, T. S., & McCrady, R. E. Automated finger praxis training with a cerebral palsied adolescent. *Mental Retardation*. 1975, 13(4), 75.

Ball, T. S., McCrady, R. E., & Hart, A. D. Automated reinforcement of head posture in two cerebral palsied retarded children. *Perceptual and Motor Skills*, 1975, 40, 619-622.

Ball, T. S., Sibbach, L., Jones, R., Steele, B., & Frazier, L. An accelerometer-activated device to control assaultive and self-destruction behaviors in retardates. *Journal of Behavior Therapy and Experimental Psychiatry*, 1975, 6, 223-228.

Barrett, B. H., & Lindsley, O.R. Deficits in acquisition of operant discrimination and differentiation shown by institutionalized retarded children. *American Journal of Mental Deficiency*, 1962, 67, 424-436.

Barton, E. S., Guess, D., Garcia, E., & Baer, D. M. Improvement of retardates' mealtime behaviors by timeout procedures using multiple baseline techniques. *Journal of Applied Behavior Analysis*, 1970, 3, 77-84.

Benson, H., Shapiro, D., Tursky, B., & Schwartz, G. E. Decreased systolic blood pressure through operant conditioning techniques in patients with essential hypertension. *Science*, 1971, 173, 740-742.

Bijou, S. W. A systematic approach to an experimental analysis of young children. *Child Development*, 1955, 26, 161-168.

Bijou, S. W. Methodology for an experimental analysis of child behavior. *Psychological Reports*, 1957a, 3, 243-250.

Bijou, S. W. Patterns of reinforcement and resistance to extinction in young children. *Child Development*, 1957b, **28**, 47-54.

Bijou, S. W. A child study laboratory on wheels. *Child Development*, 1958a, 29, 425-427.

Bijou, S. W. Operant extinction after fixed-interval schedules with young children. *Journal of the Experimental Analysis of Behavior*, 1958b, 1, 25-29.

Bijou, S. W. Learning in children. *Monographs of the Society for Research in Child Development*, 1959, **24**(5), (Whole No. 74).

Bijou, S. W., & Sturgis, P. T. Positive reinforcers for experimental studies with children-consumables and manipulatables. *Child Development*, 1959, 30, 151-170.

Deitz, D. E. D., Repp, A. C., Mitchell, M. E., Deitz, S. M., & Repp, C. F. Retarded students as behavorial technicians. Paper presented at a meeting of the Southeastern American Association on Mental Deficiency, 1975.

Elder, S. T., Ruiz, Z. R., Deabler, H. L., & Dillenkoffer, R. L. Instrumental conditioning of diastolic blood pressure in essential hypertensive patients. *Journal of Applied Behavior Analysis*, 1973, **6**, 377-382.

Ferster, C. B., & Skinner, B. F. *Schedules of reinforcement*. New York: Appleton-Century-Crofts, Inc., 1957.

Gorman, P. J., & Kamiya, J. Biofeedback training of stomach pH. Paper presented at the Western Psychological Association Meeting, 1972.

Hall, R. V., Lund, D., & Jackson, D. Effects of teacher attention on study behavior. *Journal of Applied Behavior Analysis*, 1968, 1, 1-12.

Hawkins, R. P., & Dobes, R. W. Behavioral definitions in applied behavior analysis: Explicit or implicit. Paper presented at a meeting of the American Psychological Association, 1973.

Hersen, M., & Bellack, A. S. A multiple-baseline analysis of social-skills training in chronic schizophrenics. *Journal of Applied Behavior Analysis*, 1976, 9, 239-245.

Orlando, R., & Bijou, S. W. Single and multiple schedules of reinforcement in developmentally retarded children. *Journal of the Experimental Analysis of Behavior*, 1960, 3, 339-348.

Patterson, G. R., Cobb, J. A., & Ray, R. S. Direct intervention in the classroom: A set of procedures for the aggressive child. In F. W. Clark, D. R. Evans, and L. A. Hamerlynck (Eds.), *Implementing behavioral programs for school and clinics: The proceedings of the third Banff International Conference on Behavior Modification*. Champaign, IL: Research Press, 1972.

Repp, A. C., Deitz, S. M., & Speir, N. C. Reducing stereotypic responding of retarded persons by the differential reinforcement of other behavior. *American Journal of Mental Deficiency*, 1974, **79**, 279-284.

Skinner, B. F. *Science and Human Behavior*. New York: Macmillan, Inc., 1953.

Sobell, M. B., & Sobell, L. C. A brief technical report on the Mobat: An inexpensive portable test for determining blood alcohol concentration. *Journal of Applied Behavior Analysis*, 1975, 8, 117-120.

Tate, B. G. An automated system for reinforcing and recording retardate work behavior. *Journal of Applied Behavior Analysis*, 1968, 1, 347-348.

Walker, H., & Buckley, N. K. Investigation of some classroom control parameters as a function of teacher dispensed social reinforcers. *Journal of Applied Behavior Analysis*, 1971, 5, 209-224.

Weiss, T., & Engel, B. T. Operant conditioning of heart rate in patients with premature ventricular contractions. *Psychosomatic Medicine*, 1971 33, 310-321.

Werry, J. S., & Quay, H. Observing the classroom behavior of elementary school children. Paper presented at the Meeting of the Council on Exceptional Children, 1968.

Welgan, P. R. Learned control of gastric acid secretions in ulcer patients. *Psychosomatic Medicine*, 1974, 36, 411-419.

Whitehead, W. E., Renault, P. F., & Goldiamond, I. Modification of human gastric acid secretion with operant-conditoning procedures. *Journal of Applied Behavior Analysis*, 1975, 8, 147-156.

Wilson, C. W., & Hopkins, B. L. The effects of the intensity of noise in junior-high home economics classes. *Journal of Applied Behavior Analysis*, 1973, 6, 269-276.

5

Methods of Direct Recording

CHARACTERISTICS

Direct versus Indirect

From the behavioral insistence on defining behaviors in a manner that allows observation and measurement, we could infer that a behavioral system is based on direct observation, and we would be correct. Direct observation means that the target behavior is concurrently being observed and recorded. For example, if we were interested in measuring a child's competence in brushing teeth, we would record data on the skills *while* we were watching the child brush. Indirect observation, on the other hand, is a system in which the target behavior is not being concurrently observed and recorded. Many[1] inventories (e.g., Vineland Social Maturity Scale, the Adaptive Behavior Scale) are indirect in that the observer does not record while observing the behavior. For example, an inventory question might be "How well does the child brush his teeth," and the answers could be "(a) without assistance, (b) with some assistance, or (c) must be totally done by someone else." Inventories of this type usually have several hundred items which are to be completed in one or two sessions by someone who knows the child. They are not, however, complete while the child is engaging in the task and as such are subject to many influences that could make the data suspect. While direct observation and recording are not without error, it is a system that seems to have less error and to be more precise.

---

[1] But not all (e.g., Balthazar Scales of Adaptive Behavior).

The goal of direct observation is to arrange conditions so that we will reliably react to each occurrence of the response. The goal of direct recording is to make a direct record of this reaction. Both of these movements involve a series of behaviors so both can be sources of error. We know that observations beyond a few minutes can become tiring or simply boring, so all behavioral systems have a problem with "observer fatigue." We also know that observers tend to alter the written definition, developing a slightly different one by which they decide whether to record a response occurrence, and with this problem we have a phenomenon termed "observer drift" (O'Leary & Kent, 1973). We also know that observers change the way in which they record behavior when they know that they themselves are being observed (O'Leary & Kent, 1973; Romanczyk, Kent, Diament, & O'Leary, 1973); they generally become more accurate. So direct observation and recording is not without its own problems; it is not a perfect system. But it is a system that will generate data that are more valid and reliable[2] than an indirect system.

Types of Observational Data

Data generated from recording observations are usually of three types, some of which are direct and some of which are indirect; these are (1) narratives, (2) ratings, and (3) checklists (Brandt, 1972). Narrative data are supposed to be exact reproductions of behavioral occurrences and should not include interpretations of data. The most common forms of *narrative* data are (1) anecdotes, which describe certain episodes of behavior over long periods of time (e.g., tantrums since birth); (2) ecological descriptions, which report a comprehensive itemizing of the environment (e.g., room size, number and arrangement of chairs, tables, books, and toys, etc.); and (3) running narratives, which describe behavior continuously over a short period of time. The running narrative is particularly useful in applied behavior analysis when we are unfamiliar with the setting. In applied behavior analysis, the running narrative takes a particular form consisting of three columns, which list the events that are antecedent to responding, the behaviors following the antecedents, and the events that are consequences of the behavior. An example of a running narrative is provided by Bijou, Peterson, and Ault (1968, pp. 178-179) in their description of a child's behavior in a play yard.

Running narrative: *Timmy is playing by himself in a sandbox in a play yard in which other children are playing. A teacher stands nearby. Timmy tires of the sandbox and walks over to climb the monkeybars. Timmy shouts at the teacher, saying, "Mrs. Simpson, watch me." Timmy climbs to the top of the apparatus and shouts again to the teacher, "Look how high I am. I'm higher than anybody." The teacher comments on Timmy's climbing ability with approval. Timmy then climbs down and runs over to a tree, again demanding that the teacher watch him. The teacher, however, ignores Timmy and walks back into*

---

[2] While there are precise mathematical definitions of each of these terms, validity will be used here to refer to the degree to which we are *actually* measuring what we believe we are measuring, and reliability will be used to refer to the degree to which we are consistent in measuring behavior.

the classroom. Disappointed, Timmy walks toward the sandbox instead of climbing the tree. A little girl nearby cries out in pain as she stumbles and scrapes her knee. Timmy ignores her and continues to walk to the sandbox.

A traditional running narrative of the situation would begin: *Setting: Timmy (T.) is playing alone in a sandbox in a play yard in which there are other children playing. T. is scraping sand into a bucket with a shovel, then dumping the sand into a pile. A teacher, Mrs. Simpson (S.), stands approximately six feet away but does not attend to T.*

However, to provide information that can be more rapidly assimilated, the running narrative was cast into the antecedent—response—subsequent event form, which in this case was:

Time	Antecedent Event	Response	Consequent Social Event
9:14		1. T. throws bucket and shovel into corner of sandbox.	
		2. . . . stands up.	
		3. . . . walks over to monkeybars and stops.	
		4. . . . turns toward teacher.	
		5. . . . says, "Mrs. Simpson, watch me."	
			6. Mrs. S. turns toward Timmy.
	6. Mrs. S. turns toward Timmy.	7. T. climbs to top of apparatus.	
		8. . . . looks toward teacher.	
		9. . . . says, "Look how high I am. I'm higher than anybody."	
			10. Mrs. S. says, "That's good, Tim. You're getting quite good at that."
	10. Mrs. S. says, "That's good, Tim. You're getting quite good at that."	11. T. climbs down.	
		12. . . . runs over to tree.	
		13. . . . says, "Watch me climb the tree, Mrs. Simpson."	
			14. Mrs. S. turns and walks toward classroom.
	14. Mrs. S. turns and walks toward classroom.	15. T. stands, looking toward Mrs. S.	
9:18	16. Girl nearby trips and falls, bumping knee.		

Time	Antecedent Event	Response	Consequent Social Event
	17. Girl cries.		
		18. T. proceeds to sandbox.	
		19. . . . picks up bucket and shovel.	
		20. . . . resumes play with sand.	

Rating scales provide a second form of observational data, and although not prevalent in ABA, they are the most common form throughout psychology and education. Ratings are often very observer biased and as such are of limited value. Although they form a primary data for many studies (e.g., social psychology), they are never used as primary data in ABA and serve only as "additional information" (e.g., Hersen & Bellack, 1976).

Checklists provide a third type of observational data. They require us to note or catalog certain events or behaviors, and they occur in one of two forms: (1) static descriptions or (2) action checklists. The former refers to nonbehavioral characteristics which are highly stable and which relate to the individuals who are being studied. Such items as age, sex, degree of retardation, and family income, are examples of static descriptions. They are not behaviors; they are, instead, conditions. The action checklist, however, is used to provide records of actual behavior and, as such, it is the basic unit in applied behavior analysis. While the data take different forms depending upon the method of recording, all types of action checklists require the observer to mark instances of behavior.

Major Methods for Recording Data

Continuous observation refers to observations that allow us to record behavior without imposed interruptions of time. For example, if we were to record all occurrences of behavior for 30 minutes, we would have a case of continuous observation and continuous recording. If we were to record for 30 minutes the next day, we would have another session with continuous recording. The sessions themselves are discontinuous, but the method itself is not. Discontinuous observation presents data that are discontinuous not because of convenience but because of the method itself. For example, if we were to record whether or not behavior were occurring every sixtieth minute and ignored behavior for the intervening 60 minutes, we would have a case of observation and recording that was discontinuous; the method itself required a break in recording.

The major methods of recording behavior from continuous observation are (1) frequency recording, (2) duration recording, and (3) interval recording. While each of these is similar to the others in several aspects, there are differences in the datum deployed and in precautions we must take while using each. The major methods of recording behavior from discontinuous observation are (1) time sampling, and (2) task sampling.

FREQUENCY RECORDING

Definition and Datum.   Frequency recording is a very simple procedure in which we merely write the times at which the recording period begins and ends, and then mark each occurrence of responding. The datum used depends

Day *Wednesday*	0₁ _A R_	Teacher _Pat C._	Location _EMR_
Date _6/1/78_	0₂ _D D_	Teacher _____	Activity (a) _writing_
Session _12_	IOA _100%_	Teacher _____	(b) _free time_
			(c) _art_

student-behavior		student-behavior		student-behavior	
John L. - app. social		*Corey L. - app. social*		*Mike E.*	
Time	Responses	Time	Responses	Time	Responses
8:30	2 2	8:30	0 0	8:30	1 1
8:40	2 4	8:40	0 0	8:40	3 4
8:50	0 4	8:50	0 0	8:50	0 4
9:00	0 4	9:00	0 0	9:00	1 5
9:10	1 5	9:10	0 0	9:10	2 7
9:20 (b)	8 13	9:20 (b)	1 1	9:20 (b)	4 11
9:30 (c)	1 14	9:30 (c)	0 1	9:30 (c)	4 15
9:40	0 14	9:40	0 1	9:40	1 16
9:50	2 16	9:50	0 1	9:50	1 17
10:00	stopped recording	10:00	stopped recording	10:00	stopped recording

ΣR = _16_	ΣR = _1_	ΣR = _17_
ΣT = _90_	ΣT = _90_	ΣT = _90_
Rate or count = _10.67/hour_	Rate or count = _0.11/hour_	Rate or count = _11.33/hr._

Figure 5-1. An example of a form appropriate for frequency recording. The upper set of information identifies when the data were collected, by whom (0₁), the extent to which two observers (0₁ and 0₂) agreed on the data (IOA), the staff present, the location, and the activities in which the students were engaged while being observed. The second set of information includes the data from the recording session, which has been divided into segments to indicate whether the responding has been equally distributed across the session.

upon the definition of the response, the length of the recording period, and the teacher's objectives; and the datum can be count, rate, or percent. Count is the simplest datum and only requires that we sum the data for each recording period. Rate is also a simple datum and represents the count per unit time (e.g., mean responses per minute or mean responses per hour). Percent is another datum commonly used in frequency recording, and it is particularly useful when we are summarizing the proportion of responses that fall into a certain category (e.g., the percent of all responses that are correct or the percent of students who attended school today).

Appropriate Use

While frequency recording is a ubiquitous procedure, there are two considerations before choosing it as a recording procedure: (1) the duration of the response and (2) the rate of the response. Most of us record responding of short duration by frequency recording, because responding of short duration (i.e., a few seconds) is relatively constant by definition.

The second concern we must have about the response before choosing frequency recording is its rate. Responses of extremely high rate, perhaps 40 or 50 per minute, can be recorded by the frequency method, but the rate is so high that the method leads to observer fatigue and, therefore, to inaccurate data. In situations with high rates of responses, like some forms of stereotypy, most behaviorists choose a method other than frequency recording.

Practical Use

Figure 5-1[3] is a sample form for recording the verbalizations of three students, and it indicates some of the data we should have while recording ongoing behaviors: (1) *identifying information* should include the day, date, session number, teachers' names, recording location, activity in session, target subjects' names, response labels, primary observer, and interobserver agreement scores; (2) *recording information* should include time intervals, a tally of each response occurrence, the sum of response occurrences, the sum of time, and the overall rate or count for the entire session.

INTERVAL RECORDING

Definition and Datum.   In this procedure, a session is divided into a number of small intervals, the observer is cued by a timing device at the end of each interval, and then the observer marks the presence or absence of a response in the preceding interval. There are two major variations in this procedure: (1)

---

[3] Figure 5-1 is a sample data sheet used to record ongoing responding as opposed to trial responding, which requires a teacher to present material to a student before a response can occur. Modification of this form is appropriate even for ongoing responding, but it should serve as a resource for us in planning our own data-collection sheets.

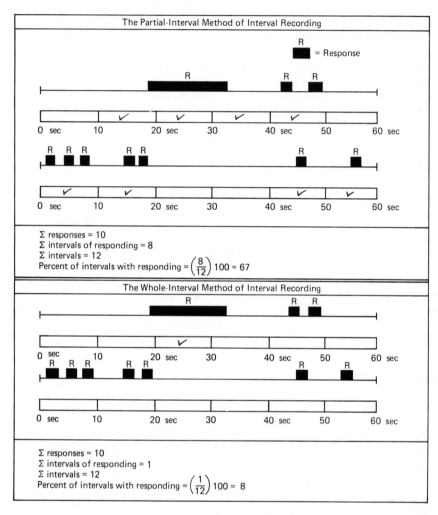

Figure 5-2. An example of two methods of interval recording. In the partial-interval method, an interval is scored as one of responding (✓) if a response occurs in any portion of it. In the whole-interval method, an interval is scored as one of responding only if a response occurred during the whole interval. In this example, both methods are used on the same record of responding (indicated by ■) to indicate the differences in the data they provide.

what constitutes an interval of responding and (2) whether a recording-only period is included. The two choices in the first variation are to record responding if a response occurred at *any time* in the interval or to record responding only if a response occurred for the *entire* interval. Generally called *partial-interval recording*, the first is by far the most used, while the second, generally called *whole-interval recording*, is used in special cases. An example of each is given in the section on appropriate use of interval recording. Figure 5-2 is an example of data collected by the partial-interval method and by the whole-interval method. If the upper lines represent responding, then in the first 60 seconds there were three responses and in the second 60 seconds there were seven. The number of intervals that contained at least one response was eight, so the percent of intervals in which responding occurred is (8/12)100 = 67, according to the partial-interval method. The lower set of lines and blocks refers to the whole-interval method, and they are *identical* to the information in the partial-interval example. However, only one response (in the third recording block) met the definition of an interval of responding, so according to this method, the percent of intervals in which responding occurred is (1/12) 100 = 8.

The second choice is whether or not to include a record-only period in the method. In this approach, we would have a period of observation, e.g., 10 seconds, followed by a period of recording without observation, e.g., 5 seconds. The alternative is to observe for 10 seconds and to record at the end of the tenth second. As both methods provide very similar data (Repp, Roberts, Slack, Repp & Berkler, 1976), the choice is based on how complex the recording procedure is, i.e., the number of students being observed and the number of behaviors being recorded at one time.

Appropriate Use

Unlike frequency recording, interval recording can be appropriately applied to responses that vary in duration and to responses that have short, moderate, or long durations. The reason is that we are reporting the percent of *intervals* that contain responding; we are not reporting a percent of *responses*. As such, the responses do not have to be uniform; the intervals, however, have to be uniform and they always are (e.g., all intervals are 5 seconds, or 10 seconds, or 60 seconds).

Interval recording does, however, have one major restriction; one that is not involved in the decision of whether the method is appropriate, but one that becomes involved once the choice has been made. This restriction is on the size of the interval relative to the rate, duration, and pattern of responding. Put most simply, we can say that several studies (e.g., Hawkins & Dotson, 1972; Repp, Roberts, Slack, Repp & Berkler, 1976) have shown that interval recording provides a poor reflection of behavioral occurrences when intervals contain more than one response. The reason for this is obvious: as interval recording describes only the percent of intervals in which responding occurs, it equates intervals with 1, 2, 5, or 10 responses. The solution to the problem is also obvious: we should sample responding before formal data collection begins and then choose an interval that does not contain more than one response.

Another consideration for interval recording is whether to use the partial-interval or the whole-interval method. The whole-interval method is appropriate when the target behavior is of some duration and is a response one would normally want to increase. For example, we used interval recording to examine the on-task behavior of students and chose the whole-interval variation. Choosing the partial-session variation would make little sense, because a student who was on-task for 1 second of each interval would be on-task 100% of the time, and obviously this type of data is misleading. The whole-session method would not be appropriate for most programs to decelerate behavior, because any occurrence of inappropriate responding should be reflected in the data.

Page 1	Activity (a) _spelling_	O$_1$ _R. R._	Interval _5 sec_
Day _Thursday_	(b) _____	O$_2$ _—_	Started _9:10_
Date _11/30/77_	(c) _____	IOA _—_	Ended _9:12_
Session _12_	Location _Classroom A_	Staff _R. T._	Staff _S. S._

Interval _5 seconds_

Subject Ø — behaviors: on-task / in seat / approp. verbal
(columns numbered 0 1 2 3 4 5 6 7 8 9)

Subject — behaviors: on-task / in seat / approp. verbal / inapp. verbal / writing / descriptive
(columns numbered 0 1 2 3 4 5 6 7 8 9)

Subject — behaviors: on-task / in seat / approp. verbal / inapp. verbal / inactivity
(columns numbered 0 1 2 3 4 5 6 7 8 9)

TS#1 ( )

Subject 1 (rows 1–10), Subject 2 (rows 1–10), Subject 3 (rows 1–10) — interval recordings with Ø and 0 marks.

Codes:
- Subject 1: T S V
- Subject 2: T S V⁺ V⁻ W D
- Subject 3: T S V⁺ V⁻ I

TS#2 ( )

Subject 1 (rows 11–20), Subject 2 (rows 11–20), Subject 3 (rows 11–20)

Codes:
- Subject 1: T S V
- Subject 2: T S V⁺ V⁻ W D
- Subject 3: T S V⁺ V⁻ I

TS#3 ( )

Subject 1 (rows 21–30), Subject 2 (rows 21–30), Subject 3 (rows 21–30)

Summary:

	Subject 1	Subject 2	Subject 3
ΣR	20 30 6	8 17 3 10 4 6	22 28 7 1 4
ΣI	30 30 30	30 30 30 30 30 30	30 30 30 30 30
%	67 100 20	27 57 10 33 13 20	73 93 23 03 13

Figure 5-3. An example of a form appropriate for recording multiple responding through interval recording. The upper set of information identifies when the data were collected and by whom (O$_1$), the extent to which two observers (O$_1$ and O$_2$) agreed on the data (IOA), the staff present, the location, the activities in which the students were engaged while being observed, and the size of the interval. The second set of information identifies by coded number the subjects being observed, the behaviors being recorded,

Practical Use

Because we do not have to count or time each occurrence of a response, partial-interval recording is easier to use than frequency or duration recording when observing more than a few responses or persons. Similarly, interval recording is easier when observing behaviors that are of very high rate (e.g., 30, 40, 50 rpm) or behaviors that do not have a very easily observed beginning or ending (e.g., some forms of stereotypic responding). In none of these cases are other procedures a wrong choice, but in each case interval recording is the more practical choice. Figure 5-3 is an example of a form used for recording multiple behaviors of up to three persons per page. The top of each page again provides identifying information, which in this case includes (1) the day and date, (2) the times at which the observation period began and ended, (3) the activity in which the subjects were engaged while being observed, (4) the location of the observation, (5) the session number, (6) the name of the primary observer, (7) the name of the secondary observer whose data are used to compute interobserver agreement scores, (8) the size of the observation interval, (9) the page number of this sheet for that day's recording, and (10) the staff present.

DURATION RECORDING

Definition and Datum. *Duration recording is a procedure in which we record the duration of each response and the total time of the session.* If the total time of each session is the same, one can use count as the datum and simply report the total duration across all sessions. If the sessions differed in length, or if the teacher were interested in the percent of time the student spent engaging in the behavior, the appropriate datum would be percent, and we would multiply the total time responding by 100 and then divide by the total observation time.

Appropriate Use

Duration recording is in some respects similar to both frequency and interval recording, but its use is so different that it should be considered distinct. It is similar to frequency recording in that we are counting; the difference is that we are counting the number of seconds in a response (and usually the number of responses as well) instead of just the number of responses. It is similar to interval recording in that both are actually estimates of the percent of the total time in which responding occurred. In interval recording, the formula

$$\frac{\text{intervals in which responding occurred}}{\text{intervals of observation}} \times 100 = \%$$

is used to report the percent of intervals in which responding occurred. Although no one reports it as a percent of the total time in which responding occurred, it is generally interpreted as a rough estimate of that ratio. The preference shown for

---

and again identifies the interval size. The third set of information provides the data. The nine sets of 100 boxes are the data from interval recording, while the nine TS# boxes are the data from time sampling.

interval recording is a reflection of its greater ease in recording multiple responses. For example, to obtain simultaneous duration records of 10 responses, we would have to locate 10 timing devices and then we would have to coordinate

Page 1/1	Activity (a) reading	O_1 A. C.	Staff Terry R.
Day Thursday	(b) writing	O_2 C. C.	Doug C.
Date 7/6/78	(c) _____	IOA 92%	
Session 31	Location EMR classroom		

Recording began ___9:18___   Recording ended ___10:08___

Subject-behavior				Subject-behavior			
Susan G. – out of seat				Toby S. – on-task			
Began Ended Dur. ΣD		Began Ended Dur. ΣD		Began Ended Dur. ΣD		Began Ended Dur. ΣD	
9:21 9:24 180 180				9:18 9:19 70" 70"			
9:27 9:28 20 200				9:19 9.24 310 380			
9:31 9:31 10 210				9:24 9:26 110 490			
9:40 9:41 33 243				9:27 9:32 316 806			
9:42(b) – – –				9:34 9:35 50 856			
10:01 10:02 140 353				9:36 9:41 290 1146			
				9:42(b) – – –			
				9:42 9:51 550 1696			
				9:52 9:53 83 1779			
				9:53 9:56 191 1970			
				9:58 10:02 255 2225			
				10:03 10:08 310 2535			

Σ responses ___5___	Σ responses ___11___
Σ time responding ___353 sec___	Σ time responding ___2535 sec___
Σ time recording ___3000 sec___	Σ time recording ___3000 sec___
% time responding ___12%___	% time responding ___85%___
Duration/response ___71 sec___	Duration/response ___231 sec___

Figure 5-4. An example of a form appropriate for recording two behaviors through interval recording. The upper set of information identifies the date of the recording, who (O_1) recorded the behaviors, the extent to which two observers (O_1 and O_2) agreed on the data (IOA), the staff present, the location, and the activities in which the students were engaged during the recording. The second set of information indicates when the recording session began and ended, who the students and what the behaviors were, time each behavior began and ended, the duration and the cumulative duration of each response. The final set of information is a summary of the session's data and includes the number of responses, the total time responding, the total time recording, the percent time responding, and the mean duration of each response.

these to each of the behaviors we are counting. While relating 10 devices to 10 behaviors can be complicated, purchasing 10 timing devices is usually more complicated and even prohibitive. To gather data on the same behaviors through interval recording, we would only need a single timing device to signal the end of each interval and a single form with 10 columns corresponding to the 10 behaviors.

Duration recording is really appropriate for gathering information on any ongoing responding, but it seems much too burdensome for behaviors that are of short duration or that are of moderate or high *and* constant duration. In these cases, it should be rejected in favor of frequency recording, which is much easier to use. The value of duration recording is in providing accurate information on responding that varies in duration.

Practical Use

Figure 5-4 represents a sample data-collection form for recording the duration of one response by each of two persons. The identifying information is the same as the basic identifying information on other forms, but the data entries are quite different. The first two entries indicate the times recording began and ended, and together they indicate the length of the recording session. The next entries identify the students and the behaviors to be recorded. In this case, one behavior of each of the subjects is being recorded. The major portion of the sheet is for recording and indicates the time each behavior began and ended, as well as its duration. The fourth column provides a cumulative total and is used only if we want to check the addition of each of the durations.

TIME SAMPLING

Definition and Datum. Unlike frequency, interval, and duration recording, time sampling is not a continuous measure of behavior within a session; it is a discontinuous measure. *In time sampling, the observer ignores the behavior for a relatively long period* (e.g., 60 minutes), *and then after a signal, quickly scans the situation and records the behaviors being observed.* There are really two types of time-sampling procedures, although the first listed is generally considered the only type: (1) multiple time samples and (2) single time samples. The distinction is quite simple: in the first, time samples are repeated several times per session, while in the second, the sample occurs only once per session. In either case, the datum used is the same. At the end of the session, we multiply by 100 the number of observations in which responding occurred, divide by the number of observations, and report the result as the *percent* of observations in which responding occurred.

Appropriate Use

The major disadvantage of time sampling is that the data it produces to describe behavioral occurrences are greatly affected by the frequency of behavior, the duration of responding, the pattern of responding, and the number of time samples per session. Quite simply, the more rapid the rate of responding, the longer the duration of responding, the more even the pattern, and the more frequent the time samples, the greater the chance that time sampling will produce data that are identical with data produced by continuous measures of responding (Repp, Roberts, Slack, Repp & Berkler, 1976). The reason for the problem is obvious: the method only samples the time period in which responding occurs, so a considerable amount of responding might be ignored. The more frequent responding is, the more likely the time sample will detect it at a proportion similar to the proportion of time it is occurring in the entire session; the greater the duration of responding, the more likely that detection will occur; the more consistent responding is across the session, the more likely a sample will be representative of the whole session; and the more frequent the time samples, the more likely an appropriate proportion will be reported. Because the frequency, duration, and pattern of responding are independent of the method of recording, the only choice we have to reduce error is to make the interobservation times as small as possible. The contribution of time sampling is that it does not require constant observation, freeing the teacher (or the nonteaching observer) to do other things. But we know that this period of nonobservation distorts the data to some extent, so there must be a trade-off between inaccuracy of data and time required for other responsibilities. There is no resolution to the problem, and we should simply record as often as possible.

Practical Use

Time sampling is clearly more practical than duration, interval, or frequency recording when we are trying to record the behavior of a student while teaching several others. Its practical advantages seem to be that (1) it allows the teacher more time for other activities; (2) it is the easiest to use, since it really requires only a mark indicating *yes, the behavior did occur,* or *no, the behavior did not occur;* (3) being the easiest and least interfering method, it is more likely to be maintained when a single person must be the observer, the recorder, and the teacher; and (4) it can be flexible in its demands on time. Although most time samples have a constant interobservation period, they do not need to have one. Observation could be set at 9:00, 9:10, 9:30, 10:00, 10:30, 10:40, and 11:00 if these times are the most convenient. When varying these times, the most important consideration is that the times *must be set prior* to the session and not left to "when I remember." The latter, "remembering," is most likely to happen when there is a cue for it to happen, and such cues are generally related to the behavior. Data collected in this manner are generally unfair to the students; "bad children" are much more likely to be noticed being "bad," and hypotheses become confirmed through the data.

In the section on *definition and datum,* two types of time samples were briefly described, one which provides multiple samples and one which provides only a single sample per session. Figure 5-5 is a sample form useful for the multiple-time-sample method. In the upper section, it provides identifying information similar to that provided by other forms described in this chapter. In the middle section, it identifies the time between samples and then provides room for the observer to record whether or not responding occurred during each

Page ___1___   Activity (a) _playtime_   Observer₁ _R. S._   Staff _Terry R._

Day _Wednesday_   (b) _____   Observer₂ _J. S._   _Mike E._

Date _4/5/78_   (c) _____   IOA___100 %___   _____

Session ___3___   Location _classroom_

Time-sample _1 minute_	Time-sample _____

Student _Mark_   Behavior _independent play_   Student _____   Behavior _____

Time	Response	Time	Response	Time	Response	Time	Response	Time	Response	Time	Response
8:30	Yes	8:44	No								
8:31	Yes	8:45	No								
8:32	No	8:46	No								
8:33	No	8:47	Yes								
8:34	Yes										
8:35	No										
8:36	Yes										
8:37	No										
8:38	No										
8:39	Yes										
8:40	Yes										
8:41	No										
8:42	No										
8:43	Yes										

Responding observations __8__
Total observations _____18_____
% observations responding _44 %_

Responding observations _____
Total observations _____
% observations responding _____

Figure 5-5. An example of a form appropriate for recording the behavior of two students through time sampling. The upper set of information identifies when the recording occurred, who (0₁) recorded the data, the extent to which two observers (0₁ and 0₂) agreed on the data (IOA), the staff present, the location, and the activities in which the students were engaged during the observation. The second set of information identifies the time between the samples, the students and the behaviors, the time at which each sample was taken, and whether behavior occurred (+) or did not occur (−) during each sample. The third set of information is a summary of the total number of observations in the session, of the number of observations in which responding occurred, and of the percent of observations in which responding occurred.

observation. The last section includes a summary of the total number of observations in a session, the total number of observations in which responding occurred, and the percent of observations in which responding occurred.

Figure 5-6 is an example of the single-time-sample method of recording, and in this format it is usually called a checklist. The author (James Favell, 1977) and his associates (e.g., Judy Favell, 1977) have developed a number of forms to monitor (1) the conditions in which the retarded people at Murdoch Center in North Carolina live, and (2) the manner in which they are treated. This form

ROADRUNNER BATHROOM CLEANING AND LINEN EXCHANGE CRITERIA AND CHECKLIST

Week beginning: _____

Routing: 1. Supervisor checks after AM bathing and PM diapering.
2. Supervisor gives completed checklist to External Monitor weekly.

Code: / = OK; X = No; NA = Not Applicable

	Mon.		Tues.		Wed.		Thurs.		Fri.	
Day:	AM	PM	AM	PM	AM	PM	AM	PM	AM	PM
Staff Responsible:										
Observer:										
Bathroom Cleaning										
1. Tables, counters, and carts free of stickiness, food, or spots along tops, edges, and legs.										
2. Slab, sink, and hopper free of stickiness or spots on inside (PM), outside and rim (AM only).										
3. Net is dry to the touch.										
4. On Wednesdays, after morning cleaning, slab, tub, and commode free of stains and dirt inside and outside.										
5. After morning cleaning and PM cleaning, bathroom floor free of dirt, water puddles, piles of hair, or lint.										
6. Netting over slab free of stains, dirt, and BM.										
7. Hair brushes clean.										
Linen Exchange										
1. Mesh diaper bag in garbage can, containing fewer than four dirty items.										
2. Linen bag in hamper containing fewer than six dirty items.										
3. Under the diaper table, all of the following: a. Enough towels to make one pile about 30 inches high.										
b. Enough washcloths to make one pile about 30 inches high.										
c. Enough diapers to make a pile about 30 inches high.										
d. As many plastic pants as possible (maximum of 15).										
4. In linen storage area, all of the following: a. Enough sheets, pillowcases, and bedspreads to change each bed if necessary.										
TOTALS /										
X										

Figure 5-6. An example of a checklist, the data for which are collected through a single time-sample each day (Favell, 1977). The upper section identifies the week, what becomes of the data, and the code for the data entries. The next section provides information on the cleanliness of the bathroom, while the final section provides information on the linen situation. At the bottom of the form, summaries are provided of the appropriateness (/) and inappropriateness (X) of the environment.

monitors the bathing area for nonambulatory retarded persons. The upper section, *bathroom cleaning*, indicates whether the bathing area is as clean as it should be if these individuals were able to live in their homes rather than in an institution. It assesses the cleanliness of the tables used for bathing, of the net used to hold the individuals (so they will not have to lie on a cold surface), of the brushes, and of the general area. The lower section, *linen exchange*, assesses the cleanliness of the diapering area and the preparation of the area for bathing and clothing all residents. The latter is to ensure that no student would be left unattended in the bathing area while staff looks for linens, a situation that is dangerous for physically disabled persons lying on a table or in a net (on or in which they will be bathed).

Checklists of this type have become extremely popular in service areas although they have, of course, been in use for many years. They are quite useful in providing information on the state of the physical environment, as well as on teaching behaviors that are to be sampled only once. As such, they provide a system for accountability that is quite useful in facilities that are understaffed and truly do not have staff who can record data for more than a few minutes a day. The type of items naturally vary according to the purpose of the data, but they all share the common characteristic of being appropriate for a single assessment per observation session.

TASK SAMPLING

Definition and Datum. *Task sampling occurs in two forms. In one, the teacher simply evaluates the child's performance on a task* (e.g., sewing a button on a shirt) *to determine whether the student can complete it correctly or whether it should be added to the list of learning objectives.* In this situation, we count the number of correct and incorrect responses.

In the other form of task sampling, we look at performance on graduated steps in a single task rather than at the completion of the entire task. Much current work with retarded and with other populations involves breaking a task into its subcomponent parts and teaching the subcomponent behaviors in some prescribed manner.[4] There are two typical ways in which data are collected in task analyses, with both ways aimed at assessing the quality of the task analysis. Some teachers record the number of correct and incorrect responses on each component of the analysis. Others teach a specified number of trials per day and record the number of sessions to reach criterion for each subcomponent. This number is then compared with the number of trials to criterion for every other component in the program to determine whether any component requires an abnormally large number of trials to complete. If some components do, the data will identify them and allow the teacher to reanalyze that component to deter-

---

[4] Analyzing a task to determine its subcomponents is called task analysis and will be discussed in detail in Chapter 10. The manner in which the subcomponent behaviors are linked to each other involve one or more of the teaching procedures called forward chaining, shaping, backward chaining, or graduated guidance, each of which will be discussed more fully later.

mine whether it is too complex. The datum used to summarize the data can be either percent or count.

Appropriate and Practical Uses

Task sampling of either type is dictated by the purposes of the teacher, so each is always appropriate when directed to that end. Figure 5-7 is a sample of a large number of teaching tasks in a program designed to teach adolescents and young adults skills necessary for independent or semi-independent living. This particular form briefly describes 11 tasks in a program teaching some sewing skills. While no information on teaching that task is on the evaluation form, it would be included in the task-analysis programs kept separately by the teachers. The form provides four types of information, each separately coded: (1) an E means that the student was evaluated on the task, but did not perform it at criterion level; (2) an E-C means that the student was evaluated once and did complete the task at criterion; (3) a √ means that the student is now learning the task; and (4) C means that the student performed the task at criterion after being involved in a program to teach that specific behavior. A form of this type is very simple, requires only a few seconds to complete, and provides an easy-to-read summary of the student's progress across a wide variety of tasks.

Figure 5-8 is an example of a form useful for analyzing the number of responses or sessions necessary to complete an instructional objective taught through a task-analysis approach. The upper portion of the form identifies (1) the *student*, (2) the *task by name*, (3) the *task by number* (tasks are coded by curriculum, area within curriculum, and number so that a teacher can quickly locate the form which indicates how the task is to be taught), (4) the *step criterion* (in a task analysis, there should be a criterion for moving from one step to the next in a sequence, such as 10 consecutive correct responses; when the student completes the criterion, the teacher moves to the next most difficult step in the program), (5) the *task criterion* (there should also be a criterion which indicates when the student has mastered the task and can move to another task in the program; such a criterion could be 30 consecutive correct responses, (6) *trials per session*, and (7) the *teachers* involved in the program. While only one teacher may be involved in the program, often other people are, including teachers' aides, students who are not retarded, or volunteers.

A summary of each day's progress is entered into the lower portion of the form by entering the date on which the step was taught and the number correct and incorrect. In this section, each column represents a step in the program, and each row represents the number of sessions required to progress to any step in the program. When the numbers of sessions required to move from one step to another are compared, we can quickly determine whether progress is uniform or whether some steps require considerably more time to complete. In this example, step 1 required two sessions to complete, as did step 2; step 3 required only one session. Step 4, however, required three sessions, which was atypical for the program. Such information can be valuable for assessing the steps written for a program nd reanalyzing the task when necessary.

Student: John J. Date	6/1/77	7/1/77	8/1/77	9/1/77	10/1/77	11/1/77	12/1/77	1/1/78	2/1/78	3/1/78	4/1/78	5/1/78	6/1/78
FAATE Sewing													
1. Threading a large eye needle	E-C												
2. Threading a small eye needle		E	C										
3. Knotting a threaded needle		E✓	C										
4. Knotting end of thread				E	✓	C							
5. Sewing a straight stitch on needle point canvas			E	✓	C								
6. Sewing a straight stitch on lined cloth			E	✓	✓	✓	C						
7. Sewing on buttons								E✓	✓	✓	C		
8. Sewing on hooks and eyes								E✓	✓	✓	C		
9. Simple mending				E				✓	✓	✓	✓	✓	✓
10. Cutting a straight line on material		E✓	✓	✓	✓	C							
11. Cutting a shape on material		E✓	✓	✓	✓	✓	✓	C					

Figure 5-7. An example of task sampling in which the student's performance on a task is evaluated. The upper portion identifies the student and the evaluation dates, while the lower portion summarizes the evaluation results through a variety of codes: (a) E, which indicates that the student did not perform the task at criterion level; (b) E-C, which indicates the student was evaluated and did perform the task at criterion; (c) ✓, which indicates that the student performed the task at criterion after being involved in a program to teach that specific behavior.

125

Student _Jimmy W._   Step-criterion _10 consecutive_   Teacher (a) _Cheryl_

Task name _buttoning_   Task-criterion _30 consecutive_   (b) _____

Task number _EMR-SH-12_   Trials/session _10_   (c) _____

SESSIONS		Steps																	
20																			
19																			
18																			
17																			
16																			
15																			
14																			
13			Task completed																	
12																			
11																			
10																			
9																			
8			10^+ 7/22																	
7			8^+ 7/21																	
6			5^+ 7/18																	
5		10^+ 7/17																		
4	10^+ 7/16																			
3	6^+ 7/14																			
2	10^+ 7/11																			
1	8^+ 7/10																			
Steps	1	2	3	4	5	6	7	8	9	10	11	12	13	14	15	16	17	18	19	20

Figure 5-8. An example of a form used to indicate the number of sessions required to master each step in a task analysis. The upper portion identifies the student, the task by name and number, the criteria for mastering each step as well as the complete task, the trials per session, and the teachers. The lower portion is a graph representing the number of sessions required to progress to any point in the program; it is completed by entering a line after each session at each step. The information below the line is the date as well as the number of correct and incorrect responses for that date.

INTEROBSERVER AGREEMENT

Interobserver agreement is a measure of the extent to which observers agree that responding has occurred. It is a standard procedure in research, and none of the better journals publish studies unless they have a number of sessions in which two observers' measurements were compared. It is not a standard procedure in teaching for at least two reasons: (1) it requires two persons to record responding and there is not usually a second person available for this purpose, and (2) teachers do not consider it a practical advantage for their instructional strategies.

The first objection is often valid, but there are two means to resolve the problems that are helpful in some but not all cases. The first is to involve other persons in the area with you, whether they be teachers, aides, or other students. While there often are no other staff available, there *have to be* students available, and they can often participate by collecting data themselves, with the teacher or other students collecting data for interobserver agreement checks. While some might argue that retarded persons cannot perform such tasks, arguments of this type are simply continued prejudices against the underestimated capabilities of retarded persons. While certainly some types of retardation preclude data collection, most do not. In one program, we taught persons classified as severely retarded to collect data accurately, so there is little reason that the vast majority of retarded persons, functioning at higher levels, cannot do so. Data collection can be structured by the creative teacher to perform a number of purposes, including (1) providing a means to teach some students basic arithmetic as it relates to what they do rather than just being work in a textbook, (2) being fun, prestigious, etc., and a rewarded responsibility for the good student, and (3) freeing the teacher for other duties.

Other than serving as a stimulus for incorporating administrators, parents, volunteers, students, etc., in your program, interobserver agreement checks do have an important function in a data-collection system: they serve to assess whether we are reliably measuring what we are supposed to be measuring. In many circumstances, such as those in which students write answers, reliability is easy to assess. However, behaviors which are not so easy to record present a problem because the observer's behavior may be changing independently of the student's behavior. The point has been well summarized by Baer, Wolf, and Risley (1968) in which they note that

> A useful tactic in evaluating . . . a study is to ask not merely, was *behavior* changed? but also *whose* behavior? Ordinarily, it would be assumed that it was the subject's behavior which was altered; yet careful reflection may suggest that this was not necessarily the case. If humans are observing and recording the behavior under study, then any change may represent a change only in *their observing and recording responses, rather than in the subject's behavior* [italics added]. Explicit measurement of the reliability of human observers thus becomes not merely good technique, but a prime criterion of whether the study was appropriately behavioral. (p. 93)

The problem is important in many respects insofar as a researcher at a university is concerned, but insofar as a teacher is concerned, it is most important at the beginning of instruction, when the response is being defined and data collection is being planned. A good way of checking the thoroughness of the definition is to ask someone else to spend a few minutes with us observing the behavior. We will talk about every response either of us believes occurred, suggesting why we think it should be recorded. After observing 20 or 30 occurrences and discussing them, we should find whether our definition was adequate or whether it needed some revision. Because poor definitions may be the most significant contribution to recording errors, 15 or 20 minutes of joint observation could prevent considerable time wasted from using poor definitions of behaviors throughout programs for months on end.

Methods for Calculating Interobserver Agreement

Just as there are several means of recording responding, so there are several means of calculating agreement scores. Some of these are specific to one data-collection method, while others go across methods. Because the agreement methods are related to the data-collection methods, we will discuss them under headings of the recording methods.

Frequency Recording. Interobserver agreement scores for frequency recording can be calculated in three ways.[5] The first involves ongoing responding which two observers independently count throughout the session. The smaller number recorded is multiplied by 100 and then divided by the larger number, and the result represents the percent of interobserver agreement. For example, if a teacher recorded 37 correct verbal responses by her class during the language period, and the aide recorded 40 responses, the percent of interobserver agreement would be 93%, from $(37/40) \times 100$. This method, which has been labeled the *whole-session* method (Repp, Deitz, Boles, Deitz & Repp, 1976) is very popular because it is so simple. It has, however, been criticized because there is no inherent designation of the times at which responding was recorded, and high agreement scores could be produced even if there were little agreement on *when* responding occurred. For example, the teacher could have recorded 37 responses during the first half of the language period and none during the second, while the aide could have recorded none during the first half of the period and 40 during the second, yet the agreement score would be 93%.

An alternative to the whole-session method is the *partial-session* method (Repp, Deitz & Roberts, 1976), which involves parcelling the session into a number of intervals, arranging the numbers of responses into fractions with the smaller number as the numerator, adding all numerators, adding all denominators, and dividing the former sum by the latter sum. The result is then multiplied by 100 and reported as the percent of interobserver agreement. For example, if a teacher recorded 12 correct social responses by her class the first half of the period and 10 the next, while a student teacher recorded 11 and 11, the agreement would be 91%, from $(11 + 10)/(12 + 11) \times 100$. If agreement had

---

[5] Coefficients of reliabilities can be calculated, but they will not be discussed here for two reasons: (1) they are theoretically inappropriate (Baer, 1977), and (2) they are impractical; practitioners have little interest in locating and using statistics books for reliability scores, especially when far easier means are available.

been calculated by the whole-session method, the score would have been 100%, from $(12 + 10)/(11 + 11) = 1000$.

In an effort to be still more exacting, other researchers have employed another procedure for calculating agreement, which has been called the *response-by-response* method (Repp, Deitz & Roberts, 1976). An example of this method is provided by Van Houten and Sullivan (1975), who marked instances of teacher praise on recording sheets having a space provided for each second of each minute of the sessions. The number of responses was counted in each session, and the data were plotted as responses per minute, a very typical procedure. Their recording procedure, however, allowed for a very atypical assessment of observer agreement by defining agreement as observer-marked responses which did not differ by more than 2 seconds. Percentage of interobserver agreement was calculated by multiplying 100 times the number of agreements and dividing by the sum of the agreements and disagreements. A similar attempt at reducing the probability of this type of error was made by Bailey and Meyerson (1970) and Gladstone and Sherman (1975), whose observers recorded responding on event recorders which provided permanent paper records of responding and of time. They defined agreement as an instance in which the two observers engaged the event recorder relays with n seconds (1 second for the former study and 5 seconds for the latter), with this determination being made by inspecting the event recorder tapes.

Interval Recording.   Interobserver agreement scores calculated on data collected through interval recording reflect the agreement between observers that reponding did or did not occur. The basic procedure is to compare the number of intervals in which both observers agreed with the total number of intervals observed:

$$\frac{\text{interobserver}}{\text{agreement}} = \frac{\text{intervals of agreement}}{\text{intervals of agreement} + \text{intervals of disagreement}}$$

For example, if the data in Figure 5-9 represent two observers' record of on-task responding, the percent of interobserver agreement could be calculated by adding the number of intervals in which the two observers agreed either that responding did or did not occur (14 intervals), by adding the intervals in which the two observers did not agree that responding did occur (6 intervals), and by dividing the former by the sum of the former and the latter (14 + 6). The percent of interobserver agreement in this case equals 70% $[14/(14 + 6)]$ and suggests a moderate agreement score that could probably be improved by better response definitions or by training observers more carefully. Some, however, mght object to this conclusion, arguing instead that considerable work still needs to be done before the data collected could be used for assessment. The basis for this argument is the contention that agreement scores should reflect agreement *only* on intervals in which responding did occur; i.e., "agreement" means "agreement on responding having occurred." With this approach, the formula for calculating interobserver agreement ratios is

$$\frac{\text{interobserver}}{\text{agreement}} = \frac{\text{intervals of agreement on responding}}{\text{intervals of agreement on responding} + \text{intervals of disagreement}}$$

Interval	Observer A	Observer B	Agree Using All Intervals	Agree Using Response Intervals Only
1	✓	✓	Agree	Agree
2			Agree	---
3			Agree	---
4			Agree	---
5	✓		Disagree	Disagree
6		✓	Disagree	Disagree
7		✓	Disagree	Disagree
8			Agree	---
9			Agree	---
10			Agree	---
11	✓	✓	Agree	Agree
12	✓	✓	Agree	Agree
13			Agree	---
14			Agree	---
15			Agree	---
16	✓		Disagree	Disagree
17			Agree	---
18		✓	Disagree	Disagree
19	✓		Disagree	Disagree
20			Agree	---
			Agree = 14	Agree = 3
			Disagree = 6	Disagree = 6

Agreement using all intervals $= \left(\dfrac{14}{14+6}\right) 100 = 70\%$

Agreement using all intervals in which responding was recorded $= \left(\dfrac{3}{3+6}\right) 100 = 33\%$

Figure 5-9. A display of data gathered by observers A and B through interval recording. Checkmarks (√) indicate that a response was recorded; the *Agree Using All Intervals* column indicates whether observers agreed that responding did or did not occur; and the *Agree Using Response Intervals Only* column indicates whether there was agreement on those intervals in which at least one observer recorded responding. Calculations at the bottom of the figure indicate the percent of interobserver agreement derived (a) when using all intervals and (b) when using only intervals containing at least one response.

With this formula, we add the number of intervals in which both observers agreed that responding occurred (3 intevals), add the number of intervals in which the observers disagreed that responding did occur (6 intervals), and then divide the former by the sum of the former and the latter (3 + 6). The percent of agreement *on response occurrence* is only 33% [(3/9)100] and supports the position that considerably more work needs to be done before one can use the data collected in this system.

Duration Recording.   Agreement scores for duration recording can be calculated like agreement scores for frequency recording. Using the whole-session method, we would sum the durations recorded by each observer, multiply the smaller by 100 and divide by the larger, and report the result as the percent of observer agreement. For example, if one observer recorded 500 seconds of on-task responding in 30 minutes and another recorded 600, the percent of interobserver agreement would be 83% [(500/600)100].

Time Sampling.   In time sampling, the observer simply records whether or not responding occurred at the time of observation. As such, the data on the recording form are not unlike the data gathered through interval recording; both simply express the percent of observations in which responding occurred. Caculating interobserver agreement for time sampling is similar to calculating agreement for interval recording, and we can either report agreement scores on all observations or only on those observations in which at least one observer recorded responding.

Task Sampling.   In task-sampling, the observer notes whether or not the student can complete either an entire task or a step of a task. For the purpose of assessing agreement, the two are treated identically and are subjected to the response-by-response method from frequency recording. After the data are recorded, we compare responses by the observers on each task or step evaluated. If both agree that the student can or cannot complete the behavior, there is one agreement; if the observers disagree, there is one disagreement. The agreements are summed, the disagreements are summed, the agreements are divided by the sum of the agreements and disagreements, the result is multiplied by 100, and the product represents the percent of interobserver agreement.

GRAPHS

After gathering data, we have the problem of bringing them together into a single form that will allow a rapid and meaningful inspection by a reader. The simplest way is to table the data, and Figure 5-10 is an example of such a format. The table summarizes a student's rate of correct and incorrect responding on arithmetic problems under three conditions, one of which is repeated. The conditions are usually referred to as phases, and in this study (1) phase 1 consisted of no special consequence for correct or incorrect responding and lasted 15 days, (2) phase 2 consisted of the teacher praising the student for every correct response and lasted 20 sessions, (3) phase 3 repeated the conditions for

Correct and Incorrect Arithmetic Problems per Hour Under Three Conditions:
No Contingency, Praise, and Free Time

Condition	No Contingency															
Session	1	2	3	4	5	6	7	8	9	10	11	12	13	14	15	Mean
Rate Correct	3	2	4	6	1	3	2	5	2	1	4	4	6	3	3	3.27
Rate Incorrect	2	0	1	1	3	0	1	2	1	1	1	2	1	0	2	1.20

Condition	Praise																				
Session	16	17	18	19	20	21	22	23	24	25	26	27	28	29	30	31	32	33	34	35	Mean
Rate Correct	2	6	4	8	7	5	4	6	7	5	9	7	8	6	7	5	8	7	9	8	6.40
Rate Incorrect	2	1	1	3	2	0	1	0	0	1	2	1	0	0	1	0	0	1	0	0	0.80

Condition	No Contingency										
Session	36	37	38	39	40	41	42	43	44	45	Mean
Rate Correct	8	9	3	4	4	6	2	3	4	4	2.35
Rate Incorrect	2	0	3	2	1	2	3	2	1	2	0.90

Condition	Free Time																				
Session	46	47	48	49	50	51	52	53	54	55	56	57	58	59	60	61	62	63	64	65	Mean
Rate Correct	4	2	6	4	3	5	2	3	4	6	8	5	5	3	6	7	5	5	4	6	4.65
Rate Incorrect	4	3	1	0	2	1	2	2	2	1	1	0	0	0	2	1	0	0	2	0	1.25

Figure 5-10. A table of a student's correct and incorrect responding on arithmetic problems under three conditions: (a) no contingency for correct or incorrect responding, (b) praise for correct responding, and (c) free time for correct responding.

phase 1 and lasted 10 days, and (4) phase 4 consisted of 10 minutes of free time for five or more correct responses.[6]

The problem with a table such as this is obvious. When there is even a moderate number of data points, tables do not allow the reader to summarize easily what changes occurred from day to day and from condition to condition. As a result of this problem, graphs are most often used to present data in applied behavior analysis, as well as in other fields. While there are many graphs, three types predominate: (1) the time-series graph, (2) the histogram, and (3) the step graph.

Time-Series Graph

The *times-series graph* is one of many types of line charts and is by far the most popular graph in our field. It is *a graph in which the x-axis* (also called horizontal axis or abscissa) *represents time and the y-axis* (also called vertical axis or ordinate) *represents the number of occurrences of the dependent variable*. There are two choices with time-series graphs that must be made before the graphs can be constructed. The first is whether to make the y-axis cumulative or noncumulative from session to session. The second is whether to make the y-axis re-

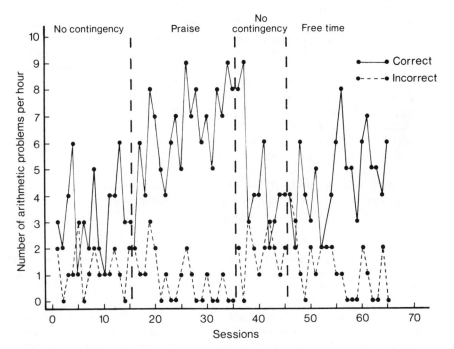

Figure 5-11. The data from the table in Figure 5-10 plotted as a noncumulative time-series graph.

---

[6] Certainly there is much more to know about this teacher's assessment of her pupil's responding, including the arrangement of the consequences, the curriculum, the setting, etc.; but for the purpose of this example of data presentation, this information is sufficient.

present an interval scale or a logarithmic scale. While the philosophies adopted by the proponents of each alternative may be complicated, the graphs themselves are very elementary and easy to understand.

Cumulative and Noncumulative Graphs.   In a noncumulative graph, we begin from the zero point each session in determining the y value for that session. For example, in the first five sessions of data represented in Figure 5-10, the values of correct responding are 3, 2, 4, 6, and 1. In a noncumulative graph, the value of the y-axis is 3 for the first session, 2 for the second, 4 for the third, 6 for the fourth, and 1 for the fifth. In a cumulative graph, on the other hand, we begin from the last session's y value in determining the y value for any particular session; i.e., we add the value of the present session to the cumulative value through the last session. Using the prior example, the plots for the first five sessions would be 3, 5 (from 3 + 2), 9 (from 5 + 4), 15 (9 + 6), and 16 (15 + 1).

Figure 5-11 is an example of a noncumulative time-series graph representing the data presented in Figure 5-10. Note that for each session, the value plotted is the number for that day and it is independent of the value from the prior day. Figure 5-12 is an example of a cumulative graph of the same data. Note in this case that the value plotted for any session is the number for that day plus the cumulative number through the prior session.

The noncumulative graph is by far the most popular, but the cumulative is just as correct and is particularly appropriate in certain circumstances, one circumstance is when a total number of units completed by the student is really the objective. For example, if a student is to complete 50 reading units in four months, a cumulative graph is more appropriate because it will indicate immediately how many units have been completed at any point in time. A second circumstance occurs when reading the graph is easier if the data are plotted in a cumulative fashion. One such situation occurs when two or more responses do not differ appreciably in occurrence but are being plotted on the same graph. For example, if a child's correct and incorrect (n) academic responses were 5 (5), 4 (6), 3 (7), 4 (6), 5 (5), 6 (4), 5 (5), 5 (5), 5 (5), and 6 (4), then data plotted in a noncumulative fashion would be difficult to read because the points are equivalent on so many of the days. When these data are plotted cumulatively, the overall, as well as the daily, differences are easier to identify.

Equal Interval and Semilogarithmic Graphs.   Most graphs in applied behavior analysis have an equal-interval scale; i.e., the distances on the graph between any two pairs of points is proportionate to the difference between their values. For example, the distance on the graph between values of 50 and 55 is the same as the distance between 60 and 65 or 82 and 87 or 3 and 8; and the distance between 10 and 20 is twice the distance between 5 and 10. In semilogarithmic graphs, such as the one in Figure 5-13, the y-axis is in a logarithmic scale. Quite simply, this means that the distance between any two points that are expressed as a fraction is equal to the distance between any two other numbers that describe the same fraction. For example, because 2 is twice 1, and 10 is twice 5, the distance on the graph between 1 and 2 is the same as the distance between 5 and 10 (or 2 and 4, or 3 and 6, or 4 and 8, etc.). Similarly, the distance between pairs that form different fractions is proportionate to the relationship between those frac-

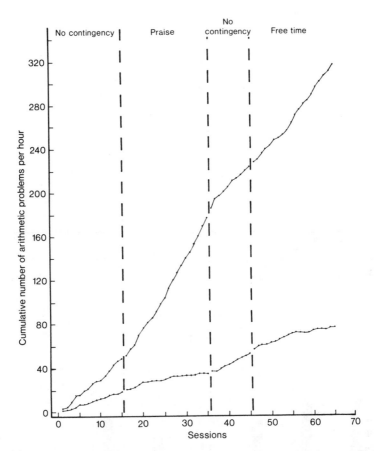

Figure 5-12. The data from the table in Figure 5-10 plotted as a cumulative time-series graph. The line labeled "slope" refers to the angle of a line drawn through the majority of the data points in a phase. Note that there are two slopes generated by the data in the last phase.

tions. For example, the distance from 1 to 2 is one-half the distance on the graph from 1 to 4, or 2 to 8, or 1.5 to 6, etc. When this relationship is identified by the reader, a semilogarithmic graph is quite easy to read.

Histogram

The most common type of histogram is the bar graph, and it is the type most commonly used in ABA. The major advantage of the bar graph is that it allows a rapid examination of a summary of data across several subjects or sessions. Its major disadvantage is that it does not provide a continuous, perhaps daily, representation of data; it presents instead only a summary of continuous data. Figure 5-14 is a bar graph that shows the performance of autistic/retarded children when being taught either alone, with one other child, or with seven other children (Koegel & Rincover, 1974). In this study, the children were

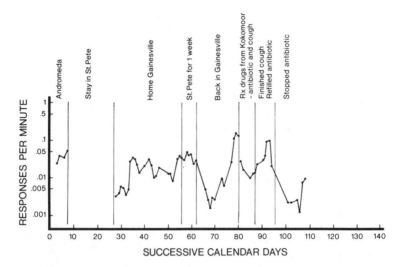

Figure 5-13. The rate of a child's coughing in two different cities and under different medications. Note that the *y*-axis is logarithmic.

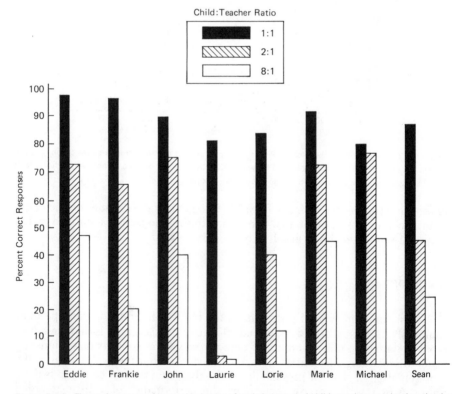

Figure 5-14. The performance of learned behavior of autistic/retarded children when taught alone by the teacher (1:1), with one other child (2:1), or with seven other children (7:1). From Koegeland Rincover, 1974, p. 52.

taught in a one-to-one situation certain verbal and nonverbal behaviors until they reached a criterion of 80% mastery. Their behavior was then measured when being taught by the teacher in two other group sizes. Figure 5-14 combines their performance of the verbal and nonverbal behaviors and indicates that the children showed a decrease in correct responding as the size of the group increased.

Step Graphs

Since the 1930s, a procedure labeled task analysis has been employed in a number of settings intended to train nonhandicapped persons. In the late 1960s, this method of analyzing what is to be taught has been very popular in teaching retarded as well as other developmentally disabled persons. The procedure,

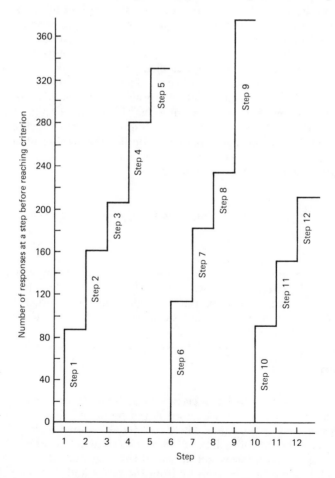

Figure 5-15. A step graph displaying the number of responses required to meet a criterion of seven consecutive correct responses at each of 12 steps in a task analysis. When steps 5 and 9 were completed, the count was begun and the zero line for steps 6 and 10.

which will be discussed in detail in Chapter 10, involves breaking a complex task into a number of steps or components, each of which is at a level easy enough for the student to master without too much difficulty. The purpose of a step graph is to make an assessment of the components to determine whether the student has progressed through each step of the task analysis without difficulty and at about the same rate. To determine the amount of time required to move from one step to another, we must set a step criterion that is the same for each component. This step criterion indicates the level of mastery required at any step before progressing to the next and can be such statements as "10 consecutive correct trials," or "20 correct responses, with at least the last 10 being consecutive." Once this criterion is determined, the step graph provides a simple and rapid means of determining how long a student required to complete each step at the criterion level. While Figure 5-8 is actually a step graph, Figure 5-15 is presented here is a form more typical of graphs. This figure is a step graph of a task with 12 components and a criterion of 7 consecutive correct responses for each step. A glance at the graph shows the reader that the number of responses required to reach criterion on steps 6 and 9 was excessive. With this information, the teacher can ask questions such as: (1) were there circumstances that contributed to atypical behavior during this period (e.g., a change in medication, illness, family problems)? and (2) is the decrement in correct responding during these two steps repeated across individuals (e.g., did Johnny also require more responses in these than in other components to reach criterion)? If this situation occurs, then the teacher should reanalyze the troublesome components, possibly breaking them into subcomponents. Such information underlies the significant advantage of data collection: when procedures are inappropriate, too complex, etc., we can identify a problem and begin to correct it.

DATA COLLECTION: THE INITIAL OBSERVATION

This section offers an example of how we could collect data in a teaching situation with five students, none of whom the data collector had ever seen before. It is divided into five steps, each of which could be followed in any situation we first observe; these steps are (1) observing, (2) defining behaviors, (3) choosing a method of recording and a datum, (4) developing a data-collection form, and (5) recording.

Observing

The situation was described as a classroom with one teacher, an aide, and five retarded adolescents, each of whom displayed problem behaviors. The first few minutes were used to determine where the students were taught, where an unobtrusive place for recording data would be, and what behaviors were of concern to the teachers. This information indicated that the students were taught at a table or while seated in chairs away from the table, and that the behaviors of concern could be labeled as "hands," sleeping, sitting at table, and noncompliance.

Defining Behaviors

After finding an appropriate place for data collection, the next step was to write definitions for each of the four behaviors. This was done by writing notes on what constituted an occurrence, as well as the absence of responding, and produced the following tentative definitions: (1) *Susan's hand behavior:* hand or finger(s) touching lips or in mouth, *or* hands touching each other while flicking one or more fingers. Any other responding did not constitute hand behavior; (2) *Brian's sleeping behavior:* eyes closed, *or* head on table, *or* head on hands and elbows on table; (3) *all students' correct sitting behavior:* (a) head is up and facing teacher *and* (b) eyes are open, *and* (c) both feet are on the floor, *and* (d) hands are not in the mouth, above the head, or in general anywhere but on the table, on materials, in the lap, or by one's side, *and* (3) elbows and forearms are not on the table (notice that all five conditions need to be met for sitting to be recorded as being correct); and (5) *John's compliance behavior,* which was defined as moving from one place in the room to another when requested by the teacher or the aide. Excluded from compliance/noncompliance was any situation which involved a request (e.g., Johnny, point to the red one) that could be met without moving from one place to another in the room.

Choosing a Method of Recording and a Datum

The first requisite of choosing methods of recording was that all behaviors could be recorded during the recording period rather than recording one behavior the first portion of the period, another behavior the next, etc. This choice was made in case the behaviors occurred primarily during situations which happened only once or twice per day. The following methods of recording were chosen: (1) for Susan's hand behavior, 15-second time sampling because the behavior occurred for enduring periods and was of high rate and because frequency (the behavior was of long and varying durations), interval (too many other very different behaviors were to be recorded simultaneously), and duration (no stopwatch, too complicated with other behaviors being recorded) recording were inappropriate; (2) for Brian's sleeping behavior, 15-second time sampling for the same reasons offered in the prior example; (3) for all five students' sitting behavior, 30-second time sampling for the same reasons offered above previously (a 30-second period was chosen instead of a 15-second period to reduce the possibility of observer fatigue); and (4) for John's compliance behavior, frequency recording, as we should be recording both the number of requests for movement and the number of compliances. Because in each of the four cases the number of observations (for hand, sleeping, or sitting) or the opportunities for responding (for compliance) would vary from day to day, percent was used as the datum by which the data would be expressed.

Developing a Data-Collection Form

The major consideration in designing a form is that it should make data collection easy. One potential problem when recording several behaviors of several persons simultaneously is that if the forms are on different pages, the recorder will be unnecessarily encumbered. Figure 5-16 shows an attempt to eliminate this problem by placing all the information needed on a single sheet of paper. The upper left area is for recording Susan's hand behavior and Brian's sleeping behavior. A circle is used if an observation indicates that neither student was engaged in these responses; / indicates that Susan was engaged in hand activ-

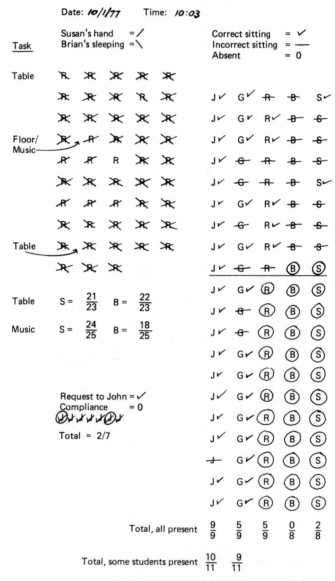

Figure 5-16. A recording sheet on which (1) the sleeping behavior of Brian (\) and the hand-in-mouth behavior of Susan (/) are recorded while they are at a *table* and while they are on the *floor* during *music*; (2) the *requests* to John (√) and John's *compliance* with requests; and (3) the *correct sitting, incorrect sitting,* and *absence* of John, Gerry, Robert, Brian, and Susan. All the behaviors except requests to John and John's compliance are recorded by time sampling; those two behaviors are recorded by frequency recording.

ity; \ indicates that Brian was sleeping; and X indicates that both students were emitting responses. The "task" designation on the far left indicates where the student was located when data were recorded. The area on the bottom left indicates the requests for John to move (Ⱦ) and the compliances (Ⱦ). The area on the right represents a seating chart describing the order in which the students are seated at the table (John, Gerry, Robert, Brian, and Susan). A check mark (✓) indicates correct sitting; — indicates incorrect sitting; and 0 indicates that the student was not at the table. With this kind of form, which can be developed in 3 or 4 minutes, the observer should find recording quite simple.

Recording

Recording the occurrences of two low-rate behaviors, such as the teachers' instructions and John's compliances, is of course quite simple. But recording two behaviors every 15 seconds and five additional behaviors across five subjects every other 15 seconds is somewhat more complicated. The simplest way to accomplish this task accurately is to develop a ritual. For the time-sampling procedure in this example we would (1) test to determine whether we can paraphrase each of the definitions, (2) record data for at least several minutes at untimed intervals to determine whether we can identify the occurrence or nonoccurrence of each behavior of each subject, and (3) develop the ritual for recording the data that will be used. In this case, that ritual could be (1) if right-handed, place the watch to your left and the recording paper to your right; (2) look down at the watch and at 0:10 seconds read the names of the students whose behavior you will record in the order in which you will look at them; (3) at 0:15 seconds look at Brian and say "Brian" or say nothing and at Susan and say "Susan" or say nothing; (4) look down and mark on the recording sheet whether Brian was sleeping ("Brian") or not, and whether Susan was "handing" or not; (5) at 0:25, read the names of the students whose sitting behavior you will record, and whose sleeping and hand behaviors you will record, being sure to have the names on the data sheet in the order in which they are seated; (6) at 0:30, look at the sitting behavior of John and say "John" or nothing, on through Gerry, Robert, Brian, and Susan while repeating the name of the students who *are* responding; (7) then continue looking at Brian (for sleeping) and Susan (for "handing") and say their names if they are responding; (8) look down at the recording sheet and record the behavior of those students whose names you have said. If a student has not responded, designate this a few seconds later so that the total number of observations (responding plus no responding) can be determined. This cycle is then repeated at the 0:45 and 1:00 times. With a few practice trials, you would soon find the work quite simple provided the ritual is followed; when it is not, competing behaviors (e.g., "daydreaming") occur and inaccuracy results.

SUMMARY

This chapter presents (1) characteristics of direct and indirect recording, (2) types of observational data, including narratives, ratings, and checklists, (3) major methods of recording data directly, including their definition, datum, and a discussion of their uses, (4) methods of calculating interobserver agreement for each of the methods of recording, (5) time-series graphs, histograms, and step graphs, and (6) an example of collecting data when in a situation for the first time.

Chapter 6 will present information on two very different types of evaluations: (1) the operant designs for evaluating treatment procedures on a session-to-session basis, and (2) checklists for determining intermittently whether a child can complete a task.

REFERENCES

Baer, D. M. Reviewer's comment: Just because it's reliable doesn't mean that you can use it. *Journal of Applied Behavior Analysis,* 1977, **10,** 117–119.

Baer, D. M., Wolf, M. M., & Risley, T. R. Some current dimensions of applied behavior analysis. *Journal of Applied Behavior Analysis,* 1968, **1,** 91–97.

Bailey, J., & Meyerson, L. Effect of vibratory stimulation on a retardate's self-injurious behavior. *Psychological Aspects of Disability,* 1970, **17,** 133–137.

Bijou, S. W., Peterson, R. F., & Ault, M. H. A method to integrate descriptive and experimental field studies at the level of data and empirical concepts. *Journal of Applied Behavior Analysis,* 1968, **1,** 175–191.

Brandt, R. M. *Studying behavior in natural settings.* New York: Holt, Rinehart and Winston, 1972.

Deitz, D. E. D., Roberts, D. M., & Slack, D. J. *An analysis of the effects of various strategies and conditions for observing staff behavior in an instructional setting.* Paper presented at a meeting of the Southeastern Psychological Association, 1976.

Favell, J. E. *Maintaining quality care and treatment in a comprehensive developmental environment for profoundly multi-handicapped individuals.* Paper presented at the Spring Conference on Staff Training and Motivation in Treatment Services for the Developmentally Disabled. Northern Indiana State Hospital, South Bend, Indiana, 1977.

Favell, J. E., Jr. *An institution-wide evaluation and feedback system.* Paper presented at the spring Conference on Staff Training and Motivation in Treatment Services for the Developmentally Disabled. Northern Indiana State Hospital, South Bend, Indiana, 1977.

Fichter, M. M., Wallace, C. J., Liberman, R. P., & Davis, J. R. Improving social interaction in a chronic psychotic using discriminated avoidance ("nagging"): Experimental analysis and generalization. *Journal of Applied Behavior Analysis,* 1976, 9, 377–386.

Gladstone, B. W., & Sherman, J. A. Developing generalized behavior-modification skills in high-school students working with retarded children. *Journal of Applied Behavior Analysis,* 1975, 8, 169–180.

Hawkins, R. P., & Dotson, V. A. *Reliability scores that delude: An Alice in Wonderland trip through the misleading characteristics of inter-observer agreement scores in interval recording.* Paper presented at Kansas Conference on Behavior Analysis in Education, May 1972.

Hersen, M., & Bellack, A. S. A multiple-baseline analysis of social-skills training in chronic schizophrenics. *Journal of Applied Behavior Analysis,* 1976, 9, 239–245.

Johnson, S. M., & Bolstad, O. D. Methodological issues in naturalistic observation: Some problems and solutions for field research. In L. A. Hamerlynck, L. C. Handy, and E. J. Mash (Eds.), *Behavior change: Methodology concepts, and practice.* Champaign, IL: Research Press, 1973.

Kent, R.N., Kanowitz, Jr., O'Leary, K. D., & Cheiken, M. Observer reliability as a function of circumstances of assessment. *Journal of Applied Behavior Analysis,* 1977, 10, 317–324.

Koegel, R. L., & Rincover, A. Treatment of psychotic children in a classroom environment: I. Learning in a large group. *Journal of Applied Behavior Analysis,* 1974, 7, 45–59.

O'Leary, K. D., & Kent, R. N. Behavior modification for social action: research tactics and problems. In L. A. Hamerlynck, P. O. Davidson, & L. E. Acker (Eds.), *Critical issues in research and practice.* Champaign, IL: Research Press, 1973.

O'Leary, K. D., Kent, R. N., & Kanowitz, Jr. Shaping data collection congruent with experimental hypotheses. *Journal of Applied Behavior Analysis,* 1975, 8, 43–51.

Repp, A. C., Deitz, D. E. D., Boles, S. M., Deitz, S. M., & Repp, C. F. Differences among common methods for calculating interobserver agreement. *Journal of Applied Behavior Analysis,* 1976, 9, 109–113.

Repp, A. C., Deitz, D. E. D., & Roberts, D. M. *A comparison of methods for assessing interobserver agreement in frequency recording.* In A. C. Repp (chair), Methodological considerations in data collection. Paper presented at the 10th Annual Meeting of the Association for Advancement of Behavior Therapy, 1976.

Repp, A. C., Roberts, D. M., Slack, D. J., Repp, C. F., & Berkler, M. S. A comparison of frequency, interval, and time-sampling methods of data collection. *Journal of Applied Behavior Analysis,* 1976, 9, 501–508.

Romanczyk, R. G., Kent, R. N., Diament, C., & O'Leary, K. D. Measuring reliability of observational data: A reactive process. *Journal of Applied Behavior Analysis,* 1973, 6, 175–184.

Thompson, C., Holmberg, M., & Baer, D. M. A brief report on a comparison of time-sampling procedures. *Journal of Applied Behavior Analysis,* 1974, 7, 623–626.

Van Houten, R., & Sullivan, K. Effects of an audio cueing system on the rate of teacher praise. *Journal of Applied Behavior Analysis,* 1975, 8, 197–201.

PART

III

6

Evaluation of Behavior and Behavior Change Programs

Evaluation of Behavior

BEHAVIORAL VERSUS TRADITIONAL EVALUATIONS

Behavioral evaluations are quite different from traditional evaluations, and, according to behaviorists at least, their recent development has been an important contribution to the analysis of human behavior. The primary difference is that the traditional test usually compares the individual to other people, while the behavioral test compares the individual to himself over different times. For example, a traditional intelligence test seeks to determine how each of us answers certain questions and solves certain problems, and then it attempts to compare us with people in the normative sample based upon our test responses. Similarly, a traditional personality test seeks to determine how we would behave in certain situations generally by asking us to say how we might behave in those situations. The results are then analyzed, the people answering the questions are categorized and labeled, and differences among the people taking the test are then discussed. Behavioral assessments on the other hand are more concerned with defining intelligent behaviors or certain social behaviors and then determining the conditions under which they do and do not occur.

A second major distinction is that traditional assessments view behavior as signs of broader dispositions that are lasting and general, whereas behavioral assessments view behavior as a sample of comparable behavior that is lasting but specific (Cone, 1975). As Goldfried and Spafkin (1974) have noted in a text on a behavioral approach to personality assessment, "behaviorally oriented psychologists have not completely eliminated the concept of personality . . . [however], an individual's behavior is not seen as being a function of his personality, but rather the reverse" (p. 3); i.e., what we call a person's personality is a general statement based on our assessment of what he or she does. If a child engages in frequent arguments, pushes and hits other students, etc., we might use the label "aggressive" to describe him; or if a child waits quietly in line, says "thank you" and "please," opens doors for others, picks up dropped books, asks friends if he might help them, we might use the label "polite" to describe him. In either case, the label we choose to describe the child is based upon our informal assessments of his behavior.

A third major distinction between these assessments is that behavioral tests assess certain behaviors and encourage us to teach or treat those behaviors that are tested, while traditional tests assess certain behaviors and encourage us to generalize beyond those tested behaviors to teach or treat behaviors other than those tested. For example, a behavioral evaluation on self-help skills might assess with one of its items whether a child can unbutton a three-button sweater. If she cannot, the child is taught that task. A traditional evaluation instrument concerned with intelligence on the other hand might have a card with pictures of objects on it. The tester might ask, "Show me which one we cook on," or "Show me what we carry when it is raining." If the child does not answer correctly, he is not to be taught that response later in his class. Rather, he is presented "an enriched environment" to increase his "intelligence." With traditional assessments, teaching answers to test items is called unfair. With behavioral assessments, teaching answers to test items is called teaching to objectives.

The intensity of the staunch behaviorist's opposition to traditional assessment has been demonstrated by Gold (1974) in his argument for the abolition of diagnosis and formal evaluation:

> We're like Procrustes of Greek mythology who had an inn with one bed. He would bring people in and make them fit his bed either by stretching them or cutting off their legs. And that's what we are doing. We construct categories and then force people into them. After we've got them there, we make judgments about what they can and cannot do. The problem with our present system of diagnosis and evaluation is that D & E activities are separated from treatment activities. [Evaluation should not be separated from training; instead we should] decide what a student needs to know and find a way to train him to know what we want him to know. (p. 3)

Although there are thousands of traditional evaluations, intelligence tests are the ones most closely associated with mental retardation. For many years, scores on intelligence tests were the sole criterion for being or not being declared mentally retarded. While these test scores are no longer used as the sole criterion, they are still used as one of the primary criteria in the definition by most persons in this field (e.g., the definition of the American Association on Mental Deficiency, Grossman, 1973).[1]

---

[1] See Chapter 1.

Behaviorists believe that performance on an intelligence test is a function of the individual's history with events that shape cognitive performance. Bijou's (1969) analysis of the difference between the retarded and the intellectually accelerated child is relevant to this concern. He views the developmentally retarded individual

> as one who has a meager repertory of cognitive behaviors as a consequence of restrictions in his interactional history. Among the limiting conditions are: (a) mild to gross abnormal anatomical structure and physiological functioning, (b) inadequate programming of reinforcement and discriminative stimuli, (c) consequences of strong and frequent contingent aversive stimulation, (d) reinforcement of inappropriate behavior, and (e) the weakening of behavior through the loss of stimulus control, extinction, random reinforcement, time-out from positive reinforcement,[2] and the like. (p. 19)

Bijou views the intellectually accelerated individual as one who has

> a history characterized by a preponderance of conditions which foster the development of extensive repertories of cognitive behavior. Among these conditions are: (a) normal to superior anatomical structure and physiological functioning, (b) availability of stimuli for cognitive learning, and (c) high saturation of interactions with parents, teachers, and others who place a high value on cognitive achievement, who arrange contingencies for effective cognitive learning, and who provide positive reinforcement which maintains the cognitive behaviors acquired. (p. 19)[3]

An analysis of the differences between accelerated and undeveloped behavior supports one of the reasons behaviorists tend to ignore intelligence tests. There simply is more concern in this field with learning how to arrange learning conditions for retarded persons that promote learning, as the learning conditions for the more intelligent students have done. The basic behavioral program is directed toward that end. It includes (1) a definition of the goal for the target behavior, (2) a statement of the present level of functioning, and (3) a suggested means for moving from the present level of functioning to the goal. Because traditional tests do not allow a precise enough analysis of any of these steps, other evaluations have been developed which are either in part or in whole satisfactory. The next section will present a discussion of some of these.

INVENTORIES

While there is sometimes overlap, most behavioral evaluations are intended to provide information in one of two areas: (1) primarily on the behavior of the individual, or (2) primarily on the success of treatment strategies as measured

---

[2] These will be discussed in ensuing chapters.

[3] This analysis of accelerated cognitive development has been compared by Bijou to the findings of Terman (Terman, 1925; Terman & Oden, 1959).

through changes in the behavior of the individual. Evaluations with the first purpose will be discussed in this section under the heading Inventories; those with the second purpose will be discussed in the next section under the heading Evaluation of Behavior Change Programs.

There are numerous inventories used to measure developmentally retarded behavior, and representatives of these will be discussed in this section. While they can be categorized according to various criteria, the distinction made in this section is whether (1) they measure directly or indirectly the behavior of the individual (these tests typically provide for someone very familiar with the individual to be interviewed, and the results of the interview are used in lieu of direct measurement), or (2) are curriculum-based inventories that measure whether a student can complete a curriculum task at a criterion level, i.e., criterion-referenced tests.

Direct Measures of Student Behavior

Inventories that directly measure behavior are those that provide for the performance by the student of each of the behaviors listed in the inventory. For example, if one item questions whether the child can write the correct answer to $1 + 1 = x$, then the child would be asked to write the answer. If the criterion for "child can write the correct answer" is three of three presentations, then the problem is presented to the child three times. At no time, however, is the teacher, parent, or attendant asked to say whether the child can answer that test item; the child provides the answer. Although there are several tests of this type, two will be discussed as representative of the field.

Balthazar Scales of Adaptive Behavior. The Balthazar scales are direct measures and, in his introduction, Balthazar indicates his concern for this procedure:

> information should be provided by directly observing and studying the subject before one formally measures his performance. Accurate measures are *not* obtained by asking others what his eating and dressing behaviors are like. The only exception to this is provided by the interview procedure in the Toileting Scales [although when possible one should] observe some of the individual's toilet behaviors before conducting the interview. (1971b, Part II, p. 7)

The Balthazar Scales of Adaptive Behavior for the profoundly and severely mentally retarded are in two sections. The Scales of Functional Independence (BSAB-I) (Balthazar, 1971a) test the ambulatory student's skills in three areas of independent functioning. The Eating Scales cover five classes of behavior (dependent feeding, finger foods, spoon usage, fork usage, and drinking), with each of these classes broken into 9 or 13 subclasses. In the subclasses, the behaviors are defined and scored according to how many times the individual emitted the behavior in 10 opportunities. The Dressing Scales cover a standard clothing list in eight categories according to the clothing (shoes, socks, briefs, t-shirt/undershirt, regular shirt or blouse, pants, skirt, dress). These categories are broken into two sections, putting on or taking off, and then the behaviors

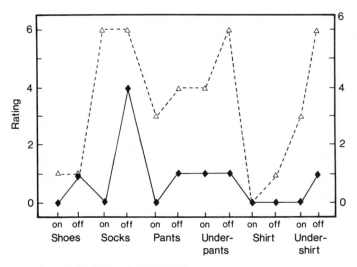

Student: J.R. Hansen (261-60-0041)
Baseline: 9/3/77
Second Observation: 11/3/77
Evaluator: R.B. Evans (Psy.)

Figure 6-1. The performance of a student on the dressing scale in the Balthazar Scales of Adaptive Behavior before and after a two-month training program. The rating scale is from 0 (no participation) to 6 (independent, perfect performance), and the ratings were made on September 3 and November 3, 1977.

necessary to complete each are listed. The behaviors are then scored on a seven-point rating scale according to the degree of independence displayed while engaging in the behavior; the higher the rating, the greater the independence. The Toileting Scales cover a number of items involved in toileting and rely on the questionnaire format. In each case, questions are phrased to elicit a numerical answer from zero to 10 and follow the general format "For an average 10 times that Johnny . . ., how many of those times did he . . .?"

The Balthazar Scales of Social Adaptation (BSAB-II) (Balthazar, 1971b) are similar, and they also provide both a means for evaluating adaptive behavior and a means for programming. The scales represent the student's present level of functioning, his or her baseline skills. The scale items can then be used either as direct objectives for the student to learn, or they can be used as measures of the student's progress in a general program. Figure 6-1 shows how the scale can be used to indicate quickly and in general where progress has been made, how much progress has been made, and what are the strengths and weaknesses in the student's behavioral repertoire.

The Behavioral Characteristics Progression. The Behavioral Characteristics Progression (BCP)[4] (1973) is an enormous inventory, being much larger and covering many more items than the Balthazar scales. It consists of 59 *strands*

_____

[4] The BCP is said by its authors to be a criterion-referenced test. However, because it does not accompany a collection of task analyses to teach each of the tasks, it does not meet the criterion used in this book or by Cone (1975) for a criterion-referenced test.

or classes of behaviors, including basic self-help skills, simple visual tracking, reading, music skills, and homemaking. Within each strand are various behavioral characteristics generally numbering 40 or 50 and totaling 2,400. Each strand has a list of *identifying behaviors* that focuses on particular problems the student might have with a particular strand (e.g., for the strand *social eating*, there are 16 identifying behaviors, including eating too fast or too slow, taking another's food, eating with mouth open, etc.). The evaluator marks the identifying behaviors that are relevant for a student for each strand. With this addition, the BCP can describe several tens of thousands of behavioral combinations on 59 pages of test paper. These behavioral characteristics allow the BCP to serve three functions: (1) an assessment tool to identify individual strengths and weaknesses, (2) an instructional tool to provide a meaningful number of instructional objectives for retarded students, and (3) a communication tool to show a student's progress from year to year through a multiplicity of programs.

Each strand of the BCP is scored in the same manner and each item is scored in one of six ways: (1) the behavior was not displayed but there was no opportunity for display (e.g,, self-entry onto school bus could not occur because the aide's job was to assist every student), (2) opportunity offered but behavior not displayed, (3) behavior displayed, but less than 75% of the time, (4) behavior displayed at least 75% of the time, (5) behavior cannot be displayed because of physical handicap, or (6) behavior cannot be displayed because materials necessary for occurrence are not present. The results of the evaluation can then be used to monitor the student's progress.

Indirect Measures of Student Behavior

Indirect measures of behavior are those which provide data on the individual not through direct observation of his behavior but through the remembrances of persons familiar with the individual. Because they are so much easier to administer than tests that measure directly, indirect tests are quite popular. They all suffer, however, from inherent error, because they do not insist that data taken directly on the student's behavior be used. While there are many such inventories, the most popular is the AAMD Adaptive Behavior Scale (ABS), so it will be discussed as representative of this kind of evaluation.

AAMD Adaptive Behavior Scale. The ABS (Nihira, Foster, Shellhaas & Leland, 1975) is a two-part rating scale for mentally retarded, emotionally disturbed, and developmentally disabled persons, and is intended to provide an objective description of their adaptive behavior. Part One is organized to represent increasing developmental levels, and it covers 10 behavior domains and 21 behavior subdomains. The domains are independent functioning, physical development, economic activity, language development, numbers and time, domestic activity, vocational activity, self-direction, responsibility, and socialization. Part Two of the ABS is not developmentally arranged, concentrating as it does on maladaptive behavior related to social expectations that communities and institutions have placed on these individuals. It comprises 13 behavior domains and one condition (medications) and includes violent and destructive behavior, antisocial behavior, rebellious behavior, untrustworthy behavior, withdrawal, stereotyped behavior and odd mannerisms, inappropriate interpersonal manners, unacceptable vocal habits, unacceptable or eccentric habits, self-abusive behavior, hyperactive tendencies, sexually aberrant behavior, psychological disturbances, and use of medications.

The test is administered by an evaluator asking questions of the person who spends the greatest number of waking hours with the individual. The ABS manual recommends three types of administrations: (1) first-person assessment, where the evaluator knows the individual well enough to complete each item of the scale, (2) third-person assessment, where the evaluator seeks responses to each of the items from various persons, such as parents, teachers, or attendants, or (3) interview method, where the evaluator interviews someone familiar with the student. Interestingly, the ABS manual recommends this "third-party assessment" because it can be completed in 15 to 20 minutes. The manual does point out, however, that data gathered from the interview method are not exactly comparable to data gathered from the first two methods. Answers to the test items are scored and then summarized on the Profile Summary Sheet that is used to relate the individual to national norms established for mentally retarded persons living in institutions in the United States. A number of investigators are currently trying to determine norms for community rather than just institutional persons, so that the profile would be more useful. Others argue against such norms, saying that the progress of the individual is more important than her or his behavioral competencies relative to others.

Curriculum-Based Inventories

Curriculum-based inventories are direct measures of student behavior on items in a curriculum through which the student is taught. They differ from other direct measures like the Balthazar scales, because they are directly related to a curriculum. Inventories of this type usually ask one of two questions: (1) can the student display mastery of the task? or (2) to what degree can the student complete the task? The first simply asks the question "Is the student competent at the task?" and answers with a "yes" or "no." The second is much more complex and relies on specified components of complex behaviors that allow more than a simple "yes" or "no." This kind of inventory might indicate that a student can complete 12 of the 16 components of a self-help task or eight of the 10 components of a preacademic task. Such an evaluation must rely on good descriptions of the components of complex tasks or behaviors, a descriptive product that results from task analyses.[5]

A brief example of a classroom inventory can be taken from the curriculum checklists developed by Turnbull, Strickland, and Brantley (1978). Figure 6-2 presents eight items from the intermediate-level arithmetic portion of their checklist for classroom academics. In this section, the student's skills at counting, reading, and writing numbers is assessed, and the teacher can immediately tell where the student's strong and weak points are.

---

[5] Task analyses will be explained in Chapter 10.

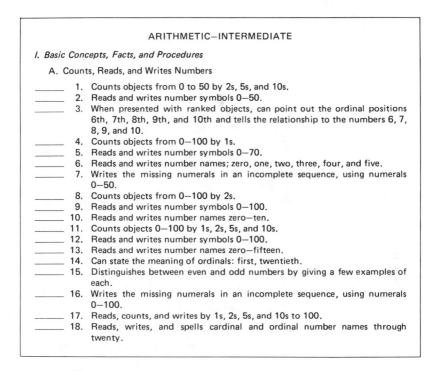

ARITHMETIC—INTERMEDIATE

I. Basic Concepts, Facts, and Procedures

  A. Counts, Reads, and Writes Numbers

_____ 1. Counts objects from 0 to 50 by 2s, 5s, and 10s.

_____ 2. Reads and writes number symbols 0—50.

_____ 3. When presented with ranked objects, can point out the ordinal positions 6th, 7th, 8th, 9th, and 10th and tells the relationship to the numbers 6, 7, 8, 9, and 10.

_____ 4. Counts objects from 0—100 by 1s.

_____ 5. Reads and writes number symbols 0—70.

_____ 6. Reads and writes number names; zero, one, two, three, four, and five.

_____ 7. Writes the missing numerals in an incomplete sequence, using numerals 0—50.

_____ 8. Counts objects from 0—100 by 2s.

_____ 9. Reads and writes number symbols 0—100.

_____ 10. Reads and writes number names zero—ten.

_____ 11. Counts objects 0—100 by 1s, 2s, 5s, and 10s.

_____ 12. Reads and writes number symbols 0—100.

_____ 13. Reads and writes number names zero—fifteen.

_____ 14. Can state the meaning of ordinals: first, twentieth.

_____ 15. Distinguishes between even and odd numbers by giving a few examples of each.

_____ 16. Writes the missing numerals in an incomplete sequence, using numerals 0—100.

_____ 17. Reads, counts, and writes by 1s, 2s, 5s, and 10s to 100.

_____ 18. Reads, writes, and spells cardinal and ordinal number names through twenty.

Figure 6-2. A curriculum-based inventory from a small part of the curriculum checklist of Turnbull, Strickland and Brantley, 1978.

Direct Measures of Staff Behavior

Along with an interest in evaluating the behavior of those who are taught, many administrators and teachers have an interest in evaluating the behavior of those who are doing the teaching, by evaluating how often teachers engage in various behaviors or how well they are progressing in a training situation.

The first objective was addressed by Bourgeois (1975), who was interested in how attendant-level personnel in an institution distributed their behaviors. To begin the task, 33 staff members were each followed for an entire 8-hour shift. The observers, who informed the staff of the purpose of the observations, wrote descriptions of their work behaviors. From these descriptions, 15 categories were identified and labeled as communication with other attendants, communication with supervisors and other administrative staff, communication with residents, communication with charge, personal needs of staff, preparation for residents, daily scheduled program activities, resident assistance, disciplining residents, reinforcement, extinction, observing or supervising residents, general activities, cleaning and housework, preparing or administering medication. From the observations, data were collected to indicate how much time was spent on each activity across all three shifts during weekdays and during weekends. Figure 6-3

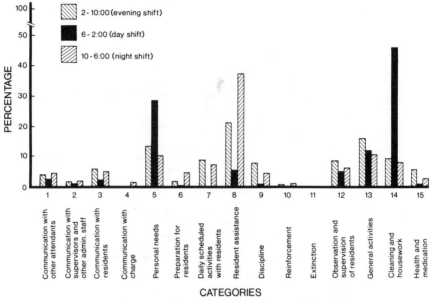

CATEGORIES
Percent-time of behaviors observed during weekdays

Figure 6-3. The percent of attendants' behaviors distributed across 15 categories (Burgeosis, 1975).

indicates the percent of time staff engaged in each of the 15 behaviors. Such an evaluation can be very valuable in determining strengths and weaknesses and in selecting objectives for training or instruction. For example, the graph indicates that the day shift has very little communication with the particular residents to whom they are assigned, and that the evening shift has no communication with these particular residents. Such information points out the immediate need for communication with the residents to whom staff are assigned. In addition, some training in the type (vocal, sign language, nonvocal, etc.) and level of communication might also be appropriate. The graph further indicates residents are virtually never reinforced for appropriate responding. The need for a training program in this area is apparent, and its success could be measured by continuing assessments at convenient intervals.

Evaluation of Behavior Change Programs

All behavioral work has two goals, which in their simplest form are (1) to change behavior and (2) to determine whether behavior changed because of the program we instituted. The first goal cannot always be met; there are, however, a number of behavior change procedures that can increase the probability of success, and these are discussed in ensuing chapters. The second goal is actually easier to attain, although it too is not always attainable. In this section, however, we will discuss designs that allow us to attempt to determine whether behavior change is due to a program we instituted, or whether it is due in whole or in part to other events.

DEPENDENT AND INDEPENDENT VARIABLES

There are two types of variables in behavioral research and application: dependent and independent variables. The value of the dependent variable is said to *depend* upon the value of the independent variable, hence the two names. One example of this relationship can be found in the work of counselors teaching retarded children. Suppose that the dependent variable was the frequency with which the counselors praised the students and that the independent variable was whether or not the counselors were trained through a simple modeling procedure to praise the students. The question then is, would praising be greater, the same, or less when the independent variable was changed from no training to training? One study (Gladstone & Spencer, 1977) demonstrated that four of five counselors increased their praise statements when the modeling procedure was instituted. In this case, for most of the counselors, the value of the dependent variable (praising) *depended* on the value of the independent variable (being trained to praise).

Most of the examples of this relationship in our field are not concerned with what staff are doing; they are concerned instead with what retarded persons are doing. For example, Garcia and Trujillo (1977) found that the number of imitative responses of three retarded children were dependent upon the teacher's facial orientation. Azrin and Armstrong (1973) found that students' correct eating increased as a function of a particular training package. Bailey and Meyerson (1970) found that a child's self-injurious behavior decreased as a function of vibratory stimulation being applied when self-injurious responding did not occur. Kazdin and Erickson (1975) found that students increased the number of instructions they followed when they were praised and given food for correct responding. White, Nielsen, and Johnson (1972) found that, on the average, time-out durations of 15 and 30 minutes were more effective than a time-out duration of 1 minute. Examples of this kind of relationship are considerable in number, and the sections in this book on procedures to change behavior contain many of them. Regardless of the procedure involved, however, they all have one basic similarity: each is concerned with determining whether or not the value of the dependent variable is a function of the value of the independent variable.

An objective, then, of all applied behavior work is to determine whether the dependent variable changes as a function of the value of the independent variable. When it does, a *functional relationship* is said to exist; when the dependent variable does not change as a function of the independent variable, a functional relationship does not exist. The problem, then, of this type of work is to determine whether or not a functional relationship exists; and to determine whether it does, there are certain rules we must follow. One of these rules is that the data must be reliable, and this rule is addressed through the various procedures used to assess interobserver agreement. Another rule is that the relationship must be established according to certain methods of having and of not having the independent variable present. These rules are the operant designs for evaluating behavior change procedures that will be discussed in this chapter, and they are the reversal, multiple baseline, multielement, and changing criterion designs.

THREE TYPES OF INDEPENDENT VARIABLES

One classification system for independent variables is time based and classifies stimuli as occurring either before, after, or during the dependent variable. The first type is called *antecedent stimuli* and refers to those stimuli that occur before and in a sense occasion the behavior that is the dependent variable. Examples of antecedent stimuli include instructions, or modeling, or any curriculum. A specific example of the latter would be "4 + 4 = _____" on a worksheet; it is the stimulus that is antecedent to the written response, "8." A picture of a cow and the instructions "Tell me the name of this animal" can be considered antecedent to the student's verbal response "cow"; or when a teacher writes a "7" on the board and asks a student to write the same number next to it, then the modeling response along with the instructions are antecedent to the student's writing a "7." The second type of stimulus that can be an independent variable is an event that occurs after the response and is called, interchangeably, a *subsequent event* or a *consequence*. Examples of subsequent events are praising correct responding, scolding incorrect responding, smiling after someone smiles at you, or thanking someone who offers you a soda. A third type of stimulus that can be an independent variable is one which exists before, during, and after the dependent variable occurs. Such stimuli are usually conditions such as temperature, size, or color of room or number of children in the classroom, and these conditions are usually called *setting events*. Together, these three constitute classes of stimuli that are temporally related to the dependent variable. Whether they are called independent variables is determined by an analysis of their effects on changes in the dependent variable; and whether the dependent variable can be said to have changed as a function of these stimuli is determined by the correct use of one or more of the various types of designs for evaluating treatment programs.

SINGLE-SUBJECT DESIGNS

Collectively these designs are called the single-subject or within-subject designs and they are contrasted with the group or between-subject design. *The essential feature of the single-subject design is that all conditions are applied to the same subject, and the results of a change in behavior are analyzed with respect to that individual.* Although there are probably hundreds of variations, many group studies have as a common property the application of one condition to one group and another condition to another group. Differences in the conditions are analyzed by comparing one group's performance with that of the other group. For example, if we wanted to assess through a single-subject design the effects of praise on correct responding, we would assess responding of the same student under conditions of no praise and of praise. If we wanted to assess these effects through a group design, one of the alternatives would be to compare the responding of a student whose correct responding is being praised with the responding of a student whose correct responding is not being praised. Although the words "group" and "single subject" appear to imply different requirements on the number of subjects in each group, there is no upper limit. Each might have 50 students involved in a study comparing praise and the absence of praise. However, every student in the study conducted by the single-subject design would experience both the praise and the no-praise conditions.

There are both advantages and disadvantages of the single-subject design. A major advantage is that it is free from between-subject variability, a term that refers to differences in results that are caused by differences in the individual and not by differences between conditions. This design circumvents that problem because each individual is exposed to all conditions of the study. Another advantage is that conclusions can be drawn about individuals, because each individual's behavior is measured across time and conditions. Properly conducted, the study will allow us to understand something about why someone behaves as he or she does. The traditional group design, however, does not provide conclusions about individuals, because data are not presented on individuals. Rather, data are summed for each group, and then one group's data are compared with the other group's data. Other advantages of the single-subject design are that it rules out for the most part contributions toward behavior change from sources other than the independent variable.[6] These sources include events that occur simply as a result of time, developmental growth of the subject, *systematic* changes in measurement (e.g., measurement that consistently overestimates), selective loss of subjects (e.g., in a group design, loss of only those students in the treatment condition who are doing poorly), and selective effects from repeated testing (Campbell & Stanley, 1963).

There are, however, some disadvantages to this design. One is that its external validity, i.e., the extent to which the results from one study can be generalized to other groups or settings, is precarious. Another is that the study itself may have an effect on behavior, perhaps in a small measure or perhaps in a great measure. For example, if a teacher is recording a student's correct responding to test the effects of special praise, the mere fact of having behavior recorded might be changing the student's behavior more than the praise. Three other disadvantages have been discussed by Kazdin (1973): (1) One is that it does not allow comparison of the effects of one treatment program relative to a traditional and different one (e.g., behavior therapy vs. psychoanalysis). (2) Another is that it does not allow us to assess the *initial* introduction of two different programs. For example, since we know that effects can be additive across time, a four-month program that has one month each of program A, program B, program A, program B may not allow us to generalize the results of just applying program B to different students. (3) Another is that it does not allow a full understanding of long-term effects. For example, if there were a program for children from 4 to 6 years old that produced large gains in academic behavior

---

[6] This effect is particularly true of the reversal design, which is discussed in this chapter.

at ages 5 and 6, we would like to know whether these gains continued through ages 8, 9, or 10, etc. Such information would have to be gained through comparison of the children in this program with children who were not in the program.

Despite its limitations, the single-subject design is a most useful design for those who want to know whether what they did had an effect. Its use is particularly important in education and health professions, where the concern for the individual is paramount. The single-subject design allows us to ask questions about what will work in *our* setting and it allows us to answer those questions in a relatively short time.

DISCOVERING PRINCIPLES OF BEHAVIOR

Many of us are concerned with whether what we did actually caused a change in behavior of the person we are teaching or helping. One of the reasons for this concern might be to answer the question "Why?" But a more important reason is so that we will have a firmer basis for decision of what to do the next time we are faced with a similar problem. When we are questioning whether to face the same problem with the same procedure, we are questioning whether directly to replicate a prior finding. When we do implement the same procedure and find the same results, we are producing principles of behavior. When we produce principles, we are building a science. When we build a science of teaching retarded persons, and when we build a science of teaching those who teach retarded persons, we will be increasing the self-sufficiency and the self-esteem of the retarded.

Purposes of Single-Subject Designs

Thousands of questions have been asked by teachers, social workers, paraprofessionals, professors, etc., and have been answered through the use of these designs. All revolve around the question of whether a particular independent variable caused the change in behavior, and most seem to have diverse objectives. Bailey (1978), however, has noted a number of similarities among these objectives and has noted a number of common purposes, five of which are (1) solving problems, (2) demonstrating the effectiveness of a particular set of procedures, (3) comparing several procedures with each other, (4) providing a parametric analysis, and (5) analyzing the components of a package of procedures whose effectiveness has already been demonstrated.

Regardless of the purpose we have while trying to determine the effects of the independent variable, there are only a few designs which have been developed to assess these effects. Of these few, the two primary ones are the reversal and the multiple baseline designs; the others are less often used, but their use may be increasing.

FOUR SINGLE-SUBJECT DESIGNS

Reversal Design

Reversal designs[7] *are those consisting of at least three phases with at least two of them having behavior occurring at about the same level because the same specific procedures were used in these two.* When behavior is systematically *reversed* in this manner to a prior level, then the design is said to be a reversal. The intent of this design is obvious; it is to show that, when a certain procedure is in effect, behavior is at a certain level, and when the procedure is not in effect, behavior is not at that level. When this type of relationship between behavior and procedures is demonstrated, then a *functional relationship* is said to have been demonstrated. Functional relationships established through reversal designs are said to be quite powerful; that is, when effects are demonstrated, we can be quite sure that the procedures used have caused the behavior change. The importance of this demonstration is considerable as it allows us to be sure that what we are doing is affecting our student's behavior. With this information, we know something we can do that will continue to help this particular student learn; in addition, we might have identified something that could help other students learn. When we have established the same relationship between this particular procedure and another student's behavior, we have identified something that will help him or her to learn.

There are a number of types of reversal designs. They all, however, have two elements in common: they begin with a baseline period, and they successfully reverse behavior to a prior level because of a particular procedural change. The baseline period is essential to this and all other operant designs. It is a description of the conditions existing during the initial period of observation; it is called the first phase of a study; and it provides a standard against which the effects of the manipulation of the independent variable can be measured.[8]

As all operant designs have a baseline period, they all share a common objective: to determine when to change from the first phase to the second phase. In

---

[7] Although generally called the reversal design (Baer, Wolf & Risley, 1968), this procedure is sometimes referred to as the equivalent time samples (Campbell & Stanley, 1963), intrasubject replication (Sidman, 1960), or ABAB (Kazdin, 1973).

[8] Many people consider baseline to be synonymous with a pretreatment condition. It is considered to be such, because most studies follow the initial observation period with a period in which an independent variable is applied. But this need not be the case, as an independent variable could just as well be subtracted as added. For example, if a teacher normally nagged students who did not begin assignments promptly or finish them within the allotted time, and if the teacher wanted to measure the effects of his nagging, the first phase of investigation could be a measurement of student behavior under the present condition of nagging, while the second phase could be under the condition of "no nagging." In this case, the first phase would be considered the baseline period; it happens, however, to be the phase in which the independent variable is present. If another teacher did not nag her students, but wanted to determine what kind of effects nagging had, she could follow an observation period consisting of her regular teaching procedures with a period that included nagging. In this case, the first period would also be called the baseline period.

practice, this change is based upon a number of idiographic reasons, such as the number of days in which to complete the study or changes forced by administrative decisions. In theory, however, change should be based upon (1) *stability* or (2) behavior changing in a *countertherapeutic* direction. *Stability* refers to behavior that meets some criterion of sameness from day to day. For example, behavior could be said to be stable if, for any five consecutive days, behavior for one day does not vary from the mean of those five by more than 20%. *Countertherapeutic direction* refers to (1) behavior that is increasing if the purpose of the next phase is to decrease behavior, or to (2) behavior that is decreasing if the purpose of the next phase is to increase behavior.

All reversal designs then have the same first two phases, baseline followed by some change. After that, however, there are several variations. The most basic reversal design follows the second phase with a third that reinstates the conditions of the first phase. Such a design, labeled ABA, is not a particualrly good one for two reasons: (1) if the behavior reverses to its initial level, we are left with behavior occurring at a level that was unacceptable in the first place; (2) if behavior does not reverse, remaining instead somewhere near the level in the B phase, we have successfully achieved a carrryover effect, but we have not successfully demonstrated that B actually caused the change. Other factors could have come into play at about the same time the second phase began and could, in reality, have caused the change. Faced with these potential problems, most researchers using this type of design have chosen the ABAB reversal procedure in which both conditions are repeated, and the client's behavior is left at an improved level.

Figure 6-4 is an example of an ABAB design (Twardosz & Sajwaj, 1972) in which two basic conditions were alternated. In the first and third phases, the teacher gave this student and all others the same command ("It's time to play at the table"), but no additional prompts. During the second and fourth phases, the teacher ignored the student when he was not in his seat, but praised him and sat him down when he returned to his chair; in addition, she praised him and gave him tokens while he remained sitting. Although the program was only applied to the child's sitting behaviors, four of his other behaviors were also measured to determine whether they were affected by the change in his sitting behavior. These other behaviors were labeled posturing (which included lying on the floor, running, jumping, skipping, and hopping), walking or standing still (but not sitting), playing with or holding toys, and proximity (being within 2 feet of another child for at least 2 seconds). Figure 6-4, which indicates the percent of 10-second intervals in which these behaviors were occurring in whole (sitting, use of toys) or in part, demonstrates that these behaviors also changed when the sitting program was in effect.

Variations.   Although the basic ABAB design is the most common, there are several variations of what is done in the first and third phases. One is to have an extremely short baseline, a procedure that is followed when we are quite certain the student cannot emit the behavior. This variation is quite common in all academic programs where the teacher is teaching students to do something they have never before done, such as adding certain number combinations or spelling certain words. The basic question to ask when considering whether to

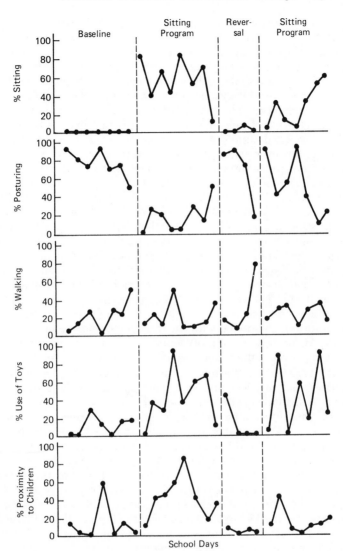

Figure 6-4. The percent of intervals in which Tim's sitting, (inappropriate) posturing, walking, use of toys, and proximity to children during free-play occurred as a function of the teacher ignoring him when he did not obey a command to sit down (baseline and reversal) and the teacher prompting him and reinforcing his sitting behavior (sitting program). (Twardosz & Sajwaj, 1972, p. 75.)

use this variation is whether the objective is to teach the student to do something he or she never does, or whether it is to teach the student to do something more or less often than he or she presently does. When the answer to the question is the first option, then this alternative is appropriate.

A second variation involves typical first, second, and fourth phases, but an atypical third phase. In this phase, the consequence is applied to the omission of the response for a prescribed interval, and the procedure itself is interchangeably labeled DRO[9] or omission training. For example, if in the first phase no special contingencies were in effect for a child's naming colors, and if in the second phase the child were praised for correct naming, and if in the third phase a DRO procedure were employed, the child would be periodically reinforced in the third phase if for a prescribed interval he or she either emitted no responses or emitted only incorrect responses. The use of DRO in this manner seems to make little sense, as the *absence* of behavior that has been improved is being rewarded; however, all reversal designs share that same problem. The use of this procedure is appropriate, however, when (1) the programmer wants to show a reversal in behavior in order to strengthen the argument that a particular contingency is the reason behavior has changed; (2) the behavior in question is unlikely to return to the baseline level if the only change is the absence of the contingency in the third phase (such a possibility is probable when the behavior is one of acquisition, such as spelling or typing), and (3) the programmer wants to demonstrate the reversal effect very quickly, preferring to shorten the length of the third phase. That the DRO procedure will reverse behavior rapidly has been demonstrated by Goetz, Holmberg, and LeBlanc (1975), who compared the effects on a three-year-old preschooler's compliance of (1) contingent praise and proximity by the teacher (condition A), (2) noncontingent praise, which involved praising various other behaviors (condition B), and (3) DRO in which the child was praised for not complying with the teacher's requests (condition C). Using an ABACABAC design, the authors found that behavior was reduced in the B phases, but that it was reduced more rapidly and to a lower level in the C phases.

A third variation of the reversal design incorporates typical second and fourth phases, but atypical first and third phases. In the latter phases, the contingency is made available regardless of the particular behavior that is occurring. In this procedure, which is generally termed a noncontingent procedure, we make available to the individual what his or her behavior produced in the second and fourth phases. For example, if we were interested in the effects of tokens on correct spelling behavior, we could (1) give a number of tokens to the student at the beginning of class each day of phase 1, (2) allow the student to earn tokens with correct spelling behavior during phase 2, (3) during phase 3, give the student at the beginning of each class the same number of tokens that were earned as an average during the last portion of phase 2, and (4) during phase 4, allow the student to earn tokens again as in phase 2. The first and third phases provided tokens noncontingently, while the second and fourth phases provided tokens contingent on correct responding. So in this case, the third phase is one in which the teacher attempted to reverse behavior to an earlier level through noncontingent reinforcement.

Advantages and Disadvantages.   There are a number of advantages and disadvantages to the reversal design. *The major advantage of the ABAB reversal is that, when behavior is reversed in the second A phase (A_2) and again in the second B phase (B_2), we have produced a very strong argument against extraneous*

---

[9] The differential reinforcement of other behavior (DRO) is defined as a procedure in which reinforcement is delivered if a particular response does not occur for a prescribed interval.

factors producing the change. The chance that other factors would coincide with the introduction of B_1, would be removed with the introduction of A_2, and would again coincide with the introduction of B_2 is indeed very small. With the use of an ABAB reversal design, teachers can be quite certain that their procedures were in fact responsible for the improvement in their students' behaviors.

There are a number of disadvantages to the reversal design; among them are (1) ethics, (2) time, (3) irreversible behaviors, and (4) nonstable behaviors. The problem of *ethics* is the major problem for this design. When the behavior is of importance to the individual or to society, then reversing to an earlier level of responding that was unacceptable does not seem to be ethical. There are individual cases that might argue that using the procedure is ethical, such as when no other design is available and when the procedure is so valuable in terms of helping other individuals that it must be demonstrated as the single source of behavior change. When the behavior is of little *immediate* importance to an individual or society, then use of the design would generally be ethical; but much of our work with retarded persons does not fall into this category. Another disadvantage of the reversal design is the *length of time* required to make the reversal. This problem is related to the one of ethics, as it too is concerned with a period of time in which the client is not receiving treatment believed to be valuable. The problem of *irreversibility* refers to those behaviors for which baseline levels of responding are not able to be recovered. An attempt to solve this problem is made by using the DRO variation in which the absence of the target behavior for a particular period is reinforced. However, not all behaviors can be reversed with a DRO procedure, and DRO is not appropriate for all situations. *Nonstable* refers to behavior which during the first baseline is not stable.[10] Such a situation causes evaluation of behavior change to be more difficult than when the behavior is stable, and it has produced the rule of thumb that, when behavior is not stable during baseline, the change during treatment must be greater than it would have to be if behavior is stable.

Multiple-Baseline Design

The multiple baseline design (Baer, Wolf & Risley, 1968) is an attractive alternative for those situations in which the reversal design is inappropriate because (1) the target behavior will not reverse to the baseline level, (2) a reversal is unethical, or (3) we want to examine the effects of the teaching program across several behaviors of the same individual, across the same behavior of a number of individuals, or across a number of settings.

The latter reason describes the basic form and variations of the multiple baseline design. *Basically, it is a design in which (1) at least two baselines are kept beginning the same day, (2) these baselines are kept on different behaviors, different individuals, or in different settings, and (3) the independent variable is applied at a different time to each baseline.* The latter is the element that

---

[10] The problem of nonstable behavior during baseline is lessened when behavior is changing in a countertherapeutic way during this period. However, this pattern of change is not predominant.

differentiates multiple baselines from simple AB designs that are placed across a number of elements: the baselines must be staggered in time for the design to be a multiple-baseline design. The intent of this design is to show that behavior changes only when the independent variable is being applied. When behavior changes once, there is some belief that the particular procedure just introduced caused the change; however, other factors could have caused the change. When the same effect, however, is repeated at a different time, then the belief is strengthened; and when the same effect is repeated at a still different time, then we can be even more sure that the procedure being used is why students are improving. The reason we stagger baselines is that, when the same change can be shown to occur at different times only with the introduction of the independent variable, then we can be more certain that extraneous factors, such as personal events in the student's life perhaps unknown to the teacher, are not causing the change. With such assurance, a teacher can be more certain that what she or he has done has, in fact, helped the student and can have some indication of what *might* help this and other students with similar problems.

Regardless of the particular type of multiple baseline in use, all share the common problem of when to terminate each of the baselines. The first one can be terminated, and the independent variable can be introduced when behavior is stable or when it is changing in a countertherapeutic direction. The second baseline can be terminated when the condition for terminating the first baseline has been met and when the independent variable has demonstrated a stable effect on the first behavior. The third, fourth, fifth, etc., baselines can be terminated when similar conditions are met. The problem for the teacher is to decide before the program begins what all these conditions should be. While this may at first seem to be a confusing decision, it really is not. Once the behaviors in question have been defined and once a few sample measures have been taken, there is little problem in deciding what these conditions should be.

Variations. *Multiple baseline across behaviors of the same individual.* As its name implies, *this design examines several behaviors of a single individual with each being brought sequentially into contact with the independent variable.* If each of the behaviors changes only during its second phase, then the argument that behavior changed only as a function of the particular procedure in use is strong. Figure 6-5 represents a multiple baseline design across four behaviors of retarded persons during a program in which social skills were taught to four mildly retarded persons (Bates, 1980). The social skills were broken down into four categories: (1) introductions and small talk, (2) asking for help, (3) differing with others, and (4) handling criticism. After two weeks of pretesting, the students were taught skills in "introductions and small talk" through a group-instruction procedure that included verbal instruction, modeling, role playing, feedback, contingent incentives, and homework. A week later, the instruction package was applied to "asking for help"; a week later, to "differing with others"; and finally, a week later, to "handling criticism." Results showed that these behaviors improved when and only when the training package was used.

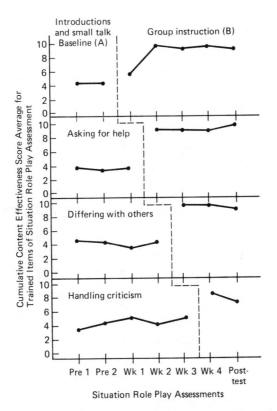

Figure 6-5. On a scale from 0-10, the extent to which four students mastered four social skills. (Bates, 1980, p. 244).

Multiple Baseline Across Subjects.   In this multiple-baseline design, *the behavior remains constant across persons, but the independent variable is introduced to individuals or groups at different times.* Figure 6-6 depicts this design as it was used to study the effects of role-played social interactions on five behaviors: the time an individual looked at the person to whom she or he was talking, the number of irrelevant comments, the number of hostile comments, the number of inappropriate requests, and the number of appropriate requests (Frederiksen, Jenkins, Foy, & Eisler, 1976). Although this may seem like a multiple-baseline-across-responses design, it is not because the training program attempted to affect all five recorded behaviors at the same time. It is an across-subjects design, because, as Figure 6-6 indicates, the training program began at different times for the two persons who were being taught to decrease their verbal outbursts by increasing their social skills. As the figure shows, the behaviors changed very systematically only after training began. Such a demonstration allows one to support such a training program as the cause of the behavior changes and to support its use in the present or perhaps individually modified form for other persons who need to learn the same skills.

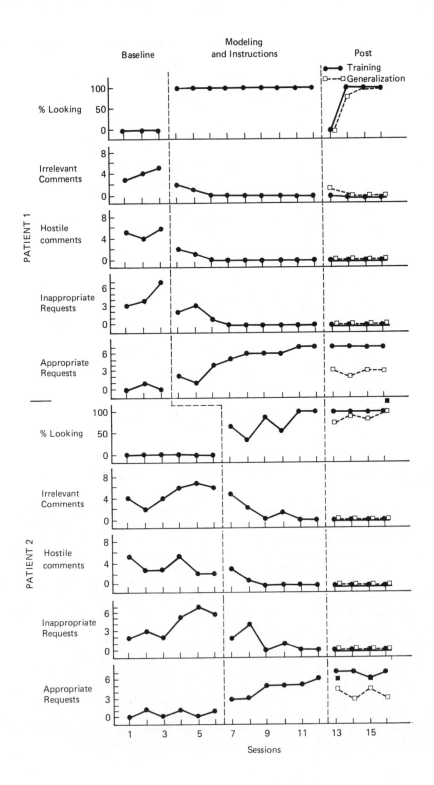

Multiple Baseline Across Settings with the Same Subject and Behavior. As the name indicates, *only the setting varies in this design.* Figure 6-7 is an example of this design (Seymour & Stokes, 1976). In the portion on the left, the percentage of Michelle's behavior that was work behavior in the workshop and in the office is indicated across three conditions: (1) baseline, when she received tokens for work, (2) a second phase, in which she recorded her own work while still earning tokens for working, and (3) a third phase, in which she self-recorded but no longer received tokens. In the portion on the right, the same design was used to study Michelle's number of work units produced in the office and the workshop. Both graphs are examples of this design, because the self-record/tokens condition was instituted sequentially in the workshop and the office.

Multiple Baseline Across Settings with the Same Behavior but with Different Subjects. *In this design, only the behavior remains constant, as both the subjects and settings vary across baselines.* This design can be used across individuals or across groups of individuals. For example, Hobbs and Holt (1976) examined the behaviors of 125 adjudicated delinquent males, many of whom were labeled retarded, in a residential setting. In one of their investigations, they measured four behaviors (following rules of group games, completing chores, following cottage rules, and following instructions of cottage supervisors) under baseline and token conditions. All behaviors earned tokens at the same time for the residents in each of three cottages. However, the time at which all behaviors began to earn tokens differed across the three cottages; hence, a multiple baseline across individuals (or across groups in this case) and situations was used to assess the effects of the token program. Results showed that appropriate behavior during baseline and token conditions increased for cottage A from 66 to 92%, for cottage B from 47 to 81%, and for cottage C from 73 to 94%.

A similar application of this design to group behavior was made by Switzer, Deal, and Bailey (1977), who looked at the effects of a group contingency applied sequentially to the stealing behavior of three classrooms of second graders. In this contingency, children were (1) given extra free time if no thefts occurred, (2) allowed regular amounts of free time if stolen items were returned, and (3) punished with loss of free time if the stolen items were not returned while the teacher left the room for 2 or 3 minutes. The stealing behavior of each class decreased only when that class was consequated for stealing, not when the other classes were consequated. As a result, the time at which behaviors changed and the degree of change supported the use of this procedure to reduce the stealing behavior of these youngsters (the mean number of items stolen per day during baseline and group contingency periods reduced for the three classes from 1.46 to 0.08, from 2.87 to 0.37, and from 1.91 to 0.22).[11]

Figure 6-6 (opposite page). Frequency of the five target behaviors emitted by each patient during role-played interactions. Behavior in Training scenes is represented with a solid line. Behavior in Generalization scenes is represented by a broken line. (Frederiksen, Jenkins, Foy, & Eisler, 1976, p. 122.)

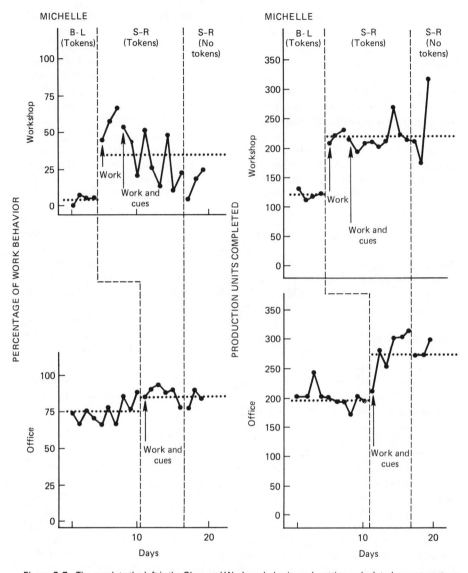

Figure 6-7. The graph to the left is the Observed Work each day in each setting, calculated as a percentage of the combined categories of Work, Interrupted Work, and Nonwork. The average work units during baseline and combined self-recording conditions is shown by the horizontal dotted line. The graph to the right is the number of work units produced each day in each setting. The average work units during baseline and combined self-recording conditions is shown by the horizontal dotted line. (Seymour & Stokes, 1976, p. 51.)

[11] Irrelevant to the discussion of multiple baselines, but humorous to those with children or who work with children, is a variable introduced between the baseline and group contingency conditions for two of these classes. For these children, the teacher lectured on good behavior every five days, saying to the children, "I know that you all want to be good boys and girls, and to be good boys and girls, it is important to remember that you should not take things that do not belong to you, should not tell stories that are not true, and should not take answers from others' papers" (p. 269). When the amounts of stealing during baseline and during the period of lectures on honesty were compared, the teacher found that stealing *increased* from a mean of 1.46 to 3.36 per day for one class and from a mean of 2.87 to 4.00 per day for the other class.

Advantages and Disadvantages.   The primary advantages of the multiple baseline design are (1) when behaviors change successively only when the independent variable is applied, the design provides a very strong argument for ruling out other factors which might cause the behavior changes; and (2) unlike the reversal design, we do not have to reverse improved behavior to demonstrate the effectiveness of the procedure. The multiple-baseline design also has several disadvantages: (1) One disadvantage is that if behaviors are interrelated, the design is useless. This problem focuses on the core of this design; for it to be effective, a change in one behavior must not cause a change in other behaviors; all behaviors must be independent. Independence may not be particularly easy to achieve, particularly in the across-responses and the across-subjects designs. Changing a child's on-task behavior is likely to change a number of his appropriate and inappropriate behaviors, so an across-behaviors design could be questionable with behaviors like these. Similarly, if the child is bothering other students while he or she is off-task, then changing on-task behavior is likely to change some behaviors of some of the other students in the class. In this case, the across-subjects design might not be appropriate, because the behaviors being recorded might be interrelated. (2) A second disadvantage is that the length of the baselines, particularly for the second, third, fourth, etc., behaviors in question, can be disturbing. Obviously, in this design some behaviors must be under baseline conditions longer than others. If this delay is serious in terms of the immediate importance of a change in the behavior, then a multiple-baseline design is inappropriate. When using this design, then, we should assign priorities to the behaviors and apply the treatment condition to the most important behaviors first. If such a ranking would still leave some behaviors untreated too long, then we should either question the need for being certain that the procedure is causing the effect, or we should choose another design.

MULTI-ELEMENT DESIGN

The multi-element design is the applied version of the multiple schedule described by Ferster and Skinner (1957) and used in so many laboratory studies. *The basic design uses a number of highly discriminable stimuli, correlates a different procedure with each stimulus condition, and should show different responding under each of the conditions.* Unlike the reversal and multiple-baseline designs, all conditions are present each day in the multi-element design.[12] This does not, however, mean that there cannot be a condition analogous to the baseline condition of the other designs; there could be one, but it would remain throughout the study.

For example, in one study (Repp, Klett, Sosebee, & Speir, 1975) four conditions were used to investigate different variables in classroom token systems. In a matching-to-sample task involving papers with four color codes but the same items each day, retarded adolescents responded in four conditions. In the blue-color condition, all correct answers were followed by tokens, exchangeable for

---

[12] Some authors (e.g., Sulzer-Azaroff & Mayer, 1977) use this label to refer to designs which have only one condition per day but have a different condition each day. This type of design is a variation of the multi-element design.

food, while all incorrect responses were ignored. In the red-color condition, all correct responses earned exchangeable tokens, while all incorrect responses lost tokens on a 1:1 ratio. In the white-color condition, all correct responses earned tokens but the tokens were not exchangeable for food, while all incorrect responses were ignored. In the green-color condition, all responses were ignored. The sequence of the conditions varied daily so that there would be no order effects. This procedure allowed an assessment of the effects of the loss of tokens (incorrect responding decreased but correct responding did not increase), as well as an assessment of two typical baselines in token studies: no tokens or nonexchangeable tokens (there was more responding in the nonexchangeable-token component indicating that studies which measure the effectiveness of token programs against nontoken programs are confounding the effects of the teacher attention that accompanies the delivery of tokens).

A multi-element design has also been used by Redd (1969), who investigated the extent to which adults who reinforce the behavior of retarded youngsters affect the behavior of those youngsters when they are present. Four conditions were present each day, the last three of which were randomly sequenced. In condition 1, the target subject was in a room without an adult but with four other boys. In condition 2, an adult praised the student and gave him candy when he engaged in cooperative play. In condition 3, a different adult reinforced the child regardless of his behavior. In condition 4, a different adult reinforced cooperative play during half the period, and praised the student and gave him candy regardless of his behavior the other half of the period.[13] A test of the child's behavior was then made by comparing whether cooperative play occurred during the first 45 seconds each adult entered the room. When the adult who had previously reinforced cooperative play ("good" behavior) entered the room, the child played with the other children. When the adult who had indiscriminantly reinforced the child entered the room, there was no change in his behavior. When the adult who reinforced cooperative play part of the period entered, the child did not play. If, however, he did not receive praise and food after a while (as from that portion of the period in which this adult indiscriminantly provided praise and food), he began cooperative play. This study, using a multi-element design in which different adults were correlated with different conditions, clearly shows that the way we treat retarded children will affect the way they behave in our presence, even when that target behavior is an interaction with someone else and not with us.

There are a number of advantages to the multi-element design: (1) although there can be (and should be for the clearest results) a baseline condition, there need not be; (2) all behaviors can be treated from the first day; (3) there is no problem with irreversible behaviors; (4) it allows the comparison of several procedures at one time, indicating perhaps that one is clearly better than others; (5) it allows a component analysis of a complex procedure, something other operant designs do not do very well; and (6) without a baseline, it has a greater probability than the reversal or multiple-baseline designs of producing an early improvement in behavior. Some problems with this design are (1) that having multiple conditions occurring within the same day is neither pragmatic nor

---

[13] These last two conditions are analogous to different degrees of careless or indiscriminant reinforcing that we all do.

necessary in most cases, as we often are interested simply in whether some addition to our program is better than what we now have; (2) when different behaviors are in each of the conditions, they may be interrelated, and if they are, we will have no clear indication of the contribution of the procedure used in any one condition if it were to be the only procedure used throughout the day. The ultimate purpose of this design *in a purely applied situation* is to determine which of several procedures will help our students improve more rapidly. But when the contribution of a single procedure is either increased or decreased by the presence of another procedure used during the same day, we cannot know what its contribution would be when we apply it by itself.

CHANGING CRITERION DESIGN

The changing criterion design is a very different design, bearing little resemblance to the reversal, multiple-baseline, or multi-element designs. *Its essential features are (1) a baseline phase, followed by (2) implementation of a procedure, which (3) establishes a criterion for responding to be consequated, with (4) the criterion changing from one phase to the next. The intent of the design is to demonstrate that behavior changes when the criterion changes.* As Hartmann and Hall (1976) have summarized, "each treatment phase is associated with a stepwise change in criterion for the target behavior. Thus, each phase of the design provides a baseline for the following phase. When the target behavior changes with each stepwise change in the criterion, therapeutic change is replicated and experimental control is demonstrated" (p. 527).

As with the reversal and multiple-baseline designs, we have the problem of deciding when to terminate the first phase, and as with these other designs, the decision is based on either (1) stability or (2) change of behavior in a countertherapeutic direction. The next decision in this design is the choice of the first criterion. This is solved in simple fashion by basing the criterion for the second phase on responding during the first phase. For example, if the number of responses per hour during five sessions of baseline were 8, 10, 7, 7, and 8, we could use the mean average (8) as the first criterion. Using a criterion similar to the present level of responding, of course, offers a very fair criterion for the client to achieve, which is the most important factor in any program. We might want to use a criterion a little greater than or less than the mean level, depending upon whether the goal is to increase or to decrease responding. Such a choice is quite acceptable as long as the value chosen is one the student will attain in two or three sessions, the point being that since we believe that the contingency selected will affect the individual's behavior, we must be certain that the behavior can, in fact, come in contact with the contingency. Selecting an initial value that is too different from the present level to allow the student to reach it may actually promote antagonistic behaviors and, in fact, be worse than no additional program at all. Succeeding changes in criteria can be handled in similar fashion, making them the same, a little more, or a little less than representative behavior of the prior phase. As you may notice, this design, unlike others, has a treatment component to it. The design is interwoven with the objective of shaping the student's behavior to the criterion level.

Another factor influencing the length of each treatment phase is the requirement that the phases (1) must be of unequal length or (2) if of equal length, they must be preceded by a baseline phase longer than any of the treatment phases (Hartmann & Hall, 1976). This requirement helps to rule out naturally occurring events as the cause of behavior change from one level to the next.

Figure 6-8 is an example of a changing criterion design in which the number of times students changed the topic during an academic classroom discussion was decreased (Deitz & Repp, 1973). When the students made fewer than the specified number of responses during each of the first four days of the week, they earned free time. When the requirement was that responding be less than or equal to a particular criterion, responding decreased successively during the four phases in which the criteria were successively decreased. This particular study also indicates a variation within this design: the incorporation of a reversal phase. When the intent of the teacher is at some time to eliminate the program, then the conditions of the final phase can be similar to the conditions in the first baseline phase.

Advantages of the changing criterion design are that (1) it does not require a reversal phase to demonstrate a functional relationship, (2) it requires only a short baseline, and (3) it is the closest of the designs to what should be a natural teaching technique, that being to start at the present level of functioning and to change gradually to an improved level. Whether the intent is to increase or to decrease behavior, the changing criterion design allows a teacher to begin at the present level and to move toward improved levels of responding, whether improvement is in terms of the amount or the complexity of responding. Disadvan-

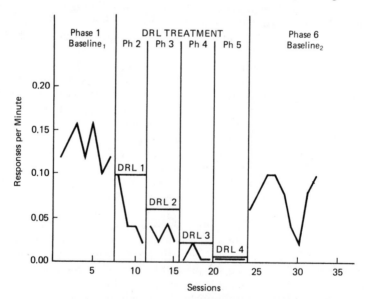

Figure 6-8. The rate of subject changes for a class of high school senior girls during baseline 1, treatment, and baseline 2 phases. "Free" Fridays could be earned by the group if they made fewer than the specified number of responses for each of the first four days of the week. The limit for the first treatment week was five or fewer responses during the 50-min. sessions (DRL 1). DRL 2 required three or fewer responses. DRL 3 required one or fewer responses, and DRL 4 required zero responses. (Deitz & Repp, 1973, p. 461.)

tages of this design are that it (1) does not allow one procedure to be compared with another, (2) does not allow a component analysis to determine what portions of the procedure are most responsible for improvement, and (3) deals with only one behavior at a time. Criteria could be established for a number of behaviors at a time; however, none of the advantages of the multiple baseline design in showing that behavior changes only when a procedure is implemented are available. Criteria could be intially introduced at different times across behaviors, settings, etc., but the overall design then is a multiple-baseline design.

DETERMINING THE EFFECTIVENESS OF BEHAVIOR CHANGE PROCEDURES

The single-subject designs discussed in this chapter do not in and of themselves determine the effectiveness of treatment procedures. Instead, they provide an argument for ruling out contributions from other sources, and they allow us to determine the effectiveness of a procedure either by observing graphs or by making a few calculations. Calculations are of two types: (1) statistical or (2) arithmetical. The statistical analyses are plentiful, but their use in behavioral work is debatable (Hartmann, 1974; Kazdin, 1976; Keselman & Leventhal, 1974; Kratochwill, Alden, Demuth, Dawson, Panicucci, Arntson, McMurray, Hempstead & Levin, 1974; Michael, 1974a, b; and Thoresen & Elashoff, 1974). Several reasons for not using statistical analyses have been discussed by Michael (1974b): (1) in terms of training and time, they are expensive judgmental aids, (2) there is no basis for selelction of particular significance levels, with the selection of the most popular level of 0.05 (i.e., there is a 5% chance of error in our judgment that the independent variable caused the change in the dependent variable) seeming to have been random, (3) statistical procedures are used in place of good, competent control of irrelevant sources of variation, (4) statistical analyses generally call for large number of individuals, none of whom is usually treated for a prolonged period, (5) statistical designs dictate how we should study behavior, and the designs are often counterproductive to important social change, and (6) statistical studies wait until the study is completed before analyzing data, therefore making for a very inflexible system. This last criticism is critical to mental retardation, where we should be sensitive to the day-to-day changes in our client's behavior, altering our treatment procedure at any moment the client's behavior shows us that our present procedure is inadequate. A different focus on the argument against extensive statistical analyses have been offered by Sulzer-Azaroff and Mayer (1977), who have written that when behavior has changed as a result of an intervention an important question to ask is the following:

> "Of what significance is this demonstrated relation?" One traditional approach has been to base interpretations of significance upon probability theory, asking "What is the likelihood that these results could have been obtained by chance alone?" If it is concluded that chance was unlikely to have accounted for the outcome, then the data are more likely to be accepted as "statistically significant." *In applied behavior*

analysis, however, the emphasis is more on **social, personal,** *or* **clinical** *significance than on statistical significance* [emphasis added]. The applied behavior analyst asks the question "What importance does the demonstration of this functional relation have for particular individuals and their society?" (p. 471)

Arithmetical determinations of the effectiveness of behavior change procedures are much less controversial among behaviorists, although there is some disagreement about what type to use. The basic arithmetical determinations are (1) a statement of the means or medians of each phase in the study, (2) a comparison of the means or medians between any two phases, with the comparison usually expressed as a percent of change, and (3) a statement or comparison of the ranges (i.e., the low and the high values) of each phase. While none of these is "sophisticated" in the sense of being complex, each provides us immediate information on the change in behavior brought about by a change in conditions.

Two nonmathematical means for judging behavior across conditions are offered by Kazdin (1976); these are (1) nonoverlapping data and (2) different trends. The former refers to data points in one phase which are not in the range of data points of a different phase. When no data points are in that range, the data are said not to overlap, and when the effect of nonoverlapping data is replicated through designs like the ABAB reversal or the multiple baseline, there is little question that the difference in conditions between phases caused the changes in behavior. The second method discussed by Kazdin is to compare trends between phases. For example, if the trend in one phase is stability (the slope of the line is horizontal) and the trend in the next phase is that behavior has increased by a factor of 5, one has a good argument for differential effects of the two conditions. Obviously, the more different the trends, the more certain we can be in judging that behavior has changed as a function of changes we have made in the environment.

SUMMARY

This chapter considers two types of evaluations: (1) instruments which evaluate behavior and (2) operant designs which allow the evaluation of the effectiveness of procedures used to change behavior. Evaluations of behavior include direct and indirect measures of student behavior, curriculum-based inventories, and direct measures of staff behavior. Evaluations of operant designs include the reversal, multiple-baseline, multi-element, and changing criterion. Strengths and weaknesses of each design are discussed as well.

REFERENCES

Azrin, N. H., & Armstrong, P. M. The "mini-meal"—a method for teaching eating skills to the profoundly retarded. *Mental Retardation*, 1973, 11, 9-13.

Baer, D. M., Wolf, M. M., & Risley, T. R. Some current dimensions of applied behavior analysis. *Journal of Applied Behavior Analysis*, 1968, 1, 91-97.

Bailey, J. S. *A handbook of research methods in applied behavior analysis.* Tallahassee: Florida State University Press, 1978.

Bailey, Jr., & Meyerson, L. Effects of vibratory stimulation on a retardate's self-injurious behavior. *Psychological Aspects of Disability*, 1970, **17**, 133-137.

Balthazar, E. E. *The Balthazar scales of adaptive behavior. Section I: The scales of functional independence.* Champaign, IL: Research Press Company, 1971a.

Balthazar, E. E. *The Balthazar scales of adaptive behavior. Section II: The scales of social adaptation.* Champaign, IL: Research Press Company, 1971b.

Bates, P. The effectiveness of interpersonal skills training on the social skills acquisition of moderately and mildly retarded adults. *Journal of Applied Behavior Analysis*, 1980, **13**, 237-248.

Behavioral characteristics progression. Palo Alto, CA: Vort Corporation, 1973.

Bijou, S. W. *Environment and intelligence.* Paper presented at the Conference on Contributions to Intelligence, University of Illinois, 1969.

Bourgeois, A. E. *Job analysis of attendant-level staff.* Paper presented at the American Psychological Association, 1975.

Campbell, D. T., & Stanley, J. C. Experimental and quasi-experimental designs for research and teaching. In N. L. Gage (Ed.), *Handbook of research on teaching.* Chicago: Rand-McNally, Inc., 1963.

Cone, J. D. *What's relevant about reliability and validity for behavioral assessment.* Paper presented at the meeting of the American Psychological Association, 1975.

Deitz, S. M., & Repp, A. C. Decreasing classroom misbehavior through the use of DRL schedules of reinforcement. *Journal of Applied Behavior Analysis*, 1973, **6**, 457-463.

Ferster, C. B., & Skinner, B. F. *Schedules of reinforcement.* New York: Appleton-Century-Crofts, Inc., 1975.

Frederiksen, L. W., Jenkins, J. O., Foy, D. W., & Eisler, R. M. Social-skills training to modify abusive verbal outbursts in adults. *Journal of Applied Behavior Analysis*, 1976, **9**, 117-125.

Garcia, E. E., & Trujillo, A. The effect of facial orientation during imitation maintenance. *Journal of Applied Behavior Analysis*, 1977, **10**, 95.

Gladstone, B. W., & Spencer, C. J. The effects of modeling on the contingent praise of mental retardation counselors. *Journal of Applied Behavior Analysis*, 1977, **10**, 75-84.

Goetz, E. M., Holmberg, M. C., & LeBlanc, J. M. Differential reinforcement of other behavior and noncontingent reinforcement as control procedures during the modification of a preschooler's compliance. *Journal of Applied Behavior Analysis*, 1975, **8**, 77-82.

Gold, M. W. *Train, don't test.* Unpublished manuscript, 1974.

Goldfried, M. R., & Spafkin, J. N. *Behavioral personality assessment.* Morristown, NJ: General Learning Press, 1974.

Grossman, H. J. (Ed.) *Manual on terminology and classification in mental retardation.* Washington, D.C.: American Association on Mental Deficiency, 1973.

Hartmann, D. P. Forcing square pegs into round holes: Some comments of "an analysis-of-variance model for intrasubject replication design." *Journal of Applied Behavior Analysis*, 1974, **7**, 635-638.

Hartmann, D. P., & Hall, R. V. The changing criterion design. *Journal of Applied Behavior Analysis*, 1976, **9**, 527-532.

Hobbs, T. R., & Holt, M. M. The effects of token reinforcement on the behavior of delinquents in cottage settings. *Journal of Applied Behavior Analysis*, 1976, **9**, 189-198.

Kazdin, A. E. Methodological and assessment considerations in evaluating reinforcement programs in applied settings. *Journal of Applied Behavior Analysis*, 1973, **6**, 517-531.

Kazdin, A. E. Statistical analyses for single-case experimental designs. In M. Hersen & D. H. Barlow (Eds.), *Single case experimental designs: Strategies for studying behavior change.* Elmsford, NY: Pergamon Press, Inc.: 1976.

Kazdin, A. E., & Erickson, L. M. Developing responsiveness to instructions in severely and profoundly retarded residents. *Journal of Behavior Therapy and Experimental Psychiatry*, 1975, **6**, 17-21.

Keselman, H. J., & Leventhal, L. Concerning the statistical procedures enumerated by Gentile *et al.*: another perspective. *Journal of Applied Behavior Analysis*, 1974, **7**, 643-645.

Kratochwill, T., Alden, K., Demuth, D., Dawson, D., Panicucci, C., Arntson, P., Mc-Murray, N., Hempstead, J., & Levin, J. A further consideration in the application of an analysis-of-variance model for the intrasubject replication design. *Journal of Applied Behavior Analysis*, 1974, **7**, 629-633.

Michael, J. Statistical inference for individual organism research, some reactions to a suggestion by Gentile, Roden, and Klein. *Journal of Applied Behavior Analysis*, 1974a, **7**, 627-628.

Michael, J. Statistical inference for individual organism research: mixed blessing or curse? *Journal of Applied Behavior Analysis*, 1974b, **7**, 647-653.

Nihira, K., Foster, R., Shellhaas, M., & Leland, H. *American Association on Mental Deficiency Adaptive Behavior Scale.* Washington, D.C.: American Association on Mental Deficiency, 1975, revised.

Redd, W. H. Effects of mixed reinforcement contingencies on adults' control of children's behavior. *Journal of Applied Behavior Analysis*, 1969, **2**, 249-254.

Repp, A. C., Klett, S. Z., Sosebee, L. H., & Speir, N. C. Differential effects of four token conditions on rate and choice of responding in a matching-to-sample task. *American Journal of Mental Deficiency*, 1975, **80**, 51-56.

Seymour, F. W., & Stokes, T. F. Self-recording in training girls to increase work and evoke staff praise in an institution for offenders. *Journal of Applied Behavior Analysis*, 1976, **9**, 41-54.

Sidman, M. *Tactics of scientific research.* New York: Basic Books, Inc., 1960.

Sulzer-Azaroff, B., & Mayer, G. R. *Applying behavior-analysis procedures with children and youth.* New York: Holt, Rinehart and Winston, Inc., 1977.

Switzer, E. B., Deal, T. E., & Bailey, J. S. The reduction of stealing in second graders using a group contingency. *Journal of Applied Behavior Analysis*, 1977, **10**, 267-272.

Terman, L. M. *Genetic studies of genius.* Stanford, CA: Stanford University Press, 1925.

Terman, L. M., & Oden, M. *The gifted child grows up.* Stanford, CA: Stanford University Press, 1959.

Thoresen, C. E., & Elashoff, J. D. An analysis-of-variance model for intrasubject replication design: Some additional comments. *Journal of Applied Behavior Analysis*, 1974, **7**, 639-641.

Turnbull, A. P., Strickland, B. B., & Brantley, J. C. *Developing and implementing individualized education programs.* Columbus, OH: Charles E. Merrill Publishing Co., 1978.

Twardosz, S., & Sajwaj, T. Multiple effects of a procedure to increase sitting in a hyperactive boy. *Journal of Applied Behavior Analysis*, 1972, **5**, 73-78.

White, G. D., Nielsen, G., & Johnson, S. M. Timeout duration and the suppression of deviant behavior in children. *Journal of Applied Behavior Analysis*, 1972, **5**, 111-120.

PART

IV

Reinforcement

In Chapters 2 and 6, there were brief discussions of *three-term contingencies,* a phrase that refers to the relationship between environmental events and behavior. We have alternately referred to it as the A-B-C paradigm, and it includes (1) *antecedent events* (A), i.e., those events that come before the response and affect the probabilitiy that behavior will recur, (2) the *response* (B), and (3) *consequences* (C), i.e., those events that come after the response and affect the likelihood that the behavior will recur. When either or both of these types of events are systematically shown to affect behavior, a contingency has been demonstrated. When events are shown not to affect behavior, a contingency has not been demonstrated and these events are said to be neutral. This is an extremely important concept that has considerable theoretical and practical relevance to our field. The theoretical relevancy is that learning by retarded persons is assumed to be influenced by antecedent and subsequent events, and that if we can learn to arrange these events in a certain fashion, learning by our students can be more rapid. The practical relevancy is that time after time, certain arrangements of events have reliably been shown to increase the rate at which our students can learn, can become more independent, and can have a better chance at coping in a less structured, protective, and restricted world.

The behaviorists' preoccupation with data-based demonstrations really comes from the concept of three-term contingencies. Learning is not something to be presumed or something at which we guess; learning is demonstrated acquisition of skills, an acquisition that can be affected by the way we arrange the learning environment for our students.

Some of those aspects of the learning environment are antecedent events and have been discussed in prior chapters under different headings. These include (1) curriculum, which quite obviously affects what the student will at least have an opportunity to learn, (2) instructional objectives, which describe the conditions under which responding is to occur, and (3) task analyses, which generally identify the conditions for responding, the procedures by which a sequence of behaviors will be taught, and the order in which the successive response components of the goal behavior will be taught.

Another way in which these aspects of the environment have been discussed is as independent variables, i.e., those events that constitute either the first or the third term of the contingency. The determination of independent variables has been discussed in Chapter 6 under the section on operant designs, which included the reversal, the multiple baseline, changing criterion, and multi-element. In many cases, indpendent variables are nonhuman events that antecede and affect responding, things such as curriculum and materials, or the number of students in the classroom, or even attributes of the room itself such as color, size, or shape. One current area of investigation in the last category is the effect of lighting on hyperactive behavior. In one study (Colman, Frankel, Ritvo, & Freeman, in press), eight children who were labeled autistic were observed individually under conditions of either fluorescent or incandescent lighting in the same room. In both conditions, each child engaged in nonpurposeful repetitive behaviors, but during the fluorescent lighting periods, these behaviors increased by 70%. While this particular study does not necessarily mean that students will engage in more nonpurposeful activity in a room with fluorescent illumination than in a room with incandescent illumination, it does show that conditions existing irrespective of the student can affect the student's behavior.

Antecedent events can also be programmed directly to affect behavior. In one study investigating the degree to which television newscasts would affect retarded students' discussions of current events, Keilitz, Tucker, and Horner (1973) provided an opportunity for the students to earn tokens and praise for correct verbalizations about current events. They found that when the videotaped news broadcasts were shown without interruption there were fewer verbalizations than when each broadcast was interrupted after each specific news item. In this case, a simple change in the way in which the antecedent event was presented affected the students' behaviors.

In other cases, independent variables can be human events, i.e., behaviors of the individual himself or of other persons that occur either before or after the target behavior. For example, if we were interested in the greeting behavior of a student as he enters a classroom, various kinds of behaviors of other people could affect whether or not the student says "hello" or "good morning" when entering. Such behaviors include whether the teacher said hello or just ignored him, or whether other students greeted him, or whether his older brother just yelled at him, or whether his mother told him to have a nice day at school and to be sure to say hello to his teacher.

Some behaviors are also more or less likely to occur depending upon prior behaviors of the individual himself. A student in one of our TMR classes occasionally engaged in extraordinary 20- or 30-minute episodes of shadow boxing and cursing at an imaginary opponent. These very violent episodes occurred randomly every few weeks with no apparent relation to anything teachers or students had said, and they had been occurring for several years. One teacher, however, noticed that the student became muscularly tense before an episode. After one particular occurrence, the teacher began to place this student in a series of isometric exercises whenever the muscle tension was noticeable. When the particular chain of behaviors by this adolescent was interrupted, the violent fighting episodes stopped. The tensing behaviors apparently prompted the fighting behaviors, and once they were interrupted, fighting ceased. Certainly, prosocial behaviors occur in the same way. When we enter a room in which there are two people, we are more likely to say "hello" to the second person we see if we have greeted the first than if we have not greeted the first person.

The manner in which retarded people are grouped may also have an effect on their behavior. Various works (e.g., Ardrey, 1966; Lorenz, 1966; Poluck & Esser, 1971) have shown that hierarchies of aggression develop within various species including humans, and that within these hierarchies, dominant subjects consistently aggress toward less dominant subjects. Using this generality, Grot and Randolph (1975) examined the amount of aggressive behavior of profoundly retarded institutionalized males. In their study, the aggressive behaviors of one group of seven and of another group of eight residents were recorded while they were in a large dayroom with other residents with whom they were regularly housed. These two particular groups were considered to be aggressive, while the residents with whom they were housed were considered to be passive. After several weeks of observation, the seven and the eight residents were separated from the others for more than a year. The changes were dramatic. For one group in which six persons remained in the institution the total period, the number of aggressive behaviors in the months before and after regrouping changed from 574 to 129. Following a period of reductive procedures, such as those that will be discussed in later chapters, the behavior reduced to 21 in a month. For the second group, the change was similar in pattern, from 1,003 to 644 to 149. While placing aggressive persons together can produce an extremely volatile situation and is certainly not universally promoted, Grot and Randolph achieved considerable success in this particular area with a simple grouping change. The conditions for aggression were changed, and the incidence of aggression changed collaterally.

That certain behaviors or events prompt or set the occasion for certain responses is obvious, and one of our objectives in working with retarded people is to learn what does precede and affect responses. Other behaviors, however, are equally or perhaps even more influenced by events that follow a response. If a student greeted us each morning, but if we frowned and did not smile or nod or reply for five or six consecutive days, the student would probably stop greeting us for a while. Or if we returned the greeting each time, the student would probably continue to greet us most mornings. Similarly, if we totally ignore a child when he's being good, but talk to him and ask him why he's misbehaving after he has just done so, the child is likely to learn that the only way he receives our attention is by acting inappropriately. Or if a young child is cold and she learns that, but pushing a button, she can be warmed by a heater in front of her, she is likely to push that button the next time she is in that situation.

All these events could change the likelihood or the probability that a response will recur. Some events or changes in the environment increase the likelihood of recurrence, and this process will be called *reinforcement*. Others decrease the likelihood of recurrence, and this process will be called *punishment*. Still others have no effect on behavior whatsoever, and these events will be called *neutral*. In this chapter, reinforcement will be discussed in a variety of ways, including its types and ways to maximize its effectiveness.

REINFORCEMENT[1]

Reinforcement is a very important procedure in this field, and the term has a particular meaning. To reinforce something means "to strengthen" it. The suffix "-ment" refers to a procedure or process, so reinforcement will refer to a procedure for strengthening something. In our field, that "something" will always be behavior, so reinforcement will refer to a procedure by which behavior is strengthened (i.e., increased in probability). Anytime behavior changes, whether it increases or decreases, it must change as a function of something. In the case of reinforcement, behavior increases as a function of a change in stimulus conditions. So our formal definition of reinforcement must include two elements: the element of behavior change and the element of stimulus change. The definition of *reinforcement* then is *a procedure in which a response produces a stimulus change and as a result becomes more probable.*[2] When we smile at the student who greets us, that stimulus change from no smile to smile might have reinforced his greeting. Or when the temperature changed from cold to warm, the child was reinforced for pushing a particular button on a heater. The examples are countless, and their occurrences are frequent in the lives of all of us. In each case, a response occurs, the environment changes, and behavior becomes more probable. However, in not every case does the environment change in the same way; and the way in which it changes will determine whether the term is labeled *positive reinforcement* or *negative reinforcement.*

Positive and Negative Reinforcement Defined

In arithmetic, the word "positive" means to add something while the word "negative" means to subtract or take away something. When those adjectives are applied to the word reinforcement, the two types of stimulus changes can be described: positive reinforcement refers to stimuli that are produced or added, while negative reinforcement refers to stimuli that are removed or subtracted. The formal definition of *positive reinforcement* then is *a procedure in which a response produces a stimulus and becomes more probable,* while the formal definition of *negative reinforcement* is *a procedure in which a response removes a stimulus and becomes more probable.* Many people interchange the terms negative reinforcement and punishment, presumably because they believe that *negative* refers to a reduction in *responding.* It does not; it refers instead to a reduction in *stimulus* conditions. The word *reinforcement* refers to *responding,* and its description of responding is that responding has increased.

---

[1] In many of the chapters in this book, new terminology will be introduced. At first, the terminology may seem excessive and confusing, but most of the terms are quite functional in that they are descriptive of the procedures they represent. As such, you should try to identify the meaning of each term before you read its definition. In most cases, you will probably find that the definition you give to the word is not so different from the definition given to you in this text. Try the word *reinforcement.* What does "reinforce" mean? What does "-ment" mean? If you have said that "reinforce-" means "to strengthen" and that "-ment" generally means "action" or "process," then you have most of the definition of reinforcement: the process of strengthening.

[2] A special type of reinforcement is called adventitious reinforcement or superstitious conditioning. In this procedure, the response does not actually *produce* the stimulus, although the behavior increases as if it does. Baseball players go through all sorts of gyrations while waiting to hit a pitch, simply because those gyrations are sometimes followed by a hit even though the gyrations do not really produce it. Similarly, some gamblers have favorite phrases or motions before throwing die.

Although punishment is discussed in ensuing chapters, the distinction between punishment and reinforcement can perhaps be made clear at this point through reference to Figure 7-1. Reinforcement refers to an increase in responding, while punishment refers to a decrease in responding. *Positive reinforcement* refers to a procedure in which responding increases (reinforcement) as a result of producing (positive) a stimulus, while *positive punishment* refers to a procedure in which responding decreases (punishment) as a result of producing (positive) a stimulus. In the same fashion, *negative reinforcement* refers to a procedure in which responding increases (reinforcement) as a result of removing (negative) a stimulus, while *negative punishment* refers to a procedure in which responding decreases (punishment) as a result of removing (negative) a stimulus. Note that in each and every case a definition describes a functional relationship between behavior and the environment; i.e., the behavior (the dependent variable) is a function of the environment (the independent variable). In no case is a procedure labeled before the fact, i.e., before the resultant change in behavior. Reinforcement must show an increase in behavior; punishment must show a decrease. The importance of this point is that many people presume certain events will be reinforcers for everyone. Candy is often said to be a reinforcer, but something cannot be a reinforcer in and of itself. It can only be a reinforcer for a *person* if it results in an increase in that person's behavior. For some people candy is a reinforcer for certain behaviors at certain times; for other people it is not. Similarly, most people presume praise is a reinforcer. But, again, it is

	and if responding increases	and if responding decreases
if a stimulus is produced	then the procedure is *positive reinforcement*	then the procedure is *positive punishment*
if a stimulus is removed	then the procedure is *negative reinforcement*	then the procedure is *negative punishment*

	and if responding increases	and if responding decreases
if a stimulus is produced	then the stimulus is a *positive reinforcer*	then the stimulus is a *punishing stimulus* (or *aversive stimulus*)
if a stimulus is removed	then the stimulus is a *negative reinforcer* (or *aversive stimulus*)	then the stimulus is a *positive reinforcer*

Figure 7-1. The upper portion identifies the procedure that describes the effect on behavior of a particular stimulus change. In the table, a row should be read, then a column, and then the intersect. For example, "if a stimulus is produced, and if responding increases, then the procedure is positive reinforcement."

The lower portion identifies the label for the stimulus that has changed with the resultant effect on behavior. The lower portion of the table is read in the same manner as the upper portion. For example, "if a stimulus is produced, and if responding increases, then the stimulus is a positive reinforcer."

not a reinforcer in and of itself. It is a reinforcer for some, but not all, behavior of some people. It is not a reinforcer for all people (in fact, some children are labeled autistic because social behaviors are not reinforcing for them).

Examples of Negative Reinforcement

In this paradigm, the behavior must increase its probability of recurrence because an *aversive stimulus* is removed. To find examples of this procedure, then, we must simply identify situations in which behavior removes or decreases a stimulus, and increases in probability. When we are warm and being warm is aversive, we can decrease or change the condition by a variety of responses, such as taking off clothes, turning on an air conditioner, jumping in a pool, or fanning ourselves. Or when we are cold, we can put on more clothes, or go inside, or turn on a heater. When a child takes out the garbage only to stop his parent's nagging, his behavior is negatively reinforced. When you brush your teeth regularly to avoid having the dentist drill your teeth, brushing is being negatively reinforced. Or when you return home for your umbrella and raincoat before it is raining but while the skies are darkening and you hear thunder, your behavior is also being negatively reinforced.[3]

There are a number of ways in which negative reinforcement operates in school situations. Some are unfortunate and include situations in which class is aversive to students who learn they can get out of class and go to the principal's office by acting out, or who learn they can be excused from class by being ill, or who learn they can bring assignments late if they fabricate a story about themselves or their family. In many of these situations, negative reinforcement actually increases a behavior that is undesirable. But this need not always be so. All reinforcement procedures, and all punishment procedures for that matter, describe relationships between behavior and events irrespective of the value we place upon the behaviors. Behaviors we would like to increase as well as behaviors we would like to decrease can be increased through reinforcement procedures regardless of the value we as individuals or society as a whole place upon these behaviors.

Some studies, however, have used the escape or the avoidance paradigm of negative reinforcement to deliberately increase particular behaviors of retarded persons. Greene and Hoats (1969) used both the escape and avoidance conditions of negative reinforcement to increase the production-line task behavior of a mildly retarded young adult placed in a program for behavior problems. In this task, the student was required (1) to discriminate between two data-processing cards, (2) to pull one of two levers, (3) to insert the correct card partially into one of two slots, and (4) to discard the card into one of two containers. The series of discriminations seemed to be well within this individual's repertoire of behaviors, but he was not producing so rapidly as seemed appropriate for his

---

[3] These examples actually describe two types of negative reinforcement. In one, a stimulus that is already present is being removed or reduced. In this case, one is escaping from the aversive stimulus, so the paradigm is called *escape*. In the other type, the aversive stimulus is not yet present, but it is signaled. In this case, that stimulus is avoided, so the paradigm is called *avoidance*.

demonstrated capabilities. To determine whether his rate of production could be increased through a negative reinforcement paradigm, the authors placed in the working area a television which could be manipulated so that both the sound volume and clarity and the picture steadiness could be altered. After a baseline period with undistorted television which was used to measure the student's production rate, an avoidance paradigm was instituted whereby the student could avoid television distortion as long as he completed one four-step unit of work within a specified time (an interval that was reduced from 15 to 4 seconds as the student's rate of production increased). If the student did not complete a unit of work, the sound and picture distortion began; he could, however, escape from this situation if he completed a unit of work. So two situations, avoidance of and escape from television distortion, existed and were totally within the control of the student's behavior. The question then is "were these conditions negatively reinforcing?" That question was answered through an ABAB design by comparing the rates during baseline with the production rates during the television periods. In each case, responding increased in the distortion period relative to the preceding no-distortion period. Because of these changes, television distortion was an aversive stimulus for this student's behavior in this situation. If the changes had not occurred, distortion would not be considered an aversive event for this student.

Note that a condition *prior* to responding was changed (in the escape condition) or avoided (in the avoidance condition). Television distortion occurred because of the absence of responding with a response being defined as a production unit completed within a specific time. Distortion could also be used following behavior, but in such a situation it could not be considered an example of negative reinforcement, because the stimulus condition could not be made to go away through responding. Greene and Hoats (1969) did in fact use the same system of television distortion to consequate a mildly retarded girl's gross hyperactivity. In this situation, any one of a number of responses produced distortion. Because distortion reduced her behavior, it is said to be an aversive stimulus, but the procedure is called punishment. Note that when this condition, television distortion, was considered to be part of an example of negative reinforcement, distortion was *eliminated* or *avoided* because responding occurred.

Screven and LaFond (1973) similarly used the avoidance portion of negative reinforcement to increase the work production of retarded persons in a sheltered workshop. Students were required to place finished work products on a small metal box which had a springed top and a counting mechanism to ensure that a finished product was indeed placed on it. The mechanism also had a timing device which could be adjusted from 5 to 90 seconds, depending upon the capabilities of the worker. When work was not completed, a white light and a buzzing sound came on at the end of the prescribed interval, and the student lost part of an accumulated bonus or credit for a few finished work products. Whenever the worker needed a break, or whenever there were other reasons for work interruption, the timing mechanism was simply stopped. When the mechanism was in use, production rate was about twice what it was during preceding and subsequent baseline levels. The program was one of avoidance that could be used to teach retarded persons increased rates of working that might be transferable to nonsheltered work areas. With an adjustable timing device, the program could be individualized, allowing all students to succeed. The authors addressed this advantage in stating that

> in the case of trainees who were more prone to emit emotional outbursts when involved in a frustrating experience, the above results depended on extremely careful shaping of the avoidance procedure. During initial shaping, large time intervals were allowed to assure initial success [and] the light-buzzer condition [was] clearly correlated with non-productive and time-consuming irrelevant activity. (p. 15)

Spiro and Shook (1973) also used an avoidance paradigm to address an entirely different problem. They discussed the problem of formalized mental testing as it related to retarded persons, many of whom delay answering questions for long periods of time. When the latency of responding exceeds the time limit proscribed by the standardized test, the examinee is presumed not to know the answer. However, the child may be able to answer questions correctly but not within the correct time. As the authors suggested,

> with the extension of mental testing procedures to mentally retarded and culturally deprived populations, the validity of the relationship between response latency and response adequacy suggests a more serious question. Such children may have had little experience with games requiring quick verbal responses, and their social backgrounds may not have developed a strong generalized capacity by the approval of adults such as those who administer various tests. Under these circumstances, it is difficult to interpret a long latency. (p. 384)

The authors examined this situation with a retarded 17-year-old who delayed responding to Peabody Picture Vocabulary Cards. In a reversal design, baseline alternated with an avoidance condition in which the student could avoid admonishment by responding within 10 seconds to the question, "Ricky, what is this picture?" After the initial session in each avoidance condition, latency reduced to less than 10 seconds. During baseline, latencies had been more than 25 seconds.

Both these studies used negative reinforcement to increase appropriate responding. But each also added reinforcement procedures to maintain responding. Later in the Screven and LaFond study, appropriate responding resulted in various events that were presumed to be positive reinforcers. Similarly, in the Spiro and Shook study, the avoidance procedure was replaced by one in which the student was praised when he responded within the 10 seconds. Latency was maintained at the low level established by the avoidance procedure. These changes from using an aversive procedure to using a positive procedure suggest a very important ethical point when using negative reinforcement, as well as any other punitive procedure. Some behaviors will simply not change when only positive approaches are used. If this is the case *and* if an aversive procedure is warranted, then the aversive procedure should eventually be eliminated and replaced with a positive approach. In all cases, positive approaches are the most desirable.

Examples of Positive Reinforcement

To iterate, *positive reinforcement is a procedure in which a response produces a stimulus and increases in probability as a result of producing that stimulus.* So all examples of positive reinforcement must show an increase in behavior as a result of a stimulus being produced by that response. For example, in an ABAB design, Hall, Lund, and Jackson (1968) examined the effects of teacher attention on six primary students' study behavior. During the second and fourth phases, whenever a student was studying, the teacher moved by the student's desk, verbally commented on her or his appropriate behavior, and gave general nonverbal approval, such as pats on the back. Although the amount of studying varied among the children, attention in general doubled the amount of studying. For a sixth student, who was studying about 70% of the time during baseline, the behavior was increased to about 90%. In this example, attention can be labeled a positive reinforcer because the behavior which produced teacher attention was shown to increase systematically when it did produce this stimulus condition. Because most teacher attention combines verbal and nonverbal approval, Kazdin and Klock (1973) sought to determine whether just the nonverbal factor would serve as a reinforcer for a class of moderately retarded elementary school students. In an ABAB design, the attentive behaviors of each student were measured during a daily handwriting period. During the entire study, five types of contingent teacher attention were measured: the nonverbal behaviors were smiling or physical contact, while the verbal behaviors were verbal approval alone, verbal approval with smiles, or verbal approval with physical contact. During the first phase, the teacher's five types of attentive behaviors as well as each child's attentive or inattentive behaviors were recorded. During the second phase, the teacher was instructed to maintain the level of verbal statements of approval but to increase her use of smiles and physical contact following attentive child behavior. During this phase, feedback was given to the teacher so that her rates of verbal and nonverbal relative to baseline were appropriate. In the reversal phase, the teacher was told to return to her previous classroom practices without any special effort toward parceling her verbal and nonverbal attention. In the last phase, the teacher was again asked to increase positive nonverbal consequences for student attentiveness without increasing her verbal approach.

Figure 7-2 shows that the student's attentive behaviors systematically increased when the teacher was asked not to change her verbal approval but to increase her nonverbal approval. As such, it would appear that the teacher's nonverbal approval functioned as a reinforcer for student attention to task. However, before that conclusion can be reached, one would have to demonstrate that the teacher's nonverbal attention actually increased while the verbal attention remained at the same level. The reason for this demonstration is, once again, the requisite of the definition of a reinforcer for these students' behavior. One must show that their behavior actually increased as a result of producing something in the environment that was not previously there in that amount. Figure 7-2 simply demonstrates that student behavior increased when the teacher was asked to increase her nonverbal attention; it does not show whether the teacher actually increased her rate of nonverbal approval for student attentiveness.

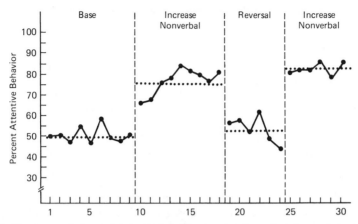

Figure 7-2. The percent of observations in which students in a class for moderately retarded persons were being attentive. During baseline, the teacher consequated attentive behaviors of the 12 students during a handwriting period in her regular fashion. During the second and fourth phases, she was asked to increase her rate of nonverbal approval (smiles or physical contact) for the students' attentive behaviors (Kazdin & Klock, 1973, p. 650.)

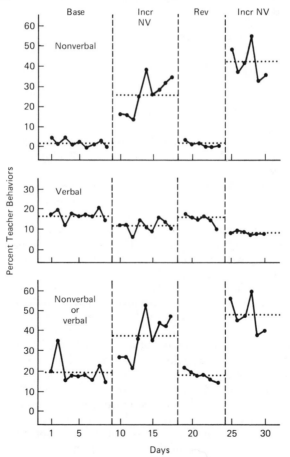

Figure 7-3. The percent of opportunities in which the teacher approved of her students' attentiveness in either a verbal or a nonverbal fashion (Kazdin & Klock, 1973, p. 649).

Figure 7-3, however, does address this issue. It shows that, during the periods in which the teacher was asked to increase nonverbal approval, she did indeed increase her nonverbal approval rate while essentially maintaining her verbal rate. As a result, one can conclude that nonverbal attention in the form of smiles and physical contact was an effective reinforcer for student attention during the class period devoted to handwriting. The importance of this study for our work with this population is that it demonstrates that a single teacher in a room with a dozen retarded elementary school students has the opportunity to increase significantly her students' appropriate learning behaviors. It also shows that this increase could be done quite simply and efficiently; in fact, it is difficult to find any procedure that could be considered much simpler than smiling or patting students on the back when they are doing well. There are many other examples of reinforcers, but these will be presented in the next section in which classifications and types of reinforcers will be discussed.

REINFORCERS

Classifications of Reinforcers

There are many ways by which reinforcers could be classified, but in this section three different ways of classifying reinforcers will be discussed. These are whether they are positive or negative, natural or artificial, or primary or conditioned. These classifications are not mutually exclusive with respect to each other; i.e., a reinforcer could be negative, and natural, and conditioned. Neither are they inclusive of all types of classifications; rather, for different reasons, they represent convenient ways of considering reinforcing stimuli.

Positive versus Negative Reinforcers. Remember that "positive" and "negative" do not refer to our value of stimuli; rather they refer to whether a particular stimulus condition increases behavior when it is produced or when it is removed by that response. If a response increases when it is consequated by a particular event, then that event is a positive reinforcer. In the study by Kazdin and Klock (1973), we have seen that nonverbal attention can increase the behavior that it consequates; hence, in this situation, it would be termed a positive reinforcer. We should also be careful not to apply the term "positive" to the behavior in question. Certainly, we attempt to increase only those behaviors we value positively, but a contingent stimulus can increase behavior whether or not we value that behavior. Certainly, many students whose curriculum does not allow them to succeed very often direct a good deal of their time toward acting out. If we attend to those behaviors, and if the student is not given the opportunity to earn our attention through appropriate behaviors, attention might serve to reinforce and maintain a behavior that would certainly not be considered positive. The problem is that positive reinforcers *work*; they increase behavior by definition through the principle of reinforcement. The social and the academic behaviors of retarded persons can be increased. But whether these behaviors are considered appropriate or inappropriate is a different matter altogether.

Similarly, "negative" refers neither to the value of the stimuli nor to the value of the behavior. Negative reinforcer refers simply to a stimulus which when removed or avoided by behavior increases the probability that that behavior will recur. We have discussed examples of negative reinforcers being used to increase entirely appropriate workshop behavior. Similarly, negative reinforcers can increase behavior we would not like to have increased, such as acting out by a student who is then released from class. Such behavior might well tell us something about the quality of that learning environment, but the behavior is not one we would like to have continued and carried over to other situations.

In addition, stimuli should not be considered to be positive or negative reinforcers in and of themselves. They may be reinforcers for certain behaviors of certain people in certain situations. They may not be reinforcers for the same behaviors of the same people in other situations. Stimuli may also serve as positive reinforcers in some situations and as negative reinforcers in others. For example, many of us go through a long series of behaviors just to be exposed to the light of the sun for an hour or two. But when we come out of a movie theater or some other dark room, that same light may first be very aversive, and we may put on sunglasses, cover our eyes, etc. In that condition, sunlight serves as a negative reinforcer.

Natural versus Artificial Reinforcers.   Another way of classifying reinforcers is whether they are natural or artificial to the learning environment. Our intent, of course, should be to move to reinforcers that occur naturally in a student's environment. Perhaps the most natural events in any classroom are the behaviors of the teachers and the other students. When a teacher directs attention, praise, or smiles toward appropriate learning, and when these behaviors are reinforcers, then they are a good choice because they are natural. Similarly, when the attention of peers might be reinforcing, the teacher should direct peer attention toward appropriate behaviors. With some of the population with which we work, we might have to teach the students to discriminate between the behavior to be praised and all other behaviors; or we might have to serve as a model for the praise behavior itself; or we might have to guide some young or more involved students physically through behaviors such as clapping. Approving of others may be a behavior that has to be taught. Yet praising a companion or a peer is very natural and should be encouraged.

Other reinforcers natural to learning environments are the activities regularly occurring in the classroom. For some students, certain academic activities are quite enjoyable and can serve as reinforcers. We have used access to working on arithmetic problems as a reinforcer for other academic activities, like improved spelling or writing. Such situations are not so infrequent as we might at first believe, particularly for retarded persons who fail or do not do particularly well in some areas, but who through careful teaching sequences, or perhaps just plain luck, do very well in certain areas and are able to earn considerable attention. The key to making certain activities fun and reinforcing may well be careful programming of curriculum that allows the student to make significant progress with minimal errors.

Other stimuli are natural in some situations and artificial in others. While some argue that we should use whatever works to accelerate responding, reinforcers such as money for correctly spelling words in a primary classroom are quite artificial. Using money for workshop production, on the other hand, is quite natural; in fact, it is always an ethical and usually a legal requisite. Artificial reinforcers, however, should not be neglected altogether. They should merely be avoided when a natural and equally potent reinforcer is available. When behavior can best be accelerated rapidly through the use of artificial reinforcers, their judicious use can be recommended. But a program should not retain them if at all possible, and we should incorporate more natural consequences into the environment while fading out the artificial consequences.

Primary versus Conditioned. Primary reinforcers are those which, for a particular individual, do not require any history of conditioning (learning). They are naturally reinforcing and include for most people light or darkness, warmth or coolness, food, water, etc. Whether something is a primary reinforcer for a retarded person we are trying to teach, however, is really of little importance. More relevant is simply whether something is reinforcing regardless of whether it is primary or conditioned. *Most reinforcers in fact are conditioned;* i.e., *their reinforcing properties depend upon a history of pairing with stimuli that are already reinforcing.* The latter may be primary or they may be conditioned. For our purposes, whichever they are does not really matter. All that does matter is that they are already reinforcing.

In trying to establish stimuli as conditioned reinforcers, we really have several tasks: (1) to find something that already is a reinforcer, (2) to pair the neutral stimulus with the reinforcing stimulus, and (3) to reduce the frequency of the original reinforcer while employing the conditioned reinforcer. Finding a reinforcer is a matter sometimes of guessing, of observing, or asking, and of testing. Pairing stimuli is much more straightforward. There are three options to pairing: (1) to immediately precede the reinforcer with the presently neutral stimulus, (2) to present both simultaneously, or (3) to follow the reinforcer with the neutral stimulus. The first option is the only one that produces conditioning of this type and is the procedure we should follow. The next objective involves reducing the relative frequency of the initial reinforcer, and this procedure involves gradually and irregularly reducing the number of times the original reinforcer is paired with the conditioned reinforcer. These pairings should lessen in occurrence while the conditioned reinforcer begins to maintain responding by itself. Figure 7-4 describes a means of establishing a stimulus as a conditioned reinforcer through pairings with a stimulus that is already reinforcing. It also provides an example of how the relative frequency of both the original and the conditioned reinforcer can be reduced. This example should be taken just as that, and not as the only way to use this procedure. While involved in this conditioning process, we should be recording data to determine the effect of each step in the procedure. If responding decreases in rate, or quality, or topography, etc., a number of factors could be responsible, one of which might be the means by which this procedure was established. In that case, we could return to an earlier step until behavior stabilizes and then progress through the other steps at a slower pace.

In Figure 7-4, the first phase is an attempt to accommodate the student to the learning situation and to determine whether what we thought was an extant reinforcer is in fact one for this behavior. This phase could involve only 5 or 10

ESTABLISHING A CONDITIONED REINFORCER		
Phase	Operation	Purpose
1	$R \to S^R$ $R \to S^R$ etc.	(a) to allow the student to accommodate to the situation (b) to test whether S^R is really a reinforcer
2	$R \to S^N \to S^R$ $R \to S^N \to S^R$ etc.	(a) to pair the neutral stimulus with the reinforcing stimulus
3	$R \to S^r \to S^R$ $R \to S^r \to S^R$ $R \to S^r$ $R \to S^r \to S^R$ $R \to S^r$ $R \to S^r \to S^R$ $R \to S^r$ $R \to S^r$ $R \to S^r \to S^R$ $R \to S^r$ $R \to S^r$ $R \to S^r \to S^R$ $R \to S^r$ $R \to S^r \to S^R$ $R \to S^r$ $R \to S^r$ $R \to S^r$ $R \to S^r \to S^R$ $R \to S^r$ $R \to S^r$ $R \to S^r$ $R \to S^r \to S^R$ $R \to S^r$ $R \to S^r$ $R \to S^r \to S^R$ $R \to S^r$ $R \to S^r$ $R \to S^r$ $R \to S^r$ $R \to S^r \to S^R$ etc.	(a) to increase the ratio of S^R to S^r (b) to increase the ratio of S^R to S^r in a successive but irregular pattern
4	$R \to S^r$ $R \to S^r$ $R \to S^r$ etc. $R \to S^r$ $R \to 0$ $R \to S^r$ $R \to 0$ $R \to S^r$ $R \to 0$ $R \to 0$ $R \to S^r$ $R \to 0$ $R \to S^r$ $R \to 0$ $R \to 0$ $R \to 0$ etc.	(a) to increase the ratio of S^r to R (b) to increase the ratio of S^r to R in a successive but irregular pattern

Figure 7-4. A means of introducing an originally neutral stimulus (S^n); of providing it with reinforcing properties (S^r) through pairing with a primary reinforcer (S^R); of reducing the relative frequency of the original reinforcer; and of reducing the relative frequency of the conditioned reinforcer.

trials if the student is familiar with the situation and if the stimulus is a powerful reinforcer that demonstrates an increase in responding. The purpose of the second phase is to pair the neutral stimulus (S^N) with the reinforcer a number of times. Again, there are no rules for how many pairings are necessary, with this figure depending upon properties of the stimulus itself, properties of the reinforcer, the response, and the level of functioning of the student. For some, 10 or 20 trials may be sufficient, but for others several hundred pairings may be necessary. In the third phase, there are two objectives. The first is to decrease the number of times the original reinforcer is paired with what should not be the conditioned reinforcer. The reasons we reduce this ratio are that continued presentations of the original reinforcer will lead to satiation, and that continued presentation of it was not the objective, or else we would never have sought to replace it with the conditioned reinforcer. The second objective is to decrease this pairing in a successive but irregular pattern. That is, the ratio of S^R to S^r should go from 1:1 to 1:2 to 1:3 to 1:4, etc., but the 1:2 ratio and all other ratios should present an average, not a repeating ratio. For example, the 1:2 ratio could be an average of 1:1 + 1:2 + 1:3 + 1:2. This type of pattern makes reinforcement less predictable, and actually helps to support better responding than a regular pattern.[4] In the fourth phase, the ratio of the conditioned reinforcer is increased, again in a successive but irregular pattern. The reasons are to increase responding through a variable relation between reinforcement and responding, to reduce effects of possible periods of extinction (a period in which responding is no longer reinforced), and to make teaching easier for the instructor. This is exactly the procedure we use when we first use an artificial reinforcer like candy, but then move to social praise as the reinforcer.

There are literally thousands of experiments on conditioned reinforcers in basic research. There are also several with retarded persons that are applied or semiapplied. Lauten and Birnbrauer (1974) tested whether the principle of pairings (classical conditioning) established in basic research with a number of species would hold with mildly retarded persons learning a discrimination. In a group study, the relationship of the verbal stimulus "right" with a primary reinforcer (candy) was tested with three groups. For one group, the students were told they were "right" before they were given the candy. For another group, "right" accompanied candy, while for a control group, "right" and candy were programmed independently. Results showed that learning was promoted only when "right" reliably preceded candy. These results support the notion that a neutral stimulus must precede a reinforcer in order for it to become a conditioned reinforcer, and it shows that this is the procedure we should follow when establishing conditioned reinforcers for the students we are teaching.

When selecting neutral stimuli to establish as conditioned reinforcers, we should select those that can be maintained in the environment in which the student will be learning. For example, if a student is to be with us for two or three weeks, and will then be returning to a former classroom, we should not try to establish tokens as conditioned reinforcers if tokens are not going to be used in the other classroom. We should be practical and explore the environment into which the student will be going. If, on the other hand, the student will be with us

---

[4] Through the principle of resistance to extinction and through an analogy to the principle of variable ratios of reinforcement, two topics that will be discussed in other sections of this book.

for a year or so, we have considerable more choice. In this case, we could establish conditioned reinforcers which might not predominate a year or two from now, as we would have time to bring the student's behavior under the control of reinforcers that will be in the future environment. This problem of environmental maintenance is why behaviorists tend to work so hard at establishing verbal and nonverbal praise as conditioned reinforcers. Praise can be natural to any environment and hence be maintained. With this advantage, the student's progression through different programs could be easier in terms of continued responding in new environments.

Types of Reinforcers

One way to classify reinforcers is to label them conditioned or primary (unconditioned) as has been done. Within each, however, there are many various kinds or types of reinforcers, such as edibles, tokens, praise, and activities. In this section, examples of these and other popular reinforcers will be given, regardless of whether they are conditioned or unconditioned.

Edibles. Various kinds of food were often used as reinforcers for retarded persons in the 1960s, in part because food is reinforcing for most people and in part because applied behavior analysis was quite a new field which proceeded tentatively. In many cases, edibles were used inappropriately in the sense that they were not natural to the learning environment. The result was an "M & M syndrome" in which behavior modification was equated with giving students candy for correct responding. There are, however, appropriate uses of food as reinforcers, including those situations in which food is the only apparent reinforcer suitable, or those in which food is being faded out and replaced by more natural reinforcers, those in which an expeditious change in behavior was necessary and food appeared to be the most powerful reinforcer, or those in which earned snacks were very appropriate to the environment. In many cases, more nutritious foods, such as fruits, could be used instead of candies.

Hopkins (1968) demonstrated how to use and then reduce the use of candy while reinforcing the smiling of an eight-year-old retarded boy who typically did not smile or make any other change in facial expression when encountering or being greeted by people around his school. During walks around the school, Hopkins counted the number of times the student encountered people and what proportion of those opportunities he smiled. In the baseline period, the youngster did not smile during a single encounter, so a contingency was established in which the child would receive a piece of candy if he smiled. But during these walks, the child never smiled, so the possibility of reinforcement never occurred. This example represents a significant, obvious, but sometimes overlooked problem in "reinforcement programs" that fail. If the reinforcement does not occur, either because responding occurs at such a low rate naturally or because the response demands are too high or complex, then the program will fail because the behavior will not have sufficient opportunities to come into contact with the contingency. In these cases, we typically use either verbal or physical prompts in order to allow the behavior to occur often enough for the principle of reinforcement to take effect. In this particular case, Hopkins used verbal instructions ("Smile!" or "Smile when you say hello to _____") in order to develop at least some level of responding. After several days of instructions, the contingency of candy for smiling was reinstated, and each time the student smiled during an encounter he received a piece of candy. The contingency now resulted in a substantial increase in responding so that the student smiled most of the times he met someone on his walks. During this period, the child was given candy continuously, i.e., after each response (which of course is inappropriate for more than a short period). To reduce the ratio of candy to correct responses, Hopkins began to reinforce the student intermittently and on an irregular or variable schedule. First, the child was reinforced on the average of every 1.2 responses[5] (e.g., reinforcement could occur after 1 response, after 1 response, after 1 response, after 2 responses, and after 1 response). After eight sessions at that value, the ratio was increased across 39 sessions from 1.67 to 2.5 to 5.0 to 7.5. After this last value, which means that on the average the child was given candy after every 7.5 times he smiled during an encounter, candy was no longer provided. Efforts were then made to bring the greeting behavior under social control so that others talked with him only when he smiled when meeting them during his walks. The greeting behavior of the child, once at an absolute zero level, was then brought to an entirely acceptable and normal level of occurrence and maintained under conditions natural to his environment. As such, Hopkins' study demonstrates a means of fading out the use of edible reinforcers when they are not natural to the environment.

Stolz and Wolf (1969) used edibles to reinforce a number of behaviors by a moderately retarded adolescent who was also labeled emotionally disturbed, brain damaged, and visually impaired. The neurological report suggested that prenatal brain damage resulted in damage to the optic nerve with probable associated atrophy. However, his vision was also reported as inconsistent, with his being able to see some small objects but not being able to see larger objects. Stolz and Wolf sought to determine whether this student, considered to be organically blind, could emit some visually based behaviors if they were environmentally consequated. For the first behavior, Stolz tested whether Fred could discriminate between a correct and an incorrect stimulus when pairs differing on different dimensions were presented: e.g., two triangles differing only in color, two triangles differing in size, blocks differing only in color, and pieces of paper differing only in color. At the beginning of each trial, the instructor indicated the correct stimulus in the pair by telling Fred "This is the right one. Look at it. Now do you see it? Point to the right one." When a correct response was made, he was praised and then given candy (in an effort to maintain or increase the reinforcing properties of praise). After more than 40 trials, Fred was still choosing correctly only at chance level, so the three-term contingency was not operating. As a result, the antecedent portion of the contingency was changed, and the discrimination task became one that could be solved using either visual or tactile cues. In these trials, a yellow piece of paper 1 by 2 inches was correct, while a red piece of paper 1 by 3.8 inches was incorrect. Praise and food still followed correct responding, but the cues for correct responding were made more visual as the red paper was made gradually closer in size to the yellow

---

[5] This schedule is termed a variable ratio 1.2, which means that reinforcement occurs irregularly but on the average every 1.2 responses.

paper until they differed only in color. After the sessions in which the added cue was faded out, correct discriminations were continued and the boy was basing his behavior on visual cues once presumed imperceptible to him. Praise and food continued to be used to reinforce correct responding during an adaptive visual acuity testing and during sessions in which Fred was taught to make eye contact.

A more natural use of food as a reinforcer was made in programs to teach Fred to eat properly and to select food independently from a cafeteria line. In the cafeteria, Fred obtained some items for himself often after feeling about for some time in their vicinity; but he was often given items by aides, other adolescents in the program, or by kitchen staff. During these weeks, there were really no consequences for visually based selections, because food would often be given to him. But Stolz began a program in which all personnel were instructed not to help Fred, who instead would have to use his vision as an aide in selecting items to eat. By the end of the program, he had increased his self-help behavior in the cafeteria so that he selected nearly 100% of the items by himself. In this case, the eventual consumption of food was probably reinforcing his selecting behaviors, and edibles were very natural reinforcers for the environment.

Many other types of behaviors have been taught and maintained through the use of food as a reinforcer. For example, Peterson and McIntosch (1973) taught retarded youngsters to ride tricycles through a system in which approach, mounting, and pedaling were shaped and reinforced by food, initially given for every correct response but gradually decreased. A number of studies have also examined the cooperative responding of retarded persons and have used food as reinforcement. Morris and Dolker (1974) trained severely retarded children to play a game requiring cooperation, and found that a shaping program in which the children were taught successively more difficult components to cooperation was beneficial, that teaching cooperation is easier when one of the children is already interacting with others, and that the shaping procedure could be enhanced through using food as reinforcement. Wiesen, Hartley, Richardson, and Roske (1967) increased what they termed a generosity response by giving children a piece of candy after they had previously given candy to other retarded youngsters. At first, the students ate the candy themselves, refusing to offer it to others. But after the children were guided through the correct response a number of times, they began and maintained generosity responding. Samaras and Ball (1975) extended this type of work to profoundly retarded persons, showing that even at this level of retardation, cooperative behaviors could be systematically developed and maintained through food reinforcement.

However, although edibles have been shown to be powerful reinforcers for certain behaviors, many teachers prefer to use a reinforcer that presents no nutritional conflicts and that is more natural to the environment. Of the several alternatives, perhaps the most frequent is attention.

Attention.   Attention can be an extremely powerful reinforcer for many students, but the effects of attention are more complex in the teaching environment than the effects of food are. One major problem is that attention exists almost all the time in a learning environment, whether that attention is from staff or from students. As such, attention is often an uncontrolled, but not necessarily uncontrollable, stimulus that can follow and reinforce inappropriate behavior just as well as appropriate. While the distinction between appropriate and inappropriate behavior seems so obvious that one would hardly expect a teacher to attend to very much inappropriate responding, such a pattern is hardly the case. Time after time we find (1) teachers attending more to students who are not behaving appropriately than to students who are, and (2) students who receive more attention for inappropriate than for appropriate behavior. Certainly, one of the most important, and perhaps revealing, investigations we can make is to classify the behaviors to which we attend in a classroom and to count how many of our attending responses follow appropriate and inappropriate behaviors. Few of us have as high a proportion in the former category as we should, and still fewer of us are willing to document that fact through a few hours of data collection. As has been discussed previously, a good deal of teacher attention actually follows nonstudy rather than study behavior (Hall, Lund, & Jackson, 1968; Patterson, Cobb & Ray, 1972; Walker & Buckley, 1971; Werry & Quay, 1968). The study by Walker and Buckley was particularly intriguing as it showed that (1) 77% of the teacher's attention was contingent upon responding of problem children, while only 23% was contingent upon responding of appropriately behaving children, and (2) of the attention directed toward the problem children, 89% was for inappropriate responding, while only 11% was for appropriate.

But systematic attention has been used to increase and maintain appropriate responding in many situations. The first work in this area tended to be centered in basic research in which the behaviors were not socially important (see Panda & Lynch, 1972, for a review). But in the late 1960s, several studies concentrated on applied work in public schools and showed that contingent teacher attention could increase study behavior of students in regular classrooms (Hall, Lund, & Jackson, 1968; Hall, Panyan, Rabon, & Broden, 1968; Thomas, Becker, & Armstrong, 1968). The same effects were demonstrated by Broden, Bruce, Mitchell, Carter, and Hall (1970) with two retarded boys in an elementary school who engaged in disruptive behavior and insufficient study behavior. When the teacher was trained to attend to and praise each student whenever she noticed he was attending in class, the appropriate behaviors of each student rose from about 30% of the time to 80%. Similar results were shown in studies of institutionalized retarded persons by Gray and Kasteler (1969), who trained foster grandparents to teach a number of skills to the residents while socially reinforcing them. The program showed that properly trained paraprofessionals could improve retarded behavior by systematically providing social reinforcement.

Foxx (1972) also used attention as a reinforcer but for an entirely different type of behavior. Previous work had shown that attention could be successful in remedying the food-related problems of anorexic[6] and obese individuals. Bachrach, Erwin, and Mohr (1965) had helped an anorexic woman gain weight by providing a social interaction contingent upon individual eating responses. In a different procedure, Ayllon and Haughton (1962) had withdrawn social interaction whenever an anorexic patient refused food. Schaeffer and Martin (1969) had worked instead with weight loss and paired social reinforcement with tokens when overweight chronic schizophrenics left portions of a meal on the plate. Foxx's study similarly dealt with weight loss, but the patient in this case was a mildly retarded 14-year-old girl who weighed 264 pounds. Prior to the reinforce-

---

[6] A psychological condition in which an individual will eat little or no food.

ment program, she had been placed on a diet, but in six months had lost only 25 pounds. The reason for the slow loss appeared to be that no contingenices controlled her behavior outside the program when she went home from the hospital, or came back from a workshop located near a canteen, or when she stole food on the ward on which she lived. Foxx noted that controlling her weight by restricting her to a closely supervised ward was antithetical to acquiring skills necessary for a successful community adjustment, that praise was an ineffective reinforcer, as were promised clothes and promised corrective surgery for a bowed leg, scheduled to begin only after considerable weight loss. But Foxx did notice that attention he paid to her seemed highly reinforcing, so trips to the canteen for conversation and low-calorie sodas were planned. When they seemed as if they were potentially reinforcing for her, trips were made contingent upon 1.5 pounds of weight loss the preceding week. In 25 weeks of this program, the girl lost an additional 71 pounds, and weight loss continued after the program continued. This program, which was so simple, required so little time, and achieved such excellent results with a very important series of weight-loss related behaviors, appears to have succeeded for a variety of reasons which include (1) successful identification of a reinforcer after prior attempts had failed, (2) making reinforcement available for small but significant results (1.5-pound loss) rather than for larger amounts that might not be met, and (3) bringing the behavior under control of natural elements in the environment: "Eating behavior has now (at the end of the program) come under the control of a wide variety of social reinforcers, since generous amounts of praise and attention from others, including a new boyfriend, allowed the experimenter to fade out as the controlling stimulus" (p. 23).

The effects of attention are not, however, always positive. When attention followed appropriate behavior and was withdrawn following oppositional behaviors, differential parent attention has been shown in some cases to be ineffective in altering oppositional behaviors (Wahler, Winkel, Peterson, & Morrison, 1965; Wahler, 1969). Similarly, O'Leary, Becker, Evans, and Saudargas (1969) found that differential teacher attention did not decrease disruptive behavior for six of seven children. But perhaps the most interesting study in this area is that by Herbert, Pinkston, Hayden, Sajwaj, Pinkston, Cordua, and Jackson (1973), which dealt independently with two parent-training projects, one at the University of Kansas and the other at the University of Mississippi Medical Center. Designed to train parents to attend differentially to on-task and deviant child behaviors, each project presumed that, when the mothers reduced most of their attention for deviant child behaviors while maintaining baseline levels of attention for task-oriented behaviors, appropriate behaviors would increase while inappropriate behaviors would decrease. But in this complex, multiphase, and well-controlled pair of studies, deviant behavior did not decrease; in fact, it increased for 67% of the children. The authors' comments are enlightening:

> In addition to the rate increases, topographies of deviant behavior appeared for all children in the differential attention conditions which were not observed in baseline conditions. For example, Jerry, Harold, Charlotte, and Edward began assaulting their mothers; Charlotte began scratching herself until bleeding oc-

curred; Joseph rammed a pencil into his nose and bled profusely; and Jerry began dangerous and unusual climbing. It can be concluded that these children were adversely affected by this "simple" behavior modification procedure. In addition, adverse side effects were noted. Although the mothers continued to attend heavily to task-oriented behavior (save Edward), this behavior was greatly reduced. Thus, not only did these four children increase the amount and kind of deviant behavior, they also decreased their appropriate, desired behaviors. Some adverse side effects appeared at home. Edward became more enuretic and Joseph began urinating out his bedroom window, which was facing a busy street. (p. 26)

Additional confusion is added when the data are examined further. For five of the students, maternal attention was shown to be a punishing event; deviant behavior increased under conditions of decreased attention. For one of those five, material attention functioned as a punishing stimulus in the first two phases of the study, as a positive reinforcer in the next three conditions, and again as a punishing stimulus in the next three. The reasons for these puzzling results have not been identified, but the authors offered several suggestions:

(1) the presence or absence of competing activities; (2) the decreases in absolute levels of maternal attention; (3) the effects of the contingency between deviant behavior and attention; (4) the role of "extinction burst"[7] phenomenon in the increases of deviant behavior; (5) the role of intermittent schedules of attention in maintaining the deviant behavior; and (6) the discriminative functions of the ignoring procedure. (pp. 26-27)

These studies, and particularly the most intriguing one by Herbert *et al.*, are quite important reminders of our efforts to identify functional relationships between environmental events and behaviors *for individuals*. Attention is not *a priori* a reinforcer. Rather, it is a description of a procedure involving certain instructor behaviors that precede or follow certain student behaviors. For some, attention is a powerful reinforcer; for others, attention is a punishing stimulus; for still others, it is a neutral event. Rather than presuming that attention is a reinforcer for all retarded individuals, we need to demonstrate its effects when it is systematically linked to behavior. Only at that point can we determine whether we are successfully helping a retarded person learn at a faster rate than if we did not intervene. And this relationship exists whether the stimulus is food, attention, or any other stimulus presumed to be a positive reinforcer.

Tokens.   Tokens represent a recently popular alternative to other types of reinforcers and present a number of advantages as well as disadvantages. Although there will be a complete discussion of token systems in a later chapter, identification of the basic operation of a token system would be helpful in identifying the function of tokens as reinforcers. There are two components to a token system: (1) the token-production component, and (2) the token-exchange component. In the first, the student meets some stated response requirement and receives a token. In the second, the student meets some token accumulation re-

---

[7] A phenomenon in which behavior that was but is no longer reinforced actually increases. Typically, during this procedure, which is called extinction, behavior decreases.

quirement and exchanges the tokens for another reinforcer (e.g., food, free time, activities). In this section, the concern is only with that first component; in a later section, the concern will be with both. Because tokens are exchanged for something else, it is important that we understand that it is the "something else" that is initially reinforcing and that tokens are not. As such, tokens are correctly considered to be conditioned reinforcers, and they operate under the same principles as other conditioned reinforcers. They must be paired with something that is presently reinforcing; the pairing should eventually be decreased to allow ease of teaching; and their reinforcing properties must be demonstrated through a functional relationship between tokens and the behavior that produces the tokens.

The basic method for establishing tokens as reinforcers first involves instructing the student that a particular response will earn a token, and that at some time, some number of tokens can be exchanged for something else. For some students, instructions are sufficient to establish the relation between tokens and access to the terminal reinforcer. But for other students, a number of pairings might be necessary. In this case, you would first give a token to the student and allow (or physically guide) the student to exchange the token immediately either for a short duration (as in free time) or a small amount (as with food) of the reinforcer. After a number of these pairings, the time between token delivery and token exchange is gradually increased to the level appropriate when the token program is in place. As this delay is being increased, the relation between responding and token delivery is taught. The student either is allowed to make the correct response or is physically guided through the correct response. A token is delivered and exchange is allowed. After a few pairings of this sort, the delay between token delivery and token exchange is increased. In addition, the number of responses necessary to earn a token is increased from a continuous schedule of token reinforcement (i.e., one token earns one backup reinforcer).

Although basic research with tokens had been started 25 years earlier (Wolfe, 1936; Cowles, 1937), systematic applied work did not begin until 1961 when Ayllon and Azrin (1968) began their work with hospitalized schizophrenics and Staats (Staats, 1968; Staats, Minke, Finley, Wolf, & Brooks, 1964; Staats, Staats, Schultz, & Wolf, 1962) began his work with a series of language behaviors. Since that time, more than 100 articles have been published using tokens, and certainly thousands of projects have utilized tokens in classrooms and institutions to improve various behaviors of exceptional persons (see Axelrod, 1971, and O'Leary & Drabman, 1971, for reviews). Soon thereafter, many studies described token systems used to alter a number of behaviors of retarded persons, much of which has been reviewed by Kazdin and Craighead (1973). Girardeau and Spradlin (1964) used tokens to improve various behaviors of moderately and of severely retarded girls. Tokens were earned by improvement in self-care, social, and grooming skills, and they were exchanged for various items available in a "store" for the girls. The program was continued at the Mimosa Cottage at the Parsons State Hospital and Training Center in Kansas (Lent, 1967, 1968), and it was extended for behaviors related to occupational skills, personal appearance, academic skills, and social behaviors.

Other studies showed significant improvement when tokens were made contingent upon a variety of self-care behaviors, including personal appearance (Hunt, Fitzhugh, & Fitzhugh, 1968) and mealtime behaviors (Ray & Shelton

1968). Language behaviors were altered by Kazdin (1971), who suppressed psychotic talk by removing tokens whenever the student engaged in this behavior, and by Peine, Gregerson, and Sloane (1970), who made praise and tokens contingent upon proper vocabulary and upon spontaneous speech. In a series of studies discussed in Chapter 2 (Bijou, Birnbrauer, Kidder, & Tague, 1966; Birnbrauer & Lawler, 1964; Birnbrauer, Wolf, Kidder, & Tague, 1965), an experimental classroom at Ranier School in Washington used tokens to consequate social behaviors and various academic behaviors. Disruptive classroom behavior was also investigated by Zimmerman, Zimmerman, and Russell (1969), who found that for most students tokens and praise developed more instruction-following behavior than just praise, and by Perline and Levinsky (1968), who consequated appropriate responding with tokens and disruptive responding with restraint or loss of tokens.

In the last decade, studies involving tokens have become more complex, have examined many more types of behaviors, and have identified a number of steps we should follow in building token systems. The latter will be discussed in the chapter on token systems. However, at this point, a number of attributes of tokens can be identified that will allow the value of tokens as potential reinforcers to be better stated. One is that tokens allow a highly *individualized* program, even in a classroom of students with disparate skills. For example, each student may be receiving tokens for correct responses on an arithmetic program, but each student can be in a different place in the program. In addition, students do not have to produce the same number of correct responses to earn tokens, so an appropriately slower student might earn one token for every 5 correct responses, a moderate-rate student might earn one token for every 8 correct responses, while a very quick student might earn one token for every 15 correct answers. Another advantage is that *tokens do not lose their reinforcing power when more responses are required* for reinforcement as long as the change is made gradually. So when beginning a task, a student may earn one token for every correct response. But soon thereafter the student may have to make 5 responses for a token, and eventually perhaps 10. Another attribute is that *a token is a concrete, nonvarying source of feedback* that can be quite valuable because of its nonambiguity. Several years ago, when we first began to use tokens with profoundly retarded students, we were told that tokens were too abstract for this population and that more traditional reinforcers should be used. However, the opposite is probably true, because the token (whether it is a marble or a chip from a Peabody kit or a checker) is tangible, discrete, and has nonvarying properties of color, size, and form. As such, it should be much easier to develop as a conditioned reinforcer than social praise, which, in terms of smiles, hugs, and verbalizations, differs so much from day to day and from adult to adult. Another attribute is that *tokens are quite easy to pair with attention* which may not be initially reinforcing, but which should always be developed as a conditioned reinforcer. Probably all token problems should have as their objective their own demise, to be replaced as a reinforcer by attention, activities, and other reinforcers more natural to learning environments. An attribute similar in context is that *tokens can be easy to administer, providing reinforcement without disrupting the learner's activities.* If a child were reinforced with candy, he or she might well disrupt work to eat the candy; or if a child is to be reinforced with free time, then reinforcing immediately after correct responding would be both counterproductive and ridiculous. But token delivery can be significant but nondisruptive. If the student is disrupted, perhaps by interrupting work to play with the token, steps such as placing tokens in a translucent container should be taken. Another attribute, contained in part in the last one, is that *token reinforcement can occur immediately after correct responding*. Many studies have shown that delayed reinforcement is not so effective as immediate reinforcement. But tokens can be delivered immediately and serve to bridge the time gap between responding and the eventual reinforcer. Another attribute and an extremely important advantage of tokens over other reinforcers is that it can be given the properties of *generalized conditioned reinforcers*. A generalized conditioned reinforcer is one which is paired with a number of reinforcers, rather than with just one or two. Tokens lend themselves to this arrangement, and we should allow a number of options for the student in the token-exchange component. The power of generalized conditioned reinforcers, as contrasted with conditioned reinforcers, is that they are far less likely to lose their power over time, particularly when a number occur within a relatively short period of time. This temporary decrease in reinforcer effectiveness due to repeated deliveries is known as *satiation* and can be a powerful effect. But because token systems should provide a number of options at exchange, satiation on more than a few of the options is unlikely. Hence, the token itself should be relatively constant in its reinforcing properties and not be subject to the temporal vagaries of satiation. Another advantage within the same context is that *the token system allows not only variation in reinforcers for the same student, but it also allows variation in the eventual reinforcer across students*. If one student likes music, another likes candy, while a third likes to sit quietly and rest for a few minutes, then individual reinforcers for each can be made available through the token exchange.

Feedback.   Within all token systems, there is an element of feedback in the sense that token delivery provides information that appropriate responding has occurred, while token removal provides information that inappropriate responding has occurred. Feedback is also present when other forms of reinforcement are provided, such as verbal praise or a hug. But feedback can be used independent of other established reinforcers. When feedback alone is effective, it probably is so because it has been developed as a conditioned reinforcer through its prior association with the delivery of other reinforcers (Kazdin, 1975). Because of poor histories of reinforcement, however, the value of feedback alone with retarded persons is equivocal. For example, Jens and Shores (1969) found that feedback on the number of completed work units did not increase workshop production. However, when feedback was paired with public charting of work rates, production did increase. Similarly, Salzberg, Wheeler, Devar, and Hopkins (1971) found that only when feedback was paired with access to play was it effective in improving handwriting of kindergarten children. Brown, Van Deventer, Perlmutter, Jones, and Sontag (1972) found equivocal results. For some children, feedback in the form of charting increased the production rates of retarded and severely emotionally disturbed students in a public school workshop; for other students, there was no effect. A similar study was completed by Zimmerman, Stuckey, Garlick, and Miller (1969), who in the feedback phase did tell the clients how many units they had completed and how many points they would have earned if points had been available. Performance in this case did increase. When points were later given and were made exchangeable as tokens, performance increased even more.

These studies seem to indicate that for some people feedback in and of itself can serve as a reinforcer, but for other people it does not. This relationship, of course, is no different than that between other events and behavior: for some people, some contingent events will reinforce some behaviors in some situations. But feedback does not seem to be a powerful reinforcer for very many retarded individuals. It is, however, very appropriate and natural to learning situations when it is a conditioned reinforcer. As such, it could be developed just like any other reinforcer through repeated pairings with existing reinforcers. Such a program, with eventual decrease in the rate of presentation of existing and perhaps more obtrusive reinforcers, would seem to be an appropriate goal for any person concerned with teaching.

Auditory and Visual Stimuli

Various types of music, paintings, pictures, movies, etc., are reinforcing events for all of us. We go through some physical effort to arrive at a theater, gallery, or symphony hall, and we exchange our tokens for entry into these events. Of course, such events can be and should be used as reinforcers for retarded persons; they are natural, generally relaxing, sometimes educational, and a pleasant experience available to others of us, so they should be made available to this population. Occasionally, however, such stimuli are brought to the learning environment itself and made immediately contingent upon responding. For example, Chandler and Adams (1972) worked with an eight-year-old spastic diplegic[8] and mentally retarded child who would walk only if placed on his feet and given assistance. During baseline, the child was given nine walking trials each day during which he was verbally encouraged to take as many steps as he could in each 1-minute trial. Then, after the parents indicated that the child was fond of music, a program was begun in which any time he exceeded the number of uninterrupted and unassisted responses during baseline (an average of 20 per trial) he was reinforced with 30 seconds of music from a portable radio carried by the therapist. This showed a dramatic initial increase, which was, however, transitory. When the number of steps began to decrease, a different procedure was employed in which the radio was turned on when the child started walking and demonstrated balance. When he stopped walking or lost control of his balance, it was turned off. This procedure also showed a dramatic increase, doubling the baseline level and going slightly above the phase 2 level. But this effect was also transitory, with contingent music seeming to lose its reinforcing properties after 10 days, but then showing some recovery. The procedure was continued for five days with one additional consequence: each time he exceeded the base rate by at least one step, he received candy. The number of steps again increased and showed inconsistent results. Although within each phase the number of steps was irregular, the number had increased from each of the phases

---

[8] Spasticity refers to a condition in which one or more limbs are rigidly immobilized by constant muscular contractions; diplegia refers to a condition in which there is major physical involvement in the lower limbs and minor physical involvement in the upper limbs.

to the next so that, on the final day, he had walked 89 steps in 1 minute. At this point, the contingent music and candy were removed and responding continued, not only in the therapy sessions but also at home and in the classroom. This study contains a number of interesting points that could be extended to other programs and other types of reinforcers: (1) There is an extreme difference between behavior that does not occur because of motivational difficulties and behavior that does not occur because of learning difficulties. In the former case we need only investigate contingent events, while in the latter case we also need to investigate the steps in the teaching program. In this case, the child could walk and the problem was motivational. In the work by Horner (1971), the skills of a spina bifida[9] child necessary for ambulation with crutches had to be taught through a carefully analyzed sequence of components. (2) Another point is that events may be reinforcing only for short periods of time, and the instructor may need to be prepared with other alternatives should this effect occur. The unstable effect in this study may have been a result simply of novelty, or of satiation, or of many other identified procedures. (3) A third is that the presentation of reinforcement *during* responding (as in phases 3 and 4) rather than after responding presents an interesting alternative. This procedure is generally labeled conjugate reinforcement (Lindsley, 1961), but it has remained quite unexplored. It may well, however, be a means of increasing responding quite efficiently.

Music was also used as a reinforcer by Ball, McCrady, and Hart (1975), who made music contingent on the head orientation of each of two retarded and quadriplegic persons. A mercury switch circuit was connected to standard earphone held in place on the ear by a wire cradle and adhesive tape. The switch was adjusted to remain closed when the student held his head upright or tilted backward. When the person was seated upright, and when his or her head dropped, the switch opened. Ten-minute sessions were held twice daily, and the student was told that he or she would be given the opportunity to listen to music from a transistor radio. To determine whether music would reinforce holding the head upright, there were two conditions: (1) *contingent music*, in which music played through the earphone only when the head was held upright, and (2) *noncontingent music*, in which music played irrespective of head position. Results showed that one student held her head up 10% of the time during baseline, but 90% of the time during treatment; another student displayed similar change. A similar program was instituted by Ball (1971), who used contingent music to control a blind retarded girl's head dropping. A mercury switch was attached to a ribbon in her hair. It activated a portable radio when she held her head in a normal position, and it terminated the music when she dropped her chin to her chest. An earphone and a portable transistor radio allowed the apparatus to be used in a classroom without interrupting other children.

Visual stimuli are inherent in many activities used as reinforcers such as attendance at the circus and movies. In addition, some books or instructional materials maintain student behavior more frequently than other materials simply because of the design and artwork. But visual stimuli do not seem to be frequently planned as reinforcers. Rynders and Friedlander (1972) studied preferences of visual stimuli by institutional retarded persons and showed that they

---

[9] Spina bifida is a condition in which there is a defect in the closure of the spinal column.

preferred color motion pictures to black and white slides of the same subject. But this study was in the basic research idiom and serves only to substantiate what we might have guessed. The study did use, however, equipment analogous to teaching machines, and facilities that have automated teaching devices utilizing slides, motion pictures, television, etc., could certainly employ various forms of visual stimuli as reinforcers. This field seems remarkably unstudied with our population and almost curiously so, as most teaching involves reading letters or numbers or responding to various geometric shapes. Why we would know so little about how to arrange these stimuli to provide more interest is quite striking.

Tactile Stimuli

Tactile stimuli in their various forms are highly reinforcing for many people. But response-contingent tactile stimulation, like visual reinforcement, seems to be a field in which there has been little investigation. One basic research study (Ohwaki, Brahlek, & Stayton, 1973) did investigate tactile stimuli and compared it with visual stimuli. Interestingly, there was a relation between the reinforcing properties of vibration as a reinforcer and mental age. For a group of students labeled profoundly retarded, vibration was the preferred reinforcer; for a group labeled severely retarded, vibration and visual stimuli were equally preferred; and for a group labeled moderately retarded, visual stimuli were preferred to tactile stimulation. This study again indicates that whether something is reinforcing to a person is a highly individualistic relation between that stimulus and her or his behavior. But is also suggests that at different levels of development various stimuli might be differentially reinforcing when a group is considered *in toto*. This means that, if we are working with a profoundly retarded child and we do not know what we should be reinforcing, we might begin by determining whether vibration would be reinforcing. It does not mean that vibration will be reinforcing for that individual; it does mean that vibration might be an intelligent choice on our part if we have no other information on the individual's preferences. Vibration has been shown, in fact, in a few studies to be an effective reinforcer for nonretarded infants (Schaeffer, 1960), for ambulatory severely or moderately retarded persons (Rehagen & Thelan, 1972), and for a nonambulatory profoundly retarded child (Bailey & Meyerson, 1969). Bailey and Meyerson (1970) completed additional work with vibration as a reinforcer, utilizing it for a different purpose than the previously mentioned works. The child with whom they worked was seven years old, self-injurious, and restrained to a crib because of physical problems. The self-injurious behavior was described by the authors: he "engaged almost constantly during his waking hours in self-stimulatory and self-injurious behavior unless he was physically restrained. The self-injurious behaviors, which resulted in visible tissue damage, were chewing on fingers and hands, and hitting head or feet against the bars of his crib" (p. 134). The authors connected a vibrator to the crib and used it to reinforce the child when he was operating a manipulandum and not being self-injurious.[10] A similar approach was taken by Nunes, Murphy, and Ruprecht (1977), who worked with two self-abusive youngsters. For one, a vibratory stimulus was

---

[10] Plans for building such an apparatus with a chair have been provided by Doughty (1976).

withdrawn whenever he engaged in self-abusive behavior. For the other person, a vibrator was placed on her back when she was on-task and not engaging in self-injurious behaviors. These uses of reinforcing stimulus to consequate the absence of a response or to consequate a particular response that is incompatible with the self-injurious behavior are examples of a large group of studies generally termed "reducing responding through reinforcement," which will be discussed in a later chapter.[11] The use of vibration as a reinforcer for these procedures would seem to be quite promising.

ACTIVITIES

Most of the reinforcers discussed to this point have been made available by someone else and are part of the environment, such as food, a teacher's attention and feedback, and auditory, visual, or tactile stimulation. Another type of reinforcer is something that the person, himself or herself, actually does, like singing or coloring or even sleeping. When these activities are made contingent upon other behaviors, they may increase the other behaviors. This relation between behaviors is known as the *Premack principle*, having been suggested by Premack in 1959 when he commented that a difference in rates between two behaviors is a necessary and sufficient condition for reinforcement. The formal statement of that relation was that "Any response A will reinforce any other response B, if and only if the independent rate of A is greater than that of B" (p. 220). This statement means that behavior itself, and not just stimuli external to us, can be reinforcing; and as behavior is always occurring, it means that in any learning situation potential reinforcers are present—it is almost as if every student brings with him his own reinforcer.

Beginning with the original applied work, the Premack principle has utilized behaviors one would traditionally not think to use as reinforcers. In that first applied study, Homme, deBaca, Devine, Steinhorst, and Rickert (1963) investigated a classroom of three-year-old children who were often unruly, running around the room, pushing chairs, yelling, or sometimes quietly completing jigsaw puzzles.

> Taking Premack seriously, such behaviors were labeled as high probability behaviors and used in combination with the signals for the reinforcers. These high probability behaviors were then made contingent on desired behaviors. For example, sitting quietly in a chair and looking at the blackboard would be intermittently followed by the sound of the bell, with the instruction: "Run and scream." The children would then leap to their feet and run around the room screaming. At another signal they would stop. At this time they would get another signal and an instruction to engage in some other behavior which, on a quasi-random schedule, might be one of high or low probability. At a later stage, they earned tokens for low probability behaviors which would later be used to "buy" the opportunity for high probability activities. (p. 544)

---

[11] The concept of reducing responding through reinforcement might seem confusing at first, as we have been discussing an increase in responding through reinforcement. But in all these programs, something other than the behavior to be reduced is actually being reinforced.

With this procedure, the students came under control almost immediately, to the extent that the authors suggest that a visitor would almost certainly have concluded that extreme aversive control was used to alter the children's behavior. The sight of the alteration of good learning behaviors and planned bedlam has always seemed amusing, but an imaginative study like this has a number of things to suggest for itself: (1) it worked!, (2) the children were their own reinforcers, (3) nothing aversive was ever used, and (4) the teacher was not afraid to deviate from our excessive belief in the doctrine that children should be passive, quiet, and docile in the classroom, that only on the playground could these behaviors be appropriately displayed.

Another unusual use of the Premack principle has been demonstrated by Mitchell and Stoffelmayr (1973), who worked with patients labeled schizophrenic and who had been hospitalized more than 15 years. Two of these individuals were extremely inactive, spending much of their time sitting. During morning work periods, they averaged working only 7% of the time, so a contingency was arranged so that units of work completed lead to free periods for sitting; i.e., a high probability behavior was made contingent upon a low probability behavior. At first each had to complete a portion of a unit while standing before being allowed to sit. Then a whole unit and finally several units had to be completed before sitting was allowed. This very simple procedure, based on the Premack principle, was extraordinarily effective, changing work behavior to 80% of the time for one person and to 90% of the time for the other, and thus changing essentially inactive persons to active persons for this period. A similarly different approach was offered by Lewinsohn, Weinstein, and Shaw (1969), who worked with depressed patients, who virtually by definition have few sources of reinforcement available to them. They do, however, often engage in "depressed" talking at high rates, and that behavior could be established as a contingency for low rate and socially important behaviors. When high-rate depressed conversation was made contingent on important career-related behaviors, the important behaviors increased.

Holt (1971) used this system in working with academic behavior of two retarded persons described as hyperactive and nonattentive. The behaviors of the individuals were observed for 23 hours, and the high-rate behaviors selected were coloring, cutting out, playing with dolls, and embroidering. The students were then told that when they completed a particular task they would be able to go to an adjoining room for 5 minutes to engage in the activity of their choice. The materials used included various first- through sixth-grade reading books and mathematics problems from the Science Research Associates programmed arithmetic series. The data collected to determine whether access to play time would increase academic behavior were different from the others discussed. The duration of responding was measured during baseline and during the period of the contingency. The response was "solving with 90% accuracy all problems on two pages of the SRA program, or reading with 90% accuracy two pages of the text materials." If the student did not meet the criterion, she repeated the task until she met criterion, so the measure was of how long responding occurred before it met criterion. The results for both students were similar and quite successful. During baseline, the students averaged 28 minutes to complete the reading and mathematics tasks, spending much of their time engaged in "hyperactive" and nonattending behaviors. But during the period of contingent free time for those activities, the time decreased to an average of 8 minutes, with most of this time being spent on-task. This was truly a remarkable change that cost nothing in terms of extra materials or teacher time. In addition, other related behaviors changed. When the program began, the students took about three-quarters of a minute to go from the classroom to the adjoining room and about the same length of time to return from that room to the task area. But as the days passed, this time decreased to about one-quarter of a minute, indicating a substantial decrease in dawdling behavior and an observable increase in interest in completing academic tasks. This series of alternating access to high-probability behaviors contingent upon completing academic tasks seems to be an extraordinarily easy plan that could be incorporated in almost any learning situation. The tasks may vary, the initially high-probability behaviors would vary, but the system of making the latter contingent upon criterion performance of the former could easily transfer across situations.

Access to free time is often used as a reinforcer and can sometimes be synonymous with the Premack principle. When the free time allows or provides materials for high-probability behavior, it can be an example of this principle. When it does not allow these behaviors to occur, free time may be simply a rest period or, for some students, a period of boredom. Busse and Henderson (1972) used free time as a consequence in a public junior high school special education class for educably mentally retarded students. The 13 students in the class had an academic history of low rates of performing reading responses, so this was the behavior that was consequated. Reading materials were from the *Webster New Practice Readers* (Grover, Kinkead, Anderson, Stone, & Burton, 1960), and the students reading progress was measured in two ways: (1) scores on the *Iowa Silent Reading Tests*. Elementary Edition (Greene & Kelley, 1942), and (2) each individual's daily rate of correct and incorrect reading. The rate correct formed the basic data for the study and was based on each student's oral and written responses. Each child was required to read orally 10 sentences in each day's assignment. The number of correctly read words was divided by the time required to read the words, resulting in a measure of rate correct. Written responses included writing letters, writing words, circling the correct words, and underlining the appropriate word or sentence. During baseline, the rates of correct reading and writing responses were recorded, but no external contingencies were in effect. During treatment, however, the students were told that they could earn more than their usual 5 minutes of free time by increasing their daily reading rate. Free time was defined as a period during which students could work at a number of activities presented to them. These activities contained a good sample that could be considered high-rate behaviors, and included sets, puzzles, mosaic works, card games, chess, checkers, carom boards for playing games like pool and bowling, an electric football game, leather-craft materials to make belts, purses, billfolds, and knife sheaths, a record player, records, headphone set, and a film-strip viewer. The list of items allowed the teacher to solve the problem of satiation and of changing interests in activities. The students were told during the treatment phase the importance of being correct and careful in their work, that their graphs of reading rates would be posted to give them feedback, and that each could earn extra minutes of free time according to increases over their individualized baselines. The teacher added a daily rate expectation chart that clearly indicated to each child what his or her performance could earn. The chart consisted of each student's name and how many minutes of free time

Subject	Baseline Mean	Reinforcement Mean
A	60	140*
B	62	125
C	31	86
D	50	89
E	70	145*
F	60	130
G	53	150*
H	29	101*
I	69	230*
J	57	150*
K	39	99
L	39	82
M	52	175*

*Material increased one grade level in difficulty.

Figure 7-5. The individual overall increases in daily reading rates for each of the students described in the study by Busse and Henderson, 1972, p. 72.

are available for each student's rate of correct reading. The determination of each day's requirement allowed for individual changes as it was based on the previous day's rate. This continuing change in criterion is an excellent way to avoid rigid criteria that do not allow for changes in reading materials and continued changes in successful performance.

Figure 7-5 shows for each individual the change in reading rate from baseline to reinforcement. The changes in response rate are absolutely remarkable as are the changes in achievement scores measured by the *Iowa Silent Reading Tests*. At baseline, the students were reading at a grade placement score of 3.98, but during the program they were reading at a mean grade placement of 5.18. For these students, who normally did not gain one year in reading level for each year in school, the reinforcement program increased their reading achievement scores by more than one grade in about one-third of a year. In addition, increases in daily reading rate did not decrease comprehension; the number of comprehension questions answered incorrectly during baseline and reinforcement did not vary. Seven of the 13 students were then placed in a regular reading class appropriate for their grade level, and all seven did quite well in the new setting according to the regular class teachers. The utilization of behavioral principles in a manner like this is really the essence of mainstreaming programs, i.e., preparing individuals for entry into a less restricted and restrictive program by increasing their skills in deficit areas.

SUMMARY

In this chapter, we discussed the definitions of positive and negative reinforcement and provide examples of each. From that section, you should be able to differentiate between reinforcement and reinforcers, both positive and negative, and you should be able to identify when reinforcers are and are not being used. In the next section, we discussed types of reinforcers. From this section, you should be able to identify these types and, more importantly, you should use the examples provided as sources for possible use in your programs.

In the next chapter, we will present 11 means by which we can use reinforcers effectively. This is an important section for practical use, and you should combine the information from that chapter with the information from this chapter so that you can more effectively motivate the retarded students that you are teaching.

REFERENCES

Ardrey, R. *The territorial imperative.* New York: Atheneum, 1966.

Axelrod, S. Token reinforcement program in special classes. *Exceptional Children*, 1971, **37**, 371-379.

Ayllon, T., & Azrin, N. H. *The token economy: A motivational system for therapy and rehabilitation.* New York: Appleton-Century-Crofts, Inc., 1968.

Ayllon, T., & Haughton, E. Control of the behavior of schizophrenic patients by food. *Journal of the Experimental Analysis of Behavior*, 1962, **5**, 343-352.

Bachrach, A. J., Erwin, W. J., & Mohr, J. P. The control of eating behavior in an anorexic by operant conditioning techniques. In L. Ullmann and L. P. Krasner (Eds.), *Case studies in behavior modification.* New York: Holt, Rinehart and Winston, Inc., 1965.

Bailey, J., & Meyerson, L. Vibration as a reinforcer with a profoundly retarded child. *Journal of Applied Behavior Analysis*, 1969, **2**, 135-137.

Bailey, J., & Meyerson, L. Effect of vibratory stimulation on a retardate's self-injurious behavior. *Psychological Aspects of Disabilities*, 1970, **17**(3), 133-137.

Ball, T. S. Comments: Blindism. In T. S. Ball (Ed.), *A guide for the instruction and training of the profoundly retarded and severely multihandicapped child.* Santa Cruz, Ca: Santa Cruz County Office of Education, 1971.

Ball, T. S., McCrady, R. E., & Hart, A. D. Automated reinforcement of head posture in two cerebral palsied retarded children. *Perceptual and Motor Skills*, 1975, **40**, 619-622.

Bijou, S. W., Birnbrauer, J. S., Kidder, J. D., & Tague, C. E. Programmed instruction as an approach to teaching of reading, writing and arithmetic to retarded children. *Psychological Record*, 1966, **16**, 505-522.

Birnbrauer, J. S., & Lawler, J. Token reinforcement for learning. *Mental Retardation*, 1964, **2**, 275-279.

Birnbrauer, J. S., Wolf, M. M., Kidder, J., & Tague, C. E. Classroom behavior of retarded pupils with token reinforcement. *Journal of Experimental Child Psychology*, 1965, **2**, 219-235.

Broden, M., Bruce, C., Mitchell, M. A., Carter, V., & Hall, R. V. Effects of teacher attention on attending behavior of two boys at adjacent desks. *Journal of Applied Behavior Analysis*, 1970, **3**, 199-203.

Brown, L., Van Deventer, P., Perlmutter, L., Jones, S., & Sontag, E. Effects of consequences on production rates of trainable retarded and severely emotionally disturbed students in a public school workshop. *Education and Training of the Mentally Retarded*, 1972, **7**, 74-81.

Busse, L. L., & Henderson, H. S. Effects of contingency management upon reading achievement of junior high educable mentally retarded students. *Education and Training of the Mentally Retarded*, 1972, **7**, 67-73.

Chandler, L. S., & Adams, M. A. Multiply handicapped child motivated for ambulation through behavior modification. *Physical Therapy*, 1972, **5**, 399-401.

Colman, R. S., Frankel, F., Ritvo, E., & Freeman, B. J. The effects of fluorescent and incandescent illumination upon repetitive behaviors in autistic children. *Journal of Autism and Childhood Schizophrenia*, in press.

Cowles, J. T. Food-tokens as incentives for learning by chimpanzees. *Comparative Psychology Monograph*, 1937, **14** (5, Series No. 71).

Doughty, N. R. An inexpensive electro-mechanically operated chair for the delivery of vibratory stimulation. Cambridge Area Developmental Rehabilitation and Education Center, Cambridge, MN, 1976.

Foxx, R. M. Social reinforcement of weight reduction: A case report on an obese retarded adolescent. *Mental Retardtion*, 1972, **10**(4), 21-23.

Girardeau, F. L., & Spradlin, J. E. Token rewards in a cottage program. *Mental Retardation*, 1964, **2**, 345-351.

Gray, R. M., & Kasteler, J. M. The effects of social reinforcement and training on institutionalized mentally retarded children. *American Journal of Mental Deficiency*, 1969, **74**, 50-56.

Greene, H. A., & Kelley, V. H. *Iowa silent reading tests*. New York: Harcourt Brace Jovanovitch, 1942.

Greene, R. J., & Hoats, D. L. Reinforcing capabilities of television distortion. *Journal of Applied Behavior Analysis*, 1969, **2**, 139-141.

Grot, J., & Randolph, R. The effects of grouping on aggressive behavior among profoundly retarded adult males. Paper presented at a meeting of the American Association on Mental Deficiency, 1975.

Grover, C., Kinkead, E., Anderson, D., Stone, C., &Burton, A. *Webster's new practice readers*. New York: McGraw-Hill Book Co., 1960.

Hall, R. V., Lund, D., & Jackson, D. Effects of teacher attention on study behavior. *Journal of Applied Behavior Analysis*, 1968, **1**, 1-12.

Hall, R. V., Panyan, M., Rabon, D., & Broden, M. Instructing beginning teachers in reinforcement procedures which improve classroom control. *Journal of Applied Behavior Analysis*, 1968, **1**, 315-322.

Herbert, E. W., Pinkston, E. M., Hayden, M. L., Sajwaj, T. E., Pinkston, E. M., Cordua, G., & Jackson, C. Adverse effects of differential parental attention. *Journal of Applied Behavior Analysis*, 1973, **6**, 15-30.

Holt, G. L. Systematic probability reversal and control of behavior through reinforcement menus. *Psychological Record*, 1971, **21**, 465-469.

Homme, L. E., deBaca, P. C., Devine, J. V., Steinhorst, R., & Rickert, E. J. Use of the Premack principle in controlling the behavior of nursery school children. *Journal of Exerimental Analysis of Behavior*, 1963, **6**, 544.

Hopkins, B. L. Effects of candy and social reinforcement, instructions, and reinforcement schedule learning on the modification and maintenance of smiling. *Journal of Applied Behavior Analysis*, 1968, **1**, 121-129.

Horner, R. D. Establishing use of crutches by a mentally retarded spina bifida child. *Journal of Applied Behavior Analysis*, 1971, **4**, 183-189.

Hunt, J. G., Fitzhugh, L. C., & Fitzhugh, K. B. Teaching "exit-ward" patients appropriate personal appearance by using reinforcement techniques. *American Journal of Mental Deficiency*, 1968, 73, 41-45.

Jens, K. E., & Shores, R. E. Behavioral graphs as reinforcers for work behavior of mentally retarded adolescents. *Education and Training of the Mentally Retarded*, 1969, 4, 21-28.

Kazdin, A. E. The effect of response cost in suppressing behavior in a prepsychotic retardate. *Journal of Behavior Therapy and Experimental Psychiatry*, 1971, 2, 137-140.

Kazdin, A. E. *Behavior modification in applied settings*. Homewood, IL: Dorsey Press, 1975.

Kazdin, A. E., & Craighead, W. E. Behavior modification in special education. In L. Mann and D. A. Sabatino (Eds.), *The first review of special education*, Vol. 2. Philadelphia: Buttonwood Farms, 1973.

Kazdin, A. E., & Klock, J. The effect of nonverbal teacher approval on student attentive behavior. *Journal of Applied Behavior Analysis*, 1973, 6, 643-654.

Keilitz, I., Tucker, D. J., & Horner, R. D. Increasing mentally retarded adolescents' verbalizations about current events. *Journal of Applied Behavior Analysis*, 1973, 6, 621-630.

Lauten, M. H., & Birnbrauer, J. S. The efficacy of "right" as a function of its relationship with reinforcement. *Journal of Experimental Child Psychology*, 1974, 18, 159-166.

Lent, J. R. A demonstration program for intensive training of institutionalized mentally retarded girls. Progress report, January 1967, U.S. Department of Health, Education, and Welfare.

Lent, J. R. Mimosa Cottage: Experiment in hope. *Psychology Today*, 1968, 2(1), 50-58.

Lewinsohn, P. M., Weinstein, M., & Shaw, D. Depression: A clinical research approach. In R. D. Rubin and C. M. Frank (Eds.), *Advances in behavior therapy*. New York: Academic Press, Inc., 1969.

Lindsley, O. R. Conjugate reinforcement. Paper presented at the meeting of the American Psychological Association, 1961.

Lorenz, K. *On aggression*. New York: Harcourt Brace Jovanovitch, 1966.

Mitchell, W. S., & Stoffelmayr, B. E. Application of the Premack principle to the behavioral control of extremely inactive schizophrenics. *Journal of Applied Behavior Analysis*, 1973, 6, 419-424.

Morris, R. J., & Dolker, M. Developing cooperative play in socially withdrawn retarded children. *Mental Retardation*, 1974, 12, 24-27.

Nunes, D. L., Murphy, R. J., & Ruprecht, M. L. Reducing self-injurious behavior of severely retarded individuals through withdrawal of reinforcement procedures. *Behavior Modification*, 1977, 1, 499-516.

Ohwaki, S., Brahlek, J. A., & Stayton, S. E. Preference for vibratory and visual stimulation in mentally retarded children. *American Journal of Mental Deficiency*, 1973, 77, 733-736.

O'Leary, K. D., Becker, W. C., Evans, M. B., & Saudargas, R. A. A token reinforcement program in a public school: A replication and systematic analysis. *Journal of Applied Behavior Analysis*, 1969, 2, 3-13.

O'Leary, K. D., & Drabman, R. Token reinforcement programs in the classroom: A review. *Psychological Bulletin*, 1971, 75, 379-398.

Panda, K. C., & Lynch, W. W. Effects of social reinforcement on the retarded child: A review and interpretation for classroom instruction. *Education and Training of the Mentally Retarded*, 1972, **7**, 115-123.

Patterson, G. R., Cobb, J. A., & Ray, R. S. Direct intervention in the classroom: A set of procedures for the aggressive child. In F. W. Clark, D. R. Evans, & L. A. Hamerlynck (Eds.), *Implementing behavioral programs for schools and clinics: The proceedings of the third Banff International Conference on Behavior Modification.* Champaign, IL: Research Press, 1972.

Peine, H. A., Gregerson, G. F., & Sloane, H. N. A program to increase vocabulary and spontaneous speech. *Mental Retardation*, 1970, **8**, 38-44.

Perline, I., & Levinsky, D. Controlling maladaptive classroom behavior in the severely retarded. *American Journal of Mental Deficiency*, 1968, **73**, 74-78.

Peterson, R. A., & McIntosch, E. I. Teaching tricycle riding. *Mental Retardation*, 1973, **11**, 32-34.

Poluck, R. J., & Esser, A. H. Controlled experimental modification of aggressive behavior in territories of severely retarded boys. *American Journal of Mental Deficiency*, 1971, **76**, 23-29.

Premack, D. Toward empirical behavior laws: I. Postive reinforcement. *Psychological Review*, 1959, **66**, 218-233.

Ray, E. T., & Shelton, J. T. The use of operant conditioning with disturbed adolescent retarded boys. Paper presented at the 20th Mental Hospital Institute, Washington, D.C., 1968.

Rehagen, N. J., & Thelan, M. H. Vibration as positive reinforcement for retarded children. *Journal of Abnormal Psychology*, 1972, **80**, 162-167

Rynders, J. E., & Friedlander, B. J. Preferences in institutionalized severely retarded children for selected visual stimulus material presented as operant reinforcement. *American Journal of Mental Deficiency*, 1972, **5**, 568-573.

Salzberg, B. H., Wheeler, A. A., Devar, L. T., & Hopkins, B. L. The effect of intermittent feedback and intermittent contingent access to play on printing of kindergarten children. *Journal of Applied Behavior Analysis*, 1971, 4, 163-171.

Samaras, M. S., & Ball, T. S. Reinforcement of cooperation between profoundly retarded adults. *American Journal of Mental Deficiency*, 1975, **80**, 63-71.

Schaeffer, H., & Martin, P. L. *Behavior therapy.* New York: McGraw-Hill Book Co., *Analysis of Behavior*, 1960, 3, 160.

Schaeffer, H., & Martin, P. L. *Behavior therapy.* New York: McGraw-Hill Book Co., 1969.

Screven, C. G., & LaFond, R. J. An application of an avoidance procedure to a sheltered workshop. *Psychological Record*, 1973, **23**, 13-16.

Spiro S. H., & Shook, G. Reduction of long latency verbal responding in a multiply handicapped adolescent utilizing an avoidance positive reinforcement procedure. *Psychological Record*, 1973, **23**, 383-389.

Staats, A. W. A general apparatus for the investigation of complex learning in children. *Behavior Research and Therapy*, 1968, **6**, 45-50.

Staats, A. W., Minke, K. A., Finley, J. R., Wolf, M. M., & Brooks, L. O. A reinforcer system and experimental procedure for the laboratory study of reading acquisition. *Child Development*, 1964, **35**, 209-231.

Staats, A. W., Staats, C. K., Schultz, R. E., & Wolf, M. The conditioning of textual responses using "extrinsic" reinforcers. *Journal of the Experimental Analysis of Behavior*, 1962, **5**, 33-40.

Stolz, S. B., & Wolf, M. M. Visually discriminated behavior in a "blind" adolescent retardate. *Journal of Applied Behavior Analysis*, 1969, **2**, 65-77.

Thomas, D. R., Becker, W. C., & Armstrong, M. Production and elimination of disruptive classroom behavior by systematically varying teacher's behavior. *Journal of Applied Behavior Analysis*, 1968, **1**, 35-45.

Wahler, R. G. Oppositional children: A quest for reinforcement control. *Journal of Applied Behavior Analysis*, 1969, **2**, 159-170.

Wahler, R. G., Winkel, G. H., Peterson, R. F., & Morrison, D. C. Mothers as behavior therapists for their own children. *Behaviour Research and Therapy*, 1965, **3**, 113-124.

Walker, H., & Buckley, N. K. Investigation of some classroom control parameters as a function of teacher dispensed social reinforcers. *Journal of Applied Behavior Analysis*, 1971, **5**, 209-224.

Werry, J. S., & Quay, H. Observing the classroom behavior of elementary school children. Paper presented at the Meeting of the Council on Exceptional Children, 1968.

Wiesen, A. E., Hartley, G., Richardson, C., & Roske, A. The retarded child as a reinforcing agent. *Journal of Experimental Child Psychology*, 1967, **5**, 109-113.

Wolfe, J. B. Effectiveness of token rewards for chimpanzees. *Comparative Psychology Monograph*, 1936, **11** (5, Series No. 60).

Zimmerman, E. H., Zimmerman, J., & Russell, C. D. Differential effects of token reinforcement on instruction-following behavior in retarded students instruction as a group. *Journal of Applied Behavior Analysis*, 1969, **2**, 101-112.

Zimmerman, J., Stuckey, T. E., Garlick, B. J., & Miller, J. Effects of token reinforcement on productivity in multiply handicapped clients in a sheltered workshop. *Rehabilitation Literature*, 1969, **30**, 34-41.

8

The Effective Use of Reinforcers in Reinforcement Programs

The previous chapter described seven types of reinforcers and, in so doing, made occasional suggestions about how to use reinforcers to maximize their effectiveness. In this chapter, several of those suggestions will be restated and amplified while a number of other suggestions will be made. Many of these are not restricted just to reinforcement programs of the type discussed here, but are relevant to a number of teaching and maintenance programs.

SELECTING REINFORCERS

There are a number of ways to select potential reinforcers. One is to observe how a student does throughout various periods of the week to determine whether there are any high-rate or high-interest behaviors that could be used in the Premack paradigm. Another is simply to ask the student, an approach which is too often ignored. The student could be asked to list a number of activities or events that she or he believes would be worth working for in class to earn. We, of course, have to be aware of one very important consideration; what we say we will do and what we actually do are not necessarily the same, in fact, they are often not (to wit: the venerable New Year's resolution). Again, reinforcers are portions of the environment that demonstrate a functional relationship with behavior; they increase or later maintain responding. But asking the client's help in selecting potential reinforcers is a good starting point, and several reinforcement surveys have been developed to help the instructor. Cautela and Kastenbaum (1967) developed the *Reinforcement Survey Schedule* primarily to deal with populations in a clinical situation, but there is no reason that a good portion of it could not be adopted for our use, particularly with retarded individuals functioning in the mild range of retardation. The schedule is divided into four sections. The first consists of items that can be presented to the person, such as edibles and beverages. Section II consists of items that for the most part can only be presented through facsimile or imagination. The third section differs from the other two in that it presents situations, rather than discrete activities or objects, and asks how one would react in these situations. The last section asks the individual to list things he or she does or thinks about fairly frequently, and it is an attempt to list behaviors to be used in accord with the Premack principle. Sections I and II could be helpful in determining preferences for some of our students; they are represented in Figure 8-1 (see pp. 216-221). The student is simply asked to respond to questions about how much each of the items might be pleasurable. When the sections are completed, the teachers should have several alternatives from which to select those that are most appropriate for that particular learning environment.

A similar approach has been taken by Rotatori and Switzky (1977), who developed the *Reinforcement Survey Hierarchy* for severely and for profoundly retarded students. The survey employs 11 reinforcement categories and uses an indirect preference technique by asking parents and teachers to rate each category according to the degree to which they believe the student would like that event. The information can then be used by the instructor as a basis for choosing possible reinforcers. Figure 8-2 (see pp. 222-223) contains the survey, which can be adapted for students functioning at levels higher than the severely or profoundly retarded level the authors suggest.

IMMEDIACY

One suggestion for effective use of reinforcers has been documented so often and so reliably in basic research that it has come to be known as a *principle;* it is that immediate delivery of the reinforcer is more effective than delayed delivery of the reinforcer. The basic reason for this phenomenon has been discussed by Reynolds (1968), who sugested that

> delayed reinforcement is not as effective as immediate reinforcement, partially because it allows the organism to emit additional behavior between the response we wish to reinforce and the actual occurrence of the reinforcer; thus, the intervening behavior is also reinforced, with the result that what is reinforced is the response followed by some other behavior rather than just the response alone. (1968, p. 29)

REINFORCEMENT SURVEY SCHEDULE

The items in this questionnaire refer to things and experiences that may give joy or other pleasurable feelings. Check each item in the column that describes how much pleasure it gives you nowadays.

	Not at All	A Little	A Fair Amount	Much	Very Much

Section I

1. Eating
   a. Ice cream
   b. Candy
   c. Fruit
   d. Pastry
   e. Nuts
   f. Cookies
2. Beverages
   a. Water
   b. Milk
   c. Soft drink
   d. Tea
   e. Coffee
3. Alcoholic beverages
   a. Beer
   b. Wine
   c. Hard liquor
4. Beautiful women
5. Handsome men
6. Solving Problems
   a. Crossword puzzles
   b. Mathematical problems
   c. Figuring out how something works

Figure 8-1. Sections I and II of the Reinforcement Survey Schedule developed by Cautela and Kastenbaum. 1967. pp. 1118-1121.

	Not at All	A Little	A Fair Amount	Much	Very Much
7. Listening to music					
a. Classical					
b. Western country					
c. Jazz					
d. Show tunes					
e. Rhythm & blues					
f. Rock & roll					
g. Folk					
h. Popular					
8. Animals					
a. Dogs					
b. Cats					
c. Horses					
d. Birds					

Section II

	Not at All	A Little	A Fair Amount	Much	Very Much
9. Watching sports					
a. Football					
b. Baseball					
c. Basketball					
d. Track					
e. Golf					
f. Swimming					
g. Running					
h. Tennis					
i. Pool					
j. Other					
10. Reading					
a. Adventure					
b. Mystery					

Figure 8-1. Continued.

	Not at All	A Little	A Fair Amount	Much	Very Much
c. Famous people					
d. Poetry					
e. Travel					
f. True confessions					
g. Politics & history					
h. How to-do-it					
i. Humor					
j. Comic books					
k. Love stories					
l. Spiritual					
m. Sexy					
n. Sports					
o. Medicine					
p. Science					
q. Newspapers					
11. Looking at interesting buildings					
12. Looking at beautiful scenery					
13. T.V., movies or radio					
14. Like to sing					
a. Alone					
b. With others					
15. Like to dance					
a. Ballroom					
b. Discotheque					
c. Ballet or interpretive					
d. Square dancing					
e. Folk dancing					
16. Performing on a musical instrument					
17. Playing sports					
a. Football					
b. Baseball					

Figure 8-1. Continued.

	Not at All	A Little	A Fair Amount	Much	Very Much
c. Basketball	___	___	___	___	___
d. Track & field	___	___	___	___	___
e. Golf	___	___	___	___	___
f. Swimming	___	___	___	___	___
g. Running	___	___	___	___	___
h. Tennis	___	___	___	___	___
i. Pool	___	___	___	___	___
j. Boxing	___	___	___	___	___
k. Judo or karate	___	___	___	___	___
l. Fishing	___	___	___	___	___
m. Skin-diving	___	___	___	___	___
n. Auto or cycle racing	___	___	___	___	___
o. Hunting	___	___	___	___	___
p. Skiing	___	___	___	___	___
18. Shopping					
a. Clothes	___	___	___	___	___
b. Furniture	___	___	___	___	___
c. Auto parts & supply	___	___	___	___	___
d. Appliances	___	___	___	___	___
e. Food	___	___	___	___	___
f. New car	___	___	___	___	___
g. New place to live	___	___	___	___	___
h. Sports equipment	___	___	___	___	___
19. Gardening	___	___	___	___	___
20. Playing cards	___	___	___	___	___
21. Hiking or walking	___	___	___	___	___
22. Completing a difficult job	___	___	___	___	___
23. Camping	___	___	___	___	___
24. Sleeping	___	___	___	___	___
25. Taking a bath	___	___	___	___	___

Figure 8-1. Continued.

	Not at All	A Little	A Fair Amount	Much	Very Much
26. Taking a shower					
27. Being right					
a. Guessing what somebody is going to do					
b. In an argument					
c. About your work					
d. On a bet					
28. Being praised					
a. About your appearance					
b. About your work					
c. About your hobbies					
d. About your physical strength					
e. About your athletic ability					
f. About your mind					
g. About your personality					
h. About your moral strength					
i. About your understanding of others					
29. Having people seek you out for company					
30. Flirting					
31. Having somebody flirt with you					
32. Talking with people who like you					
33. Making somebody happy					
34. Babies					
35. Children					
36. Old men					
37. Old women					
38. Having people ask your advice					
39. Watching other people					
40. Somebody smiling at you					

Figure 8-1. Continued.

	Not at All	A Little	A Fair Amount	Much	Very Much
41. Making love	___	___	___	___	___
42. Happy people	___	___	___	___	___
43. Being close to an attractive man	___	___	___	___	___
44. Being close to an attractive woman	___	___	___	___	___
45. Talking about the opposite sex	___	___	___	___	___
46. Talking to friends	___	___	___	___	___
47. Being perfect	___	___	___	___	___
48. Winning a bet	___	___	___	___	___
49. Being in church or temple	___	___	___	___	___
50. Saying prayers	___	___	___	___	___
51. Having somebody pray for you	___	___	___	___	___
52. Peace and quiet	___	___	___	___	___

Section III—Situations I Would Like To Be In

How much would you enjoy being in each of the following situations?

1. You have just completed a difficult job. Your superior comes by and praises you highly for "a job well done." He also makes it clear that such good work is going to be rewarded very soon.

   not at all ( )   a little ( )   a fair amount ( )   much ( )   very much ( )

2. You are at a lively party. Somebody walks across the room to you, smiles in a friendly way, and says, "I'm glad to meet you. I've heard so many good things about you. Do you have a moment to talk?"

   not at all ( )   a little ( )   a fair amount ( )   much ( )   very much ( )

3. You have just led your team to victory. An old friend comes over and says, "You played a terrific game. Let me treat you to dinner and drinks."

   not at all ( )   a little ( )   a fair amount ( )   much ( )   very much ( )

Figure 8-1. Continued.

REINFORCEMENT SURVEY HIERARCHY FOR
SEVERELY AND PROFOUNDLY MENTALLY RETARDED INDIVIDUALS

Name _____ Date of Birth _____

Age _____ Date Completed _____

Rater _____

Relationship _____

Intelligence Test Data

Name	Date of Test	I.Q.	M.A.
_____	_____	_____	_____
_____	_____	_____	_____

Please rate each item in regard to how much pleasure you feel the individual being rated receives, using the below listed point scale.

1-none 2-same 3-a fair amount 4-much 5-very much N.O.-no opportunity

I. Eating of
1. potato chips _____
2. fruit _____
3. dry, sweet cereal _____
4. sweet candy _____
5. M&M's _____
6. cookies _____
7. pudding _____
8. ice cream _____
9. raisins _____
10. applesauce _____
11. cake _____
12. lollipops _____
13. pickles _____
14. pretzels _____
15. chewing gum _____
16. popsicles _____
17. olives _____
18. buttered bread _____
19. graham crackers _____
20. pastries _____

II. Drinking of
21. juice _____
22. Kool-Aid _____
23. white milk _____
24. chocolate milk _____
25. sucking ice _____
26. lemonade _____
27. coffee _____
28. sweet carbonated water _____
29. soft drink _____

III. Listening to
30. radio
  1. rock n' roll _____
  2. country western _____
  3. show tunes _____
31. TV _____
32. sing-along _____
33. story telling _____
34. tape of own voice _____

35. music box _____
36. tape of student-made noise _____
37. musical mobile _____
38. records
  1. Sesame Street _____
  2. movement records _____
39. rhythm instruments _____
40. musical instruments _____
41. nursery rhymes _____
42. noise-maker _____
43. bells _____
44. clocks or watches _____

IV. Looking at
45. view master _____
46. catalogs _____
47. flashing lights _____
48. kaleidoscope _____
49. colored cellophane _____
50. show 'n' tell _____
51. lights _____
52. magazines _____
53. looking out window _____
54. bright colors _____
55. mobiles _____
56. shining objects _____
57. flashlights _____
58. faces _____
59. films
  1. cartoon _____
  2. nature scenes _____
  3. animal _____
  4. home movies of children in class _____
60. TV _____
61. Picture books _____
62. mirror _____
63. pictures of self _____
64. shadow box _____

V. Playing with/on/in

65. moon-walk _____
66. piano _____
67. puzzles _____
68. clay, putty _____
69. water (soap suds) _____
70. sandbox _____
71. dress-up clothes _____
72. scotch tape _____
73. drum _____
74. wearing jewelry _____
75. rocking horse _____
76. flashlights _____
77. finger puppets _____
78. stacking towers _____
79. rhythm instruments _____
80. water bed _____
81. swinging in net _____
82. toys
   1. pop-up _____
   2. stuffed animals _____
   3. blocks _____
   4. rattles _____
   5. beads, necklaces _____
   6. slinky _____
   7. musical _____
   8. push-up toys _____
   9. rings and pole _____
  10. dolls _____
  11. cars _____
83. straws _____
84. balloons _____
85. crayon and paper _____

VI. Academic activities

86. coloring book _____
87. pasting pictures in scrapbook _____
88. watering classroom plants _____
89. running errands _____
90. taking pictures with camera _____
91. drawing on black-board _____
92. painting with brush _____
93. drawing _____
94. scribbling _____
95. marking attendance on blackboard _____
96. teacher's helper (holding things) _____
97. finger painting _____

VII. Home living-area chore activities

98. pushing mop across floor _____
99. sweeping with broom _____
100. running vacuum cleaner _____
101. watering plants _____
102. rearranging furniture _____
103. dusting with mop _____
104. dusting with cloth _____
105. feeding fish _____

106. wheeling a food cart _____
107. clearing off carts _____
108. wiping tables _____

VIII. Touching/feeling of

109. pat on back _____
110. holding hands _____
111. wet sponges _____
112. texture boxes _____
113. clay _____
114. colored water _____
115. pet animals _____
116. wet paint _____
117. cooking dough _____
118. fur squares _____
119. moisture cream _____
120. Astro Turf rugs _____
121. patty cake _____
122. felt objects _____
123. squeeze soft toys _____
124. string _____
125. towels _____
126. sheets _____
127. vibrating objects _____
128. brushes _____
129. carpets _____
130. stroking by person _____

IX. Social

131. verbal praise _____
132. physical contact _____

133. medals, ribbons, plaque _____
134. first in line _____
135. hug _____
136. applause _____
137. being carried piggy-back _____
138. rough housing _____
139. tickling _____
140. hide n' seek _____
141. kiss _____
142. sit on lap _____
143. being held _____
144. smiling _____
145. shaking hands _____
146. pat on back or head _____
147. laughing _____

X. Smelling of

148. perfume _____
149. hand lotion _____
150. soap _____
151. after shave _____

XI. High-frequency behaviors

152. rocking in chair _____
153. crinkling paper _____
154. flicking lights _____
155. mouthing objects _____
156. hand clapping _____

Figure 8-2. The Reinforcement Survey Hierarchy for Severely and Profoundly Retarded Individuals (Rotatori and Switzky, unpublished). Each item is to be rated by someone who knows the individual well, and the highest rated items can first be used as possible reinforcers in a program.

This effect is extremely important with retarded persons, and we would expect particularly so as the degree of functioning decreases and the link between the correct reponse and the reinforcer is difficult to bridge. Delivering reinforcement immediately after every response is certainly difficult at best, and usually disruptive. For example, if the reinforcing event is 5 minutes of free time, it cannot be delivered after every correct answer to arithmetic problems written on a sheet of paper.

To solve this apparent dilemma, three approaches are taken. The first is to build a *gradual delay* between the response and the contingent event. This operation can be done quite simply by beginning with immediate reinforcement, shifting to a short delay, and continuing to shift to successively larger delays. There are no formulas for selecting the successive interval sizes; those seem to be a function at least of the student, the behavior, the reinforcer, and competing responses in the student's repertoire. However, whether a shift is too great is very simple to determine. We need only look at a graph of the child's behavior; if it is not continuing at the same level as it previously was, then *one* reason could be that the increase in delay could have been too great (this, however, need not be *the* reason, as many other factors operate). If this is the case, we could simply shift back to the previous size, determining then whether behavior will recover its previous level. We must, however, be careful about backtracking in this as well as in other procedures we employ, for at this point we might have taught the student that the best way to avoid a continuing delay in reinforcement is by decreasing the quality and/or quantity of his or her work.

A second approach to the problem of instituting delays of reinforcement is to *bridge the time* between the response and the eventual reinforcer with a conditioned reinforcer, like praise or a token. The function of these kinds of stimuli, of being reinforcing while being nondisruptive, is quite important and is one reason that these kinds of reinforcers are so popular and so powerful in maintaining responding. Examples of this function are found in each of the studies involving tokens and in many of the studies involving social reinforcement.

A third approach is to *schedule* the relation between responding and reinforcement so that reinforcement does not occur each time a response does. Any arrangement between responding and reinforcers is called a schedule of reinforcement. It will be discussed briefly in the next section and more extensively in a later chapter.

SCHEDULES OF REINFORCEMENT

Schedules of reinforcement constitute a rule that describes the relation between responding and reinforcement. The rules describe this relationship in terms of time, or of number, or of time *and* number. The rules can be divided into two sections: reinforcement is *nonintermittent* or *intermittent*. Two examples of nonintermittent reinforcement are *continuous reinforcement* and *extinction*. In continuous reinforcement, every single response is reinforced. In extinction, no responses are reinforced, although previously in the person's history of learning at least some of these responses had been reinforced. Examples of intermittent reinforcement schedules would seem to be practically endless, but only a few have been studied. Some that have been were identified and discussed by Ferster and Skinner (1957) in a 739-page monumental book devoted solely to describing what happens to behavior when it is related to reinforcement in a certain way.

Without entering into an extended discussion of intermittent schedules, we can say that in teaching we should (1) often reinforce every response during the initial teaching trials, (2) gradually change so that not every response is reinforced, (3) increase the ratio between responding and reinforcement, (4) add a conditioned reinforcer if necessary to bridge the delay between responding and the terminal reinforcer, and (5) attend to data so that we can determine whether changes we have made have been too rapid. The ways in which these changes can be made, the effects of various schedules of reinforcement on behavior, and the ways we can change from one schedule to another will be discussed in Chapter 9.

NOVELTY

The arrangement of reinforcers that are either unusual, unexpected, or unavailable in other parts of the student's environment may be reinforcing solely because they are novel. A number of studies in basic research have shown that organisms will respond for novel situations. In our own lives, we certainly pay more for vacations to "different places" or for tickets to see novel or exceptional performers, and we do many things just to break our routine. Novelty itself can make a reinforcer even more effective than it would normally be. Such a program is described by Sulzer-Azaroff and Mayer (1977), who commented on the clever use of novelty in a classroom.

> A surprise box was prepared, with slips of paper containing all sorts of different directions: Draw a picture of a cow; wash the blackboard; get a drink of water; write a paragraph describing your pet; five minutes of free time; tutor a friend in reading, and so on. The students could draw slips from the box when they had completed their assignments. Not knowing what the slips might contain added lots of excitement to the game. (p. 137)

From their description, this program seemed successful, and the events seemed to be much more reinforcing than if they were expected. Such a program would seem to have a good chance of succeeding if the teacher were enthusiastic and made the game fun for the students, and if the teacher made sure that there were no disappointments.

Others have worked with novelty in a more formal sense to determine whether it did enhance reinforcing effectiveness. Zeaman and House (1963), in their brilliant discussion of the role of attention in learning by retarded persons, suggested that novelty was a highly discriminable dimension, that it enhanced the student's attention during learning tasks, and that it was a preferred dimension. The latter was supported by Dickerson and Girardeau (1970), who found that retarded persons preferred the novel stimulus when presented along with a series of identical stimuli. An interesting analog of this effect was discussed by Altman, Talkington, and Cleland (1971), who noted that the sometimes high rates of verbal encouragement and praise might make these events less reinforcing through overuse. The possibility of this effect is particularly evident when we notice that generally there are very few phrases or words we use as social reinforcers. For the most part, we probably use no more than a dozen at any significant rate while praising our students, choosing instead the stock ones such as "good," "that's great," "that pleases me," and "you're doing very well." To test their hypothesis, Altman *et al.* verbally praised students for completing the Sequin Form Board in one of two ways: either (1) with the adult next to the student, providing praise for his work, or (2) with the adult in the next room, looking at the student through a one-way mirror, and using the same praise statements but delivering them through a speaker recessed in the ceiling of the student's room. While we might expect that the latter's "impersonalized" delivery would be less reinforcing, it actually was more reinforcing than the traditional way. Presumably, this effect occurred because the speaker-delivery system was unique for these students.

This study should not at all be interpreted to mean that we should be delivering praise thorough a speaker system while situated in another room. It does mean, however, that we should take more care than we probably do to change our form of encouragement and praise. Words or phrases can be changed; inflections can be changed; students can be taught to cheer and clap for one another. There are many ways we can change our delivery so that what once was reinforcing either (1) does not lose its effectiveness or (2) can be made even more powerful through a novel presentation. This approach provides a few dilemmas for us, however. Some students have a very limited base for receptive language and cannot discriminate between a changed praise statement and other nonmeaningful words. On the one hand, we want consistency for the individuals in this population; but on the other hand, we know that novelty can possibly help them motivationally. Another dilemma is that by praising[1] students frequently, we are also reinforcing their behavior and providing them important feedback for correct responding. So while we are reducing the effectiveness of praise by repetition, we are probably providing valuable information that should increase correct responding and decrease errors. There are too many public school and institutional classrooms in which there is virtually no praise for correct responding and considerable attention for inappropriate (particularly social) behavior; they seem to be "dead" environments for learning, promoting nothing but ennui, and we certainly do not want the active classrooms to regress to that level. The option, then, appears to be for the teacher to attempt to arrange novel ways of providing feedback and reinforcement for students. Some of them can be traditional reinforcers, while others can even be silly events that would provide fun, laughter, and good breaks from on-task behavior.

SATIATION AND DEPRIVATION

Satiation and deprivation are phenomena that are generally synonymous with the absence or presence of novelty. *Satiation is the temporary decrease in performance due solely to the repeated presentation of the reinforcer. Depriva-*

---

[1] Praise is used as a consistent example in this discussion, but the same problems should hold for any other type of reinforcer.

tion refers to a temporary increase in the effectiveness of a reinforcer due solely to the passage of time since it last was present. Satiation and deprivation obviously affect the way we behave, particularly with respect to primary reinforcers like food, water, sex, and temperature. But these effects can also occur with conditioned reinforcers like praise or like tokens with inadequate backups. Some tokens such as money are generalized conditioned reinforcers, exchangeable for very large numbers of reinforcers. The value of tokens like these is that the person is generally never satiated, instead being in a deprivation state for something at any one time. For example, if we are interested in classical music and buy a number of records by Mozart, Haydn, Gluck and other composers of *classic* music, we may become satiated after listening to only them daily for a month. But we would not be satiated with regard to that generalized conditioned reinforcer money, so we could, in turn, buy and listen to recordings of *modern* composers like Gershwin, Copeland, or Britten; or we could listen to jazz by Davis, Coleman, or Brubeck; or we could listen to popular music. It is for this reason of maintaining deprivation that we use token systems with large numbers of backup reinforcers—the behavior of retarded persons in learning situations stands a better chance of being motivated at any particular time of learning.

The classic study in the applied use of satiation was done by Ayllon (1963), who worked with a psychiatric patient who hoarded towels in her room. The patient had been discouraged by the nurses from collecting the towels, but their entreatment seemed to have no effect. The only recourse appeared to be removing the towels from her room, a practice followed twice weekly by the nurses. To determine the extent of this problem, baseline data were collected for several weeks. These data showed that, despite the fact that the nurses kept removing the towels, 19 to 29 were in her room at the various times of counting. The routine of removing towels was then reversed; the nurses gave the patient a towel when the nurse was in her room, simply handing it to her without any comment. At first, she was given an average of seven towels per day, but by the third week she was being given 60 towels per week. When the number of towels reached 625 in her room, the patient stopped collecting them and began removing them herself. After they had been removed, she kept an average of 1.5 towels in her room at any time during the next 12 months while data were being collected. Although there was nothing funny about the difficulties associated with this patient's various problems, the slides Ayllon has of a relatively small bedroom with 625 towels are humorous and provide a rather dramatic indication of why this woman did become satiated.

Satiation is a phenomenon that may be most related in our work to the use of food as reinforcement. As Kazdin (1975) has discussed, the effectiveness of food as a reinforcer is directly related to the deprivation state of the individual. He goes on to note that

> the strength of food or another consumable as a reinforcer is maximized by depriving the individual. If the individual is not at least partially deprived, it may only serve as a weak reinforcer. [As such] . . ., many investigators sometimes use food reinforcement prior to mealtime or during mealtime itself (Barton, Guess, Garcia & Baer, 1970). In addition, light meals may be given throughout the day so that slight deprivation is maintained and food will be reinforcing continuously (O'Brien, Bugle & Azrin, 1971). Even if the individual is deprived of food before the training period, as training proceeds on a given day the reinforcing value of food may be

reduced. The number of times food can be delivered and the quantity delivered after a response are limited because of the possibility of satiation. To forestall satiation, some investigators have delivered small portions of the consumable item, such as a bite of food, a few pieces of popcorn, or half a cigarette (Ayllon & Azrin, 1968; Risley & Wolf, 1968). Nevertheless, food and consumables are still readily subject to satiation. (p. 116)

Kazdin's summary explains a number of the approaches we usually take while using reinforcers to motivate learning by retarded persons, and these include the following: (1) When consumables are necessary, deliver only small amounts at any one time; hence, you will find even M & M's broken into three or four pieces, or crackers broken into several pieces; (2) Alternate consumables to enhance their effectiveness; we are always surprised to see instructors just giving food or just giving soda. A more practical approach is to alternate bits of salty foods like potato chips with small amounts of soda. (3) Distribute the delivery of reinforcers over as much time as possible while still maintaining performance. (4) Substitute something else, like tokens, that will not lead to satiation so rapidly. (5) Increase the number of responses required for reinforcement. (6) Build conditioned reinforcers out of events, activities, attention, and other matters that are both more natural to the environment and less likely to produce satiation. (7) Allow the client when possible to choose a particular reinforcer for that day. Even if food is to be used, several types could be available for her or his choosing.

MOVE TO NATURAL REINFORCERS

Stressed throughout various sections has been the need to move to natural contingencies for the maintenance of behavior. Such efforts may take weeks or months, but they should be made. The overriding reason for this approach is that as the student moves from the present learning environment, he or she is less likely to find an artificial contingency in two consecutive environments than to find a natural contingency in two consecutive learning environments. This problem seems particularly pertinent with the present population, with which response building often takes so long, response maintenance is not so expected as it is with nonretarded people, and response reacquisition takes so much longer than with the nonretarded population. To this end, the goals of any program involving nonnatural reinforcers should be (1) to produce a behavior change that will allow the individual to live in a less restrictive environment, and (2) to eliminate the artificial contingencies such as food or tokens, replacing them with more natural contingencies such as praise that will allow behavior to continue in new environments.

The manner in which artificial reinforcers are replaced is analogous to the manner in which conditioned reinforcers are created. The natural event should initially be paired with the artificial event at every occurrence. Then the artificial one should be presented intermittently, perhaps every other time, while the natural event continues to occur each time. Then the intermittency is altered so that the artificial event occurs fewer and fewer times. Finally, this event is eliminated altogether. Such a program may not, however, be so automatic as it might seem. Suppose, for example, that you are now using candy as a reinforcer, believe that praise should be used, and have four weeks before this student moves to another classroom in which only teacher attention is used to motivate students. So a plan of fading out the candy over the next two weeks is designed, leaving two weeks with only praise in use. But what if praise cannot be developed as a conditioned reinforcer either in that time or at all? There would not be sufficient time to try other alternatives. Plans then should be made well ahead of anticipated times of student movement to incorporate natural contingencies, allowing time to select among the most effective of the various natural reinforcers available.

Perhaps the ultimate in natural contingencies can be arranged through self-control[2] in which a person determines whether or not he or she is doing something, keeps a record of these observations, and maintains improved behavior solely because of the feedback itself. There is a considerable amount of study being done on self-control, but the persons involved are not generally mentally retarded. There are, however, a few presumptions that we can make that have been demonstrated in other areas. One is that feedback may be insufficiently reinforcing to produce behavior change. In this case, we may first have to combine it with something presently reinforcing, which would then be faded out of the environment. Another is that feedback may not be sufficient to maintain behavior change once the appropriate level has been achieved. In this case, social attention, special events, and so forth can be arranged intermittently. While this type of program would not be self-control in the strictest sense, trying to operate an environment without other sources of feedback, fun, and reinforcement would be foolish. Another potential problem is that with behaviors that do not produce permanent products, reliability may be difficult. While reliability for the sake of reliability is not important, reliability for the sake of avoiding delusion or illusion is. If a child is asked to manage a record of her own social behaviors, if she reports later to the teacher that she's "been social 100% of the chances," if she's only behaved appropriately 50% of the opportunities, and if the teacher congratulates her, then instead of teaching the child some form of self-management, we have taught the child to lie.

Another problem arises with the types of behaviors which cannot be counted through frequency recording, either by virtue of the behavior or by virtue of the method being impractical. The problem then is how to determine when to record whether or not the behavior is occurring. One way was suggested by Broden, Hall, and Mitts (1971), who were interested in the effects of self-recording on the classroom behavior of eighth-grade students. For one of the students who was not studying enough, a slip of paper was printed with 30 small boxes. In each box, she was asked to enter a + or a − to indicate whether or not she was studying. The student was told what constituted studying and was told to record her behavior " 'when she thought of it' during her history class sessions" (p. 193). While such a procedure is quite simple and efficient, it suffers

---

[2] There is considerable debate currently about whether what is generally termed self-control is really different than any other type of control. To avoid that *theoretical* issue and to remain concerned with *applied* issues, we will use *self-control* to refer to behavior change occurring in the presence of one's own feedback and in the absence of any *extra* contingencies provided by others.

from being biased by the antecedents to recording. Certainly, the likelihood of someone recording his own behavior is not the same for most people when he is responding and when he is not responding. To circumvent this problem, there should be a neutral way of signaling that the student should record his own behavior. The teacher, for example, could set a kitchen timer at random intervals. When it rings, the student is to record his behavior.

An interesting alternative that allows total portability has been offered by Hart and McCrady (1977). They have designed components for a small box about 3 by 2 by 0.6 inches which can be set at various intervals of time. When that time expires, the device vibrates quietly and provides a cue to record behavior. The device costs only a few dollars and can be held in the hand, placed in a pocket, clipped to a belt, etc. Being portable, it can provide cues to a child in the classroom, on the bus, on the playground, etc. Various alternatives like this can be found which can be designed by the teacher to be amusing, somewhat of a game, and also to help the student learn how to manage his or her own behavior.

MANIPULATING ANTECEDENTS

A major method of manipulating antecedents to produce more behavior by retarded persons is *response priming*, which is a method in which the first steps of a behavior the client can emit are "primed" or initiated. It differs from procedures that teach new behaviors in that it is used to initiate those behaviors already demonstrated in the repertoire. The basic need for priming has been discussed by Kazdin (1975) and others and involves the principle of immediacy of reinforcement. Quite simply, the closer a response is in time to its reinforcer, the more likely it is to recur. Many behaviors, of course, are comprised of a number of readily identifiable components. Putting on a pullover shirt involves a number of arm, head, and trunk movements; eating with a fork involves many movements from picking up the fork to placing food in the mouth and withdrawing the fork; going to the store could involve getting dressed, finding keys, walking to the car, and so forth. The problem with some of these behaviors is that they simply are never begun. We even have cliches for this situation: "Once I begin" or "If I can only get started . . . ." Response priming helps to initiate the first few components of the response, and it can do so in a number of ways.

One method of priming involves a signal that the client learns is related to the behavior. The device by Hart and McCrady (1977), for example, could be used to cue behaviors themselves, rather than just cueing the recording of other behaviors. Students whose toilet training includes "trip-training" could place such a device in their shirt pocket and use it as an antecedent and a reminder for walking to the bathroom; or students who constantly "forget" to put away materials could use it as a cueing device. Such uses would have to be faded from the environment over time, but they would allow students to be reminded to do something without the teacher's attention being contingent upon the student's not doing something. Azrin and Powell (1969) used another type of device to prompt taking pills for someone who is on self-medication. Their literature review showed that with out-patient care failure to take medications has ranged from 20% to 70% for psychiatric, arthritic, and tubercular patients. The rationale given for their procedure provides a good explanation of response priming:

> The taking of a pill was analyzed as a behavioral sequence in which swallowing was the final response that was always preceded by the response of holding the pill and the pill container in one's hand. Holding the pill was selected as the response to be reinforced. The rationale was that the final response in a sequence would be more likely to occur if an earlier response in the sequence could be reinforced. (p. 39)

They designed an ingeniously simple device which held pills and which sounded a tone at a time the pill was to be taken. The tone, however, remained on until a knob was turned. Two events then occurred: (1) the tone was terminated, so turning the knob was negatively reinforced, and (2) a pill was ejected, so the first response in the sequence could be initiated. This approach was compared with a portable alarm timer and the conventional wristwatch, and it was found to be much more efficient. As so many retarded persons are medicated to reduce seizures and to provide other benefits, and as so many retarded people on medication are going to public schools that do not have the medical attention some institutions do, clever ideas such as Azrin and Powell's could serve to help with the problem of maintaining self-medication.

Priming is often used in a physical way to begin various kinds of self-help training, particularly with profoundly retarded or with younger students. Dressing sequences are often primed as the teacher touches the arm, leg, etc. Eating skills are often primed by touching the student's wrist or hand. Maintenance tasks such as workshop assemblies, puzzle assemblies, or matching tasks are also often prompted by touching the student's body. Such prompts, of course, should be reduced over time so that the student can display the skill independently. Fading this type of prompt is again a teaching skill that requires gradually removing the prompt while carefully watching for any response decrement.

Another use of prompts for priming behaviors is that suggested by Turner and Vernon (1976), who were concerned with the number of people who did not keep appointments at their mental health center. In the baseline period, 32% of the more than 1,000 clients failed to keep appointments, offering a variety of excuses. The procedure employed was simply a telephone call from a mental-health center worker who, one to three days beforehand, reminded the patient of the appointment. The change was dramatic, reducing the missed appointments to 11% of all scheduled appointments. This change is remarkable in two respects: (1) of the 11% absent, not all were reached by telephone, and (2) the cost-effectiveness of the project was enormous. The total cost of the telephone contact was $162; the cost of out-patient therapy time per hour was estimated at $27, meaning that only six appointments needed to be kept instead of broken in order for the program to meet costs. But the data, through extrapolation, suggest that about 150 fewer people missed appointments during the prompting periods (a reversal design was used) than during the nonprompting periods. With very large numbers of retarded persons being released from institutions to the community, the number of client-to-professional contacts per year for medical services, social services, etc., is staggering. One approach is to go to the home of the individual, but cost for that plan would be enormous. Much more practical would be for the clients, sometimes accompanied, to come to the places in which the service provider works. At this point, these people are analogous to out-patients, and there is no reason to suspect that their rate of no-show would be significantly different than the rate reported here, or the 40% of a psychiatric population reported by Rosenberg and Raynes (1973), the 50% of mental-health-center outpatients reported by Gottesfeld and Martinez (1972), or the 52% of pediatric patients reported by Nazarian, Mechabar, Charney, and Coulter (1974). The problem of unkept appointments seems to go across populations, and it seems to be a problem that will increase for our field.

Another approach was taken by Newkirk, Feldman, Bickett, Gipson, and Lutzker (1976), who were interested in the attendance at a variety of activities by residents of an extended-care facility. They looked at a number of easily manipulated variables affecting attendance and found that choosing an activity room that was centrally located rather than one that was peripherally located and announcing the names of people who attended activities significantly increased attendance. What could be easier as a method of achieving behavioral change? A similarly simple approach was taken by Wheeler and Wislocki (1977), who were concerned with the relative social isolation of institutionalized persons. They found that in many instances retarded persons do not interact with each other. Such behavior seems appropriate to promote, so they considered reinforcing peer interactions but rejected this procedure because (1) the constant vigilance needed to reinforce social behaviors would be impossible in most institutions, and (2) the act of reinforcement could disrupt continued peer interactions. In a workshop activity of their program, interaction was noted to occur primarily between staff and residents, rather than between residents and other residents. As a first step, they merely removed the attendant and found that peer interactions increased threefold; the attendant had been functioning as an antecedent for staff-client interactions, and removing him acted as an antecedent for increased peer interactions. Over time, the attendant was faded back into the work environment, and the interactions continued. This very simple change coupled with careful attention to behavioral changes serves also to comment on the "help-the-retarded-to-do-everything" syndrome, in which many self-help skills, social skills, and academic skills are not developed or maintained because staff come to be antecedents for nonbehavior.

REINFORCER SAMPLING

Reinforcer sampling is similar to the prior procedures in that something prior to the response is manipulated. In this case, *limited access to the reinforcer is made available, and the initial response during reinforcement activities themselves are primed.* In essence, the individual samples that portion of the environment which should later provide reinforcement. This procedure is, of course, common in our lives. Automobile dealers let us sample the pleasures of their automobiles before buying them in an attempt to induce us to buy their product. To estimate the effects of this form of reinforcer sampling, imagine two car dealers who sell the same brand. One allows test driving, but the other does not. From whom would you buy the car? Similarly, supermarkets often allow representatives of food companies to provide free samples of their products. Record companies send records by mail before the response of buying occurs. Movie companies show excerpts of their movies as previews. The list goes on, and all are attempts to influence our responding.

The first reported systematic analysis of reinforcer sampling in the mental-health field was provided by Ayllon and Azrin (1968a, b) in their analyses of token systems in a mental hospital. In one, patients were not using contingent events as often as possible. One problem could be that the events were not reinforcing; another could be that reinforcer use needed to be primed. Ayllon and Azrin chose the latter as being more probable, so they required each patient to engage in the event for a limited period each time it was available, hence the term reinforcer sampling. The procedure was evaluated for three events: attending a music session, walking, and watching a movie. Results showed that patients used each of the reinforcers more when the sampling procedure was in effect and that they used them to a greater extent. In addition, overall increases were due not just to a few persons moving from extremely low use to high; even those who had been participating some increased their participation. Attendance of individuals at religious services, social events, and recreational events was also increased by the same procedure: a few minutes of initial attendance increased overall attendance.

These procedures were developed to increase the effects of events used as backup reinforcers in token systems. But reinforcer sampling need not be limited to token programs. Children who can earn free time before lunch can be given a few minutes of free time just before the period in which that free time could be earned. Or a teacher whose children who can earn a trip to the zoo in two weeks for improved academics could use reinforcer sampling in a way that could be fun and educational. On various days before the trip, a few minutes could be devoted to the zoo experience. Slides could be shown and interesting questions could be asked of each student. Each could pick a pet animal that they would be sure to feed. The bus or automobile ride to the zoo could be planned along the most interesting route. Slides could be shown of particular land, trees, buildings, etc., with each child being given "my tree" or "my building" to identify during the trip. Events like trips lend themselves very much to opportunities for pleasure and learning, perhaps even pleasurable learning, that make the event much more than passive attendance.

LABELED PRAISE

Labeled praise or specific praise is a procedure in which the behavior itself is named and praised. It has been shown to be more effective than unlabeled praise (Bernhardt & Forehand, 1975), and it is a procedure we have used for some time. Examples of labeled praise would be, "Johnny, I like the way you are *printing those letters,*" or "Sherie, you're doing a good job of *passing out the paint brushes,*" or "I like the way you are *standing straight* today, Diane." Each praise statement identifies the behavior that is being praised, and this procedure is important for two reasons. One is that the student learns quite clearly that something she or he is able to do pleases someone. For retarded persons who so frequently find failure, such statements can be quite pleasant. Another reason is that the behavior can be separated from the individual, so *a statement of disappointment about someone's performance can be made about the behavior rather than about the individual.* As a result, the teacher is not in a situation in which he or she dislikes the student; rather, the teacher dislikes the behavior. Again, for retarded people who fail so often in our society, this distinction could be very important for them to learn. Conversely, however, the praise statements should seem to be about the person as well as the behavior; the teacher is pleased with John because of what *he* has done.

VICARIOUS REINFORCEMENT

Vicarious reinforcement is a term that in some areas has replaced the term modeling. *It is a situation in which one's behavior increases in probability as a result of observing the consequences of someone else's behavior.*[3] It is a procedure that we used extensively in programming both social and academic behaviors in early childhood classes, prevocational and vocational classes, TMR, and EMR classes. The basic procedure involves three simple elements: (1) identifying a child engaging in the appropriate behavior, (2) indicating that this child is engaging in the behavior by specifically praising that child and the behavior (e.g., "I like the way Jerry is working on her math assignment"), (3) intermittently providing for that child something that would be reinforcing for the children not engaging in the behavior. In many cases, this "something" would be the praise itself, and that should be the goal. If, after the statement is made, the other children begin the behavior immediately, then praise is probably reinforcing for them. A fourth step sometimes used is praising or reinforcing the children once they come into compliance; but there is a note of caution associated with this approach. We should be sure not to praise the child just after switching from not emitting the behavior to emitting the behavior; otherwise, the child will be reinforced for "switching" rather than for "on-task" *per se*. The alternatives then are to wait a few minutes and, if the response is continuing, reinforce the child at that point, or not to reinforce the child for switching, waiting instead until the child is responding without being prompted by the praise given to another child. During these opportunities, this child could serve as the model and his or her appropriate behavior could be praised.

A number of articles have shown this phenomenon. For example, Broden, Bruce, Mitchell, Carter, and Hall (1970) examined the vicarious effects of teacher attention on the attending behavior of two boys who were seated at adjacent desks and who were described as the most disruptive students in the classroom. Their behaviors included talking to other students, talking to the teacher out of turn, waving papers, high rates of looking around the room, getting out of the seat and disturbing others, failing to do assigned work, looking out the win-

---

[3] The opposite process, of course, can also occur; i.e., one's probability of responding can decrease as a result of observing the consequences of someone else's behavior. This procedure is labeled *vicarious punishment*.

dow, and laughing at the other boy. When the teacher was trained to systematically direct her attention toward one of the boys when he was attending, both his and the other boy's behavior improved, although the latter's did not improve as much. When the conditions were reversed, attending increased for the boy who had not increased his attending behavior as much, while the attending behavior of the boy who had previously been directly reinforced declined somewhat. These results suggest at least two relations that may generalize to other situations in which vicarious reinforcement is used. The first is that the attending behavior of several highly disruptive students can be improved at once by a single teacher through systematic use of her own attention. Being in a class of disruptive students does not mean that it is unmanageable and that the teacher must fail. Instead, the teacher could select one or two students and systematically reinforce them with something that would *also be reinforcing* to other students in the class. Rather than taking a shotgun-in-despair approach with her attention toward the whole class, the teacher could be very systematic and thorough with a small number of students in the class. The second relation is that direct reinforcement is more potent than vicarious reinforcement; each of these students did better under direct reinforcement. This suggests that we could start with vicarious reinforcement, but that we should change to direct reinforcement for all the students involved.

Kazdin, Silverman, and Sittler (1975) made another important point for us in their study of the effects of vicarious reinforcement on the attending behaviors of two pairs of students in a class of 17 children in a laboratory demonstration school. They noted that approval can be verbal or nonverbal, and that there may be differential effects with each as nonverbal is less noticeable to onlookers. They found that nonverbal teacher attention could be a powerful reinforcer for the student being directly reinforced, but that it had little effect on the behavior of others. However, when nonverbal approval was paired with verbal approval, the behavior of both the target and the nontarget students improved; and when nonverbal approval of the target student was paired with a verbal prompt to the other students (e.g., "Class, look at Tina"), nonverbal approval had the typical effect of vicarious reinforcement. These results indicate to us that, if we use this approach, direct reinforcement of the target student must be noticed by the other students in order for vicarious reinforcement to have an opportunity to occur. The issue is not so much with *verbal* approval as it is with *salient* approval, and an approach such as noticeable token delivery could be just as effective.

Other work by Kazdin (1973a, b, 1977) has suggested that a great deal of the effect in this procedure may be due to the cue value of praise rather than to the modeling effect *per se*. These studies showed that the behavior of both the target and the nontarget students increase when the target student is reinforced directly. However, these studies also show that the behavior of the nontarget student will *increase* when the target student is being reinforced for a behavioral *decrease*, hence the concept of cues (or discriminative stimuli). For example, in one study in a sheltered workshop, the work rates of both students increased when one student was reinforced for fast work rates. However, the work rate of the nontarget student also increased when slow work rates of the target student were reinforced. The point of these three studies is that the nontarget subjects are not responding so much to the peer's behavior as to the cue value of the reinforcing stimulus; for these people, praise of another person is a cue that they will soon be praised for appropriate behavior for which they have previously been praised. The effect of these results for those of us involved in programming has been suggested by Kazdin: "one cannot recommend to individuals in rehabilitation settings simply to reinforce one or a few individuals with the idea that this will increase performance of observers (peers). The effect of approval of one person on the behavior of another may depend upon the fact that it is often followed by reinforcement of the *observer*" (1973a, p. 10). In essence, although vicarious reinforcement is excellent to prime the behavior of nontarget students, direct reinforcement must be used intermittently for that behavior change to be maintained.

PEER CONTINGENCIES

In vicarious reinforcement, the contingency on one person's behavior affects the behavior of a peer. With peer-related contingencies, the contingency on one person's behavior is maintained by his or her peers. Although this section is primarily concerned with reinforcement, peer-related contingencies can take the form of antecedent and/or subsequent events. For example, Harris and Sherman (1973) trained fourth- and fifth-grade students to tutor classmates in arithmetic, while Johnson and Bailey (1974) trained fifth graders to teach arithmetic to kindergarten students. Peers have also been trained to categorize responding as appropriate or inappropriate or to consequate those behaviors. Surratt, Ulrich, and Hawkins (1969) worked with attending behaviors and trained a fifth-grade student to modify the nonstudy behaviors of four first-grade students in a classroom. Greenwood, Sloane, and Baskin (1974) trained peers in a "behavior-disorders" classroom to use point reinforcement, social reinforcement, and response cost in a programmed math section of the class. In a different setting but with a related population, Bailey, Timbers, Phillips, and Wolf (1971) made points contingent on predelinquent males' detections of articulation errors, while Phillips, Phillips, Wolf, and Fixsen (1973) trained a peer to award points for appropriate and to remove points for inappropriate clean-up behaviors in a home for the same population. Retarded youngsters have also been shown to be quite adept with peer contingencies by Deitz, Repp, Deitz, Mitchell, and Repp (1975), who taught severely retarded students to teach each other, to consequate correct and incorrect responding, and to record data.

There is obviously no question as to whether peers can accurately arrange antecedent and subsequent events, and there seem to be a number of advantages, including (1) serving as an earned consequence for their own good behavior, (2) serving as a prompt to increase the social interactions of students who normally interact with their peers at a low rate, (3) changing their own behavior so that they do not reinforce with their own attention the inappropriate behaviors of their classmates, (4) helping the teacher to provide more individualized learning experiences for children in the class, (5) providing some sources of responsible behavior for peers, and (6) being fun.

GROUP CONSEQUENCES

Most behavioral programs involve consequences for the behavior of an individual, but many situations are amenable to providing consequences for a group of individuals whose behavior is taken as a unit. For example, Deitz, Repp, and Deitz (1976) worked with 14 EMR students in a class described as the most disruptive one in the school. Instead of making events contingent upon each individual's behavior, the group was treated as an individual and earned tokens when the group's rate of disruptive behavior was less than a particular level. Wodarski, Hamblin, Buckholdt, and Ferritor (1973) compared individual consequences with group consequences and found that group-shared consequences, contingent upon the behavior of the bottom four performers, produced the highest incidence of peer tutoring and produced the greatest improvement in arithmetic performance.

While the contingencies for a whole class can be based upon the performance of all members of the class, contingencies for a whole class can be made contingent upon the performance of only a few of its members. Evans and Oswalt (1968) found that discontinuing regular classroom duties for an entire class contingent upon the behavior of underachieving children in one fourth-grade and in another sixth-grade class produced significant academic gains for the underachieving students. Such a program can be great encouragement and motivation for some students, but care must be taken to avoid any undue peer pressure that would make the whole situation traumatic. Some care in making the initial response requirement one that a student can meet would seem to be a good beginning. Then the complexity and rate, or whatever, of the response can be increased as the student's skills increase. In this manner, the student is never given excess pressure by making his or her requirement too difficult, yet the student's behavior can be shaped to greater levels. Sulzer-Azaroff and Mayer (1977) note a number of advantages of group contingencies; among them are (1) increased social responses, like encouragement, among classmates; (2) facilitation of peer tutoring with subsequent increased gains in academic performance; and (3) less student concern solely with their own performance and more concern with the performance of their peers. Several of these could be adapted for our population, particularly those functioning at a higher level.

SUMMARY

This chapter concentrates on the topic of reinforcement, a term that describes the relation between behavior increase and subsequent stimulus change. In *positive reinforcement*, behavior increases because a stimulus is subsequently added to the environment, while in *negative reinforcement*, behavior increases because a stimulus is subsequently removed from the environment. While some stimuli are reinforcing in a variety of settings, all reinforcers can be more effective if the instructor provides for one or more of the following considerations: (1) *selecting stimuli* that based upon observation appear likely to be reinforcing, (2) initially reinforcing behavior *immediately* and moving to *delayed* reinforcement only as quickly as the behavior of the student indicates is tolerable, (3) initially reinforcing *every occurrence* of correct responding, but moving as rapidly as possible to *intermittently* and seemingly irregularly presented reinforcement, (4) maximizing the use of *novel* stimuli as reinforcers, (5) avoiding the possibility of *satiation*, a term referring to a temporary decrease in reinforcer effectiveness due solely to repeated presentations, (6) increasing the likelihood of behavior maintenance by moving to *natural* contingencies if artificial ones were ever used, (7) manipulating *antecedents* through such techniques as response priming, (8) allowing the student briefly to *sample the reinforcer* before the learning session begins, (9) identifying for the student the behavior as it is being reinforced through *labeled praise*, (10) using the reinforced behavior of some students to cue appropriate behavior of other students through *vicarious reinforcement*, (11) teaching *peers* how to develop contingencies, and (12) with care, making the *consequences for a group* contingent upon the behavior either of the whole group or of a few members of the group.

This chapter deals with reinforcers themselves. The next chapter will discuss the temporal and/or numerical relation between behavior and reinforcement, and it will do so in three classifications: (1) as single schedules, (2) as combinations of schedules, and (3) as schedules of schedules, which for our purposes will be limited to token systems.

REFERENCES

Altman, R., Talkington, L. W., & Cleland, C. C. Effects of novelty on verbal reinforcement effectiveness with retardates. *Psychological Record*, 1971, **21**, 529-532.

Ayllon, T. Intensive treatment of psychotic behavior by stimulus satiation and food reinforcement. *Behaviour Research and Therapy*, 1963, **1**, 53-61.

Ayllon, T., & Azrin, N. H. Reinforcer sampling: A technique for increasing the behavior of mental patients. *Journal of Applied Behavior Analysis*, 1968(a), **1**, 13-20.

Ayllon, T., & Azrin, N. H. *The token economy: A motivational system for therapy and rehabilitation*. New York: Appleton-Century-Crofts, Inc., 1968(b).

Azrin, N. H., & Powell, J. Behavioral engineering: The use of response priming to improve prescribed self-medication. *Journal of Applied Behavior Analysis*, 1969, **2**, 39-42.

Bailey, J. S., Timbers, G. D., Phillips, E. L., & Wolf, M. M. Modification of articulation errors of pre-delinquents by their peers. *Journal of Applied Behavior Analysis*, 1971, **4**, 265-281.

Barton, E. S., Guess, D., Garcia, E., & Baer, D. M. Improvements of retardates' mealtime behaviors by timeout procedures using multiple-baseline techniques. *Journal of Applied Behavior Analysis*, 1970, **3**, 77-84.

Bernhardt, A. J., & Forehand, R. The effects of labeled and unlabeled praise upon lower and middle class children. *Journal of Experimental Child Psychology*, 1975, **19**, 536-543.

Broden, M., Bruce, C., Mitchell, M. A., Carter, V., & Hall, R. V. Effects of teacher attention on attending behavior of two boys at adjacent desks. *Journal of Applied Behavior Analysis*, 1970, **3**, 199-203.

Broden, M., Hall, R. V., & Mitts, B. The effect of self-recording on the classroom behavior of two eighth-grade students. *Journal of Applied Behavior Analysis*, 1971, 4, 191-199.

Cautela, J. R., & Kastenbaum, R. A reinforcement survey schedule for use in therapy, training, and research. *Psychological Reports*, 1967, 20, 1115-1130.

Deitz, S. M., Repp, A. C., & Deitz, D. E. D. Reducing inappropriate classroom behavior of retarded students through three procedures of differential reinforcement. *Journal of Mental Deficiency Research*, 1976, 20, 155-170.

Deitz, D. E. D., Repp, A. C., Deitz, S. M., Mitchell, M. E., & Repp, C. F. Retarded students as behavioral technicians. Paper presented at the Southeastern Association on Mental Deficiency, 1975.

Dickerson, D. J., & Girardeau, F. L. Oddity preference by mental retardates. *Journal of Experimental Child Psychology*, 1970, 10, 28-32.

Evans, G. W., & Oswalt, G. L. Acceleration of academic progress through the manipulation of peer influence. *Behaviour Research and Therapy*, 1968, 6, 189-195.

Ferster, C. B., & Skinner, B. F. *Schedules of reinforcement*. New York: Appleton-Century-Crofts, Inc., 1957.

Gottesfeld, H., & Martinez, H. The first psychiatric interview: Patients who do and do not come. *Psychological Reports*, 1972, 31, 776-778.

Greenwood, C. R., Sloane, H. N., & Baskin, A. Training elementary aged peer-behavior managers to control small group programmed mathematics. *Journal of Applied Behavior Analysis*, 1974, 7, 103-114.

Harris, V. W., & Sherman, J. A. Effects of peer tutoring and consequences on the math performance of elementary classroom students. *Journal of Applied Behavior Analysis*, 1973, 6, 587-597.

Hart, A. D., & McCrady, R. E. A unique electronic cueing device providing a tactile signal for behavior monitoring of self or others. *Behavior Therapy*, 1977, 8, 89-93.

Johnson, J., & Bailey, J. S. Cross-age tutoring: fifth graders as arithmetic tutors for kindergarten children. *Journal of Applied Behavior Analysis*, 1974, 7, 223-232.

Kazdin, A. E. The effect of vicarious reinforcement on performance in a rehabilitation setting. *Education and Training of the Mentally Retarded*, 1973a, 8, 4-11.

Kazdin, A. E. The effect of vicarious reinforcement on attentive behavior in the classroom. *Journal of Applied Behavior Analysis*, 1973b, 6, 71-79.

Kazdin, A. E. *Behavior modification in applied settings*. Homewood, IL: Dorsey Press, 1975.

Kazdin, A. E. Vicarious reinforcement and direction of behavior change in the classroom. *Behavior Therapy*, 1977, 8, 57-63.

Kazdin, A. E., Silverman, N. A., & Sittler, J. L. The use of prompts to enhance vicarious effects of nonverbal approval. *Journal of Applied Behavior Analysis*, 1975, 8, 279-286.

Nazarian, L. F., Mechabar, J., Charney, E., & Coulter, M. P. Effect of a mailed appointment reminder on appointment keeping. *Pediatrics*, 1974, 53, 349-352.

Newkirk, J. M., Feldman, S., Bickett, A., Gipson, M. T., & Lutzker, J. R. Increasing extended care facility residents' attendance at recreational activities with convenient locations and personal invitations. *Journal of Applied Behavior Analysis*, 1976, 9, 207.

O'Brien, F., Bugle, C., & Azrin, N. H. Training and maintaining a retarded child's proper eating. *Journal of Applied Behavior Analysis*, 1972, 5, 67-72.

Phillips, E. L., Phillips, E. A., Wolf, M. M., & Fixsen, D. L. Achievement place: Development of the elected manager system. *Journal of Applied Behavior Analysis*, 1973, 6, 541-562.

Reynolds, G. S. *A primer of operant conditioning.* Glenview, IL: Scott, Foresman & Company, 1968.

Risley, T. R., & Wolf, M. Establishing functional speech in echolalic children. In H. N. Sloane, Jr., & B. D. MacAuley (Eds.), *Operant procedures in remedial speech and language training.* Boston: Houghton Mifflin Company, 1968.

Rosenberg, C. M., & Raynes, A. E. Dropouts from treatment. *Canadian Psychiatric Association Journal*, 1973, 18, 229-233.

Rotatori, A. F., & Switzky, H. A reinforcement survey hierarchy for use in educational programming for the severely and profoundly mentally retarded. Unpublished manuscript. Northern Illinois University, 1977.

Sulzer-Azaroff, B., & Mayer, G. R. *Applying behavior analysis procedures with children and youth.* New York: Holt, Rinehart and Winston, Inc., 1977.

Surratt, P. R., Ulrich, R. E., & Hawkins, R. P. An elementary student as a behavioral engineer. *Journal of Applied Behavior Analysis*, 1969, 2, 85-92.

Turner, A. J., & Vernon, J. C. Prompts to increase attendance in a community mental-health center. *Journal of Applied Behavior Analysis*, 1976, 9, 141-145.

Wheeler, A. J., & Wislocki, E. B. Stimulus factors effecting peer conversation among institutionalized retarded women. *Journal of Applied Behavior Analysis*, 1977, 10, 283-288.

Wodarski, J. S., Hamblin, R. L., Buckholdt, D. R., & Ferritor, D. E. Individual consequences versus different shared consequences contingent on the performance of low-achieving group members. *Journal of Applied Social Psychology*, 1973, 3, 276-290.

Zeaman, D., & House, B. J. The role of attention in retardate discrimination learnings. In N. R. Ellis (Ed.), *Handbook of Mental Deficiency.* New York: McGraw-Hill Book Co., 1963.

9

Schedules of Reinforcement

SCHEDULES OF REINFORCEMENT

In chapter 8, reinforcers were discussed in terms of their classifications, types, and ways in which they could be made more effective. One way involved the manner in which they were *scheduled*, i.e., the relation between responding and reinforcement. In some cases, this relation involves a particular response producing a reinforcer; in other cases, this relationship involves the absence of or a reduction in responding, which then produces reinforcement. While these opposing functions may seem confusing at first because we tend to associate reinforcement only with a procedure of increasing responding, they should not be confusing if *schedule of reinforcement* is considered to refer to *the rule describing the relation between responding and reinforcement.* One rule could be "every verbalization will earn a token"; another rule could be "if no verbalization occurs for five minutes, a token will be earned." Both statements are schedules of reinforcement because they describe the rule between responding and reinforcement. Quite obviously, the intent of the instructor is different in these two cases. In the first, a therapist may be trying to teach a child to begin to talk. In the second, a teacher may be trying to teach an excessively verbal child to be quiet for short periods of time. Nevertheless, both state a rule between responding and environmental change.

There are many ways to classify schedules and several will be used here.[1] The major classification used in this chapter will be whether the schedule is (1) a first-order schedule, (b) a combination of schedules, or (3) a second-order

---

[1] For an extraordinary study of reinforcement schedules, see Ferster and Skinner (1957), as well as many of the papers in the *Journal of the Experimental Analysis of Behavior*, 1958 to the present.

schedule. *First order* refers to a single rule between the reinforcer and the behavior; e.g., every tenth correct response will earn a token. *Compound* refers to two or more rules; e.g., if you finish your arithmetic worksheets by Tuesday, you will earn a token for every 10 correct answers, but if you do not finish them until Wednesday, you will earn a token for every 12 correct answers, and if you do not finish until Thursday, you will earn a token for every 14 correct answers. *Second order* refers to two rules. The first rule is that of the first-order schedule, and the second rule is a rule about that first-order rule. For example, if the first-order rule is that every tenth correct response will earn a token, the second rule could be that the fifteenth token collected will earn 30 minutes of free time. The rule about the number of tokens necessary for free time is really a higher-order rule; it is a rule about token collection.

CONTINUOUS AND INTERMITTENT SCHEDULES

Whether schedules are first- or second-order, they can be either continuous or intermittent. *Continuous reinforcement* is a *schedule in which every response occurrence is reinforced. Intermittent reinforcement* is *any schedule in which not all responses are reinforced.* Traditionally, continuous reinforcement is suggested as the procedure to follow when beginning a reinforcement program. With profoundly and severely retarded persons, this schedule may be necessary for anywhere from a few to a large number of responses. With some moderately and with mildly retarded persons, continuous reinforcement may be necessary; for others, it may be unnecessary and can be replaced by instructions and an intermittent schedule. The "trick" in a sense is to use continuous reinforcement only long enough to establish for the client the link between response and reinforcement. When the client's behavior, through an increase in rate, duration, complexity, or whatnot, indicates that such a link has been established, we can move to intermittent schedules.

For example, when we were teaching previously unsupervised, profoundly and severely retarded youngsters, who essentially had had no programming for their 10 or 15 years, we at first used primary reinforcement and praise for every correct response, because not having been in educational programs before, they did not make very many correct responses in areas like self-dressing, toileting, or even sitting down. Later, these behaviors were placed on intermittent schedules of reinforcement. At that same time, we were implementing programs for students in EMR and TMR classes. For many of the behaviors of many of the students, continuous reinforcement was not necessary as long as instructions and feedback were properly used.

The point is that we do not need to use continuous reinforcement in all programs we are beginning; in many cases, alternatives are just as good. But why the concern with not using continuous reinforcement? There are several reasons. One was discussed in Chapter 8, and that involves the problems associated with *satiation.* Quite obviously, if a child is responding at a moderate rate and is being continuously reinforced, the reinforcer is likely to lose its effectiveness after it is presented a number of times. When the reinforcer is not presented every time, it will reach the point of satiation more slowly. A second reason is that the delivery of reinforcement may *interfere* with responding and in that sense be counterproductive. For example, if we are praising a child by hugging her when she finishes the first step of a dressing task, we would not want to keep doing so while she is progressing through step 2.

Another reason is what may at first seem the improbable finding that within limits someone will *respond more quickly* on an intermittent than on a continuous schedule of reinforcement. While there are presumptions made as to why this happens, they are unimportant for our purposes. The point is simply that, if a child has to finish 10 spelling problems to earn a token, she or he will finish those 10 problems more quickly if not given a token after each of the 10 responses.

Another reason for not maintaining continuous schedules very long involves the phenomenon called *resistance to extinction*. Extinction refers to a period in which behavior decreases as a result of a prolonged period in which it is no longer reinforced. Resistance to extinction refers to the extent to which the behavior resists a decrease while it is not being reinforced. While the problem may seem esoteric, it really is not and it arises in two general situations. One occurs when a teacher was able to concentrate on a task yesterday, reinforcing the student for every correct response, but is unable to provide her attention today because another student is acting out, or she has materials to prepare, etc. In that sense, correct responding today is under extinction. As a result, some of the gains made yesterday may be lost. If the student had been on an intermittent schedule, the possibility of any losses today would be lessened. Another situation occurs when a child moves from one program to another or when the teachers in the program are changed. Often such changes are not accompanied by a thorough maintenance of programming, as each instructor incorporates his or her own ideas for programming. If responding had been under an intermittent schedule, it would be maintained for a longer period in the new situation. An additional reason for changing from continuous to an intermittent schedule is simply to conserve *teacher time*. When an instructor is distributing reinforcement, whether that be praise or something tangible, there is some loss of time. When those deliveries are centered about one child, other students may not be receiving the attention and feedback they deserve and need. Intermittent reinforcement for all students simply allows more students to be reinforced.

When switching to intermittent reinforcement, we should do so in a manner that allows improvement to continue, and the only way of assessing such progress accurately is to record data on the student's responding. As a cliche, we often say "the data will tell you," and the data will. If you have reduced the density of reinforcement too rapidly, data should indicate a decrease in responding. For example, if we would like a student to copy words from a worksheet more quickly than he now does, we might praise him for every sentence copied. If his rate increases, we might praise him for every two sentences completed. If his rate of copying either is maintained or continues to increase, then we might require five completed sentences before he is praised. This is a simple shaping procedure, but one which does require some care. If this jump from two to five sentences is too large an increase, his rate might decrease, and we may have to adjust the requirement.

But such a situation can cause a problem. For example, during continuous reinforcement, the child may have been completing one sentence per minute.

During the first intermittent schedule, the child may also have been working at the same rate, but during the second intermittent schedule, her rate may have dropped to 0.5 sentences per minute. If we drop the requirement back to "two sentences produce praise" and if the child's rate goes back to one sentence per minute, what have we taught her?—That a *decrease* in her responding produces a greater density of teacher attention, praise, proximity, etc.

PROGRAMMING FIRST-ORDER SCHEDULES

Schedules to Increase Responding

In this section, we will discuss the basic schedules, what kind of responding occurs within each, how each is programmed, and how a teacher can move from one to another in an attempt to motivate appropriate responding by all students while making a reinforcement system manageable for the teacher. The basic first-order schedules dealing with increasing responding are fixed ratio, variable ratio, fixed interval, variable interval, and limited hold. The basic difference among them in terms of definition is whether they are based on number or whether they are based on *number and time*. Those in the first category are ratio schedules; those in the second category are interval and limited hold schedules.

Fixed Ratio. A *fixed-ratio schedule (FR) is "a schedule of intermittent reinforcement in which a response is reinforced upon completion of a fixed number of responses counted from the preceding reinforcement"* (Ferster & Skinner, 1957, p. 727). The word *ratio* refers to the ratio between the number of responses necessary to produce reinforcement and reinforcement. If a child receives a token for every 15 completed problems, then the ratio between completing problems and tokens is 15 to 1; if a child receives a nickel for taking out the garbage twice, then the ratio between taking out the garbage and nickels is 2 to 1. The word *fixed* refers to the stability of the ratio. If it is the same every time, then the ratio is said to be fixed. If, for example, the child receives a token for every 15 completed problems, no matter how many he or she does, then the rule for reinforcement is a fixed ratio 15 (FR15). If, however, the child receives one token for 15 problems one time, a token for 12 problems the next time, and a token for 18 problems the next time, then the ratio is not fixed; it is varied.

The fixed-ratio schedule generally produces consistent rates of responding with few long pauses and rates of responding that are quite good. As such, it is an excellent schedule to use when motivating students. An added advantage to this schedule, as mentioned in the discussion of intermittent schedules, is that within limits, the *higher* the ratio, the *higher* the rate of responding; i.e., when the child has to do more in order to produce reinforcement, the child will respond more quickly. A study by Stephens, Pear, Wray, and Jackson (1975) demonstrates this effect quite nicely. Retarded children involved in a picture-naming task were reinforced for correct responding by verbal approval and by candy according to various schedules. Figure 9-1 indicates the cumulative number of pictures

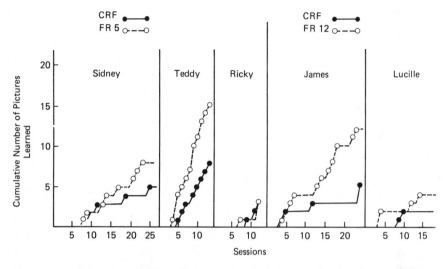

Figure 9-1. The cumulative number of pictures learned (named correctly to criterion) by retarded children responding under two different schedules of reinforcement. For Sidney, Teddy, and Ricky, the two schedules were continuous reinforcement and FR 5. For James and Lucille, the two schedules were continuous reinforcement and FR 12. Note that responding tends to be better under intermittent reinforcement (Stephens, Pear, Wray, & Jackson, 1975, p. 439).

learned by each child under each pair of schedules.[2] For Sidney and Teddy, more pictures were learned when they were reinforced for every five responses than when they were reinforced for every response; for Ricky, there was no difference in responding under the two conditions. For James and Lucille, more pictures were learned when they were reinforced for every 12 correct responses than when they were reinforced for every correct response. These data quite clearly show that, for four of these children, an intermittent fixed-ratio schedule was more effective than a continuous schedule, and that for a fifth student, there was no difference. If these data are generalizable to other children's behaviors, and there is no reason to presume they are not, they suggest that a teacher should move to intermittent fixed-ratio schedules of reinforcement for the child's benefit (and quite obviously for the teacher's as well). Other data from this study show the effects of various fixed-ratio schedules on the performance of two of these children. During the first 15 sessions, Teddy learned six more pictures under an FR10 schedule than under an FR5 schedule; in the next 20 sessions, he learned about twice as many pictures in the FR15 than in the FR5 condition. For the other child, the pairs of schedules in each condition were FR5-FR10, FR5-FR15,

---

[2] This experiment is also a good example of the single-subject design in which all independent variables are experienced by the same individual. Note that the authors did not compare the responding of Sidney, Teddy, and Ricky under a condition of continuous reinforcement with the responding of three other children under a FR5 schedule. If they had, any differences might have also been attributable to differences between the two groups. In the single-subject design, one can quite clearly see that for two of the three students the FR5 schedule produced more responding, and that for the third student there was no difference in responding under the two conditions.

FR5-FR20, FR5-FR25, and FR5-FR15. In each pair, the number of pictures learned in one condition was greater than or equal to the number learned in the FR5 conditions. These results suggest that not only are intermittent schedules more effective than a continuous schedule, but also that a higher-valued FR schedule is at least as effective as a lower-valued FR schedule (within limits, of course).

There are certain characteristics of FR schedules with which we should be familiar before systematically employing them. These include the general finding that (1) FR schedules produce fairly consistent responding between pauses, so if we would like a student to work at a fairly consistent pace without too much daydreaming or other self-imposed interruptions, an intermediate FR may be appropriate; (2) the higher the FR, the higher the rate of responding at low or intermediate FR values, so we may increase FR schedules somewhat without a great risk of response loss and with some savings in teacher time; (3) as the FR requirement becomes high for that child's behavior, pauses develop between responses, so we have to be careful to watch for this effect; and (4) as an FR requirement increases, the probability of pauses after reinforcement increases and the lengths of these pauses increase. This effect could be analogous to off-task or "break" behavior that we and our students experience as summarized in our general complaint that "I've worked so hard I deserve a break!" If breaks of some length are appropriate in the learning situation, then there is no problem; if such breaks lead to disruption of other students, then there is a problem. While we usually do not identify this effect, it has occurred with all of us in one way or another. When we have to read 200 pages for a class, we are more likely to take a long break than when we have to read only 20; and when we have written a 100-page paper, we are more likely to take a long break than when we have just written a 10-page paper. There is little reason to suspect that this sort of relation between output and pauses does not exist for retarded learners as well. The amount of responding before taking a break may certainly be less than it is for us, and it may not be very large at all, but being able to identify the amount should help us learn how to arrange the teaching environment in still better fashion.

Variable Ratio. A *variable-ratio schedule (VR) is "a schedule of intermittent reinforcement under which reinforcements are programmed according to a random series of ratios having a given mean and lying between arbitrary extreme values"* (Ferster & Skinner, 1957, p. 734). Like an FR schedule, a VR schedule provides a number that describes the ratio between responses and reinforcements. Unlike an FR schedule, however, that number describes an average rather than a fixed ratio, as the ratio in a VR schedule varies from time to time. For example, if a child is being reinforced with a token for *every* 15 correct responses, an FR15 schedule is in effect. But if the child is reinforced *on the average* for every 15 correct responses, a VR15 schedule would be in effect. To define the VR15, it is necessary to describe its components, which in a way can be considered to be a mixed series of FR schedules. For example, in a VR15, a child could be reinforced for the 10th, then the 20th, then the 10th, then the 15th, and then the 10th response. Or the child could be reinforced for the 2nd, then the 8th, then the 20th, then the 15th, then the 20th, then the 15th, then the 30th, and then the 10th response. In both cases, the child would be earning tokens according to a ratio schedule, the ratio would vary, the ratios would have as their mean a value of 15, and the schedules would both be labeled VR15.

Variable-ratio schedules, of course, are quite related to fixed-ratio schedules. Each produces high rates of responding because each tends to provide reinforcement after clusters of high-rate responding rather than after a response or two following a long pause. Each produces a deterioration in responding if jumps in values are made too rapidly. Each produces response decreases during extinction, although VR schedules tend to be more resistant to extinction. VR schedules tend to eliminate the pauses of FR schedules, particularly at high ratio values (see Ferster & Skinner, 1957), and thus have considerable extra value for classroom situations. These schedules tend to reinforce very stable responding without the "breaks" that could lead to disruptive behaviors. Again within reason, each of the ratio schedules tends to produce higher rates of responding as the ratio increases, a benefit for both student and teacher.

Variable-ratio schedules are quite easy to program and, because they do produce more consistent responding, they are sometimes preferred in teaching situations. When switching from an FR to a VR schedule, we should at first maintain the same ratio value. After behavior is stable under the VR schedule, changes in mean values can be made. VR schedules should be composed of a fairly large number of values in mixed order so that the pattern of reinforcement delivery is not easily discernible. Choose a number of values and scramble them so that a series of these values produce the desired VR mean. A few of these series can be constructed in 2 or 3 minutes, and these series can be scrambled to be used across days. While determining the values for the VR mean seems easy, operating a VR schedule may seem difficult. Generally, however, it is not. When there are permanent products, such as written answers, there is no problem because they are usually scored at a later time. At this time, the teacher can circle every 15th, 12th, 18th, etc., response and inform the child that he or she is earning something for each of those circles. When the behaviors are transient, the situation may be a little more difficult, but it is generally solvable by using some sort of prompt. For example, when teaching groups of five or six children, we could prepare a stack of cards, chips, paper strips, etc., for each child. Most pieces would be the same, but an occasional one would be distinguishable by color, shape, etc. The teacher simply arranges the odd piece in each child's stack so that it fits the VR schedule. For each correct response, the top piece is removed; when the odd piece arrives, the child is reinforced. For some children, a game can be made of "making the yellow card appear," and that alone could be the reinforcer if the teacher is skilled enough at arranging such situations, including having all children cheer each other in an appropriate way, seeing how fast each can make the yellow card appear. Various kinds of systems like this, which allow the instructor to systematically reinforce students, can be arranged with a little ingenuity.

Fixed Interval.   Interval schedules, unlike ratio schedules, are based upon time as well as number. In all cases, the number of responses required for reinforcement is one. In all cases, however, that key response must occur *after* the stated value of the interval schedule. As with ratio schedules, there are two types of interval schedules: fixed interval and variable interval. *A fixed-interval schedule (FI) is "a schedule of intermittent reinforcement in which the first*

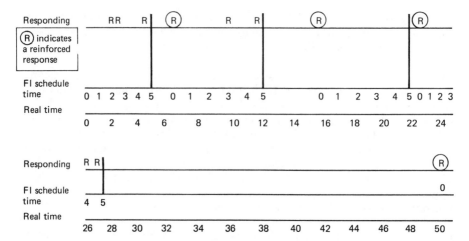

Figure 9-2. Diagram of an FI 5-minute schedule in which the first response *after* 5 minutes is reinforced. The upper line indicates when responding occurred (R) and when reinforcement occurred (Ⓡ). The middle line indicates the fixed interval of 5 minutes. Note that once the interval expires, it does not begin again until reinforcement occurs. The lower line represents real time as indicated by a clock separate from the FI timer.

response occurring after a given interval of time, measured from the preceding reinforcement, is reinforced" (Ferster & Skinner, 1957, p. 727). There are two particularly important aspects of this definition, each illustrated in Figure 9-2, and these are that (1) it is the first response *after* the interval expires that is reinforced, and (2) an interval is begun *after reinforcement*, not after the last interval expired.[3] Note in Figure 9-2 that the first three responses had no effect on reinforcement; they occurred before the 5 minutes specified in the FI 5-minute schedule. The fourth response, however, has two effects: (1) it produced reinforcement, and (2) it started the next interval. This diagram shows also that there is no preset relation between the minimum number of reinforcers delivered and the time that has elapsed. If a person made a first response after 20 minutes, then only one reinforcement could have occurred, despite the fact that it could have occurred at any time.

The problem with this schedule is obvious: because responding within the interval is not consequated, it tends to be minimal. As such, responding tends to increase as the interval begins to expire. Figure 9-3 is a graph of the number of bills passed by the 87th to 90th congresses of the United States. The behavior of the congresspersons is quite similar to that of typical FI behavior of pigeons in Skinner boxes in laboratory experiments. There simply is not a great deal of behavior during the first portion of the 12-month interval. As the interval approaches the point of expiration, behavior increases sharply. Another situation analogous to FI schedules that we have all experienced is our own study or writing behavior for college classes. If an examination is scheduled 4 weeks from now, we are likely to do as much studying in the final week as we have done in all

---

[3] Although as Ferster and Skinner (1957) note, the schedule could be programmed either way, they chose the present way "so that no instance occurs of a response being reinforced after less than the designated fixed interval" (p. 133).

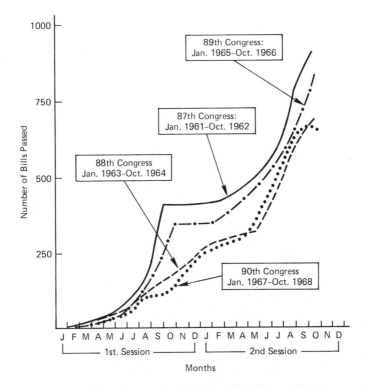

Figure 9-3. The cumulative number of bills passed by the 87th, 88th, 89th, and 90th Congresses. The data represent a finding similar to that of subjects in laboratory studies reinforced on FI schedules: responding occurs at a higher rate during the last quarter of the interval than during other quarters (Weisberg & Waldrup, 1972, p. 95).

of the first three. Similarly, if a paper is due at the end of a semester, we are likely to do most, if not all, the work in the last few weeks of the term. Occasionally, we are able to break that pattern, distributing our work fairly evenly over a time period. In such cases, we have probably set contingencies, whether implicit or explicit, along the way. This type of pattern is much more efficient for performance as it avoids the long periods of little behavior, the relatively short period of practically exhaustive behavior, and the following long period of little behavior. FI schedules are simply inefficient and poor schedules with respect to classroom behaviors. If we are forced into them, then we should combine them with other schedules that reinforce a more even distribution of behavior within the interval.

If you have students who are developing projects that are due in a few weeks, every few days prompt portions of the project. When the students begin those portions, praise their efforts. Later you can shift your attention to their completing portions of the project, and you will probably be able to generate work fairly evenly distributed across the weeks; and you may be able to avoid the emotional behaviors associated with having to complete a lot of work in a short time. With many of the students in our population, producing large amounts of work in short time is either impossible or a behavior pattern that has never been learned. As such, it seems unwise to structure classroom or workshop behaviors on large FI's without considerable pretraining on our part. Too often, we seem to make shifts from other implicit schedules to FI schedules too abruptly. When we are training students for gainful employment, we generally use frequent praise, tokens, feedback, instructions, etc., and then transfer the student to a job in which little of this exists and the only powerful reinforcer is a paycheck, generally not really contingent upon the work behaviors themselves and generally far removed in time from those behaviors.

Variable Interval. Variable-interval schedules offer an attractive alternative to fixed-interval schedules and can be considered a mixed series of FI schedules. *In VI schedules, the first response after the interval expires is reinforced, but the interval is not the same each time.* For example, if a teacher wants to reinforce a child's on-task behavior on a VI 5-minute schedule, a kitchen timer can be set for the following series of minutes: 1, 5, 9, 8, 3, 5, 6, 1, and 7. In this series, the teacher would be responsible for three simple operations: (1) setting the timer, (2) reinforcing the first on-task behavior *after* the interval expires, and (3) setting the timer at the next interval value at the time of reinforcement.

Figure 9-4 illustrates a VI 5-minute schedule and once again demonstrates the relation between schedule time, real time, and responding. In so doing, it again demonstrates the weakness of the interval schedule: no behavior is required *during* the interval, so periods of pausing will be reinforced. The value of the variable-interval as opposed to the fixed-interval schedule is that there is less chance for these pauses to be reinforced because there are intervals of short duration in which pausing will be punished. This should tell the teacher that two factors in VI schedules are important: (1) they should contain a number of short intervals, so the instructor merely needs to construct them that way; and (2) they

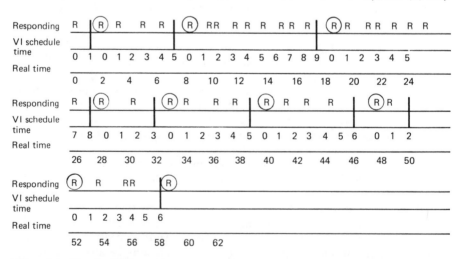

Figure 9-4. Diagram of VI 5-minute schedule of reinforcement in which, *on the average*, the first response after 5 minutes is reinforced. The actual intervals comprising the schedule are 1, 5, 9, 8, 3, 5, 6, 2, and 6 minutes. Note that although reinforcement was available after a total of 45 minutes (9 reinforcement × 5 minutes as an average), the schedule took 58 minutes to complete.

must be unpredictable, for if they are not, they will actually be a series of identifiable FI schedules to the student. As such, they may produce the problems associated with FI schedules. Fortunately, the solution is obvious and simple: we need only spend 20 or 30 seconds each day arranging a series of numbers that varies from the series used yesterday, and we need to use some timing device that does not serve as a signal to the student that the interval has elapsed.

There are some advantages and disadvantages to VI schedules. Relative to VR schedules, they produce a lower rate of responding (Ferster & Skinner, 1957). However, when used carefully, they need not produce a low rate of responding. In addition, they are moderately resistant to extinction, particularly when a few long values are included in the values that comprise the VI schedule. There are, however, two major advantages to this schedule. One is that they tend to generate *very consistent* and even distributions of *responding*. This pattern, again, is essential to anyone in a teaching situation. If one person is teaching 10 moderately retarded students, and if variable schedules of reinforcement have been used so that all 10 are responding at moderate but sustained paces with minimal disruptions, the teacher will be able to offer individual attention without having to contend with off-task behaviors of the other students. This is a tremendous advantage for both students and teachers in any learning environment. A second advantage of this schedule relative to ratio schedules is that it is *easy to implement*. We do not have to count all responses; we only have to count a single response after the interval has expired. This is a tremendous advantage for us.

Given the classroom advantages of VI schedules with behaviors that are not permanent products, the question becomes how do we apply them? The general progression involves first using continuous reinforcement for as short a period as is required. Then we carefully move through successively larger FR schedules, stopping at a point that is convenient to the teacher and to the learning environment, and that produces a high rate[4] of responding. Then an equal-valued VR schedule can be employed to generate behavior patterns that are more consistent and with shorter pauses. Then the teacher can institute an easily operable VI schedule that would produce the same amount of reinforcement for the student that the VR schedule did. This equivalency can be easily reached by averaging the number of reinforcers the student earns each day, dividing that average by the number of intervals that should occur each day, and distributing that number of reinforcers for the first response after each interval expires. For example, if on a VR schedule the student is averaging 30 tokens per day and the teacher decides to use 10 intervals per day in the VI schedule, then 3 tokens could be distributed for each response following each interval.

Limited Hold. A limited-hold (LH) schedule also relies on time and number and is defined as "*a short period during which a reinforcement arranged by an interval schedule is held available. At the end of the limited hold, a response will not be reinforced until another reinforcement has been set up*" (Ferster & Skinner, 1957, p. 729). It is similar to the interval schedules in that on-

---

[4] Although the word "rate" is used, the same relation should hold for behaviors whose importance lies in other measures, such as duration or percent correct.

ly a single response is required, but it differs from them in that the response must occur *within*, not after, the interval. It is from this relation, that of reinforcement being *held* available for a *limited* time, that the schedule derives its name.

The purpose of limited-hold schedules is to reduce pauses in responding so that a single response following a long pause will not be reinforced. We all use limited-hold schedules without formally studying them. The arithmetic assignment is due Friday, and only if it is completed on time can you receive an A. A child is being taught a two-step command; but only if the two steps are completed within 1 minute will the child be praised. The major problem with our informal use of this schedule is that we do not use it systematically. When teaching a child or a developmentally delayed adolescent, we should specify the interval so that there is no ambiguity. "Thirty seconds" in which to follow a command is a time that most of us can approximate; but when we say "30 seconds," "quickly," "in a short time," etc., to a retarded person, we may be conveying information that is not particularly discrete and helpful. In some cases, devices could be used to indicate time in a clear manner. For example, in age-appropriate classes, one of six marks on the blackboard could be erased every five seconds; or a thick line across the blackboard could be erased on a continuous basis, proportional to the passage of time. Again, with clever and enthusiastic teachers, such devices can be made into games in which all students are either directly involved or are encouraging their peers. In addition to a clear specification of the time, proper use of limited-hold schedules would include a systematic increase in the response requirement. In ratio schedules, we systematically shaped an increase in the number of responses required for reinforcement from 1, to 2, to 3, etc. An analogous approach can be used with limited-hold schedules. We should begin with an interval that the student can meet without much difficulty; then the length of the interval can be systematically decreased until a suitable goal is reached. In this way, the student does not initially have to perform the behavior at the goal level; but we can start at a level at which the student succeeds and change systematically to the level most appropriate to him or her.

Differential Reinforcement of High Rates.   In the limited-hold schedule only one response was necessary within the interval to produce reinforcement. *In the differential reinforcement of high rates of responding (DRH), a number of responses greater than or equal to some minimum within the interval is necessary for reinforcement.*[5] For example, a child could earn a token if he completes 10 or more problems during the math period. Next week, he might be required to complete at least 11 problems; and the following week, perhaps 12. In each case, rates at or higher than a minimum are reinforced, hence the term "reinforcement of high rates." This is an especially excellent schedule for teaching developmentally disabled persons to work more quickly, because the initial requirement can be set at the client's present level of functioning. In this manner, persons who do not perform particularly quickly are not penalized; they are simply taught over time to work more quickly.

---

[5] While there are other ways of programming DRH schedules, the way in which we program it in applied work with retarded persons will be the only way discussed here. See Ferster and Skinner (1957) for a laboratory analysis of DRH.

The ways in which DRH schedules can be used for many types of classroom behaviors should be obvious. Simply define the behavior carefully, record its occurrence during a baseline period, and then reinforce rates greater than or equal to the baseline rates. Some of the behaviors with which DRH schedules can be used are not so obvious and require some ingenuity. For example, Wilson and McReynolds (1973) were concerned with the poor voice quality of hard-of-hearing and deaf speakers. Among the consistent problems found was poor speech rhythm, often associated with speech generated at too slow a rate. The problem with training speech at a natural rate often involves the lack of feedback and of antecedent prompting; i.e., how does one who cannot hear others talk identify how rapidly to talk himself. To provide such information, the authors used a mechanical device that provided pulses to each student's palm at 1.2, 1.4, 1.6 . . ., and 2.8 rhythmic pulses per second. The children were then given materials to read orally at a pace equal to that provided by the mechanical device. In the first training session, the instructor first read alone while sharing the oscillator pulse with the student. The instructor then gradually faded his prompting until the student was reading along in synchrony with the pulse. When the student read at the proper pace, tokens were earned; and when the pace was maintained for 10 lists of words, the next higher pulse rate was used. The results showed that the program was quite successful in differentially increasing the rate of the students oral reading.

Schedules to Decrease Responding

Although reinforcement schedules are typically used to increase responding, they can also be used to decrease responding. In Chapter 11 these schedules and other reinforcement-based procedures will be discussed in detail. In this section, however, three of these will be introduced briefly.

Differential Reinforcement of Other Behavior. The *differential reinforcement of other behavior (DRO) is a schedule in which reinforcement is delivered if a particular response does not occur for a prescribed interval.* The difference between this schedule and those intending to increase responding is quite straightforward: reinforcement is delivered for response *omission* rather than for response *emission*. Because this requirement of response omission is for a particular period of time, a DRO schedule is essentially the opposite of a limited-hold schedule in which a response must occur within the interval. Examples of this schedule would be praising a child for not talking out during the whole music period, or for not hitting another child for the entire day, or for not throwing papers during the study period.

Figure 9.5 shows the power of DRO schedules in reducing stereotypic responding (which is any form of high-rate, repetitive, nonsocial behavior). It is almost always found with infants, but it is also often found beyond that age with persons labeled autistic, severely retarded, or profoundly retarded. Each of the three behaviors in this study (Repp, Deitz, & Speir, 1974) were occurring at extraordinary rates, and each was interfering with our teaching purposeful activities. One of the students was moving her fingers across her lips about 80 times

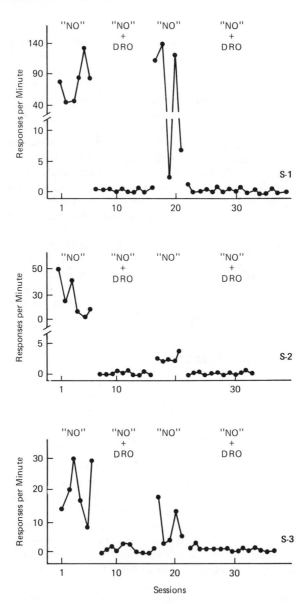

Figure 9-5. The rate of stereotypic responding during baseline and treatment (DRO) phases. The behaviors were "lip flapping" (S-1), rocking (S-2), and waving hand in front of one's face (S-3) (Repp, Deitz, & Speir, 1974, p. 281).

per minute; another was rocking back and forth about 27 times per minute; while the third was moving his hand horizontally back and forth in front of his face about 20 times per minute. With each of the individuals, the same general

DRO procedure was followed. When the behavior did not occur, the teacher praised and hugged the student for a few seconds. Gradually, the requirement for response omission was increased from a second or two to about a minute for each of the students, while the behaviors continued to decrease.

The intricacies of programming DRO will be discussed in Chapter 11, but the basic element to a successful DRO program is the same as that of other reinforcement schedules. A requirement that the student can now meet should be chosen first. In this case, that requirement is an interval of response omission. Then the requirement for reinforcement should be changed in a systematic manner toward the eventual goal. Again, the value of a careful use of reinforcement schedules is particularly evident with our population. The initial requirement need never be "beyond the student's capabilities," for the initial requirement can be the present level of responding. A careful movement toward the eventual goal will allow the student to succeed all along the way, a result that is probably even more important for a handicapped than a nonhandicapped population.

Differential Reinforcement of Low Rates. The *differential reinforcement of low rates of responding (DRL)*[6] *is a schedule in which responding less than or equal to a particular rate is reinforced.* As such, it is essentially the opposite of a DRH schedule when it is used in applied settings. In using a DRL schedule, we typically set a limit, and deliver reinforcement when the number of responses is less than or equal to some limit. For example, in one classroom of "extremely disruptive" TMR students in a special classroom within a public school, we (Deitz & Repp, 1973) attempted to reduce the rate of talk-outs by the entire class. Talk-outs included making statements not related to the ongoing class discussion, talking to oneself, singing or humming, and talking to the teacher or classmates without the teacher's permission.[7] After an analysis of the baseline data, the teacher told the students that each would receive a choice of edibles if the group made five or fewer talk-outs within a 50-minute period. When this DRL contingency was invoked, behavior reduced immediately and stayed below that level both while the DRL schedule was in effect and after it was removed. The DRL limit of five per 50 minutes suggests one of the advantages of this schedule, which is that the goal does not have to be complete response suppression. Rather, it can be a limit that allows some off-task behavior, some acting out, etc., but not so much that it interferes with the progress that all the individuals in the class should be making. In essence, the students do not have to be "perfect angels"; they merely need to be good enough most of the time to allow them to learn what they are in a class to learn.

---

[6] DRL is also a procedure that can be programmed in several ways (Dietz & Repp, 1974). In this section, however, the way in which it is programmed in applied situations with our population is discussed.

[7] Unfortunately, these and other descriptions of classroom and individual behavior are quite "antiseptic," lacking the flavor of what is really happening. Such of our work has been with students described as "hell-raisers," "behaviorally disturbed," "the worst I've ever seen," "about to kill himself by his head-banging," etc.

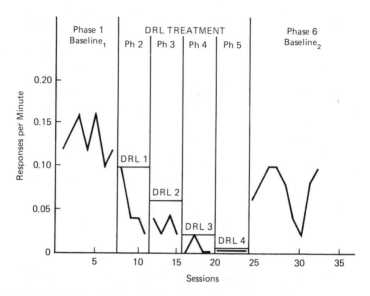

Figure 9-6. The rate of subject-changes for a class of high school senior girls during baseline 1, treatment, and baseline 2 phases. "Free" Fridays could be earned by the group if they made fewer than the specified number of responses for each of the first 4 days of the week. The limit for the first treatment week was five or fewer responses during the 50-minute sessions (DRL 1). DRL 2 required three or fewer responses. DRL 3 required one or fewer, responses and DRL 4 required zero responses (Deitz & Repp, 1973, p. 461).

Another important aspect of DRL schedules, similar to other schedules, is that it allows us to progress gradually to the terminal goal rather than imposing it from the beginning. Figure 9.6 demonstrates an orderly progression through a series of subgoals to the final goal. In this study, a group of high-school seniors engaged in a high rate of "subject-changes," probably in part to taunt the teacher and to disrupt her teaching procedures. Subject-changes were considered to be a change in the ongoing academic discussion to another, usually social, topic. After a baseline analysis of the rate of responding, the teacher instituted a DRL contingency such that free time could be earned on Friday if the class made fewer subject-changes than the DRL limit for each of the first four days of the week. Initially, the DRL limit was five or fewer responses during the 50-minute class period, but the limit was successively decreased to 3, 1, and then zero. While the contingency was in effect, behavior was maintained at this low level, and the discussions for the most part pertained to the classroom objectives. There are, of course, many analogous uses in other classroom areas for this schedule. While some of its intricacies will be discussed later, the basic idea is to set the initial DRL rate limit near the baseline level so that each student can succeed. Then an orderly series of changes can be made to reach a final goal satisfactory to all.

Differential Reinforcement of Incompatible Responding. In *the differential reinforcement of incompatible responding (DRI), a response topographically incompatible with the target behavior is reinforced.* The attempt, of course, is to increase the occurrences of the incompatible response to such a level that the inappropriate response simply does not occur. For example, for out-of-seat behavior, we could reinforce in-seat behavior; for sleeping in class, we could reinforce writing answers to problems; for social isolation, we could reinforce cooperative play. The types of behaviors for which this procedure could apply are, of course, enormous, but the basic procedure is generally the same for all. Generally, on either a ratio or an interval schedule, the instructor reinforces the incompatible behavior while recording the occurrences of both the behaviors. The same basic approach is followed in a DRI program as is followed in all other schedules: start with a requirement that the student can now meet and move to a requirement that is in keeping with other requirements of the learning environment.

Figure 9-7 demonstrates the power of this schedule in decreasing incompatible behavior. Favell (1973) worked with three retarded youngsters who were engaging in various stereotypic behaviors at high rates. She chose as an incom-

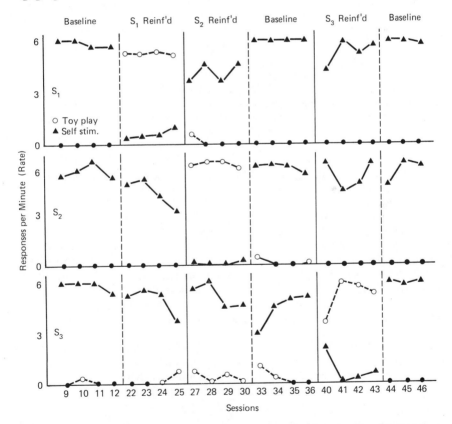

Figure 9-7. The rate of 10-second intervals per minute in which stereotypic responding or toy playing was occurring. The design is a multiple baseline in which only one student in a phase was reinforced for toy play, a behavior incompatible with these particular forms of stereotypic responding. During phases 1, 4, and 6, none of the children was reinforced for toy playing. During phases, 2, 3, and 5, only subjects 1, 2, and 3, respectively, were reinforced for toy play. The study demonstrates the effects of differentially reinforcing incompatible responding (Favell, 1973, p. 22).

patible response "playing with a pegboard" and reinforced each of the students in an across-subjects multiple baseline design. Throughout the study, the rate of 10-second intervals per minute in which responding was occurring was measured (six per minute would be the maximum). In the first phase, no special contingencies were in effect. In the second phase, toy play by the first subject only was reinforced. It immediately increased, while intervals with stereotypic responding reduced almost to zero. In the third phase, toy play by the second child only was reinforced. His responding reduced almost to zero, while the stereotypic responding of the third child remained high and that of the first child returned to a high level. In the fifth phase, toy play of the third child was reinforced, and it increased with results similar to those of the other two students. In the fourth and sixth phases, baseline conditions were reinstated. Although the study showed no carryover, it did show quite clearly that toy play could be increased to high levels and that, when it was, stereotypic responding occurred at a low rate. The problem of carryover, however, is inherent with all our work and should not be construed as a criticism of this schedule, particularly as this project was designed more to demonstrate the effect than to produce lasting change. The project does, however, suggest the major problem of this schedule: when the incompatible response cannot be made (e.g., when for this study the pegboard is not available), the inappropriate behavior is likely to return as it has never been directly consequated (as it would be in DRO and DRL schedules). The point to remember then is that we will build a weakness into the schedule when we reinforce behaviors that require manipulanda that will often not be present at the same time the response is likely to occur.

PROGRAMMING SCHEDULES WITH COMPOUND REQUIREMENTS

There are a number of schedules that have compound requirements in a manner different from those of the differential reinforcement schedules. While they have been studied in laboratory experiments, they have been barely if at all studied in applied work. The purpose of this section, then, is not so much to present schedules whose successful use has been demonstrated, as it is to present schedules that may suggest to the reader practical uses. The import of this approach should be apparent. If a teacher need spend no extra time reinforcing a child's behavior, or preparing materials, or urging a principal or a superintendent to buy curricula; if a teacher need do no more to increase responding and promote student achievement than simply to select an appropriate schedule of reinforcement, then we should have in our repertoire as many schedules as possible. In this section, we will briefly illustrate a few of these schedules; they are labeled *alternative, conjunctive,* and *interlocking* schedules.

Alternative Schedules

Alternative schedules are defined as ones *"in which reinforcement is programmed by either a ratio or an interval schedule, whichever is satisfied* **first**. *Thus, in an alternative FI5-FR300 the first response is reinforced: (a) after a period of 5 minutes provided 300 responses have* **not** *been made; or (b) upon* *completion of 300 responses provided 5 minutes has* not *elapsed"* (Ferster & Skinner, 1957, p. 5). An alternative schedule thus provides *alternative* ways in which to earn reinforcement. While the way in which it has been defined requires an interval and a ratio schedule, we can certainly generalize the concept of an alternative to other conditions. For example, a child could be given 10 tokens if he or she correctly completes at least 90% of the 50 homework problems or correctly completes 20 during study period. There are quite obviously a number of extensions that can be made of this basic concept. The important approach for those of us working with retarded individuals is not so much to try to fit some of our work to the alternative schedule paradigm as it is to take the alternative concept and to test it for such questions as is the student's behavior improved simply because of the use of such an arrangement? or is such an arrangement difficult for an instructor to implement? or is such an arrangement preferred by students to other arrangements?

Conjunctive Schedules

Where the word alternative implies that one of at least two requirements be met, the word conjunctive implies that all requirements be met. Ferster and Skinner have used the term to describe a schedule *"in which reinforcement occurs when both a ratio and an interval schedule have been satisfied. For example, a response is reinforced when at least 5 minutes have elapsed since the preceding reinforcement* **and** *after at least 300 responses"* (p. 6). Again, although the definition includes both a ratio and an interval schedule, we should not limit our inventiveness to these two schedules. We could require that a student finish at least 20 problems and with at least 90% accuracy during class; or we could require that the student make three or more social interactions with peers during playtime and that all be positive; or that a student run 100 meters in less than 11 seconds, high jump at least 6 feet, and pole vault at least 12 feet, etc., in order to qualify for the high school decathalon.

The examples, of course, can go on and on. But the immediate value of each remains constant: we are placing a requirement on each of the defined behaviors before a single reinforcing event is to occur. As such, we immediately reduce the problem of satiation. At the same time, we can more easily deal with building complex requirements and behaviors. In applying these combinations systematically to the study of retarded persons' behaviors, we may well find some totally unanticipated advantages.

Interlocking Schedules

An interlocking schedule locks together time and number. It is defined as a schedule in which a person *"is reinforced upon completion of a number of responses; but this number changes* **during** *the interval which follows the previous reinforcement.* For example, the number may be set at 300 immediately after reinforcement, but it is reduced linearly, reaching 1 after 10 minutes. If the organism responds very rapidly, it will have to emit nearly 300 responses for reinforcement. If he responds at an intermediate rate, he will be reinforced after a smaller number—say, 150. If he does not respond at all during 10 minutes, the first response thereafter will be reinforced. Many different cases are possible, depending upon the way the number changes with time" (Ferster & Skinner, 1957, p. 6). The analog of this schedule for applied use should be apparent. We can simply require more responding if the student takes longer to respond. For example, we can tell a student that 15 responses are necessary for reinforcement now; if he chooses, however, he may have 20 minutes of free time. In that case though, 25 completed problems will be due this afternoon. In essence, we are allowing the student to choose his or her own requirement relative to time. The student can do so many problems now, or she or he can do more if he or she chooses to wait. The problem with making large increases in requirements over time can, however, be considerable. Reynolds (1968) has discussed this issue quite vividly.

> The increasing interlocking-schedule is[8] particularly dangerous, since the requirement for reinforcement becomes prohibitively large after a short time. Thus, responding may never be reinforced if it does not begin at a high enough rate. If a group of organisms were subjected to this schedule, they would very rapidly separate into two distinct groups: those who initially responded rapidly enough to allow the schedule to maintain their responding and those who initially responded so slowly that reinforcement never occurred. The first group would continue to respond rapidly, and the latter group would soon not respond at all. This is the sort of insidious schedule that exists in cumulative educational systems in which, as time passes, the requirements for success become larger and larger. It is, for example, extremely difficult to perform well in the third grade if very little was learned in the first and second. Such an educational system develops and maintains a separation of students which appears to be dictated by nature but which actually depends primarily on their initial performance. (p. 85)

Reynold's remarks relate quite directly to our educational history of passing students through grades for "social reasons," and to our pushing some students through mainstreamed classes without having well-developed individualized curricula. Interlocking schedules do present the problem of the student becoming so far behind that he or she can never catch up, thus experiencing a series of failures. However, judiciously used in the classroom, we do not have to make increments in requirements over time so great that they would lend themselves to failure. They could be quite appropriately used by now allowing the total length of time to be very long in the first place and by using such techniques as response priming and reinforcer sampling. The comparative value of interlocking schedules was demonstrated by Stephens, Pear, Wray, and Jackson (1975) when they compared that schedule with an FR schedule in the picture-learning task for retarded children. The data were presented in several ways, but the data in Figure 9-8 indicate the differences between these schedules quite effectively. The study was conducted in four phases. In phase 1, an FR5 was compared with an interlock in which 5 responses were required in t minutes. If 5 were not made, 2 more were required in t more minutes; if these 2 were not made, 2 more were required in t more minutes, etc., up to 15 total responses. The time t was gradual-

---

[8] This author would substitute "can be" for "is."

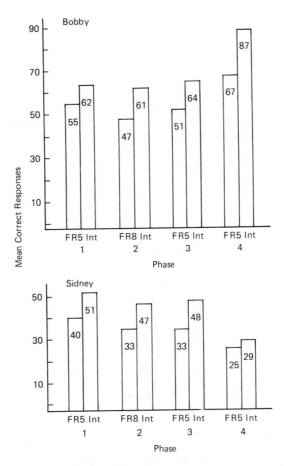

Figure 9-8. The mean number of correct responses under conditions of an FR or interlocking schedule by two retarded children on a task of "picture learning." The response requirements for the interlocking schedule are shown in Figure 9-10 (adapted from Stephens, Pear, Wray, & Jackson, 1975).

ly decreased in this phase from 2 minutes to 1. In phase 2, the FR value was increased to 8, which was the average number of responses made in the interlocking schedule in the prior phase. In phase 3, the FR5 condition of the first phase was repeated. In phase 4, the FR value was 5, but the time t for the interlocking schedule was decreased to 0.5 minute. Figure 9-9 shows the requirement for the interlocking schedule for the final value of t for each of the phases. The results in Figure 9-8 show the large difference in mean correct responding that was produced *just by the difference in scheduling.* The teacher had to do nothing other than change the schedule of reinforcement; no additional reinforcers, materials, etc., were required. The importance of such an effect, due solely to instituting a particular schedule of reinforcement, cannot be overemphasized; *nothing else needed to be done to improve performance,* and with our population, often displaying such difficulties in performance, this is a critical effect.

A similar effect with a variation on this schedule was demonstrated by Lovitt and Esveldt (1970). In the typical interlocking schedule, the *number of responses* necessary for reinforcement changes as a function of *time*. In this variation, the *number of reinforcers* changed as a function of the *rate of responding*. In one of their demonstrations, the authors were concerned with the math performance of a student labeled behaviorally disturbed. During the baseline period, the student was given problems of the type 50 + 22 = _____, where the sum was ≤ 198. The student was capable of answering these problems, and he did so. But the rate at which he finished problems was thought to be too low. During the first phase of the study,[9] the student earned one point exchangeable for 1 minute of free time in a "high-interest" room for every 20 correct mathematics answers. During the second phase, a multiple band contingency was instituted in which the student could earn: "(a) no points for 0 to 44 responses, (b) three points for 45 to 59 responses, (c) six points for 60 to 74 responses, and (d) 15 points for more than 75 responses" (p. 264). The relation of this schedule to an interlocking schedule is demonstrated by comparing Figure 9-10 with Figure 9-9. In the study by Lovitt and Esveldt, the number of reinforcers that could be earned increased as the rate of responding increased. In the study by Stephens *et al.*, the number of responses required for reinforcement increased with time. As Figure 9-11 indicates, a change to this schedule had a dramatic and continuing effect. When the second phase was in operation, correct math responding almost doubled while the error rate decreased to one-third its prior level. When the conditions were reversed in this ABAB design, the same effect was repeated. These results indicate again the enormous power of schedules in changing behavior. All the teacher had to do to increase significantly this student's academic responding was to tell him that by

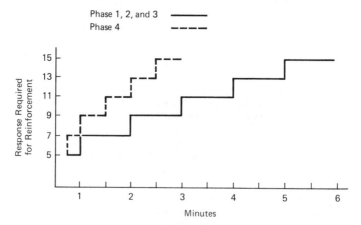

Figure 9-9. The number of responses required in an interlocking schedule used by Stephens, Pear, Wray, and Jackson, 1975. In phases 1, 2, and 3, five responses within a minute lead to reinforcement. If five had not occurred within 1 minute, seven were required within 2 minutes. If seven had not occurred within 2 minutes, nine were required within 2 minutes, and so forth. In phase 4, the length of time was changed from 1 minute to 30 seconds, so that five responses were required in the first 30 seconds. If five had not occurred within that time, seven were required by the end of 1 minute, and so forth.

---

[9] This discussion is of Experiment II.

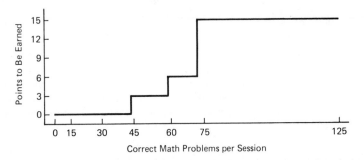

Figure 9-10. The number of points that could be earned for each band of correct mathematics problems per session. For less than 45 problems, no points were earned; for 45-59 problems, three points were earned; for 60-74 problems, six points were earned; and for 75 or more problems, 15 points were earned. While not meeting the definition of an interlocking schedule, this schedule is quite similar in concept (adapted from Lovitt & Esveldt, 1970).

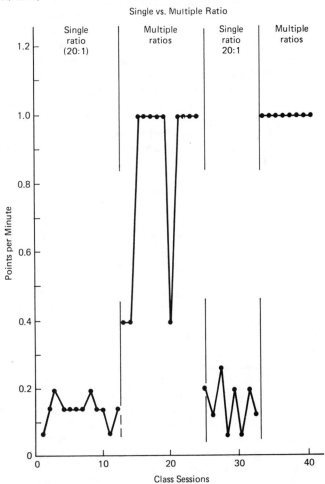

Figure 9-11. The rate of correct and incorrect math performance under two conditions. In phases 1 and 3, one point could be earned for every 20 correct responses. In phases 2 and 4, more points could be earned for rates of correct responding that were higher than the rates in phases 1 and 3 (Lovitt & Esveldt, 1970, p. 265).

263

working more rapidly he could earn a few more minutes of free time. The behavior of this child, which was considered far too low in rate, was thus increased at absolutely no expense in terms of time or materials. When we normally have to go to extreme lengths to improve the performance of retarded youngsters, we should not pass by such extremely easy means of improvement as schedule control.

PROGRAMMING SECOND-ORDER SCHEDULES (TOKEN SCHEDULES)

Second-order schedules are those in which schedules are scheduled. For example, a student might earn a point worth 1 minute of free time for every 20 correct math problems, but the student might have to earn five of those points before he or she can use them. In this case, the mathematics performance would be on an FR20 schedule, but the exchange of points for free time would be on an FR5 schedule. Or a student might earn a token if he or she follows an instruction within 30 seconds, but the student might not be able to exchange the tokens for a variety of items until Thursday at 3:00. In this example, a limited-hold schedule is itself scheduled according to some interval at which the tokens can be exchanged. Certainly not all second-order schedules involve tokens. In reality, probably relatively few do. But our understanding of the applied nature of this schedule is limited for the most part to token programs. In view of their extreme popularity in recent years, they will be discussed as an example of second-order schedules.

Token Schedules

A token program is a two-component chain. In the *token-production component*, the student simply earns tokens according to some schedule of reinforcement. In the *token-exchange component*, the student simply exchanges the tokens for backup reinforcers according to another schedule of reinforcement and according to some exchange ratio.

Token economics have been present for thousands of years with various forms of money used as tokens in our general societies. Within our educational societies, however, token economies are a relatively new phenomenon, occurring predominantly in the last 15 years. There were, however, examples of token programs long before the advent of behavior analysis, or even of psychology. Kazdin (1977) has discussed several of these in a book devoted solely to token economies. One of the first was that of Joseph Lancaster, who in the early 1800s developed the monitorial system in England. At that time, Lancaster had initiated free education for the poor, a movement that swelled the enrollments and crowded facilities. Without enough teachers, Lancaster began a system in which students acted as monitors for groups of students. There were several types and duties of monitors (e.g., teaching, examining, keeping attendance records), but the system in general seemed to revolve around the principle we now call reinforcement. Kazdin describes the reinforcement system as one

> based upon competition. As students were taught in their groups, while standing in a semi-circle around the monitor, each wore a number which indicated his or her relative position in the group in order of merit. As individuals performed in the

group, the standing of each was changed as a function of their responses relative to others. For correct responses (e.g., reading) one moved up and for incorrect responses one moved down in the ranking. The top individual in each group earned a rank of 1 and received a leather ticket of merit. Also, he wore a picture pasted on a small board and suspended on his chest to indicate his excellent performance. If his performance was surpassed by someone else in his group, he forfeited the honor of having the ticket and wearing the picture and the highest ranking number. Yet, he received another picture as a reward for having earned first place. Individuals were periodically examined by someone other than their monitor to determine whether they could be promoted to a higher group. When a student knew the lesson and earned a promotion, he received a prize. His monitor also received a prize of the same value. (p. 31)

Other procedures were used to promote other appropriate behaviors. Students who excelled in attending to their studies or in helping others received silver medals to wear about their necks. The Lancaster system was brought to New York, which in 1805 made free education available to the poor. This was perhaps the first token system used in American education and, as Kazdin notes, it extended the English system and is quite similar to present token economies. Using the same basic monitoring system as Lancaster had, the New York City system also used fixed numbers of tickets for performance; but it also allowed greater flexibility by giving the teacher discretionary use of more than 1,000 tickets per month for special achievements. The system also advanced the idea of token loss for inappropriate classroom behavior, replacing with it the physical punishment system used before and since.[10]

Token systems certainly continued in one form or another, but they were never systematically studied in order to determine how to make them more successful and with what particular behaviors and populations they would be successful. Curiously, within a year of each other, two studies of basic research were published in the 1930s (Cowles, 1937; Wolfe, 1936), but interest in tokens remained dormant for many years. A few decades later, another curiously singular series of events began. Prior to this time, applied work had really been direct applications of methods and principles found in basic research. But in 1961, applied work with tokens began before very much basic research had been completed with token systems.[11] Then in 1961, Staats began his work with tokens

---

[10] There are remarkable commonalities between this system and the means by which many of us advocate teaching should be arranged at present. The practice of rewarding a student for correct responding is, of course, central to *reinforcement*. Changing the status of student standings requires *continuous measurement*. Using monitors is the same as our use of *peers* to teach, reinforce, and provide informative feedback. Having the student tested by someone other than a monitor is analogous to our insistence on *reliability*. *Rewarding the teacher* (monitor) as well as the student is a program attempted by many of us. Either *eliminating* the use of *punishment* altogether, as advocated by Skinner, or at least replacing personally involved punishment with impersonal systems like token loss, is a common rule of behaviorists. Perhaps the only procedure mentioned in the quotation from Kazdin not commonly used is competition between students. While it is sometimes used, it is generally rejected in favor of a system in which the student in essence competes with himself. This is the central idea to all of our evaluation systems, whether they be tests like criterion-referenced ones or experimental designs like reversals or the changing criterion.

[11] Some basic work with tokens had been completed by Kelleher (1957a, b) and a great deal of work had been completed with conditioned reinforcement, a much broader category; but very little in terms of a systematic study of tokens had been done.

and language and Ayllon and Azrin began their large-scale work with tokens and psychiatric patients (Ayllon & Azrin, 1968; Staats, 1968; Staats, Minke, Finley, Wolf & Brooks, 1964; Staats, Staats, Schultz & Wolf, 1962). From that point, an enormous amount of applied study with token economies began.

In our field, Birnbrauer and Lawler (1964) published the first report of work with a token system in a special education classroom. Of their 37 students, 14 had never attended school, 3 had been dismissed from school because of "incorrigibility," and 4 were "severe behavior problems." Birnbrauer, Bijou, Wolf, and Kidder (1965) used a token system to support their programmed instructional materials for teaching academic and practical tasks like reading, writing, arithmetic, and telling time. The success of token systems with academic and social behaviors in classrooms was demonstrated in this and in a continuing series of studies by these authors (Bijou, Birnbrauer, Kidder & Tague, 1966; Birnbrauer, Wolf, Kidder & Tague, 1965). The success of token systems in institutions was also being demonstrated with social behaviors primarily at the institution in Parsons, Kansas (Girardeau & Spradlin, 1964; Lent, 1967, 1968). With these studies as a basis, teachers, psychologists, aides, and many others became seriously involved in the application of token systems as motivation and feedback devices for retarded persons in a very wide variety of settings. Some of this work was research oriented, designed to learn more about the reasons for successes and failures with tokens. Some of the work was simply direct application of what had already been demonstrated, but it did serve to validate the efficacy of these programs across settings, behaviors, staff, and retarded individuals. From all this work, we have learned a number of procedures to follow to increase the likelihood that token systems will work. The next section will describe some of these procedures.

Factors to Consider in Programming Token Economics

In this section, we will discuss some of the factors relating to token systems, and we will do so in a number of sections: (1) considering whether to implement a token program, (2) considerations before starting a program, (3) physical aspects of the token economy environment, (4) suggestions to follow while implementing a token program, and (5) removing the token economy.

Considering Whether to Implement a Token Program. The initial question to ask about a token program is whether we should even both to implement one. There are several areas we need to consider before answering that question. One is *whether present conditions are sufficiently motivating* or are changes in conditions necessary. The traditional motivating system used in public schools has been grades. For some students, this is an adequate reinforcer. But for other students, grades do not affect behavior. With our population, there are two general and often separate problems with grades: (1) for some of our students, a mark on a card is simply meaningless, and (2) the delay between classroom responding and the delivery of a grade is simply too long. For a delayed response-contingent grade to be effective, the student would at least have to have been through a careful series of increased delays, but this, of course, seldom happens. Given then that grades are usually not reinforcers, do we have other systems for reinforcement operating with sufficient frequency? Are students given immediate feedback on their performance and, if so, is feedback reinforcing? Are students frequently given praise and other forms of attention for their correct work and, if so, are these acts social reinforcers? Are peers reinforcing to each other? If so, to what extent do they reinforce each other for appropriate or inappropriate behaviors? Are activities, free time, etc., present in the environment and are they now arranged in such a way that students do not need to link with tokens their performance to reinforcing activities? There are many such questions to ask, but they all revolve about the question of whether the learning environment is presently sufficiently reinforcing so that tokens would add nothing to the students' performance and learning. A similar consideration is *whether the environment needs so little change that the appropriate changes could be made without implementing a token system.* This is similar to the problem discussed by Drabman and Tucker (1974) of "using a cannon where a BB gun would do just as well" (p. 185). Some classrooms need only a little more consistency or a few more reinforcers to be more successful. In situations like these, token economies may simply require time and money that are not necessary to effect the changes desired.

Another question is *whether the program would be physically possible to implement.* This question should be considered in two areas. One is the class size. If a class is large, a teacher may simply be unable to consequate with tokens more than one or two simple behaviors. If this is the case, other types of reinforcement programs might be used just as effectively on those behaviors (one of the advantages of praise, of course, is that it does not require a great deal of movement by the teacher; delivering tangible tokens often requires more movement). As Drabman and Tucker (1974) have suggested, one alternative is to use group contingencies instead of individual contingencies when the group size is prohibitive. Consequences can be made contingent upon the group average or upon the behavior of an individual (e.g., the person with the lowest score must have a score of at least 10 in order for the group to receive a token). However, when the class is highly divergent, this type of program may either be impossible or may make little sense to most of the class members. A second consideration on the physical possibility of a token system is whether the reinforcers to be used for exchange involve any costs. Generally, we try to use classroom activities as reinforcers, but tangibles such as games, toys, and tickets to ballgames are often very powerful reinforcers. Before implementing a program, one then has to identify the potential reinforcers to be used in the token exchange, at what rate they will be earned, and what the cost of the entire program will be.

A final consideration is that token economies require a change in the teacher's behavior in order to change the student's behavior. The question then becomes *will your behavior be changed?* Many people consider token programs to be efforts directed solely at changing the behaviors of students; but that change is really only the final product. For years, we have been struck by the way in which token programs can change the behavior of teachers. Student behaviors tend to be more rigorously defined by teachers; teacher attention is more frequently contingent upon appropriate behavior and less frequently contingent upon inappropriate behavior; each student tends to receive more feedback and attention than he or she previously did; often objective and more frequent data are collected in order to assess student progress; and more decisions of a programmatic nature are based on data. But many of the changes in teacher behavior also require feedback, attention, and praise. Is there someone who will help you through the problems and share with you the successes? Excellent programs can and certainly have been developed by individuals alone, but the first time one is establishing a program, aid is certainly helpful.

Considerations before Implementing a Program.   After one has decided to implement a token program, there are several issues to resolve before actually beginning. Perhaps the most important is whether there is *approval from the administrator, the teacher, and all other staff involved.* Some token programs fail because adminstrators, psychologists, consultants, and others force token programs on staff without properly explaining the rationale and obtaining their approval. When staff do not approve of the program, it will probably fail unless there is a rapid and dramatic improvement with some of the clients. When staff do not approve but an administration is adamant, an adminstrator should be in the program, initially on a full-time basis, to provide guidance, encouragement, feedback, and reinforcement for the staff. Very little will sabotage a program so rapidly as an outsider demanding something be done without providing the support necessary for its implementation. On the other hand, staff who implement a program despite lack of enthusiastic administrative support need to provide the administrator with feedback on student progress, as well as encouragement to visit their program. Support and approval should also be sought from the *parents.* There is nothing so disarming as an enraged parent who, after walking all over you, goes to the adminstration and tries to stop your program. There really is no need to endanger a potentially successful program by failing to inform parents of your plans before you begin. Be honest and be specific with them. If you are going to remove tokens for inappropriate responding, don't just tell them of that portion of your program in which correct responding will be rewarded with programs. Be sure to specify exactly what behaviors will earn (or lose) tokens, how many responses are required per token, and how many tokens are required to exchange for each item. Finally, and most importantly, *discuss the program with the student.* A system implemented without proper forewarning is simply not fair. Explain to them what behaviors will be consequated with token gain (and perhaps loss); explain when they can exchange tokens for backup reinforcers; explain how many tokens each exchange item requires; seek the student's approval and cooperation; and be certain that you test whether the student has comprehended the rules of the economy. Sometimes verbalizations may be enough; sometimes you will need to model some of the behaviors; and sometimes you may just have to wait until the program has been implemented before you can test whether the student has comprehended the relation between responding and consequences. This type of program represents a *behavioral contract,* which can be drawn up in a classroom, at home, in a sheltered workshop, etc. It is an agreement between the client and another person on a goal and a procedure for reaching that goal.

A second consideration is *how long each day the program will be in effect.* Certainly, the longer the program is in effect each day, the more chance it has of succeeding. But implementing it for long periods each day from the start may doom the program itself for no other reason than teacher fatigue. Being personally reinforcing, being as consistent as we should be, maintaining records, providing exchanges, etc., can be fatiguing, particularly at the start of a program. In such cases, we should start slowly, gradually increasing the length of the program and the demands on ourselves as we become more accustomed to the various roles we must assume. Such a shaping program to ourselves may require only two or three weeks, and we can sometimes make the system easier to operate and even use our students to help. Many teachers use posters or blackboard charts with checks, stars, or "happy faces." These correspond to the tokens earned and can be posted by children who can then discuss their successes.

As we shape our own behavior into being more complex and varied in this program, we should be making gradual changes in the complexity of the students' behavior. Such a plan requires that we *write the details of the program before it is started.* This writing should include the following: (1) Definitions of the behaviors that will now be consequated. (2) Definitions of the behaviors that are expected to become more complex in such areas as topography before they will be consequated over time. If for one week a child is to earn tokens for eating a certain way, but if more independence, manners, etc., are required the second week, then these changes in skill levels should be specified. (3) Statements for each student of what level of behavior is required for tokens. One of the advantages of token systems is that they can be highly individualistic. Mike might earn a token for every three correct answers; Doug might earn one for every eight correct answers; and Susan might earn one for every twelve correct answers. But to be fair to the students and to lessen confusion, all these schedules of token reinforcement should be written before the first day of the program. (4) Written schedules for token exchange. Because the schedules for token delivery can be individualized, the schedules for token exchange can be the same for all students. They merely need to be written once and then posted.

A final and very important consideration is that *all staff should be trained* in response definitions, token delivery and exchange procedures, data collection, and all other facets of the program before it begins. In addition, checks to ensure that all are following the procedures correctly should be scheduled and explained beforehand. Staff inconsistencies can be very damaging to any program, regardless of whether it is a token program; and like all programs, staff problems are not eliminated just by its implementation. Bath and Smith (1974) have discussed this issue noting the "profound effect that inconsistencies among personnel had on performances. Though there was some drop in positive behavior during the periods of inconsistency, the most marked result was the sharp increase in undesirable behaviors" (p. 43). The authors go on to note a problem when facilities have substituted employees, remarking on anecdotal information that the students had complained that some staff were unfair in dispensing tokens, and that staff complained that they need not bother to learn a system when they were only substituting. They concluded that "the apparent effects of personnel inconsistency observed here point out the need for having extra trained staff available to fill absences during token program implementation" (p. 43). Certainly, we should not believe that preimplementation staff training will prevent all problems. But it is another area of preparation that can help to reduce problems.

Physical Aspects of the Token Economy Environment.   The token environment requires quite a few physical arrangements by staff. For example, we need to *identify where the tokens are to be kept.* For primary areas, some teachers wear carpenter's or change bags and dispense tokens from these. If they are chips of a sort, they may need to be coded to prevent stealing. In other cases, tokens may be marks on a paper or on the blackboard, so the task may be easier for the teacher. We also need to *identify a place for token exchange.* The usual choice is some part of the room that is used primarily for this purpose and that has sufficient space. When exchange is for activities, free time, etc., the exchange procedure can take place wherever the student happens to be, and special places are unnecessary. *Schedules of token exchange* should be posted as close as possible to the area of token exchange. When appropriate, students can be encouraged to read the amount necessary for exchange, to count the number of tokens they have accumulated, and to determine whether they have enough. Token systems lend themselves quite nicely to the practice of math skills, and we should not let this opportunity pass. One of the problems with teaching arithmetic skills is that they are generally not maintained by the student's environment outside the time he or she is being taught the specific tasks. Token accumulation and exchange can be arranged as relevant features of a child's life with a little imagination. *Rules of the token economy* should also be posted. They should include consequences for each of the target behaviors, exchange ratios and times, and all the various features indigenous to individualized programs. Arrangements also need to be made for *record keeping.* Many students enjoy posting on public charts the number of their correct responses and the number of tokens they have earned each day. Again, this opportunity for maintaining math skills should not be overlooked. If we have no aversive aspects in our program, posting charts on walls is an excellent method for allowing each student to demonstrate and be proud of her or his accomplishments for the day. At the end of various periods in which tokens can be earned, students can post their own earnings, discuss their achievements, learn to applaud each other for appropriate responding, and learn the social skills associated with being polite while other people are talking. *Token programs can and should be used to teach many more behaviors than the system itself directly consequates.*

Another aspect of the physical environment is the *token itself;* what will it be? Some of the choices are limited by the behaviors or possible behaviors of the students themselves. Small plastic or metal objects should not be used with individuals who are likely to chew or swallow them. Similarly, paper tokens should not be given to persons who are likely to destroy them. Two very different experiences with matching tokens with clients have been described by Sulzer-Azaroff and Mayer (1977): A

> token that we have found particularly useful is a construction-paper coin. Developmental Learning Corporation[12] manufactures rubber-stamp impressions of 1-cent, 5-cent, and 10-cent coins. They can be stamped on squares cut from construction paper. Such tokens serve a dual function—as tokens and for compu-

---

[12] Developmental Learning Corporation, 3805 North Ashland Avenue, Chicago, IL, 60657.

tational skills. One teacher of a combination second- and third-grade class set up a program in which students could earn "1 cent" by engaging in behaviors like getting their work cards, "5 cents" for following directions, and "10 cents" for choosing an activity. They could earn five minutes of free time for "$1.50," the opportunity to be cashier for "$1.00," the chance to be first out for recess for "$1.00," writing on the blackboard for "$1.85," or helping the teacher for "$1.75."[13] In a study by Thomas, Sulzer-Azaroff, Lukeris, and Palmer (1977), many of the clients could neither write nor count. But they could figure out the price of an object from the "price tag." The tag was a sheet of cardboard on which the outlines of the requisite number of tokens were drawn. The client then had only to fill in the outlines with her tokens to pay the correct amount. (p. 397)

Aspects of the token itself have been discussed by Wolff and Gray (1973), who identified six types of tokens most frequently employed in the economies. These were (1) *poker chips,* usually the colored plastic type found in drug and game stores, (2) *coins,* generally of a foreign currency less expensive than the cost of poker chips, (3) *check marks,* usually on cards given to each student, (4) *points,* often posted or kept by the instructor, and differing from the other tokens in that they are not tangible objects retained by the student, (5) *credit cards,* using the same system all credit-card companies use, and (6) *special paper money,* printed somewhat like monopoly monies but often with an area for the students name, the behavior, and the date to be written. Some advantages and disadvantages of each of these have been summarized by Wolff and Gray, and they appear in Figure 9-12. The comments hold for most places in which each type of token would be used, although some of the disadvantages listed for each can be overcome.

Just as tokens are an aspect of the physical environment, so are backup reinforcers. Three general concerns arise. These are (1) what to use as backup reinforcers, an issue addressed by those factors discussed in Chapter 8 on selecting reinforcers; (2) what not to use as backup reinforcers, a legal and ethical issue usually answered by distinguishing between "rights" and "privileges" (see Budd & Baer, 1976, for a discussion of some legally defined rights and privileges); and (3) how to obtain backup reinforcers. A number of very good suggestions have been made by Sulzer-Azaroff and Mayer (1977) for obtaining backups at either no cost or at low cost. Some of these are the following:

1. To ask community stores for discards, rejects, excess parts, etc., that can be used to construct objects. They have obtained broken cookies and day-old goods from wholesale bakeries, imperfect dolls from a factory, scraps from a lumber yard, and spools from a thread manufacturer.

2. To ask parents, co-workers, clubs, and other community members for "white elephants" and discards such as magazines and old toys.

3. To obtain junk-mail giveaways and promotional items such as catalogs, free samples, and calendars; also, *The Whole Kid's Catalogue* (Cardozo, 1975) and the *Salisbury Catalog of Free Teaching Materials.*

---

[13] Note that the backup reinforcers were activities; none had to be bought.

PHYSICAL ATTRIBUTES OF TOKENS

Types of Reinforcers Employed

Characteristics	Poker Chips	Coins	Checks	Points	Credit Cards	Play Money
Negative:						
Can be lost	Yes	Yes	Yes	No	No	No
Can be stolen and spent	Yes	Yes	No	No	No	No
Can be counterfeited	Yes	Yes	Yes	No	No	No
Can be hoarded	Yes	Yes	Yes	Yes	Yes	Yes
S can live beyond means	No	No	No	No	Yes	No
Positive:						
Can be dispensed mechanically	Yes	Yes	No	No	No	No
Can be delivered without attracting "much" attention	Yes	Yes	Yes	Yes	No	No
Easily transported to other areas	Yes	Yes	Yes	No	No	Yes
S can quickly determine present balance	Yes	Yes	Yes	Yes	No	Yes
Can be delivered in less than 5 sec	Yes	Yes	Yes	Yes	No	No
Automatically yields data on how each S earns reinforcers	No	No	No	Yes	Yes	Yes
Automatically yields data on how groups earn reinforcers	No	No	No	Yes	Yes	Yes
Automatically yields information on S's rate of reinforcement	No	No	Yes	Yes	Yes	Yes
Automatically yields information on T's use of reinforcement	No	No	No	Yes	Yes	Yes

Chips, coins, and checks have the common positive attribute of being tangible and can be delivered immediately after the emission of the behavior. Tangibleness may be particularly important with nonverbal Ss. However, in terms of the quantity and quality of data which they automatically yield, they are distinctly inferior to the point and credit card systems. Special paper money is tangible, yet it provides data concerning the operation of the system. Unfortunately, there is an inherent response-reinforcement delay, for T must record the information on the reinforcement before delivering it. Also, S must spend the reinforcement before the data can be analyzed.

Figure 9-12. A listing of several advantages and disadvantages of six items commonly used as tokens (Wolff & Gray, 1973, p. 677).

4. To find items for "collections" such as Christmas cards, postcards from a particular country or region, pictures of animals, etc.[14]
5. To rent rather than give items permanently to the students. For example, instead of 10 tokens being sufficient to "buy" a toy, 10 tokens could only rent a toy for a month. At that time, the student could rent the item

---

[14] Suggesting a collection of similar items would seem to be a means of making a single item much more reinforcing than it would otherwise be. Stamp collectors, automobile collectors, and many others emit behaviors in pursuit of a particular item for their collection that they would never emit for other items. There is no reason why the same class of collection-earning behaviors could not operate in a classroom.

again, or if he or she finds something else more reinforcing at the time, the student could choose that. Our likes and dislikes obviously change over time, and many items a student buys will soon be discarded. A rental system could return these items to the economy, to be rented again, thereby providing extra backup reinforcers at no cost to the economy.

6. To buy objects in bulk from companies that supply vending machines.
7. To enlist the aid of those peripherally associated with the program. Ask administrators, parents, and others to help you locate backup reinforcers; we may find this interchange to be a good vehicle to discuss other matters in our program that are of concern to all.

Suggestions to Follow When Implementing a Token Program.   Token economies involve the behaviors of at least two groups of persons: staff and students. We usually presume the concentration of our efforts will be directed toward the students, and it should be. But much of our efforts should be directed toward ourselves and our own behaviors. To that end, this section provides a number of suggestions on general procedures that should help you operate a token economy. These include (1) being consistent, (2) adding social reinforcers, (3) programming reinforcement delays, (4) using reinforcement rules like sampling, (5) programming natural consequences, (6) considering economic factors, (7) involving the group, (8) consequating inappropriate behaviors, (9) choosing whether to consequate social or academic behaviors first, (10) altering rules only after consulting data, (11) providing data on staff behavior, (12) buying tangibles, and (13) following the many rules provided by the extensive work by Ayllon and Azrin (1968).

Consistency may be the most critical factor of any program, and with developmentally delayed individuals, its importance is emphasized. In general, we label people retarded because their behavior is retarded. That is, their rate of learning for many behaviors is simply slower than the rate of learning demonstrated on the same tasks by people not labeled retarded. The problem then becomes one of eliminating as many factors as possible that inhibit or interfere with their rate of learning. One of the most obvious interfering factors is lack of consistency in the learning environment. When we lavishly praise a student the first time or two she or he points to the correct color card in a new learning program and then offer no feedback for the next five responses, we have presented an ambiguous environment. When we ask a child to point to her mouth, praise her when she does on the first trial, and then do not provide her differential feedback when she touches her nose and then her mouth on the second trial, we have presented an ambiguous environment. When we state that cleaning the blackboard will earn a token, forget the tokens on Tuesday, and then don't give Harold a token for cleaning the boards, we have presented ambiguity. In so doing, we have not provided the type of environment in which these students can learn appropriate behaviors at an appropriate rate. The rules for providing a good learning environment must be maintained. The rules of the token system itself must also be maintained. Drabman and Tucker (1974) have warned us of the occasional attempts of students to cajole or coerce the teacher.

It is reasonable that students should try to minimize their work while maximizing their reinforcement. They will often make self-serving suggestions and threats (e.g., "I will not work unless you give me my points first," or "You gave Marjie 10 points and I was better than she, but you only gave me seven points. I won't work until you give me three more points"). Teachers should not reward this behavior by paying attention to it. A teacher must always keep in mind that the teacher is the manager of the classroom and that within that context the teacher-student roles should be defined clearly. (p. 183)

In our work, we have never had the kind of problems described by Drabman and Tucker. Perhaps the reason is that our populations differed; or perhaps the reason is that the situations they described are those in which the teachers emphasized the tokens too much. Minimize the importance of the token itself and maximize the importance of the social aspects of the token system. The token economy itself should be fun. It should not be something in which the student is reinforced for verbalizing about the importance of tokens *per se;* rather it should be a vehicle for two objectives: (1) to provide very clear feedback for responding, and (2) to provide a base for building social reinforcers. The terminal objective for most large-scale token programs should be their own programmed demise. Despite the similarity of tokens to our monetary system, most token programs are artificial, and they should be replaced by social reinforcers operating in the environment. Token programs may be needed to establish order, to rapidly produce significant gains by the students, and to develop more natural reinforcers. But they should all include a careful program of increasing the reinforcing properties of our social behaviors. To that end, *pair all token exchanges and token deliveries with your social approval and, when appropriate, with the social approval of peers.*

The delay between responding and token delivery and the delay between token delivery and token exchange can be critical. If they are initially long, most token programs will fail. The initial delay, of course, depends upon the student, the behaviors involved, the teachers, and other aspects of the environment. In its simplest form, we have taught the token system to young retarded children in a preschool program in just a few steps. Initially, we arrange a number of known reinforcers near us. Then a token is placed in the student's hand. After a few seconds, we ask the student to give us the token. Immediately after complying, the child is given a small portion of the assembled reinforcers. If the child does not comply with the token-exchange request, she or he is physically guided through placing the token back into the teacher's hand. These steps are repeated a few times until the child has the meaning of this part of the token system. "Meaning" simply means that the child opens his or her hand to receive the token, that the child returns the token upon request, orients toward the reinforcer area, accepts what we presume will act as a backup reinforcer, and will engage in each of these behaviors without exceeding a latency of a few seconds. Then we alter the situation so that the student comes closer and closer to emitting the behavior we would like token delivery to reinforce (at present, it would only be reinforcing the child's behavior of holding out his or her hand for the token). This may require only a single step in which the child is returned to the area in which the target behavior is to be performed. When the child does, he or she is given a token and token exchange begins.

At this point, delay is introduced into the system. We must recognize that there are different ways in which delay can be programmed. One involves only a time dimension and requires that the time between the response and the token delivery be increased, and that the time between token delivery and token exchange be increased. This procedure is *not* the one to follow. An alternative is to *program delays in reinforcement by utilizing adjusting schedules of reinforcement*. Adjusting schedules are simply those in which we increase the number of responses necessary for reinforcement after the last reinforcement. In this procedure, we would simply require two tokens for exchange, then three, then four, etc. Then we would alter the delay pattern by requiring two correct responses for token delivery, then three, then four, etc. In this manner, correct behavior is still being consequated, but delays in reinforcement are being programmed. If we delayed simply on a time dimension between correct responding and token delivery, then we would not be immediately reinforcing correct responding, and as the token delivery must be following some behavior of the student, we may, in fact, be reinforcing some behaviors we would prefer not to reinforce. As the ratios are increased, and as the delays are thereby increased, variations of interval schedules can be used to make token exchange more convenient to the classroom operation. We should remember, however, that interval schedules are often not so effective as ratio-based schedules, so we should move to time-based exchanges only after responding is occurring at a good rate. To check whether our progression through various schedules of reinforcement has been correct, we need only check the data to determine how well the student is responding.

The degree to which we need to go through small steps to teach the meaning of a token system, of course, varies with the student we are teaching. Since our students vary widely in developmental level at any chronological age, there can be no rule that will tell us how quickly to progress through particular values while increasing delays. The rules are more general, and they include being consistent, progressing in an orderly manner, and checking the data to determine how well the student is performing.

Another suggestion is to *use the rules for making reinforcement more effective* that were discussed in Chapter 8. Some of these include (1) reinforcing immediately, (2) using intermittent schedules of reinforcing, (3) finding novel reinforcers, (4) avoiding reinforcing satiation through having many backup reinforcers available, (5) incorporating at some time reinforcers that will be available in the student's future environment so that behavior will be maintained, (6) use response priming if necessary to provide the opportunity for behavior to be consequated, (7) label the behavior we are reinforcing with tokens, (8) use vicarious reinforcement by distributing tokens only to those students responding correctly and by labeling the behaviors we are reinforcing loudly enough for all students to hear, (9) ask student peers to distribute tokens and help in the exchange or in the data collection, and (10) use group consequences when appropriate.

Using natural reinforcers have been mentioned several times as a very important aspect of reinforcement programs for two reasons:)1) there is more opportunity for the behavior to be reinforced in different environments each day, hence the probability for generalization is increased, and (2) there is more opportunity for the behavior to be reinforced after the student leaves your program, hence the probability for carryover is increased. Token systems are inherently artificial, because receiving tokens for appropriate behavior is something that does not occur in many environments. But the backup reinforcers do not have to be artificial. They can be natural for that individual student and/or they can be natural for that learning environment. There are, of course, significant individualized differences with us all. One of those differences is that some things are reinforcing for one child and not reinforcing for another child. We should use those activities or events that seem most naturally reinforcing for each child and, within reason, use them as reinforcers. Within classrooms, we can use the Premack principle and arrange favored sections of the curriculum as reinforcement for good performance in less favored sections, whether the curriculum is academic, vocational, or social.

Economic factors of the token economy itself can affect the success of the entire program, just as economic factors can affect behavior in our buying world. In a number of articles, Winkler (Kagel & Winkler, 1972; Winkler, 1971a, b, 1973) has discussed the token system as a closed economy, with purchasing trends that may be similar to those experienced in our own economic society. He has shown that psychiatric patients tend to produce the same relationship between buying and spending as is found in economic research. In general, patients with low income spent more than their income and patients with high income spent less than their income. Winkler (1973) has also shown that high savings of tokens produced poor performance while low savings improved performance. Furthermore, the effect of savings was so great that it practically eliminated any effects one would expect from changes in the amount of reinforcement.

A similar problem with institutionalized retarded persons was found by Brierton, Garms, and Metzger (1969), who found sudden drops in performance during the fifth week of their token program. Checking the data, they found that during this week more than 700 tokens had been accumulated. They concluded with an assumption that individuals with high savings would not expend much effort to obtain more (this effect is, of course, similar to satiation).

Schroeder and Barrera (1976a, b) have undertaken a systematic analysis of the relation of earnings to spendings with retarded persons. They discussed the importance of learning how to control expenditures, with these skills certainly being something we should teach our clients. In one study (1976a), clients in a sheltered workshop earned tokens in two ways: (1) based upon the actual work output, and (2) based upon social and societal behaviors in the workshop (e.g., "each employee earns a weekly salary based on seniority, including sick leave, paid vacation, merit increases, etc. He may earn additional tokens daily for the following: punctuality, grooming, having a clean workspace, finding defects in work, performing constructive tasks without prompting, initiating positive social interactions, and reporting promptly when he has finished a task," p. 21). Careful records were kept of each client's earnings and expenditures. Results showed that for the group, spending was less than half of earned income, and that as income increased, the percent of earned income spent decreased. Furthermore, differential spending occurred for expendable and less expendable items. "As income increased, the relative amount spent on expendable items increased and the relative amount spent on less expendable items decreased" (p. 23). As the authors indicated, their results are similar to those found in the general population and at variance with the apparent myth that retarded persons are impulsive spenders who will not budget their incomes. Continuing their work (1976b), they examined the *elasticity* of items (i.e., items whose demand decreases as its price increases) upon the premise that many fixed-price economies fail because they ignore the rules of supply and demand and are, therefore, unrealistic simulations of economic systems they purport to represent. They found that items were differentially elastic. Beverages were less elastic than food items, and both were less elastic than luxury items. Again, institutionalized retarded persons demonstrate money-managing skills, spending less on luxuries as the price for them rises. When these results with institutionalized persons are extrapolated to noninstitutionalized and often more skilled persons, the effects of supply and demand in token programs in classrooms and community centers seem foolish to ignore. The relevance of Schroeder and Barrera's work is quite clear:

> Accurate information on *elasticity of demand* [italics added] of diverse commodities within the token economy allows for careful economic planning and the prevention of potentially serious mishaps. For example, once buying by clients reaches asymptotic level, token managers may resort to artificial inflationary practices, in the belief that this will stimulate more purchasing and increase the rate of kinds of behavior by which clients earn tokens and commodities. The present analysis, however, suggests that *this sort of manipulation may easily backfire*, in the sense that *raising prices across the board may selectively suppress consumption of highly elastic items, thus decreasing* [italics added] rather than increasing the *appeal* of such commodities and thereby reducing clients' willingness to engage in higher rates of working or purchasing behavior. Under those conditions, clients will tend to narrow their selection of items to a small category of inelastic goods, defeating the manager's purpose of offering and stocking a large variety of commodities. (1976b, p. 179).

The authors go on to point out that the problem may be even more serious with small economies like those in classrooms in which most items (e.g., toys, trinkets) are highly elastic; when prices are raised in an effort to *increase* motivation and responding, responding is actually most likely to *decrease*. As a result, we need to be extremely careful in setting the initial costs of items. We should determine whether items would tend to be elastic or inelastic if we attempted to increase the price of highly popular items, and we should be sure not to make across-the-board increases in all items in the economy. If we were to do the latter, items that are presently reinforcing may become overpriced to the point that they are no longer reinforcing, and our whole purpose would have been contravened. One approximation to the economy's eventual supply-and-demand characteristics would be to initially price tangible items in the token program according to their retail cost on the larger economy under which we all live. Simply choose an appropriate relation between tokens and currency, such as *one token = one penny*. Then require a number of tokens equal to the token-to-penny ratio. In this example, a $1.00 magazine would cost 100 tokens, a $15 radio would cost 1,500 tokens, etc. Some of us who have used such a system find it quite helpful.

Group consequences may be more effective than individual consequences in token programs. Tokens can be delivered contingent upon group performance (e.g., if all students finish their work by noon, each student will earn five tokens) or upon individual performance (e.g., a token for each student who finishes the assignment by noon or loss of a token for each talk-out in the lunch line). But consequences can be delivered contingent upon the group's accumulation of tokens. For example, all students could go to the movie Friday if the class earned four tokens this week by finishing their work on time (or if each student has earned at least four tokens by finishing the assignment on time). Group consequences can often be used to promote cooperation, peer approval, more interest in progress of friends, etc., and to decrease inappropriate competition between students. By the same token, however, group consequences can provide undue pressure on some students whose performance may be marginal and who thus are the most important determinant in whether the group earns the consequence. This problem is particularly apparent when the group is heterogeneous with respect to the target behavior, and the staff has not designed individualized response requirements. To apply group consequences, then, the teacher should be quite attentive to the nontarget as well as the target behaviors of the students. One strong point of token programs is that they can be highly individualized; to destroy this strength by making the same requirement for token production for all students in all cases is unfortunate and seems to result from confusing *group token-exchange criteria* with *group token-production criteria.*

Token programs tend to be very positive in that they award tokens for appropriate behaviors and often ignore inappropriate behaviors. But there is sometimes cause for *consequating inappropriate responding* as well. Drabman and Tucker (1974) have made a point that many of us forget when we are using ignoring as a procedure to reduce inappropriate responding.

> Although ignoring is a very powerful technique with young children . . ., it loses its potency as the children get older . . . and peer reinforcement replaces teacher reinforcement as the most powerful social reinforcement in the classroom. To ignore undesirable behavior in these circumstances is *not* an extinction procedure; it simply allows other reinforcers to act upon the behavior in an unobstructed manner. (p. 184)

In these cases, the use of direct consequences for inappropriate responding may be necessary. The two most common procedures are (1) *response cost*, in which tokens are removed after inappropriate responding and (2) *timeout*, in which the student and the token-earning environment are separated for a brief period in which the student cannot earn tokens. Drabman and Tucker warn that these procedures should only be used as a last resort, and advocate first trying a simple reminder that the student will either lose tokens or not be able to earn tokens if the behavior persists. If occasional reminders are not sufficient, then we do not continue to comment or else we might be reinforcing the inappropriate response through our attention. Instead, we deliver the consequence immediately but with as neutral an air as possible; we should try to teach the child that it is his or her behavior and not the teacher that really caused the consequence. If we use more than occasional reminders, we are also instituting a system of verbalized but undelivered consequences, and we will be undermining the whole token program. Again, we *must* be consistent.

When we begin with less complex programs and shape ourselves to be able to consequate more behaviors with tokens, we are always faced with the question of what behaviors to consequate first. Often this question becomes one of

whether to apply tokens first to socially disruptive or to academic behaviors.
Many people suggest that the socially disruptive behaviors be consequated first
with tokens given for appropriate behaviors and tokens taken away for disruptive
behaviors. This plan seems to be a logical one, but it does have the problem of ignoring additional contingencies for academic behavior while the social behaviors
are being arranged. An interesting alternative has been offered by Ayllon and
Roberts (1974), who suggest eliminating disruptive behavior by concentrating
only on academic behavior. They selected as target subjects 5 students
designated as the most disruptive in a classroom of 38 students. The teachers
then established a token economy in which tokens could be exchanged for many
backup reinforcers but could be earned in only one manner: 80% correct on
reading workbook assignments earned two points and 100% correct earned five
points. Two classes of behaviors were then measured during the daily reading
period: (1) correct answers in the daily performance on reading materials, and (2)
disruptive behaviors, including being out of seat without permission, talking out,
and physically interfering with another student's studying. Results were presented in terms of the percent of correct responding on the reading assignments
and the percent of observations in which the students were disruptive through an
ABAB reversal design. In the first and third phases, no tokens were administered.
In the second and fourth phases, the students earned two or five points according
to the prearranged schedule. In no phase, however, were socially disruptive
behaviors consequated. Across the four phases, academic responding changed
from about 45% correct to 70 to 50 to 85%, demonstrating a very orderly relation
between correct academic behavior and contingent tokens. A very orderly relation was also demonstrated between disruptive behavior and the phases despite
the fact that disruptive behavior was never consequated by token loss. Across the
four phases, the percents of observations in which the students were disruptive
were 45, 15, 40 and 5%. This study demonstrates that at least some socially disruptive behaviors can be reduced simply by reinforcing *alternative* behaviors,
such as academic behaviors, to the point that they are occurring at a high rate—
in essence, the children will be too busy being good to have any time to be bad.
(Because this procedure reinforces *alternative* behaviors, it is called the differential reinforcement of alternative responding. It will be discussed in Chapter 11.)

All token systems should be flexible: some behaviors will need to be added
to the system, and some may need to be dropped for the sake of efficiency; some
schedules of token production may need to be changed; and some schedules of
token exchange may need to be altered. But in making changes, the teacher
should be able to identify the antecedent to his or her own change behaviors.
Reasonable requests by students should always be respected, but cajoling should
not be. We must listen to our students; they will often be telling us the sources of
strengths and weaknesses in our program; but we listen also to what our data say.
We *consult our data* before making changes in our program; changes should be
empirically based. If your data suggest that there is not enough progress, then we
make changes. If our data indicate good progress, we respect our students'
wishes and rights, but continue to maintain contact with the data and continue to
monitor progress after the changes are made.

In addition to obtaining data on our students' behaviors, we try to *obtain
data on our own behaviors.* This objective is usually more difficult to meet, and it
is sometimes impossible. But if it can be done, the results will always be reveal-

ing; either we are doing quite well, which is great to know, or we need a little more practice, which is also very good to know. If we can have an aide, another teacher, an administrator, a parent, or a volunterring friend record data for a little while, we will be able to answer some very important questions. For example, how often did we consequate appropriate and inappropriate behaviors appropriately? or inappropriately? or not at all? We all need feedback, and even a little can be quite helpful.

Many token programs use tangibles, a practice that should be lessened over time in favor of noncostly and more natural activities. In many cases, tangibles can be obtained at no cost, but in most cases there will probably be some costs. In that event, *buy and stock as few tangibles as possible.* With some students, only being able to see the actual item in the situation will be reinforcing. With other students, pictorial representations will be sufficient. When the latter occurs, use catalogs from Sears, J.C. Penney, and other large merchandisers; or use a trip to a store to select items to be earned but not yet purchased. There are two reasons for taking this approach: (2) preferences change, and by the time a student has earned the required number of tokens his or her choice of a backup reinforcer may have changed, and something a token economy does not need is unwanted backup "nonreinforcers." (2) Purchasing or ordering items from a store can be a perfect time to practice social skills, as well as a great deal of fun (and perhaps be even more reinforcing than the backup reinforcer itself). These are opportunities to take students out of the classrooms and institutions and "into the streets"; such opportunities should not be wasted.

A large number of suggestions for token economies have been made by Ayllon and Azrin (1968) based upon their continuing study of token programs. Some of these have been discussed in other sections, but several have not. One is the *relevance of behavior rule*, which states that we should teach only those behaviors that will continue to be reinforced after training. Many institutional and some classroom programs tend to teach behaviors that have little chance to occur or be maintained after training. A great deal of time is often spent teaching severely retarded persons to identify shapes, certain colors, etc., under the guise of a "readiness program"; but these are learned behaviors that are seldom required outside that particular classroom experience. More time should be spent on the behaviors that are relevant to increased independence at any particular developmental level.

Two reinforcer suggestions are the *probability of behavior rule* and the *verbal request rule*. The former suggests that we observe what the individual does, particularly in unstructured situations, as these behaviors may serve as reinforcers at some time. This rule is a restatement of the Premack principle, which suggests that behaviors which are emitted at high rates can serve as reinforcers for behaviors which occur at low rates. Some students may finish problems very quickly, with high accuracy, and obviously enjoy talking about their accomplishments; the same students may not do so well in social studies. This rule would suggest that the time at which they can begin math and have a chance to "show off" could be made contingent upon a particular quality of work during the social studies period. The verbal request rule suggests that we note the verbal requests a student or client makes, as they may suggest reinforcers.

We can guess that, if a student "talks all the time about the Chicago White Sox," then a program booklet about the team or a trip to Comisky Park could be effective reinforcers. Obviously, we have to accept these "verbalized reinforcers" as tentative ones; they may, in fact, not be reinforcing for the behavior change we would like. But verbal requests are a good means of selecting among the many stimuli and events that might be reinforcing.

Two other reinforcer rules are related to the phenomenon of extinction. These are the *variation of reinforcement rule* and the *multiple reinforcer rule*. While these rules may seem to be the same, they really are not. The first suggests a wide variance *within* the reinforcer class and says that we should use many variations of a known reinforcer. For example, if football cards are used as reinforcers, have 100 available as opposed to 10; if attendance at football games is a reinforcer, have available the choice between seeing one of several teams; if watching television is used, have a few choices available. The second rule suggests a wide variance *between* reinforcer classes, and says that we should use many different types of reinforcing stimuli with each individual. This rule addresses the problem of satiation when only a few backup reinforcers are available. The number that can be present is limited, but we should try to make as many available as possible. We should also try not to lock the student into choosing an item and "working for" that item for a long time. Some token programs begin by asking a student to choose an item for which she or he will exchange tokens. Some students will choose a high-priced item that may take one or two months to earn. The danger of changing preferences, or perhaps access to that reinforcer through parents or others, is always present. There is certainly nothing wrong with long-range choices, but the student should occasionally be reminded that he or she can be working toward a watch for 1,500 tokens, or can right now buy a subscription to a magazine, or in a week can take a friend to the movies. Do not work against the student's learning to work toward long-range goals—that lesson is an important one to learn, but on the other hand, attend to preferences that change over time.

Three other rules discuss the client's contact with the reinforcers. The *compatability of reinforcer rule* suggests that reinforcing activities be scheduled to occur at different times so that they are temporally compatible. For example, if an institution has access to backup activities such as bowling, swimming, going to the movie, and others all available only at 4:00 on the 15th of each month, and if several of these activities are reinforcing, then the institutional program is losing an opportunity to motivate more behaviors by not making access to the events possible at different times. The *reinforcer sampling rule* has been discussed before with regard to reinforcement in general. It states that before using an event as a reinforcer we should sometimes require sampling of the reinforcer before the task is to begin. If we are using free time as a reinforcer for a class of children, this rule suggests that we might allow them a few minutes of free time in the toy area of the classroom before they begin to work in the token program. The *reinforcer exposure rule* suggests that we display all stimuli that will be available during exchange. There are also suggestions that these displays not be static: "As marketing experts have long known, novelty and change play a great part in the desirability of a piece of goods. Window displays are changed frequently to capitalize on this effect. In our token economies, we shifted the back-up reinforcers each week or two, so that some novel items were always available" (Sulzer-Azaroff & Mayer, 1977, p. 392).

Three rules relate to administrative matters and to accountability. The *time and place rule* suggests that we specify (1) the time and the place in which the token-producing response is to occur and (2) the time and place for token exchange. This is an excellent rule for two reasons. It specifies part of the responsibilities of the staff, and it helps to avoid arguments with the students. This problem may arise in classrooms in which token programs are in force only part of the day, and the behavior can also occur during other parts of the day. It may also arise in institutions in which students are programmed by various teachers in various settings. For example, the special education and the music education teachers may provide tokens for various "polite" behaviors, while the recreation teacher may not. The same class of behaviors can occur in all three situations, but it may be reinforced by tokens in only two. This difference should be clearly specified for the student. The *individual responsibility rule* suggests that a supervisor should assign one and only one individual to be responsible for token delivery or exchange for a given occasion. When several are appointed and the responsibility is kept by none, there is too much room for excuses of the type "but, I thought he was going to . . . ." According to the *direct supervision rule*, we should provide systematic and direct observation of the token delivery and exchange. Such observation can serve three purposes: (1) it can provide feedback that may reinforce correct staff behavior, (2) it can identify weaknesses that can be changed, and (3) it can serve as a vehicle to bring supervisors and staff together, a ubiquitous complaint from teachers being that their supervisors do not see them enough.

The *multiple reinforcing agents rule* encourages us to use different individuals to implement the delivery of tokens as well as the exchange. At first, this rule may seem to contradict the individual responsibility rule, but it does not. That rule indicates that one person should be responsible for any particular day or occasion. This rule says that when possible the person who is responsible for reinforcing the student should be changed from day to day. When just beginning a program, a good idea is to have the same person responsible for the same portion of the program for a week or two. At that point, any problems should have been identified, and there should be consistency on the part of the teacher in token delivery and exchange. Then if other teachers, aides, etc., are available, they should become involved in the program in order to promote *generalization* (stimulus generalization is a term that refers to the extent to which the same response occurs under varying stimulus conditions). Obviously, we do not want the student to be polite, helpful, studious, etc., just in the presence of Mrs. Miller. We would like the same behaviors to occur in the presence of Mrs. Switzky. One way of moving toward that goal is to have other people interact with the student in the program. In that way, they may become antecedent stimuli who increase the probability of correct responding, and they may become conditioned reinforcers who increase the probability that this behavior will recur.

Three rules concern methods for increasing the probability that complex behaviors will occur. The *response exposure rule* suggests that we have the learner observe another individual who performs the task and receives tokens.

This rule is simply the vicarious reinforcement paradigm applied in token programs. For example, if we are having problems with one or two students who are off-task, disruptive, etc., we might reinforce the appropriately behaving individual. The *response sampling rule* is based on the assumption that the chances of having a complex response emitted are increased if the initial portions of the target behavior are performed. We might prompt a student verbally to begin working on a project, or we might physically guide a client through the first steps of a self-help skill he or she can already perform but is not presently doing. The *response shaping rule* is more concerned with behavior that has not yet been demonstrated; it states that in developing a complex chain of responses, we should begin by reinforcing an existing response that has a component relation and shape the complex chain by successive approximations.

Removing the Token Economy.   Most of the preceding rules and suggestions should be helpful in designing and implementing token programs. There is one final consideration, however, and that is removing the token economy. The primary reason for removing the economy is to bring the behaviors under the antecedent and reinforcing control of a more normalized environment, and there are a number of ways in which this can be done. One is to alternate periods of tokens and no tokens within the same day. Perhaps from 9 to 10 tokens could be earned through academic behaviors only; then from 10 to 11 through social behaviors only, etc. Then periods could be inserted in which tokens cannot be earned. Another way is to increase the schedules of reinforcement gradually but substantially. Tokens could be produced on higher and higher ratio schedules, while tokens could be exchanged at intervals increasingly further apart. At this time, however, it is essential that the staff replace the tokens with other forms of reinforcement. Praise, approval, attention, etc. should have been paired frequently enough with token delivery that they will be powerful reinforcers. At the time that reinforcer *density* (i.e., the ratio of reinforcers to responses) and reinforcer *rate* (i.e., the number of reinforcers per minute) decrease, the teacher must provide these other forms of reinforcement. Another way of reducing the token economy is simply to leave the tokens as an excellent, concrete form of feedback, but to eliminate the token exchange.

If we try to phase out a token program at the time students will be leaving our program, we could try any one or a combination of these methods. The basic concerns are to make gradual changes and to refer to the data on student responding; these data should serve as feedback to us on the effectiveness of our token removal progress.

SUMMARY

This chapter discusses schedules of reinforcement, a term referring to the relation between responding and reinforcement. Three types of schedules are presented. First-order schedules are those that are based on number or on number and time. First-order schedules which depend only on number are fixed- and variable-ratio schedules; those which depend on both number and time are fixed interval, variable interval, limited hold, and the differential reinforcement of high rates of responding. All these schedules are intended to increase responding, but other first-order schedules are intended to decrease responding. These include the differential reinforcement of (1) other behavior, (2) low rates of behavior, and (3) incompatible responding. A second class of schedules is the compound schedule in which a single response is reinforced when the requirements of one or more schedules of reinforcement have been met. Some of these are alternative, conjunctive, and interlocking schedules. Another class of schedules is labeled second order; these are complex schedules, which are really schedules of schedules. While there are many types of second-order schedules, the type most used in our field is the token economy, the programming factors of which are discussed in this chapter.

The next chapter will include discussions of methods for generating complex behaviors the individual does not presently emit. These include shaping, chaining, fading, imitation, and graduated guidance. In addition, methods for teaching the maintenance of these behaviors in appropriate situations will be discussed. These include generalization, discrimination, and carryover. Finally, these methods will be discussed as they are combined in larger programs dealing with academics, language, and self-help skills.

REFERENCES

Ayllon, T., & Azrin, N. H. *The token economy: A motivational system for therapy and rehabilitation.* New York: Appleton-Century-Crofts, Inc., 1968.

Ayllon, T., & Roberts, M. D. Eliminating discipline problems by strengthening academic performance. *Journal of Applied Behavior Analysis,* 1974, **7**, 71-76.

Bath, K. E., & Smith, S. A. An effective token economy for MR adults. *Mental Retardation,* 1974, **12**, 41-44.

Bijou, S. W., Birnbrauer, J. S., Kidder, J. D., & Tague, C. E. Programmed instruction as an approach to teaching of reading, writing and arithmetic to retarded children. *Psychological Record,* 1966, **16**, 505-522.

Birnbrauer, J. S., Bijou, S. W., Wolf, M. M., & Kidder, J. D. Programmed instructions in the classroom. In L. P. Ullmann & L. Krasner (Eds.), *Case studies in behavior modification.* New York: Holt, Rinehart and Winston, Inc., 1965.

Birnbrauer, J. S., & Lawler, J. Token reinforcement for learning. *Mental Retardation,* 1964, **2**, 275-279.

Birnbrauer, J. S., Wolf, M. M., Kidder, J. D., & Tague, C. E. Classroom behavior of retarded pupils with token reinforcement. *Journal of Experimental Child Psychology,* 1965, **2**, 219-235.

Brierton, G., Garms, R., & Metzger, R. Practical problems encountered in an aide-administered token reward cottage program. *Mental Retardation,* 1969, **7**, 40-43.

Budd, K. S., & Baer, D. M. Behavior modification and the law: Implications of recent judicial decisions. *Journal of Psychiatry and Law,* a special reprint, Summer 1976, 171-244.

Cardozo, P. *The whole kid's catalogue.* New York: Bantam Books, Inc., 1975.

Cowles, J. T. Food-tokens as incentives for learning by chimpanzees. *Comparative Psychological Monographs,* 1937, **14**, No. 71.

Deitz, S. M., & Repp, A. C. Decreasing classroom behavior through the use of DRL schedules of reinforcement. *Journal of Applied Behavior Analysis*, 1973, 6, 457-463.

Deitz, S. M., & Repp, A. C. A description and analysis of three ways to program schedules of reinforcement requiring the differential reinforcement of low rates of responding. Paper presented at a meeting of the American Psychological Association, 1974.

Drabman, R. S., & Tucker, R. D. Why classroom token economies fail. *Journal of School Psychology*, 1974, 12(3), 178-188.

*Favell, J. E. Reduction of stereotypes by reinforcement of toy play. *Mental Retardation*, 1973, 11, 21-23.

Ferster, C. B., & Skinner, B. F. *Schedules of reinforcement.* New York: Appleton-Century-Crofts, Inc., 1957.

Girardeau, F. L., & Spradlin, J. E. Token rewards in a cottage program. *Mental Retardation*, 1964, 2, 345-351.

Journal of the Experimental Analysis of Behavior. Bloomington, In: Society for the Experimental Analysis of Behavior, Inc., 1958.

Kagel, J., & Winkler, R. C. Behavioral economics: Areas of cooperative research between economics and applied behavioral analysis. *Journal of Applied Behavioral Analysis*, 1972, 5, 335-342.

Kazdin, A. E. *The token economy: A review and evaluation.* New York: Plenum Publishing Corp., 1977.

Kelleher, R. T. A comparison of conditioned and food reinforcement on a fixed ratio schedule in chimpanzees. *Psychology Newsletter*, 1957a, 8, 88-93.

Kelleher, R. T. Conditioned reinforcement in chimpanzees. *Journal of Comparative and Physiological Psychology*, 1957b, 50, 571-575.

Lent, J. R. A demonstration program for intensive training of institutionalized mentally retarded girls. Progress report, January 1967. Washington, D.C.: U.S. Department of Health, Education, and Welfare.

Lent, J. R. Mimosa Cottage: Experiment in hope. *Psychology Today*, 1968, 2, 50-58.

Lovitt, T. C., & Esveldt, K. A. The relative effects on math performance of single- versus multiple-ratio schedules: A case study. *Journal of Applied Behavior Analysis*, 1970, 3, 261-270.

Repp, A. C., Deitz, S. M., & Speir, N. C. Reducing stereotypic responding of retarded persons by the differential reinforcement of other behavior. *American Journal of Mental Deficiency*, 1974, 79, 279-284.

Reynolds, C. S. *A primer of operant conditioning.* Glenview, IL: Scott, Foresman & Company, 1968.

Salisbury catalog of free teaching materials. P. O. Box 1075, Ventura, CA, 93001.

Schroeder, S. R., & Barrera, F. How token earnings are spent. *Mental Retardation*, 1976a, 14, 20-24.

Schroeder, S. R., & Barrera, F. J. Effects of price manipulations on consumer behavior in a sheltered workshop token economy. *American Journal of Mental Deficiency*, 1976b, 81, 172-180.

Staats, A. W. A general apparatus for the investigation of complex learning in children. *Behavior Research and Therapy*, 1968, 6, 45-50.

---

* This reference was incorrectly made in the original journal article as Flavell, J. E. The correct reference is Favell, J. E.

Staats, A. W., Minke, K. A., Finley, J. R., Wolf, M., & Brooks, L. O. A reinforcer system and experimental procedure for the laboratory study of reading acquisition. *Child Development*, 1964, **35**, 209-231.

Staats, A. W., Staats, C. K., Schultz, R. E., & Wolf, M. The conditioning of textual responses using "extrincis" reinforcers. *Journal of the Experimental Analysis of Behavior*, 1962, **5**, 33-40.

Stephens, C. E., Pear, J. J., Wray, L. D., & Jackson, G. C. Some effects of reinforcement schedules in teaching picture names to retarded children. *Journal of Applied Behavior Analysis*, 1975, **8**, 435-447.

Sulzer-Azaroff, B., & Mayer, G. R. *Applying behavior-analysis procedures with children and youth*. New York: Holt, Rinehart and Winston, Inc., 1977.

Thomas, C. M., Sulzer-Azaroff, B., Lukeris, S., & Palmer, M. Teaching daily self-help skills for "long-term" maintenance. In B. Etzel, J. LeBlanc, & D. Baer (Eds.), *New developments in behavioral research: Theory, method and application*. Hillsdale, NJ: Erlbaum Associates, 1977.

Weisberg, P., & Waldrop, P. B. Fixed interval work habits of Congress. *Journal of Applied Behavior Analysis*, 1972, **5**, 93-97.

Whitehead, W. E., Renault, P. F., & Goldiamond, I. Modification of human gastric acid secretion with operant-conditioning procedures. *Journal of Applied Behavior Analysis*, 1975, **8**, 147-156.

Wilson, M. D., & McReynolds, L. V. A procedure for increasing oral reading rate in hard-of-hearing children. *Journal of Applied Behavior Analysis*, 1973, **6**, 231-239.

Winkler, R. C. Reinforcement schedules for individual patients in a token economy. *Behavior Therapy*, 1971a, **2**, 534-537.

Winkler, R. C. The relevance of economic theory and technology to token reinforcement systems. *Behavior Research and Therapy*, 1971b, **9**, 81-88.

Winkler, R. C. An experimental analysis of economic balance, savings, and wages in a token economy. *Behavior Therapy*, 1973, **4**, 22–40.

Wolfe, J. B. Effectiveness of token-rewards for chimpanzees. *Comparative Psychological Monographs*, 1936, **12**, No. 60.

Wolff, R., & Gray, J. J. Physical attributes of tokens: A comparison. *Psychological Reports*, 1973, **32**, 675–678.

10

Behaviorally Based
Teaching Methods

There are a number of behavioral methods for teaching skills to retarded and nonretarded persons that are quite common across many types of curricula areas, such as self-help, language, recreation, etc. Some of these methods are called *shaping, chaining, fading,* and *imitation.* Although in many programs designed to teach particular skills, several of these methods are often used simultaneously, they will first be discussed individually. Then they will be discussed in combination through a few teaching programs in self-help and in language.

SOME BASIC CONCEPTS

Chains

The basic premise for all these methods is that the behaviors with which we are working are a *chain* of "subresponses." For example, when a child says the letters of the alphabet, there is a chain of at least 26 subresponses. Or when a child is self-feeding, there are a number of responses such as picking up a spoon, scooping food, bringing the spoon to his mouth, etc. The concept of chains is, of course, indigneous to writing task analyses. When writing what the student will be doing in each step of the task, we are writing each of the subcomponents as that student will be taught them. This is a critical concept, and the ways in which we teach retarded persons will be directed toward establishing the subcomponents of a chain and finishing the task with the subcomponents in the proper order. The way in which we choose to arrange those subcomponents, however, determines the method which we will be using. If the student does not presently emit many of the subcomponents, we will have to teach or *shape* them. If the student can emit them individually but not sequentially, we could choose to teach the sequence beginning with the last member of the chain, then with the next to last, etc.; we would be using a *backward chaining* procedure. If the student cannot now emit most of the subcomponents, we may wish to physically guide the student through the sequence and then lessen our guidance as the lesson progresses; in that case, we would be using *graduated guidance*. If the student can now emit the behavior, but does so in an inappropriate context (e.g., he says "three" when asked what number is on a card with a five), we may only change the way in which antecedent events are presented, allowing him to continue to make the same response. For example, we could present cards with a very large "5" and a small "3," and then we could prompt the correct answer. Gradually we would make the numbers the same size while removing our prompt. This procedure is called *fading*. Finally, we may teach a chain of behaviors in a less direct way by having the student observe someone else; this procedure is generally labeled *imitation training* or *modeling*.

Stimulus Control

Another concept that is very important in a behavioral analysis of learning and performance is *stimulus control*, a term that refers to the extent to which an antecedent stimulus determines the probability that a particular response will occur. *When there is a high probability that a response will occur in the presence of a particular stimulus and no others, we say that stimulus control has been demonstrated* (i.e., the stimulus has influenced or "controlled" the probability of responding). Conversely, when the probability of a response occurring in the presence of a particular stimulus is low, we say that stimulus control has not been demonstrated. Once past the jargon, we should realize that most of the behaviors we are trying to teach can be conceptualized in terms of stimulus control. When the student is asked to point to the number 6 when it is among several others, we would like for the 6 to come to "control"[1] the child's pointing response; we would not like for the child to point to a 7. Or when we ask the student to read the printed word *car*, we would like that word to come to control the response "car" and not to occasion other responses like "blue," or "dog," or "food." Similarly, when we ask children to begin working on their assignment in class, we would like the instruction to come to control on-task behavior; we would not like the instruction to occasion throwing books, jumping up and down, shouting "car" or "six." We really are trying, in all our teaching, to arrange conditions so that our students will learn to link certain behaviors with certain stimulus events; that goal, along with how we progress toward it, is really the essence of teaching.

By now you will have recognized that the basis for stimulus control is the three-term contingency or A-B-C paradigm discussed in other chapters. Under

---

[1] Control in this sense does not at all imply any forced or aversive type of control; it merely means that the probability of responding is controlled by an antecedent stimulus.

particular Antecedent events (the instructions "point to the number 6" and the number 6 on a card along with several other numbers on other cards), a particular Behavior (pointing to the correct number) will be Consequated ("that's right, John!"). Our problem, then, in a general sense, is twofold: (1) to decide what responses should occur in the presence of a limited number of stimuli, and (2) to determine the best method for teaching stimulus control. Regardless of the primary method for teaching stimulus control, whether it involves a single response or a sequence of responses, there is a common procedure inherent in all, and that is *differential reinforcement*. This is, quite simply, a procedure in which three operations exist: (1) *a particular response is reinforced if it occurs in the presence of a particular stimulus*, (2) *that response is not reinforced in the absence of the appropriate stimuli*, and (3) *other responses are not reinforced in the presence of these particular stimuli*. The procedure itself should seem quite easy to apply, and it often is. We praise a student who says "b" when asked what letter *b* is; we certainly do not praise him when he says "p" when the letter is *b*, nor do we praise him when he says "b" and the letter is *a*. The problems that we have usually involve feedback, consistency, and reinforcement schedules. For all our students, feedback for correct and for incorrect responding is necessary. But for some of our students, either because of medical problems or developmental level, the general feedback of the type "yes—no" is insufficient, and teacher creativity is warranted.

Consistency is also a problem, sometimes without our realizing so. Occasionally, we do not signal correct responding, sometimes we provide the signal of correct responding for incorrect responding, and sometimes we simply forget to provide the signal for incorrect responding. Recently, we watched a teacher trying to teach a student to touch her nose on command. The teacher would give the instruction, watch the child randomly touch her cheek, lips, eyes, and nose, and then scream with apparent delight when the student eventually touched her nose. While the teacher thought the student was learning to touch a body part on instruction, the student was more likely learning that "touch your nose" means "put your hand somewhere on your face." We need, in this case, to reinforce consistently the correct chain of behaviors involved in touching a particular body part; and we need to learn never to reinforce a chain that includes such obviously incorrect responding (and, in fact, we should even interrupt such a chain not only so that it will not be reinforced, but also so that it will not even occur).

Tied in with feedback and consistency is the use of intermittent reinforcement. When we are reinforcing a student after every three or four correct responses, then we must be very sure that incorrect responding is consequated or else we will not be using differential reinforcement correctly. Let us suppose we are asking a student to point to a stimulus card, and the following sequence of events occurs: correct response, correct response, incorrect response, correct response, reinforcement. This kind of sequence, which happens much more than we probably realize, has just been reinforced *in toto*, and the student will not be learning very rapidly to differentiate correct from incorrect responding. We simply must provide feedback for incorrect responding, and the feedback probably needs to be even more evident when we use intermittent reinforcement than when we use continuous reinforcement.

In stimulus control and differential reinforcement, there are three common functions of the antecedent stimuli. One function is to signal that a particular (i.e., correct) response will be reinforced. So, for example, when the student hears the instruction "Please line up," and is praised when he follows the instruction, then he learns that the instruction is a signal that the response will be reinforced in the presence of that stimulus. The stimulus is said to be discriminative in the sense that it indicates what will be reinforced. It is called a *discriminative stimulus*, abbreviated S^D, and is formally defined as a *stimulus in the presence of which a response will be reinforced*. Just as some stimuli signal reinforcement, other stimuli signal that responding will not be reinforced. For example, the stimulus "3 + 2 =" can become a discriminative stimulus for the response "5," but (1) the response "5" will not be reinforced in the presence of stimuli like "3 + 3 =," and (2) the response "6" will not be reinforced in the presence of "3 + 2 =." *Stimuli in the presence of which there is no reinforcement for responding* are not, of course, called discriminative stimuli; instead, they *are called S-deltas* ($S^{\Delta}s$). In teaching stimulus control, we are interested in arranging events so that the child (1) learns the components necessary to emit a particular behavior, (2) learns to emit the response in the presence of $S^D s$, and (3) learns not to emit the response in the presence of $S^{\Delta}s$. The basic analysis is quite simple, and when we apply the type of analysis to teaching situations, we are often able to be quite specific about what both the student and we should be doing.

In teaching chains, we ascribe a third function to antecedent stimuli, that being *conditioned reinforcement*. Let us consider the simple task of rote counting from 1 to 10. Although there certainly can be many subcomponents, let us consider the components in the chain to be just the verbalizations "1, 2, 3, . . ., 10." Through the results of many studies in experimental psychology (e.g., see Hendry, 1969), stimuli in a chain such as this are considered to be discriminative stimuli for the next response in the chain. For example, let the instruction from the teacher be "Mike, please count from one to ten."[2] The instruction serves as the discriminative stimulus for one and only one response by Mike: saying "one." The stimulus "one" in turn is a discriminative stimulus for the response "two," which in turn is a discriminative stimulus for the response "three," and so forth; each member of the chain is a discriminative stimulus for other members of the chain. From the results of these studies in experimental psychology, we also know that each of these discriminative stimuli plays another role, that of a conditioned reinforcer. In a chain such as this, we say that the reinforcer for "one" is "two," that the reinforcer for "two" is "three," etc. Similarly, in reading a sentence, the reinforcer for reading the first word is the appearance of the second word, and so forth. Members of chains then serve two purposes: (1) discriminative stimuli for the next response and (2) conditioned reinforcers for the prior response. The important point of this analysis stems from several points that were made previously: (1) that conditioned reinforcers are conditioned through repeated pairings with events that are already reinforcing, (2) that the conditioned reinforcers in a chain would probably have gained their reinforcing properties through pairings with whatever reinforcer followed the last component of the chain, and (3) that the more delayed reinforcement is, the weaker the effects of the reinforcer. From these points, it should be obvious that the first

---

[2] As mentioned before, either the responses of oneself or of others can be considered to be stimuli in one's environment; we should not use the word to refer only to tactile or tangible stimuli such as tokens. In this example, both the teacher's behavior and the student's behavior functioned as stimuli for the student.

members of the chain would tend to be the weakest because they and their conditioned reinforcers are more distant in time from the terminal and presumably stronger reinforcer. As such, we may need to do two things when teaching longer chains: (1) occasionally reinforce the first few components in the chain with the terminal reinforcer when it can be done unobtrusively (as with tokens, smiles, nods, whispers, etc.), and (2) prime or prompt the first response components when they are slow to start. With these procedures, we should be able to overcome some of the problems associated with teaching chains of behaviors.

Stimulus Generalization

Another objective, which in some ways may be considered the antithesis of stimulus control, is teaching *stimulus generalization*. Basically, this is a term that *describes the extent to which a response trained in the presence of one stimulus occurs in the presence of another.* There should be no value judgment placed on the term, for sometimes stimulus generalization is appropriate while at other times it is not. It is simply a neutral term that describes a relationship between responding and certain stimuli. Academic responses serve to make that point quite well, so let us again consider the task in which the student points to a requested numeral when several are available. If the request is "point to the 2," and the numbers 1, 2, 3, 4, and 5 printed on cards are presented to the student, then our objective would be for no stimulus generalization to occur on this trial. We do not want the student to point to just any stimulus that is a numeral; we want the student to point only to the 2. However, we would like the student also to point to the number 2 when it is on another card, perhaps smaller in size, written by the teacher instead of printed by a curriculum company, and colored red instead of black. In this case, our objective is to teach stimulus generalization across the numerals 2 regardless of how they appear. We are trying to teach that the numeral is one with a particular line configuration regardless of size, color, background, location, etc. We should not be trying to teach that the numeral is a 2 only when it has that configuration *and* is black *and* is 3 inches high *and* is presented on a 4- by 4-inch white paper background, *and* occurs around 2:00 P.M. during math period.[3] We are, in essence, trying to teach an abstraction.

---

[3] An incident during one of the years I was an administrator of programs for retarded persons makes this point well. Some of the staff worked very hard in a very tiring job and had insufficient time for lunch and a rest break, so I asked them to leave a group of students with me for a period each day during which the tasks they were teaching would be continued. One of the tasks was teaching numeral identification, and I continued it with a group of students for three or four days and found them to be performing quite well, with the best student identifying the numerals 1 to 10 about 95% of the trials. The next day I came to the room in a hurry and could not find the company-manufactured numeral cards, so numbers were quickly written in black ink on some quickly cut construction paper. To introduce the cards gradually to the rest of the group, to allow some modeling to occur, and to provide some vicarious reinforcement, I began with the girl who had been doing so well and who I was sure would answer all questions correctly. Intending to go through all ten numbers first with her before asking any of the other five girls at the table, I asked her to identify numbers for three trials and then stopped; she answered incorrectly each time. Obviously, she had not been taught the abstraction of pointing to a numeral; her behavior was under very tight stimulus control and "correctly pointing to a numeral" was under the control of only those numerals printed in a certain way by a manufacturer. This example dramatically taught us all a lesson about planning for stimulus generalization.

Stimulus generalization is an important concept, and we often have it as an objective while trying to increase the number of responses made to stimuli in the presence of which we have not taught the response. One of the areas in which this phenomena is valuable is self-help skills. For example, while teaching a child to put on a coat, we might use only one or two different coats; yet we would like the response to generalize so that the child will be able to put on a coat independently regardless of the type of coat to be put on. Another area in which stimulus generalization is important is language. For example, although we might have taught a student to name the color red in the presence of a red block, a red piece of paper, and a red book, we would like the response to generalize so that the student will be able to say that a red car is "red" or that a red wall is "red." A great deal of work with language acquisition has been done by Baer, Garcia, Guess, and Sailor. Much of their work has been concerned with stimulus generalization, and some of it will be discussed later in this chapter. An important point to remember, however, is that stimulus generalization is sometimes a very valuable relationship between the environment and responding. It is not, however, an effect that we should presume will happen; rather, it is an objective we should attempt to teach by including varied forms of the antecedent stimulus in our teaching program.

TEACHING METHODS

Shaping

Shaping is a procedure designed to teach new behaviors that the individual cannot now emit. It does so in an orderly manner, progressing from what the person can do now through a series of steps that culminate in the more complex target response. The procedure is defined as *the differential reinforcement of successive approximations to the terminal objective* and employs two subprocedures: (1) *successive approximations*, which refers to a continuing change in response complexity that is required for reinforcement, and (2) *differential reinforcement*, which refers to reinforcement being delivered only for correct responding. The basic idea is that a response which was at one time sufficient for reinforcement is no longer, and that a more complex form of the behavior is now necessary. In this way, more and more complex behaviors are taught.

Shaping involves a number of concepts discussed in previous chapters. Basically, it is a changing-criterion design that requires behaviors to change so that they become more and more like the goal behavior. The "changed" criterion reflects the idea that what once was sufficient for reinforcement is no longer. Shaping also involves a task analysis, whether one writes it formally or informally. The basic steps are to (1) define the terminal or goal behavior, (2) define a behavior the person can now emit that is linked to the terminal behavior, (3) write a sequence of responses that, when taught, will allow the person to progress from the behavior presently in his or her repertoire to the terminal behavior, and (4) determine a criterion of success at each step that will indicate to you that it is time to progress to the next step in the program. These elements have been described very well by Horner (1971) in his program to teach a mentally retarded spina bifida child to use crutches for self-ambulation. Prior efforts by a physical therapist to encourage the student to participate in gait training on parallel bars and with crutches had been met by six months of tantrums and sustained physical resistance, so Horner designed a program relying heavily on shaping. The teaching procedure consisted of two elements, use of parallel bars and use of crutches. First, each of the components was analyzed according to the steps necessary for proceeding from what the child could now accomplish to what the child needed to accomplish in order to complete the task. Use of parallel bars was broken into six steps, beginning with what the student would now do. The steps were the following:

Step 1: Sitting on stool and gripping left parallel bar with left hand and right parallel bar with right hand.

Step 2: Step 1 plus pulling to a standing position on parallel bars and maintaining standing position long enough to consume one tablespoon of root beer (a reinforcer for this child).

Step 3: Steps 1 and 2 plus taking one step using parallel bars for support before being reinforced.

Step 4: Same as step 3 except that three steps must be taken using parallel bars for support before being reinforced.

Step 5: Same as step 3 except that five steps must be taken using parallel bars for support before being reinforced.

Step 6: Same as step 3 except that 10 steps must be taken using bars for support before being reinforced.

In this section, Horner carefully increased the complexity of the behavior while changing the criterion of response complexity necessary for reinforcement. In addition, a criterion for changing from one step to the next was instituted so that there could be an objective basis for proceeding through the program. During each session, 25 trials were conducted, so the criterion was based on that number, and it became "23 or more successful trials per session for three consecutive sessions." The change from one response requirement to another occurred between sessions and represents the shaping program. Within each session and each trial, other procedures were also employed. During each trial, the instructor modeled each response and gave a verbal request appropriate to the step in the program. The student was then given 1 minute in which to complete the response (a limited-hold schedule). If he emitted the response within 1 minute, he was reinforced with root beer; if he did not, he was not reinforced (a differential reinforcement procedure).

After this part of the program was completed, the second component, which was the use of crutches, was taught. An analysis of the response components produced 10 steps:

Step 1: Crutches secured to hands by elastic bandages to prevent throwing crutches; instructor stands behind child and reinforcer is delivered for imitating the modeled response of placing the crutches on dots marked on the floor 18 inches in front of and 18 inches from each side of center line bisecting starting point.

Step 2:   Crutches secured to hands; teacher stands behind child and delivers reinforcer when step 1 is completed and when he swings his body to a crutches-supported erect position with total assistance provided by instructor through underarm pressure. Erect position maintained 15 seconds before reinforcer is delivered.

Step 3:   Crutches secured to hands; instructor stands behind child and delivers reinforcement contingent upon completion of step 1 and swinging his body to a crutches-supported erect position with assistance provided by the instructor through pressure under the arms only to prime initial movements.

Step 4:   Crutches no longer secured to hands by elastic bandages, and initial assistance no longer provided; reinforcement contingent upon independently swinging his body to a crutches-supported erect position.

Step 5:   Reinforcement contingent upon completion of step 4, maintaining balance with instructor's hand placed on child's back, and placing crutches in forward position.

Step 6:   Reinforcement contingent upon completion of step 5 plus swinging feet toward an imaginary line connecting crutch tips, maintaining balance with instructor's hand on child's back, and placing crutches in forward position.

Step 7:   Reinforcement contingent upon completion of step 6 plus one additional cycle of placing crutches in forward position, maintaining balance with instructor's hand on child's back, and placing crutches in forward position.

Step 8:   Reinforcement contingent upon completion of placing crutches in forward position, etc., with gradual fading of instructor's support during balancing.

Step 9:   Reinforcement contingent upon completion of eight cycles of placing crutches in forward position, maintaining balance without instructor's assistance, and placing crutches in forward position.

Step 10:   Reinforcement contingent upon completion of 12 cycles of placing crutches with forearm clamps (Lofstrand crutches) instead of crutches providing underarm support.

Horner's work is an excellent example of how a complex task can be broken into its components and of how a person can be taught increasingly more difficult and complex behaviors through a shaping procedure. The basic idea of moving from simple to more complex is useful with all individuals at all levels of learning. It also seems to be especially useful when teaching retarded persons who sometimes need a well-defined sequence of steps in a teaching program in order to learn new skills. As a result of its practicality, shaping has been used in a wide variety of settings. We all teach speech through a process of shaping in which sounds correctly imitated are reinforced, then more selective sounds are reinforced, then words (generally nouns and pronouns), then simple sentences with a noun and a verb, and so forth. We all also teach arithmetic in the same manner, progressing from very simple identification, correspondence, rote counting, etc., to extraordinarily complex operations.

Many of the shaping programs are combined with graduated guidance to teach physical skills such as self-feeding, dressing, ambulation, etc. Others are combined with fading procedures in which antecedent stimuli change over time. There are many of these programs, some of which will be discussed later in this chapter. But one of them will be presented here because it involves an academic skill and is somewhat different from Horner's. Skinner and Krakower (1968) developed a program to teach handwriting that involved *shaping* as it moved from reinforcing approximations to reinforcing total production of letters, *fading* as it provided successively fewer cues for correct responding, *immediate feedback* as it indicated correct and incorrect responding for each response, and *differential reinforcement* as only responses meeting the minimal requirements were reinforced. The authors describe the program as one which

> shapes successively closer approximations of writing by immediate differential reinforcement of the correct response and by gradual attentuation of the controlling stimulus. The controlling stimulus is a letter which the child traces. Portions of the letter are gradually faded out, and the child composes increasingly more of the letter freehand until he is writing the whole letter himself. Immediate differential reinforcement is provided by a special ink and a chemical treatment of the paper. The child writes with a pen which makes a black mark when the letter is properly formed, but which turns the paper orange when the pen moves from the prescribed pattern. The child thus *knows as he is writing* whether or not he is drawing the letter correctly, and he can immediately correct a response by moving the pen so that it makes a black mark. Under these conditions, the children learn quickly; they learn to write well; and they love it. (1968, p. 57)

Chaining

Chaining is a term used to describe two different procedures for teaching a person to sequence behaviors involved in a response chain; these are (1) forward chaining and (2) backward chaining. In *forward chaining, the components are taught in a forward fashion, i.e., beginning with the* **first** *link in the chain. In backward chaining, the components are taught in a backward fashion, i.e., beginning with the* **last** *link in the chain.* The distinction between shaping and chaining may at first seem unclear, but the distinction has been made by many, including Kazdin (1975), who noted that

> It may be unclear what the differences are between shaping and chaining and the different conditions which dictate choosing between these techniques. *Generally, shaping is used to develop new behaviors.* Cues such as instructions and gestures may be used as discriminative stimuli combined with direct reinforcement (e.g., praise) for responses that approach the terminal goal. Chaining usually is used to develop a sequence of behaviors using responses that are already present in the individual's repertoire. To obtain a chain of responses consisting of discrete behaviors, shaping may be used first to develop component behaviors. Certainly,

the major difference (between backward chaining and shaping) is that chaining proceeds in a backward direction beginning with the last response and building prior behaviors, whereas shaping works in a forward direction. Moreover, in shaping, the goal is to develop a terminal response. The behaviors along the way toward the goal usually are not evident when shaping is completed. In chaining, behaviors developed early in training are still evident when training is complete. (p. 40)

The choice of using a chaining procedure leaves us with the further choice of whether to use forward or backward chaining, each of which has several variations. One is to guide the student either physically or with prompts through the chain, and then to teach him to emit independently one portion of the chain. For example, if we were trying to teach a child to write his name, "James," we could in some circumstances have him trace his name on sheets we had already prepared. Gradually, we would fade out the prompts from each of these letters so that the behavior was emitted independently. We could proceed in several ways, three of which are as follows: (1) First fade out just the letter J, then the letter a, etc. If we followed this procedure, we would be using forward chaining. (2) First fade out just the letter s, then the letter e, etc. If we were to follow this procedure, we would be using backward chaining. (3) Fade all letters simultaneously. This procedure may be the simplest, quickest, etc., but for some students, it may represent too much stimulus change at one time. If we were to follow one of the first two procedures, however, we would be using forward or backward chaining. Of course, there are several ways in which these procedures could be implemented, but one example to help make the distinction can be found in Figure 10-1.

Chaining can also be used to teach a sequence of behaviors when the student can emit each of the components but simply does not do so in sequence. For

Forward Chaining:	Backward Chaining:
Antecedent Stimulus	Antecedent Stimulus
James	James
James	James
James	James
ames	Jame
ames	Jame
ames	Jame
mes	Jame
mes	Jam
mes	Jam
mes	Jam
es	Jam
es	Ja
es	Ja
es	Ja
s	J
s	J
s	J

Figure 10-1. An example of teaching a child to write his name through forward chaining and through backward chaining. The column to the left represents the antecedent stimulus for the student while the column to the right represents a correct response by the student. At each step, there would be a number of trials to criterion before the next step would be begun.

example, we have had students who have trouble beginning their work. They can emit each of the components of "working at their desk," but they simply do not begin. In these cases, we typically list the behaviors involved, such as walking to the shelf with the work papers, bringing them back to the desk, bringing a sharpened pencil to the desk, and so forth. Physical, gestural, and/or verbal prompts are used at each component, and then they are faded from the beginning (in forward) or from the last (in backward chaining).

Many of the tasks in which backward chaining is used involve manipulative behaviors. In the ubiquitious puzzle task, backward chaining is quite appropriate and increases the rate of acquisition. For the sake of brevity, let's presume that a puzzle has three large pieces and we are trying to teach the student to put all three pieces in the appropriate place (our overall goal may, of course, be more general, such as remaining on task for 60 consecutive seconds; but it can be addressed through a task like this). In the first step, the teacher would leave two of the pieces in place and remove the third perhaps only an inch from its correct position. Then she would push the piece back into its place, serving as a model for the child. After two or three demonstrations, the teacher would again remove the piece slightly; but this time she would instruct the student to complete the puzzle. If he did, she would reinforce him appropriately. If he did not, she would physically guide his hand through the response, and then reinforce him. After a criterion of consecutive corrective independent responses was met, the teacher would begin the next step of the task by removing the same puzzle piece an additional inch or so from its correct final position. At this point, a verbal prompt might still be necessary, but a physical prompt might not be. This portion of the task would continue until the first puzzle piece had been completely removed and placed on the table. Then a second piece would be slightly removed, and the same general procedure would be followed for this and for the third piece.

Traditionally, backward chaining has also been used to teach many self-help skills such as dressing. For example, in the task of pulling on pants, the child might begin with the pants on, but 2 inches below the waist. With physical guidance and prompting when necessary, the child learns to pull the pants up. This task is continued with the pants removed successively more from the student's body. Depending upon the child, the task may involve 5, 10, or even 15 discrete steps, but finally he will be completing the task beginning with the pants completely removed. In this type of self-help task, as well as in the puzzle-completion task, the student both (1) began to learn independently to emit the last step of the task before any other step, and (2) emitted only the last step of the chain. While something called backward chaining must involve the first of these elements, it need not involve the second. For example, the student could be guided physically through all components of the chain except the last. When independent responding on the last component has met criterion, responding would be physically guided through all but the last two components of the chain, and so forth. An example of this procedure could be teaching a child to self-feed with a spoon. We have often physically guided the student through the scooping and movement components, letting him, however, complete the last component independently. Unlike the way in which the puzzle-completion and the dressing tasks were described, this task would have the student going through the entire sequence each trial. Obviously, there are some advantages to this approach to backward chaining.

Azrin, Schaeffer, and Wesolowski (1976) demonstrated the advantage of using forward sequencing in an article that presented an alternative to the backward chaining procedure for teaching dressing skills to profoundly retarded individuals. They referenced a number of studies (e.g., Ball, Seric, & Payne, 1971; Bensberg, Colwell, & Cassel, 1965; Bensberg & Slominski, 1965; Horner, 1970; Minge & Ball, 1967) that have been considered to be classic examples of how to teach self-help skills through backward chaining. Their description of the procedures common to all these reports is excellent, and it provides us with a clear picture of the work done with thousands of retarded persons in the 1960s and 1970s:

> Food snacks or praise serve as the reinforcers; reinforcement is given at the completion of the act of taking off or putting on a specific garment; an instruction is given to start each trial for a given garment; "backward chaining" is used for each garment whereby the instructor himself puts on or takes off the garment almost entirely, allowing the student to complete only the final portion; the student learns to deal with one article of clothing before proceeding to the next; finally, the instructor fades out the instructions and the reinforcers. Brief training sessions of about 15 minutes are used over a period of many weeks or months. (p. 29)

The procedures by Azrin *et al.* represent a very different approach to this, the most prevalent procedure for teaching self-dressing to retarded persons of all ages. Because this procedure has been quite successful and can be generalized to other teaching objectives, the differences between the most predominate method and the one suggested by Azrin, Schaeffer, and Wesolowski will be listed. The authors mention nine such differences:

1. A forward instead of a backward chaining procedure is used and, as a result, the student participates in the initial as well as the final components of each task on each trial.
2. Instead of teaching undressing (or dressing) skills with one garment at a time, the instructors taught the skills with all the garments normally involved.
3. Oversized garments were initially used.
4. Reinforcers intrinsic to dressing, verbal praise, and physical praise were used instead of snacks and praise exclusively.
5. Initially, instructions were given nearly continuously rather than just at the beginning of each trial.
6. Manual guidance was a major rather than a secondary teaching component.
7. Manual guidance was faded through graduated guidance and intermittent guidance procedures.
8. Training was intensive, using, instead of one or two 15-minute sessions per day, two 2- or 3-hour sessions per day.
9. To reduce confusion, all undressing skills were taught before any dressing skills were taught (undressing skills were deemed easier than dressing skills).

The actual methods used are quite important, because they have been demonstrated to facilitate teaching self-help skills, because they demonstrate the use of many of the standard behavioral principles and methods, and because many of them can be generalized to teaching academic, social, other self-help, and many other types of skills. The major elements to this program are the following:

1. *Reinforcers.* Attendants were interviewed to provide lists of reinforcers for each student, and the reinforcers were divided into three classes. *Noninterrupting* ones, such as praise and back-stroking, were given virtually continuously; *short-duration but obtrusive* ones like snacks were given after each garment was put on or removed; and *longer duration interruptive* reinforcers, such as naps or walks, were provided only at the completion of total sequences.

2. *Positioning.* To reduce competing responses from unsteadiness, students were seated in a chair with a back rest.

3. *Both hands used.* To reduce interference from a nonused hand and to reinforce behaviors incompatible with inappropriate responding, students were taught to use both hands to dress.

4. *Fading clothing sizes.* Initially, garments were two sizes too large. As the student progressed, smaller sizes were used.

5. *Types of garments.* Five garments were used: underpants, shoes, socks, pants, and shirt. Again, to make correct responding more probable, all were slip-on garments without laces, buttons, zippers, snaps, or belts.

6. *Sequencing.* Students were first taught to undress themselves in a natural sequence from shoes to socks to pants to underpants to the more difficult shirt. After each sequence, the staff dressed the student; and after undressing skills were mastered, dressing skills were taught.

7. *Forward sequencing.* Students learned to dress or undress in a normal forward sequence rather than in an interruptive backward chaining sequence.

8. *Session length.* In accordance with Azrin's preference for massed practice in other programs he has devised, intensive 3-hour sessions were used.[4]

9. *Attending prompts.* If the student did not follow directions, his name was called, the instruction was repeated, and if necessary his head was directed toward the task.

10. *Reason for reinforcement.* Students were told what behaviors lead to reinforcement.

11. *General to specific instructions.* Instructions proceeded from general ("get undressed") to specific ("take off your shoes") to allow the student to follow the more general instruction if he could.

---

[4] It is interesting that the individuals in this study had standardized test scores of less than 1.5 years mental age and 1.6 years social age. As such, they are in the group of individuals usually excused as having short attention spans and as being unable to work for more than 15 or 20 minutes. The authors attribute part of their success with 3-hour sessions to intensive reinforcement procedures.

12. *Prompts.* The prompts became increasingly directive if the student did not comply. The first prompt was a verbal instruction. If that did not result in compliance within a few seconds, the instructor pointed to or touched the garment. If that did not work, the verbal instruction was repeated, and the student's hands were molded around the garment. If that did not result in compliance, the instructor guided the student through all the movements while describing each one of them. In this manner, students were allowed to demonstrate independent functioning, but were not allowed noncompliance; all trials resulted in responding.

13. *Delayed manual guidance for passive learners.* For students who had learned the skill but were passive and did not comply, instructions were repeated every 10 seconds for 1 minute before manual guidance was used.

14. *Multiple instructors.* Two instructors were present at the beginning and until the student could be easily managed by one instructor. (This assistance is congruent with all the other steps that are consistently directed toward maximizing success and removing interfering conditions.)

15. *Graduated guidance.* Students were gently guided in the initial stages of all tasks. The instructor's hands were molded around the student's hands and provided guidance. If there was resistance, the student was not forced, and guidance began once the student was again relaxed. As the student began to respond, guidance was lessened.

16. *Intermittent guidance.* As training progressed, guidance became intermittent and was used lightly only when the student was not responding or was having difficulty.

17. *Verbal praise and stroking.* Praise and stroking were used to differentially reinforce compliance behaviors. When the student followed instructions, she or he was reinforced; but when the student did not follow instructions or resisted guidance, reinforcement stopped.

18. *Intensive training on one garment.* In line with the massed practice theory, intensive training began on single garments if the student was having difficulty with one or two garments. This procedure interrupted the forward sequence that included all five garments, but intensive training on a single garment still followed the forward sequence rather than backward chaining.

The results of this study were very good. But more importantly for our purpose, the work provides examples of forward chaining, of graduated guidance, of proper utilization of reinforcers, of starting with antecedent stimuli (oversized garments without belts, snaps, zippers, etc.) that maximize the probability of success, of sequencing, of massed practice, of differential reinforcement, of labeled praise, of intensive practice on components with deficiencies, and of other factors useful in teaching many different types of tasks.

Fading

Fading is an extraordinarily useful procedure in which we attempt to maximize the probability of successful responding by particular artificial arrangements of antecedent stimuli. Then, through careful sequencing, the arrangements are changed until behavior is under the control of stimuli natural to the learning environment. The definition offered by Sulzer-Azaroff and Mayer (1977) describes the procedure quite well: *"the gradual removal of (usually artificial or intrusive) discriminative stimuli such as directions, imitative prompts, physical guidance, and other cues and prompts"* (p. 516). In this sense, fading is very similar to shaping. In the three-term contingency, shaping involves the successive approximation of responding (the second term) to its final form, while fading involves the successive approximation of the antecedent stimulus (the first term) to its final form.[5]

There are many forms of fading, but for our purposes we will consider them to be in one of two classifications: (1) teacher aid is faded, or (2) the physical properties of objects are faded. Teacher aid can be of many types. For example, we might initially use verbal prompts at the beginning of each member of a three-component chain in which we would like each student when entering the classroom to hang up his or her coat, sit down, and begin to work. If one of our students has a problem with his sequence, we might use three instructions such as "Johnny, hang up your coat," then "Please sit down now," and finally "It's time to put your worksheet and pencil on your desk, so please do so." Because we would like "entering the classroom at 8:30" to be the antecedent event for this sequence, the verbal prompts are artificial to the final environment; so we would fade them gradually from this environment. As the later portions of chains are more likely to occur than earlier portions, prompts should first be faded from the last component. In this problem, we have several options. One is to drop the last half of the last prompt, while retaining all of the first two prompts. The last prompt could be something like "It's time for your worksheet and pencil." Then the whole prompt could be faded. If the chain is still properly occurring, the second prompt would be faded in a similar fashion; and then the first could be faded. The basic idea is to maximize success by adding prompts, then to withdraw them gradually and systematically while the behavior is still occurring. Stimulus control is then transferred from an artificial but helpful environment to a more natural environment.

In this example, physical prompts such as pointing could also be used. They too would be faded out as behavior came under control of the antecedent stimulus of entering the classroom. Physical prompts can also be used in many other ways, and as the example by Azrin, Schaeffer, and Wesolowski (1976) demonstrates, the fading of physical prompts through *graduated guidance* is an extremely useful method to teach retarded persons very definite skills. One of the areas in which this method has been most frequently used is self-feeding, but it is

---

[5] The third term of the contingency, the consequence, also undergoes a systematic change to its final form. An example would be when we initially reinforce a child for every correct response, then for every two correct, etc., until we arrive at the final schedule we would like to use.

frequently used in many others. A single program for guidance was used by O'Brien, Bugle, and Azrin (1972) to teach a profoundly retarded six-year-old girl to feed herself with a spoon. First the task was divided into six steps. Then the teacher provided manual guidance for each of the steps in the following manner:

> (1) The handle of the spoon was placed in the child's right hand, which was then held by the teacher's right hand. (2) Guiding the hand, the spoon was dipped into the food, and with food on the spoon, it was lifted to about 1 in. above the bowl. (3) The spoon was lifted to within 2 in. of the child's mouth. (4) The teacher placed her left hand on the child's chin and gently opened the child's mouth. (5) The spoon was gently guided into the child's mouth. (6) The child's hand was guided upward and outward resulting in the food being removed from the spoon by the child's upper teeth or lip. (p. 69)

Then as the student began to emit the components of this chain, guidance was faded. The same general procedure can be applied to hundreds of tasks related to physical skills such as handwriting, walking, putting on clothes, assembling components in a workshop, and so forth. The basic procedure to be abstracted across all teaching tasks utilizing graduated guidance includes (1) writing the components of the response, (2) identifying the order in which physical prompts are to be faded, and (3) determining a criterion that indicates when a prompt should be faded.

Other types of fading involve gradual changes in the physical properties of objects that act as antecedent events. One of the more clever uses of fading was offered by Westing (unpublished) while working with a four-year-old boy who typically regurgitated any solid foods. The preschool which the student attended became the site of a fading program intended to teach him to eat solids, as well as to teach him to eat independently. Three factors were considered as possibly contributing to the problem; these were the use of solid foods, attempts to "force feed" the child, and the presence of other children. Four tactics were concurrently implemented to address the problem. The first instituted a feeding program that started with yogurt, which was a food the child would eat without fighting or regurgitating. After he was eating yogurt, other foods eaten by fellow students were thoroughly pureed with the yogurt. At first, the blended solids constituted 10% of the mixture, but its contribution was increased every few days (from 10 to 20, 30, 45, 50, 60, 65, 75, 85, 95, and 100%). Then the food-blending procedure was discontinued, as the solids were first chopped fine and then cut into bite-sized pieces. The second concurrent tactic involved graduated guidance to teach the student independent feeding. The procedure was like that described by O'Brien, Bugle, and Azrin (1972) and involved decreasing guidance along the task-analyzed components. The third tactic was concerned with the possibility that other children were signals (discriminative stimuli) and reinforcers for the inappropriate behavior. If this were the case, then the program could be helped initially by removing the student from the other children during the eating period. So during the first seven days of the program, just this student and the teacher were together during mealtime. Then for nine days one student joined the student during this period. A second student was added, then a third, a fourth, and finally a fifth to produce the normal-sized seating arrangement. A final tactic was to provide extra sessions each day so that correct responding could be practiced. The program was in effect for 43 days during which there were no episodes of vomiting. At this time, the child was returned to the regular eating practices of his classmates, which included a snack and lunch. Four months later, Westing had a follow-up conversation with the child's mother, who reported that he continued to feed himself independently, that he was eating a good variety of cut-up foods, that she had been very surprised at her child's cooperation in eating such foods, and that no episodes of regurgitation had occurred. Because there was no experimental design to the study, one has no indication as to whether each of the components contributed to the success of the program or whether, in fact, any of the four tactics contributed to the success.[6] The tactics remain, however, appropriate ones for situations like these.

Many examples of fading are based upon strategies to teach academic or quasi-academic skills. In the early 1960s, an excellent series of studies by Terrace (e.g., 1963a, b, c, 1964a, b, 1966) in laboratory situations established the basic fading procedure for discriminations by moving systematically from very easy discriminations to the more difficult one that would be required in the end. Moore and Goldiamond (1964) took Terrace's basic procedures and applied them to a human learning situation as they compared fading and nonfading procedures for teaching a delayed matching-to-sample task to preschool children. In this task, which involved geometric forms, a triangle was presented briefly as the sample. It was then withdrawn and three triangles were placed on three small windows in a panel before the student. One of the three triangles was just like the one that was removed, while the other two were rotated slightly. The child's task, then, was to choose the triangle that matched the one that was just removed. A trial then might look like this:

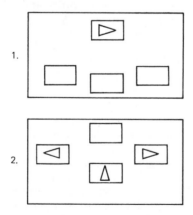

In the *nonfading procedure*, the sample window was lighted with *full intensity* (110 volts). It then went off, and the three "matching" windows below it went on at full intensity (110 volts). The student then chose which of the three stimuli matched the figure that had just disappeared. The procedure, which is identified with our typical teaching procedure in the sense that we traditionally do not use

---

[6] That is, there were only two phases to this study, the baseline phase and the phase in which all four tactics were employed. All the procedures, however, are good ones that demonstrate fading from an artificial to a natural environment while the behavior is still being maintained.

fading techniques, proved very difficult and resulted in performance at about the chance (33% correct) level. In the *fading procedure*, the sample was also presented at full intensity and then withdrawn. But the three "matching" windows were presented in a different fashion. Initially, only the window with the match was lighted; the windows with the incorrect alternatives were not lighted. After three trials, these windows then became progressively lighted as the voltage of the incorrect windows was increased through various percentages of full voltage.[7] In this procedure, matching behavior was quickly established; it was also retained throughout the fading series virtually without error as stimulus control was transferred from a brightness dimension to a form dimension. Thus the *same* students had (1) trouble during nonfading periods of presentation,and (2) no trouble learning during the fading periods of stimulus presentation. These results are produced in virtually all fading studies that employ a basic teaching procedure that we can generalize to many of our teaching situations: (1) *initially make the distinction between the correct stimulus* (the S^D) *and the incorrect stimulus* (the S^Δ) *as great as possible; then* (2) *gradually make this distinction less apparent until both the correct and the incorrect stimuli appear in their final form.*

This basic procedure has been adopted by many people to teach tasks that are more directly academic. For example, Egeland (1975) taught preschool children to discriminate between pairs of similar letters by first distinguishing important aspects of the letters in color and by then fading out the colors. Corey and Shamow (1972) went beyond individual letters and tested the efficacy of a fading program in teaching students to read words. They noted that the popular "sight" method for teaching reading (Heilman, 1961) was essentially a non-fading method. It involves superimposing printed and verbal or pictorial stimuli, which are then rather abruptly dropped. They sought then to compare a *fading* program with the more typical *superimposition* program to teach "sight" reading. Both procedures involved photographic slides of Milton Bradley "Picture flash card words for beginners" (apple, ball, horse, dog, elephant, and book). The superimposition procedure consisted of two picture-word combinations presented five times, followed by presentation of the word alone for one trial. This sixth presentation constituted the test for the effectiveness of the superimposition procedure in teaching a child to read a word. The fading procedure also consisted of six steps. The first was the same as that of the other procedure. The next four steps, however, involved fading the picture of the object which was acting as a supplemental cue. The sixth step again involved a test of the procedure. After this sixth step was completed for each of the words used in the two procedures, a cumulative test was given in which each child was tested on all the words used. Results showed that on the (sixth-trial) initial test on the words taught by the fading procedure the children averaged *5.67 words correct out of 6;* for the same test on the words taught by the nonfading or superimposition procedure, the children only averaged *0.33 words correct out of 6 words.* In the review or cumulative test, the children averaged *3.00 correct* on the words taught by the fading procedure and only *0.83* correct on the words taught by the

---

[7] The series was 35, 40, 50, 60, 65, 70, 75, 80, 83, 86, 88, 90, 92, 94, 96, 98, and 100%. The reason the voltages did not increase by even increments was that the authors took into account the phi-phenomena effect, an effect unimportant to our point.

nonfading procedure. These differences are remarkable; *almost all* the children learned to read *all* the words correctly when taught to read by the *fading* method, while *most* of the same children *could not read any* of the words when taught by the nonfading method.

The same basic procedure was repeated by Dorry (1972) and by Dorry and Zeaman (1973, 1975); the first two studies demonstrated a possible added advantage of fading. The study by Dorry involved nonretarded children and again demonstrated the significant advantage of using fading to teach children to acquire vocabulary. In addition, however, the study found that with these children, "vocabulary acquisition pretraining using a fading procedure significantly affected later learning using the standard method of simultaneous presentation" (Dorry and Zeaman, 1973, p. 3). Quite simply, this means that, for these children and this task, (1) acquiring vocabulary initially by the fading method was more efficient than by the nonfading method, and (2) once having learned by the fading method, students learned better on the same type of task taught by the nonfading method. As this is an important but puzzling finding, the study by Dorry and Zeaman sought to confirm it, and the study did. Eighteen nonreading retarded persons participated in the study and were divided into two groups. For one, eight words (cow, pie, bus, monkey, apple, duck, tree, corn) coupled with pictures were presented in the typical fading procedure. For another group, the eight words and pictures were presented in the typical nonfading manner. After a few presentations, the groups were tested on just the words. Results showed that the fading group had learned on the average 3.6 words, while the nonfading group learned only 1.2 words. These results and procedures are similar to those of the other studies. Now, however, the interesting variation was begun. A second list of words (car, pig, bed, rabbit, chair, door, goat, shoe) was then presented to *both groups* in the nonfading manner. Results of the test trials showed (1) that the group which has learned the first list by the fading method and the second list by the nonfading method averaged 4.1 words correct, and (2) that the group which had learned both lists by the nonfading procedure averaged only 1.7 words correct on the second list. The reason for these results may be that the fading program forces the student to focus attention on the relevant stimulus, i.e., the word (Dorry, 1976).

These studies indicated that there may be effects from learning by a fading procedure that carry over to tasks learned through a nonfading procedure. The opposite question can also be posed: are there carryover effects to a fading program once an individual has been exposed to a nonfading program? In a classic and brilliant series on the fading procedure, Sidman and Stoddard (1966, 1967; Stoddard & Sidman, 1967) produced results relevant to this question, but results which neither answered nor were intended to answer this question. Nineteen retarded persons participated in the study, which required the individuals to discriminate a circle from seven ellipses. Each student was tested individually and sat in a room facing a panel with eight operative keys. A projector in an adjoining room provided stimuli on each of the keys, and the students' task was to press the key with the circle. Figure 10-2 represents a portion of the fading program presented to ten of the students. Note that in this procedure only the correct image (the circle) was initially available. The seven incorrect images (the ellipses) were added onto the keys over many trials. This group may have been responding initially to a "bright *vs.* dark," then to a "form *vs.* no-form," and

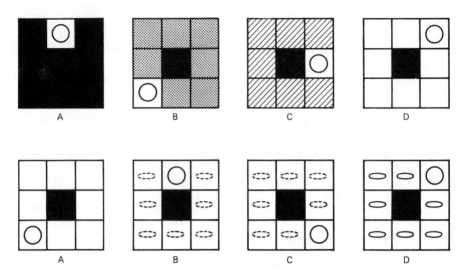

Figure 10-2. The upper figure is a schematic illustration of a few steps in the background-fading portion of the program. The correct key always had the circle on a bright background. The incorrect keys were dark at first (A) and gradually became brighter (B, C, D). The lower figure is a schematic illustration of a few steps in the ellipse-fading portion of the program. The ellipses appeared gradually (B, C, D), on the bright backgrounds of the incorrect keys. (The ellipses were not actually dotted; they were drawn that way here for convenience in reproduction.) (From Sidman & Stoddard, 1967, p. 6.)

finally to a "circle *vs.* ellipse" discrimination. Of the ten students in this group, seven learned the discrimination. The other group, consisting of nine students, was presented the discrimination on the same number of slides according to a nonfading format in which the circle and the seven ellipses were presented in their final form from the very first trial. Of these nine students, only one learned the discrimination. When these students were then brought to a level at which the fading group was performing partway through the fading program, they still made more errors than the students in the fading group. The performance of one of the students typified the problem: he developed an error pattern in which he systematically touched keys around the matrix until finding the correct key. This pattern is not at all unlike the "guessing" responses of retarded students who are asked to indicate (by pointing, naming, etc.) the one correct stimulus among several incorrect ones (e.g., identifying the red square when presented with a red, a blue, and a yellow square). While not answering the question of whether being presented a task by a nonfading procedure will counteract the positive effects of being presented the same task by a fading procedure, this series of studies does suggest that such a sequence may have counterproductive effects; the students may develop error patterns that require additional programs to correct.

Many of these studies have taught discriminations by using electronic equipment. Some of it (e.g., Sidman and Stoddard's) is extremely sophisticated, expensive, and unrealistic for classroom use. Other pieces are not, however, and classroom application can be easily arranged. Most schools have access to slide projectors, and slides are quite simple to make. One method of fading out the added cues was described by Corey and Shamow (1972). They mounted their negatives in plastic slide holders and covered the faded pictures with varying amounts of translucent tracing and typing papers. An even simpler procedure is to cover the faded material before photographing with varying amounts of translucent materials. Such procedures are quite simple, require no special artistic or photographic skills, and can even be used as reinforcing activities for appropriately trained individuals in special or regular classrooms. A similar, but nonphotographic procedure was used by Haupt, Van Kirk, and Terraciano (1975), who taught arithmetic functions like addition, subtraction, and multiplication by covering answers with increasing layers of cellophane until the students were responding only to the natural cue—the arithmetic problem. Some tasks we teach can incorporate a fading procedure that does not require overlays of any type. These tasks include virtually any kind of identification task in which a student is required to indicate one particular stimulus among several that are present. For example, suppose that our task is to teach the student to touch on 20 consecutive trials the red square when presented with a red, a blue, and a yellow square. We have four decisions to make. The *first* is how to consequate an appropriate response. Let us suppose that for this student, our smiling, praising, and touching is reinforcing. So, after every correct response, we will reinforce the student with the most suitable, natural, and noninterruptive form of attention. The *second* decision is how to consequate error responding. For many retarded persons, feedback for errors must be made quite distinct from feedback for correct responses. So we will schedule four consequences for an incorrect response: (1) a "No!" said in a gentle tone that is nevertheless quite distinctive from the tone of our praise statements, (2) a brief timeout period of about 5 seconds in which we withdraw the materials for the student, do not give attention in the form of eye contact, and do not talk, (3) a correction trial (i.e., the trial is repeated until a correct response is made), and (4) after the correction response, a return to the prior step in the sequence. Such a return provides a student with a good opportunity for a correct response so that the aversive aspects of an error are less likely to recur immediately, and it also provides us with another opportunity to present whatever concept we were trying to teach on that trial. The *third decision* involves a choice of the fading sequence, while the *fourth decision* involves how to teach beyond these particular stimuli (i.e., how to teach an abstraction). The actual steps in a task like this can be quite large, usually numbering about 50. They can be summarized in a few "phrases," however, that incorporate steps with a similar objective. Figure 10-3 describes these phases.

Imitation

One form of changing behavior that involves prompting and fading is *imitation, a procedure in which a model's behavior acts as a prompting stimulus that controls the behavior of the observing student.* While chaining and shaping are generally considered ways to teach new forms of behavior, and while fading is generally considered a way to bring a current behavior under the control of new forms of stimuli, imitation really has two different functions. One function is to affect *learning*, i.e., to teach the student through observation new forms of

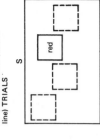

S

T

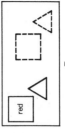

S

T

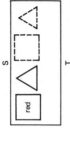

S

T

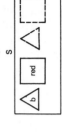

S

T

PHASES:

Phase 1: Teach the student correct response (i.e., to touch an object).

Phase 2: Teach S to touch the red square (S⁺) when another object (S⁻) is present but not approximate.

Phase 3: Teach S to touch the red square when it and S⁻ are equidistant from S.

Phase 4: Teach S to touch the red square as S⁻ becomes more like S⁺ in every dimension but color.

Phase 5: Teach S to touch the red square when a blue square is present.

TEACHER BEHAVIORS

For four or five trials, the teacher (T) places a red square at various places on the table and asks the student to touch the red one. Correct responses reinforced. Physical guidance used if necessary to teach touching response. (At this point, the student is only learning to touch an object, not to touch a red object, so these trials are small in number.) (Pointing is not used because it is a response that can be rapidly changed from one object to the next.)

T presents another object of a different shape, size, and color. It is presented with the square and precedes the instruction. The incorrect object (e.g., a small blue triangle) is presented as far from S as possible. T's hand remains close to the incorrect stimulus (S⁻) and covers it if the student seems to be reaching for it.

T moves S⁻ closer and closer to the student on succeeding trials. T's hand is moved farther and farther from S⁻ as the touching response comes under the control of the red stimulus.

T introduces other forms of S⁻ that have already been cut from construction paper. One option is to make the triangle successively larger in three or four gradations until the altitude (height) of the triangle is the same as the side of the square.

T presents blue objects that are successively similar to the red object until the blue object differs from the red one only in color.

308

Phase 6: Teach S to touch the red square when a blue square and a yellow square are present.

Phase 7: Teach S to touch the "red one" as opposed to the "red square."

T repeats Phases 2-5 with the yellow stimulus with it eventually being presented as a yellow square the same size as the red and blue ones. Instructions are still to touch the red one.

1. (At this point, the student may well be responding to "red square" rather than to "red," and if presented with a red circle, he may respond incorrectly.) T places a red object of another shape in front of S and gives the usual instruction.

2. The incorrect stimuli (blue and yellow squares) are withdrawn for a few trials. They are then moved successively closer to S as correct responding occurs.

3. The correct stimulus is again changed in shape and presented singly.

4. The incorrect stimuli are faded in.

5. Many forms of S⁺ are presented. The correct stimuli are retained in shape, while the blue and yellow stimuli gradually become the same shape.

6. Stimuli are randomly presented without regard to size or shape.

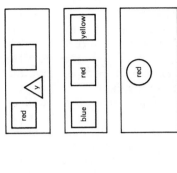

Figure 10-3. A task that incorporates fading techniques to teach a student to touch a red square when presented a red, a blue, and a yellow square on a table and the instructions "touch the red one."

behaviors. The other function is to affect the *performance* of behaviors the student has already learned to emit. Making this distinction allows us to determine more appropriately the correct use of this method. Imitation (also called modeling and sometimes called observational learning) is simply not an appropriate method to teach even simple tasks to retarded students who are functioning at a low developmental level. For example, a skill like buttoning a shirt is an inappropriate skill to teach only through modeling. Certainly, showing the student how to perform any skill is appropriate, but teaching such skills without the added aid of guidance, shaping, chaining, etc., is inappropriate. Many teachers probably incorporate modeling in such a context without realizing they are so doing. They *expect* a student to kick a ball, or to say words, or to write letters during work time because *other* students are engaging in these behaviors. Such an expectation incorporates the concept of imitation, i.e., that one student will learn to do something because she or he sees other students doing it. But such an expectation fails to include three very important factors: (1) the skill level of the student relative to the complexity of the task, (2) observable consequences of the model's behavior, and (3) consequences of the observer's behavior.

When a student has already learned to emit appropriate forms of behavior, then modeling is a procedure that only affects performance, and it does so through two procedures, vicarious reinforcement and vicarious punishment. *Vicarious reinforcement is a procedure in which reinforcement of an individual's or a group's behavior increases the performance of that behavior by others who are not directly reinforced.* There have been many formal studies of this effect. For example, Kazdin (1973a) showed that, when students were praised for fast rates of production in a sheltered workshop, their rates of production increased. In addition, however, the work rates of students who were not praised also increased, thus the vicarious reinforcement effect. A number of other studies have shown the same effect (e.g., Broden, Bruce, Mitchell, Carter & Hall, 1970; Christy, 1975; Kazdin, Silverman & Sittler, 1975). However, in the Kazdin study, there was an interesting additional effect that may be unexpected. When *slow* work behavior of the target subjects was directly reinforced, the work behavior of the observing workers again became *faster*. This effect has been demonstrated by Kazdin in other settings (Kazdin, 1973b, 1977), and in one of these, he has offered a reasonable explanation of this effect:

> [the] behaviors of the target and nontarget children usually change in the same direction. That is, reinforcing attentive behavior of the target subject increases that behavior in both target and nontarget subjects. Thus, it appears that the nontarget subject performs the behavior that (s)he sees reinforced in the target subject. In some situations, the nonreinforced peer may *not* perform the behaviors for which the target subject is praised. For example, in one classroom study, providing verbal praise to target subjects for *either* attentive or inattentive behavior increased attentive behavior in adjacent nontarget subjects (Kazdin, 1973b). Changes in the nontarget subjects' behavior did *not* appear to be related to the specific behaviors reinforced in the target subjects. Possibly, delivering approval to one child *signals* other children that the reinforcing agent is monitoring behavior and may deliver reinforcing consequences. Praise to the target subject may serve as a discriminative

stimulus (S^D) to the nontarget children that their behavior may be reinforced. Thus *hearing* the praise rather than *observing* the behavior of the target subject might be sufficient to achieve changes in the nonreinforced subject. In the previous study, the target subjects initially received verbal approval for attentive behavior and later for inattentive behavior. The consistent improvements in attentive behavior of the nontarget subjects across both contingencies may have resulted from first associating approval of the target subject with attentive behavior. Put another way, the order of the contingencies in the previous study may have contributed to the results. (1977, p. 58)

For our purposes, these results suggest that if we consistently reinforce the students in our class, three effects are likely to occur: (1) those behaviors of the "model" that are directly reinforced will increase, (2) the same behaviors will be increased by the observers, and (3) behaviors of the observers *other than those reinforced for the model* will increase. The first two effects are expected to occur and are quite beneficial to our programs. The third effect, however, is unexpected, but its benefits are at least as important. The third effect means that if we have been consistently reinforcing our class, the reinforcers we use will act as cues[8] for behaviors of the observers that have previously been reinforced; these behaviors do not have to be the same as the behavior for which the target student is being reinforced. If we are careful not to reinforce inappropriate behaviors, then when we praise a student that praise will serve as a cue *only for appropriate* behaviors of other students in the class.

The second procedure in which modeling affects performance is *vicarious punishment, a procedure in which punishment of an individual's or a group's behavior decreases the performance of that behavior by others who are not directly punished.* While there is not enough work on vicarious reinforcement to allow us to understand how best to utilize its effects, there is unfortunately even less work on vicarious punishment. A few studies, however, have at least demonstrated that we can control the behavior of some students by punishing others. In one study, we (Repp, Samuels & Boles, 1975) were interested in investigating some methods of token loss (a procedure called response cost)[9] that could be managed by a single teacher in a TMR classroom. In a multiphase design, we looked at the effect of an inappropriate set of instructions and of four manageable procedures that were based on vicarious punishment. In the first procedure, instructions had no effect on appropriate sitting. In a second procedure, the teacher removed tokens from only one particular student on occasions of inappropriate sitting. The same student was observed throughout the period, and the same student was observed from day to day. This is obviously an easy system, which only requires that the teacher be particularly attentive to the special behavior of one student. This procedure successfully reduced the behavior of the target student, but it had only a transient effect on the other stu-

---

[8] This effect occurs because conditioned reinforcers have a second function, that of discriminative stimuli (see the discussion on chains).

[9] A procedure in which a response results in the loss of accumulated reinforcement (e.g., a fine for speeding).

dents. For the first few days, their behavior decreased; but after this period, it returned to its prior level. Obviously, although this procedure was easy to implement, it was not effective in terms of vicarious effects. So a second procedure was used in which one student was the target student each day, but the target student changed from day to day. This procedure also effectively reduced inappropriate sitting for the target student for that day. But the students soon learned that the first loss of the day signaled who would lose tokens that day, so the reduction of the behavior on the class as a whole was only transient. Another procedure was then tried in which a different student was the target subject every few minutes. Thus each student was in the response-cost condition each day, but the procedure was still easy for the teacher. In this case, responding increased substantially but not totally. In effect, each student was under direct punishment on an intermittent schedule (just those periods in which he or she was the target student), as well as under vicarious punishment on an intermittent schedule (because not all responses of all other students resulted in token loss; they resulted in token loss only when that student was the target student). This procedure, which is manageable for most teachers, is effective and appropriate when we are not concerned with reducing all occurrences of inappropriate responding, preferring instead just to reduce it to nondisruptive levels. We followed this with what is often too time-consuming a procedure: taking away tokens for each response by each student on each occurrence. This procedure immediately reduced responding. All along we were providing instructions to students on appropriate and inappropriate sitting, so we wanted to determine whether just instructions would maintain low rates of responding, and we found that it did. While this study does not separate in its later phases the effects of vicarious from direct punishment, it does suggest a number of points: (1) for students who had never received punishment of this type for other behaviors in the classroom, the cue value of vicarious punishment was only transient, (2) that the more frequently vicarious punishment is linked with direct punishment, the more effective it will probably be, and (3) that the cue value of instructions can be enhanced by direct association with consequences.

As we have seen from these studies, the effect of a model on the observer's behavior is much like the effect of other stimuli. If other children are punished, an observing child is much less likely to emit that particular response. If other children are reinforced, an observing child is more likely to emit that particular response or other responses that have previously been reinforced. To some extent, then, the model can be treated like any other stimulus, and some of its properties relative to its environment can be examined to determine what affects the occurrence of the modeled response. Sulzer-Azaroff and Mayer (1977) have discussed a number of these. One is the *similarity of the model to the observer*. In general, the more *similar* the model to the observer, the more likely the observer will imitate. For our students functioning at a moderate or high developmental level, this effect could be important, as it suggests to us that there are certain individuals who would have more effect on classmates than others. We should be careful to select those students to reinforce directly who would have the greatest vicarious effect on the students whose behaviors most need to be changed.

When teaching imitation, we need to be sure that these are *appropriate consequences* both for the model's and the observer's behavior. We should determine reinforcing events for the observer and use these events as consequences for the model's behavior. For example, if we are interested in increasing a child's rate of appropriate social behavior (like saying "thank you," or "please"), we could (1) arrange the model's behavior by offering someone who usually does say "thank you," etc., something he needs or wants, and (2) consequating his "thank you" with something we believe will be reinforcing for the observing child (praise, a token, etc.). In a way, this procedure shares some aspects of the reinforcer sampling and response priming procedures, terms which generally describe direct rather than indirect intervention. The observing child vicariously (visually and/or auditorally) samples the reinforcer. In addition, the child's behavior may be "primed" by the scene he or she has just observed. After arranging this sequence with one or two models, we should immediately arrange such a sequence with target subject. If we wait too long, there may be no effect.

One advantage of imitation training is that the behavior learned is sometimes generalized. This acquisition can take two forms. One is that *imitation itself* can be a learned response; i.e., the student learns to imitate a variety of behaviors. One of the first studies of this effect with retarded persons was by Baer, Peterson, and Sherman (1967). They worked with severely and with profoundly retarded persons who had neither vocal nor motor imitative behaviors. Initially, the students were asked to imitate a series of behaviors modeled by the instructor. When they did not imitate, the students were guided through various physical movements (e.g., raising left arm, tapping table with left hand, standing up). When the imitative response occurred, it was consequated with praise and food. Imitative chains were then modeled and reinforced in which old and new imitations were chained together first in two-response, then in three-response, etc., chains. This study demonstrated several important results. First, as more behaviors were imitated, immediate imitation of new demonstrations increased greatly. This effect suggests that although our first imitation sessions may require considerable shaping and guidance, the latency of new imitations will decrease. Second, as imitation training progressed, certain new imitations were never reinforced. Yet as long as other imitative behaviors were reinforced, these nonreinforced behaviors continued. This effect indicates that the students learned the behavior of imitation itself and generalized it across other stimuli. This result suggests that in teaching imitation we should use varying stimuli to promote generalization, but that we would not have to provide a reinforcement program for each new imitation. Third, the study showed that imitation can go across modalities. After imitation of the motor responses was taught, imitation was used to establish initial verbal repertoires for some of the students.

The second type of generalization is that of the learned behavior itself. For example, Garcia, Guess, and Byrnes (1973) taught a retarded student through imitation to label items either singly ("That is one _____") or in plural ("These are two _____"). In probe trials, however, items were displayed without any preceding labeling response from the instructor. Results showed that the student generalized the appropriate labeling response to these new items. Similar results have been produced by others. For example, Lutzker and Sherman (1974) taught retarded persons to use sentences with correct subject-verb pairings of two forms: (1) plural subject and the verb "are" or (2) singular subject and the verb "is." When generalization probe pictures were presented to them, some of the students produced novel and untrained sentences. Thus, the responses generalized to novel stimuli.

EXAMPLES OF TEACHING PROGRAMS

There are many teaching demonstrations of fading, shaping, etc., with retarded individuals. Most of these have been replicated, so we are quite certain that these procedures work. There are, however, very few comprehensive programs to teach a number of sequenced or related skills. In this section, though, we will briefly discuss a few programs that do represent systematic efforts to teach skills in two areas: (1) language and (2) self-help. These two have been chosen because they represent tasks appropriate for the various levels of mental retardation.

Language Programs

There are several language-based programs that incorporate behavioral principles. Some of these have been discussed by Dudzinski (1977) and these include the programs by (1) Guess, Sailor, and Baer, (2) Bricker and Bricker, (3) Gray and Ryan, and (4) Kent. The program by Guess, Sailor, and Baer has been developed over a number of years through their research with language acquisition by retarded persons, and it has been reported in a number of papers (e.g., Guess & Baer, 1973; Guess, Sailor & Baer, 1974, 1976, 1977; Guess, Sailor, Keogh & Baer, 1976). The program includes a number of individual training steps that are designed to move a student from no speech to modest conversational speech. The program is based on three considerations:

> (a) the program must emphasize the functionality of speech and language—that is, it must rapidly bring children into contact with the potential of speech as an effective mode of controlling the environment; (b) the structure of the training sequence must emphasize the teaching of skills which allow children to expand their own language repertoire; and (c) the sequence of instruction must allow flexibility in reordering the content areas to be trained, in accordance with ongoing data analysis. (Guess, Sailor, Keogh & Baer, 1976, p. 305)

The teaching sequence is divided into 10 areas. Two of the areas (*Persons and Things* and *Persons and Things and Actions*) are taught to all students. After those areas, the remaining areas are divided into two tracks. One track, **Preacademic,** is divided into five content areas (*Possession, Color, Size, Relation,* and *Morphological Grammar*). The other track, **Community Living,** is divided into three tracks and is designed for those students needing training to function in their home, in a community sheltered workshop, a halfway house, a nursing home, or in other such community settings. The areas for this track are *Social Skills, Help-Seeking,* and *Conversational Speech.*

The sequence of training steps within any of the 10 content areas is organized through five dimensions:

1. *Reference.* In this dimension, the student is taught that certain sounds (words) represent either objects and events or attributes of objects and

events. In this area, the student is taught names of these objects and events, descriptions of actions, ownership (my/your), color, and relations (size, position).

2. *Control.* Here the student is taught that language can be used to control the environment to some extent as she or he acquires the skills to make requests. The authors make the important point that, since the purpose of this dimension is to teach that one can manage one's own environment, we should be certain to reinforce this behavior and to provide a means for the individual to broaden the scope of language by introducing labels for those parts of the environment for which language has not been acquired. To this end, an extended control repertoire is taught.

3. *Self-extended control.* Students are taught to request more specific information that allows them to interact more effectively with their environment. The requests are based upon the student's own separation of what he or she does not know from what he or she does know. In the Control dimension, the student learns to produce language concerned with things or actions; e.g., "I want (*action or thing*)," "I want (*action plus thing*)," or "I want you to (*action plus thing*)." In the Extended Control dimension, the student learns to extend his or her vocabulary by initiating the acquisition of new labels; e.g., "What (is) that?" "What (are) you doing?"

4. *Integration.* The dimensions of reference, control, and self-extended control are integrated so that the student will interact appropriately with the environment, speaking about things she or he knows, and asking for more information on that which she or he does not know. This section has two objectives: (a) to teach the student when to ask questions and when to respond to questions and (b) to teach the student dialogue.

5. *Reception.* While the other dimensions have referred to expressive language, this one teaches skills at the receptive level. The curriculum follows particular behavioral procedures, including (a) specific contingencies for correct, partially correct, incorrect, and no answers, (b) specified teaching procedures, (c) description of how the instructor should use prompts, modeling, and shaping, (d) a format for programming generalization, (e) ways to extend the technology across other behaviors, such as the nonoral language system used with communication boards and signing, and (f) a description of data-collection procedures, including scoring forms.

Bricker and Bricker (1970) have also developed a language training program based on research efforts. Their language components include:

1. *Operant audiometry.* In this phase, students are tested through behavioral procedures to determine whether they have severe hearing losses.

2. *Receptive vocabulary.* The child is taught (and tested for) receptive language in a two-item presentation series in which he or she is reinforced for picking the named object and for not picking the unnamed object.

3. *Imitation.* In an hierarchical shaping program, the student is taught a series of imitations in the typical manner from motoric responses, through speech sounds, words, phrases, and sentences.
4. *Naming.* Having acquired imitation skills and some receptive language, the student is now taught expressive language skills. An object is placed before the student, and he is asked to name it. If he does so, he is reinforced. If he does not, the instructor names it and the student is guided through imitating it. As names of new objects are taught, names of previously taught objects are reviewed.
5. *Sentence production.* Initially, the student is taught two-word combinations that are useful and natural to his or her environment. Word sequences as well as their appropriate uses are then taught.

The program has been revised and explained on occasion (e.g., Bricker & Bricker, 1974; Bricker, Ruder & Vincent, 1976), and it has 43 phases in its intervention strategy. Part 1 is designed to teach the student to construct three-word phrases consisting of an agent, an action word, and an object. Part 2 is designed to extend the student's skills allowing him or her to modify this basic three-part construction.

The initial skills to be taught involve three basic responses: (1) sitting quietly in a chair, (2) directing eye contact with the instructor's face, and (3) imitating simple behaviors on command. From this point, all 43 phases are taught according to a format that describes (1) the setting and teaching materials, (2) baseline probes, (3) training procedures, (4) data collection, (5) training probes, and (6) generalization training. The format is easy to follow and is an aid both to the teacher and the instructor.

Gray and Ryan (1973) have also developed a language program for non-language children. Theirs is comprised of a series of steps that follow a shaping program from less to more complex and difficult. Nine factors are considered in their training program:

1. *Response.* Stress on the importance for the instructor to define objectively the response, whether it be oral or nonoral.
2. *Stimulus.* Visual and/or auditory stimuli comprise the set of events that act as discriminative stimuli for language behaviors.
3. *Reinforcer.* While the immediate consequence for appropriate responding can be quite varied, this program relies heavily on tokens, primarily perhaps because token systems do not require a language base to be successful.
4. *Criterion.* Criteria are specified for correct responding so that the instructor will have an objective referent for moving from one step in a program to the next. This is analogous to the step criterion provided in task analyses.
5. *Reinforcement schedule.* Continuous reinforcement is initially scheduled, and the child is given a token after every correct response. As the student progresses, the token schedule is thinned until it is no longer present, having been replaced with praise.
6. *Response mode.* Although the response mode can be either oral or nonoral, Gray and Ryan's program is oral, so it concentrates on that mode.

7. *Stimulus mode.* The stimulus mode is either visual (e.g., pictures, objects, actions) or auditory (e.g., a verbalization by the instructor).

8. *Model.* This word refers to the type of prompt used to help the student respond correctly. The degree of aid is faded as the students begin independently to produce the response. The five models are (a) immediate/complete, in which the child is given completely what he is to say just before he is to say it; (b) delayed/complete, in which the child is given completely what he is to say but he must delay repeating it; (c) immediate/truncated, in which the child is given only a portion of what he is to say immediately before he is to say it; (d) delayed/truncated, in which the child is given only a portion of what he is to say and he must delay responding; and (e) no model, in which no prompts are given to the student.

9. *Complexity.* This describes the relationship between the model and the response.

The program is divided into three sections: core, secondary, and optional. Figure 10-4 lists the 41 sections of the language curriculum, each of which is based on the nine factors and is presented in a common format that provides needed information for the teacher. The format includes (1) the step number, (2) the stimulus to be presented to the student, (3) the model, (4) the response, (5) the schedule of reinforcement, (6) the placement of an object (when appropriate), and (7) the branching index, which indicates the steps to use if a child is failing a step. The authors present some data on the program's success with various nonlanguage populations. Although its extensive use of codes makes the

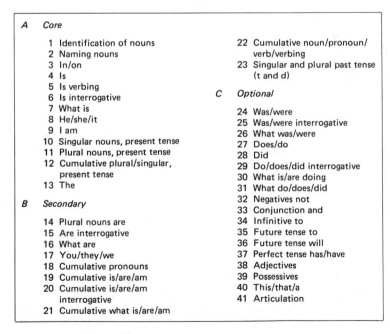

A   Core

1 Identification of nouns	22 Cumulative noun/pronoun/
2 Naming nouns	verb/verbing
3 In/on	23 Singular and plural past tense
4 Is	(t and d)
5 Is verbing	
6 Is interrogative	**C Optional**
7 What is	
8 He/she/it	24 Was/were
9 I am	25 Was/were interrogative
10 Singular nouns, present tense	26 What was/were
11 Plural nouns, present tense	27 Does/do
12 Cumulative plural/singular,	28 Did
present tense	29 Do/does/did interrogative
13 The	30 What is/are doing
	31 What do/does/did
B Secondary	32 Negatives not
	33 Conjunction and
14 Plural nouns are	34 Infinitive to
15 Are interrogative	35 Future tense to
16 What are	36 Future tense will
17 You/they/we	37 Perfect tense has/have
18 Cumulative pronouns	38 Adjectives
19 Cumulative is/are/am	39 Possessives
20 Cumulative is/are/am	40 This/that/a
interrogative	41 Articulation
21 Cumulative what is/are/am	

Figure 10-4. The 41 programs of the language curriculum developed by Gray and Ryan (1973, p. 27).

program difficult to follow during the first session, it quickly becomes easy to interpret and is a valuable instructional and sequenced referent for the language teacher.

Another language program has been developed by Kent and her associates (Kent, 1974; Kent, Klein, Falk & Guenther, 1972) following eight years of research. The program is in three sections. The *preverbal* section teaches attending behaviors and motor imitation, the *verbal-receptive* and the *verbal-expressive* sections teach instruction-following, expressive and receptive object and body-parts identification, verbal imitation, and language relationships of various types. The program relies heavily on reinforcement principles, using shaping, imitation, promoting, guidance, fading, data, and criterion-referenced progressions. The program also has an adaptation for hearing-impaired and deaf children, so it can allow one to produce a total communication program.

With total communication being the current vogue, there has been increased interest recently with the use of signing for retarded individuals. While not developing a modified system for teaching signing, Dayan, Harper, Molloy, and Witt (1977) have discussed the issue briefly and have offered some suggestions, which include (1) choosing signs for activities in which the child is engaged, (2) saying the word while signing, (3) checking that signs are reliably made, (4) exaggerating signs at the beginning of the program, (5) using only a single sign for each word and training all staff to adhere to that sign, (6) using signs as praise statements (e.g., good, thank you). (7) reinforcing the student for using signs to express himself, (8) using shaping techniques to build expressive language, (9) providing daily training sessions, and (10) using communication boards (such as pictures of objects or Blissymbols) for students who cannot use their hands in the manner required in signing.

More traditional behaviorally based language programs have been developed commercially that deal with reading printed language. The *Sullivan Programmed Reading Series* was not designed for retarded children, but rather for children who are performing at a prereading level. Nevertheless, the series has become extremely popular as a basis for teaching retarded students to read. The *programmed reading* approach grew from the work by Cynthia Dee Buchanan, who had been associated with some of the research in programming taking place at Harvard in the 1950s, and of M. W. Sullivan, who was the head of the Modern Language Department at Hollins College. In 1957, the authors experimented with teaching machines to present their materials. Field testing proved unsuccessful as the children participating in the program did not seem motivated. After a few more years of testing, teaching machines were dropped in favor of a printed series in booklet form published by McGraw-Hill Book Company. The series, however, still contained two important contributions used in teaching machines: (1) the series is programmed so that the student at any level will be able to perform well because he or she has been taught the prerequisite skills, (2) immediate feedback is provided, (3) observable responses are recorded, and (4) the student progresses at his or her own pace. The 21 workbooks in the series are expendable, and the student is expected to write in answers rather than just checking them against correct answers as in other programs. As Aukerman (1971) has suggested, writing letters and words tends to reinforce the reading behavior itself, providing one of the advantages of the series. Figure 10-5 demonstrates the response requirements as well as the feedback. The student

sl**e**d		Sam has Nip on the sl___d.
p**a**st		It slid p___st Ann.
slid		It ___lid past Tab.

Figure 10-5. An example of the Sullivan reading series (page 12, Book 3, Series 1).

looks at the second column and writes in answers. Then, the student uncovers the first column and checks whether the answer is correct.

Series I consists of seven workbooks which present the five short vowels as well as consonants in a variety of settings or positions. It provides continued practice through 5,000 frames on 13 vowel sounds and 26 consonant sounds. Series II and III also contain seven workbooks each. They provide new sounds, so that by the end of the series the student should be reading more than 3,000 words. In each of the workbooks, testing occurs after every 50 frames of material. Results from this information allow the teacher to assess the student's progress quite frequently so that any difficulty can be quickly identified. The value of individualized pacing and built-in testing has been described by Neisworth and Smith (1973):

> [The Series] automatically pinpoints the level at which a child should be placed within the reading program. No longer does the teacher need to speculate about a child's ability before deciding where to start to help him. The Series also simplifies the problems incurred by children having been absent; they begin where they left off upon returning to school. The teacher can quickly check on the extent to which prerequisite skills have been forgotten while the child was at home by requiring the child to review previous selections or to take the previous test. (p. 193)

In addition to the workbooks, the program provides a series of "Storybooks" describing the adventures of Sam and Ann. While we need to be careful about such stories when they are not age-appropriate, the stories have been enthusiastically reviewed by many:

> The Storybooks are by far the most fascinating materials produced within the format of linguistically controlled vocabulary. The interesting stories are embellished by equally interesting and extremely clever illustrations in color which tickle youngsters (and oldsters, as well). . . . It should be observed that the story lines provide fun for the reader to an extent not found in most other linguistics-phonemics approaches. (Aukerman, 1971, pp. 191-193.)

Another reading program frequently used with, but not developed specifically for, retarded persons is *Distar* (Direct Instruction Systems for Teaching Arithmetic and Reading). This project began in 1964 at the Institute for Research on Exceptional Children at the University of Illinois and was headed by Bereiter and Englemann. When Bereiter left Illinois, Becker took his place on the project. The approach is controversial, being very popular with some and unpopular with others. Its popularity results from the fact that it works. Its unpopularity with some results from the fact that it puts demands on the teacher in a no-nonsense fashion. It is a teacher-centered program rather than a child-centered program. This does not mean that it is not concerned with the individual; rather, it means that if the child is performing at a lower level, it is the *teacher's responsibility to teach* the student so that she or he can learn to perform at a higher level. Because it has explicit directions for teachers, it is viewed by some as restrictive. But the program is one that has been directed to teaching disadvantaged children for whom time is essential; as such, it does not allow teaching time to be wasted.

The program is divided into three parts, moving from basic skills in determining what particular symbols mean to reading for new information. Throughout, the system relies on a number of assumptions:

(a)   Goals must be objectively stated.
(b)   The teacher's behaviors must be directed toward these goals.
(c)   Tasks should be analyzed into their components.
(d)   One concept should be learned at a time.
(e)   Continuous evaluation should be employed.
(f)   Current psychological theories offer too many generalities and should be replaced by objective analyses of what is to be learned.
(g)   Student learning is the responsibility of the student.
(h)   Direct instruction will produce specific skills.

The results of Distar have been extraordinary from the start. In 1967, a Distar group was compared with a conventional Head Start program in Canton, Ohio. On the Pre-school Inventory Test, the Distar group gained 126 points while the Head Start group gained 70 points. On the Concept Inventory Test, the Distar group gained 158 points, while the Head Start group gained 65 points (Young, 1968). In a report by Karnes (1968), the Distar group was shown after two years to move from a mean Binet IQ of 97 to a mean Binet score of 120. The gains have continued to be demonstrated over the years and have been summarized in a number of places. One (Becker, in press) describes in detail the results of Follow Through, which is a federally funded program designed to test the effectiveness of various approaches to the economically handicapped in kindergarten through third grade. Sponsors provided full programs for early childhood education for what came to be 75,000 low-income children annually in 170 communities. The data from these sponsored programs were collected by Stanford Research Institute, and they were analyzed by Abt Associates of Cambridge, Massachusetts (1976, 1977). Although there were 20 "sponsors," there were large amounts of data for only nine. These sponsors covered a wide range of philosophies, from Freud to Skinner. The nine have been divided into three groups by Becker.

The first group is based on the subjective theories of Piaget, Freud, and Dewey. They have in common individualized approaches (i.e., teaching strategies), whole-person goals, and child-initiated activities. The models were as follows:

1. *Open Education Model*, sponsored by the Education Development Center (EDC). The model attempts to teach the child responsibility for his own learning. One teaches a desire to communicate instead of directly teaching reading and writing, and child-directed choices and flexible schedules are advocated.

2. *Tucson Early Education Model (TEEM)*, sponsored by the University of Arizona. This program teaches intellectual processes with content considered secondary.

3. *Cognitively Oriented Curriculum*, sponsored by the High/Scope Educational Research Foundation. This program is based on a Piagetian model of strengthening underlying cognitive processes that *allow* one to learn. Child-directed choices about what he is to do each day are stressed.

4. *Responsive Education Model*, sponsored by Far West Laboratory. This model used theories of Deutsch, Moore, and Montessori. It tries to build an environment that is responsive to the child and concentrates on building self-esteem.

5. *Bank Street College Model*, sponsored by Bank Street College of Education. It takes support from the theories of Freud, Piaget, and Dewey, and advocates the philosophy developed by Head Start. It seeks to help the child become inventive, confident, and productive.

The second group is based on the behavioral approach of B. F. Skinner, and it emphasizes teaching students particular skills they will need to optimize their chances of success in school and other aspects of life. Two models represented this group:

1. *Behavior Analysis Model*, sponsored by the University of Kansas. This model, under the direction of Don Bushell, uses typical behavioral methods of systematic praise and tokens for positive reinforcement, sequenced tasks presented in small steps, task monitoring, and careful teacher training.

2. *Direct Instructional Model*, sponsored by the University of Oregon. This model used the Distar programs developed by Bereiter, Englemann, Becker, and associates. It emphasizes sequenced lessons in reading, arithmetic, and language, small-group lessons, careful staff training, and monitoring of progress.

The third group has some commonalities with the other two but remains different enough to have been separated by Becker. This group includes the following:

1. *Florida Parent Education Model*, sponsored by the University of Florida and based on the work of Ira Gordon. The program concentrates on teaching parents of disadvantaged children and utilizes

them part of the time in the classroom. The focus is on cognitive, language, affective, and psychomotor instruction.

2. *Language Development (Bilingual Model)*, sponsored by the Southwest Educational Developmental Laboratory (SEDL). The focus is on language, and the model borrows from many theories, behavioral as well as nonbehavioral.

Children participating in the study were tested upon entry and every spring thereafter through third grade. Tests included the Metropolitan Achievement Test (MAT) (1970), the Raven's Color Progressive Matrices (1956), the Coopersmith Self-Esteem Inventory (1967), and the Intellectual Achievement Responsibility Scale (Crandall, Katkowsky & Crandall, 1965). In a program of this sort, there is, of course, an extraordinary number of tables and graphs. Figure 10-6 however, is an overall summary of the many subsummaries and ranks all the programs. It shows quite clearly that Distar was the highest ranked in *basic skills*, in *cognitive* measures, and in *affective* measures, all three measures of the report. As Becker notes, Distar was expected to do well in the basic-skills area, but not in the other two. It was, however, one of only two programs (Southwest Lab) to have positive scores in this area. Those programs which were intended to improve cognitive-conceptual skills simply did not! Distar results show that, if basic skills are well developed, cognitive skills can also be well developed. The difference between the Behavior Analysis Model and the Direct Instruction Model is attributed by Becker to his assumption that *curriculum as well as systematic reinforcement is necessary* to overcome the inability of schools to teach language to economically disadvantaged children. Perhaps the biggest surprise for its detractors is that Distar was ranked highest in the affective measure. Critics had contended that its stress on controlled instruction would lower children's self-esteem. But the Distar and the Behavior Analysis models ranked highest on this dimension, higher than those which purportedly had as their major objective developing self-esteem! Apparently, systematically telling children they are doing well and that you are pleased with their work makes children express good feelings about themselves.

Normative performance measures for disadvantaged children are also available for total reading, total math, spelling, and language. These data show

Model	Basic Skills	Cognitive Measures	Affective Measures	Average Rank
Direct Instruction	1	1	1	1
Southwest Lab	2	2	4	2
Parent Education	3	3	3	3
Behavior Analysis	4	6	2	4
Bank Street	5	4	7	5
Responsive Education	7	5	6	6
TEEM	6	7	9	7.5
Cognitive Curriculum	9	8	5	7.5
Open Education	8	9	8	9

Figure 10-6. Ranks of nine programs designed to teach disadvantaged children. Contrary to expectation, the Distar program was first on the cognitive and the affective measures (from Becker, in press). (The Ravens was dropped from the scoring by Abt as a test that does not adequately measure cognitive skills.)

the Direct Instruction Model is clearly the highest, and that it elevates the performance of disadvantaged students in their program to national norm levels. Area results show that (1) in math, Distar is far above all others, (2) in spelling, only Distar and the Behavior Analysis model approach national norms, (3) in reading, only Distar, Behavior Analysis, Bank Street, and Responsive Education approach national norms, and (4) in language, Distar is again far ahead of all others.

The controversy about this model will continue. But these data show clearly that Distar is a highly successful program whose benefits to students probably far outweigh the structure some teachers dislike. The results from the five models in the first group of the Follow Through study show, however, that lack of teacher-directed structure can be disastrous. These results are of further importance to us as they demonstrate success with children with IQ scores of less than 80 and with children from economically disadvantaged environments, a setting that is greatly overpopulated by persons labeled mentally retarded.

Self-Help

The second area in which we will present an example of a program using fading, chaining, and shaping is that of self-help. As reviewed briefly in Chapter 2, there has been a large number of published works concerned with teaching self-help skills to retarded persons. In addition, there have been thousands of unpublished efforts directed toward teaching the same skills. The problem with the unpublished efforts is that they lack generalizability; i.e., because they are unavailable to more than a few workers, they cannot be used with clients other than those for whom they have been specifically developed. Many of the published works, on the other hand, have been directed toward only one or two skills. As they were solely intended to teach those few skills, these works certainly have met their objective. But because they have been developed by single groups of workers, they do not account for differences across educational programs.

To meet these problems, the U.S. Office of Education sponsored Project MORE, which was an effort to develop a group of standardized task analyses for various self-help skills (e.g., hair rolling, ironing, showering). The task analyses were tested according to two designs. Multiple baselines provided some assurance that other factors were not contributing to the clients' progress. Pretest-posttest comparisons provided some measure of each client's overall progress. Each step of the task was analyzed for its effectiveness along four dimensions: (1) mean rating on all days of training, (2) mean rating on the last six days of training, (3) number of students who required no help for training, and (4) number of training errors for each student. Data allowed steps to be revised in the program if (1) 50% or more of the students scored less than criterion on all days or on the last six days of training, (2) there was more than 10% trainer error, or (3) the reliability on a step was less than 85%.

Each of the self-help skills is described in a similar manner, progressing through the various steps. Labels for two of the programs are toothbrushing (Horner, Billionis & Lent, 1975) and handwashing (Stevens, Ferneti & Lent, 1975).

TOOTHBRUSHING

1. *Pick up your toothbrush.* The subject is required to start each session by first turning on the water and then picking up the toothbrush by its handle.
2. *Wet your toothbrush.* The subject holds the toothbrush, placing the bristles under the running water for at least five seconds. The subject then turns off the running water and lays the toothbrush down.
3. *Take the cap off the toothpaste.* The subject places the tube of toothpaste in his least preferred hand, unscrews the cap with the thumb and index finger of his preferred hand, and sets the cap on the sink.
4. *Put the toothpaste on your brush.* The subject picks up the toothbrush by its handle, holds the back part of the bristles against the opening of the toothpaste tube, squeezes the tube, moves the tube toward the front bristles as toothpaste flows out on top of the bristles, and lays the toothbrush on the sink with the bristles up.
5. *Put the cap back on the toothpaste.* The subject picks up the toothpaste cap with the thumb and index finger of his preferred hand, screws the cap on the toothpaste tube, which he is holding in his least preferred hand, lays the tube of toothpaste down with his preferred hand.
6. *Brush the outside surfaces of your teeth.* The subject brushes the outside surfaces of his upper and lower teeth on both sides and in the center of the mouth, using either an up and down or back and forth motion for at least thirty seconds.
7. *Brush the biting surfaces of your teeth.* The subject brushes the biting surfaces of his upper and lower teeth on both sides and in the center of the mouth, using a back and forth motion for at least thirty seconds.
8. *Brush the inside surfaces of your teeth.* The subject brushes the inside surfaces of his upper and lower teeth on both sides and in the center of the mouth, using a back and forth motion for at least thirty seconds.
9. *Fill the cup with water.* The subject lays the toothbrush down, picks up a cup, places it under the faucet, turns on the cold water, fills the cup, and turns off the cold water.
10. *Rinse the toothpaste from your mouth.* The subject spits out any excess toothpaste foam, takes a sip of water, holds it in his mouth, swishes it around in the mouth, and spits it out. If any toothpaste foam is still present in the mouth, this procedure is repeated.
11. *Wipe your mouth.* The subject picks up a hand towel and dries his mouth.
12. *Rinse your toothbrush.* The subject picks up his toothbrush by its handle, turns on the water, and places the bristles under the running water until the bristles are free of toothpaste, turns off the water, and lays the toothbrush down.
13. *Rinse the sink.* The subject turns on the water and rubs his hand around the inside of the sink to wash any residue of toothpaste or toothpaste foam down the drain. He then turns off the water and dries his hands on a hand towel.
14. *Put your equipment away.* The subject puts the toothpaste in the proper storage place along with the towel and toothbrush (Horner, Billionis & Lent, 1975).

HANDWASHING

1. *Turn the cold water on.* The subject rotates the cold water faucet one-quarter of a turn or until a steady stream of water flows into the sink.
2. *Turn the hot water on.* The subject rotates the hot water faucet one-quarter of a turn, or until the combined flow of hot and cold water produces a heavy stream without splashing over the sides of the sink.
3. *Adjust the water to warm.* The subject adjusts the flow of cold and hot water until the flow of water is warm to the touch and does not splash over the sides of the sink. The subject tests the temperature by quickly running his fingers through the water.

Figure 10-7. Definitions of the responses involved in the steps of two self-help skills from Project MORE.

4. *Wet your hands.* The subject places his hands directly under the stream of water, and turns the hands palms up then palms down until the hands are thoroughly covered with water.

5. *Pick up the soap.* The subject picks up the soap with his preferred hand and holds the soap under the stream of water for a few seconds.

6. *Work the soap into a lather.* While holding the bar of soap under the stream of water, the subject grasps the soap with both hands and turns it in the palms of the hands until a lather begins to form. The subject removes his hands from the stream of water and continues to turn the soap until the inside surfaces of both hands are completely covered with lather.

7. *Put the soap down.* Using either hand, the subject returns the soap to the back of the sink or to the soap dish if one is available.

8. *Scrub the palms and backs of your hands.* The subject cleans his palms and the inside surfaces of his fingers and thumbs by vigorously rubbing the palms and fingers together for approximately five seconds. The subject then vigorously rubs the back of his left hand with his right palm for the same amount of time. This procedure is repeated with the left palm rubbing the back of the right hand.

9. *Scrub between your fingers.* The subject places his hands palm-to-palm with fingers spread slightly apart, then lightly interlocks the fingers and rubs them vigorously back and forth for approximately five seconds.

10. *Scrub your fingernails.* With his right hand open palm up, the subject scrubs the fingernails and thumbnail of his left hand by rubbing them across the palm of the right hand for approximately five seconds. He repeats the procedure for the fingernails and thumbnail of the right hand.

11. *Rinse the soap from your hands.* The subject holds his hands under the stream of water and then turns the hands palms up then palms down several times until all the soap is removed.

12. *Rinse out the sink.* The subject places one hand under the stream of water and swishes the water around the sink until the soap residue is washed down the drain.

13. *Turn the water off.* The subject turns the hot and cold water faucets to the off position.

14. *Dry your hands.* Using a hand towel, the subject wipes his hands until all of the water is removed.

15. *Dry the counter.* The subject uses the towel to wipe the counter and the edges of the sink until all the water is removed. It is not necessary to dry the inside of the sink.

16. *Hang up the towel.* The subject folds the towel neatly and hangs it on a towel rack near the sink. (Stevens, Ferneti & Lent, 1975).

Figure 10-7. Continued.

The steps are taught with four degrees of aid: (1) no help, (2) verbal help, (3) demonstration, and (4) physical help. These labels describe the degree to which the client can independently master any of the steps in the program. When each of the degrees is given a different numerical value (i.e., 1, 2, 3, or 4), the steps can be rated for their effectiveness. The general definitions for these levels of assistance are as follows:

No help: The individual is allowed to perform the step without assistance. If he cannot perform the step correctly within 5 seconds, then *verbal help* is given.

Verbal help: The individual is reminded of the response required to finish the step. If he performs correctly, he goes to the next step and is given *no help.* If he does not respond or if he responds incorrectly, then he is given the next level of assistance, *demonstration.*

Purpose: To evaluate proficiency in using Project MORE programs.

Instructions: For each item rate the trainer on the five point scale below.

Trainer _____ (1) never

Student _____ (2) seldom

Rater _____ (3) about half the time

Program _____ (4) most of the time

Date _____ (5) every time

BEHAVIOR	RATING
Preparation	
1. Arrived promptly for training session.	
2. Brought program to training session.	
3. Greeted student before training.	
Teaching Procedures	
4. Got student's attention before initiating training.	
5. Trained one step at a time.	
6. Trained steps in the designated sequence.	
7. Gave opportunity for occurence of behavior before intervention.	
8. Provided verbal cues only when opportunity (7) failed.	
9. Provided verbal cues prior to visual cues.	
10. Provided concrete verbal cues rather than general ones.	
11. Provided no more than three verbal cues before proceeding to next strategy.	
12. Provided visual cues only when verbal cues failed.	
13. Provided visual cues prior to providing physical assistance.	
14. Provided clear appropriate visual cues.	
15. Provided no more than three visual cues before proceeding to next strategy.	
16. Provided physical assistance only when visual and verbal cues failed.	
17. Allowed 5 to 10 seconds for behavior to occur after each procedure.	
18. Physical assistance was given in a positive, helpful manner, not in a punitive or coersive one.	
19. Trained only behaviors listed in program.	
20. Determined appropriateness of behavior, using behavioral definitions.	

BEHAVIOR	RATING
Reinforcement	
21. Provided verbal or physical reinforcement immediately after an appropriate performance.	
22. If used verbal reinforcement, stated what the student did correctly.	
23. Gave verbal reinforcement enthusiastically.	
24. Varied the nature of the verbal reinforcer.	
25. Gave physical reinforcement enthusiastically.	
26. Used both physical and verbal reinforcement.	
27. Gave reinforcement contingently.	
General	
28. Ignored inappropriate behavior not interfering with training.	
29. Handled inappropriate interfering behaviors, enabling resumption of training.	
30. Spoke in clear, understandable tone of voice.	
31. Used visual and verbal prompts enthusiastically.	
32. Used student's name.	
33. Interacted courteously with student.	
34. Asked about student's progress and/or kept track of student's progress.	
35. Maintained self-control even when student misbehaved.	
36. Insured student attention during training by placing self near student and/or between student and distractors.	
37. Kept student on task by not introducing irrelevant cues (e.g., conversation) during training.	
38. Demonstrated in voice and manner the importance of this task to the student.	
39. Informed student of his progress.	

Figure 10-8. A training proficiency scale to test the teaching skills of those training clients with the Project MORE program (Horner, 1973).

Demonstration: The instructor shows the student how to respond (modeling) and verbally assists the client through the step. Verbal assistance is paired with the physical so that in the future *verbal help* will become more effective and perhaps preclude the use of *demonstration*. If the student responds correctly, the instructor goes to the next step at the *no help* level. If the student fails to respond within 10 seconds or responds incorrectly, the instructor provides the next level of assistance, *physical help*.

Physical help: The instructor provides *verbal help* and physically assists the client through the step. If the client responds correctly, the instructor goes to the next step and provides *no help*. If the client is still unable to perform the step correctly after being physically guided, the instructor does not give the student the opportunity to perform the step again until the next training session. Instead, the instructor moves to the next step at the *no help* level.

The labels of the steps provide the instructor with an easy means of following the steps of the programs. However, to provide the teacher with a complete description and to allow some consistency from day to day with the same client, as well as across different clients, each of the labels is defined as a response. Figure 10-7 provides definitions of the responses involved in each of the steps in these programs. (These definitions are taken from S.M. Freagon, unpublished manuscript.) To check how well each of the tasks is taught, the instructor's performance is rated from the beginning to the end of the training session. Figure 10-8 presents a training proficiency scale (Horner, 1973) that was used to test the performance of instructors while teaching clients these self-help skills.

SUMMARY

This chapter discusses some of the major behavioral methods for teaching retarded persons. These include shaping, chaining, fading, and modeling that lead to the development of single behaviors or chains of behaviors. In some cases, these behaviors are taught to occur within restricted stimulus conditions, such that considerable stimulus control is demonstrated (e.g., saying "food" when asked "What does f-o-o-d spell?"). In other cases, these behaviors are taught so that they will occur across a very wide variety of situations so that stimulus generalization occurs (e.g., saying "thank you" to anyone giving you something). These methods were discussed in terms of their application for teaching retarded persons particular skills. In addition, programs which reflect a combination of these methods were presented across two areas, language programs and self-help programs.

Chapter 11 will discuss methods of decreasing behavior. These include the punishment-based procedures of positive punishment, overcorrection, timeout, and response cost, and the nonpunishment procedures of extinction and the differential reinforcement of (1) low rates of responding, (2) incompatible behavior, (3) other behavior, or the complete absence of the target behavior, and (4) alternative behavior.

REFERENCES

Abt Associates. *Education as experimentation: A planned variation model (Vol. III).* Cambridge, MA: Abt Associates, 1976.

Abt Associates. *Education as experimentation: A planned variation model (Vol. IV).* Cambridge, MA: Abt Associates, 1977.

Aukerman, R. C. *Approaches to beginning reading.* New York: John Wiley & Sons, Inc., 1971.

Azrin, N. H., Schaeffer, R. M., & Wesolowski, M. D. A rapid method of teaching profoundly retarded persons to dress by a reinforcement-guidance method. *Mental Retardation,* 1976, **14**, 29-33.

Baer, D. M., Peterson, R. F., & Sherman, J. A. The development of imitation by reinforcing behavioral similarity to a model. *Journal of the Experimental Analysis of Behavior,* 1967, **10**, 405-416.

Ball, T. S., Seric, K., & Payne, L. E. Long-term retention of self-help skill training in the profoundly retarded. *American Journal of Mental Deficiency,* 1971, **76**(3), 378-382.

Becker, W. C. The national evaluation of Follow Through: Behavior-therapy-based programs come out on top. *Education and Urban Society,* in press.

Bensberg, G. J., Colwell, C. N., & Cassel, R. H. Teaching the profoundly retarded self-help activities by behavior shaping techniques. *American Journal of Mental Deficiency,* 1965, **69**(5), 674-679.

Bensberg, G. J., & Slominski, A. Helping the retarded learn self-care. In G. J. Bensberg (Ed.), *Teaching the mentally retarded: A handbook for ward personnel.* Atlanta, GA: Southern Regional Education Board, 1965.

Bricker, D. D., Ruder, K. F., & Vincent, L. An intervention strategy for language-deficient children. In N. G. Haring & L. J. Brown (Eds.), *Teaching the severely handicapped, Volume 1.* New York: Grune & Stratton, Inc., 1976.

Bricker, W. A., & Bricker, D. D. Program of language training for the severely language handicapped child. *Exceptional Children,* 1970, **37**, 101-111.

Bricker, W. A., & Bricker, D. D. An early language training strategy. In R. L. Schiefelbusch & L. L. Lloyd (Eds.), *Language perspectives: Acquisition, retardation, and intervention.* Baltimore: University Park Press, 1974.

Broden, M., Bruce, C., Mitchell, M. A., Carter, V., & Hall, R. V. Effects of teacher attention on attending behavior of two boys at adjacent desks. *Journal of Applied Behavior Analysis,* 1970, **3**, 199-203.

Christy, P. R. Does use of tangible rewards with individual children affect peer observers? *Journal of Applied Behavior Analysis,* 1975, **8**, 187-196.

Coopersmith, S. *The antecedents of self-esteem.* San Francisco: W. H. Freeman & Co., 1967.

Corey, J. R., & Shamow, J. The effects of fading on the acquisition and retention of oral reading. *Journal of Applied Behavior Analysis,* 1972, **5**, 311-315.

Crandall, V. C., Katkowsky, J. K., & Crandall, V. J. Children's beliefs in their own control of reinforcements in intellectual-academic achievement situations. *Child Development,* 1965, **36**, 91-109.

Dayan, M., Harper, B., Molloy, J. S., & Witt, B. T. *Communication for the severely and profoundly handicapped.* Denver: CO: Love Publishing Company, 1977.

Dorry, G. W. The effects of faded pretraining on later reading acquisition. Unpublished Master's thesis, C. W. Post College, Long Island University, 1972.

Dorry, G. W. Attentional model for the effectiveness of fading in training reading-vocabulary with retarded persons. *American Journal of Mental Deficiency*, 1976, 81, 271-279.

Dorry, G. W., & Zeaman, D. The use of a fading technique in paired-associate teaching of a reading vocabulary with retardates. *Mental Retardation*, 1973, 11, 3-6.

Dorry, G. W., & Zeaman, D. Teaching a simple reading vocabulary to retarded children: Effectiveness of fading and nonfading procedures. *American Journal of Mental Deficiency*, 1975, 79, 711-716.

Dudzinski, M. *Language acquisition in severely retarded: A behavioral approach*. Unpublished manuscript. Department of Special Education, Northern Illinois University, 1977.

Egeland, B. Effects of errorless training on teaching children to discriminate letters of the alphabet. *Journal of Applied Psychology*, 1975, 60, 533-566.

Freagon, S. M. The effects of houseparents training severely and profoundly handicapped group home residents. Unpublished doctoral dissertation. University of Wisconsin, 1977.

Garcia, E., Guess, D., & Byrnes, J. Development of syntax in a retarded girl using procedures of imitation, reinforcement, and modeling. *Journal of Applied Behavior Analysis*, 1973, 6, 299-310.

Gray, B. B., & Ryan, B. P. *A language program for the nonlanguage child*. Champaign, IL: Research Press, 1973.

Guess, D., & Baer, D. M. Some experimental analyses of linguistic development in institutionalized retarded children. In B. Lahey (Ed.), *The modification of language behavior*. Springfield, IL: Charles C. Thomas, 1973.

Guess, D., Sailor, W., & Baer, D. M. To teach language to retarded children. In R. Schiefelbusch & L. Lloyd (Eds.), *Language perspectives: Acquisition, retardation, and intervention*. Baltimore: University Park Press, 1974.

Guess, D., Sailor, W., & Baer, D. M. *Functional speech and language training for the severely handicapped*. Lawrence, KS: H & H Enterprises, Inc., 1976.

Guess, D., Sailor, W., & Baer, D. M. A behavioral-remedial approach to language training for the severely handicapped. In E. Sontag, J. Smith, & N. Certo (Eds.), *Educational programming for the severely and profoundly handicapped*. Reston, VA: Council for Exceptional Children, 1977.

Guess, D., Sailor, W., Keogh, W. J., & Baer, D. M. Language development programs for severely handicapped children. In N. G. Haring & L. J. Brown (Eds.), *Teaching the severely handicapped (Vol. 1)*. New York: Grune & Stratton, Inc., 1976.

Haupt, E. J., Van Kirk, M. J., & Terraciano, T. An inexpensive fading procedure to decrease errors and increase retention of number facts. In E. Ramp & G. Semb (Eds.), *Behavior analysis: Areas of research and application*. Englewood Cliffs, NJ: Prentice-Hall, Inc., 1975.

Heilman, A. W. *Principles and practices of teaching reading*. Columbus, OH: Charles E. Merrill Publishing Co., 1961.

Hendry, D. P. *Conditioned reinforcement*. Homewood, IL: Dorsey Press, 1969.

Horner, R. D. Establishing use of crutches by a mentally retarded spina bifida child. *Journal of Applied Behavior Analysis*, 1971, 4, 183-189.

Horner, R. D. *Training proficiency scale: Project MORE*, University of Kansas, Bureau of Child Research, 1973.

Horner, R. D., Billionis, C. S., & Lent, J. R. *Project MORE: Toothbrushing*. Bellevue, WA: Edmark Associates, 1975.

Karnes, M. B. A research program to determine the effects of various preschool intervention programs on the development of disadvantaged children and the strategic age for such intervention. Paper presented at the meeting of the American Educational Research Associates, 1968.

Kazdin, A. E. The effects of vicarious reinforcement on performance in a rehabilitation setting. *Education and Training of the Mentally Retarded,* 1973a, **8,** 4-11.

Kazdin, A. E. Role of instructions and reinforcement in behavior changes in token reinforcement programs. *Journal of Educational Psychology,* 1973b, **64,** 63-71.

Kazdin, A. E. *Behavior modification in applied settings.* Homewood, IL: Dorsey Press, 1975.

Kazdin, A. E. Vicarious reinforcement and direction of behavior change in the classroom. *Behavior Therapy,* 1977, 8, 57-63.

Kazdin, A. E., Silverman, N. A., & Sittler, J. L. The use of prompts to enhance vicarious effects of nonverbal approval. *Journal of Applied Behavior Analysis,* 1975, **8,** 279-286.

Kent, L. *Language acquisition program for the severely retarded.* Champaign, IL: Research Press, 1974.

Kent, L. R., Klein, D., Falk, A., & Guenther, H. A language acquisition program for the retarded. In J. E. McLean, D. E. Yoder, & R. L. Schiefelbusch (Eds.), *Language intervention with the retarded: Developing strategies.* Baltimore: University Park Press, 1972.

Lutzker, J. R., & Sherman, J. A. Producing generative sentence usage by imitation and reinforcement procedures. *Journal of Applied Behavior Analysis,* 1974, 7, 447-460.

Metropolitan Achievement Test. New York: Harcourt Brace Jovanovitch, Inc., 1970.

Minge, M. R., & Ball, T. S. Teaching of self-help skills to profoundly retarded patients. *American Journal of Mental Deficiency,* 1967, **71**(5), 864-868.

Moore, R., & Goldiamond, I. Errorless establishment of visual discrimination using fading procedures. *Journal of the Experimental Analysis of Behavior,* 1964, 7, 269-272.

Neisworth, J. T., & Smith, R. M. *Modifying retarded behavior.* Boston: Houghton Mifflin Company, 1973.

O'Brien, F., Bugle, C., & Azrin, N. H. Training and maintaining a retarded child's proper eating. *Journal of Applied Behavior Analysis,* 1972, **5,** 67-72.

Raven, J. C. *Colored progressive matrices.* Dumfries, England: Crichton Royal, 1956.

Repp, A. C., Samuels, R. T., & Boles, S. M. An analysis of the effects of various response cost procedures in a TMR classroom. *Mental Retardation,* 1975, 13, 44-45.

Sidman, M., & Stoddard, L. T. Programming perception and learning for retarded children. In N. R. Ellis (Ed.), *International review of research in mental retardation (Vol. II).* New York: Academic Press, Inc., 1966.

Sidman, M., & Stoddard, L. T. The effectiveness of fading in programming a simultaneous form discrimination for retarded children. *Journal of the Experimental Analysis of Behavior,* 1967, **10,** 3-15.

Skinner, B. F., & Krakower, S. A. *Handwriting with write and see.* Chicago: Lyons and Carnahan, 1968.

Stevens, C. J., Ferneti, C. L., & Lent, J. R. *Project MORE: Handwashing.* Bellevue, WA: Edmark Associates, 1975.

Stoddard, L. T., & Sidman, M. The effects of errors on children's performance on a circle-ellipse discrimination. *Journal of the Experimental Analysis of Behavior,* 1967, **10,** 261-270.

Sulzer-Azaroff, B., & Mayer, G. R. *Applying behavior-analysis procedures with children and youth.* New York: Holt, Rinehart and Winston, Inc., 1977.

Terrace, H. S. Discrimination learning with and without "errors." *Journal of the Experimental Analysis of Behavior,* 1963a, **6**, 1-27.

Terrace, H. S. Errorless transfer of a discrimination across two continua. *Journal of the Experimental Analysis of Behavior,* 1963b, **6**, 223-232.

Terrace, H. S. Errorless discrimination learning in the pigeon: Effects of chlorpromazine and imipramine. *Science,* 1963c, **140**, 318-319.

Terrace, H. S. Wavelength generalization after discrimination learning with and without errors. *Science,* 1964a, **144**, 78-80.

Terrace, H. S. Wavelength generalization of stimuli correlated with different schedules of reinforcement. Paper presented at meetings of the Psychonomic Society, 1964b.

Terrace, H. S. Stimulus control. In W. K. Honig (Ed.), *Operant behavior: Areas of research and application.* Appleton-Century-Crofts, Inc., 1966.

Westing, D. The elimination of vomiting through the systematic alteration of food consistency and other variables. *Unpublished manuscript.*

Young, B. W. A new approach to Head Start. *Phi Delta Kappan,* 1968, LX 386-388.

11

Decreasing Behavior

For much of the last 150 years, the inappropriate and maladaptive behaviors of retarded persons have been accepted as concomitants of retardation, as if being retarded were the cause of these problems. In the last two decades, however, we have learned that retardation seldom causes behavior problems, and that even when it does, we can often do a great deal to help the individual. As we have become more concerned with teaching retarded persons to behave adaptively, we have identified two objectives that are easy to state but sometimes difficult to meet; they are (1) to identify through research and application effective procedures for reducing various behaviors, and (2) to protect the clients' rights when these procedures are applied. In the first area, we have made some progress, but there must be a great deal more to learn. In the second area, we have made much less progress, but we have made some efforts. In part, the lack of progress may be due to this being a more subjective area and therefore a more difficult one in which to reach agreement. In part, however, it is because we often cannot provide guidelines until we know what we are guiding; in these cases, the guidelines or suggestions follow the development of the procedures.

In this chapter, three different types of reductive procedures will be discussed. The first includes the reinforcement-related reductive procedures, such as (1) the differential reinforcement of other behavior, (2) the differential reinforcement of low rates of responding, (3) the differential reinforcement of incompatible responding, (4) the differential reinforcement of alternative behavior, and (5) extinction. The second type of reductive program includes the aversive procedures such as (1) positive punishment, (2) timeout, and (3) response cost. The third type of reductive program is drug-based, and this type will be discussed briefly, although it is a medical and very definitely not a behavioral procedure (as with so many nonbehavioral procedures, however, its effectiveness can be assessed through behavioral measurements and designs). But before the procedures themselves are discussed, problems associated with training persons to use reductive procedures will first be discussed.

TRAINING FOR ALL REDUCTIVE PROCEDURES

When reading in journals and books of the success of various persons with reductive programs, we may come to believe that these programs are quite easy to institute and that they will always work. But neither of these assumptions is particularly true. Books and journals are extremely biased reports of programs for several reasons: (1) they generally do not publish reports of programs that fail, (2) they often report results from programs that are supported with unusually low student-to-staff ratios, and (3) because they are research efforts, they are usually better able to reduce extraneous problems (such as other staff who will not cooperate in the program). These criticisms do not in any way discredit the "goodness" of the procedures or programs themselves; they should, however, help us to consider that implementation may not be so simple and straightforward as it first appears. From our years of experience with serious behavior problems, we have come to discriminate between the procedure itself and the conditions under which the procedure will be implemented. The procedure may have been shown to have worked on hundreds of occasions with the same behavior, but the conditions for implementation may not be favorable; as a result, the program may fail for reasons not attributable to the procedure itself. One of the most common problems we have found has been that of training: for one reason or another, the conditions for training staff in the careful use of procedures have not been present. In this section, there will be a discussion of some of the conditions which support successful training and which, therefore, increase the likelihood of successful programming.

Commitment by Administrators to Training

Basic to any training program is the need for a commitment by administrators to the success of the program. In our own experiences, we have not found the active support of the top-level administrator to be critical, although it certainly is nice to have. Of critical importance, however, is the active and enthusiastic support of the day-to-day, front-line administrator: the person who is present every day and who can arrange time for training and all the other conditions that allow training and implementation to progress smoothly and with quality. One duty of this administrator should be appointing a qualified person who is held accountable for (1) writing special-procedure programs, (2) training staff to implement them, (3) monitoring implementation, and (4) ensuring both that data are properly recorded and analyzed and that program changes are made accordingly.

An administrator's commitment to training must extend beyond acquiring competent personnel and should include providing time for the staff to be trained. Public schools schedule an initial work period for teachers before students report in the fall as well as workdays throughout the school year, and some training could occur at this time. But in institutional settings, removing staff for training while maintaining adequate student coverage is more difficult. An important objective for administrators is to make the necessary program changes to provide staff training before the work assignment begins and then to maintain that training over time. The long-term advantages of a well-trained staff far outweigh the disadvantages of a few weeks of limited programming.

Deciding Who Should Be Trained

Before developing a system for training, one must decide who should receive training. In public school settings, identifying staff to train is easier as students usually come in contact primarily with their teachers and teachers' aides. But within an institution, many more staff generally interact with the residents. In this case, all staff who come into contact with the residents—all professional staff, all residential-care staff, and all support staff within the unit—should be trained. The need to educate the child to control behavior across settings and staff demands such extensive training programs. In residential and public facilities, parents should also be trained, but this procedure is usually far more difficult. Because we know, however, that even rare inappropriate consequences can ruin a program, training should be as extensive as possible.

Training Staff to Implement Reductive Procedures

Assuming that a viable training system is established (and recognizing that assumption to be optimistic), there are many considerations in training staff to implement reductive procedures; some of these are as follows:

1. There are a large number of ethical issues in the implementation of programs, including what behaviors should be changed, how those changes should be generated, who should participate in those decisions, etc., that must be considered before programs can be initiated. These should be addressed to the mutual protection of the rights of both students and staff (see Repp & Deitz, 1978b, for a review of ethical issues involved with reducing responding of institutionalized persons). In some facilities, these rights are protected by committees comprised of people who do not work directly with the student. This approach is sometimes beneficial, but at other times committee reviews present inordinate delays.

2. The trainer should write the reduction program in detail, with great care being given to response definitions, specification of a concrete program goal, response contingencies, the schedule of reinforcement, the system for response measurement, phase-change criteria, provision of an appropriate response to replace the undesirable behavior, and plans for generalization. The trainer should then discuss the program with all staff who come in contact with the client and should make sure

that copies of the program are available at all times. To hold staff accountable for program implementation, trainers should ask each individual to sign a statement saying that he or she has read and understood the proposed program, has a clear definition of his or her responsibilities, and will implement the procedures according to the written program.

3. The trainer must be certain that all staff participating in the program agree on the presence and absence of responding. Observer agreement checks can then be made between staff members to determine the extent to which they agree on the response definitions. If we are not consistent in our judgments about whether a response has or has not occurred, then we cannot be consistent in delivering consequences. As a result, the student will receive "mixed messages," with behavior being consequated in one fashion one time and in another fashion another time.

4. The trainer should model implementation using other staff as subjects. Each staff member should then be required to model the procedure until she or he is comfortable with the procedure and consistently performs it correctly. An implementation checklist, as well as staff performance criteria, should be established for each reduction procedure. After staff have instituted the procedure correctly using their fellow staff in place of the student, they should implement the procedure with the student.

5. Training for a reduction program should give staff specific alternatives for *every conceivable* situation. Reduction programs, especially those using positive procedures, rarely prepare us for aggressive or uncooperative behavior, seeming instead to presume that students on the program will never become angry and act out. Even punitive procedures are often written as though the subject will be happy to comply with the consequences, ignoring the fact that most students will not be happy about losing 10 tokens in a response-cost program or brushing their teeth with Listerine for 15 minutes in an overcorrection program. Providing staff with procedures for handling possible side-effect behaviors increases the probability that a reductive program will succeed.

6. Trainers should be sure of adequate numbers of staff to implement a procedure. If staff coverage is questionable, one might postpone a program rather than have it carried out sporadically and eventually terminated as unsuccessful. For those programs which demand tiring work, such as some forms of overcorrection, there should be a special-procedures team which provides backup staff. Each program should include a plan for staff shortages, and when there is a shortage, arrangements should immediately be made to cover the program.

7. The trainer should always assign specific staff to each aspect of procedure implementation at specific times. There should be *no* opportunity for staff to escape accountability if some facet of the procedure is not carried out appropriately, and assignments should be designated on paper (e.g., "Ruth is responsible for implementing the DRL procedure

for Sheila from 1:30-2:15 on Thursday," or "David is resonsible for recording DRO data on Robert from 9:00-10:00 on Monday"). *Someone must be held accountable for each component of a procedure at all times.*

8. Another objective before implementing reductive programs is to design the most functional data system that still yields all necessary information. Specially designed recording sheets may be necessary and should be developed. The importance of objective, data-based decisions should be explained to staff in two areas: (1) to provide a basis for choosing the best program and for determining when the present program is and is not working, and (2) to meet the requirement of most human rights committees that there be documentation on the failure of positive methods to reduce inappropriate behavior before punitive approaches can be approved.

9. Program coordinators must provide feedback to staff concerning the effectiveness of treatment. This should be done as often as possible and with the feeling that a particular program is a group effort with everyone sharing equally in its success or failure.

10. Another objective is to determine the times for treatment to be implemented. With low-rate behaviors, procedures may be implemented 24 hours a day, at school and at home. But with very high rate behaviors which demand one-to-one staffing, the facility may not be able to implement the program continuously. In these cases, the trainer must decide the activities in which staff should institute treatment. The program should specify the treatment schedule as well as how staff should respond to target behaviors when treatment sessions are *not* in progress.

11. Monitoring staff performance during program implementation is another consideration. Following those guidelines already specified in this section should help to increase accountability, which is part of any monitoring system. In addition, implementation checklists developed to rate staff in training can be used to rate the staff's performance during implementation. These checklists are easily made by listing all the observable and measurable behaviors involved in implementing a program. If staff responsibilities are specified on paper, a trainer can enter a setting with a copy of the implementation checklist and the assigned responsibility, list and simply check off whether or not staff are performing each item correctly. Monitoring checks should be made within each program several times a day for the first week and then several times a week for the duration of the program.

These recommendations cover training in general, regardless of the procedure. Some recommendations are specific to the procedure, and these will be discussed in the following sections, which will define the procedures, provide a few examples, and provide some programming recommendations for successful implementation. The first section will be concerned with reinforcement-related reductive procedures; the second, with punishment-related procedures; and the third, with drugs.

REINFORCEMENT-RELATED REDUCTIVE PROCEDURES

In prior chapters, the term reinforcement has been used to describe a procedure in which a response produces a change in the environment and becomes more probable because of that change. Because reinforcement describes a response *increase*, its use in programs to *decrease* responding may at first seem puzzling. But the procedures themselves are directly related to the reinforcement of some behavior. In one (DRO), the student is reinforced if he or she does anything else except the target behavior for a specified period of time. In another (DRL), the student is reinforced if he or she decreases how often something is done. In a third (DRI), the student is reinforced for doing something topographically incompatible with the target behavior. In a similar procedure (DRA), the student is reinforced if he or she engages in a behavior that is an alternative to the target behavior but is not necessarily incompatible. In a final procedure (extinction), the student is no longer reinforced for a response for which she or he was previously reinforced. Reinforcement-related reductive procedures have several advantages over punishment-related procedures and should almost always be tried first. They tend to be more compatible with the natural ongoing environment; most of them do not precipitate arguments, tantrums, etc. (the exception is extinction, which sometimes does); they are not associated with aversive consequences, so the client does not learn to regard the learning environment as aversive;[1] and they are less restrictive in a learning sense and sometimes in a physical sense than punitive procedures. They should not, however, be regarded as a guaranteed means of eliminating behavior problems. With severe behavior problems such as self-abuse and with situations in which the person's rights have been protected, punishment may be quite appropriate (Repp & Deitz, 1978b.)

Differential Reinforcement of Other Behavior

Definition. The differential reinforcement of other behavior (DRO) is a procedure in which reinforcement is delivered if the target behavior does not occur for a specified period of time (Reynolds, 1961). When this procedure is used alone, the client is permitted to emit any behavior other than the target behavior; hence the phrase "reinforcement of other behavior." The programming for this procedure is quite simple. If a response occurs, the person will not be reinforced and the interval is begun again; if a response does not occur during the interval, reinforcement is delivered and the interval is begun again. The programming objective for this procedure is also straightforward. We should

---

[1] Earlier, developing conditioned reinforcers by pairing neutral stimuli with stimuli that are already reinforcing was discussed. In quite the same way, some neutral or even positive stimuli that are paired with aversive stimuli may acquire the properties of a conditioned aversive stimulus. For this reason, teachers who apply aversive procedures, or the classrooms in which the aversive procedures are applied, may themselves become aversive to the client. Conditioning of this type is certainly something we should try to avoid, although total reliance on positive procedures is not always possible. We should also stress that developing conditioned aversive stimuli in complicated environments like a classroom is not a simple and unrelenting result. But conditioning of this type is a natural phenomenon, and it is one of which we should be aware.

begin with a small interval and then progress gradually to an interval size that is more manageable for the staff involved. When we begin with an interval size that is not small enough, the program will not be so successful as it would have been had the interval been small (Repp & Slack, 1977).

While we do not have any definitive information on how to determine the initial size of the interval, some guesses can be made. The best would seem to be based on making the probability of reinforcement for not responding greater than the probability of reinforcement for responding. While this statement may seem complicated, in reality it is not. For example, one student with whom we worked (Repp & Deitz, 1974) emitted various aggressive behaviors (throwing objects, hitting others, spitting, and several others) in a classroom. Baseline data indicated that these behaviors occurred about 12 times per hour. If the child was reinforced by attention or anything else every time he responded, then the maximum rate of reinforcement would be about once every 5 minutes (from 60 minutes ÷ 12 responses per hour). So that the student could be reinforced as frequently for *not* responding as he could possibly be reinforced for responding, we chose to set the initial DRO interval at 5 minutes. With another student, we (Repp, Dietz & Speir, 1974) found stereotypic responding to be occurring about 27 times per minute. The initial DRO interval was set at 2 seconds (from 60 seconds ÷ 30 responses per minute), so that the student would be reinforced as frequently for not responding as he could possibly be for responding. While there are probably more sophisticated ways for determining the initial interval size, this procedure has been a successful one and might be followed to give an estimate that is based upon the client's behavior. Regardless of how the interval is calculated, we must remember that there are only two components to a DRO procedure: (1) the reinforcer, with its strength as a reinforcer for that individual being critical, and (2) the DRO interval size, with its length and its relation to baseline responding also being critical.

Examples.   While it can be used alone, DRO has more often been used in conjunction with other procedures and has helped to reduce a wide variety of inappropriate behaviors. Several studies have shown that DRO, when paired with other procedures can generally be successful as a package treatment[2] to reduce self-injurious behavior. For example, Ragain and Anson (1976) made food contingent on periods in which a 12-year-old girl did not scratch herself or bang her head. They used an adjusting DRO schedule in which the girl was first required to refrain from self-abuse for 5 seconds; later in the program, she was required to omit this response for 30 seconds before food was provided. A longer extension of the DRO period was made by Repp and Deitz (1974), who worked with several institutionalized persons. One young girl had been confined to arm splints for several years, because she scratched her face severely and frequently when released (about 16 times per minute during the brief periods she was released). During the first portion of the treatment phase, the child was taken to a room where other students would not interfere and was consequated in two

---

[2] We should be aware that in such "packaged treatments" the individual effects of each of the treatments involved in the package cannot be assessed; some of the procedures may, in fact, have had no effect at all. This type of approach is generally tried when we face a difficult problem and want to amass as strong a procedure as possible in order to quickly reduce the behavior.

ways. If she did not scratch herself, she was given a small portion of an M & M and was praised verbally and through back and arm rubbing. If she moved to scratch herself, she was told "no" and her hand was pulled down to her side. At first, the DRO interval was only 1 second long; this short period was used to provide a large number of opportunities for her to learn not to scratch herself. Then the period was increased gradually, until it was 120 minutes. Concomitantly, two other fading procedures were used. Initially, the 25-minute sessions were conducted away from the child's regular programming area where there were other staff and students. After the program was shown to be effective, the child was brought back to the regular teaching room a few of the 25 minutes, with this period being extended gradually until the whole program was being conducted in that room. Then the 25-minute periods were extended to 2 hours.

DRO has also been used to reduce stereotypic responding by retarded persons. Chitraker and Buel (1976) worked with two children who engaged in stereotypic hand licking and handclapping. One child was praised and received tactile reinforcement, while the other child received food for 5-second periods without the target behaviors having occurred. The DRO interval was increased and the behaviors decreased considerably during the program for each of the children (from more than 80% of the recording intervals to less than 10%). Repp, Deitz, and Speir (1974) also reduced stereotypic responding with this procedure. During baseline, three clients engaged in "lip-flapping with fingers" (80 rpm), in rocking (27 rpm), or in hand movements in front of his face (20 rpm). For each of the individuals, a timer was set at a short interval that was related to baseline responding. If the client did not respond, the teacher hugged and verbally praised him or her. If the client did engage in a form of stereotypic responding, the teacher continued the "No!" which she had been using to consequate responding during baseline. In each case, the DRO interval was increased while the behavior reduced to an almost zero level.

DRO has also been use to decrease inappropriate classroom behaviors. Dandy, Oliver, and Kaprowy (1976) began with 15-minute intervals in which tokens were delivered for periods without boisterous and other disruptive behaviors. When the interval was increased to 30 and then to 60 minutes, the student maintained his improved work behavior. Deitz, Repp, and Deitz (1976) reduced the shouting and talking-out by a 13-year-old boy in an EMR classroom by awarding him a token for every 3 minutes in which he did not engage in the disruptive behavior. In addition, four other students earned free time for periods in which they did not talk-out on topics unrelated to the subject being discussed in class.

Programming DRO.   There are a number of strengths and weaknesses of DRO schedules, as well as programming choices one must consider while programming these schedules. Some of these are as follows:

1. DRO can be a totally positive approach; i.e., it need not incorporate any aversive aspects during its use. As such, it is a nonrestrictive procedure and should be considered before using any aversive procedure.
2. DRO can be used to eliminate a wide variety of behaviors. As the examples indicated, it can be used both with very serious as well as with

fairly innocuous behaviors. We should, however, be quite cautious about using it with self-abusive behavior even though a number of studies have demonstrated success.

3. From our experiences, DRO appears to provide immediate feedback to the staff, because it tends either to work very quickly or not at all.[3] As such, there appears to be little need to use it for several weeks in hopes that its effects become more pronounced over time.

4. One of the problems as well as advantages of DRO is that it is a fairly weak procedure; i.e., there is really little consequation for responding, the only consequation being the postponement of reinforcement. The advantage is that this reduces any aversive aspects of the program, while the disadvantage is that it presents a weak consequence for responding. The critical issue then becomes how important the resulting delay of reinforcement is and how powerful the reinforcer is for that individual. Perhaps, as with so many other schedules, DRO tends to work either quickly or not at all because the matter for the individual is really quite simple: is the consequence for and history of emitting a response greater than the consequence for not emitting that response? This paradigm suggests that the selection of the reinforcer is critical, and that we should take great care in selecting something which is believed to be a powerful reinforcer for that individual in that situation.

5. Another problem with DRO is that it can be quite time consuming. As some of the examples have indicated, initial DRO intervals should not necessarily be considered a reason for rejecting this program, as the seriousness of the problem may fully warrant such care. It is, however, something we should consider before implementing the procedure so that the other students can receive adequate programming. One way around this problem has been suggested by Sulzer-Azaroff and Mayer (1977), who discussed a quasi-DRO schedule in which one ignores behavior during the interval and delivers reinforcement at the end of the interval if responding is not occurring at that moment. This procedure, which we might term *momentary DRO* for its similarity to momentary time sampling, should certainly not be so effective as a DRO schedule, because its requirements are so much less stringent. It may, however, prove to be a suitable alternative when the occurrence of a response is more a bother than a cause for real concern.

6. *Behavioral contrast* is a phenomenon that presents a problem for DRO, as well as for every other reductive procedure.[4] It refers to a situation in which a response decrease in one situation (e.g., Mr. Cullinan's class) is accompanied by a response increase in another situation (e.g., Mr. Epstein's class). Reynolds, who has demonstrated this phenomenon, has discussed the difference between behavioral contrast and generalization:

---

[3] This effect is one mentioned only from personal experience with perhaps 30 or 40 examples, and it should not be regarded as a carefully studied and demonstrated phenomenon.

[4] However, to avoid repetition, behavioral contrast will be discussed only in this section.

In generalization, the rates of responding in the presence of two stimuli both change in the same direction. In behavioral contrast, the rates in the presence of two stimuli change in opposite directions. . . . We have an example of generalization when a child's unruly behavior extinguishes more slowly than usual at home, because it is reinforced on the playground; we have an example of behavioral contrast when the extinction of unruly behavior at home makes for increasingly frequent unruly behavior on the playground. (1968, p. 45)

The effects described in behavioral contrast are extremely important for any reductive program. The phenomenon can occur when previous reinforcement for responding in the presence of one stimulus condition becomes less probable (e.g., in Mr. Cullinan's class where out-of-seat behavior no longer results in attention, but where 15-minute periods of in-seat behavior earns tokens), while reinforcement for the same response in another stimulus condition remains just as probable (e.g., Mr. Epstein's class in which out-of-seat behavior still results in the teacher's attention). In many cases, we would like generalization to occur; i.e., we would like improvement to occur in all situations. Behavioral contrast, however, suggests to us that generalization is something for which we should plan rather than something which we should expect.

7. In programming DRO schedules, there are also a number of considerations. One is that baseline data should be recorded not only to describe behavior, but also as a means to determine the size of the initial DRO interval. As discussed before, this choice should be based on data so that we can optimize our chances of helping the individual reduce his or her inappropriate behavior. Our best guess at present is to make that interval smaller than the inverse of the average rate of responding in baseline.

8. In all cases, we will want to increase the DRO interval so that the student's behavior will come under control in a more natural environment. Changing interval size should also be as objective as possible, although we do not have objective steps for making these changes. There are two considerations. The first is the amount by which we will increase the interval size at each change. Unfortunately, we do not know the answer to this question. For example, we do not know whether improved behavior is more likely to maintain if we increase the present interval by 10%, by 100%, or by the difference between the present and prior interval. We have two conflicting objectives at this point: (1) to make the interval change large so that the program can quickly be faded out, and (2) to make the change small so that the behavior maintains at its improved level. The only answer at present is to make a subjective guess, to watch the data so that any regression can be quickly noted, and to react to the data. The second consideration is when to make the change. Again, we have no basis for this decision and we are caught in a subjective-objective puzzle. The procedure we have used can, however, be adopted with whatever alterations are

necessary. Typically, we have set some arbitrary standard and made changes only when this criterion has been met. For example, in working with stereotypic responding, we have often used as a criterion "90% of the DRO intervals have successfully been met for two consecutive days."

9. Another programming consideration is whether responding should be consequated just with delayed reinforcement (produced by the interval being reset) or whether to add another contingency. DRO has been coupled with punitive methods, such as response cost or timeout,[5] and the results have been quite good. In such a case, however, the program loses its nonaversive aspects. The decision should probably be based on the severity of the response as well as the anticipated reactions of the individual involved. If such additional procedures would quite likely lead to physical resistance and aggression, then we should be quite cautious in their use.

10. We should also be certain that reinforcement is not delivered following a grossly inappropriate response even if the DRO interval has expired without the target response having occurred. This problem is obviously one met by common sense and is readily dismissed by providing a delay between the scheduled reinforcement and the occurrence of this second inappropriate response.

11. When programming DRO for several students in a classroom, we could have a problem of insufficient staff to operate separate intervals for all students involved. In these cases, if the baseline responding of each is not too disparate, we could use the same DRO for each individual. Such a procedure would require the teacher to set just one kitchen timer or to note the time on a clock and make the operation much easier. In addition, such a procedure could allow group consequences if all students met the requirement. Obviously, we would have to be careful that such a program would be fair to all students involved.

Differential Reinforcement of Low Rates of Responding

Definition. The differential reinforcement of low rates of responding (DRL) is a schedule that is designed to decrease responding to an acceptable level, and it usually reaches a final acceptable level through a few intermediate steps. For example, an acceptable rate of talk-outs may be ten per hour one week, eight per hour another week, and finally six per hour for the remainder of the year. In this sense, DRL schedules can, like DRO schedules, be analogous to a shaping program in which requirements for correct responding change in an orderly fashion. DRL schedules can be programmed in three ways. One is the *interresponse-time* or *spaced-responding* method developed in laboratory studies of infrahuman and human behavior. The purpose of these studies was often to produce a low stable rate of responding against which the effects of independent variables like drugs could be assessed. To achieve these rates, the

---

[5] These methods are discussed in this chapter.

experimenters *reinforced a response if and only if it followed a prior response by a particular time period;* hence these interresponse times were reinforced. The difference between this and a DRO schedule is that in DRL a response had to occur before reinforcement could be delivered, while in DRO a response could not occur if reinforcement was to occur. An example of this procedure would be praising a child who usually asked for help quite frequently and unnecessarily when he was supposed to be working mostly on his own, but who now waited. In this case, we might say something like, "Thank you, Terry, for working on your own so long; now may I help you with your question" (you raised your hand to ask). Because we are attending to an inappropriate response, this program should be used for behavior that is inappropriate only because it is occurring at too high a rate. Examples of appropriate behaviors for this procedure would be question asking or handraising, while examples of behaviors not appropriate for this procedure would be throwing pencils at classmates or hitting someone.

A second method of programming DRL is the *full-session* method (Deitz & Repp, 1973, 1974 a, b) *in which reinforcement is delivered if the rate of responding for the whole session is below a limit.* An example of this procedure would be praising a class if no more than three errors were made on all the arithmetic problems answered.

A third method is the *interval method in which the session is broken into a number of intervals, and reinforcement is delivered at the end of each interval if responding is less than a particular level for that interval.* For example, the three-hour morning class might be divided into three 1-hour intervals. Then the class could be praised if there were less than four disruptions by the end of each hour. This procedure is simply a variation of the whole-session method, and the reason for its use should be obvious. If a student exceeds in the first 10 minutes the limit set for 3 hours, then the chance for reinforcing appropriate levels of responding the last several hours is lost. Dividing long periods into shorter intervals deals with this problem.

Examples.   Most of the DRL studies with retarded individuals have been in classrooms, although its use need not be restricted to that setting. These studies have generally concentrated on disruptive behaviors and have applied contingencies both to groups and to individuals. For example, Deitz, Repp, and Deitz (1976) worked with a 12-year-old boy who was classified as EMR and who was considered the most disruptive student in the class. The behaviors in which he engaged were "(1) talking when not called upon by the teacher, (2) talking about a subject other than classwork, (3) leaving his seat, and (4) yelling at other students in the class" (p. 157). In an ABAB study, the baseline phases constituted no special treatment, while the treatment phases allowed the student to go to the library for 10 minutes if he emitted two or fewer disruptive responses during the class period. In the library, he was allowed to watch television, play games, read comics, or engage in similar activities. The results, shown in Figure 11-1, indicate that in the two treatment phases, the student exceeded the DRL limit of two responses on only one occasion, and that he had little trouble managing his own behavior.

A second project reported in this study dealt with a class of 14 EMR students whose average age was 13 years. The students engaged in no dangerous behaviors, but they constituted what both the teacher and the principal

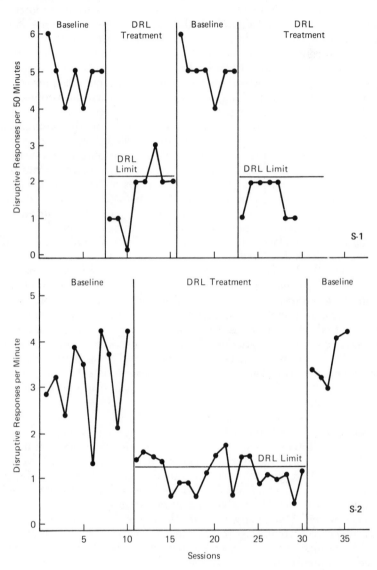

Figure 11-1. Disruptive responses per 50-minute session for S-1 (top) during four phases of DRL experiment 1. During treatment, staying below the DRL limit earned S-1 10 minutes free time in the library. Disruptive responses per minute for Ss-2 (a group of 14 EMR students) during three phases of DRL experiment 2 (bottom). During treatment, staying below the DRL limit of 1.3 rpm earned Ss-2 exchangeable tokens (Deitz, Repp, & Deitz, 1976, p. 157).

described as the most disruptive class in school. The disruptive behaviors in which they engaged were "(1) talking aloud, (2) being out of one's assigned seat, (3) making loud noises, (4) hitting or shoving other students, and (5) throwing objects" (p. 159). An ABA design was used, and in the second phase tokens were earned when the students had a disruptive rate of less than 1.3 responses per minute averaged over the classroom period. This rate was chosen by the teacher as something which she believed would not be too restrictive but which would not interfere with the classroom instruction. The class was already on a token program, so the same tokens and backup reinforcers were used to consequate lowered rates of disruptive behavior. The backup reinforcers again were activities rather than tangible items and included going to the library, reading or playing games in the classroom, and playing supervised games outside. Figure 11-1 shows that the class met the DRL limit on 60% of the days, and that on the other days the disruptive behaviors were very near the limit. Both these studies showed good control by the DRL contingencies. Each, however, in the reversal phases showed that behavior did indeed reverse to its pretreatment levels. Such a reversal is something we should attempt to prevent by fading out the contingencies over time. In each of these cases, however, the last day of data was also the last day of school before vacation.

A variation of this DRL program has also been used in classrooms and has been called the Good Behavior Game (Barrish, Saunders, & Wolf, 1969; Fishbein & Wasik, 1981; Harris & Sherman, 1973; Medland & Stachnik, 1972). Although there are variations within the game itself, the basic procedure involves dividing the class into two or more groups, letting them compete against each other or against a (DRL) standard in terms of who has been good, and reinforcing the team(s) that has behaved well. The work by Medland and Stachnik (1972) describes some of the details of the program. They were concerned with a class which had been divided into two reading groups in the morning and which had become for the month of the reading program "virtually uncontrollable." There were many kinds of disruptive behaviors during this period, and they were combined into four categories: out of seat, talking out, motoric disruptions (e.g., hitting), and not raising hand for permission to engage in some activities. The Game has a number of components explained at the beginning of reading class by the teacher to the students. The instructions were that

> (a) what they were about to do was play a game in which each reading group would try to win and that the game was to be played in reading class only; (b) when a team or teams won the game, the team or teams would receive certain privileges (it was made clear that both teams could win); (c) there were certain rules that the teams had to follow to win the game (the rules were read to both groups and were based on the behavioral definitions used to record the target behaviors); (d) whenever one of the team members broke one of the rules there would be a mark against that team; (e) a team or teams would win if they received five or fewer marks per day; (f) winning would entitle them to three minutes of extra morning recess. If a team received 20 or fewer marks for a week, they would be awarded extra activity time the following Monday afternoon from 2:20 to 3:20 p.m.; a losing team would continue their scholastic assignments (this did not cut into class time very much because 40 minutes of that hour were previously for an end-of-day study time and recess); (g) if a team had an individual who precluded winning by getting four or

more marks in one day, the group could vote to exclude that person from the group for a day, thus causing the person to miss participation in any activities won by the team that week. The individual would be put behind a screen in the back corner of the room on the next day to study alone (this timeout component was installed in order to avoid the problem children encountered by Barrish *et al.*, 1969. In that study, two students were dropped from the game and the marks were not imposed on their teams). (p. 47)

The rules for this particular implementation of the Good Behavior Game account for some potential problems and can be used as a basis for implementing the procedure in any classroom setting. Modifications can certainly be made as needed in order to make the program more appropriate for an individual teaching environment. But allowing both teams to win instead of just the team with the fewest marks would seem to be a suggestion that should be followed; so too should some consequence for an individual member of the team who has caused almost by himself the team to lose.

As mentioned before, when the DRL contingency has been used with retarded individuals, it has traditionally been used in classrooms. Such a restriction is of course not necessary. For example, a large number of projects has been devoted to such behaviors as cigarette smoking, and the basis for such programs can easily be adapted for retarded individuals. In these, baseline data are recorded for a few days, and then the first DRL contingency is imposed at a level slightly lower than the baseline level. With reduced cigarette smoking as a goal, one might find during baseline that 30 were smoked each day. The first DRL limit might be 25 per day. When behavior stabilized at this level, the limit could be further reduced, perhaps to 20 per day. Reductions could continue until such a goal is reached. In this way, a DRL program *in toto* could be viewed as a shaping procedure that utilizes a changing criterion design. There is no reason why such a program could not be adapted with developmental-appropriate feedback for a variety of responses by retarded individuals.

Programming DRL.   Regardless of the type of DRL program used (i.e., interresponse-time, full session, or interval DRL), there are a number of strengths and weaknesses as well as programming choices we must consider while programming these schedules. Some of these are as follows:

1. DRL, like DRO, can be a totally positive approach in the sense that no aversive contingencies need be programmed. As such, we should consider its use before employing any aversive techniques, all of which are more restrictive. In another sense, DRL can be a negative approach in that its consequences are related to inappropriate responding. The "trick," then, is for the teacher to deemphasize the fact that any inappropriate responding was occurring and to emphasize how much improvement the student or class has demonstrated. The emphasis then usually is on the *improvement* in responding rather than on the behavior itself.

2. DRL need not be a procedure aimed at total reduction of responding. Rather, it can focus on behavior occurring at levels that are appropriate and do not interfere with learning adaptive behaviors. In this way, DRL

does not tell the student that he should never get out of his seat, that he should never talk to the person next to him, or that he should never "let off steam." It says instead to the student that we all do these sorts of things, and that such behavior can be tolerated as long as it does not occur so often that it interferes with the learning that he or other students should be accomplishing. In short, students do not have to be "still, quiet, and docile" (Winett & Winkler, 1972); they just need to learn to be considerate of others.

3. DRL has a unique property that other procedures do not share, which is that the procedure itself can be the design by which it can be evaluated. Although DRL programs can retain only one DRL value in the end, they usually involve a stepwise chain from baseline levels to acceptable levels of responding. When they do, they are utilizing the changing criterion design, and the effectiveness of the program can be evaluated by the parameters for evaluation by this design (Hartmann & Hall, 1976). This benefit is an excellent one as it precludes the necessity for reversal phases (in the ABAB design) or for extended baselines (in the multiple baseline design), while at the same time providing us with some information on how well our intervention has worked.

4. Because DRL does allow some amount to responding and, in essence, approves that amount by delivering reinforcement for it, DRL is appropriate only for behaviors that can be allowed, such as mild disruptions or errors on worksheets. It makes little sense to apply it to behaviors that are unacceptable at any level, such as physically aggressive disruptions or self-injurious behaviors. We should simply not be providing praise or other forms of feedback or reinforcement in these cases (e.g., "Good Elliot, you only punched Terry in the nose seven times today, and that's an improvement over yesterday"). As such, DRL should be judiciously limited to those behaviors which we want to reduce or eliminate (e.g., smoking), but whose reduction can be programmed over a few weeks or months.

5. A problem DRL shares with DRO is that reinforcement must incorporate an element of time and therefore must also incorporate some delay between good behavior (or at least the absence of inappropriate behavior) and reinforcement. DRL is, after all, a procedure that provides reinforcement for a lowered *rate* of responding, so it cannot be delivered until some period of time elapses. For example, if we provide tokens if the class has no more than four disruptions in the morning, then a great deal of appropriate behavior would be separated from reinforcement by several hours. This type of delay is certainly something which we want as a goal in the program, but it is not necessarily something with which we want to begin a program. If it is not, then the interval could be initially small and repeated several times during the day.

6. Because there is a delay, and because it is a strictly reinforcement-based procedure, the effectiveness of the program relies heavily on the power of the reinforcer for the individuals involved, as well as on how carefully that reinforcer is scheduled. Thus we should be certain that the contingent event is indeed a reinforcer for the individual or the

group, and we may need to be a little more creative than just selecting traditional events, like free time or token delivery.

7. As with DRO, the selection of the initial DRL schedule may be critical. The value should reflect some level which the student can meet and therefore should be based on the baseline level of responding. If we are using the full-session method, then we can begin a little below the mean rate of responding for baseline. If we are using the interval method and want to allow only one response per interval, then we can simply divide the mean rate of responding for baseline into the length of the session. For example, if the mean rate of disruptions during baseline were 6 rph and if the class were 1 hour long, each interval could initially be 10 minutes (60 minutes ÷ 6). If we are using the interresponse time method, we could use the overall mean during baseline as representative of the mean time between responses. The calculations in this case would be the same as in the interval method, but the programming would be different. For example, if a student averaged raising his hand 20 times per hour during baseline, then we could say that an estimate of the average time between responses could be 3 minutes (60 minutes ÷ 20). If we wished to use that figure as the first value for the interresponse time, then we could answer the student's question each time he waited at least 3 minutes since last asking a question.

8. Because DRL schedules tend to have their values changed over time, as in the changing criterion design, we need to determine both a criterion for when to change and a criterion for how much the change should be. If we began by reinforcing five or fewer disruptions per hour, we would need to determine when to change to a lesser value. Again, as with DRO, there are no rules for making this change, but we can set arbitrary but objective criteria, such as "meets requirements for four consecutive days." Similarly, there are no rules for determining what values should be used next, except that it should be less than the value in the prior phase when criterion was met. For example, if during those "four consecutive days," the student averaged 3.5 responses per hour, then the next DRL limit might be set at 3.0 responses in an hour.

9. One value of a DRL schedule is that it can be made meaningful for most of the students we service, regardless of their language competencies. If we have taught them the concept of zero, and if we have taught them "less versus more," then the program can be instituted with various prosthetics. For example, if the DRL limit is five, then five tokens could be placed on a child's desk or five marks could be placed on the board. Each response could result in a token being removed or in a chalk mark being erased. If the period ends and there are no tokens or marks left, the student does not win. Devising such mechanisms for teaching students the meaning of this program is really quite simple and can be highly individualized to the student's level of functioning.

10. Other advantages of DRL schedules are that they are quite easy to use and that they can be extended to groups. As Medland and Stachnik

(1972) have indicated, consequences can be made for groups, and games can be designed that allow groups to compete with each other and with a standard that allows all groups to win. This advantage is quite significant and somewhat unusual, as many behavioral procedures are difficult to employ with more than a few students.

Differential Reinforcement of Incompatible Responding

Definition. The *differential reinforcement of incompatible responding (DRI) is a program in which a response* **topographically** *incompatible with the target behavior is reinforced.* The premise for this procedure is that as the incompatible behavior increases, the inappropriate behavior must decrease. A further supposition, although not always found true, is that as the inappropriate response decreases in rate, it will become even less likely to recur because there will be fewer opportunities for the behavior to be reinforced by whatever has been maintaining it previously. This schedule generally operates in one of two ways, depending upon the target behavior involved. When that behavior is discrete and of short duration, then it is reinforced after some number of responses (1, 10, etc.) according to some type of interval or ratio schedule. For example, if the inappropriate response were "errors on math worksheets," then we could praise the child for every correct response while ignoring errors. However, when the target behavior continues for some duration, it is generally reinforced either if the behavior occurs for some specified duration or if the behavior is occurring at some specified moment. For example, if our problem were that a child is out of seat, running around the room, and fiddling with books, pens, etc., at the side of the room, we could choose as an incompatible target behavior "in seat." If we chose to praise the child for in-seat behavior, we could not do so on a continuous basis, but we could easily do so by one of two methods: (1) if he were in his seat for a specified duration, e.g., 10 minutes, or (2) if he were in his seat at a particular time of observation, e.g., at random observation times of 9:12, 9:18, 9:27, 9:30, 9:46, and 9:50.

Examples. There are many variations of the DRI procedure, as well as many types of behaviors with which it has been used. Hall, Lund, and Jackson (1968) worked with a number of students, two of whom were somewhat disruptive in the classroom. One displayed the typical repertoire of nonaggressive disruptive behaviors so familiar to all who have worked with this type of problem:

> behaviors included beating his desk with a pencil, chewing and licking pages of books, moving his chair back and forth in unison with a classmate, banging his chair on the floor, blowing bubbles and making noises while drinking his milk, and punching holes in the carton so that the milk flowed onto the desk. He would also gaze out the window or around the room and would say, "This is too hard," "Shoot, I can't do this," and "How did you say to work it?" (p. 7)

Studying was the behavior topographically incompatible with these disruptive behaviors that was chosen as the target behavior to increase. In this program, someone aided the teacher and signaled when the student had engaged in study behaviors for six consecutive 10-second intervals (the recording system was a partial-interval one utilizing 10-second intervals). At this point, the teacher attended to the child by moving to his desk, making some verbal comments, patting him on the shoulder, or the like. With this program, studying behavior increased markedly, and almost all disruptive behavior disappeared. A similar objective was used for another student in a different classroom who "disturbed the class by making loud noises, by getting out of his seat, and by talking to other students" (p. 9). In this case, the student's studying behavior was relatively high, so no one else was used to cue the teacher when to attend to the student. When the teacher's attention was contingent on studying behavior, the studying behavior increased to more than 85% of the time, and his disruptive behavior decreased to less than 1% of the time.

Deitz, Repp and Deitz (1976) also worked with disruptive behavior and teacher attention, but the DRI schedule was programmed in a different manner. In their study, the student was a 14-year-old boy in an EMR classroom who engaged in "talk-outs" that did not occur at a high rate (about four per hour), but which were of the type that frequently disrupted the entire class, sometimes for as much as 10 minutes. In the baseline phase of the study, the teacher reprimanded each occurrence of the target behavior as she had done prior to the study. During the second phase, she ignored the disruptive behavior and attended to appropriate academic behaviors. In this case, a predetermined series of numbers was written for the teacher in order to signal her to be certain to reinforce the first academic response after the classroom clock passed that number (a variable interval schedule of reinforcement). During this phase, the disruptive behavior decreased to one-third of its prior level. In the third phase, the DRI contingency was withdrawn, but the teacher continued to ignore disruptive behaviors in order to determine whether the ignoring procedure was responsible for the entire reductive effect. As behavior returned to near-baseline levels, a fourth phase was instituted in which the DRI contingency was used again. Because the variable-interval 3-minute schedule (VI 3 min) was somewhat cumbersome for the teacher, the VI schedule was increased gradually over 12 days until it was 15 minutes. This level was retained for a long period as the teacher should be attending to appropriate work behaviors that often occurred regardless of whether a special program was in effect.

Favell (1973) also used the DRI procedure, but consequated a different behavior. In her study, three institutionalized children were observed to engage in various forms of stereotypic responding a great deal of the time. In an effort to decrease this behavior while increasing an appropriate response, Favell used graduated guidance, reinforcement, and stimulus fading to teach the children how to play with toys. The results, displayed in Figure 11-2, show through a combination multiple baseline and reversal design that as the children's play behavior increased, their stereotypic behavior decreased. Thus, through a DRI procedure, a maladaptive behavior was decreased while an appropriate response was increased. A problem, however, for this type of target behavior to be used as a DRI procedure in a totally applied teaching situation is that the behavior (toy play) cannot easily transfer across situations, because it is dependent upon the presence of a particular stimulus condition (i.e., toys). When our objective is

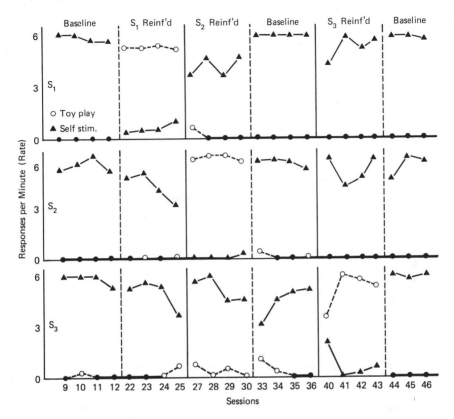

Figure 11-2. The rate of toy play and stereotypic responding by three children. During baseline phases, the incompatible response (toy play) was not reinforced. During the "Reinf'd" phases, either the first (S₁), the second (S₂), or the third (S₃) child was reinforced for toy play (Favell, 1973, p. 22).

teaching as opposed to testing procedures through research (as Favell's objective appropriately was), we should be quite careful about selecting an appropriate incompatible target behavior.

Programming DRI. There are several advantages, disadvantages, and considerations that DRI shares with DRO and DRL, so these will not be discussed here. However, some that are more indigenous to DRI are as follows:

1. The target behavior should be one that can occur across many of the situations in which the inappropriate response is occurring. If it does not, then any decrements during the DRI program are not particularly likely to generalize to the other situations in which the student's behavior should be decreased. This problem is not a major one in facilities where there is a great deal of active programming, but it is a major problem in facilities where little active programming occurs (e.g., some institutions with insufficient numbers of staff and with insufficient supplies).

2. A decision must be made about whether to *consequate* responses exceeding some *duration* criterion (e.g., 5 consecutive minutes of studying), or whether to *consequate* responses *on occurrence* (e.g., answering problems correctly), or whether to consequate enduring responses at prescribed intervals (e.g., in-seat behavior if it is occurring at 10:11, 10:29, and 10:52). These decisions are in part determined by the choice of the target behavior, but we should be careful to choose as a target behavior that which will be possible, in terms of other classroom responsibilities, for the teacher to reinforce.

3. Once the type of requirement for reinforcement is determined, the particular and exact schedule should be determined. As with DRO and DRL schedules, this decision is probably best made when based on the level of responding during baseline. We should probably begin with a schedule in which the student is reinforced more often for the appropriate response than she or he could be for the inappropriate response. After the program has stabilized, reinforcement can be provided less frequently by increasing the requirement.

Differential Reinforcement of Alternative Behaviors

Definition. *The differential reinforcement of alternative behaviors (DRA) is a procedure like DRI except that it does not require the target behavior to be incompatible with the inappropriate response. As such, it can be defined as a procedure in which an appropriate response is increased in rate to the extent that an inappropriate response is decreased in rate.*

Examples. The difference between what we are labeling DRA and DRI is quite small, but the difference is quite clear. In DRI, the behavior must be topographically incompatible with the inappropriate response, while in DRA it is not. For example, if we were concerned with a child being out of his seat too much, we might in a DRI procedure reinforce him every fifth minute if he is in his seat; in a DRA procedure, we might reinforce him if he finishes 30 math problems between 10:00 and 10:30. The basic premise of the DRA procedure is that if an individual has enough to do, and if he is reinforced for doing it, he will not have time to get into trouble. Ayllon and his colleagues have provided several examples of this procedure. In one (Ayllon, Layman, and Burke, 1972), the four worst students in an EMR class considered to be "the most unmotivated, undisciplined and troublesome in the school" (p. 316) were chosen. The major problem was the amount of disruptive behavior, which included walking or running around the classroom; throwing objects; talking out loud to oneself or to other students; calling out to the teacher; ringing, whistling, or humming; tapping or pounding objects, feet, or fingers; dropping objects; and snapping fingers. One way to have dealt with these behaviors would have been to consequate them directly, either by punishing their presence or rewarding their absence. Another, however, is to have selected some appropriate behaviors for programming. The authors chose the latter alternative and chose a program in which reading and arithmetic would be consequated. In the first phase of the study, the teacher engaged in her regular routine. During these days, the students were disruptive in 98% of the 10-second intervals in which they were observed. In the next phase, the teacher divided the class time into two consecutive 30-minute periods. In one, the teacher instructed the students in math for 5 minutes, then presented them with a 2-minute test, and then repeated the instruction-test cycle until it had occurred four times. In the next 30 minutes, the teacher distributed materials to the students to be read. At the end of each 5 minutes, a 1.5-minute timed test was given over the material just read. This cycle was also repeated until it had occurred four times. During this phase, the disruptive behaviors reduced to 17% of the observations. Then four phases occurred in which either the math or the reading answers were consequated with one token for each correct response. The results were astonishing and they demonstrate the value of this approach: (1) disruptive behavior remained depressed, and (2) academic performance increased tremendously. "Within less than 20 hours of the reinforcement procedures, two children improved in reading from preprimer to second grade. The other two children improved from first to fourth grade" (p. 321). In addition, apparently because the token/no-token program was alternated across the math and reading periods, the children continued to perform quite well when tokens were no longer used for the math performance, as the teacher in one adroitly used consequences that were natural to the classroom environment.

These results are very important for several reasons. One is that these children had been labeled mentally retarded, but they had been allowed to function at a much lower academic and social level than was necessary. Perhaps if a program like this had been provided for them before they reached the ages of 12 or 13, they could have functioned in a less restrictive environment and at a much higher level. Another important aspect of these results is the way in which they differed from other reductive procedures. If a DRO, DRL, or DRI procedure had been used, the disruptive behaviors may well have been decreased to a similar low level. But academic achievements would have been fortuitous as they would never have been directly consequated. The twofold benefits of this approach are substantial and make it a very attractive alternative. As Ayllon, Layman, and Burke (1972) have noted,

> The impressive progress made by all four children suggests that the time has come for behavioral engineers to be satisfied with nothing less than academic objectives. If academic progress, such as that reported here, can be made with these so-called educable mentally retarded children, then it is time for the same procedure to be applied to assist in the education of the slow, the underachiever, and the undisciplined child. While disruptive behavior and discipline in the classroom are the major, and often the immediate, objectives of the classroom teacher, behavioral applications cannot in good conscience be exploited to foster classroom conformity. On the contrary, the classroom teacher must come to realize that behavioral techniques enable her to rededicate herself to her noble professional objectives: the teaching of the young. (p. 322)

Programming DRA. Because of its similarities to DRI, this procedure has many of the benefits, restrictions, and programming requirements of DRO, DRL, and DRI. Its major attractiveness relative to the other techniques is that it allows us to concentrate on appropriate behaviors, whether they be academic or social. As such, it is an excellent program for classrooms. Its major disadvantage is that it does not directly consequate inappropriate responding, and as such it may not reduce inappropriate responding as much as it should. For example, students would still be throwing objects, shouting, humming, etc., and completing their work. While the behaviors in that case would not be "disruptive" by definition, they would certainly still be socially inappropriate. There appear to be two solutions to this potential problem: (1) simply add a DRO or DRL procedure if the data suggest one would be necessary, and (2) give the students enough work to do and enough attention for completing it that they simply do not have enough time or the incentive to be disruptive.

Extinction and Ignoring

Definition. *Extinction is* used here as a term that refers to *a procedure in which a response that was previously reinforced is no longer reinforced. Ignoring is a procedure in which one does not provide attention contingent upon responding.* While these two definitions are similar, they differ in a very important way. Because extinction means that a previously reinforced response is no longer reinforced, we must identify what is reinforcing or maintaining a behavior before we can know we are using extinction. That sort of exercise, however, can be quite difficult. Many people instead simply ignore behavior under the impression that their attention was maintaining the inappropriate behavior, and they then call this procedure extinction. There is a major problem here, however, and the problem is not the technically correct or incorrect use of jargon. The problem is that many inappropriate behaviors are not maintained by our attention. They may be maintained physiologically, or they may be maintained by other aspects of the environment, which we either cannot identify or could not change if we could identify. To confuse ignoring with extinction in these situations is quite important, because in this confusion we would be denying treatment to our client under the mistaken impression that we are correctly providing a behavioral procedure. Indeed, some people label certain children autistic when, among other things, they do not respond well for attention. To ignore inappropriate behavior when human attention is not reinforcing in the first place is to fail to provide treatment for individuals who should be provided treatment.

Examples. Most behavioral programs, indeed most teaching programs that are consistent and objective, use extinction or ignoring while teaching a student new behaviors. We generally guide, instruct, or prepare the student in some way to emit a correct response; if an incorrect response occurs, we generally ignore it under the presumption that our attention either maintained the behavior in the past or might maintain it now. But some procedures involve events other than our attention that would be powerfully reinforcing. For example, O'Brien, Bugle, and Azrin (1972) demonstrated the effects of a graduated guidance program designed to teach a girl to feed herself with a spoon. When manual guidance was not used, the child could eat food from her hand or use the spoon incorrectly in some other way, and because food was the reinforcer, all those responses would be reinforced. So instead of allowing these behaviors to be completed, the authors interrupted the chain, not allowing the child to eat the food and thus put these behaviors under extinction. Because these chains of inappropriate responding were no longer reinforced, they soon were eliminated.

A clear demonstration of extinction has been provided in an ABABAB study by Pinkston, Reese, LeBlanc, and Baer (1973), who demonstrated the relationship between teacher attention and the aggressive attacks of a three-year-old boy on his playmates at school. In the A phases, the teachers responded to the child's aggressive behavior in their regular fashion, which included verbal admonitions such as "Cain, we don't do that here," or "Cain, you can't play here until you're ready to be a good boy!" In the B phases, the teachers did not attend to the aggressive behaviors, except to separate him when needed from his target. Whenever Cain was attacking a child, they attended to that peer with statements such as "I'm sorry that happened to you. Why don't you play with this nice truck?" In these phases, the attacking behaviors declined rapidly, averaging less than 5% of the time in the last few sessions of the extinction periods compared with more than 25% of the time during the A phases. Because there was such a clear difference in responding in each of the successive phases of this study, the teachers' attention was quite clearly maintaining the behavior and the phases in which it was reduced were quite clearly extinction phases.

Laws, Brown, Epstein, and Hocking (1971) provided an example of ignoring inappropriate behaviors displayed by three boys in a special day-care program. The behaviors included various stereotypes; inappropriate comments, squeals, giggles, moaning, and screeching; out of seat; looking away from task; and head bobbing accompanied by heavy breathing. The authors used an ignoring procedure in which any of the inappropriate social behaviors resulted in the therapist's turning away from the student. Although there were insufficient controls on the therapist's attention to determine whether this was extinction, the label does not matter as the procedure was the same general one used in extinction and it was successful.

Programming Extinction and Ignoring. Because neither of these procedures consequates inappropriate responding with an active program, they can be weak procedures and, as such, they are often used in combination with other procedures. But whether they are used singly or in combinations, there are several considerations that apply. The first several are properties of extinction, some of which have been demonstrated in laboratory research but not very often in applied settings. The second set are more related to the actual use of the procedure.

1. Extinction is sometimes (but not always) a slow process, in that behavior takes many days or weeks to reach an eventual low point. As such, when used *alone*, it is appropriate for nonaggressive low-rate behaviors whose occurrence we can tolerate but would prefer to be less frequent. It is not appropriate, however, for behaviors which we cannot tolerate occurring at all.

2. Occasionally, extinction results in an initial increase or burst of responding. As such, we should be prepared for this possibility, and we should be using it only with behaviors for which this phenomenon is not a catastrophe or for behaviors that we can prevent by physical restraint. Because of this and the previously mentioned property of extinction, it

may not be an appropriate procedure to use along with large adolescents in aggressive behavior or with other such cases.

3. The extinction period is sometimes accompanied by an initial outburst of aggression, regardless of the nature of the target behavior involved. Two common nontherapeutic examples occur with grades in school and with vending machines. When we receive a low grade on a test, we have not been reinforced for studying, and we often curse the professor, throw our books down, and engage in other foolish but natural aggressive behaviors. A second example occurs when we put coins in a vending machine and find they have not registered but have been lost. Because this behavior has been reinforced in the past with the delivery of food, it is now under extinction and it is often accompanied by an aggressive act like kicking or hitting the machine. The extent to which extinction-induced aggression occurs in behavioral programs is unknown, but it probably does occur some times. The important factor for us is not so much that it does or does not occur; rather, it is to be prepared for it and to predict whether a student's particular form of aggression is typically verbal or physical.

4. Another characteristic of extinction demonstrated in laboratory studies is spontaneous recovery, a phenomenon which suggests that, after a month or two of zero occurrences, the behavior may occur several times for a day or two. Whether this would happen in applied settings where appropriate behaviors could be reinforced to high rates is equivocal. However, the point again is that we should be prepared for its occurrence. Because this is a phenomenon that occurs over time, we should be particularly careful to apprise any new staff of the behavior and what to do if it occurs.

5. There are several considerations with extinction that interweave with its characteristics. One is the type of program for which an extinction procedure *by itself* is appropriate. Because the procedure can take some time, can have associated aggression, spontaneous recovery, and an initial increase in behavior, extinction is an inappropriate procedure when used alone for very serious problems such as self-injurious behavior. With some behaviors, in fact, extinction is an inappropriate procedure even when used in combination with other procedures. For self-injurious behaviors like head-banging, we should not ignore the response; we should restrain the individual from responding. To allow it to occur through extinction is really quite unnecessary in most situations.

6. Another consideration with extinction is consistency, and the problem is quite interesting. In essence, the greater the degree of consistency up to perfection, the worse the problem can be. With a few examples, this perhaps unexpected relationship should be less surprising. Suppose we had three circumstances of extinction: (1) one in which the teacher makes a mistake and attends to the inappropriate response about every fifth occurrence, (2) another in which the teacher makes a mistake about every tenth occurrence, and (3) another in which the teacher makes a mistake about every fifteenth occurrence. While these three situations represent increasing consistency in ignoring behavior, the

behavior theoretically will be increasingly worse as the consistency increased. The reason is that these three situations represent three schedules of reinforcement: (1) VR5, (2) VR10, and (3) VR15. As we may remember, with increasing reinforcement ratios, responding tends to increase in rate. So when we only occasionally make a mistake and reinforce an inappropriate response, we may actually be strengthening that behavior.

7. A third problem with extinction, but not with ignoring, is that we must first identify whatever is reinforcing the behavior. To do so actually requires an ABAB design, an objective that contradicts the objective of treatment. The alternative is to presume that something is maintaining the behavior and then to prevent it from occurring. That, however, can be a precarious approach to use when not combined with another procedure that does not require this presumption.

PUNISHMENT PROCEDURES

Punishment refers to a procedure in which responding produces a stimulus change and as a result of this change becomes less probable. There are two types of punishment: (1) in positive punishment, the stimulus change is one in which something is added to the environment, while (2) in negative punishment, the stimulus change is one in which something is taken away from the environment. There are two predominant procedures in each of these types of punishment. In one positive-punishment procedure that is usually referred to as *aversive conditioning*, the student is punished by some aversive event (a "No!," a spanking, etc.) if the student makes an inappropriate response. In another positive-punishment procedure, *overcorrection*, the student is required to practice excessively the appropriate form of the behavior and is required to restore the environment if he has disrupted it (e.g., cleaning the entire classroom for one hour if he has thrown over a desk during a tantrum). In one form of negative punishment, *timeout*, the reinforcing environment and the student are separated for some period of time as a result of an inappropriate response. In the other common form of negative punishment, *response cost*, the student loses something she or he has accumulated (e.g., tokens) as a result of a response.

Regardless of the type of punishment procedure used, there are a number of relevant factors: (1) considerations prior to choosing an aversive procedure, (2) considerations in choosing an aversive procedure, and (3) considerations after choosing an aversive procedure. The first consideration is *whether there are objective data that suggest the need for intervention*. Since we are in the era in which clients' rights should be protected, we should use objective data to support our actions. It is unfair to the client to punish her or him for a behavior that we subjectively believe is more intense or frequent than it really is. The methods involved in objectively defining and measuring behavior are well known and are taught in hundreds of university classes. In addition, the reliance on subjective information to support any type of program is currently at variance with federal regulations (e.g., Public Law 94-142; Federal Regulation 45CFR249.13, 1977, Regulations for ICF Services for Mentally Retarded or Persons with Other

Related Disorders), as well as ethically unwise. The presentation of verified data should be the first requisite to a program using any form of punishment.

A second consideration is *whether nonaversive procedures have been tried.* Clearly, ruling out these procedures before choosing an aversive one is incumbent upon us. A number of nonaversive procedures have been proved effective with inappropriate behaviors of retarded persons, and these procedures include DRO, DRL, DRI, and DRA. Data demonstrating that these procedures have failed should be available before one tries an aversive approach. Implicit in this demonstration is the assumption that these procedures have been used in a thorough and not in a haphazard manner. Teachers should have been properly trained, and programming must have been provided in a manner that is congruent with the latest technology.

A third question is *whether the behavior is injurious to this client or to other students.* When the student is engaging in self-injurious behavior, and damaging sight, hearing, limbs, etc., then we must consider the strongest program available to eliminate that behavior. In addition, when a student's behavior includes physical assaults on others, those persons have a right to freedom from abuse. In these cases, we may be quite justified in using punitive programs. To refuse to do so and to fail to eliminate the behavior in other ways is simply not fair to the other students.

After we have decided to implement an aversive procedure, there are many other considerations. One is *whether the proposed treatment procedure is a commonly used one or an experimental one.* As Martin (1975) has suggested, a client who is being provided an experimental (i.e., new) procedure is more at risk than a client who is being provided a commonly used procedure. This problem does not mean that we should refrain from developing procedures that could eventually help hundreds of individuals, but it does mean that in such cases we must exercise even more caution than usual in protecting the rights of the clients. In addition, it means either (1) that we should try common procedures first and experimental procedures only after the traditional ones have failed, or (2) that we should have quite supportable reasons why we believe the novel approach would be better for the client than the traditional approach. The point is that we should not be confusing research with treatment and that our first obligation is to provide treatment.

Another consideration is *whether the appropriate committees have recommended that the procedure be used.* Because of some cases of the inappropriate use of reductive procedures, many facilities and even states have established human rights and/or behavior modification committees. The purpose of these committees is to protect the rights of the clients to treatment in the most fair and judicious manner possible. These committees have veto power over experimental programs and over most positive-punishment procedures; and their power is very important. Although most states recommend such committees, not all facilities have them. Those that do not should seek guidance in forming one from facilities that have one.

An important consideration is *whether notice has been served.* The facility should have written rules describing what behaviors will lead to what punishment procedures under what conditions. These rules should be available to the students, their parents, and any other appropriate representatives. In addition, a clear description of the punitive procedure should be presented to the client and parents, and they should be informed that such a procedure will begin if the student does not discontinue the inappropriate behavior.

When unusual procedures are used, *informed consent should be obtained from the client and the parents.* Informed consent presents a number of problems in that it means more than (1) that the persons have been informed of what will happen and (2) they have consented. Martin (1975) has addressed this issue and has made several suggestions for properly obtaining consent: (1) the facility should have written consent procedures; (2) the consent proceeding should be in the family's native language, at a level of comprehension appropriate to the family, and the consent papers should be delivered in oral as well as in written form; (3) the individual(s) giving consent should have been tested for their capacity to consent; (4) efforts should be made to reduce the implied coercion inherent in proceedings of this type (e.g., if you do not comply, we will remove your student from our program); and (5) the participants should be informed of risks and benefits of both the proposed and alternative procedures.

The procedure should be documented, and a description of it should be written in such a manner that allows staff training. Whoever is responsible for the procedure should read texts, research publications in journals, and other sources for strengths, weaknesses, possible problems, and the proper manner in which the procedure should be implemented. Staff should be trained and then tested to determine whether they can implement the procedure correctly. In training, the staff should be required to define the behaviors to be punished, prove through reliability checks that they can identify both when the behavior occurs and does not occur, model the implementation, complete the data-collection process, and perform the many functions indigenous to particular procedures. Through the training program, we should be able to eliminate most errors that would be unfair to the retarded individual we are trying to help.

After training, we should be certain that *implementation of the procedure is witnessed as frequently as possible.* This objective could be achieved in a number of ways. If the procedure necessitated approval by a committee, members of that committee should check periodically that the procedure is being followed correctly. Videotape recordings can also be made in many schools that have the necessary equipment. This is an excellent procedure for two reasons: (1) it provides a permanent record that can be used if persons unfairly criticize the program and say we are doing things we are not, and (2) it provides feedback for the staff who can, perhaps in a calmer moment, determine whether they are implementing the procedure the way they would describe their implementation. Another way is to ask an administrator to witness or even to help with the procedure. Be certain that she or he has been fully informed of the procedure and has approved it beforehand, but then ask for occasional assistance (this can be another way to increase your supervisor's understanding of the problems classroom or institutional teachers have—numbers and reports can have more meaning for administrators under these circumstances).

While implementing the program, we should determine *whether a goal for the termination of the program has been met.* These goals are of two types. One is for the successful completion of the program and would be a statement like "does not hit any other children for 20 consecutive days." Another is for failure of the program. This goal should recognize a point at which the program should be replaced by another, because it has not been as effective as anticipated. An appropriate statement could be "If after the first five days of treatment, John hits other children more than 10 times in 10 days, the program will be terminated and replaced by another."

A related concern is *whether an alternative procedure has been chosen should the present one fail.* While we should not convey an impression of imminent failure, we should have prepared a description of an alternative procedure should the present one fail. In this situation, we could immediately move to an alternative procedure if the present one meets our criterion of failing, and we would not have to waste time during which our client is not receiving a program for the problem behavior.

Inherent in any program is the need to *provide for generalization.* Often, programs first need to be conducted only part of the day during optimal conditions for success (e.g., when student-to-staff ratios are lowest). However, once behavior has been decreased in this area, the procedure should be implemented throughout the day in diverse areas in an attempt to bring the student's behavior under the control of various aspects of the natural environment. If the student is served by several teachers in different classrooms throughout the day, we must be very careful that all people are willing to cooperate and that they have been trained.

A final consideration is *whether an alternative response has been increased.* Many forms of inappropriate responding are either directly or indirectly related to appropriate forms of responding. In such cases, programs to reduce responding through punishment should incorporate procedures to increase appropriate responding through reinforcement (e.g., a child being punished for hitting other students should be reinforced for related appropriate social behaviors toward these students). Such combinations certainly increase the probability that reductive programs will succeed.

Aversive Conditioning[6]

Definition.   Aversive conditioning is one form of positive punishment, *a procedure in which a response produces an aversive stimulus and as a result becomes less probable.* In this sense, it is exactly like positive reinforcement in that it produces a stimulus; its difference, of course, is that punishment reduces responding, whereas reinforcement increases responding. Positive punishment occurs most frequently in one of two forms: (1) the response produces an aversive event in the environment, or (2) the response produces excessive additional response requirements. The first procedure will be discussed under this section; the second will be discussed under Overcorrection.

Examples.   Aversive conditioning has been used in a variety of settings, with a variety of behaviors, and in varying forms. It can be something as mild as a "No" when a child points to the number 5 when asked to point to the number 4, or it can be something as severe as electrical shock when a child violently bangs his head on a concrete floor. Quite obviously, the adage "the punishment should

---

[6] This procedure is somewhat different than the classical conditioning procedure called aversive conditioning and used in behavior therapy for alcohol, drug, sex, and other problems.

fit the crime" should be used as a reference; we should not be using highly aversive procedures for mildly inappropriate behaviors.

Punishment is a procedure that must be defined functionally; i.e., it must describe a reduction in behavior as a result of some contingent stimulus. Too often, we presume *a priori* that something will be punishing for someone because it has been for others. For example, if we verbally correct someone's inappropriate behavior, we might presume that we could reduce that behavior. Madsen, Becker, Thomas, Koser, and Plager (1968) tried just such a procedure while using "Sit down!" commands as a consequence for out-of-seat behavior. When the incidence of "sit down" commands increased, however, the incidence of out-of-seat behaviors also increased. A similar, although perhaps even more dramatic result, was found by Corte, Wolf, and Locke (1971), who worked with four retarded persons who had extreme self-destructive behaviors. Because DRO or extinction was either ineffective or inappropriate, the authors used electrical shock contingent upon the self-abusive responses. For three of the clients, a particular shocking device was effective. For a fourth, however, when it was first used

> the rate increased markedly, with 84 responses occurring in approximately 4.5 minutes of the session. This increase in the rate prompted substitution of . . . [a second device for the first] . . . because the former delivered higher wattage and subjectively "felt" more aversive. With the punishment of only a single response (with this device), no more responses occurred in the remaining 30 seconds of the period. The response rates obtained on the next three days were six, three, and two, respectively. Thereafter, the behavior recurred on only one occasion. (p. 210)

Electrical shock has been used on a number of occasions by behaviorists, and unfortunately the publicity surrounding its use is thousands of times greater than its incidence. With the publicity, many people have come to associate behaviorism with punishment, despite the fact that its leading proponent, B. F. Skinner, has opposed the use of punishment in our society. It has, however, been used quite effectively with very severe behavior problems, generally only of a self-abusive nature. For example, before the work by Corte *et al.*, Lovaas and his associates were working with some of the most difficult self-injurious autistic children in the country. In one study (Lovaas, Freitag, Gold, & Kassorla, 1965), they were able to control self-abusive behavior by considering it to be a learned behavior under social consequences, thus susceptible to such procedures as extinction and the reinforcement of incompatible behavior. In other situations, however, electrical shock has to be used to eliminate massive self-injurious responding (e.g., head-hitting at a rate of 30 times *per minute*). While the results are impressive and important, perhaps the rationale for using a few applications of punishment with incredibly self-destructive children who had been in restraints for a year or more is more instructive. Previously, Lovaas *et al.* (1965) found that self-destructive behavior could be suppressed by building incompatible behaviors. perhaps this would be the most humane procedure, since it involves exposing the child to minimal pain. However, the children to be treated here came from, and were to be returned to, state hospitals where maintaining incompatible behaviors was judged unfeasible. The wards were understaffed (a particular nurse having to deal with as many as 20 children) and were staffed by personnel unfamiliar with reinforcement procedures. In fact, the failure of the ward environment to provide reinforcement for alternative behaviors (coupled with the attention paid to the self-destruction) may have originally created, maintained, and increased the self-destruction. The viable alternatives, then, center on extinction by "ignoring *versus* suppression with severe aversive stimulation" (p. 144). However, extinction

> is not immediately effective and temporarily exposes the child to the danger of severe damage from his own self-destruction, which is particularly intense during the early stages of the extinction run. In some cases of severe self-destruction, it is ill-advised to place the child on extinction. Marilyn, for example, could have inflicted serious self-injury or possibly even killed herself during an extinction run. (p. 155)

Another interesting and important description of the effects of electrical shock has been provided in an excellent research and treatment study by Risley (1968). The child with whom he worked in the study was six years old, mentally retarded, labeled autistic, and brain damaged (from pneumococcal meningitis). There were many problems, but two were primary and they have been aptly described by Risley. She "would strike her three-year-old brother with an object, push him down the stairs, *etc*. . . . three or four times a day" (p. 29). In addition,

> her predominant behaviors in all situations were climbing in high places (on furniture, window sills, trees, houses, etc.), alternating with sitting and rocking rhythmically. Her climbing was a constant source of concern to her parents due to the threat to her life and limb (her body bore multiple scars from past falls; her front teeth were missing, having been left imbedded in a 2- by 4-inch molding from which she had fallen while climbing outside the second story of her house), and the attendant destruction of furniture in the house. She had attended several schools for special children but had been dropped from each because of these disruptive behaviors and her lack of progress. (p. 22)

Her parents had miraculously resisted institutionalization, believing that because of her behavior she would have to be kept in constant physical restraint on a custodial ward. However, because she was becoming so much larger, her climbing and her physical assaults on her brother caused the parents to consider institutionalization as a serious alternative. Risley began working with the child in a room in a clinic, free from the distractors typical of other environments. After unsuccessfully using timeout, extinction, and the reinforcement of incompatible behaviors, he tried electrical shock and found it to be successful in this situation. It did not, however, generalize to the home, and the mother had to use it in that environment before the behavior was eliminated. In his article, Risley makes many excellent points about the use of punishment, some of which will be discussed in the next section.

Although these studies are important and they probably used the only method that would have worked with these severe cases, they represent a very small portion of behavioral work in general. Indeed, punishment itself is not used very often in behavioral work.[7] When it is used, it is of the more common variety used by parents. The difference between the behavioral and the traditional uses of punishment is that the behavioral is more systematic and attempts to identify the effects on the target behavior and perhaps on other behaviors as well. A good illustration of this use of punishment has been provided by Koegel and Covert (1972), who used a "No!" and an occasional slap on the hands to suppress excessive stereotypic behaviors of children diagnosed autistic. Figure 11-3 shows the amount of self-stimulation under baseline and punishment conditions for two students. In both cases, stereotypic responding was eliminated. Perhaps more interesting as well as important, however, is the relationship between stereotypic responding and a learned discrimination. During the baseline phase, the mean occurrence of stereotypic responding for the first child was 60% of the time, while the mean percent of correct trials was consistently below 40%. When the inappropriate behavior was suppressed, the

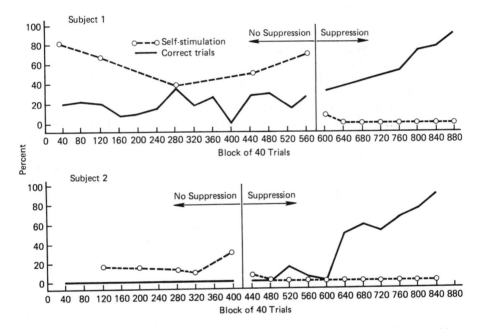

Figure 11-3. The relationship between self-stimulation and correct responding on a discrimination task by two autistic children. In each case, stereotypic responding was decreased in the suppression phase (in which the instructor said "No!" and occasionally slapped the hands after stereotypic responding). Also, in each case, the performance on the discrimination task increased markedly as soon as the stereotypic behavior was eliminated (Koegel & Covert, 1972, p. 383).

---

[7] A brief survey of the first 10 volumes of the *Journal of Applied Behavior Analysis* shows that about 2% of the articles dealt with timeout, response cost, overcorrection, or aversive conditioning. When one considers that the work in this area is usually quite dramatic and involves significant behavior problems, this publication rate of 2% probably exceeds the rate in the nonpublication world of behaviorism.

criterion of 85% correct was reached rather quickly. For the second child, the percent of stereotypic responding during baseline was 17%, while the percent of correct responding was 0%. When stereotypic responding was suppressed, this child also rather quickly reached the criterion of 85% correct within a given block of 40 trials. This study shows very clearly the value of any ethical procedure in reducing inappropriate responding that interferes with learning adaptive behaviors. When we can reduce the hyperactive behaviors, the stereotypic responding, the self-induced seizures, etc., we have a much better opportunity for teaching individuals how to live more adaptively.

Programming Aversive Conditioning. While there has been substantial work with punishment in applied settings, this work has not been directed toward advancing our understanding of what to consider while programming punishment; instead, and rightly so, it has been directed toward rapid and effective treatment. Laboratory research, on the other hand, has been able to progress more leisurely and systematically in ferreting out principles or guidelines for the use of punishment. From the work of Azrin, Holz, Hutchinson, Hake, and their colleagues, a great deal of information has been gathered about the characteristics of punishment and about the ways to maximize its effectiveness. This information is extremely important, because if we are punishing a retarded person for doing something, we are not using punishment in an ethical manner if we are not using it in a manner that will most effectively reduce the behavior. We do have a responsibility to free the individual from the punishment process as quickly as possible.

Azrin and Holz (1966), in one of the finest reviews on an operant procedure ever written, have provided us with considerable information on the characteristics and effective use of punishment. These will be discussed briefly, followed by some additional considerations developed from applied work.

1. The punishing stimulus should be arranged in a way that does not allow the student to escape from it. If it did, the student would not be lessening the frequency of inappropriate behavior, the "trick" of escaping from the teacher's proposed punishment may become a behavior that is highly reinforced, and the student may be able to repeat the target behavior in a context that earns even more reinforcement. These problems would seem to be inherent in social behaviors like stealing, cheating, disruptions, etc.

2. The punishing stimulus should be as intense as possible. We often do the opposite, trying to be kind to the student. But several studies suggest the possibility of a very important relationship between gradually increasing the severity of punishment and the point at which responding would cease. These studies showed that if we started at a low intensity and progressed through four or five values before locating the one that would eliminate behavior, that final value would be higher than the value that would have eliminated responding if we had used it initially. To illustrate, let us suppose that we decided to punish a child for talking-out by removing tokens after each response. We might have started with a cost of 1 token and found that we had to progress through a cost of 2, 4, 6, 8, and finally 10 tokens before we eliminated the talk-

outs. If, however, we had begun with a cost of 6 tokens per talk-out, we might have eliminated the behavior at that value. This suggestion does not mean that we should start all programs with maximum punishment intensities; that procedure would often be an example of behavioral overkill and could be cruel. It does mean, however, that we should be cautious not to shape a child into being more and more resistant to punishment. The issue has been discussed by Lovaas and Simmons (1969) with respect to the self-abusive children with whom they have worked:

These children have demonstrated, through their self-destruction, that they will apparently withstand considerable pain to get attention, and that they may have considerable experience with pain adaptation. To avoid selecting a neutral shock, or a weak one to which the children could adapt quickly, we have used a strong shock which guaranteed quick suppression. (p. 156)

3. The punishing stimulus should occur immediately after the response, and it should occur after every response. A few applied studies have suggested that variable-ratio punishment schedules can be effective, but again we should be trying to be maximally effective in order to keep the punishment period as short as possible.

4. We should be very careful not to associate the delivery of punishment with the delivery of reinforcement; otherwise, the punishing stimulus might acquire the properties of a conditioned reinforcer. This is a very practical problem with some adult-child interactions in which the child's primary means of gaining attention is through acting in a manner that will lead to punishment. This leads to the associated suggestion that we should make available an alternative response that will produce at least as much reinforcement as the punished response. In our situations, we should be certain that we are providing a great deal of attention for appropriate academic and social behaviors, and that we are giving no attention other than that inherent in the punishment process for the inappropriate behavior.

5. A reduction in positive reinforcement can be used when aversive conditioning is impractical for ethical, legal, or practical reasons. In these cases, Azrin and Holz suggest the use on timeout or response cost, two procedures that will be discussed in following sections of this chapter. This suggestion is an important one to follow, for we should use the least aversive procedure necessary to provide the desired results.

6. Additional considerations for programming punishment have been offered in the applied literature; one of the foremost is that which is needed to program generalization. Just as conditioned reinforcers are developed through pairings with reinforcers, so are conditioned aversive stimuli; and just as conditioned reinforcers function as antecedent stimuli (S^Ds), signaling that responding will be reinforced, so do conditioned aversive stimuli function as antecedent stimuli signaling that responding will be punished. Other environmental stimuli tend to alter behavior in the same way only to the degree that they are similar to these stimuli that are the reinforcing or punishing stimuli. This relation-

ship presents an obvious problem for punishment: punishment behaviors tend to be suppressed when the student is near the person who administers the punishment, but they may not be suppressed when that person is not present (indeed, there is even a contrast phenomenon in which behavior decreases in the presence of the conditioned aversive stimulus but increases in its absence). Risley (1968) found that the climbing behaviors that he decreased in his clinic did not decrease at home until the mother also punished her daughter's climbing. Corte, Wolf, and Locke (1971) found similar problems. When self-injurious clients were punished only in a particular room, their behaviors decreased substantially in that room, but they did not decrease in the cottages in which they lived. The authors discussed another aspect of generalization relative to one of the clients whose

rate of self-injurious behavior decreased in the presence of a fourth observer without shock, after shock was administered by three other observers. This demonstration of programmed generalization has important implications. Apparently, after punishment by three adults, the student spontaneously generalized to the fourth adult. On the other hand, the student still did not spontaneously generalize to those occasions when no observers were in view. . . . The highly specific and discriminated nature of the effects of the punishment demonstrates that profoundly retarded children can make discriminations when strong consequences are applied. (p. 212)

The same conclusion has been reached by Lovaas and Simmons (1969), who discussed the situation-specific nature of punishment, with respect both to the adults present and the other physical properties of the environment. They argue that for punishment to be maximally effective, it should be administered by more than one person in more than one setting. These findings, replicated elsewhere, provide us with some guidelines in using aversive conditioning. Clearly, for that procedure to be necessary, the behavioral problem must be a significant one, and our arrangements must provide for its maximum effectiveness. To provide only for short training sessions with no punishment scheduled the rest of the day may be research, but it can hardly be considered complete treatment.

7. In applying aversive conditioning, we should also be aware of the possibility of behavioral side effects, and we should be prepared for them. Although the adults become conditioned aversive stimuli in these situations, and although we would expect some withdrawal behaviors to be evidenced, quite the opposite often happens. Risley (1968) found increases in eye contact. Hamilton, Stevens, and Allen (1967) found their children "to be more socially outgoing, happier, and better adjusted in the ward setting" (p. 856). White and Taylor (1967) found their clients "to be more aware of and interact more with the examiner" (p. 32). Lovaas, Schaeffer, and Simmons (1965) reported similar findings and have recorded on film positive social changes that have impressed many of us.

8. Some children, however, do evidence the expected negative side effects. Several studies (e.g., Simmons and Lovaas, 1969; Meerbaum, 1973) found that the child became quite fearful of the punishing stimulus, while others reported different types of changes in the student's behavior. For example, Bucher and Lovaas (1968) reported that a child when punished would also cry and shiver, while Bucher and King (1971) reported that their child became quiet and sullen. Risley (1968) demonstrated the contrast effect for punishment when he punished the girl for climbing a bookcase and found that she increased her rate of climbing on a chair. When this behavior was punished, it too decreased rapidly. The importance of these effects is as a warning that there may be undesirable side effects for which we should be prepared. Perhaps some of these problems could be prevented or reduced by providing plenty of warmth and attention for appropriate behaviors while the inappropriate behavior is being punished.

9. A final consideration relates to the administration of the punishing stimulus itself. Be certain that the stimulus is no more than that which the child's IEP program team believes is necessary. If a "No!" is sufficient, then use just that. If you use any form of corporal punishment, be certain (1) that the failure of all other techniques has been documented, (2) that informed consent and notice have been given, (c) that all appropriate committees have agreed upon the procedure, (4) that the procedure is witnessed and that occasional videotapes are made where possible, and (5) that you have experienced the punishing stimulus yourself. If you are going to slap a child on the hand, have someone slap you harder; if you are going to ask a registered psychologist to shock a child, have someone apply the same shocking stimulus to you a number of times.

Overcorrection

Definition. Overcorrection is a punishment procedure that has gained considerable popularity this decade under the presumption that it is an educative as well as a punishment procedure. There are two components to an overcorrection program, although both are not always possible. *Restitutional overcorrection requires the individual to restore the environment she or he has just disrupted to a "better-than-before" condition.* For example, a student who throws over his chair and desk might have to put them back, straighten all chairs and tables in the room, wash each of them, wash the walls, and clean the blackboards. *Positive-practice overcorrection requires the individual to practice excessively the topographically correct forms of a behavior he or she has just emitted.* For example, a child who uses toys in a stereotypic, self-stimulatory manner might be manually guided through several minutes of appropriate toy play. The positive-practice procedure typically has four straightforward components:

(a) a verbal warning to stop engaging in the act, (b) physically stopping the episode, (c) forced practice of appropriate forms of behavior, and (d) release from forced practice. According to its originators (Azrin, Kaplan & Foxx, 1973; Foxx & Azrin, 1973), positive practice overcorrection has two functions: first, to suppress stereotypic behavior and, second, to teach and motivate the occurrence of more appropriate forms of behavior. (Wells, Forehand, Hickey, & Green, 1977, p. 679)

Examples. Azrin and Foxx and their co-workers developed the overcorrection procedure and published several demonstrations of its effectiveness with diverse behaviors. Azrin and Foxx (1971) designed a toilet training program for retarded persons (later adopted for nonretarded children) that was interesting in its completeness. One electronic device was made that signaled when a client urinated or defecated in his shorts, while another device was made that signaled when a client urinated or defecated in a toilet. As a result, all recording of correct and incorrect responding was automated, and all behaviors could be consequated immediately. The program utilized massed practice, occurring 8 hours per day during which the clients drank fluids every half-hour. A DRO procedure was used in which clients were given food and praise every 5 minutes while dry. Dressing and undressing skills were taught during toileting. Modeling was utilized as clients were taught in groups. Correct toileting was positively reinforced and was maximized by initially having the client on the toilet 20 of every 30 minutes. Incorrect responses were punished by the overcorrection procedure and by a 1-hour timeout. The overcorrection procedure generally required about 20 minutes during which the client cleaned himself, his clothes, and the physical area, showered, and dressed. After the clients were toilet trained, a maintenance program was begun to ensure that all the training was not wasted. Figure 11-4 lists both the training and the maintenance programs and provides an outline of the multiplicity of procedures involved.

Azrin, Kaplan, and Foxx (1973) used the positive practice portion of overcorrection to reduce stereotypic responding of nine severely or profoundly retarded persons. Six of the individuals engaged in body-rocking; two demonstrated side-to-side head-weaving; two exhibited stereotypic head movements; and three engaged in complex finger movements (four of the nine engaged in more than one of these autistic behaviors). During the "autism reversal" program, clients were reinforced for correct incompatible behaviors and were punished by the positive practice procedure for stereotypic responding. When a stereotypic response occurred, an instructor verbally reprimanded the student, and then stood behind the client while guiding him or her through the autism reversal procedure for 20 minutes.

Residents who engaged in autistic head-weaving were required by instructions and manual guidance to maintain their heads in each of three postures: the head held upward, the head held straight, and the head held downward. Residents who rocked their body were required to practice maintaining their shoulders in two postures: shoulders forward away from the chair, and shoulders back against the chair as in a normal sitting position. Residents who engaged in autistic hand-movements consisting of hand-gazing and paper-flipping were required to maintain their hands in each of three postures: hands extended above the head, hands outstretched from the sides of the body, and hands held to the sides of the body. Autistic finger and thumb movements consisting of cloth-rolling, string-threading and pill-rolling were followed immediately by required practice in sustaining two

---

.OUTLINE OF THE TOILET TRAINING PROCEDURE

I. When no accidents occur:
1. Resident seated in chair when not seated on toilet bowl
2. Resident drinks fluids every half hour
3. Scheduled toileting of resident every half hour
4. Resident given edible and social reinforcer every 5 minutes while dry
5. Shaping of undressing and dressing during toileting
6. Resident given edible and social reinforcer following elimination in toilet bowl, and returned to chair

II. When accidents occur:
1. Trainer disconnects pants alarm
2. Trainer obtains resident's attention
3. Resident walks to laundry area to obtain fresh clothing
4. Resident undresses himself
5. Resident walks to nearby shower, receives shower, and dresses himself
6. Resident obtains mop or cloth and cleans soiled area on chair or floor
7. Resident handwashes soiled pants, wrings pants out, and hangs pants up to dry
8. Trainer removes resident's chair from use
9. 1-hour timeout procedures:
    (a) no edibles or social reinforcers every 5 minutes
    (b) no fluids every 30 minutes
    (c) chair not available
    (d) continue 30 minute scheduled toilet periods

POST TRAINING MAINTENANCE PROCEDURE

I. General procedure:
1. Advance assignment of one attendant for Toilet Responsibility each shift
2. Snack period between breakfast and lunch and between lunch and dinner
3. Resident's pants inspected at mealtime, snacktime, and bedtime (six times daily)
4. Attendant initials record sheet when resident is checked; record sheet sent directly to supervisor
5. Discontinued use of both apparatuses for detecting eliminations

II. When accidents occur:
1. Cleanliness training whenever an accident was detected:
    (a) Resident walks to laundry area to obtain fresh clothing
    (b) Resident undresses himself
    (c) Resident walks to nearby shower, receives shower, and dresses himself
    (d) Resident obtains mop or cloth and cleans soiled area on chair or floor
    (e) Resident handwashes soiled pants, wrings pants out, and hangs pants up to dry
2. Delay of meal for 1 hour if accident was prior to meal
3. Omission of snacks if accident was prior to snack
4. Attendant initials and records each accident

Minimal maintenance—starts 8 weeks after training:
1. Inspections only at mealtime and bedtime
2. Cleanliness training given for accidents

Termination of maintenance procedure—when resident is continent for at least 1 month:
1. No regular inspections for that patient
2. Cleanliness training given for accidents when detected

Figure 11-4. An outline of the teaching and maintenance programs for the Azrin and Foxx method of toilet training (Azrin & Foxx, 1971, p. 91 and p. 94).

postures: either the hands held together or the hands held apart. The residents were required to maintain their thumbs in an upright position away from their fingers at approximately a 90° angle in both positions. (p. 243)

The overcorrection procedure has proliferated since these studies and has been used with a number of different behaviors. For example, Azrin and Wesolowski (1974) worked with 34 retarded persons who frequently stole items from one another. In a correction procedure, the clients returned stolen items and apologized; this procedure resulted in about 20 thefts per day. In an overcorrection procedure, the clients returned the stolen items and gave the victim in addition an item identical to the one returned. This procedure eliminated thefts by the fourth day. Searching behaviors (carefully and thoroughly touching floors, sofas, cabinets, etc.) have been reduced by an overcorrection program of having the client wash his hands for extended periods (Rusch, Close, Hops & Agosta, 1976). Vomiting has been eliminated by requiring the client for 20 minutes to wash her face with cold water, to wash the floor, window sills, and walls, to take off her soiled clothes, and to dress (Duker & Seys, 1977). Throwing small objects into the face of other clients and of staff was reduced by a 5-minute episode involving (1) apologizing to the offended person, and (2) picking up objects and placing them in a trash can (Matson & Stephens, 1977). The list of behaviors is quite extensive, and its size is interesting as unlike other reductive procedures, overcorrection sometimes requires inventiveness in determining how to overcorrect some behaviors.

Programming Overcorrection. Overcorrection is one of the newer procedures and is undergoing a familiar evolution in which something is first viewed as very positive, but then, under scrutiny, is viewed more cautiously. In this section, we shall discuss some ways to make overcorrection more effective, as well as some cautionary notes.

1. The proponents of overcorrection believe that it is an educative procedure in which the individual learns appropriate forms of behavior through positive practice. While this point is suspect, programming an overcorrection behavior that is topographically *related* to the inappropriate behavior would seem only to have neutral or positive effects; it would not seem to have negative effects. Following this premise, we would, for example, not use the head posturing portion of the autism reversal procedure for a behavior like hand movements; that procedure instead would be used for something like head-weaving.
2. As with all reductive procedures, overcorrection should be applied immediately and after every response. Care should also be taken to maximize generalization, which could be addressed by involving more than one person in the procedure and by applying the procedure in as many locales as possible. In addition, we should be careful not to make portions of the procedure reinforcing (particularly the attention and the physical contact), or else we place the individual in the situation of gaining both punishment and reinforcement through inappropriate re-

sponding. To that end, we should provide both verbal and physical attention for appropriate behaviors, so that the client has appropriate means for gaining access to reinforcement.

3. Because overcorrection involves physical guidance by staff for extended periods, it is often a very aversive procedure to those involved. When a single individual is guiding a student through the autism reversal procedure for several 20-minute segments each day, he or she is likely to become highly intolerant of any behavior of the student. To reduce the likelihood of undue punishment associated with this procedure, we should schedule a rotation across staff every 4 or 5 minutes. If this is not possible, we should either use short overcorrection periods, or we should not use the procedure at all.

4. Short overcorrection periods are not, however, likely to be as effective as long overcorrection periods simply because the latter is more aversive. Doleys, Wells, Hobbs, Roberts, and Cartelli (1976) found that 40-second positive practice periods were not particularly effective in suppressing noncompliance. This finding does not mean that 4 or 5 minutes would also have been ineffective and that only 20 minutes would have been effective. It does, however, suggest that short periods may not be as effective as long ones. As such, intermediate or long periods might be more effective, but they would require at least one person just to work with this particular client. The effects of this requirement on other clients' programs must be analyzed before overcorrection is chosen.

5. Although overcorrection should be concerned with topographically similar behaviors if it is truly to be used as an educative process, it need not be. We can use an "overcorrection procedure" on an unrelated response and be just as effective. For example, after developing a "hand" overcorrection procedure that reduced a child's pounding objects with his hands, Epstein, Doke, Sajwaj, Sorrell, and Rimmer (1974) used the same procedure to reduce inappropriate vocalizations and inappropriate foot movements. The authors concluded that "it would be difficult to attribute the treatment effects to the development of 'positive practice' behaviors" (p. 390). Results such as these suggest that the principal effects of overcorrection might be from the aversive aspects of positive practice and/or restitutional overcorrection.

6. *Because* overcorrection may work principally *because of* a punishment component, it may represent more of an aversive procedure than is actually necessary. For example, with three clients on whom 20-minute overcorrection periods were ineffective when programmed over a two-week period, we used an aversive taste solution (reconstituted lemon juice) and immediately suppressed self-injurious behaviors. Since then we have used this procedure (in which the teacher simply squirts the solution into the child's mouth contingent upon stereotypic or self-abusive responding) several times with considerable success. The procedure is quite rapid and is much less aversive in the sense that teachers don't become irritable, and children don't cry and struggle as in the overcorrection procedure.

7. All procedures are capable of producing side effects, and overcorrection has been shown to do so. Some effects are positive; e.g., Epstein *et al.*, (1974) showed that appropriate toy play increased when inappropriate self-stimulation decreased. However, there are more reports of negative side effects than of positive ones. In the same study, Epstein *et al.* showed that inappropriate foot movements increased when inappropriate vocalizations were suppressed. This type of side effect can be "explained away," however, as simply behavior that might occur, and that could also be eliminated or perhaps even prevented by reinforcing a great deal of appropriate behavior during the days or weeks overcorrection is in effect. There are, however, other negative side effects that are indigenous to overcorrection, because it is an aversive procedure that often requires a teacher to physically guide the student through extended periods of movement. Matson and Stephens (1977) reported an overcorrection procedure in which a woman was required to pick up trash for 5 minutes in the day room or hallways and place it in a garbage can. She "was manually guided through required activities when she refused to carry them out. Guidance was discontinued after a few sessions, since she voluntarily began performing the desired response. On occasion during the first few days of overcorrection, she became so disruptive that it was impossible to guide her through overcorrection without a physical struggle" (p. 561). Rollings, Baumeister, and Baumeister (1977) found that "During the application of overcorrection procedures the student exhibited several previously unobserved behaviors. These 'new' behaviors included self-pinching, self-scratching, complex finger manipulations, and screaming. . . . In addition, head-banging was observed during the last two sessions of training. At this point, training was terminated for fear of injury to the subject" (p. 35).

8. In addition to the negative side effects, one of the major problems with overcorrection is that, being a newly developed procedure, it has not been researched as fully as we would like. This problem has been well stated by Rollings *et al.* (1977), who disagreed with the statements of Foxx and Azrin (1973) concerning the success of overcorrection relative to other procedures:

(a) overcorrection procedures, applied contingently on the occurrence of stereotyped behavior, may produce deceleration in rate of that behavior, but the magnitude of the effect varies considerably between subjects; (b) punishment and nonpunishment conditions are well discriminated by the subject, partly on the basis of trainer proximity; (c) increased collateral stereotypic and emotional responding may accompany deceleration of target behaviors; (d) no spontaneous generalization of suppression is observed from training to living areas; and (e) suppression effects obtained under the procedures employed here are not durable. In general, we may conclude that the overcorrection procedure is actually a very complex package of contingencies and that the effects on behavior may also be complex. (pp. 42-43)

Timeout

Definition. *Timeout is a procedure in which a response removes access to reinforcement for a specified period of time.* The presumption is that timeout will reduce responding, but it does not always do so. When it does, it is a punishment procedure; when it does not, it is not considered a punishment procedure for that individual in that situation. While there are a number of variations to the timeout procedure, they all differ from the positive punishment procedure in that something is removed from the environment contingent upon responding. They also differ from the extinction procedure in applied studies in that the period for no reinforcement in timeout is response contingent, whereas the period for no reinforcement in extinction does not occur as the result of a response by the client.

Examples. There are many ways in which timeout is programmed in applied settings, five of which are (1) ignoring, (2) isolation, (3) removal of materials (4) withdrawal, and (5) contingent observation. *Ignoring* involves removing adult attention for responding and is based on the assumption that attention is a reinforcer. It is a very common procedure in teaching retarded persons discriminations and involves looking away when the student makes an error. The extent to which the removal of attention is augmented by the differential feedback of a teacher looking away is unknown, but the combined procedure is easy to use and appears at least mildly effective. Other behaviors are also appropriate for this procedure. Risley and Wolf (1967) used ignoring as a consequence for temper tantrums and hyperactivity. Wasik, Senn, Welch, and Cooper (1969) directed a teacher to withhold social attention by turning away from two girls whenever they were noncompliant, passively watched others work, "checked on" what others were doing, or engaged in a variety of attention-seeking behaviors.

Isolation is similar to ignoring except that the individual is removed from the reinforcing environment for a specified period of time. It may be the most common form of timeout and has become almost synonymous with the procedure. It is also one of the most overused of the behavioral procedures, with so many schools and institutions having special timeout rooms. The procedure has been used to reduce a variety of behaviors, including out-of-seat and aggressive behaviors in a classroom (Drabman & Spitalnik, 1973), aggressive or oppositional behavior (Hawkins, Peterson, Schweid & Bijou, 1966), and children's oppositional behaviors to parental requests in the home (Wahler, 1969), to name but a few.

Removal of materials is similar in that the client cannot obtain reinforcement, but in this case the materials are removed from the client rather than the client from the materials. This is the basic home remedy of "If you don't play nicely with your toys, I'm going to take them away from you!" This procedure is, of course, often used but perhaps too frequently in an unsystematic manner. A systematic use was provided by Barton, Guess, Garcia, and Baer (1970), who removed food trays from retarded persons whenever they engaged in a variety of inappropriate eating behaviors.

Withdrawal of the environment is another variation, with the teacher being removed in this case. We have used this procedure in an early childhood class when a child has been disruptive, choosing to move the children and the teacher to another table rather than removing the disruptive child. The bases for this alternative are that removing a disruptive child from a table must include some physical attention and that removing a child while she or he is being aggressive ·can lead to further problems. A variation of this procedure has been provided by Foxx and Shapiro (1978), who developed it as an alternative to timeout procedures in which the child was removed from the learning environment. In their procedure, severely retarded children were given different-colored ribbons to wear, with a ribbon serving as a signal that the wearer would receive praise and edibles every few minutes. In the timeout period, all forms of teacher reinforcement and participation in activities were discontinued for 3 minutes; the student did, however, remain in the room. The misbehavior reduced substantially, and the procedure appears to be a very simple and efficient one.

Contingent observation, another variation of timeout, is similar to Foxx and Shapiro's technique in that it involves a period in which the student is present but does not participate. The procedure was demonstrated (Porterfield, Herbert-Jackson & Risley, 1976) with a group of children, one to three years old, who were in a day-care program and who displayed a number of inappropriate behaviors, including aggression, crying and fussing, tantruming, destructive use of toys, and creating dangerous situations (e.g., by climbing on a counter). Whenever one of these behaviors occurred, a four-part contingent observation procedure was begun in which the teacher (1) described the form and the inappropriateness of the behavior to the child, (2) moved the child to the periphery of the activity and instructed the child to observe the appropriate behaviors of the other children, (3) returned to the child after about 1 minute, asked whether he knew how to play properly, etc., and returned him to the group if he replied correctly, and (4) immediately gave him attention when he behaved properly back in the group. Contingent attention was quite effective and appears to be an attractive alternative for use with small children because it is short in duration, retains the child in the environment, and revolves in part at least about the positive aspects of behaving rather than the negative aspects of timeout.

Programming Timeout.   Because timeout is an aversive procedure, it requires many of the same precautions that aversive conditioning and overcorrection require. It is, however, a much milder procedure, and such variations as contingent observation, removal of materials, and ignoring appear to be innocuous, common sense, and without any significant deprivations. When a student is removed from the natural environment to a timeout room, however, other procedures should first have been tried, permission should have been obtained, and the other precautions for punishment should have been taken. There are, however, other considerations indigenous to timeout.

1.   Data must be taken to ensure that the timeout procedure is, in fact, a reductive procedure, for it is not always so. In fact, it can sometimes function like a positive reinforcer. In laboratory studies, Azrin (1961) showed that when response requirements were high (FR 200), the subjects responded to produce periods of timeout. A similar result was

produced by Thompson (1964), who showed again that a high response requirement (for reinforcement) can become aversive and that subjects will work to produce timeouts. These findings suggest an important consideration for us in our work with retarded individuals. When using timeout, we should be certain that the learning environment is not aversive, and that we are presenting praise, tokens, feedback, or whatever, fairly often.

A similar result has been demonstrated by Plummer, Baer, and LeBlanc (1977), who were concerned with the disruptive behaviors produced by children placed in a special class because of behavior problems. The behaviors included (1) hoarding play materials, (2) grabbing play materials, (3) leaving activities, (4) self-instructions, and (5) tantrums. In an ABA design, the A phases combined a 1-minute timeout (no teacher attention) with teacher instructions that were spaced about 2 minutes apart; the B phase involved only the paced instructions. One would expect inappropriate responding to be less during the timeout phases, but just the opposite occurred. The students apparently misbehaved in order to "timeout" teacher instructions for 1 minute. The study was replicated with the eating behaviors of a five-year-old boy diagnosed as autistic, brain damaged, and retarded. "When the procedural timeout for inappropriate eating (Condition II) was implemented, the percentage of one teacher's instructions to eat followed by inappropriate behavior increased from 8% at the end of Condition I to 50% during the last two sessions of Condition II" (p. 698). If we intended to increase a behavior, and found that it changed from 8 to 50%, we would probably be quite pleased. But to have increased an inappropriate behavior by such an amount with a procedure commonly believed to reduce responding is perhaps astounding. This demonstration should remind us that a functional analysis of the relationship between behavior and the environment should be made, and that to institute a supposedly reductive procedure without concomitant data gathering could be a serious error.

2. A consistent finding has been that timeout is either ineffective or minimally effective unless the individual has an alternative response available to obtain reinforcement (Azrin & Holz, 1966). This means that, if we suspect that a child is acting out, being aggressive, etc., in order to gain attention, we should teach that child appropriate means of gaining attention and we should be sure that attention is provided when he or she does behave appropriately.

3. The length of the timeout interval should be specified beforehand. An appropriate length is highly individualistic, but we should realize that extended timeout periods (e.g., 30 minutes) can be highly reinforcing. The child might sleep, masturbate, sing, daydream, etc., to the extent that what we believe is "timeout from reinforcement" actually becomes "time-in for reinforcement." A problem with timeout durations has been demonstrated by White, Nielsen, and Johnson (1972), who showed that (1) when 1-minute timeout periods preceded 15- and 30-minute periods in an ABACADA design, the 1-minute period was as effective as the others, and (b) when the 1-minute period followed

either the 30-minute, or both the 15- and the 30-minute periods, it increased behavior above baseline levels and actually functioned as a reinforcer.

4. Although it is not always done, some observation of what happens during timeout should be made. Finch, Wallace, and Davis (1976) consequated 16 behaviors of four individuals with brief periods of timeout. They found that timeout was effective in producing lowered rates after timeout compared to before timeout. However, for two of the individuals, the frequency of the consequated behaviors actually increased *during* the timeout period. One individual,

> when placed in timeout, would yell obscenities out the window of the timeout room or would talk in the delusioned manner which had just been consequated with timeout. [Another] . . . would also begin to yell and talk delusionally, and would increase his manipulation of clothing, rubbing of his body, and flailing of his arms. Arm flailing and loud, delusional speech were indeed those behaviors consequated by timeout. [A third individual] . . . would stand in one corner of the room and bite the thick callus on his right index finger. [He would also] . . . destroy what little property was available in the room. He kicked a hole in the wall, bent the grillwork on the windows, tore his clothes, and ripped the buttons off his shirt. (p. 412)

These behaviors quite clearly indicate that we must be careful about whom we choose to place in timeout. Such behaviors as these certainly cannot be allowed to continue; however, when we do intervene, we are providing attention that may well be reinforcing. In such cases, we should make predictions about what our clients are likely to do in timeout. Should behaviors like these be predicted with some degree of certainty, timeout is probably an inappropriate procedure.

Solnick, Rincover, and Peterson (1977) found a similar problem with behaviors occurring during timeout and found again that the procedure actually functioned like a reinforcer. They worked with a six-year-old autistic, retarded girl who during free time in the classroom and on the playground displayed 0% social behavior, 0% appropriate play, and 100% self-stimulatory behavior. During teaching sessions and in other periods of the day, she engaged in moderate-rate tantrums. To consequate tantrums, the instructor placed the child in timeout. During baseline, the child engaged in tantrums zero to three times per day, but during the timeout phase, she steadily increased tantrums to a high of 33 per day. The results were then repeated in an ABAB fashion. The authors did note, however, that during timeout the girl engaged in stereotypic responding 100% of the time. In essence, we have here an unusual demonstration of the Premack principle in which the child engaged in a low-rate behavior (tantrums) in order to gain access to a situation which would allow a high-rate behavior (stereotypic responding) to occur. The point again is that we need to observe what happens during timeout and to assess whether timeout is in effect decreasing responding.

5. Another consideration is the schedule of the timeout procedure; i.e., does it occur on an FR schedule, a VR, etc. The most effective

procedure appears to be one in which every response is consequated with timeout. However, for behaviors that have been decreased, intermittent schedules of timeout (e.g., VR3, VR4) are almost as effective as a continuous schedule (Clark, Rowbury, Baer & Baer, 1973). This would suggest that the timeout procedure, used as an intermittent schedule, might be more manageable than expected for a teacher responsible for several students.

6. Another consideration is the difference between timeout and seclusion, which is wholly inappropriate for use with our clients. Timeout involves a short period of time, whereas seclusion involves long periods of time. Isolation timeout, which is similar to seclusion, is nevertheless conducted quite differently. A client should never be locked in a room and left alone. Rather, a staff member should be just outside the room and should be able to supervise the person so that no self-injuries would occur. Timeout should also end after a short specified period of appropriate behavior, such as sitting quietly for 10 minutes. In short, timeout should be a period without reinforcement rather than a period of extended social and physical deprivation. It is not at all meant to be a cruel procedure; it is meant only to indicate to the individual that she or he has not behaved appropriately.

Response Cost

Definition. *Response cost is a procedure in which a response leads to the removal of some portion of accumulated reinforcement.* It differs from timeout in that timeout is concerned with a timed period in which one *cannot earn* reinforcement, whereas response cost is concerned with the loss of *already earned* reinforcement. It is a very common procedure in our lives and occurs in diverse areas. Football teams are penalized for rule infractions and lose reinforcement (yardage) that they have previously earned. Students who return library books late may be fined. Speeders may be fined if they are caught by police. People who cash checks for more than is in their checking account are sometimes assessed a charge by their bank. While response cost has certainly been used in our societies for hundreds of years, we have only been studying its effects in educational programs for the last 10 or 15 years.

Examples. Response cost has been used to suppress disruptions, academic errors, speech disfluencies, and practically every other type of behavior common to educational programs. It has been used alone or in combination with reinforcement, overcorrection, timeout, and many other procedures. Although it need not be restricted to such situations, response cost is most often used in token programs. This is one of its advantages, as the loss of tokens can be regulated to the student's rate of earning tokens, and the punishment system can be made quite fair to the student's own economy. Most systems require students to earn tokens (e.g., for correct academic performance) and then withdraw tokens for inappropriate responding. A few, however, provide the tokens noncontingently at the beginning of a period and then withdraw tokens for incorrect responding. An example has been provided by Greene and Pratt (1972), who throughout 11 classes for retarded persons used response cost to reduce rudeness, insulting remarks, obscenities, refusals to follow directions, and creating a disturbance. During the response cost procedure, each class was informed that

> (a) the last half hour of their school day would be reserved for a reward period in a special room where they could play records, dance, play games, etc.; (b) a cardboard "clock" would be hung at the front of each class, set for the time the reward period was to begin (either 10:55 or 2:55); (c) each misbehavior in the classroom (intentionally left somewhat vague) would cause the entire class to lose a minute of the reward period; (d) each teacher would reset his clock to demonstrate how each misbehavior delayed the starting time for the reward period and simultaneously extended the amount of time spent in academic work. (p. 34)

This procedure was particularly interesting on two counts: (1) it developed a procedure that could be used in a departmentalized program in which students did not remain with the same teacher all day, and (2) it developed a simple means for conveying the loss of time to retarded persons that was evidently quite effective. Not all examples of response cost, however, have used specific token-exchange programs. Hall, Axelrod, Foundopoulos, Shellman, Campbell, and Cranston (1972) distributed slips of paper with the boy's name at the beginning of a lesson. When a student whined, cried, or complained that he had been given an academic assignment, the slip of paper was removed. These behaviors were rapidly suppressed, and the "emotionally disturbed" students displayed fewer of the behaviors that had contributed to such a label. Most interestingly, however, the slips of paper had no exchange value at the end of the lesson. Students with slips could not exchange them for free time, special activities, trinkets, etc. Because merely having the paper at the end of the period maintained the absence of inappropriate behavior, we can presume that it had become a reinforcer. Such a finding should suggest to us that complete token economies, so prevalent today, are sometimes not necessary and represent "behavioral overkill."

Programming Response Cost. Many of the ways in which response cost should be programmed are similar to the ways other punishment procedures should be administered. Some of these include consequating each response immediately, providing for each student the rules of the economy, and providing as little social attention with the delivery of the consequence. Other considerations are particularly related to response cost.

1. Some assessment of each student's economy should be made in order to determine the amount of the fine for each inappropriate response. When students earn tokens for correct responding, we should collect two types of data during baseline: (1) the number of tokens earned per day, and (2) the number of inappropriate responses per day. Working with averages of each of these, we can calculate the maximum fine that would still leave the student with some tokens. The problem, of course, is that if a student loses more tokens than he or she has accumulated, the only way responding could be fined would be through "future tokens." This procedure is probably not a good one as the reinforcing value of these tokens might be decreased.

2. The amount of the fine should probably be as great as possible, while still within the guidelines of the first point. Burchard and Barrera (1972), for example, showed that a fine of 30 points was more effective than a fine of 5 points in reducing antisocial behaviors of five of the six retarded persons with whom they worked. For the sixth, however, the relationship was in the opposite direction. The authors suggest that the latter finding resulted from this person's particular reinforcement history. Regardless of the reason, this study suggests that stronger fines are more effective, but it also suggests (once again) that relationships between behavior of individuals and the environment are unique, and that we must regard them as unique.

3. As with other procedures, response cost can be used alone or in conjunction with other procedures (e.g., timeout, overcorrection). The most frequent question, however, is whether to use it alone or in conjunction with a reinforcement program. An answer to that question has been provided by Kazdin (1977) and his answer is a good one:

> Generally, the desirability of using a punishment system rather than a reinforcement system can be questioned. Thus, it might be useful to consider response cost as an adjunct to an overall reinforcement system. The reason for this recommendation is that punishment is sometimes associated with undesirable side effects. . . . Perhaps, however, the main reason for recommending response cost as an adjunct rather than an end in its own right is that response cost is a punishment procedure, and as such, emphasizes what the client is not supposed to do. Punishment alone is not likely to result in the development of prosocial behaviors. On the other hand, reinforcement for specific target behaviors is likely to develop prosocial responses as alternatives for the behaviors to be suppressed. (p. 73)

The addition of reinforcement to a response-cost program has indeed been demonstrated to be more effective than just response cost alone (Clark, Greene, Macrae, McNees, Davis & Risley, 1977; Phillips, Phillips, Fixsen & Wolf, 1971).

4. Another interesting aspect of combining reinforcement with response cost has been discussed by Iwata and Bailey (1974), who compared the effects of reward and response cost in an elementary special-education class. While they found both procedures to be effective, a more interesting finding was that the reward procedure resulted in an increase in the teachers' approving comments while the cost procedure did not. We have long recognized that token programs can change teacher behaviors, and this study suggests the relative importance of positive to negative procedures in this context.

5. Students can also be taught that the absence of response cost is a positive accomplishment. In what amounts to a DRO procedure, Doty, McInnis, and Paul (1974) addressed the problem of fines exceeding earnings by using proportional payoff schedules contingent upon time without new fines. This bonus system can be used regardless of whether a problem with excessive fines exists, and it would seem to be a way of making a response cost system at least a little positive.

BEHAVIOR MODIFYING DRUGS

Behavior modifying drugs are not a "behavioral" approach to changing behavior; they represent a medical approach. The term may be confusing, but it represents the interests of both groups: to change behavior to acceptable levels. The behaviorist generally prefers to engineer these changes without medications, relying instead on the effects of the natural environment. This approach is a natural one for applied behaviorists, because their training is usually concerned with events that influence learning and performance.[8] The drug-based approach is just as natural for medical professionals, as their training is usually concerned in part with the effects of drugs. The purpose of this section is not to argue the merits of either approach. Rather, it is to accept that drugs are frequently used with retarded persons and to (1) briefly describe the purposes of these drugs, (2) present a brief description of medications frequently used with our clients, (3) discuss some of the means for regulating drug use, and (4) present a few representative studies, some of which compare drug and behavioral approaches.

Purposes of Behavior-Modifying Drugs

While there are many objectives one may have for drugs administered to our clients, three of the most common are (1) to reduce learned problem behaviors, (2) to reduce "psychotic" or "neurotic" behaviors, and (3) to reduce problems stemming from organic dysfunctions (Cox et al., 1976). As learned behaviors *are learned* in the context of the environment and are, therefore, controlled by antecedent and subsequent events, the most successful way of treating them may be by environmental changes. In addition, although learning is biochemical and drugs change biochemistry, most of the corresponding brain activity is located in the cerebral cortex, which is not affected by behavior-modifying drugs. However, some behaviors (e.g., aggression) are related to areas of the brain (e.g., the limbic system) which can be affected by drugs. The effect of the medications in these cases is not to change learned behavior, but rather to lessen the chances that areas such as the limbic system will be activated when the environmental cues for those behaviors are present.

Although most retarded persons are neither psychotic nor neurotic, some display the behaviors to which psychiatrists and clinical psychologists attach these labels. In many of these cases, doctors prescribe major tranquilizers or antipsychotic drugs, which appear to decrease the frequency with which these individuals view the world in a distorted manner. While the results of these drugs are by no means perfect, they do produce the medically desired changes in most cases.

About two decades ago, the term "minimal brain damage" was a popular hypothetical construct used to explain learning abnormalities of otherwise normal children. The hypothesis of brain damage has also been applied to some

---

[8] There are, however, several behaviorists who conduct excellent basic research on the effects of drugs on molar behavior and on neural changes, e.g., Dews and his associates at Harvard University Medical School.

retarded persons with a great deal more support, since there are many medically documented cases of brain damage. With other individuals, however, there remains only the hypothesis or suspicion that some organic dysfunction exists. A great many studies have clearly shown that damage to the amygdala, the hypothalamus, and the septal region of the brain can have significant effects on behavior. With these individuals, various types of "noise" appear to lead to bizarre and aggressive behaviors. Medications used to combat these problems are believed to raise the threshold for stimulation, as well as normalize brain waves. Other retarded individuals do not have fully developed brains. With these individuals, drugs are also used to lessen the probability that certain areas of the brain will overreact and that behavioral extremes will occur.

Medications Frequently Used with Retarded Persons

Hundreds of types of drugs are administered to retarded persons. There are, however, some types that are most commonly used. These can be classified as (1) major tranquilizers, (2) minor tranquilizers, (3) antidepressants, (4) sedatives and hypnotics, and (5) analeptics. Figure 11-5 presents the types of drugs commonly given within these classifications. This listing is by no means complete; it is, however, representative.

That these and other drugs can produce or help to produce beneficial results is certainly true. However, too often there is insufficient follow-up to indicate objectively the beneficial effects as well as the side effects, despite the fact that drug manufacturers often provide clear warnings. For example, the drug Thorazine is certainly one of the most frequently used medications, yet its possible side effects are generally ignored. They include

> may impair mental and/or physical abilities, especially during the first few days of therapy. . . . Safety for the use of Thorazine during pregnancy has not been established . . . [and] the possibility of permanent neurological damage (to the test animals' offspring) cannot be excluded. . . . should be administered cautiously to persons with cardiovascular or liver disease. . . . should be used with caution in patients with chronic respiratory disorders such as severe asthma, emphysema, and acute respiratory infections, particularly in children. Because Thorazine can suppress the cough reflex, aspiration of vomitus is possible. . . . Use with caution in persons who will be exposed to extreme heat, and in persons receiving atropine or related drugs. . . . Thorazine may mask signs of overdosage of toxic drugs and may obscure conditions such as intestinal obstruction and brain tumor. . . . Drowsiness, usually mild to moderate, may occur, particularly during the first or second week. . . . Observe patients regularly for sudden appearance of sore throat or other signs of infection. . . . EKG changes— particularly nonspecific, usually reversible—have been observed in some patients. . . . Neuromuscular reactions, closely resembling parkinsonism, and motor restlessness have occurred most frequently in psychiatric patients receiving high dosages. . . . rhythmical involuntary movements of the tongue, face, mouth, or jaw [may occur] . . . and there is no known treatment. . . . Psychotic symptoms and catatonic-like states have been reported rarely. Convulsive seizes (*petit mal* and *grand mal*) have been reported . . . Avoid undue exposure to sun (allergic reactions.) Occasional dry mouth, nasal congestion,

DRUG	USES[1]
I. Major Tranquilizers	
A. Phenothiazines	
1. Thorazine[2] (chlorpromazine hydrochloride)[3]	1. psychotic disorders 2. hyperactivity or aggressiveness[4]
2. Mellaril (thioridazine hydrochloride)	1. psychotic disorders 2. moderate to marked depression 3. hyperactivity or aggressiveness[4]
3. Prolixin (fluphenazine decanoate)	1. psychotic disorders
4. Serentil (mesoridazine besylate)	1. emotional withdrawal; hallucinations 2. hyperactivity and uncooperativeness
5. Stelazine (trifluoperazine)	1. psychotic disorders 2. excessive anxiety, tension; agitation
B. Non-Phenothiazines	
1. Haldol (haloperidol)	1. psychotic disorders 2. tics and verbalizations associated with Gilles de la Tourette's syndrome
2. Navane (thiothixene)	1. psychotic disorders
II. Minor Tranquilizers	
1. Atarax (hydroxyzine)	1. anxiety; tension 2. hyperactivity
2. Vistaril (hydroxyzine)	1. anxiety; tension 2. hyperactivity
3. Equanil (meprobamate)	1. anxiety; tension; resulting sleeplessness
4. Librium (chlordiazepoxide)	1. anxiety; tension
5. Valium (diazepam)	1. anxiety; tension 2. spasticity (e.g., from cerebral palsy)

DRUG	USES[1]
III. Antidepressants	
1. Elavil (amitriptyline hydrochloride)	1. depression
2. Tofranil (imipramine hydrochloride)	1. depression
	2. childhood enuresis
IV. Sedatives and Hypnotics	
A. Barbiturates	
1. Seconal (secobarbital)	1. acute convulsive disorders
	2. anxiety; tension
2. Amytal (amobarbital)	1. anxiety; tension
3. Nembutal (penobarbital)	1. anxiety; tension
4. Luminal (phenobarbital)	1. anxiety; tension
	2. convulsions
	3. insomnia
B. Non-Barbiturates	
1. Noctec (chloral hydrate)	1. anxiety
	2. insomnia
2. Doriden (glutethimide)	1. insomnia
V. Analeptics	
1. Dexedrine (dextroamphetamine sulfate)	1. hyperactivity (with minimal brain damage)
2. Ritalin (methyphenidate hydrochloride)	1. hyperactivity (with minimal brain damage)

[1]Uses according to the *Physicians' Desk Reference.*
[2]Brand names.
[3]Generic names.
[4]Possible, but not proved, indications.

Figure 11-5. Drugs and dosages commonly administered to retarded individuals.

constipation, urinary retention . . . [occur]. Skin pigmentary changes . . . and eye changes . . . [have occurred in patients on high doses for several years]. (*Physicians' Desk Reference*, 1978, p. 1582).

Regulating Drug Use

Thorazine is not at all atypical in its list of possible side effects, and such possibilities present two problems. The first is that no matter how well a drug company tests its product, it cannot account for all the possible effects either when administered alone or in combination with other drugs. The second problem is that the person prescribing the drug (a physician) is not the person monitoring the drug's effects (a teacher or other staff members). In many cases, effects are not monitored at all, while in others they are not monitored thoroughly. In most cases, the persons working with the clients are either not familiar with the possible effects or would not have the medical experience or equipment to diagnose the effects.

In their paper on behavior modification and the law, Budd and Baer (1976) reviewed some cases that were not concerned with behavior modification programs, but which were concerned with behavior-modifying drugs. In *United States ex rel. Wilson* v. *Coughlin*, the court ruled that neither Thorazine nor any other tranquilizer could be used merely for the purposes of control or punishment. In *Nelson* v. *Heyne*, the court ruled that a specific order by a physician was required for the administration of a tranquilizing drug, that the drug had to be administered by medical personnel, and that follow-up information must be gathered. In the *Welsch* v. *Likins* ruling, the court held that the excessive use of tranquilizing drugs to control the behaviors of retarded persons amounted to cruel and unusual punishment. In the *Wyatt* v. *Stickney* case (certainly one of the most important cases for retarded persons on many accounts), the court went further and set forth specific guidelines:

> First they stated that mentally handicapped residents have a right to be free from unnecessary or excessive medication. Second, they require that drugs be prescribed by the written order of a physician and with a termination date of not more than 30 days. Third, records must be kept of the delivery of each dosage to a resident, and, for the mentally retarded, of the effects of the medication. Fourth, the attending physician must review the drug regimen for each resident at least weekly. Fifth, medication shall not be used as punishment, for the convenience of staff, as a substitute for program, or in quantities that interfere with the patient's treatment program. (Budd & Baer, 1976, p. 223)

Court decisions like these have led to drug regulations being established by many states. Among others, the state of Michigan has specified regulations with respect to behavior modifying drugs. Some of these are:

1. Record target symptoms and behaviors as a baseline against which to assess the effects of the drugs.
2. Record effects of medication at least weekly.

3. Do not initially prescribe large doses for a period of more than one week.
4. Reduce dosage to its minimum maintenance level.
5. Prescribe drug holidays during which the client is not given medication (e.g., once weekly).
6. Chronic use of anti-anxiety drugs is unwarranted.
7. Only one psychotropic drug at a time should be prescribed with only a few exceptions.
8. Periodically review each client's drug-treatment plan.
9. Each mental retardation center should develop training and retraining programs for staff.

Drug Studies

There are, of course, thousands of studies on the effects of drugs on behavior. Many of these are laboratory based and occur before the drug is released. Others are laboratory based, use human subjects, and occur after the drug has been released to the market for sale. A few are behavioral studies, are carefully monitored, occur *in vivo*, and are concerned with therapeutic improvement. While there are many single-subject designs by which the effects could be studied, most should have (1) a baseline phase, (2) a placebo phase in which the patient and others believe the drug is being administered, and (3) a drug phase. A study by Liberman, Davis, Moon, and Moore (1973) is representative of this type of design. In one of their studies, they monitored a patient's willingness to engage in 18 daily conversations with the nursing staff. Figure 11-6 shows results of this study. In the first phase, the number of refusals increased during the last four days. In the second phase, a placebo was administered and refusals occurred at about the same rate. During the third phase, 60 mg of Stelazine were given

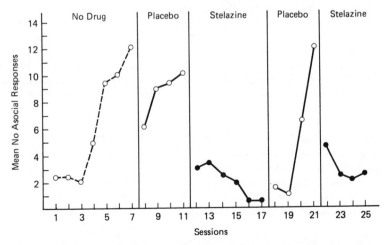

Figure 11-6. Average number of refusals to engage in a brief conversation under conditions of baseline, placebo, and 60 mg of Stelazine per day (Liberman, Davis, Moon, & Moore, 1973, p. 435).

daily, and the refusals decreased eventually to a zero level. The fourth and fifth phases constituted a reversal as the placebo and the drug were again administered. The results show quite clearly that, when compared with the placebo, Stelazine quite dramatically reduced the oppositional behavior.

Other studies have compared the effects of medication with the effects of behavioral intervention. Shafto and Sulzbacher (1977) studied the effects of Ritalin on the hyperactivity of a four-year-old child, and they found in general (1) that 5 mg of Ritalin may have increased hyperactivity slightly, (2) that 10 mg had no effect, (3) that 15 mg decreased hyperactivity, but also resulted in decreased intelligibility of speech and in insomnia, and (4) that a behavioral intervention in which the teacher reinforced the child for specific durations of appropriate play (and, hence, no hyperactivity) was by far the most successful. Ayllon, Layman, and Kandel (1975) showed that a behavioral program in which academic performance was reinforced was as powerful as Ritalin in decreasing hyperactivity. However, the performance in academics was much better when the children were off medications and were heavily reinforced for academic behavior. The results caused the authors to suggest that

> the continued use of Ritalin and possibly other drugs to control hyperactivity may result in *compliant but academically incompetent* students. . . . On the basis of these findings, it would seem appropriate to recommend that hyperactive children under medication periodically be given the opportunity to be drug-free, to minimize drug dependence and to facilitate change through alternative behavioral techniques. (pp. 144–145)

The limitations of both the behavioral and the drug approaches have been presented by Wulbert and Dries (1977), who identified the fact that we have a great deal to learn about both approaches. They measured two behaviors (aggression and ritualistic behaviors) in two settings (clinic and home). They found no drug effects in the clinic, a setting which involved a structured period; they did, however, find drug effects at home. There was more aggression but less ritualistic behavior when Ritalin was being administered. Ritualistic behaviors were decreased in the clinic through a behavioral program, but a similar decrease did not simultaneously appear at home. Specific behavior-management programs had to be designed for both the home and the clinic, as generalization was not spontaneous. A lack of an interaction effect between both these programs was also noted.

> Although clinical lore maintains that use of Ritalin and the amphetamines render hyperactive children more accessible to learning and reinforcement effects, there is little research to substantiate this notion. Arnold showed no tendency to respond more readily to a reinforcement regime when medicated than when on placebo. Hence, the present study does not support the common assumption that medication enhances learning effects.

This study does, however, support the importance of measuring what we are doing so that we can identify when our treatments are successful and when they are unsuccessful.

SUMMARY

This chapter presents a number of common ways for decreasing inappropriate behaviors of retarded persons. Some of these methods are reinforcement based in that they relate reinforcement to decreases in responding. Other procedures are punishment based in that they involve either the delivery of an aversive stimulus or the removal of a reinforcer. A third common procedure is a medical one, as opposed to a behavioral one, and it involves the use of drugs to modify behavior. In all cases, however, three issues are really more important than these specific procedures, because these issues are more pervasive. The first is that we must have clear and ethical standards by which we try to provide the best possible and the most humane services for our clients. The second is that we must be concerned with training, for these procedures are no better than the training of those who implement them. In most cases, they have been developed and researched by extremely well trained staff who have the expertise to make them successful. Their use by less well trained staff is not always so successful. The third issue is that we should be more concerned with effects data show than with the procedures themselves. To lock ourselves into using DRO, DRL, DRI, etc., is as stifling as locking ourselves adamantly into a drug or no-drug approach. We should be inventive, trying new procedures as the events call for them, and we should always be data conscious, for only then can we learn the success of our endeavors to help our retarded clients.

REFERENCES

Ayllon, T., Layman, D., & Burke, S. Disruptive behavior and reinforcement of academic behavior. *Psychological Research*, 1972, 22, 315-323.

Azrin, N. H. Time-out from positive reinforcement. *Science*, 1961, 133, 382-383.

Azrin, N. H., & Foxx, R. M. A rapid method of toilet training the institutionalized retarded. *Journal of Applied Behavior Analysis*, 1971, 4, 89-99.

Azrin, N. H., & Holz, W. C. Punishment. In W. K. Honig (Ed.), *Operant behavior.* New York: Appleton-Century-Crofts, Inc., 1966.

Azrin, N. H., Kaplan, S. J., & Foxx, R. M. Autism reversal: Eliminating stereotyped self-stimulation of retarded individuals. *American Journal of Mental Deficiency*, 1973, 78, 241-248.

Azrin, N. H., & Wesolowski, M. D. Theft reversal: An overcorrection procedure for eliminating stealing by retarded persons. *Journal of Applied Behavior Analysis*, 1974, 7, 577-581.

Barrish, H. H., Saunders, M., & Wolf, M. M. Good behavior game: Effects of individual contingencies for group consequences on disruptive behavior in a classroom. *Journal of Applied Behavior Analysis.* 1969, 2, 119.

Bucher, B., & King, L. Generalization of punishment effects in the deviant behavior of a psychotic child. *Behavior Therapy*, 1971, 2, 68-77.

Bucher, B., & Lovaas, O. I. Use of aversive stimulation in behavior modification. In M. R. Jones (Ed.), *Miami symposium on the prediction of behavior, 1967: Aversive stimulation.* Coral Gables, FL: University of Miami Press, 1968.

Corte, H. E., Wolf, M. M., & Locke, B. J. A comparison of procedures for eliminating self-injurious behavior of retarded adolescents. *Journal of Applied Behavior Analysis,* 1971, **4**, 201-213.

Dandy, M. C., Oliver, S. E., & Kaprowy, E. A. Using differential reinforcement of other behavior to reduce and maintain low levels of disruptive work behavior of a severely retarded adolescent. Paper presented at the Annual Meeting of the Midwestern Association of Behavior Analysis, 1976.

Deitz, S. M., & Repp, A. C. Decreasing classroom misbehavior through the use of DRL schedules of reinforcement. *Journal of Applied Behavior Analysis,* 1973, **6**, 457-463.

Deitz, S. M., & Repp, A. C. Differentially reinforcing low rates of misbehavior with normal elementary school children. *Journal of Applied Behavior Analysis,* 1974a, **7**, 622.

Deitz, S. M., & Repp, A. C. A description and analysis of three ways to program schedules of reinforcement requiring the differential reinforcement of low rates of responding. Paper presented at the meeting of the American Psychological Association, 1974b.

Deitz, S. M., Repp, A. C., & Deitz, D. E. D. Reducing inappropriate classroom behavior of retarded students through three procedures of differential reinforcement. *Journal of Mental Deficiency Research,* 1976, **20**, 155-170.

Doleys, D. M., Wells, K. C., Hobbs, S. A., Roberts, M. W., & Cartelli, L. M. The effects of social punishment on noncompliance: A comparison with timeout and positive practice. *Journal of Applied Behavior Analysis,* 1976, **9**, 471-482.

Duker, P. C., & Seys, D. M. Elimination of vomiting in a retarded female using restitutional overcorrection. *Behavior Therapy,* 1977, **8**, 255-257.

Epstein, L. H., Doke, L. A., Sajwaj, T. E., Sorrell, S., & Rimmer, B. Generality and side effects of overcorrection. *Journal of Applied Behavior Analysis,* 1974, **7**, 385-390.

Favell, J. E. Reduction of stereotypies by reinforcement of toy play. *Mental Retardation,* 1973, 21-23.

Fishbein, J., & Wasik, B. Effects of the good behavior game on disruptive library behavior. *Journal of Applied Behavior Analysis,* 1981, **14**, 89-94.

Hall, R. V., Lund, D., & Jackson, D. Effects of teacher attention on study behavior. *Journal of Applied Behavior Analysis,* 1968, **1**, 1-12.

Hamilton, H., Stevens, L., & Allen, P. Controlling aggressive and destructive behavior in severely retarded institutionalized residents. *American Journal of Mental Deficiency,* 1967, **71**, 852-856.

Harris, V. W., & Sherman, J. A. Use and analysis of the "Good Behavior Game" to reduce disruptive classroom behavior. *Journal of Applied Behavior Analysis,* 1973, **6**, 405-417.

Hartmann, D. P., & Hall, R. V. The changing criterion design. *Journal of Applied Behavior Analysis,* 1976, **9**, 527-532.

Hawkins, R. P., Peterson, R. F., Schweid, E., & Bijou, S. W. Behavior therapy in the home: Amelioration of problem parent-child relations with the parent in a therapeutic role. *Journal of Experimental Child Psychology,* 1966, 4, 99-107.

Iwata, B. A., & Bailey, J. S. Reward versus cost token systems: An analysis of the effects on students and teachers. *Journal of Applied Behavior Analysis,* 1974, **7**, 567-576.

Kazdin, A. E. *The token economy: A review and evaluation.* New York: Plenum Publishing Corp., 1977.

Koegel, R. L., & Covert, A. The relationship of self-stimulation to learning in autistic children. *Journal of Applied Behavior Analysis,* 1972, **5**, 381-387.

Laws, D. R., Brown, R. A., Epstein, J., & Hocking, N. Reduction of inappropriate social behavior in disturbed children by an untrained paraprofessional therapist. *Behavior Therapy*, 1971, **2**, 519-533.

Liberman, R. P., Davis, J., Moon, W., & Moore, J. Research design for analyzing drug-environment-behavior interactions. *Journal of Nervous and Mental Disease*, 1973, **156**, 432-439.

Lovaas, O. I., Freitag, G., Gold, V. J., & Kassorla, I. C. Experimental studies in childhood schizophrenia: Analysis of self-destructive behavior. *Journal of Experimental Child Psychology*. 1965, **2**, 67-84.

Lovaas, O. I., Schaeffer, B., & Simmons, J. Q. Experimental studies in childhood schizophrenia: Building social behavior in autistic children by the use of electric shock. *Journal of Experimental Research Personnel*, 1965, **1**, 99-109.

Lovaas, O. I., & Simmons, J. Q. Manipulation of self-destruction in three retarded children. *Journal of Applied Behavior Analysis*, 1969, **2**, 143-157.

Madsen, C. H., Becker, W. C., Thomas, D. R., Koser, L., & Plager, E. An analysis of the reinforcing function of "sit down" commands. In R. K. Parker (Ed.), *Readings in educational psychology*. Boston: Allyn & Bacon, Inc., 1968.

Martin, R. *Legal challenges to behavior modification: Trends in schools, corrections, and mental health*. Champaign, IL: Research Press, 1975.

Matson, J. L., & Stephens, R. M. Overcorrection of aggressive behavior in a chronic psychiatric patient. *Behavior Modification*, 1977, **1**, 559-564.

Medland, M. B., & Stachnik, T. J. Good behavior game: A replication and systematic analysis. *Journal of Applied Behavior Analysis*, 1972, **5**, 45.

Meerbaum, M. The modification of self-destructive behavior by a mother-therapist using aversive stimulation. *Behavior Therapy*, 1973, **4**, 442-447.

O'Brien, F., Bugle, C., & Azrin, N. H. Training and maintaining a retarded child's proper eating. *Journal of Applied Behavior Analysis*, 1972, **5**, 67-72.

Pinkston, E. M., Reese, N. J., LeBlanc, J. M., & Baer, D. M. Independent control of a preschool child's aggression and peer interaction by contingent teacher attention. *Journal of Applied Behavior Analysis*, 1973, **6**, 115-124.

Sulzer-Azaroff, B., & Mayer, G. R. *Applying behavior-analysis procedures with children and youth*. New York: Holt, Rinehart and Winston, Inc., 1977.

Winett, R. A., & Winkler, R. C. Current behavior modification in the classroom: Be still, be quiet, be docile. *Journal of Applied Behavior Analysis*, 1972, **5**, 499-504.

Glossary

A-B-C paradigm.   A three-term contingency in which there is (1) an antecedent stimulus which describes those events that affect responding and that antecede the response, (2) the response, which describes a single occurrence of behavior, and (3) the subsequent stimuli or consequences, which describe those events that affect responding and are subsequent to the response.

Alternative schedules.   Schedules in which reinforcement is programmed by either a ratio or an interval schedule, whichever is satisfied *first*. Thus, in an alternative F15-FR300 the first response is reinforced (1) after a period of 5 minutes provided 300 responses have *not* been made, or (2) upon completion of 300 responses provided 5 minutes has *not* elapsed.

Antecedent events.   Those events that come before the response and affect the probability that behavior will occur.

Aversive conditioning.   A form of positive punishment; a procedure in which a response produces an aversive stimulus and as a result becomes less probable.

Backward chaining.   A teaching procedure in which the task's components are taught in a backward fashion, i.e., beginning with the *last* link in the chain.

Baseline.   A description of the conditions existing during the initial period of observation; the first phase of a study; a standard against which the effects of the manipulation of the independent variable can be measured.

Behavioral contract.   An agreement between the client and another person on a goal and a procedure for teaching that goal.

Changing criterion design.   A design whose essential features are (1) a baseline phase, followed by (2) implementation of a procedure, which (3) establishes a criterion for responding to be consequated, with (4) the criterion changing from one phase to the next. The intent of the design is to demonstrate that behavior changes when the criterion changes.

Compound schedule of reinforcement.   A schedule of reinforcement with two or more rules between the reinforcer and the behavior.

Conditioned reinforcers.   Reinforcers with reinforcing properties which depend upon a history of pairing with stimuli that were already reinforcing.

Conjunctive schedule.   A schedule in which reinforcement occurs when both a ratio and an interval schedule have been satisfied. For example, a response is reinforced when at least 5 minutes have elapsed since the preceding reinforcement *and* after at least 300 responses.

Consequences.   Those events that come after the response and affect the likelihood that the behavior will recur.

Continuous reinforcement (CRF or FR1).   A schedule of reinforcement in which every response occurrence is reinforced.

Curriculum.   A set of learning objectives that are (1) specified as behaviors, (2) written in objective terms that allow observation and measurement, (3) carefully sequenced from the easiest to the most difficult, (4) descriptive of the prerequisites necessary for each objective, and (5) a result of an analysis of each task in the curriculum.

Datum.   The unit in which measurement is expressed (e.g., percent, rate).

Dependent variable.   A variable that depends upon the value of the independent variable. For example, whether a child says "you're welcome" depends upon whether we have just said "thank you."

Deprivation.   A temporary increase in the effectiveness of a reinforcer due solely to the passage of time since it last was presented.

Differential reinforcement.   A procedure in which three operations exist: (1) a particular response is reinforced if it occurs in the presence of a particular stimulus, (2) that response is not reinforced in the absence of the appropriate stimuli, and (3) other responses are not reinforced in the presence of these particular stimuli.

Differential reinforcement of alternative behaviors (DRA).   A procedure like DRI except that it does not require the target behavior to be incompatible with the inappropriate response. As such, it can be defined as a procedure in which an appropriate response is reinforced while an appropriate response is ignored.

Differential reinforcement of high rates (DRH).   A schedule of reinforcement in which responding greater than or equal to some minimum is reinforced.

Differential reinforcement of incompatible responding (DRI).   A program in which a response *topographically* incompatible with the target behavior is reinforced.

Differential reinforcement of low rates (DRL).   A schedule of reinforcement in which responding less than or equal to a particular rate is reinforced.

Differential reinforcement of other behavior.   A procedure in which reinforcement is delivered if the target behavior does not occur for a specified period of time.

Discriminative stimulus (S^D).   A stimulus in the presence of which a response will be reinforced.

Duration recording.   A method of recording in which the duration of each response and the total time of the session are recorded. The former is divided by the latter to provide the percent of time responding.

Extinction.   A procedure in which a response that was previously reinforced is no longer reinforced.

Fading.   The gradual removal of (usually artificial or intrusive) discriminative stimuli such as directions, imitative prompts, physical guidance, and other cues and prompts.

First-order schedule of reinforcement.   A single rule between the reinforcer and the behavior.

Fixed interval (FI).   A schedule of intermittent reinforcement in which the first response occurring after a given interval of time, measured from the preceding reinforcement, is reinforced.

Fixed ratio (FR).   A schedule of intermittent reinforcement in which a response is reinforced upon completion of a fixed number of responses counted from the preceding reinforcement.

Forward chaining.   A teaching procedure in which the task's components are taught in a forward fashion, i.e., beginning with the *first* link in the chain.

Frequency recording.   A method of recording in which the observer marks each occurrence of the behavior during the session. The number of responses is divided by the length of the session to provide the rate of responding.

Full-session DRL.   A procedure in which reinforcement is delivered if the rate of responding for the whole session is below a limit.

Functional relationship.   Exists when the dependent variable changes as a function of the value of the independent variable. A functional relationship is demonstrated behaviorally through operant designs such as the reversal, multiple baseline, etc.

Histogram.   A bar graph which allows a rapid examination of a summary of data across several subjects or conditions.

Ignoring.   A procedure in which one does not provide attention contingent upon responding.

Imitation.   A procedure in which a model's behavior acts as a prompting stimulus that controls the behavior of the observing student.

Independent variable.   A variable that controls the probability of the dependent variable (behavior).

Instructional objectives.   Clear statements which allow readers to agree independently on what the student will be able to do once he or she has mastered the objective; includes three components: performance, condition, and criterion.

Interlocking schedules.   A schedule in which a person is reinforced upon completion of a number of responses; but this number changes *during* the interval which follows the previous reinforcement.

Intermittent reinforcement.   A schedule of reinforcement in which some but not all responses are reinforced.

Interobserver agreement.   A measure of the extent to which observers agree that responding has or has not occurred.

Interresponse-time DRL.   (or spaced responding). A response is reinforced if and only if it followed a prior response by a particular time period.

Interval DRL.   A procedure in which the session is broken into a number of intervals and reinforcement is delivered at the end of each interval if responding is less than a particular level for that interval.

Interval recording.   A method of recording in which a session is divided into a number of equal-length intervals. The recorder then marks whether or not responding has occurred in each of the intervals. The data are summarized as the percent of observations in which responding has occurred.

Labeled praise (or specific praise).   A procedure in which the behavior itself is named and praised.

Limited hold.   A short period during which reinforcement arranged by an interval schedule is held available. At the end of the limited hold, a response will not be reinforced until another reinforcement has been set up. If a response is made during the limited hold, reinforcement is delivered.

Multi-element design.   A design in which a number of highly discriminable stimuli are correlated with different procedures. Each stimulus should show different responding, thus demonstrating the differential effects of the conditions associated with the stimuli.

Multiple baseline across behaviors.   A design that examines several behaviors of a single individual with each being brought sequentially into contact with the independent variable.

Multiple baseline across settings.   A design in which the same behavior or the same person is studied across situations. The independent variable is introduced at different times across the settings.

Multiple baseline across subjects.   A design in which the same behavior is studied across persons, but the independent variable is introduced to individuals or groups at different times.

Multiple-baseline design.   A design in which (1) at least two baselines begin the same day, (2) these baselines are kept on different behaviors, different individuals, or in different settings, and (3) the baselines are terminated and the independent variable applied at a different time to each baseline.

Negative punishment.   A procedure in which a response removes something from the environment and becomes less probable.

Negative reinforcement.   A procedure in which a response removes a stimulus from the environment and becomes more probable.

Overcorrection.   A punishment procedure that has two components. Restitutional overcorrection requires the individual to restore the environment he or she has just disrupted to a "better-than-before" condition. Positive practice overcorrection requires the individual to practice excessively the topographically correct forms of a behavior he or she has just emitted.

Positive punishment.   A procedure in which responding decreases as a result of adding a stimulus to the environment.

Positive reinforcement. A procedure in which responding increases as a result of adding a stimulus to the environment.

Primary reinforcers. Those reinforcers which, for a particular individual, do not require any history of conditioning (i.e., learning).

Reinforcement. A procedure in which a response produces a stimulus change and as a result becomes more probable.

Reinforcer sampling. A procedure in which limited access to the reinforcer is made available and the initial response during reinforcement activities themselves are primed. For example, a small portion of food is given to you as a sample in the grocery store in the hope that you will purchase the item.

Response cost. A procedure in which a response leads to the removal of some portion of accumulated reinforcement.

Reversal design. A single-subject design of at least three phases with at least two of them having behavior occurring at about the same level because of the specific procedures used.

S^Δ. A stimulus in the presence of which responding is not reinforced.

Satiation. A temporary decrease in performance due solely to the repeated presentation of the reinforcer.

Schedule of reinforcement. A rule that describes the relation between responding and reinforcement in terms of time, or of number, or of time and number.

Second-order schedule of reinforcement. A schedule of reinforcement with two rules. The first rule is that of the first-order schedule, and the second rule is a rule about that first-order rule. A token program is a second-order schedule. The first rule may be that "five correct answers produce a token." The second rule may be that "ten tokens can be exchanged for five minutes of free time."

Shaping. A procedure defined as the differential reinforcement of successive approximations to the terminal objective. It employs two subprocedures: (1) successive approximations, which refers to a continuing change in response complexity that is required for reinforcement, and (2) differential reinforcement, which refers to reinforcement being delivered for responding as well as being withheld for responding that does not meet the current definition of correct responding.

Simultaneous treatment design. A design in which a baseline is followed by simultaneous implementation of several treatment procedures as in a multi-element design. However, unlike that design, the simultaneous treatment design requires that each treatment condition be associated with each stimulus situation.

Single-subject design. A research design in which all conditions are applied to the same subject and the results of a change in behavior are analyzed with respect to that individual.

Stimulus control. When there is a high probability that a response will occur in the presence of a particular stimulus and no others, we say that stimulus control has been demonstrated (i.e., the stimulus has "controlled" the probability of responding).

Stimulus generalization. Describes the extent to which a response trained in the presence of one stimulus occurs in the presence of another.

Task analysis. A procedure of analyzing a complex task such that (1) some complex behavior is analyzed into its components, (2) these components also describe behaviors, (3) all behaviors are described in terms that allow obsevation, and (4) all analyses are intended to make learning easier for the student.

Task sampling. A method of evaluation that occurs in two forms. In one, the teacher simply evaluates the child's performance on a task (e.g., sewing a button on a shirt) to determine whether the student can complete it correctly or whether it should be added to the list of learning objectives. In the other form of task sampling, we look at performance on graduated steps in a single task rather than at completion of the entire task to determine the step (in a task analysis) at which the student demonstrates competency.

Three-term contingency. A phrase that refers to the relationship between environmental events and behavior; also referred to as the A-B-C paradigm, which includes antecedent events, response, and consequences.

Timeout. A procedure in which a response removes access to reinforcement for a specified period of time.

Time sampling. A method of recording in which the observer ignores the behavior for a relatively long period (e.g., 60 minutes), and then after a signal, quickly scans the situation and records whether responding is occurring. The number of observations in which responding was occurring is divided by the total number of observations to provide the percent of observations in which responding was occurring.

Time-series graphs. A graph in which the *x*-axis represents *time* and the *y*-axis represents *number* of occurrences of the dependent variable.

Token-exchange component. In the token-exchange component, the student exchanges tokens for backup reinforcers according to some schedule of reinforcement.

Token-production component. In the token-production component, the student earns tokens according to some schedule of reinforcement.

Variable interval (VI). A schedule of reinforcement in which the first response after the interval expires is reinforced. The interval, however, is not the same each time.

Variable ratio (VR). A schedule of intermittent reinforcement under which reinforcement is programmed according to a random series of ratios having a given mean and lying between arbitrary extreme values.

Vicarious punishment. A procedure in which punishment of an individual's or a group's behavior decreases the performance of that behavior by others who are not directly punished.

Vicarious reinforcement. A procedure in which reinforcement of an individual's or a group's behavior increases the performance of that behavior by others who are not directly reinforced.

Index